In the Ring
With
Jack Johnson

Part I: The Rise

Adam J. Pollack

WIN BY KO

Win By KO Publications

Iowa City

In the Ring With Jack Johnson
Part I: The Rise

Adam J. Pollack

(ISBN-13): 978-0-9799822-9-3

(hardcover: 50# acid-free alkaline paper)

Includes footnotes, appendix, bibliography, and index.

Cover design by Adam Pollack and Gwyn Snider ©

Manufactured in the United States of America.

Win By KO Publications
Iowa City, Iowa
winbykopublications.com

Contents

Preface: Jack Johnson

Jack Johnson was the first black fighter to challenge for the world heavyweight championship under modern-day Marquis of Queensberry rules, and the first to win it. One cannot tell the story of Jack Johnson the fighter without reference to his social significance. This book does that. Most books on Johnson focus on his social significance and out-of-the-ring life, almost to the exclusion of his fight career. Unlike the many other books on Jack Johnson, this book focuses heavily on his boxing career as well. To this extent, the book is unique and fills a void. My perspective is that if Johnson had not been a boxing champion, he would not have had the same social relevance. Hence, it is important to discuss his boxing career thoroughly and to explain how and why he became champion. That said, one cannot fully understand or appreciate Johnson's boxing career, the perspectives and analysis of it, without an understanding of the impact of race on the world and upon the sport of boxing. Context is very important. This book necessarily addresses issues of race, for it played a large role in Johnson's life and career.

Like other books in my series on the heavyweight champions of the gloved era, this book uses mostly local primary sources. Reliance on those who were there, saw the bout, and reported on it the next day will most likely provide the most accurate accounts. Review of several sources is often also very important, because like today, different observers can have varying opinions about what they saw. Since we do not have film for the majority of Johnson's bouts, and given that the films that we do have are incomplete, we must rely on these sources. Providing multiple perspectives enables this book to be as thorough, complete, and accurate as possible, and helps readers obtain a richer understanding of what took place, as well as how fans, writers, and experts perceived the performances, skills, and abilities of the fighters. Another benefit of offering multiple perspectives is that it allows the reader to draw his or her own conclusions. However, this effort necessarily requires some level of redundancy and repetitiveness that you will have to excuse as a trade-off.

Analysis and inclusion of several sources is also especially important when it comes to Johnson's career, because the added factor of racial bias, either on a subconscious or conscious level, impacted how reporters wrote about and interpreted Johnson's performances, or scouted upcoming bouts. Few writers could entirely escape the impact of the colored lenses of the racially biased world from which they emerged and took part. That said, not all criticism of Johnson was the result of racial bias. Certainly though, the inclusion of the black perspective is important, and when available, this book provides the viewpoints of black-owned newspapers.

In the late 19th and early 20th centuries, many top white fighters were unwilling to compete against black fighters, due to the social mores of the time which frowned upon competition between whites and blacks in any area of life. This norm, which mandated separation of the races, was known as the color line. Many promoters did not want to be associated with mixed-race bouts. Politicians did not care for them either, and often tried to do what they could to prevent such bouts from taking place.

As a result of the color line, black fighters were rarely allowed to engage in financially lucrative championship matches, and usually they were not paid as well as whites for the few big fights that they did have. Therefore, black boxers had to fight quite often to earn a good living. This is not to say that they did not earn more money than the average citizen. Boxing could be a financially lucrative profession for all races, which in part explains why it flourished. The public loved watching fights, regardless of race.

Despite not being willing to fight them in formal bouts, many top whites were willing to pay black fighters to be their sparring partners. Working as sparring partners for elite white fighters helped black fighters earn a living and also develop their skills.

Necessity often dictated that blacks fight each other, sometimes many times, to make good money. Consequently, many black fighters, like Jack Johnson, needed to develop good defense in order to fight as often as they did, particularly given that many fights were scheduled 20-round bouts, and they were only wearing 5-ounce gloves, with no mouthpieces. A fighter could suffer a great deal of damage in such a lengthy bout. However, one could also obtain a great deal of experience fighting so many rounds in just one fight.[1]

By fighting and sparring often, Jack Johnson was able to obtain a great deal of experience, and sharpen and improve his skills over time, eventually making him the best heavyweight in the world.

Owing to the color line, it required many years for Jack Johnson to obtain a title shot. Hence, one could argue that he was the world's best heavyweight and de facto champion much sooner than when he was able to win the championship in late 1908. Without the color line, or if Jack Johnson had been a white fighter, it is certainly possible that he could have begun his reign as early as 1903 and been champion for several more years. This is speculation for the ages.

---

[1] Some have even suggested that blacks' defensive styles were also developed in light of the need to not look too strong or good against a white opponent. If a black boxer was too dominant against a white opponent, he sometimes risked being shunned further by promoters, or whites would refuse to fight them. Some boxers felt they could defeat whites, but couldn't do so too convincingly, lest they invoke the ire of the public and promoters. Sometimes, blacks had to throw fights in order to stay in the good graces of promoters. It is not known how often this occurred. Randy Roberts, *Papa Jack*, (New York: The Free Press, 1983), 25. That general theory aside, there are plenty of instances where black fighters were aggressive and knocked out white fighters.

As a fighter, Jack Johnson became famous for his speed, almost impregnable defense, and excellent counter right uppercut. Johnson's cautious defensive style was not always the most crowd-pleasing, but it was extremely effective. He was a precursor to the frustrating styles later seen from the likes of Muhammad Ali, Bernard Hopkins, Floyd Mayweather, Jr., and Andre Ward. He posed a stylistic nightmare for most opponents. He utilized footwork, feints, abs, counters, occasional quick offensive charges, inside uppercuts, along with blocking, ducking, clinching, quick step-backs, and smothering and suppression of an opponent's offense with his gloves and arms. He could fight on the inside or the outside, sticking and moving or fighting up close, showing his versatility and skillful prowess at any range.

Johnson stood between 6'0" to 6'1½" and at his best generally fought between 190 to 210 pounds. However, he started his career as a middleweight, and for most of his early years was no bigger than a super-middleweight or light-heavyweight by today's standards.

He was nicknamed 'Li'l Artha," after his birthname, Arthur John Johnson. However, various names used to refer to Johnson throughout his career included: Arthur John Johnson, John Arthur Johnson, John James Arthur Johnson, and Jim Johnson. Reporters even used names of a racial nature, often racially disparaging, which revealed the era's and reporters' biases. These names included: Black Jack, Mistah Johnsing, Mars Johnson, Black Fitzsimmons, Colored Wonder, African, Ethiopian, Zulu, Senegambian, Ebon-Hued Giant, Big Negro, Black Animal, Ink Person, Big Cannibal, Black Peril, Black Agony, Big Shine, Smoke, Darkey, Dingy, Dinge, Dusky, Dark Cloud, Coon, Nigger, and Tar Baby.

Jack Johnson continues to be a hot-button topic of debate as much today as he was back then. He really fascinated and puzzled folks, caused a great deal of discussion and varying interpretation of him as a fighter and person, and he still does so even a century later. In fact, much of what his career reveals about American life and race to a large degree was once again revealed and replicated in the life and career of Muhammad Ali. Issues of race and the analysis of black athletes have historical underpinnings that go all the way back to Jack Johnson.

The fascination with Johnson was and is in part because of his style, lack of appreciation for the fact that fighters develop and improve over time, his personality, race bias, the era's context and culture, and also because he was simply a very unique individual.

Before there were socially significant fighters and athletes like Joe Louis, Jackie Robinson, Bill Russell, or Muhammad Ali, there was Jack Johnson. To fully understand their relevance, one must start with Jack Johnson.

This book is particularly dedicated to all those who at one time or another in their lives were picked on, put down, pushed around, or made to feel like lesser human beings. I hope you find Jack Johnson's story inspirational.

CHAPTER 1

The Color-Line in Boxing

For there is neither east nor west,
Border nor breed nor birth.
When two strong men stand face to face,
Though they come from the ends of the earth.[2]

During the era of slavery, slaves and ex-slaves often competed in bareknuckle prizefights. Those that did well enough were sometimes given freedom by their owners, who had made big money through their wagers on such contests. On rare occasions, in England, former slaves even competed against white fighters. There was no strict color-line tradition in the fight world. Former American slave Bill Richmond traveled to England and fought and lost to England's white champion Tom Cribb in a 1-hour 30-minute bareknuckle prizefight. The most famous instance of a black fighter competing against a white fighter in a championship fight was the 1810 Molineaux-Cribb prizefight. Tom Molineaux was a former slave from Virginia, and he too traveled to England to fight Cribb, who defeated him after 55 minutes. An 1811 rematch resulted in another Cribb victory after 11 rounds requiring only 19 minutes.

After the conclusion of the Reconstruction era in the post-Civil War United States, given that social and legal racial segregation predominated in the U.S., and indeed existed in varying degrees throughout the world, it is not surprising that sports were segregated as well. The general population believed that whites and blacks should not mix in any area of life on the same level, including sporting competition. Regardless of whether or not a black could defeat a white competitor, even the mere act of allowing a black person to compete with a white person symbolically gave the impression that they were on the same level and had the right to compete for the same things, which was a direct contradiction of and threat to the prevailing social order. Sport was social symbol. It reflected something about the society and the times, and many thought it should also reinforce the prevailing and desired social mores.

What is surprising is the fact that while most sports were segregated, such was not always the case, particularly with individual sports. Segregation would exist in varying degrees, given the times and the locale. Sports like

---

[2] A line one of Johnson's sparring partners used to recite. *My Life and Battles* by Jack Johnson, translated and edited from the 1911 and 1914 French versions by Christopher Rivers, Praeger Publishers, Westport, CT, 2007, page 90.

horse racing, bicycle racing, track and field, and sometimes even football oscillated at times in the degree in which integration was allowed, or which segregation was required.

While most sports eventually became totally segregated, the sport of boxing did not always follow the general social rule. This made boxing the most racially progressive of all sports. Ironically, this is in part because boxing was considered an utterly morally depraved sport, so depraved that normal social conventions did not necessarily or always apply. Fighters purportedly had no social standing, and therefore were not always expected to follow standard social norms. Essentially, those involved in the sport were considered lowlifes.

Boxing was constantly under legal attack by those who considered it to be a depraved, barbaric form of human cock fighting, and not a good influence on society, even with the race issue excepted.

However, as the sport's participants obtained popularity, economic power, and prestige, and boxing champions to some degree became social symbols, greater opposition to mixed-race bouts arose. Many fight folks wanted to elevate the sport to a higher social level, and minimize legal opposition, which meant avoidance of black champions.

Others simply felt that there was no color line in boxing, and did not have a problem with mixed-race bouts. And still others were not opposed to racially mixed bouts until there were black champions, and then their true displeasure to such a thing was revealed.

Early gloved boxing thrived at a time when the general white population abhorred the idea of mixed-race competition. Hence, many fighters drew the color line in all instances and openly refused to compete against blacks. However, some only drew the line when it came to championship bouts, which had the greatest symbolic social value. Some did not draw the line at all. Actually, non-title-fight mixed-race bouts took place more often than some realize.

What is most surprising is the fact that even in the late 1800s and early 1900s, many sports-writers openly advocated for equality of opportunity in boxing, without regard to race, which was completely opposite of the general social norm. There were plenty of fair-minded sportsmen who simply enjoyed good competition between the best athletes, and honestly wanted to see the better man win, or at least have the opportunity to fight, regardless of race. Still, some of those who advocated for equality changed their minds once blacks won championships. Then, their deep-seeded feelings emerged; sort of like folks in the second half of the 20th century being in favor integration and against the separate but equal doctrine, until their neighbors were black or their kids went to integrated schools, or their daughter brought home a black man as her date. The theory of equality was one thing; its actual application was another.

Overall, members of the fight fraternity were often quite fair, or at least fairer than one might think, when it came to decisions and analysis regarding fights, regardless of race. Merit mattered most, particularly to the writers and gamblers who backed the sport.

In fact, gamblers were a big part of the fan base and support for boxing. Discussion of wagering and odds was commonplace in newspapers. Gamblers wanted assurances of the fairness of the referee, typically the sole arbiter and decisionmaker. They often had a lot of money on the line in fights, and wanted decisions based purely on the merits. It was hard enough to pick the winner as it was. They did not want to have to factor into their analysis racial prejudice as well. They wanted assurances that the better man would win, so they would not be cheated out of their rightful earnings, nor unfairly lose their shirts. Hence, a lot of white gamblers supported fairness in decisions, without regard to color, as a result of their own financial interests.

Top referees were fair-minded in their decisions in part because they were protecting white gamblers who had wagered on black fighters and were expecting an honest decision. If a referee was not considered to be fair, he would not be used. Typically, either fighter or his manager could object to a particular referee. Clubs that wanted continued patronage made sure that they used the most qualified and fair-minded referees, and often had a house referee whom they knew was fair and honest. Gamblers also wanted referees who were not influenced by the crowd.

All that said, referees, gamblers, crowds, and promoters were still human, and so various biases, even if only subconscious, could factor into their decisions. Concerns about referee bias and subjectivity are why many purists throughout history had wanted only to wager and financially back large amounts on fights to the finish, in order to be assured that the better man won by knockout, without having to factor in referee decision-making subjectivity. This thinking in part explains why some were happy about no-decision laws, meaning that the referee would not render a formal decision unless there was a knockout or disqualification. However, some gamblers relied on the fairness of a local writer or writers whom they respected, who offered their own decision/opinions regarding who won, and the local gamblers would rely upon those opinions to decide their wagers.

Often, if a fight was very close, a referee would simply decide the bout a draw in order to protect or not prejudice the gamblers for one side or the other. In the event of a draw, no one lost, nor won their wagers. This also had financial implications to the fighters, whose purses were usually divided in such a way as to give the winner a greater share of the proceeds. If the victor was not obvious or dominant, the referee might just split the baby, so to speak, and call it a draw so that the fighters would split the purse evenly. Hence, there were a lot of draws back then.

Regardless of the fairness of many writers, they still were a product of their times, and many did not like the idea of a black champion, and could not help, either consciously or subconsciously, allowing their distaste for a black fighter defeating a white boxer to influence their comments. Sometimes, rather than laud a black contender for his performance, the writer would denigrate his defeated opponent as not being very good. Or the writer might find ways to nit-pick or criticize the performance of a black fighter even in victory. Many simply could not help allowing racial biases or stereotypes to influence their analysis of a fight or fighter. Ultimately, things were not as black and white as one might think. Hence, nowhere does analysis or consideration of sources become as important as it does when discussing black fighters of this era. Of course, it can often be difficult to delineate just where valid, fair criticism ends, and racial bias begins. Racial prejudice has its shades of grey.

For the most part, though, whites competed against whites, and blacks competed against blacks, particularly in the United States. England, Australia, France, and sometimes even Canada were not as strict regarding racial separation in prizefights. That is not to say that they did not have their own racial biases and issues.

Eventually, during the gloved era, in a few rare instances, a black fighter in the smaller weight classes would win a world title, often, but not always, in a fight held in a foreign country. Such fighters could defend their titles in the U.S., typically giving white boxers the opportunity to regain the championship for the white race, but they also fought other blacks. Primarily, though, blacks either fought each other for "colored" titles, or they fought whites in non-title bouts. The biggest prize in boxing, the heavyweight championship, remained a whites-only position.

Regardless of the color line, boxing was a profession that could generate a great deal of money for poor folks, white or black. It required no formal scholastic education or finances. Hence, it attracted a large population of participants. Blacks who had to deal with the segregation of the general society, which severely limited their economic opportunities, saw boxing as a way to make more money than they could via other professions.

The first great fighter of the gloved boxing era was John L. Sullivan. Although Sullivan never did box a black man, his stance was not always consistent. Early in his career, he had expressed himself as willing to fight a black boxer, but later, as he and the sport of boxing obtained greater social status, Sullivan openly refused to box blacks.

Some reports indicate that in 1880, while in Boston, in a large private room before paying spectators, Sullivan was about to take on a black fighter named George Godfrey, but just as they were about to begin the match, the police entered and prevented the fight. Sullivan had been willing to meet a black fighter named Johnson in 1882, but Johnson pulled out at the last minute.[3]

In 1883, when a black fighter named Charles Smith challenged Sullivan, "the champion objected to meeting Smith on account of his color." The *National Police Gazette* said, "We do not see why Sullivan should refuse to arrange a match with Smith merely because he is a colored man. Bob

---

[3] *Boston Daily Globe*, September 22, 1880; *New York Clipper*, April 29, 1882.

Travers, the great pugilist, was a colored man, and he arranged matches with and fought some of the best pugilists in England."[4]

John L. Sullivan

However, the color line was a part of American boxing, so much so that top black fighters began fighting each other for "colored" championships. In 1883, Professor Charles Hadley was known as the colored heavyweight champion, until George Godfrey stopped him.[5]

In May 1888, when George Godfrey was present in the audience at a Sullivan exhibition, the master of ceremonies tried to get them to box an exhibition. Sullivan was willing, though Godfrey was not prepared, and suggested that they fight for gate receipts at a later date.[6]

On the whole, the press did not care too much about the fact that Sullivan drew the color line, until he drew it in the late 1880s against Australia's Peter Jackson, a highly respected, admired, and well-liked black fighter. Australians did not draw the color line in boxing, and Jackson had won the Australian heavyweight championship before traveling to the United States.

After first seeing Jackson in action, the local *San Francisco Examiner* said, "Fear alone…will prevent Sullivan from meeting him…. The white fighters will draw the color line tighter than ever, now."[7]

Regarding colored champion George Godfrey, in 1888, the *Examiner* noted that "those who are recognized as the champions do not care particularly to face him, not because he has not backing enough, but because he is a man of color."[8] Then title-claimant Jake Kilrain said, "It is not customary in this country for white men to fight colored men for the championship, but I will fight any man."[9] Yet, Kilrain did not fight a black fighter during the time that he called himself champion, though he held an earlier KO3 victory over Godfrey. Eventually, on August 24, 1888 in San Francisco, Peter Jackson defeated George Godfrey in 19 rounds to become the colored world champion.

---

[4] *National Police Gazette*, August 4, 1883.

[5] *Toronto Evening Telegram*, January 26, 1883.

[6] *New York Clipper*, May 26, 1888. *Boston Herald*, May 16, 1888.

[7] *San Francisco Daily Examiner*, June 5, 1888.

[8] *San Francisco Daily Examiner*, August 25, 1888.

[9] *National Police Gazette*, January 19, 1889.

Some saw the color line as a legitimate and acceptable social barrier preventing whites from mixing with blacks, consistent with the era's social norm of racial separation. Others saw it as a mere excuse for cowardice. When it was trying to get California champion Joe McAuliffe to fight Peter Jackson, the *San Francisco Examiner* addressed the color line in sport, stating that in America, "competition is free to all." A judge was quoted as saying, "I consider if any pugilist objects to meeting him it will be merely a subterfuge and a virtual acknowledgment that the Australian is a better man, whom the other is afraid to fight." A policeman said, "The only case I know of…in which the color line was utilized is in connection with the colored pugilist Jackson. … I suppose the excuse is as good as another to avoid a dangerous man."

Peter Jackson

Some believed that the color line was "a remnant of the feeling that once existed between master and slave." However, that feeling was the predominant force in American life, despite the *Examiner's* and other semi-progressive periodicals' attempts to attack or change it, at least when it came to boxing. Many felt that McAuliffe would "degrade himself by fighting the dusky Australian."[10]

In defense of their champion, Australians criticized the American color line. The Sydney *Referee* wrote,

> The painful part of all this is that the Americans make his colour a bar to fighting him, a thing that should never have obtained in any country, least of all in the land whose sons actually went to war with their own brothers for the emancipation of these very negroes, whose descendants they now refuse to box with, eat with, or sit beside. Then there is another feature, and that is that in manner, deportment, and decency of living Peter Jackson is to Sullivan and a lot more like him as a schoolgirl is to a slum virago…. It is only these windbags, these men who don't want to meet men who mean real fight, that raise this black shield between them and the chance of defeat at the hands of a coloured antagonist.[11]

---

[10] *San Francisco Daily Examiner,* June 12, 1888.
[11] *Referee* (Sydney), August 2, 1888.

13

Eventually, Joe McAuliffe consented to fight Peter Jackson. After Jackson stopped McAuliffe in 24 rounds in San Francisco on December 28, 1888, San Francisco's black population celebrated the victory.

> The colored population of San Francisco have not had such a jubilee since Mr. Lincoln signed the Emancipation proclamation.... Every one of them had money on Jackson, but deeper even than the pleasure of winning was their joy at the victory of race.... Every one that had bet jingled coin in his pocket, and for once was disposed to dispute the superiority of any other race than his own.

Clearly, boxing had potentially powerful symbolic social implications, which explains why the color line was so important to much of the white population. Such results and their interpretation could threaten the social order. As a result, many felt that Jackson's victory was not good for boxing. "Many regret that Jackson won, on the ground that no first-class Eastern pugilist will care to fight a colored man, and they think it will have a tendency to lessen the regard of outsiders for boxing if a black man demands the championship."

Jackson wanted to fight either Sullivan or Kilrain. He said, "If they draw the color line on me I will claim the championship anyhow. That is a 'chestnut.' They cannot avoid meeting me by such a plea."[12]

San Francisco's California Athletic Club, which promoted and held his fights, supported Jackson. Its delegate said,

> He has fought his way to the front honestly and fairly, and his color must be lost sight of by those who would lay claim to championship honors. Kilrain, Sullivan, and others cannot afford to draw the color line under the circumstances. It would lay them directly open to the charge of cowardice. I do not think the color line, which the war effaced, will stand between Jackson and the championship.[13]

However, the war had not in fact effaced the color line. Rather, more and more folks were attempting to draw the line more definitively, both socially and legally.

Yet, despite the fact that the general social norm was towards separation of the races, some felt that boxing tradition differed.

> A champion of the prize ring must meet all comers. He wouldn't be any kind of a champion if he didn't, and the rules bearing upon fistic encounters, whether of the bare knuckles or of gloves, do not in the remotest way recognize color. The history of the ring shows this conclusively. England's phenomenal fighters and champions met all blacks that challenged them... Molineaux was never objected to

---

[12] *San Francisco Daily Examiner*, December 30, 1888.
[13] *San Francisco Daily Examiner*, December 31, 1888.

because of his Ethiopian skin, and he was black as the ace of spades.[14]

The New York correspondent of the *London Sporting Life* criticized Sullivan's drawing of the color line:

His flat refusal to meet Peter Jackson, on the thin excuse of his objection to fight a coloured man, was already sapping his new found popularity.... Sullivan has already put himself on record as refusing to meet a negro, and he now says that under no consideration will he meet Jackson. Many sporting men construe this as an acknowledgement of Jackson's great fighting powers.... Would it not be a curious thing if Sullivan was whipped by a nigger, and a British subject at that?[15]

On July 8, 1889, in the year's biggest title fight, John L. Sullivan defeated Jake Kilrain after 75 rounds of bareknuckle fighting that lasted about 2 hours, 15 minutes. Sullivan became inactive for the next three years.

Sullivan says that he will never enter the ring again under any consideration. He has done his share of slugging during his rather brief career in the fistic arena, and wanted no more of it. He certainly did not intend to fight the California negro, for the simple reason that he considered it entirely too degrading for a white man to place himself on an equality with a negro.[16]

Australia's *Referee* again criticized the color line:

There can be nothing more false than the idea that sneaking behind the colour-line will protect a white man from the charge of cowardice in refusing to meet a black, or enable him to hold fictitious honours. No man can call himself or be called champion while he refuses to meet and fight a black challenger.... There is no doubt but that this colour line has to go. It is against all manliness and courtesy – a fungus growth of an effete generation of self-styled champions; and the false security of these colour-line drawers has got to have the bottom knocked out of it, and that very shortly.[17]

However, in the United States, Sullivan's feelings regarding separation of the races were consistent with the majority, despite the attempts of many fair-minded sports-writers to encourage equality of opportunity without regard to race, at least when it came to the sport of boxing. Sullivan's popularity did not diminish as a result of his color line stance. Quite the contrary, he was the richest, most famous, and popular hero in all of sports.

---

[14] *Daily Alta California*, January 14, 1889.
[15] *Referee* (Sydney), February 27, 1889, quoting *London Sporting Life*.
[16] *New York Daily Tribune*, July 10, 1889; *Boston Daily Globe*, July 9, 1889.
[17] *Referee* (Sydney), September 11, 1889.

In December 1889, it was reported that a rich white widow wanted to marry Peter Jackson. "Of course a marriage between a white woman and a negro, even though it be a champion pugilist, would be unlawful, but they could get around this either by going three miles out at sea…or going to some foreign country," but "even these evasions and delays will not be necessary, for it is stated that the would-be bride herself has a strain of negro blood in her veins."[18]

In 1890 in Australia, the *Referee* continued calling Sullivan a coward, and provided an explanation for why he was then giving the illusion of moving from his color-line stance:

> From all appearances John L. Sullivan is bluffing most pronouncedly in his pretended negotiations for a fight with Peter Jackson. He was on bed rock, when in desperation, and seeing plainly that unless he came down off his cowardly color line pedestal, Jackson would be hailed Champion of the World, he suddenly coiled up the line and announced his willingness to meet the Australian Champion for a purse, if any club would give one. The California Club at once sprang into the breach and offered 15,000 dol. or 3,000 pounds, for the two to fight for. Seeing that there was an absolute danger that he would actually be matched with and have to fight the Australian champion-extinguisher, Sullivan then changed front, and with his usual braggadocio and insulting manner and language announced that he would fight any white man the club chose to match against him for 10,000 dol., or 2,000 pounds, but he wanted double for niggers…
>
> Now we are told that Sullivan has again raised his demand, and wants 25,000 dol… All this means one little word – bluff! Sullivan is frightened to death at the idea of meeting our long-armed, lithe-limbed champion, and will resort to any means, however despicable, to avoid a meeting with the man he dreads. Having withdrawn his old safeguard, the color line, he falls back on quibbling for a stake that is simply ridiculous as a means of getting out of a fight altogether…. [H]e knows perfectly well that by imposing such prohibitory stakes he evades all possibility of a meeting…. Hence Sullivan is safe, and can still boast himself champion while resorting to a mean subterfuge to avoid risking his hide and his title. The whole Press of America is against Sullivan and his cowardly and unmanly objection to fighting colored men.[19]

Seeking to become the top contender to the crown, San Francisco's James J. Corbett agreed to fight Peter Jackson. Prior to the Corbett-Jackson fight, in February 1891, when Corbett met Sullivan in Chicago, Sullivan said to him, "You're matched to fight that nigger? Well, you shouldn't fight a

[18] *San Francisco Examiner*, December 2, 1889.
[19] *Referee* (Sydney), March 6, 1890.

nigger!" Upset that he was engaging in a mixed-race bout, Corbett's own father would not speak to him for months.[20]

Corbett was the sentimental favorite in the fight, in part owing to his race. "As to prejudice, if there be any, it is all naturally on the side of the native son, as nine people out of ten in this city who take an interest in boxing would, of course, rather see the white native boy win than the colored pugilist from Australia. This is neither strange nor improper." Another said, "It seems as if national pride and a prejudice also in favor of the white as against the black, have had, so far, a good deal to do with the belief in Corbett's being able to get the best of Jackson." Regardless, few were willing to back their opinions with bets on Corbett, who was the odds underdog.[21]

James J. Corbett

On May 21, 1891 in San Francisco, in a fight to the finish, James J. Corbett fought Peter Jackson in a 61-round no-contest, the ruling made by the referee when he felt that neither fighter would be able to knock out the other, and that neither was really trying to do so at that point. The fight had lasted 4 hours.

In June 1891, Sullivan was asked about Peter Jackson. He said, "He is a nigger, and that settles it with me. God did not intend him to be as good as a white man or he would have changed his color, see?"[22]

Later that year, the *Referee* quoted Sullivan as saying,

> I vowed before the public years ago that I would never fight a colored man, because I thought, and still think, that a white man is lowering himself too much when he faces a nigger. Why, God had a view in making them black, and I earnestly believe it was because they were always doomed to be our inferiors. Leaving this aside, if I ever lower myself so much as to step into the ring with this man Jackson, his aspirations will be cut short.[23]

---

[20] James J. Corbett, *The Roar of the Crowd* (N.Y.: G.P. Putnam's Sons, 1925), 117-122.

[21] *San Francisco Chronicle*, April 27, 1891; *Daily Alta California*, May 11, 1891.

[22] *San Francisco Chronicle*, June 27, 1891.

[23] *Referee* (Sydney), September 9, 1891.

In Sullivan's eventual March 1892 public challenge, he stated, "But in this challenge I include all fighters, first come first served - who are white. I will not fight a negro. I never have; I never shall."[24]

Despite some criticism, many praised Sullivan for his color-line stance, particularly in the South. New Orleans, Louisiana's *Daily Picayune* wrote, "I think that the fact that he has faithfully kept his word by not fighting a colored man makes him deserving of much admiration."[25]

On September 7, 1892 in New Orleans, Louisiana, James J. Corbett, who had equaled Peter Jackson, stopped John L. Sullivan in the 21st round to win the world heavyweight championship.

As the biggest prize in boxing, the title with the greatest symbolic value, the heavyweight championship was the most guarded by the color line. The champions who followed Sullivan did not defend against Jackson or other blacks either.

However, lower-weight-class championships found occasional rare exceptions. Canadian-born black George Dixon had won the world featherweight championship in 1890, becoming the first black man to win a world boxing championship. The day before Corbett defeated Sullivan, Dixon, who was the first and only black world champion at the time, defeated a white fighter named Jack Skelly in New Orleans. Blacks were so enthusiastic over the victory,

> [T]hey are loudly proclaiming the superiority of their race, to the great scandal of the whites, who declare that they should not be encouraged to entertain even feelings of equality, much less of superiority. The Olympic Club management have about decided not to hold any more colored contests.

George Dixon

In New York, it was said that the hosting of a mixed-race bout had caused "sharp criticism and much indignation." It was opined that "if a white man puts himself on a level with a negro in a pugilistic contest he deserves to be thoroughly and completely thumped." Folks were upset even at the mere act of a white man entering the ring to fight a black man, regardless of the result. The mere act of fighting a black was in and of itself an attack on the racial social hierarchy, because competing with a black fighter was to concede that he had the right to compete on the same level.

[24] *Philadelphia Inquirer*, March 6, 1892.
[25] *Daily Picayune*, September 4, 1892.

Some thought that although mixed-race contests could take place in the North, "where there are very few negroes," such contests in the South would only "arouse a bitter feeling between the races which will lead to bloody affrays."[26]

The New Orleans-based *Times-Democrat* said that hosting a mixed-race bout had been a serious mistake; one that it hoped would not be repeated. Although there had been fair play, "it was a disagreeable duty to all Southern men present." It was concerned by the social message that such bouts conveyed.

> It was a mistake to match a negro and a white man, a mistake to bring the races together on any terms of equality, even in the prize ring…for, among the ignorant negroes the idea has naturally been created that it was a test of the strength and fighting powers of Caucasian and African. … [T]he colored population of this city…because of [Dixon's] victory…are far more confident than they ever were before of the equality of the races, and disposed to claim more for themselves than we intend to concede. … We of the South who know the fallacy and danger of this doctrine of race equality, who are opposed to placing the negro on any terms of equality, who have insisted on a separation of the races in church, hotel, car, saloon and theatre; who believe that the law ought to step in and forever forbid the idea of equality by making marriages between them illegal, are heartily opposed to any arrangement encouraging this equality, which give negroes false ideas and dangerous beliefs. … Some may argue that there is no race question in the prize ring. We think differently. …
>
> Mr. John L. Sullivan has set a good example in this matter. … [H]e has persistently refused to meet a negro in the ring. No one can believe that he has done this for any other reasons than his confidence that such contests place the races more or less on terms of equality.[27]

The color line was about power. Allowing blacks to compete with whites would convey the idea to blacks that they would or could have the opportunity to advance themselves to the level of whites, or even above them. That was seen as a dangerous threat to the caste system. Hence, boxing and social politics were intertwined.

William Muldoon, Sullivan's old trainer, said, "There should be colored champions and white champions, and I would like to see the line drawn once and for all."[28]

---

[26] *New York Herald*, September 3, 1892.
[27] *Times-Democrat*, September 8, 1892.
[28] *National Police Gazette*, September 24, 1892.

Immediately after defeating Sullivan, Jim Corbett's trainer/manager, Bill Delaney, a staunch color-line supporter, said,

> You can say that I am in a position to announce that Corbett will not meet Jackson again. He is averse to meeting a negro on principle; besides, all of his friends in the South do not want him to again face the black man. Jim is anxious to please them in everything, as they have proven true to him. Why should Jim fight Jackson, anyhow? He has virtually defeated him once, and that is proof positive of Jackson's inability to cope with him.[29]

Like Sullivan before him, Corbett had to absorb some criticism for not taking on Jackson. One paper wrote in late 1892,

> But does Corbett really expect the country to take stock in his sudden access of aristocratic exclusiveness, and to believe that his refusal to meet Peter Jackson springs from inherent distaste and conscious superiority? ... Such a refusal will be understood everywhere...as meaning that he is afraid of Jackson. There is no color line in professional pugilism. If Corbett avoids Jackson, after having met him once, the world will construe it as a back-out, and he will no longer be champion in any proper meaning of the term.[30]

At that time, boxing was illegal in most of the country. Politicians often pulled out all stops to prevent big fights, even when no issue of race was involved. Therefore, very few clubs were anxious to support an interracial heavyweight championship, particularly given that most legislators were staunchly opposed to allowing boxing at all, regardless of race.

In 1894, one writer noted,

> Up to date very few of the colored stars of the fistic world have gone wrong or finished second best in meetings with white men. ... It is humiliating, perhaps, but the bald pate fact seems to be that in the roped arena Africa has walked away with the top knot in nearly every encounter with the boasted "superior race." Joe Choynski and Peter Maher, in the defeats they administered to George Godfrey, are pretty much the only exceptions to the rule of recent pugilism. ... Is the cause that the white man in pugilism obstinately refuses to deny himself and to train scrupulously and be manageable like the colored one? Or is there really something in the difference of structure of the two races which makes a white man weaker in the parts above the belt that are, by the rules, made a fair target for fist smashes?

---

[29] *New York Sun,* September 9, 1892.
[30] *Referee,* November 9, 1892, quoting a Boston exchange.

Maher has toppled over Craig, Corbett should do Jackson, and Plimmer is very likely to lower Dixon's colors. A new supply of colored stock will then be needed.[31]

Certainly, there was a cognizance of race as a significant factor in analyzing the sport. Success by blacks in fights with whites posed a threat to the social order. Boxing's omnipresent legal obstacles most certainly were not going to subside should a mixed-race heavyweight championship contest take place.

However, many fair-minded sportsmen and writers wanted to see a contest between the best two fighters, regardless of color. Such fights made great copy, and intrigued fight fans, giving them a rooting interest, often making such bouts financially lucrative.

Ironically, it would be a Southern club which offered a sufficiently large purse required for a fight of the magnitude of a Jackson-Corbett championship bout. There were those willing to put race aside in order to make a match between the best.

Despite what his trainer/manager Bill Delaney said, Corbett did not openly draw the color line. He was willing to fight Jackson in the South, in New Orleans, where such a fight would be legal, but Jackson refused to box in a mixed-race bout anywhere but in the North. He was literally afraid that he might be killed were he to fight Corbett in the South, particularly if he won. However, no Northern club put up the money necessary for such a bout, and very few jurisdictions legally allowed lengthy fights. Corbett refused to fight Jackson in a limited rounds bout in the U.S., nor would he fight him overseas. Hence, Jackson never fought for the title. Most thought that Corbett would have found any excuse not to fight him anyhow, for he knew it would be a very tough fight.[32]

In 1894, while in the U.S., even English-born and New Zealand- and Australian-trained Bob Fitzsimmons, who had fought blacks in Australia, and had even received instruction from Peter Jackson while there, said that if he won the heavyweight championship, he would draw the color line. "I will fight anybody except Jackson, whom I would not meet because he is a colored man."[33]

Given that Australians had supported the right of a black man, an Australian champion in Peter Jackson, to challenge for the heavyweight championship; it was not entirely coincidental that eventually Australia would be the site of the first mixed-race heavyweight championship.

In 1895, former champion John L. Sullivan said, "No man of principle…will fight in a ring with a colored man. No man can say I ever

[31] *Buffalo Courier,* July 18, 1894, quoting *Boston Post.*

[32] *New York Clipper,* August 18, 1894.

[33] *New York Sun,* October 2, 1894; *National Police Gazette,* October 20, 1894; *San Francisco Chronicle,* November 14, 1896.

refused to fight when the time came for a fight, but I never would fight with a nigger."[34]

Bob Fitzsimmons

The ongoing antipathy towards mixed-race bouts was illustrated by a January 1897 New York news article which said that although the South generally had been more accepting of boxing than the North, there were indications that the South was shifting its position, in part as a result of mixed-race bouts. In a fight in Louisiana between a black boxer named Joe Green and a white boxer called "the terrible Swede," Green was about to knock out the Swede, and only one more blow was needed.

That blow, however, was not delivered, for at the critical moment Judge Long, one of the most prominent residents of the neighborhood, jumped into the ring with a pistol in his right hand, and with a mighty oath declared that so long as he lived "no nigger should ever whip a white man in Jefferson parish." The effect was instantaneous. The judge's remark, if not heartily applauded, certainly met with the approval of the multitude, for the fight was declared off and "the terrible Swede" spared the ignominy of being defeated by a man with a black skin...

Without desiring to be impertinent, however, and more as a matter of information than anything else, may we ask our Southern contemporaries to what, if any extent, Judge Long really reflected the sentiment of the white people of the South toward the colored brother? ... The question should be answered honestly. There is no occasion to beat bout the bush.... It must be admitted that the colored brother himself is largely responsible for the existing condition of affairs. But why be hypocritical about it? Why try to create false impressions in Northern communities as to the exact feeling entertained toward the negro by the white population in the Southern states? We must do Judge Long the credit of saying that he has the courage of his convictions. He is the representative of a type. But we do not especially admire the type.[35]

---

[34] *Brooklyn Daily Eagle*, December 10, 1895.
[35] *Brooklyn Daily Eagle*, January 25, 1897.

On March 17, 1897 in Carson City, Nevada, a state which recently had legalized boxing, Bob Fitzsimmons won the world heavyweight championship when in the 14th round he knocked out James J. Corbett with a left hook to the body. He did not defend the title until June 1899 in New York, when James J. Jeffries knocked out Fitzsimmons in the 11th round to win the crown.

James J. Jeffries

Although James Jeffries had boxed black men in non-title bouts, defeating Hank Griffin, Peter Jackson, and Bob Armstrong, in 1901, Jeffries openly drew the color line when it came to world title fights. Just as he had done with Corbett, Jeff's trainer/manager Bill Delaney insisted that Jeffries would draw the color line as champion. Hence, the heavyweight championship remained a prize for which only whites could apply.[36]

This was the world of boxing that black boxer Jack Johnson entered and endured, and from which he emerged and prevailed.

---

[36] *National Police Gazette*, December 7, 1901.

CHAPTER 2

The Legal and Social World That Jack Johnson Entered

To understand the perception about and reporting of Jack Johnson and other black fighters, and to grasp fully Johnson's struggle, impact, and historic relevance, one must understand the times from which he emerged.

In order to comprehend and appreciate the state of race in America during Johnson's life, one must go back in time and understand something about slavery, which in part formed the foundation for the world's racial beliefs. A slave was an object or chattel, a thing with no rights; a tool or piece of property to be owned and used as its owner saw fit, like a mule or horse.

Often captured and sold by fellow Africans, slaves had to survive the long walk from inland Africa to the coast, as well as the lengthy middle passage on ships to their final destinations, chained and packed in like sardines and subject to disease, starvation, and unsanitary conditions. A large percentage perished before even reaching the Americas. This was not considered human loss, but rather loss of cargo, to be analyzed economically, viewed in the same way as when some food might spoil in transit on a ship.

Slaves were seen as less than or not even human, but rather as wild beasts who needed to be controlled and tamed, and therefore entitled to no rights whatsoever. This perception helped justify their enslavement, and in order to continue to justify slavery and unequal treatment of blacks, that perception needed to be reinforced by the popular culture. Some even argued that slavery improved their lives. Yet, it was illegal to teach slaves to read or write, for educated slaves could be dangerous. Any attempts to escape or rebel were quashed with severe brutality in order to instill fear into other slaves. To harm or kill a slave was the moral equivalent of crushing a bug, or for some, a horse of some value. Slaves had economic value to their owners, as did horses, so it did not necessarily pay to maim or kill. One did not want to lose or damage valuable property, but the bottom line was that a master could do as he pleased. Ultimately, the treatment that slave-masters afforded slaves could vary from cruel to kind, as different motivational tools could be used, depending upon the individual slave-master, the slave, and circumstances.

Slavery of blacks had existed in colonial America at least since the 1600s, so for hundreds of years it was part of the fabric of American life. Therefore, beliefs about blacks as property and as being inferior to whites were deeply ingrained into the psyche of Americans. Beliefs that are deeply embedded into a society over hundreds of years are not easily changed, and often there are self-interested forces at work determined not to change them.

Concerned that United States President Abraham Lincoln and Congressmen from the North might gradually limit or even eliminate slavery, in late 1860 and early 1861 the South seceded from the Union. This led to the U.S. Civil War, the most costly war in terms of casualties in U.S. history, with well over half a million dead from various causes associated with the War. During the Civil War, on September 22, 1862 and January 1, 1863, President Abraham Lincoln issued emancipation proclamations abolishing slavery. However, slavery was not officially legally abolished until December 1865, after the Civil War was over, with the ratification of the 13th Amendment to the U.S. Constitution, which abolished slavery and involuntary servitude except as punishment for a crime. The passage of this amendment did not come without some debate and resistance.

Although slavery had ended, its abolition did not mean that blacks would have the same rights as whites. Far from it. It just meant that they were no longer slaves.

There was a relatively short period of Reconstruction, from 1865 to 1877, when some federal laws and constitutional amendments were enacted to protect the civil rights of blacks. These included the 14th Amendment's granting of citizenship to all persons born in the U.S. (including blacks, overruling the 1857 U.S. Supreme Court's *Dred Scott* decision, which held that even free blacks born in the U.S. were not citizens), and its requirement of equal protection under the law, and the 15th Amendment's requirement that the right to vote shall not be abridged or denied based upon race. During this 12-year period, many blacks became educated, financially successful, and obtained political rights. Some were even elected to political office. However, such progress did not last very long, nor did the enforcement of such rights.

Even though the Civil War's warfield battles technically had ended, another war emerged and continued. The battle over race and power had not concluded, but just shifted into another phase, where the United States had its own form of internal social war. The seeds of bitterness sown by the war continued. Southerners saw the North as having destroyed their country, their way of life, and as having taken away their valuable investments in and property rights to black slaves, without compensation. Slavery had ended only as a result of force, not as a result of folks being convinced that it was wrong. On April 15, 1865, Abraham Lincoln became the first U.S. president to be assassinated, the motive being Southern revenge.

Southerners were very concerned about what impact freed blacks would have on their post-Civil War society. Blacks technically might have been freed, but the South was determined to ensure that it ended there, that black rights would be severely limited and circumscribed. The Ku Klux Klan emerged in 1865. Other secret and not so secret societies were created, which were determined to make sure that freed blacks knew their place, which was subjugated to the white race. These reactionary societies were willing to use violence and lynchings - extrajudicial public rituals of mob violence - to enforce the social order and limit black participation in politics.

Even many Northerners who believed that slavery was wrong did not necessarily believe that freed blacks should have the same rights as whites, or that they should be treated in the same way. They just thought that blacks should not be enslaved.

Eventually, Southern politicians returned to national political power, and they were determined to limit black rights either de jure or de facto. As time passed, a significant number of Northern whites in positions of political power decided that they did not care for the ascendance of black economic or political power either, and those Northern whites who were tired of the race issue, and who wanted to gain Southern support in the 1877 presidential election, made a compromise by agreeing to withdraw troops from the South, which had to some degree ensured recognition of black civil rights.

After President Rutherford B. Hayes withdrew Union troops from the South in 1877, white Democratic Southerners quickly reversed the advances of Reconstruction. Without the presence of the military, Southern blacks would have little protection to ensure that their civil rights were not violated. For the most part, the South could do whatever it wanted.

The state governments that emerged following the troop withdrawal from the South passed legislation known as Jim Crow laws, which mandated segregation of blacks from whites. Enacted laws also made voter registration and elections more restrictive, so as to eliminate the black vote and black political power. Poll taxes, literacy and comprehension tests, and residency and record-keeping requirements limiting the ability to vote effectively disenfranchised large portions of the population that were poor or illiterate. Naturally, this included the vast majority of blacks, given that they were former slaves, most of whom had never been taught to read or write (as a result of laws making it illegal to teach slaves to read or write), or if they had learned to read and write during Reconstruction, as a great many did, they were still relatively poor and could not afford to pay poll taxes. Since schools were separated by race, black schools were usually underfunded. Furthermore, many black children had to drop out of school to help support their financially struggling families. Those who could not vote could not serve on juries. Hence, for the most part, all-white juries would decide the fates of blacks accused of crimes, as well as whites accused of crimes against blacks. Essentially, blacks would have almost no political influence or power. And it was all legal. State and federal courts upheld these laws.[37] Violence and intimidation would do the rest.

A caste system based on race was created via law and by custom. Public accommodations for blacks were invariably underfunded, inferior, and fewer. Hence, political, economic, educational, and social disadvantages for blacks predominated and were perpetuated and ingrained into the society.

During Reconstruction, the U.S. Congress had passed the Civil Rights Act of 1875. It guaranteed that everyone, regardless of race, was entitled to equal accommodations and privileges in public places such as inns, hotels, public transportation such as railroad cars, and theaters and other places of recreation. In fact, the Act was ignored.

On October 15, 1883, the U.S. Supreme Court declared the Civil Rights Act of 1875 unconstitutional. The Court held that the Act was not consistent with the U.S. Congress' powers under the 13th or 14th Amendments, and that Congress had exceeded the scope of its power. The Court said it was no infringement of those amendments to refuse to any person the equal accommodations and privileges of an inn, place of public entertainment, or the like, and to do so was not a badge of slavery or involuntary servitude implying subjugation. This was a harbinger of the poor future for black legal rights. The U.S. Congress did not pass another civil rights law until 1957.

In his lone dissent from the majority opinion, Justice John Harlan (a Kentucky lawyer) wrote,

> It is, I submit, scarcely just to say that the colored race has been the special favorite of the laws. What the nation, through Congress, has

---

[37] The U.S. Supreme Court in *Williams v. Mississippi*, 170 U.S. 213 (1898), upheld voter registration requirements for voters to pass a literacy test and pay poll taxes, and in *Giles v. Harris*, 189 U.S. 475 (1903), upheld a state constitution's requirements for voter registration and qualifications even though they had a discriminatory impact upon blacks.

sought to accomplish in reference to that race is, what had already been done in every state in the Union for the white race, to secure and protect rights belonging to them as freemen and citizens; nothing more. The one underlying purpose of congressional legislation has been to enable the black race to take the rank of mere citizens. The difficulty has been to compel a recognition of their legal right to take that rank, and to secure the enjoyment of privileges belonging, under the law, to them as a component part of the people for whose welfare and happiness government is ordained.

Black leader Frederick Douglass said the decision was "a step backward and places the United States in the rear of the civilized nations of Europe and America. Its moral effect will, he thinks, be mischievous." It was said that the decision would not actually affect the colored people in the South, because no one had obeyed the law there anyhow.[38]

Also in 1883, in deciding *Pace v. Alabama*, 106 U.S. 583 (1883), the U.S. Supreme Court upheld as constitutional Alabama's anti-miscegenation statute, which prohibited marriage, cohabitation and sexual relations between whites and blacks. States were within their rights to prevent sexual relations based upon race. The Court argued that it was the duty of the state to protect marriage as a public institution. The state had a duty to protect married couples against disturbances such as interracial relationships, because such relationships between whites and blacks "must naturally cause discord, shame, disruption of family circles, and estrangement," and therefore were incompatible with the family life that the state needed to protect. This interpretation of the constitution was the law for the next 81-plus years.[39]

In 1888, U.S. Senator John Ingalls (from Kansas), who the previous year had been elected President pro tempore of the Senate, said the "negroes are growing blacker, and that the tendency is toward segregation." He and others feared that the black population might one day outnumber whites. "He fears negro supremacy." However, the *San Francisco Chronicle* said,

> Neither the country nor the South is in any such danger. ... Instead of a gloomy view, we think the future full of hope and promise. This fine country was not conquered from the red man for the black; it will never cease to be a white man's country, unless all history is false, and the superior race shall yield to the inferior.[40]

Another San Francisco paper noted,

---

[38] *Philadelphia Press*, October 16, 17, 1883. The Court's decision was not applicable to the District of Columbia, but affected all of the states.

[39] This ruling was not overturned by the Supreme Court until 1964 in *McLaughlin v. Florida* (holding that laws prohibiting interracial cohabitation of unmarried persons were unconstitutional) and in 1967 in *Loving v. Virginia* (holding that laws prohibiting interracial marriage were unconstitutional).

[40] *San Francisco Chronicle*, December 24, 1888.

Ingalls has sounded the keynote in declaring that there is an ethnological bar to the two races dwelling together upon terms of political equality. ...

They [blacks] must demonstrate their fitness for the duties of citizenship. Then that fitness is not yet demonstrated, and yet the denial of rights which it is confessed they are not yet proved fit to exercise is ascribed to "prejudice." ... Lincoln believed that the only solution of the problem of the negroes' destiny would be found in their deportation and colonization in Hayti and Liberia, and it is opportunely recalled that General Grant thought of colonizing them in San Domingo. ...

But we begin to realize now that the colored people love the whites so much that they are determined to stay with them. The Governments of Liberia, Hayti and San Domingo are all monumental failures. The colored man cannot get along by himself.

That is to say, the colored man, wherever he attempts to govern himself, is a failure. He can't get along by himself. ...

The white man can get along by himself. ... A white minority, anywhere on earth, finally conquers a colored majority...

But we need not discuss the matter. It is getting discussion enough by the men who rightly believed that the negro did not deserve slavery, and who now confess that they were so right in that proposition that they made the mistake of omitting to see that he also did not deserve citizenship.[41]

Generally in the United States, the "negro race" was seen as an inferior, potentially dangerous and barbarous race, to be viewed with suspicion and not to be allowed to mix with whites on the same level. In 1889, Louisiana's *Times-Democrat* said, "When the negro race is left to itself it relapses into that state of barbarism in which it originally existed." The *Houston Free South* said, "[T]he young negroes – who are termed 'coons' and never knew what slavery was, are a nuisance – a curse to the South." Despite the fact that Southern Democrats were perceived as the most racist at that time, the *Williamsburg Journal* said, "It is the fixed policy of the Republican Administration to 'draw the line,' to establish a white-man's Republican Party in the South, and thus leave the colored man out in the 'cold.'"[42]

Racism and separation of the races did not just exist in the South. In 1889, the *Times-Democrat* alleged that color prejudice was actually stronger in the North, but hypocrisy tried to conceal it. It noted that Northerners were extremely upset that some blacks had been recruited recently in the South as

---

[41] *Daily Alta California,* January 4, 1889.
[42] *Times-Democrat,* July 1889; *Clarion-Ledger,* July 18, 1889, quoting *Houston Free South* and *Williamsburg Journal.*

postmasters. It called attention to the fact that Northern merchants would not hire blacks as clerks and salespersons, no matter how deserving. White Northern mechanics refused to work with negroes. Northerners would not work under a negro foreman, though this was not uncommon in the South. In New Jersey, blacks were not allowed to bathe in the ocean at the same time as whites. It asked of the North,

> Does not a colored servant cook your meal, another wait on your table, another shave your face...? Well, then, I am unable to see why it is that if you can take your breakfast from black hands, you can't also take your letters and newspapers from the hands of negro postmasters....

> There is nothing extraordinary about this particular manifestation of the color prejudice. There are other exhibitions of the same feeling, in the North as well as in the South, which are even more remarkable....

> While such things are true at the North, it is arrant hypocrisy for Northerners to prate about the "insane prejudice" of Southerners against the negro. The truth is that this color prejudice is entertained by most white people – by a great many who concede that it seems unreasonable, and yet who confess that they cannot get over it....

> We must remember that it is only about thirty years since Abraham Lincoln, in his famous joint debate with Douglas, in answering on the 18th of September, 1858, the question whether he was "really in favor of producing a perfect equality between the negroes and white people," replied:

> "I am not, nor ever have been, in favor of bringing about in any way the social and political equality of the white and black races. I am not, nor ever have been, in favor of making voters or jurors of negroes, nor of qualifying them to hold office, nor to intermarry with white people; and I will say in addition to this that there is a physical difference between the white and black races which I believe will forever forbid the two races living together on terms of social and political equality."[43]

---

[43] *Times-Democrat*, July 22, 1889. Abraham Lincoln also said in that 1858 debate, "And inasmuch as they [blacks and whites] cannot so live [together on terms of social and political equality], while they do remain together there must be the position of superior and inferior, and I as much as any other man am in favor of having the superior position assigned to the white race. I say upon this occasion I do not perceive that because the white man is to have the superior position the negro should be denied every thing. I do not understand that because I do not want a negro woman for a slave I must necessarily want her for a wife. ... So it seems to me quite possible for us to get along without making either slaves or wives of negroes. I will add to this that I have never seen, to my knowledge, a man, woman or child who was in favor of producing a perfect equality, social and political, between negroes and white men."

In 1890, Jackson, Mississippi's *Clarion-Ledger* wrote, "The declaration in the Declaration of Independence of the United States, that all men are created equal is false, utterly false in every particular." In fact, at the time of the drafting of the Declaration, slaves were not considered to be men, but rather property. Responding to then U.S. President Benjamin Harrison's attacks on the South's treatment of blacks, it defended,

> There were no Southern men engaged in the slave trade and no Southern men having slave ships…. I can point out to him and his Northern allies crimes that they have committed against the negro very lately much greater than selling him into slavery – if conspiring against his life is worse.[44]

In 1891, it was noted that although the negro population as a whole had been vastly growing, as a percentage of the total population it had been diminishing. In 1810, the negro population was 700,000 or 19% of the total U.S. population. As of the 1890 census, even though their total numbers were in the millions, they were only 11.9% percent of the population (7,488,676 blacks out of a total U.S. population of 62,947,714). "Facts such as these indicate that the negro problem will become less and less rather than more and more a political problem." The writer meant that there was less for whites to fear, owing to the fact that the black vote was being further weakened by its reduced percentage of the population.[45]

In early 1892, a black lawyer said, "[W]hite people fear the negro. They are afraid to give him a fair chance in life. … They show their cowardice by claiming his utter inferiority, and at the same time placing every conceivable barrier across his pathway."[46]

The year 1892 saw a U.S. national record 161 black lynchings (since record-keeping began in 1882). Lynching was a way to ensure that blacks knew their place and remained fearful of attempting to defy the social order. It could be used as a form of vigilante justice, without trial or due process, to punish blacks publicly for alleged crimes. It was also used as a way to intimidate blacks from voting or asserting any political power.[47]

That same year, in 1892, Homer Plessy, who was 7/8 caucasian and only 1/8 black, decided to challenge the constitutionality of Louisiana's law requiring colored folk to ride in a different railroad passenger car than

[44] *Clarion-Ledger*, January 9, 1890.

[45] *Minneapolis Tribune*, July 5, 1891. By 1900, there were 8,883,994 blacks in the U.S. During the Reconstruction era, as of 1870, Afro-American literacy was at 79.9%, but by 1900, as a result of segregationist policies, it had plummeted to 44.5%. Up to 1900, nearly 400 blacks had graduated college. *Seattle Republican*, March 23, 1906.

[46] *New York Sun*, February 14, 1892.

[47] Robert L. Zangrando, *About Lynching*, excerpt from article in *The Reader's Companion to American History*, Editors Eric Foner and John A. Garraty. Houghton Mifflin Co., 1991.

whites.[48] Although he could pass as white, he informed the conductor of his racial lineage, and then took a seat in the whites-only car. He refused to leave the car and sit in the coloreds-only car, and therefore was arrested for committing a crime. His mere presence amongst whites was a crime. Plessy was found guilty and sentenced to a $25 fine or 20 days in jail if he could not pay. His case was appealed all the way to the U.S. Supreme Court.

In 1896, the Supreme Court of the United States, deciding *Plessy v. Ferguson*, 163 U.S. 537 (1896), ruled against Homer Plessy and held that a law mandating separate but equal accommodations based upon race did not violate the 14th amendment's equal protection clause. The Court said,

> The object of the amendment was undoubtedly to enforce the absolute equality of the two races before the law, but, in the nature of things, it could not have been intended to abolish distinctions based upon color, or to enforce social, as distinguished from political, equality, or a commingling of the two races upon terms unsatisfactory to either. Laws permitting, and even requiring, their separation, in places where they are liable to be brought into contact, do not necessarily imply the inferiority of either race to the other, and have been generally, if not universally, recognized as within the competency of the state legislatures in the exercise of their police power. The most common instance of this is connected with the establishment of separate schools for white and colored children, which have been held to be a valid exercise of the legislative power even by courts of states where the political rights of the colored race have been longest and most earnestly enforced....

> [W]e think the enforced separation of the races, as applied to the internal commerce of the state, neither abridges the privileges or immunities of the colored man, deprives him of his property without due process of law, nor denies him the equal protection of the laws, within the meaning of the fourteenth amendment...

> If the two races are to meet upon terms of social equality, it must be the result of natural affinities, a mutual appreciation of each other's merits, and a voluntary consent of individuals.

In his lone dissent, Justice John Harlan, who had also dissented from the Court's decision overturning the Civil Rights Act of 1875, wrote:

> The white race deems itself to be the dominant race in this country. And so it is, in prestige, in achievements, in education, in wealth, and in power. So, I doubt not, it will continue to be for all time, if it remains true to its great heritage, and holds fast to the principles of constitutional liberty. But in view of the constitution, in the eye of the

---

[48] Although it already had a law which specified that blacks could not ride with whites in the same railroad cars, in 1890, Louisiana also passed a law requiring separate accommodations for colored (people of mixed white and black ancestry) and white passengers on railroads.

law, there is in this country no superior, dominant, ruling class of citizens. There is no caste here. Our constitution is color-blind, and neither knows nor tolerates classes among citizens. In respect of civil rights, all citizens are equal before the law....

It is therefore to be regretted that this high tribunal, the final expositor of the fundamental law of the land, has reached the conclusion that it is competent for a state to regulate the enjoyment by citizens of their civil rights solely upon the basis of race.

In my opinion, the judgment this day rendered will, in time, prove to be quite as pernicious as the decision made by this tribunal in the Dred Scott Case.[49]

It was adjudged in that case that the descendants of Africans who were imported into this country, and sold as slaves, were not included nor intended to be included under the word "citizens" in the constitution, and could not claim any of the rights and privileges which that instrument provided for and secured to citizens of the United States; that, at time of the adoption of the constitution, they were "considered as a subordinate and inferior class of beings, who had been subjugated by the dominant race, and, whether emancipated or not, yet remained subject to their authority, and had no rights or privileges but such as those who held the power and the government might choose to grant them." 17 How. 393, 404....

Sixty millions of whites are in no danger from the presence here of eight millions of blacks. The destinies of the two races in this country are indissolubly linked together, and the interests of both require that the common government of all shall not permit the seeds of race hate to be planted under the sanction of law. What can more certainly arouse race hate, what more certainly create and perpetuate a feeling of distrust between these races, than state enactments which, in fact, proceed on the ground that colored citizens are so inferior and degraded that they cannot be allowed to sit in public coaches occupied by white citizens? That, as all will admit, is the real meaning of such legislation as was enacted in Louisiana. ...

State enactments regulating the enjoyment of civil rights upon the basis of race, and cunningly devised to defeat legitimate results of the war under the pretence of recognizing equality of rights, can have no other result than to render permanent peace impossible and to keep

[49] In *Dred Scott v. Sandford*, 60 U.S. 393 (1857), the U.S. Supreme Court ruled that slaves and their descendants, whether or not they were slaves, were not protected by the Constitution and could never be U.S. citizens, and because they were not citizens, they could not sue in court, and Congress had no authority to prohibit slavery in federal territories, and that slaves, as private property, could not be taken away from their owners without due process.

alive a conflict of races the continuance of which must do harm to all concerned. ...

[C]itizens of the black race in Louisiana, many of whom, perhaps, risked their lives for the preservation of the Union, ... who have all the legal rights that belong to white citizens, are yet declared to be criminals, liable to imprisonment, if they ride in a public coach occupied by citizens of the white race. ...

If evils will result from the commingling of the two races upon public highways established for the benefit of all, they will be infinitely less than those that will surely come from state legislation regulating the enjoyment of civil rights upon the basis of race. We boast of the freedom enjoyed by our people above all other peoples. But it is difficult to reconcile that boast with a state of the law which, practically, puts the brand of servitude and degradation upon a large class of our fellow citizens, our equals before the law. The thin disguise of "equal" accommodations for passengers in railroad coaches will not mislead anyone, nor atone for the wrong this day done.

The majority's decision meant that social discrimination was legally acceptable and enforceable. States were free to enact laws requiring separation of the races in all aspects of life. It was essentially an affirmation of the prevailing public opinion. This would be the law in the United States until 1954, when the Supreme Court reversed the *Plessy* majority opinion's logic in *Brown v. Board of Education,* in that case as it pertained to school segregation. Other subsequent decisions finally ended legalized segregation upon the basis of race.

In actual application, these segregation laws led to treatment and accommodations that were usually inferior to those provided for white Americans, systematizing economic, educational, and social disadvantages. The accommodations were in fact both separate and unequal.

In 1896, the year that *Plessy v. Ferguson* was decided, a young black man by the name of Arthur John Johnson, later known as Jack Johnson, was 18 years old.

CHAPTER 3

Early Development:
Galveston and Beyond

Jack Johnson was born as Arthur John Johnson in Galveston, Texas on March 31, 1878; thirteen years after the U.S. Civil War ended, and one year after the Union withdrew its troops from the South. Galveston was a southern Texas coastal town on the Gulf of Mexico, about 50 miles southeast of Houston. The town had a thriving port, and a population of about 25,000.

Sometimes Johnson would be known by his now well-known alias, Jack Johnson, as in 'Black Jack,' while at others he would be called by his birthname, which was Arthur John Johnson. Sometimes he was even called John Arthur Johnson.

His parents, Henry and Tina "Tiny" Johnson, were both former slaves. Some say Henry Johnson was born a slave in Maryland. He traced his ancestry back to modern-day Ghana, Africa. Johnson claimed that his father fought in the Civil War. Henry was a woodcutter, laborer, saloon porter, and eventually, in 1888 he became the Galveston, Texas school janitor for the district. Jack said his father was employed as a cleaning man. Tina Johnson, generally known as Tiny, was 19 years younger than Henry. They were members of the Methodist church.

Henry and Tiny worked blue-collar jobs to raise their children. They had Lucy, Jennie, Arthur, Henry, Fannie, and Charles. Three other girls died at birth. All of the Johnson children learned to read and write. Jack possibly had some half-brothers and sisters as well.

A 1910 article gave an account of Johnson's youth. It said he was a school boy at 10, a carriage painter's apprentice at 13, amateur fighter at 16, politician at 18, and professional fighter at 19. He had three sisters and one brother living as of 1910. Jack attended school through the 10th grade, but was forced to leave school to help earn money for the family. His father had great difficulty making ends meet.[50]

Johnson's various jobs in Galveston included helping his father with the cleaning business by sweeping up with a broom, assisting a milkman by taking care of his horse and delivering milk bottles up and down staircases, for which he earned 10 cents a week, and working on the docks as a stevedore, loading and unloading ships. Other odd jobs throughout his early life included horse trainer, bread baker's assistant, porter, and barber's

---

[50] *San Francisco Chronicle*, July 10, 1910.

assistant. Johnson was also a talented bass violin player. Life was not easy in Galveston, and Johnson said the days when his stomach went empty were more numerous than the feast days. He often suffered from hunger.

There is a claim that Johnson was a prominent member of a local gang of white and black boys that roamed the docks. Johnson said he hung around the docks and in the streets, watching big boys throw dice.

Johnson said he began getting into fights with fellow Galveston dockworkers at about age 13, in the early 1890s. He fought bigger and older youths and suffered many beatings, but was capable of standing much punishment.

Some have reported that Johnson was a timid youngster who at first was a mark for the boys at school and received many a bad beating. His mother claimed that his own sister had to do some fighting for him. Enraged at this, when he was about 14 years old, his mom told him to fight his own battles, to fight the bullies back and beat them, or else she would give him a worse whipping when he returned home. From then on, Jack had courage and fought back and won.

Another story his mother told was that when Jack was 13 or 14 years old, he was beaten in a fight. She gave Jack a sound thrashing for getting beat. She told him that she would administer the same every time he allowed anyone to whip him. Thereafter, Johnson did well.[51]

The story told in 1910 was that at age 13, Jack was yanked out of school and put on a train for Houston, where his father had arranged to put him under an apprenticeship to a wagon painter by the name of Kellie.

It turned out that Kellie was a professor in the art of self-defense and gave Johnson some boxing lessons. Jack progressed rapidly. Every night after work, the two would train in the vacant barn in back of the shop, and spar in friendly fashion. Jack was only a 123-pound featherweight at the time.

Johnson enjoyed boxing a lot more than he liked painting. He was less than motivated as a painter, and eventually, after about a year, he returned to Galveston.

The story was later altered, and it was said that around the age of 15, in Dallas, Johnson became employed as an apprentice by a house-and-carriage painter, a white man named Walter Lewis. Lewis had been an amateur boxer, and he taught Johnson how to box almost every evening in the back room of his shop. Jack sparred with Lewis and others. Lewis encouraged him to pursue a career in boxing. Jack was with Lewis for about six months before returning to Galveston.

Johnson said he never sought a fight, but he never avoided one either. He took up boxing in order to be able to compete with the boys, and he attained a bit of a reputation as a fighter. Eventually, Jack had a street fight with a black boy named Jackie Morris, the neighborhood tyrant and

[51] *Richmond Planet*, January 9, 1909; *New York Herald*, December 28, 1908.

reigning bully of the docks. Johnson got his revenge. He later said, "Fights between kids give them self-confidence and are the first lesson in the struggle for survival."

Over the next several years, Johnson engaged in a number of trades. He improved the most, though, in fighting, for Kellie's lessons served him well. The neighborhood boys soon found out. He was no longer an easy mark, but became the top dog of his gang. He eventually discovered that he was the best fighter of all the local gangs.

At 16, Arthur Johnson had a street fight with a local colored tough named Dave Pierson, a grown and toughened man, who was older, heavier, and more experienced, yet Jack defeated him. People asked, "Did you hear what 'Lil Arthur' did?" Jack said that was how his nickname "Lil' Artha" was generated.

At age 16, he decided to try amateur boxing. After a try-out, he was matched against a negro boy of his own weight for a 4-round bout. Jack won with a 3rd round knockout. He received $1, of which he gave his manager 25 cents. He used the remaining 75 cents to purchase a batch of pies, which he divided amongst his crowd of admirers. From that point on, the fight fever had caught him.

Johnson was quite successful in his fights, and his reputation grew. He was an amateur middleweight champion, weighing about 156 pounds. He became popular amongst local blacks and commanded a large following.

Jack said he once stayed 4 rounds with a heavyweight boxer named Bob Thompson, who offered $25 to anyone who could last 4 rounds with him. The smaller Johnson barely made it, but he lasted the 4 rounds and earned the money. Jack said Bob had beaten him badly.

Johnson also claimed to have been a stowaway on a steamer that took him to Key West, Florida, and then to Boston. He had a number of quarrels and fights in Boston, but after the boys saw that he could hold his own, they left him alone. One fight while there stuck out, against a black boy named Lewis, who was the "cock of the walk." After a lengthy battle, spectators broke it up.

He claimed to have lived in Boston for four years before returning to Galveston. He liked to ride the rails to other cities. It has been claimed that he left home at frequent intervals, roaming around the country, taking jobs as a sparring partner or a laborer. He typically traveled as a stowaway, eventually reaching New York, Connecticut, and Chicago.

Some have said that from New York, Johnson traveled to Boston. He took a job working in the stables and found fellow black Joe Walcott, the Barbados Demon (born in British Guiana), and trained and sparred with him.

For a couple years, Johnson was a stable boy, jockey, and horse trainer. Sometimes he provided assistance in collecting bets that were made and owed. He was also a porter at a gambling parlor.

Jack was too heavy to be a jockey, so he tried bicycle racing. He won a number of races, but he was not going to be a world champion at it, and he had a rather bad fall one day, and his leg and ribs were seriously injured. That led him to give up cycling.[52]

In 1909, the *San Francisco Call* reported that Johnson fought in several battles royal on his way up the ladder. A battle royal was a fight in which several boxers all fought each other at the same time in one ring, and the last man standing won the money. It said he started fighting in about 1896 or 1897 in Galveston.

Jim Hall, the veteran Australian heavyweight, whom Fitzsimmons had stopped, was running a small club in Galveston. Hall was offered $500 to promote a show, and he signed Johnson, a tall rangy youth of about age 21 (or so he claimed). Hall asked Johnson to find someone else his own size to fight. Hall offered $100 total for them to split if they fought 10 rounds. Johnson found another black fellow who was six inches shorter, but six times bigger around the waist. They gave Hall a demonstration, and, satisfied, he told them to report to the club on the following night.

They boxed the next evening, but both were cautious and the crowd hissed. They winked at each other. Realizing that the two men had agreed to go easy on one another, Hall told Johnson that if he didn't get in and mix it that they would be locked up for faking and he would pummel them himself.

Johnson confessed that the opponent was his brother-in-law, and said he could not hit him hard or else his whole family would beat him to death. Hall said he did not care. In the 3rd round, they went at it in earnest. Johnson knocked out his brother-in-law with a right to the jaw.[53]

Most of Johnson's early career is unclear and unconfirmed, because the bouts were unreported or unrecorded. Boxing in Texas was technically illegal, so generally the fights were underground occurrences without much news coverage.

The degree to which law enforcement cracked down on boxing bouts depended on the time and the particular fight. The greater attention a bout received, the more likely that politicians would compel law enforcement to become involved. Texas Governor Charles Culberson had pulled out all stops to ensure that the scheduled 1895 Corbett-Fitzsimmons fight did not take place in Texas. Sometimes, for lower-profile bouts, they let it slide, and the fights were sold as mere exhibitions of skill without a formal decision.

Often, bouts would not be reported by newsmen, or they would not be widely advertised, lest they would obtain too much notice from politicians

---

[52] *My Life and Battles* by Jack Johnson, translated and edited from the 1911 and 1914 French versions by Christopher Rivers, Praeger Publishers, Westport, CT, 2007, 1-19; *Papa Jack: Jack Johnson and the Era of White Hopes*, by Randy Roberts, The Free Press, NY, 1983, 2-6; *Jack Johnson: Rebel Sojourner*, by Theresa Runstedtler, University of California Press, 2012, 13; Geoffrey C. Ward, *Unforgivable Blackness* (Alfred A. Knopf, New York, 2004), 13; Jack Johnson, *In the Ring and Out*, (National Spots Publishing Co., Chicago, 1927), 32-36. Johnson's autobiography neglects to mention several bouts, and the order, dates, and results are often listed incorrectly.
[53] *San Francisco Call*, January 18, 1909.

or law enforcement. Even when newsmen did a report on a boxing show, they might only report the result of the main event, and so if Johnson fought in a preliminary bout, it might not have been reported. Hence, it has been difficult for historians to track or confirm many of his early bouts.

Johnson began cleaning a Galveston gym run by Herman Bernau, known as the Galveston Athletic Club, and Jack boxed and trained there.

In 1910, Johnson claimed that his first legitimate bout fought for money was in Galveston when he was only 17 years old (about 1895) (although he later claimed he was 15), against John Lee, a skillful colored veteran boxer who weighed about 185 pounds, while Johnson only weighed 158 pounds. Because of legal concerns, they traveled 14 miles into the country and held the fight in an open field, where the ring was pitched. The sun beat down on them as they fought, and eventually Johnson knocked out Lee in the 17th round. In later accounts, Johnson said he stopped him in either the 15th or 16th round. He said this first fight was the hardest fight he ever had.

Johnson had proven that he had what it took to be a fighter. "After the fight I concluded that there was more money for me in the prize ring than in anything else I could do, and I resolved to stick to it. For a year or two I was the stalking horse in the training camps of various fighters. I trained with Dan Creedon, Tom Tracy, Joe Walcott and other fighters." He claimed to be a sparring partner for Joe Walcott for a number of years.

Johnson was determined to make prize-fighting his profession. At 19, he was growing rapidly, and even then had a lot of cleverness. He was matched with a white boxer named Curlin at Galveston and won. He fought second-rate boxers for a long while.[54]

Johnson had a number of matches in the Galveston area before traveling around again. Often times, he climbed into the ring without having eaten a thing for a full day or without anything in his stomach other than a bit of bread and buttermilk.

While he was struggling to earn money at the fight game, he also earned a living training thoroughbred horses.

Johnson even claimed to have had political aspirations, and ran for Councilman in his ward. As a result of his popularity gained through his boxing, he won. However, he was defeated a year later when he was up for re-election. Whether or not this is true is unclear.

Johnson had one older brother, whom he said was cleverer and had a harder punch than he did, and would have been a champion but for poor eyesight, which forced him to give up boxing.[55]

It is possible that Johnson did some traveling to the East Coast, fought in some smokers, and acted as a sparring partner for better-known fighters before returning to Galveston.

---

[54] *San Francisco Bulletin*, July 27, 1910; *San Francisco Chronicle*, July 10, 1910.
[55] *San Francisco Chronicle*, July 10, 1910.

In 1909, Professor James De Forest, a veteran boxing instructor and trainer, claimed that he had once taught Johnson to box in New York. He said,

> I know Johnson like a book, for I taught him how to box when he was nothing but a porter at the old Lenox A.C. in the days of the Horton law. That was ten years ago, and Johnson, a big, husky fellow, was used as a punching bag by Joe Walcott, Bob Armstrong and other fighters who trained at the club. Johnson improved rapidly once he got a start…[56]

There is a report of a bout taking place on July 25, 1895 at Billy Council's saloon at East 97th street in New York, between Jack Johnson and Julius Mack, colored. The police stopped the proceedings while the bout was in progress and arrested everyone. The question is whether this was the same Jack Johnson. If so, he was 17 years of age.[57]

Joe Walcott

Johnson claimed that for a short period of time he was a sparring partner for a black fighter named Scaldy Bill Quinn, a welterweight who was then training for a fight with Joe Walcott. However, Quinn would not pay him anything and eventually turned him away.[58]

On May 29, 1896 in Woburn, Massachusetts, Scaldy Bill Quinn lost a 20-round decision to Joe Walcott. Hence, if Johnson was working with either fighter at this time, he was probably in Massachusetts, as he claimed.

On October 12, 1896, in Queens, New York, Walcott knocked out Quinn in the 17th round. Quinn had as one of his seconds a fighter named "Jim Johnson," which very well could have been Arthur John Johnson, for newsmen often got his name wrong.[59] The then middleweight-sized Johnson was 18 years old at that point.

After the Walcott-Quinn fight, Johnson said he took part in a few minor ring bouts.

---

[56] *New York Sun*, May 23, 1909.
[57] *New York World*, July 26, 1895.
[58] *My Life and Battles* at 21.
[59] *New York Sun*, October 13, 1896.

Eventually, he became Joe Walcott's sparring partner for two months in Boston.[60] The black Walcott was a very experienced top lightweight and welterweight and future world welterweight champion. Johnson said Walcott paid for his room and board. Working with Walcott provided very good quality experience, for Joe was not only sturdy and strong, but skillful. He had been boxing as a professional since 1890.

Johnson then left and became the manager and trainer of Kid Conroy, who had a powerful punch and could nearly knock him down when they sparred. Jack lived with him at Conroy's mother's house in New Haven, Connecticut. He got Conroy into such good shape that the Kid managed to fight Jim Bradley to a draw. Conroy was a featherweight out of New Haven, Connecticut whose known record spans from 1899 to 1902.[61]

Jack also claimed to have fought in St. Louis, Sedalia, and other places, earning a few modest purses. All the while, he was learning.

> I was studying men, how they behaved in the ring, their physiognomy, learning to read the fear, anxiety, suffering, and discouragement on their faces. I figured out which ones to push and provoke until they went into a rage and which ones to fight calmly. Every man I fought taught me a new lesson. I was still a novice, but I was set in my mind that I would become a champion.[62]

Johnson said he eventually returned to Galveston.

He also claimed that he was elected president of the Republican Club of his neighborhood in Galveston. Perhaps this is what he meant when he claimed to have been a politician.[63]

On March 17, 1897 in Carson City, Nevada, 33-year-old Bob Fitzsimmons won the world heavyweight championship from 30-year-old James J. Corbett, stopping him in the 14th round with a left hook to the body.

In September 1897, in Johnson's hometown of Galveston, it was reported that statisticians, scientists, and sociologists were declaring that the negro race in America was diminishing in numbers, and therefore "declare that the negro problem will settle itself by the extinction of the race from natural causes within a century." The death-rate for blacks was exceeding the birth rate. Tuberculosis caused the most deaths. Further, "mulattoes are not a healthy class of people. The mixture of the races is attended with disease."[64]

On October 11, 1897 at the Grand Opera House in Galveston, the world-famous Joe Choynski defeated Herman Bernau when the bout was stopped in the 4th round after Bernau had been floored twice.

---

[60] Johnson, *In the Ring and Out,* at 41.
[61] *My Life and Battles* at 22.
[62] *My Life and Battles* at 23.
[63] *My Life and Battles* at 26.
[64] *Galveston Daily News*, September 5, 1897.

It is likely that Johnson served as a sparring partner for Choynski around this time, helping to prepare him for the Bernau bout, for Jack later referenced having been a Choynski sparring partner.[65]

On October 29, 1897 in San Francisco, black lightweight Joe Walcott lost his world lightweight championship bid against white boxer Kid Lavigne, who stopped Walcott in the 12th round.

On Monday November 1, 1897 in Galveston, Texas before a fair-sized audience at Professor Bernau's gymnasium, A. J. Johnson of Galveston fought a black fighter named Charles Brooks, formerly of Hannibal, Missouri, in a scheduled 15-round bout for the Texas middleweight championship. At that point, Johnson was a 19-year-old middleweight.

Johnson entered the ring at 9:20 p.m. His seconds were a man named "White" and also Tug Johnson. Brooks entered about five minutes later. He was seconded by Charles Porter and a man named "McCarthy," likely veteran fighter Australian Billy McCarthy. Kid Lewis refereed the bout, which began at 9:30 p.m.

At first, the boxers sparred for an opening. Johnson clearly had the best of matters in the 1st round. In the 2nd round, Johnson exhibited clever work and landed a blow that dropped Brooks to his knees. He rose and attacked, but Johnson decked him with another punch, and Brooks was counted out on the floor. The fight lasted about six minutes.[66]

Although technically boxing was illegal in Texas, in late 1897, a boxing enthusiast who read the law had figured out that the anti-boxing act was not violated by a glove contest to which no admission fee was charged. Friends of the fight-game exploited the legal loophole.

> Since this great discovery glove contests have regained their old time popularity. A 'vaudeville show' is given, to which admission is charged. Then, when the 'show' is out and the audience is dispersed somebody gets up and generously announces that there is to be a boxing contest, to which all present are invited. They are likewise privileged to go out upon the highways and bid other guests to come. Then a couple of 'athletes' will get up and try to hammer the stuffing out of each other.

Less than three weeks after the Johnson-Brooks bout, on Saturday November 20, 1897 at the Galveston Convention Hall, a "vaudeville" performance was given under the auspices of the "Black Diamond athletic company." It was largely attended by all classes, both white and black.

After the vaudeville show concluded, it was announced that there would be a boxing contest between "Jack Johnson of Galveston" and Ed Johnson of Pensacola for the "championship of Texas." Both fighters were black.

In the 3rd round, Texas champion Jack "shoved" Ed to the floor, and referee Australian Billy McCarthy allowed Ed to rise without counting.

---

[65] *San Francisco Call,* October 12, 1897.
[66] *Galveston Daily News,* November 2, 1897.

Twice more Jack "shoved" Ed to the floor. These "shoves" may actually have been knockdowns. In the 5th round, Jack "did it again and the Florida man was called out. The winner was too heavy for the vanquished and the event was decidedly tame, although the two men went at it hammer and tongs fashion most of the time."

Quite frankly, it sounded as if the local writer was attempting to minimize any aspect of brutality so as not to arouse the anti-boxing sentiment. Jack Johnson apparently had decked Ed Johnson several times and stopped him, but the reporter wrote, perhaps with a wink, that he "shoved" him down and the bout was tame, although at the same time in contradictory fashion saying that they went at it hammer and tongs most of the time.[67]

Over the next couple of years, Jack Johnson was primarily a local fighter, mostly boxing in obscure and unknown bouts, unrecorded and unremembered, even by Johnson himself.

In March 1898, the U.S. under President William McKinley issued an ultimatum to Spain to end its presence in Cuba. Spain refused, and on April 20, 1898, Congress declared war, starting the Spanish-American War. Eventually, Lt. Col. Theodore Roosevelt's Rough Riders were victorious in Cuba. Spain was also defeated in the Philippines. A peace protocol ended hostilities on August 12, 1898. Under the subsequent peace treaty signed at Paris on December 10, 1898, Spain relinquished title to Cuba, which became independent, and ceded Puerto Rico, Guam, and the Philippines to the United States. The U.S. also took Hawaii.

On November 10, 1898, Wilmington, North Carolina exploded in the first major race riot since Reconstruction. A large white mob killed and wounded many blacks and burned down the office and printing press of the local black newspaper, the *Daily Record*. The local white mayor and biracial city council were forced to resign and the mob installed its own Democrat white supremacist leaders. Despite pleas for assistance, President William McKinley did not respond. Essentially, more than 2,000 blacks were forced to leave the city, turning it from a black majority to a white majority city. Soon thereafter, North Carolina began passing laws that mandated segregation and restricted the ability of blacks to vote.

That same day, a race riot had also erupted in Greenwood, South Carolina, which left many whites and blacks dead and wounded. It was the result of an election row.

In February 1899, British author Rudyard Kipling's poem, "The White Man's Burden," published at the start of the Philippine-American War, urged white Americans to join Europeans in the work of empire building. It became a catchphrase, calling upon a collective white moral responsibility to civilize the world's savage people of color, in part by conquering them.

---

[67] *Galveston Daily News*, November 21, 1897.

During early 1899, Jack Johnson left Galveston heading towards Chicago, but he wound up in Springfield, 200 miles southwest of Chicago, and 100 miles northwest of St. Louis.

On Wednesday April 19, 1899 at the Central Music Hall, under the auspices of the Springfield Athletic Club in Illinois, 21-year-old Jack Johnson fought in a battle royal, wherein a number of black boxers got into a ring and fought each other all at once, with the one left standing at the end being entitled to the money.

Johnson, called a "big husky negro," got the opportunity by walking into Manager John Connors' saloon on the previous evening, April 18, and stating that he wanted to enter the following evening's battle royal as an unknown. He was accommodated. "He says he has never failed to win these contests, and declares he will make it a lively feature for the club's entertainment." The bouts started at 9 p.m.[68]

The next-day *Daily Illinois State Register*, based out of Springfield, reported,

> The show was opened by a battle royal, which was won in a punch by a large negro who called himself Jack Johnson. There were five negroes in the ring when time was called, but when Johnson hit George Williams a blow that looked like a mule kicking, there were but two left, Johnson and his partner, a little fellow. Williams and the other two got out of the ring and had enough.

> Johnson showed plainly that he is a boxer and had no business in such a place. Sam Pooler, manager of Eddie Santry, says he will make a match for him with some Chicago man. Johnson stated after the contests that he had been with Joe Walcott, the Barbados Demon, and Joe Choynski. He is a large, powerful fellow, and is fully six feet tall. He would do well against Tommy Wilson, of Athens, and no doubt would win.

The world-famous George Siler refereed the bouts that evening. James Williams was the announcer, and Frank Marvel, the celebrated jockey, was the timekeeper. The crowd contained about 500 people, who enjoyed the card.[69]

Years later, Johnson claimed he weighed 154 pounds at that time. Initially, he had gone to Chicago, but there was no demand for his services. "They didn't know me, and didn't want to." So he went to Springfield and earned $5 to win the Springfield battle royal.

After seeing him fight in Springfield, George Siler sent a telegram to a Chicago promoter saying, "Have just seen greatest natural boxer ever laid my eyes on. Sending him to you. George Siler." Such a statement got Johnson noticed, because Siler had refereed world championship bouts,

---

[68] *Daily Illinois State Register*, Springfield, April 19, 1899.
[69] *Daily Illinois State Register*, Springfield, April 20, 1899; *Springfield Journal*, April 20, 1899.

including Corbett vs. Fitzsimmons, and he had seen the world's best in action first-hand.[70]

Heavyweight Tommy Wilson, out of Athens, was supposed to fight Johnson in Springfield the first week of May, in a private bout for a purse. An offer subsequently came in from a club in Decatur, offering to host the bout there for more money.

Wilson arrived in Springfield the day he was to meet Johnson in private, and when told that the Decatur club wanted the match and would pay more, Wilson refused, saying he was prepared to fight that day, and did not want the bout postponed. Then Johnson said, "I'll meet you this afternoon, since you are so anxious to fight. If I am fortunate enough to win, I'll give you half the money. If you win, you can have it all." Wilson then got cold feet, showed a yellow streak and refused to fight the colored man, in spite of the fact that he weighed at least 25 pounds more than Johnson. Perhaps someone notified him about the local article that opined that Johnson would beat him. Or perhaps Johnson's confidence intimidated him.

John Connors began looking for another match for Johnson. He arranged to take "the big fellow" to Chicago that Saturday night, May 6, to meet Klondike. Jack was also set to meet a big man before the Decatur club on May 16.

The local Chicago papers reported that George Siler had recommended Johnson, of Springfield, to local promoters. Since Siler was a well-known boxing expert, promoter Paddy Carroll took his word and matched Johnson to meet the local black fighter, Klondike, at the large Howard theater on Desplaines street. "Johnson has something of a reputation around Springfield." He was said to weigh in the neighborhood of 200 pounds, although this was likely boosting rather than reality.[71]

Johnson briefly trained at the fairgrounds for his go with Klondike, working with Joe Bonansinga, who was preparing for his own bout set for the 16th. Of Johnson, it was said, "He is a shifty boxer and knows all about the game."[72]

According to secondary sources, 21-year-old "Klondike" John Haines (a.k.a. Klondyke Haynes), had been twice defeated by another top world-class black fighter, Frank Childs, in 1898 via LKOby6 and LKOby4.[73] Klondike's record contains at least five known victories, including an 1898 W6 George Grant; and 1899 W6 Dan Bayliff, KO2 Dick Woods, W6 Henry Baker (whom James Jeffries knocked out in 9 rounds in 1897), and KO2 Jim Fordy, but he likely had many more bouts.

[70] *Saskatoon Star-Phoenix*, April 22, 1929; *Pittsburgh Courier*, June 8, 1929.
[71] *Chicago Record-Herald, Daily Inter Ocean,* May 4, 1899.
[72] *Daily Illinois State Register*, Springfield, May 4, 1899.
[73] Boxrec.com; *Grand Forks Daily Herald*, January 9, 1898; *Sunday News Tribune*, February 27, 1898.

KLONDIKE.
(The local heavy-weight.)

The local press expected a good heavyweight fight as part of the preliminary card. "Klondike will meet a Tartar in Jim Johnson [sic] of Springfield. Johnson formerly acted as sparring partner for Joe Choynski and Tommy Ryan." If in fact Johnson had once been a Tommy Ryan sparring partner, such would have been high quality experience for him, because Ryan was a highly respected world middleweight champion.[74]

On Saturday May 6, 1899 at Chicago's Howard Theater, Jack Johnson fought Klondike, the local black heavyweight. The program was arranged by Paddy Carroll under the auspices of the Illinois Athletic Club. Malachy Hogan refereed.

At first, Johnson did well, and even dropped Klondike in the 2nd round. However, eventually Jack grew very fatigued and held incessantly. Klondike was in much better shape and consistently pounded away with solid blows, as the hurt and/or tired Johnson clinched to survive, avoid punishment, and stall. Eventually, in either the 5th or 6th round of the scheduled 6-round bout (depending on the source – two said round 6, two said round 5), at the request of the police, the referee stopped the bout. The police either thought Johnson had enough or they were simply fed up with his excessive clinching.

The local *Daily Inter Ocean* said Klondike won the fight in the 6th round, when Referee Hogan stopped the bout at the request of a police lieutenant who was close to the ropes.

It was stopped more on account of Johnson holding on than because of any rough milling. Johnson is about 6 feet 2 or 3 inches, and has a punch in either hand that would fell an ox. He could not land it fair on Klondike, although a punch in the head in the second round sent

---

[74] *Daily Inter Ocean, Chicago Record-Herald,* May 6, 1899.

Klondike to the floor. He arose immediately. After the third round Johnson tired rapidly and clung to his man at every opportunity.

The *Chicago Chronicle* said "Klondike" of Chicago was given the decision over Jack Johnson of Springfield, Illinois, before the end of the 6th round. "The bout between Klondike and Jack Johnson of Springfield was not as exciting as it should have been. Johnson had the advantage in height and reach, but before the fight had progressed midway the sledgehammer blows of his equally dusky opponent made it plain that he was not trained for punishment."

The *Chicago Times-Herald* said "John Johnson, the discovery of George Siler, proved to be a husky fighter of enormous height but of insufficient skill to win from 'Klondike,' the latter getting the decision in the fifth round after lieutenant O'Connor had called it off on account of the clinching tactics of the loser."

The *Chicago Tribune* said Klondike defeated Jack Johnson in the heavyweight class, but it did not say what the specific result was or even how many rounds the bout lasted. "Johnson, a long rangy colored man from Springfield, looking something like Fitzsimmons in black, showed up well at the start, but weakened under the steady but ponderous attack of Klondike."[75]

Johnson's debut tryout performance in Chicago had not gone very well. Although he showed early flashes of his ability, his lack of weight, inadequate nutrition, and lack of proper training led to early fatigue. He had failed to impress the locals. Although he had dropped Klondike in the 2nd round, he could not land very often. When he grew tired and/or was hurt, he simply grabbed incessantly to survive, until a police officer who felt that he had enough or was fed up with the excessive clinching requested that the referee terminate the contest. Hence, it was either a TKO or DQ loss, depending upon how you want to look at it. Klondike had proven to be a much tougher customer than Johnson had anticipated.

Regardless, contrary to the erroneous belief of some, Johnson was not dropped or knocked out, nor did he quit. Given what we later came to learn about Johnson's survival skills, it is likely that he would have lasted the full 6 rounds and lost a decision had the police not interfered.

Johnson needed to get into better shape or learn to pace himself better. Some later claimed that he was simply malnourished at that point in his life. Jack was very thin, for being poor; he struggled to earn enough money to eat well enough to be at his strongest. As he obtained more money, he ate better and put on weight.

Despite the result, the reports were not all bad for Johnson. Many still believed in him and saw his potential. Springfield's *Daily Illinois State Register* reported that Johnson was a good one, and that Johnnie Connors was pleased with his big boxer, who allegedly hailed from Hot Springs, for he

[75] *Daily Inter Ocean, Chicago Chronicle, Chicago Times-Herald, Chicago Tribune*, May 7, 1899.

did well with the respected Klondike. It said that although the bout with Klondike was scheduled for 6 rounds, the police stopped it in the 5th round.

> Johnson had an even break in the first, second and third rounds. In the latter he landed a hard right swing on Klondike's jaw that made the colored fellow totter. As is often the case, Klondike fell toward Johnson, and the latter, in not getting out of the way quick enough, spoiled his chances of winning the match at that time. Klondike caught hold of Johnson and Referee Hogan had trouble in getting him to break. Had Klondike fallen to the floor, Johnson, no doubt would have been a winner, but in the clinch Klondike had a chance to recuperate. Lovers of boxing in Chicago thought well of Connors' big colored fellow, and would like to see him meet Klondike again.

> Johnson came to Springfield the day before the last show of the Springfield club. He went into the battle royal and handed the biggest man in it such a stiff punch that the others ran from the ring. The way he handled himself at that time showed that he was a fighter and Johnnie took him up. He had no training for the go with Klondike and, after the third round, was winded. He had no steam and was unable to withstand the other fellow's strength, although Klondike failed to hurt him a bit. Manager Connors says he can put Jack into condition to whip Klondike, and offered to bet a good sum on his man, while in Chicago Saturday night, which was not taken.

> Klondike is no novice at the business, but has met some good men. He has beaten Frank Childs, who whipped Bob Armstrong. ... It now looks, from pugilistic dope, which is very uncertain, that Johnson should win from either Childs or Armstrong, and there is money in Springfield that will go up on him if he should meet either. Both Connors and Johnson speak well of the treatment afforded them by the Chicago club officials and Referee Hogan.

> Johnson is matched to meet George Grant at Decatur, May 16. ... Johnson will now go into actual training and will be trained by Connors. He had no assistance for his match with Klondike, and his good showing was really phenomenal.[76]

Perhaps others had noticed his potential as well, which is why few were willing to fight him. Once he got into proper condition, Johnson would be a risky proposition. Hence, either because local promoters were not excited to see him again as a result of the Klondike tryout, or because potential opponents feared him, lack of opportunity would push Johnson into the shadows again.

Years later, Johnson admitted that he did not live up to the wire Siler had sent out about him. He admitted that Klondike beat him in 6 rounds.

---

[76] *Daily Illinois State Register*, Springfield, May 8, 1899.

Johnson claimed to have then been only a 154-pound middleweight. He said he never was taught to box, but learned it himself through experience. Eventually, with time and more experience, Johnson would improve and prove that Siler indeed had a very good eye for raw talent. However, Johnson was not quite ready for Klondike at that early point in his career.[77]

Furthermore, Johnson was not the local prospect. Klondike was. The following week, on May 12, Klondike defeated George Grant in 6 rounds.[78]

Johnnie Connors, listed as the "clever colored heavyweight" Johnson's manager, had scheduled a Johnson bout with Chicago heavyweight George Grant, scheduled to be held in Decatur on May 16.

Johnson was training hard, and as of May 13, was appearing to be in the pink of condition. He was working at the state fair-grounds. A large number of folks had visited his training quarters and watched him box. They believed that Johnson was "clever enough to hold his own with the best of them. He is also a clever bag puncher and makes the place resound with his terrific punches and jabs at the imaginary foe." Most believed he would defeat Grant. In that event, he would be matched with Bob Armstrong, who made a good showing against Gus Ruhlin.

However, unfortunately, the Decatur mayor refused to allow the bouts to be held there. It was hoped that the card would be transferred to Springfield. Eventually, the card was cancelled, much to the chagrin of both Grant and Johnson.[79]

Johnson later said he had made more money off the Klondike fight than ever before. He saw the monetary potential in boxing if he improved. He therefore decided to make being a top fighter his goal.

According to Johnson, for the first time, he began training in earnest, and sparred with some top pros, including Dan Creedon and Tom Tracy/Tracey, who took the most interest in him.[80]

According to some, in May 1899, Johnson also served as a sparring partner for top black fighter Frank Childs, who was known as a strong

---

[77] *Saskatoon Star-Phoenix*, April 22, 1929.

[78] *Chicago Record*, May 13, 1899.

[79] *Daily Illinois State Register*, Springfield, May 13, 16, 1899; *Springfield Journal*, May 13, 1899.

[80] Johnson, *In the Ring and Out*, at 40. Australian native Dan Creedon's career included: 1891 KO5 Jim Watts, KO7 Starlight Rollins, and KO2 Australian Jimmy Ryan; 1892 KO7 Ryan; 1893 KO15 Alex Greggains; 1894 KO3 Frank Childs and LKOby2 Bob Fitzsimmons; 1895 KO2 Herman Bernau, D6 Joe Choynski, D6 Henry Baker, KO1 Billy McCarthy, KO2 Joe Dunfee, and W20 Frank Craig; 1896 KO2 Jem Smith, W20 Baker, and KO9 Dick O'Brien; 1897 KO2 Nick Burley, KO4 Charley Strong, and LKOby15 Kid McCoy; 1898 D6 Billy Stift, LKOby2 Jack Bonner, and L20 George Green; and 1899 D20 Tommy West, LKOby1 and L20 Joe Walcott. In 1900, Jack Root would stop Creedon in the 1st round. In 1901, Marvin Hart would stop Creedon in the 6th round.

Tom Tracey's career included 1893 KO19 Billy Gallagher; 1894 LKOby16 Joe Walcott; 1895 LKOby8 Tommy Ryan; 1897 LKOby9 Ryan; 1898 L20 Kid Lavigne, and September 1899 L6 Jack O'Brien.

puncher. Childs at various times claimed the colored heavyweight championship.[81]

In 1910, Johnson said,

> I worked with Childs when he was in training for several of his fights while he claimed the colored heavyweight championship of the world, and the way that fellow treated me was a shame. I didn't mind so much what he tried to do to me in training quarters, but Childs wasn't on the square with me, and I would have starved to death for all he cared.[82]

Johnson later said he even lived with Childs while he was his sparring partner, for he did not have enough money to rent a room. One night, when Childs' wife came home, Frank forced Jack to leave. Johnson had to roam the rainy cold streets that night, because he could not even afford to pay for a five-cent bed. From then on, he wanted to fight Childs and get revenge, which he later did.[83]

Others have said that while in Chicago, Johnson was a sparring partner for a number of good boxers, possibly including the respected Jack Root.[84]

On June 9, 1899 in New York, 24-year-old James J. Jeffries won the world heavyweight championship by knocking out 36-year-old Bob Fitzsimmons in 11 rounds. At that point, the middleweight-sized Jack Johnson was 21 years of age.

Johnson claimed to have fought in Pittsburgh. He might have also served as a Joe Walcott sparring partner in Boston around that time as well.[85]

Jack might have seconded Joe Walcott in a fight with Dan Creedon in New York on June 23, 1899, in which Walcott won a 20-round decision.[86]

Some claim that it was in July 1899 in New Haven, Connecticut, that Johnson helped train the white featherweight Kid Conroy.[87]

In 1910, Johnson said that in 1899, he was hiking along the roads of New Haven, Connecticut without a single cent in his pockets. He landed a job as a janitor at Becky Stanford's cigar store on Congress Avenue. For several months, he swept the store and cleaned up the poolroom, as well as practiced boxing. He sparred with Kid Conroy, then the cleverest

---

[81] In March 1899, Childs scored a KO6 over Bob Armstrong, a man who had lasted 10 rounds with Jim Jeffries. Childs obtained 6-rounds draws with Jack Bonner and Tom Stockings Conroy in Chicago on May 19 and May 26, 1899, respectively. In August and October 1899, Childs would score a W6 and KO3 over Klondike. *Police Gazette*, September 2, 1899.

[82] *San Francisco Bulletin*, July 27, 1910.

[83] *My Life and Battles* at 19-21.

[84] Roberts at 12.

[85] Johnson, *In the Ring and Out*, at 41.

[86] However, Johnson was not mentioned as one of his seconds. Ward at 30; *New York Sun*, June 24, 1899.

[87] Ward at 30.

lightweight in New Haven. Sid Cook, the Yale colored athlete trainer, gave him some ideas about physical conditioning.

Some later semi-primary sources reported that Johnson had defeated a fighter by the name of Dan Murphy (via KO10) at Waterbury, Connecticut, just north of New Haven, so it is possible that this bout took place around this time. Murphy's record included: 1897 D10, D15, and D20 George Byers; 1898 D20 and LKOby17 Tommy West, L20 and LKOby10 Dick O'Brien; and 1899 D20 Australian Jim Ryan and LKOby17 Dick O'Brien. Most all of Murphy's bouts took place in Connecticut.

Referee Billy Roche was running a boxing club near Boston. Roche said that one night, a lean, hungry-looking negro asked him to be put on as a substitute if any fighter failed to show. His clothes were in tatters and he had the appearance of being half-starved. Roche gave him a chance by putting him in with a hard-hitting give-and-take white slugger. Johnson showed his ability to dodge the swings and eventually won the fight. He became a regular at the club. He said Jack usually lost most of his money playing craps games.[88]

For the most part, during this early part of his career, Johnson was operating quietly and somewhat anonymously in the shadows, learning his craft, acting as a sparring partner, and taking lesser bouts.

On November 3, 1899 in New York, James Jeffries retained his title with a W25 over Tom Sharkey. The largest-house-ever generated over $66,000 in gate receipts, which was massive by the standards of the time.

As of January 1900, Johnson was either still in Illinois, or had returned there. It was then claimed that fighter Jack Grace was the one who the previous spring had tipped off Johnnie Connors about Jack Johnson. He had seen Johnson fight in Galveston and declared that the big black was a good one. "This assertion was afterward proven by Johnson, who is now in Chicago."[89]

For whatever reason, Johnson did not obtain fights in Chicago, and eventually, in early 1900, he returned to Galveston. He took part in numerous fights, and though he said these bouts did not particularly add to his reputation as a fighter, they did give him valuable experience.

Back in Galveston, Johnson claimed to have fought and defeated Howard Pollar and Jack Lawlor, amongst others, although the dates are unknown.[90]

On Wednesday March 21, 1900, the Galveston Athletic Club celebrated the opening of its new gymnasium on Twenty-second and Market streets. Admission was limited to club members only, and about 225 members participated in the ceremonies.

---

[88] *San Francisco Evening Post*, July 27, 1910; *Freeman*, August 6, 1910; Boxrec.com.
[89] *Daily Illinois State Register*, Springfield, January 20, 1900.
[90] Johnson at 42-43.

Jack McCormick, who distinguished himself by knocking out Kid McCoy and was in turn defeated

Because prizefighting was still illegal in Texas, the club got around the law by calling the participants instructors and the bouts exhibitions, even though they were usually actual fights and it was all done with a wink.

In the main event of the three-bout card, Detroit's Joe McCormick, a white fighter, and Arthur Johnson "(colored)" of Dallas [Jack Johnson's birth name], who were elected as club instructors, gave a demonstrative "exhibition" of the manly art of self-defense that won the club members' favor.

Most secondary sources report that McCormick was Jack McCormack (a.k.a. Jim McCormick), out of Philadelphia. If so, McCormick had a record that included over 25 bouts, such as: 1897 LKOby4 Herman Bernau; 1898 LKOby8 Gus Ruhlin and DND6 Joe Goddard; 1899 LKOby2 Tom Sharkey, WND6 Charley Strong, DND6 Jack Bonner, D6 Ed Dunkhorst, L6 Joe Choynski, KO1 and LKOby8 Kid McCoy, LKOby2 Joe Goddard, L6 Gus Ruhlin, L6 Billy Stift, and LKOby18 Jack Finnegan; and 1900 LKOby4 Tom "Stockings" Conroy, D12 George Byers, and LKOby1 Tom Sharkey, one week before the Johnson bout. In March 1899, the 190-pound McCormick had sparred with James Jeffries.

Johnson and McCormick entered the ring at 10:39 p.m. and received applause. They bowed to the crowd and took their seats. The master of ceremonies announced that they would endeavor to show members something of the art of self-defense. The bout was scheduled for 15 rounds.

McCormick had the size advantage and appeared healthy, though his flesh was soft. Regardless of appearances, McCormick was quite active and displayed gameness and considerable science. His footwork was slow, though, and he appeared slightly clumsy at times. Whenever McCormick crowded in, Johnson hit him on the body.

In the 2nd round, Johnson brought blood from his rival's nose. Early on, Johnson played on McCormick's left eye.

Nevertheless, McCormick acted as the aggressor throughout the contest, and mixed things in lively fashion. Johnson stood punishment very well and displayed splendid ducking proclivities in avoiding many vicious left swings. Still, the aggressive McCormick landed several hard taps on the chin and mouth and Johnson spat a quantity of blood. His heart was well-tested, for McCormick persistently hit him in the left chest, such that Johnson had to stretch for wind.

In the 9th and 10th rounds, McCormick had Johnson going, and his legs appeared to be weakening under the exertion. However, McCormick neglected to force matters sufficiently, so Johnson was able to gain time and recover.

Hence, when Johnson came up for the 15th and final round, he appeared fresh again, having caught his second wind. By the end of the 15th round, McCormick's discolored left eye was closed and there was considerable swelling on his left cheek.

Throughout the bout, the men broke cleanly, and "all in all the exhibition was a very pretty exchange of compliments." Essentially, it was a 15-round no-decision.

The article's writer did not render an opinion regarding what the decision would have been had one been allowed. The general impression, though, was that McCormick might have had slightly the better of matters, although it sounded as if it was a close and competitive bout and could have been a draw. Clearly, Johnson was not the puncher or finisher that someone like a Tom Sharkey was, who had twice knocked out McCormick. Furthermore, Johnson was the smaller man, not yet having fully grown into his frame. At that time, he was not much more than a middleweight.[91]

Two days later, on Friday March 23, 1900 in New York, after suffering a cut over his eye from a head butt, black lightweight Joe Gans retired in the 12th round of his title-bid against white world lightweight champion Frank Erne.

That same day, in a March 23, 1900 speech before the U.S. Senate, Senator Benjamin "Pitchfork" Tillman of South Carolina, also a former governor of that state, defended the actions of his white constituents in using violence against blacks. A fellow senator had said that since the late 1870s, blacks had their rights taken away from them, in particular by the use of violence to influence elections. Tillman proudly admitted it.

> It was the riots before the elections precipitated by [blacks'] own hot-headedness in attempting to hold the government, that brought on conflicts between the races and caused the shotgun to be used. That is what I meant by saying we used the shotgun.

> I want to call the Senator's attention to one fact. He said that the Republican party gave the negroes the ballot in order to protect themselves against the indignities and wrongs that were attempted to

---

[91] *Galveston Daily News*, March 22, 1900.

be heaped upon them by the enactment of the black code. I say it was because the Republicans of that day…wanted to put white necks under black heels and to get revenge. …

I want to ask the Senator this proposition in arithmetic: In my State there were 135,000 negro voters, or negroes of voting age, and some 90,000 or 95,000 white voters. General Canby set up a carpetbag government there and turned our State over to this majority. Now, I want to ask you, with a free vote and a fair count, how are you going to beat 135,000 by 95,000? How are you going to do it? You had set us an impossible task. You had handcuffed us and thrown away the key, and you propped your carpetbag negro government with bayonets. Whenever it was necessary to sustain the government you held it up by the Army. …

We were sorry we had the necessity forced upon us, but we could not help it, and as white men we are not sorry for it, and we do not propose to apologize for anything we have done in connection with it. We took the government away from them in 1876. We did take it. …

We did not disfranchise the negroes until 1895. Then we had a constitutional convention convened which took the matter up calmly, deliberately, and avowedly with the purpose of disfranchising as many of them as we could under the fourteenth and fifteenth amendments. We adopted the educational qualification as the only means left to us, and the negro is as contented and as prosperous and as well protected in South Carolina to-day as in any State of the Union south of the Potomac. He is not meddling with politics, for he found that the more he meddled with them the worse off he got. As to his "rights" - I will not discuss them now. We of the South have never recognized the right of the negro to govern white men, and we never will. We have never believed him to be equal to the white man, and we will not submit to his gratifying his lust on our wives and daughters without lynching him. I would to God the last one of them was in Africa and that none of them had ever been brought to our shores.[92]

On April 6, 1900 in Detroit, James Jeffries scored a KO1 over Jack Finnegan. Finnegan had knocked out Jim McCormick in 18 rounds in 1899.

---

[92] "Speech of Senator Benjamin R. Tillman, March 23, 1900," Congressional Record, 56th Congress, 1st Session, 3223–3224. Reprinted in Richard Purday, ed., Document Sets for the South in U. S. History (Lexington, MA.: D.C. Heath and Company, 1991), 147. Tillman took part in the July 8, 1876 Hamburg Riot, which was marked by the murder of a number of black militiamen who, much to the chagrin of Southern whites, were stationed in South Carolina. Tillman boasted that leading white men decided to provoke a riot so that whites could kill as many blacks as possible. Tillman used his participation to fuel his successful 1890 campaign for governor. He was the South Carolina governor for four years, from 1890 to 1894, and was elected to the U.S. Senate in 1894, where he served for the next 24 years.

Nearly three weeks after Johnson-McCormick, on Monday April 9, 1900, the Galveston Athletic Club held its regular monthly demonstrative boxing exhibitions at its gymnasium. Nearly 300 members gathered.

First up on the card was a 4-round bout between Arthur Johnson and William McNeill, "two heavyweight colored boxers of note." The bout was full of swift, hard drives and considerable mixing that pleased the audience. Weight, muscle, and science blended to yield and direct hard punches. At the bout's conclusion, both men were on their feet and comparatively fresh. It was a 4-round no-decision bout. No opinion was offered as to which boxer was the superior pugilist.

The bout had been sufficiently entertaining that the pleased spectators threw a shower of coins into the ring, which kept the boxers sliding on the sandy ground for several minutes collecting the contributions. This was the humble state of Jack Johnson's early career. Consider this when he became a wealthy self-made man years later.[93]

Two weeks later, on Friday, April 20, 1900, the Galveston Athletic Club gymnasium was again well-filled with members to watch its "instructors" give another demonstrative boxing exhibition. John Heimann, alias "Texas Jack McCormack," and Arthur Johnson, "colored," boxed in a scheduled 20-round bout for points. This was likely the same McCormack/McCormick with whom Johnson fought a 15-round no-decision one month earlier, in late March.

McCormack weighed in at 175 pounds. 22-year-old Johnson weighed 168 pounds, a mere super-middleweight by today's standards.

Jack McCormack

Johnson showed great improvement from their previous bout. The local *Galveston Daily News* said, "Johnson was the best man and outpointed his opponent at almost every turn. He was the cleverest in ducking and the most vicious in his swings, and displayed more muscle and greater staying qualities." That said, "Science was not the predominating feature of the bout." McCormack "made several clever attempts to land, but Johnson was the quicker on his feet" and almost winded McCormack by making him

[93] *Galveston Daily News*, April 10, 1900. In the main event, future Johnson opponent Jim Scanlan of Pittsburg, and Charles Fogarty of Galveston acted as "instructors" in a scheduled 20-round bout at 158 pounds. James Heiman, otherwise known as "Texas Jim McCormack," the big muscular young fellow whom Tom Sharkey knocked out in 2 rounds, officiated as referee. Scanlon stopped Fogarty in the 5th round.

miss his punches in the air. Perhaps characteristic of his future trademark manner, "Johnson aggravated his opponent by his grinning and by patting Heimann on the back when they came together in a clinch."

By the 6th round, the men lost their tempers and pushed the proposition to a real fight for blood. A concerned club President Davis was about to have the entertainment ended. However, at that point, Referee Ned Sedgwick ruled that Heimann had fouled Johnson and awarded "the negro fighter" the decision on a foul (likely a low blow). Neither man was marked from the angry spell. The "audience deeply regretted the unpleasant termination of what was expected to be a most interesting and scientific exhibition."[94]

On April 30, 1900, 500 members of the Galveston Athletic Club assembled to hear bulletins of the Jeffries-Corbett fight, scheduled to be held in New York, but the bout did not take place on that date, owing to the intervention of the police commissioners.

Instead, a scientific exhibition between two of the pupils, Cookey Defferari and Fred Heidemann, took place. Arthur Johnson was amongst those in Defferari's corner.[95]

The Jeffries vs. Corbett championship fight took place in New York on May 11, 1900, with 25-year-old Jeffries coming from behind on points to drop the 33-year-old Corbett in the 19th round before knocking him out in the 23rd round.

A couple months after defeating McCormack in a rematch, on Monday June 25, 1900, before 500 members of the Galveston Athletic Club, 22-year-old "Jack Johnson" of Galveston fought a rematch with Chicago's 22-year-old Klondike Johnny Haynes (or Haines) in a scheduled 20-round bout. It had been over a year since the two had fought the first time, when the bout had been stopped owing to Johnson's excessive clinching after he grew weary.

Both were said to be clever heavyweight boxers in prime condition. "Johnson has been training faithfully and feels confident of success. This will be the first time Johnson has been tried out before a real good man, one who has considerable science and plenty of steam behind his blows, and it remains to be seen whether he is made out of the right sort of stuff or not." The locals might not have realized that Johnson was trying to avenge his previous loss to Haynes. Certainly though, they knew that the respected Klondike would be a real test of Johnson's mettle.

---

[94] *Galveston Daily News*, April 21, 1900. McCormick would go on to spar with world champion James Jeffries again in May and August 1900. In late 1902, McCormick became a manager/trainer/sparring partner for Marvin Hart. In March 1905, 47-year-old former champion John L. Sullivan would score a KO2 over McCormick.

[95] *Galveston Daily News*, May 1, 1900. It was announced that the club was negotiating with Dan Creedon to become its chief instructor, with Jim Scanlon to be his assistant. Scanlon had defeated Jack McCarthy of St. Louis at Hot Springs on Saturday night.

According to the local *Galveston Daily News*, Klondike's knockouts included: KO3 and KO4 George Grant, KO6 Henry Baker, KO3 Joe Goddard, KO6 Grant, KO3 Henry Brum, KO6 Charley Stevens, and KO6 Ed Smith of Philadelphia, amongst others. His decisions won included W6 Billy Stift, W6 Frank Childs, W6 George Lawler, and W6 Ed Martin of Denver. However, he lost to Frank Childs in 6 rounds as well.

John "Klondike" Haines

Secondary sources report Klondike's record as including: 1898 W6 George Grant; 1899 W6 Henry Baker, TKO 5 or 6 Jack Johnson, W6 Grant, KO2 Scaldy Bill Quinn, WDQ4 Joe Goddard, L6 and LKOby3 Frank Childs (Colored Heavyweight Title Claim), W6 George Lawler; and 1900 LND6 Denver Ed Martin, WND6 Ed Smith, KO2 Henry Brum/Bram, and WND6 Charley Stevenson, amongst others.

Again it was noted that the Galveston Athletic Club got around the law by calling itself a school of boxing instruction and the bouts exhibitions designed to teach. "These exhibitions are given solely for the benefit of the club members and may be classed as a school of instruction, with the principals in the role of professors demonstrating all the fine points in the art of boxing." However, given that it was a 20-round bout, everyone knew it was a real fight.[96]

The local *Galveston Daily News* reported that Klondike Johnny Haynes of Chicago and Arthur Johnson of Galveston boxed in a dull fashion. At times the bout took on a lively spurt, but then it "tamed down to what seemed a friendly game of child's play with five-ounce gloves." To Klondike's credit, he appeared to favor a mix-up at short range, and was the aggressor throughout the bout. However, Johnson led him on a "hide-and-go-seek chase around the ring."

> On several occasions Johnson, responding to the appeals of the audience, would rush his opponent, but the rushes were scarce and extremely weak-hearted. On eleven different occasions 'Klondike' presented openings wherein it looked that Johnson could have put him out had he engaged the Chicagoan. But the combat would invariably terminate in a hugging match. For twenty rounds the two boxers wearied along and worried the audience. ... The agreement was that if the two men were on their feet at the end of the twentieth

---

[96] *Galveston Daily News*, June 24 1900; Boxrec.com.

round the contest was to be a draw. Under the terms of the bout Referee Jim Scanlan decided a draw.[97]

The tame 20-round draw was a disappointment to the 500 male spectators; for they had expected a whirlwind fight terminating with a knockout. At the pace they fought, they could have continued for another 20 rounds. It appeared that both boxers were clever and capable of putting up a good performance. Therefore, many called it a hippodrome, or fake, so far as their efforts to defeat each other were concerned.

This bout showed what would be the criticism of Johnson occasionally during his career. He was skillful and capable, but very cautious and defensive, fighting only in short spurts. This lack of fighting vim and consistency of offense caused many to underrate his ability, or they would admire his potential and skill, but not want to see him very much, owing to his less than entertaining style. It is easy to criticize when you aren't the one getting hit with 5-ounce gloves and having to pace yourself over the course of 20 rounds.

Despite the criticism, the pace for a 20-round fight typically is much slower than it would be for a bout of shorter length, so it stands to reason that Johnson might have been more cautious owing to his concern about fatigue and potentially being knocked out late in the fight when in such a state. Furthermore, often when both fighters have ability, their mutual respect and skills can offset one another and lead to a more cautious bout. They both knew that they could not win except via a knockout, but also that they could not lose unless they were knocked out. They could box to a draw and split whatever purse had been offered.

Given that his previous bout with Klondike had only lasted 5 or 6 rounds, Johnson has to be given credit for improving upon his prior performance and lasting the full 20 rounds this time, just one year later.

The next day, on June 26, 1900 in New York, Gus Ruhlin scored a KO15 over Tom Sharkey.

On August 10, 1900 in New York, Bob Fitzsimmons knocked out Gus Ruhlin in the 6th round. Fitzsimmons followed that up two weeks later on August 24 in New York with a KO2 over Tom Sharkey.

On August 30, 1900 in New York, James J. Corbett scored a KO5 over Kid McCoy. The gate receipts were over $56,000.

On September 1, 1900, the repeal of the Horton law went into effect, once again making boxing illegal in New York.

On September 8, 1900, a massive hurricane hit Galveston and destroyed most of the town. The estimated death toll was about 8,000 people, making it the deadliest natural disaster ever to hit the United States. The damage from the water and wind had left the town in shambles.

Years later, Johnson said that Billy McCarthy was with him at Galveston when the terrible cataclysm occurred and caused the deaths of so many

[97] *Galveston Daily News*, June 26, 1900.

thousands of people. "My word! We had a narrow squeak and an awful experience then."[98]

While the town was being rebuilt, Johnson temporarily took his boxing career on the road again, boxing in the South. It was around this time that Johnson might have scored a KO10 over George Lawler in Hot Springs, Arkansas. He also defeated Howard Pollar.

On Wednesday November 28, 1900 at the Phoenix Athletic Club in Memphis, Tennessee, a heavyweight fight took place between Josh Mills, champion of Ohio, who had a "good record," and Jack Johnson, champion of Texas. The local *Memphis Commercial Appeal* said Johnson's most notable achievement was a draw with Klondike, "who is possibly the best heavyweight negro pugilist in the country."[99]

The day of the fight, it was said that both Johnson and Mills weighed about 170 pounds. However, it was also said that Johnson had a 10-pound weight advantage. Frank Raggio refereed all of the bouts on the card.

> [Johnson] mixed things in the first round, and from that time on roughed it to the end. Mills, the lighter by ten pounds, tried for Johnson's wind as a means of stopping him, but he met with clever blocking. Mills was down twice in the first round, and in nearly every round thereafter he was on the floor. He did not class with the Texas negro in any respect, though he made the best showing he could. Johnson is clever a little bit, and can reach a higher point if he has wisdom and judgment. Mills is clever, too, but somewhat less than a little bit. Hence he got whipped last night. In the sixth round he was almost knocked through the ropes twice, and the referee should have stopped the fight then and there, but he did not. Mills had nothing to account for in the seventh round. He was in default when the bell sounded.
>
> Throughout both men were vicious and careless. Almost at any stage either man could have been disqualified, but the referee chose to let them hammer their way through. There were repeated cries of foul and repeated fouls, but no attention was paid them. The men were simply traveling a rough road, and the spectators were hooting and howling all the while, albeit the milling was very inartistic. Both Johnson and Mills have much to learn about boxing and a great deal more to learn about the ethics of the game. Johnson is really the better man.[100]

Mills was unable to answer the bell to start the 7th round, and retired. Therefore the local newspaper said Jack Johnson and Josh Mills fought for 7 rounds, "or rather six rounds and a fraction."

---

[98] *Sydney Daily Telegraph,* January 25, 1907; *Referee,* January 30, 1907.
[99] *Memphis Commercial Appeal,* November 26, 1900.
[100] *Memphis Commercial Appeal,* November 29, 1900.

Johnson was superior throughout the fight. Mills was game, but was never better than a 10 to 3 underdog in his chances at any stage of the bout. "Johnson won with his plenty left, while Mills had more than he cared to harbor in the line of a well-proven deficit. In every way and at every stage of the game Johnson showed his superiority. He is a threat against any negro heavyweight in the country." Clearly, Johnson had shown his gameness and strength in this one. Memphis was impressed.

One month later, on Thursday December 27, 1900, again in Memphis, Johnson fought a third match against Klondike Haynes (or Haines), the fellow black fighter. It was a scheduled 20-round bout before the Phoenix Athletic Club, where Johnson had stopped Josh Mills.

Since their 20-round draw back in June, Klondike's results included: 1900 DND6 Ed Denfass, LDQby5 Peter Maher, KO4 Jim Barnes, W6 Jim Brady, DND6 Joe Goddard, and KO4 Brady.

This time, in the 1st round, Johnson jabbed away at Klondike's left eye, which started damaging and closing it. By the 3rd round, Klondike's eyelids were closing even more.

The fight grew a little wearisome after the first few rounds, owing to the fact that heavyweights did not move as fast as lighter fighters. "They are apparently slow and sluggish without being actually so. ... The men fought prettily and observed the injunctions of the referee to the letter."

Before the end of 8 rounds, Klondike's left eye was completely closed and he could not see out of it. In spite of the disadvantage, he put up the best fight that he could under the circumstances. In the 11th round, he made things interesting, although he did not inflict any injury on Johnson.

The fight lasted 13 full rounds. When the bell rang to start the 14th round, Haines remained in his corner. Just prior to the bell, he had motioned to Referee Doc Hottum, who went over and talked with him. Klondike then got up and announced that he could not fight any more because his left eye was completely closed. "I can't fight with one eye. I can beat Johnson, and have done so. I beat him in five rounds at Chicago, but my eye is completely closed and I cannot see."

Haines had a swollen face, besides his eye being closed. He was still strong on his legs at the end. Yet, he chose to retire. The referee awarded the fight to Johnson, who danced about the ring gleefully. He had his revenge.

During the fight, Johnson was never in distress. He hardly had a bruise on him. Still, despite vastly improving upon his prior performances against Klondike and avenging his earlier loss, Johnson endured a bit of criticism for failing to achieve a clean knockout rather than a technical one by forcing his man to retire.

> He did not perform as well as he might, however. He ought to have scored a knockout. For eight rounds, at least, he was fighting a one-eyed man. Johnson lacks but one thing that is useful in his business, and that is a knockout blow. He will have to develop one before he

achieves distinction in the ring. If his hands were as fast as his feet he would be a dangerous contender for championship honors. When he met Josh Mills in this city he says he broke his right thumb on him and that hand had been bad ever since. He says he could have made a knockout of the fight last night but for this.

Some said that Klondike was probably the better fighter of the two, but for the eye injury. He had more knowledge of the business. However, "It is no excuse for Klondike to say that he would have won if his eye had not been closed. He was there to protect his eyes, as well as other parts of his body. He got hit in his eye the first round and was immediately put at a disadvantage." It was his fault for getting hit there, and to Johnson's credit for causing and enhancing the damage that handicapped him.

Regardless of his perceived lack of punching power, Jack Johnson once again showed potential. "Johnson is likely to become the best colored heavy-weight in the country. For a negro he has an intelligent face. People who are well up may say that Klondike can beat Johnson, but he didn't do it last night." It was said that club matchmaker Joe Sullivan would try to match Johnson with Frank Childs.

Doc Hottum had refereed the bouts in a satisfactory manner, which pleased the spectators. "It is hard to handle negro fighters, as they are easily rattled and disobedient."[101]

Jack Johnson had shown that he was a fighter who improved with time and experience. He had done better in each of his three bouts with Klondike, going from a loss to a draw to a victory.

Just over two weeks after his third bout with Klondike, back in Galveston again, on January 14, 1901 at the Galveston Athletic Club, Jack Johnson took on Jim Scanlan, a 26-year-old white fighter who was popular in Galveston, having fought there several times.

Scanlan and Johnson
TO-NIGHT,
Galveston Athletic Club,
Bernau's Gymnasium, Next to News Office.

Jim Scanlan's record included: 1898 D20 Jack Finnegan, D10 Australian Jimmy Ryan (over whom Marvin Hart would score a 1901 KO7), and KO11 Jack Fogarty; 1899 KO2 John Heiman (a.k.a. Jack McCormack, whom Johnson had defeated via DQ6 in 1900), KO1 Charley Brooks (against whom Johnson had scored an 1897 KO2), D20 and KO3 Paddy Purtell, KO1 Charles Lawler, LKOby2 Billy Stift, L10 Billy Lewis, and LKOby5 Jack LaFontise; and 1900 KO10 Jack Graham, KO5 Charles Fogarty (on the same card as Johnson-McNeill), L6 Jim Hall, KO6 Tim Hurley, KO5 John Cavanaugh, WDQ3 James 'Doc' Payne, and WDQ1 Dan Creedon. He had over 30 fights of experience. Scanlan had been a

[101] *Memphis Commercial Appeal,* December 28, 1900.

Galveston club "instructor," and had refereed and decided Johnson-Klondike II, so he had seen Johnson in action, up close.

The locals expected a very interesting bout. "Scanlan has greatly improved since he was here last and will probably give a good account of himself. Johnson, who is known to be very clever, will have to use his

Jim Scanlan

knowledge, box and employ the best tactics he is capable of to avoid Scanlan's vicious drives." The main event was set for 9 p.m.[102]

About 1,900 people witnessed the bout. 150 came down from Houston on a special train. Clearly, the large crowd proved that the fight had both local and semi-local appeal.

From the start of the 1st round, the bout was fierce. Johnson was the aggressor and went at Scanlan as if he intended to stop him quickly. A straight left raised a bump on Scanlan's face. Frequent "taps" on the head and body quickly followed. "Johnson seemed to find little difficulty in reaching the white man, but his blows lacked sufficient force to do much damage. The negro was fast." By the end of the round, both were sparring cautiously.

The 2nd round was all Johnson again. He landed a blow to Scanlan's nose that started the blood flowing. Johnson was able to hit him when and where he pleased. There were frequent clinches, and both men indulged in fouls. Throughout the contest, both liked to hold and wrestle, hold and hit, refuse to break, and hit on the break.

In the 3rd round, Scanlan came up fresh and showed to his best advantage. He cleverly blocked several vicious leads and landed two good body blows which caused Johnson some discomfiture. However, his success was only temporary. Both committed several fouls, and the referee was kept busy trying to check these practices, without success. At the end of the round, Johnson landed a right and left on the head and body.

At the start of the 4th round, both were cautious. For thirty seconds, each tried to get the other to lead. Johnson missed a right and they clinched. Both hit on the break and landed to the head and body. Another stiff blow

[102] *Galveston Daily News*, January 14, 1901.

to Scanlan's nose brought the blood again. They were engaged in vicious infighting at the gong.

The 5th round featured a great number of fouls, for both fighters seemed to disregard the ring rules. There were repeated clinches. They refused to listen to the referee. Things got so bad that the referee sent the men to their corners and terminated the round 45 seconds early. Still, not much damage was done.

Johnson had the decided advantage in the 6th round. He landed repeatedly to the body and head, though the blows lacked steam. Scanlan fought back hard and stood his ground, but he could not land solidly on his clever opponent. The round ended with Johnson ducking a vicious swing for the jaw.

From the start of the 7th round, the fighters commenced fouling. It became so bad that the referee once again sent them to their corners. Both complained that the other was fouling. The referee decided to terminate the contest. He had warned them repeatedly to break fair, but they refused to do so.

Initially, it was said that no decision was rendered, and the club declared it a no contest. The referee did not render a decision from the ring. Later on, he told a reporter that he had decided the contest a draw.

Regardless of the technical result, it was clear that Johnson was the superior boxer. "From almost every point Johnson had the better of the contest. Had he been the stiff puncher that Scanlan is, matters would have come to an end early in the action. He is quicker, cleverer, equally as good in ring generalship, but lacked the driving power of his white antagonist."

The light-heavyweight-sized Johnson might not have been a big puncher at that point, but he certainly was a fast and clever boxer, and strong enough to engage in wrestling tactics. Scanlon hit harder, but could not land as often.[103]

In mid-February 1901, the Jeffries-Ruhlin championship contest, set to be held in Ohio, was called off. The governor had put a stop to the bout, and a judge upheld an injunction, calling boxing a public nuisance that impeded the progress of civilization and degraded the community. These types of legal attacks were nothing new to boxing. The bigger the bout, the more the politicians came out. Jack Johnson would soon experience this.

---

[103] *Galveston Daily News*, January 15, 1901. In March 1901, Scanlon would be knocked out by Dan Creedon in 5 rounds. In May, Al Weinig would knock out Scanlon in 7 rounds.

CHAPTER 4

A Bad Night
Becomes a Bad Month

Just over one month after Johnson-Scanlan, on Monday February 25, 1901 in Galveston, Texas, a 22-year-old (one month shy of 23) Jack Johnson took on 32-year-old Joe Choynski, the biggest name and test to date in his boxing career.

Joe Choynski

The vastly more experienced "Jewish" Joe Choynski had fought three champions and nearly every top contender for over a decade of boxing. At 160-170 pounds, he fought both middleweights and heavyweights, and he had both the punch and the skill to do it.

Amongst his experiences, back in 1889, Choynski had given James Corbett a tough fight before being stopped in the 27th round. Joe had been a sparring partner for Peter Jackson in 1892 and 1894. During 1894, Choynski engaged in a war with Bob Fitzsimmons, managing to deck and badly hurt Bob at one point, though Joe grew tired and took a beating from Fitzsimmons until the bout was stopped in the 5th round. In 1897, Choynski fought a 20-round draw with a then 22-year-old James Jeffries, a man who weighed well over 200 pounds. Although Jeffries was the aggressor and dropped Choynski a couple of times, for the most part, Choynski boxed brilliantly and at one point hit Jeff so hard that his lip was forced through his teeth. Johnson probably had been a Choynski sparring partner for a brief period of time in October 1897.

Choynski had over 50 bouts of experience, most of them against solid foes. Some of his other significant results included: 1891 LKOby4 Joe Goddard; 1892 KO15 George Godfrey; 1894 D6 Bob Armstrong; 1895 KO3 Frank Childs; 1896 KO13 Jim Hall, L8 Tom Sharkey, KO4 Joe McAuliffe, and LKOby6 Peter Maher; 1897 WDQ4 Denver Ed Smith and KO4 Herman Bernau; 1898 D8 Tom Sharkey, WND6 Joe Goddard, L6 Gus Ruhlin, and W6 Ed Dunkhorst; 1899 L20 Charles 'Kid' McCoy, W6 Jack McCormick, WDQ7 Pete Everett, KO3 Jim Hall, and KO6 Steve O'Donnell; and 1900 LKOby4 Kid McCoy, W6 Peter Maher, LKOby7 Joe Walcott, LKOby3 Tom Sharkey, and WDQ4 Fred Russell.

A young Jack Johnson

Choynski was well-known for having a very hard punch, and he knew how to time it just right. Jeffries later said that Choynski and Fitzsimmons were the two hardest punchers in boxing. By 1901, Choynski was past his prime, having been stopped three times in the past year, but he was still a solid veteran, far more experienced than the decade younger Johnson, and he was still able to defeat good fighters, regardless of size.

It is fair to estimate that both Choynski and Johnson weighed about 170 pounds for this fight, as both weighed around that for fights before and after. No official weights were taken, given that it was a heavyweight bout. Johnson had slight advantages in height and reach, and of course youth, but Choynski had the vast experience advantage and was the bigger puncher.

The fight took place at the Galveston Athletic Club for the benefit of its members, and apparently every member was there. It was the first performance at Harmony Hall since the September 8 storm, which had badly damaged it. Except for the cracks and openings where the night air seeped through, it was rehabilitated, and was never better-filled.

Johnson and Choynski were engaged to give an exhibition of the manly art to the extent of 20 rounds. Sig Sass represented the club as timekeeper. Jack Simpson acted as Choynski's timekeeper, and Winter Daniels represented Johnson. Herman Bernau, the club owner who had once fought and lost to Choynski, refereed.

Choynski entered the ring at 9:34 p.m., followed by Billy McCarthy and other supporters. Five minutes later, Johnson went to his corner, followed by local boxer "Cooky" Defferari and a couple of others. They listened to Referee Bernau's instructions, selected gloves, and engaged in the usual preliminaries.

The fight began at 9:47 p.m. There was little preliminary sparring, for they immediately entered into the spirit of the big event. Choynski led with his left and Johnson "pulled down his head in beautiful style." Johnson led for the jaw and tapped it lightly. Choynski landed a considerable blow on Johnson's chin. He then "bunted Johnson on the forehead." Just before time was called Joe led hard but only touched the side of the head.

At the start of the 2nd round, each began a tattoo on the other's forehead. Johnson landed to the stomach, but he did not hit hard enough to do damage. Twice Choynski tapped Johnson's nose. Johnson tried for the stomach again but hit a glove. Joe landed a light tap on Johnson's jaw when the gong ended the round.

The 3rd round had barely begun when Johnson fell forward into Choynski's arms and gradually sank to the floor, face downward. The referee began counting and Johnson rolled onto his back. He did not rise when the ten seconds were counted, and he was called out.

This local reporter believed that Choynski had landed on his chin, but didn't seem too sure. The punch was so fast that he had not seen it. Referee Bernau said it was a feint with the left and a strike with the right on the jaw that put Johnson to sleep No blood had been spilled and neither contestant was marked.[104]

The *National Police Gazette* reported, "Both men showed up well, but it was apparent from the very beginning that Johnson was outclassed." In the 3rd round, "Choynski caught him on the jaw with a right hook and he went down and out like a log." The *New York Clipper* reported that a "right hook square on the jaw put the darkey to sleep."[105]

Johnson had met an experienced hard-punching veteran, and got caught and knocked out. Clearly, he was not yet ready for the step up to the big time. He needed more experience and time to further develop his skills. Being knocked out showed the young pugilist that he could be knocked out, which likely caused him to further improve his defense, and to develop an even more cautious style. Jack Johnson did not have a meteoric rise, but would be like a fine wine that improved with age and experience.

To make matters worse, as if being knocked out wasn't bad enough, while Johnson was laying prostrate on the canvas, out cold, Captain Brooks appeared and announced that he was a State Ranger and was placing the boxers under arrest in the good name of the State and Governor Sayers. Four rangers accompanied Brooks, and he produced warrants calling for the boxers' arrest.

Two of the rangers walked over to Choynski, who stood in his corner, to place him under arrest. They escorted him to his dressing room on the floor below.

The other two rangers "stood guard over Johnson, who lay in the middle of the ring unconscious of the new show. He awakened from a deep sleep," and at first, was confused and not sure what was going on. However, eventually his brain cleared and he learned that he was under arrest.

Some in the crowd tried to leave quickly, fearing that they might be named as witnesses, or possibly even arrested.

Colonel John Lovejoy announced that the State had designated him to represent it in the prosecution of the case. Both Choynski and Johnson were accused of violating the law against prizefighting.

The boxers were transported to the county jail and held there. Colonel Lovejoy requested that the bail be fixed at a whopping $5,000 each. Choynski and Johnson's attorneys requested that bail be set at $500, but Recorder Noah Allen agreed with Lovejoy and fixed the bonds at $5,000 each, which neither could pay. Hence, the boxers would remain in jail.

---

[104] *Galveston Daily News*, February 26, 1901.
[105] *New York Clipper*, March 16, 1901; *National Police Gazette*, March 23, 30, April 13, 27, 1901. Some Southern dispatches said a right in the pit of the stomach did the trick. However, the local account did not back this claim. *Louisville Evening Post, Louisville Times*, February 26, 1901. Sometimes Johnson later claimed that he was not knocked out, but that the police stopped the bout. This claim was at odds with the local next-day report. At times, Johnson also said it was a left hook that decked him.

Lovejoy told a reporter that Governor Sayers was determined to stop all boxing matches, no matter what the cost. The Johnson-Choynski contest had been announced for several weeks. The governor had taken notice, and it was decided to allow the contest to proceed in order to avoid any technical legal arguments that the law had not been violated by a proposed contest. Prospective warrants were obtained for a bout that had actually happened, so there was no doubt that the law against prizefighting had been violated.[106]

At the time, boxing was still technically illegal in most jurisdictions. Local politicians and law enforcement officials had been allowing real fights to occur and to elude the law's coverage by calling them instructional exhibitions of skill. However, state politicians and law enforcement officials often cracked down on high-profile fights. Johnson had been making a name for himself on the local Galveston scene. When a really big-name fighter like Choynski was brought in to box him, the contest was elevated to a higher level, with more publicity, the kind of which state politicians take note.

Deputy Sheriff Wallers Burns, Choynski, Johnson, Sheriff Henry Thomas, Jailer Frank Schreiber

Actually, the local press had attempted to minimize the publicity and advertising surrounding the Johnson-Choynski fight. They were cognizant of the fact that politicians would not be happy about the bout. However, Choynski was too big of a name for word not to spread.

Furthermore, it is likely that some of the ill-will regarding the bout might have been influenced by the fact that it was a mixed-race fight, of which the state of Texas did not approve.

---

[106] *Galveston Daily News*, February 26, 1901.

Just to provide context for the time's racial climate in the South, the same day as the Johnson-Choynski fight report was issued, the *Louisville Courier-Journal* published an article quoting an author criticizing the book *Uncle Tom's Cabin*, saying:

> [The book is] a false statement of the social conditions of the South previous to the war. It was a crime on the negroes to free them. If it had to come, it should have been gradual. 'Uncle Tom's Cabin' largely aided in bringing about this terrible injury to the negroes by falsely representing the conditions of slavery.[107]

Lending further insight into the prevailing feelings regarding racial separation, at that time, Texas legislators introduced a bill to have separate rooms for white and negro jurors.

The Johnson-Choynski fight was a hot-button political issue. In the Texas State House of Representatives, Representative Shaw of Dallas introduced a resolution calling on the Governor to provide information regarding what steps he had taken concerning the Johnson-Choynski fight. Although the newspapers had not advertised the affair, he believed the Governor had taken some action already. Representative Tarpey of Galveston moved to table the motion, but Shaw accused him of attempting to suppress information. Tarpey replied that Galveston had as capable and honest officials as any place in the state and the motion would be a reflection upon them. Mr. Bridges said it was possible to have boxing contests without violating the law, and thought that such contests were held occasionally in Dallas, where Shaw was from. He was implying that Shaw was being hypocritical in taking such an interest in Galveston affairs when boxing matches took place in Shaw's neck of the woods as well, without any such resolutions being put forth. Hence, the issue became not just about boxing, but about regional local pride and politics.

Texas Governor Joseph Sayers said he would leave it to the people of Galveston to say whether or not the prize-fight law should be enforced. He indeed had employed Mr. John Lovejoy of Galveston to represent the State in the prosecution of the prize-fight cases.

The governor had known since February 18 that the fight was to take place. Under his instructions, Adjutant General Scurry sent Captain Brooks and four other rangers to Galveston. Captain Bill McDonald, who had stopped a Choynski fight at Galveston two years ago, was not sent this time because he was too well known, which might tip off the promotion. The rangers had orders to wait and not to interfere unless the local city and county authorities failed to act.[108]

The regional battle continued. The next day, the front page of the *Galveston Daily News* commented on Representative Shaw's resolution regarding prize fighting, calling it a "cheap scheme for advertising."

---

[107] *Louisville Courier-Journal*, February 26, 1901.
[108] *Galveston Daily News*, February 27, 1901.

Politicians had often used anti-boxing fervor to get their names in the newspapers. There had been several prizefights held in Dallas, so fellow representatives did not see why Shaw should be so concerned about law and order in Galveston and this particular bout. Another representative said it was not the duty of the legislature to enforce the law, only to make laws. It was not within the province of the legislature to ask the Governor what he was doing.

To needle Shaw, other representatives called for a resolution that the Governor should also be called upon for such information as he might have touching upon the burning of people alive in Dallas, which was a more serious offense than prize fighting. Shaw declared that Dallas was God's country and there was no crime there. He did inform them that the Dallas burners had been sent to the penitentiary for life and another was soon to be dealt with.

Mr. Tarpey of Galveston said he wanted it understood that they did not have prize fights in Galveston, but only scientific boxing exhibitions.

Ultimately, by a vote of 51 to 50, the legislature adopted the resolution calling upon information from the governor regarding the Johnson-Choynski bout. The Governor said he would send a report to the legislature the following day.[109]

The state law against engaging in a prize fight carried a penalty of 2 to 5 years in the penitentiary at hard labor. This was the law that Governor Charles Culberson had facilitated in order to prevent the Corbett-Fitzsimmons fight. In the present instance, "The arrest was made at the instigation of Gov. Sayers." Many governors enjoyed the cheap notoriety they obtained when they attacked high-profile fights and fighters.

Because their pre-trial bonds were so massive and neither could pay, both Johnson and Choynski remained incarcerated for several weeks, simply for having engaged in a consensual boxing match, which may or may not have been illegal.

Choynski later said that he gave Johnson boxing lessons at the jail. While there, the two frequently put on the gloves, and Joe taught Jack a great many of the finer points of boxing. Lessons from an experienced and savvy veteran of the game did not go unheeded. Obviously, their local jailers had no issue with the sport, and probably derived some entertainment from watching them spar.[110]

Johnson said the local sheriff was a nice man who gave Joe and Jack good treatment. He allowed the club to send them boxing gloves, and every day they would box in the jail yard, surrounded by police officers and guests.

> Joe had great affection for me and to prove it, he gave me lessons, showing me the best punches anyone has ever seen in a jail yard. I

[109] *Galveston Daily News*, February 28, 1901.
[110] *San Francisco Chronicle*, July 10, 1910.

learned more in those two weeks than I had learned in my entire existence up to that point. Besides, we didn't have anything to do other than sleep, eat, box, and talk; I saw to it that the boxing part was not neglected.

So Johnson turned a negative into a positive.[111]

Governor Sayers was persistent in his efforts to punish Choynski and Johnson. When a Grand Jury failed to indict them, instead of respecting their decision as he claimed he would do, he immediately telegraphed Captain J. H. Brooks of the State Rangers, asking him to re-arrest and continue to keep the boxers in jail until another Grand Jury could be empanelled and the case again considered.

The *National Police Gazette* noted that Texas had a new way of dealing with boxing, as illustrated by the Choynski-Johnson situation. Rather than preventing the bout, they simply allowed the fighters to fight and then arrested and held them afterwards. "The mere matter of arrest will serve as a salutary warning to all fighters that they are not wanted in Texas. Thus will the object be served, and the end justify the means." Fighters would take notice of the fact that fellow boxers were being arrested and having to spend lengthy periods of time in jail for engaging in their profession, even if they were not found guilty of anything, or even indicted. Hence the deterrent effect would be obtained.[112]

Having been arrested on the evening of February 25, Choynski and Johnson were not released from jail for nearly one month, until 2 p.m. on March 22, when the Court of Criminal Appeals mandated that they be released from incarceration on a bond of $1,000 each. Bondsmen put up

---

[111] *My Life and Battles* at 32.
[112] *New York Clipper*, March 16, 1901; *National Police Gazette*, March 23, 30, April 13, 27, 1901.

the money and the boxers were released. The bondsmen asked that their names not be made public.

The original bond had been set at $5,000 each. Upon habeas corpus proceedings before Judge Allen of the Criminal Court, the bond was reduced to $2,500 each, but they still could not pay. The Court of Criminal Appeals finally reduced it to $1,000. They had been in jail for nearly 25 days.

Choynski immediately left for La Grange, Illinois. Johnson took an evening train to St. Louis, Missouri, hoping to obtain a match there in the next few weeks. Just before he left, an upset Choynski said,

> I am through with the boxing game. I shall never enter the ring again.
> … To the people in Galveston I have nothing but words of praise,
> and to Sheriff Thomas and Deputy Will Thomas and Jailers Burns,
> Schrieber and Lott I am grateful for many favors. Prison life is
> especially irksome to an active man, and a fellow, after being in
> prison 24 days, feels like a 2-year-old on a fast track when given his
> liberty. A man who has never been detained against his will don't
> know the value of freedom.

Choynski said he would return to answer any charges, but would not box in Texas again. Johnson said he was treated kindly during his imprisonment, but was glad to be free again.[113]

Eventually, the second grand jury also refused to indict the boxers. The Grand Jury felt that too much importance had been attached to the fight, "and that the moral and religious element in the State has been unduly excited by sensational and exaggerated enlargement of what otherwise, to

[113] *Galveston Daily News*, March 23, 1901.

this Grand Jury, appears to be a small affair with no motive, intent or fact to show a violation of the law." The law had not been violated, but Choynski and Johnson had lost nearly a month of their lives. Isn't the legal system lovely?[114]

The following year, in 1902, when asked if he had ever been knocked out, Johnson replied,

> I was knocked down once and dat left of Joe Choynski's did de biz for me. Dat was in Texas, and I'll sho'ly nebber forget dat night. We was boxing along all nice and fair, when 'biff and out went de lights and everything. When de referee said 'six' I kind of waked up, and den I knew it was about time for me to be getting up, but I didn't know nuffin before dat. He most sho'ly had a good left, dat Choynski.[115]

In 1908, when asked if he was ever soaked, Johnson said,

> My goodness that man Choynski caught me in my first big fight, and I thought he opened the top of my head. He hit me on the forehead over my right eye, blackened that eye, and almost broke the jaw on the other side. Oh, I was beaten, sure I was. The police jumped in and arrested us both, but I was licked anyhow. My golly, he simply knocked the brains, wind and ambition out of me. There was no more fight in me that there is in a cake of soap. I don't think anyone in the world was ever hit so hard.

> You know he hit Jeff in the mouth with a right one night, and they had to cut his lip away from his teeth with a knife. That Choynski boy was the hardest hitter that ever lived bar none.

> There's no use bluffing about not being licked, like a lot of these fellows do. I saw Caesar Attell in San Francisco once get knocked out by Congo Coon, and after they counted him out he jumped up and raved like a maniac. ... "I ain't out – I ain't out!" ... When they brought the other fellow over to Caesar to start the fight over, Attell said, "I didn't say I wanted to fight some more, Mr. Referee; I simply said that I wasn't cut."[116]

---

[114] *New York Clipper*, March 16, 1901; *National Police Gazette*, March 23, 30, April 13, 27, 1901. Choynski, clearly affected by his lengthy stay in jail, and having already been contemplating retirement, retired and did not fight again for one year. However, like most fighters, he came back to fight again. His subsequent results included: 1902 KO5 Bill Hanrahan, LKOby1 Kid Carter, KO6 Al Weinig, L6 Jack O'Brien, and W6 Frank Childs; 1903 KO2 Peter Maher, LND6 Jack O'Brien, LKOby2 and KO7 Nick Burley, DND6 Marvin Hart, and LKOby1 Kid Carter.

[115] *Los Angeles Herald*, May 10, 1902. However, the referee said it was a right that knocked out Johnson. The local account said Johnson was out cold for the 10-count.

[116] *New Zealand Truth*, April 25, 1908, quoting the *San Francisco Bulletin*.

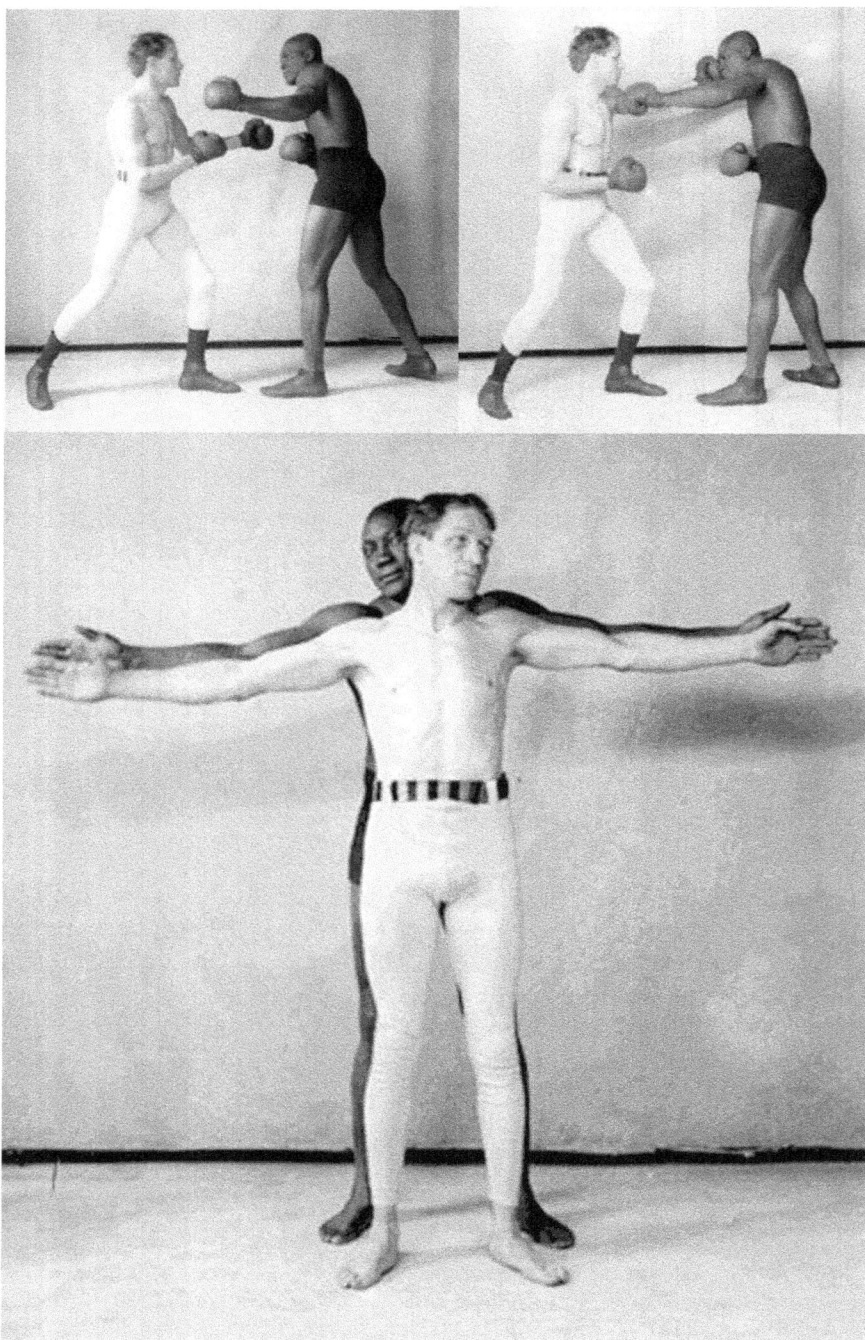

Johnson and Choynski pose in 1909

Caution in Colorado

In late April 1901, 23-year-old Jack Johnson traveled to Denver to fight another respected man in 29-year-old Billy Stift. The thickly built, strong Stift had primarily campaigned as a middleweight, though he was good enough to fight heavyweights as well. Stift had nearly 40 known bouts to that point, including: 1895 W6 Mike Brennan and D12 Frank Dutch Neal; 1896 LKOby7 Tommy West; 1897 W6 and W20 George Shrosbree, and LKOby6 Tommy Ryan; 1898 D6 Dan Creedon and WDQ5 Mysterious Billy Smith; 1899 LDQ7 Jack Root (Stift hit Root while he was down), W6 Scaldy Billy Quinn, L20 Tommy Ryan, KO3 Jim Watts, D6 George Byers, KO2 Jim Scanlan, L6 Jack Root, D6 Mysterious Billy Smith, LKOby13 Kid McCoy, and W6 Jack McCormick; 1900 KO1 Al Weinig, W6 and D10 Jack Jeffries, and L6 Dick O'Brien; and 1901 LKOby5 Dan Creedon and D10 Ben Tremble. The Tremble bout took place in Denver just one week prior to the Johnson bout.

At that time, Johnson was training and sparring with Tom Sharkey, who was also in Colorado preparing for a bout with Fred Russell. Sharkey's major bouts included 1896 W8 Joe Choynski, D4 James Corbett, and WDQ8 Bob Fitzsimmons; 1897 KO6 Joe Goddard; 1898 D8 Choynski, L20 James Jeffries, KO1 Gus Ruhlin, and WDQ9 Corbett; 1899 KO10 Kid McCoy, KO2 Jack McCormick, and L25 Jeffries in a close title bout. Since that grueling title fight, Sharkey's record included: 1900 KO4 Joe Goddard, KO2 Jim Jeffords, KO1 McCormick, KO3 Tom 'Stockings' Conroy, KO3 Joe Choynski, KO1 Yank Kenny, LKOby15 Gus Ruhlin, and LKOby2 Bob Fitzsimmons.

Having the opportunity to spar with a very strong, experienced, rough and tough, well-conditioned rushing fighter like Sharkey provided Johnson with valuable experience in dealing with an aggressive puncher. Johnson clearly had a lot of respect for Sharkey, and later called him "one of the ring's greatest fighters, though he never held a championship."[117]

Although Sharkey drew the color line and would not fight black fighters, he often paid them to be his sparring partners. Bob Armstrong, a large and clever black fighter, was Sharkey's chief sparring partner, and had sparred with Tom prior to Sharkey's 1899 championship challenge against Jeffries.

Johnson said that while in Colorado, he joined a motley crew of well-known fighters that included the world-famous Sharkey. The plan was for all of the scrappers to give exhibitions to make money.

---

[117] Johnson, *In the Ring and Out* at 44–45.

Tom Sharkey spars Bob Armstrong

On Sunday April 21, 1901 at the Sand Creek house in Denver, a big crowd gathered to watch Tom Sharkey in training. Sharkey boxed 10 fast rounds with big Bob Armstrong and Jack Johnson.[118]

The *Denver Post* called Johnson the big colored man and burly "coon" who kept Choynski company in the Galveston jail a few weeks ago. It had only been one month since Johnson was released from jail.

Johnson claimed to have defeated Klondike and all the heavyweights around Chicago. He said that he was going to send Stift home a defeated man.

The impression, though, was that Stift was the slight favorite. "The bout between Johnson and Stift ought to be on the hurricane order, and Billy will surely try to land one of his famous 'haymakers' on Johnson. If he does — well, goodby coon."[119]

In its daily hype, the *Post* anticipated that the Stift-Johnson bout would be something to talk about: a contest of the "bruising variety." "Both men are known to be sluggers and, as each is very confident of winning, there will be lots of sport for those present."

Another reason why the local paper thought it would be a good fight was because of the financial terms. "Stift wants to win enough money to make his trip to Colorado profitable. He made this match winner-take-all, Johnson readily agreed to the proposition, and the loser of this contest will have nothing but his trouble for his pains." Hence, both fighters would have a big incentive to do their utmost to win, or at least not lose. In the event of a draw, typically the purse would be split.

The local paper again confirmed that Johnson was assisting Sharkey in his training.[120]

---

[118] *Denver Post*, April 22, 1901. Sharkey's trainer, Spider Kelly, was set to fight Sam Bolan, who in turn was training Billy Stift for the Johnson fight.
[119] *Denver Post*, April 23, 1901.
[120] *Denver Post*, April 24, 25, 1901.

Billy Stift

Billy Stift had been seen before at the Colorado Athletic Club. He put James Scanlan to sleep in 2 rounds about a year prior. Johnson had been superior to Scanlan in a bout that was terminated in the 7th round and declared a draw on account of mutual foul tactics. "In Jack Johnson he meets a man who can hit as hard as he can himself and who will weigh about ten pounds more. … Something will have to give away sure. They can both hit like mules kicking." The *Denver Post* advertised in its headline that each fight on the card was about evenly matched.[121]

The local *Denver Daily News* said, "The wise ones pick Billy Stift as the winner against Jack Johnson, the big colored fighter, in their ten-round bout. Stift is anxious to make a good impression as he feels he did not do his best when he met Tremble at the Wheel club last week. George English will referee all three bouts."[122]

On Friday April 26, 1901 in Denver, Colorado, before the Colorado Athletic Club, Jack Johnson of Texas fought Billy Stift of Chicago 10 rounds to a "very tame draw." Nothing else was mentioned by the *Denver Daily News* regarding this undercard fight, likely given that the bout was boring.[123]

---

[121] *Denver Post*, April 26, 1901. Abe Attell would box Young Cassidy, and Spider Kelly would fight Sam Bolan. The doors would open at 7:15 p.m. At ringside would be celebrities who would second the various contestants on the card, including Tom Sharkey, Bob Armstrong, New York Jack O'Brien, Tommy Ryan, Young Corbett, and Fred Russell.
[122] *Denver Daily News*, April 26, 1901. Also known as the *Rocky Mountain News*.
[123] *Denver Daily News*, April 27, 1901. In the main event, Abe Attell scored a KO2 over Young Cassidy. Spider Kelly scored a KO3 over Sam Bolan.

The *Denver Post* said Stift, of whom much was expected, was a disappointment to the good-sized crowd. The 10-round bout had been hyped up, "but in a way it was quite disappointing." Referee George English called it a draw.

> Here were two big 170-pound men boxing ten rounds and neither one of them put a mark on his opponent. Not that the men weren't trying, but it shows that they have still much to learn about the game. Billy Stift has gone back woefully from what he used to be. Take him about five years ago and he would have made short work of an opponent like Johnson. Billy ties himself in a knot every time he tries to deliver that famous old haymaker of his. Instead of keeping on swinging his right and left hand continually he would swing his right and then clinch. Had he kept on swinging he might have caught Johnson with one of them and the battle would have ended. Johnson is a rather hard man to hit with the right hand at that. He assumes an awkward position, and with his long left hand manages pretty well to keep an opponent at a safe distance. In last night's contest the man who led was the one generally to land. Stift allowed Johnson time and time again to take the lead away from him. It was easy to see how Choynski knocked Johnson out. ... The big black fellow holds his right too low. Choynski just about feinted him into a lead and then swung his left to the jaw. ... Stift had the same opportunity last night, but failed to take advantage of it. Taken as a whole, it was a very tame exhibition for two big men. Not a knockdown occurred during the journey. They will have to do better than that to get main events.[124]

The *Denver Times* said Johnson and Stift put up a very bad fight at the Colorado Club.

> Stift and Johnson fought a slow ten-round draw. ... The very long and tiresome ten-round loafing match between Billy Stift and Jack Johnson put a damper on the entire affair, and there was very little enthusiasm. Johnson gained fame by eating bread and water in a Texas prison, and from the kind of fight he put up last night it will be better for him if he sticks to his trade instead of trying to break into the ring. ...

> The Stift-Johnson go is hardly worthy of a notice. Stift did not want to fight and Johnson was afraid to, so they stood up there through ten rounds, made faces at each other and fiddled the time away. Either man is capable of hitting a bull a hard enough blow on top of the head to put kinks in his tail, yet neither of them had a mark when the fight was over. Johnson led about eight times during the ten rounds and Stift about twice that many, and the remainder of the

---

[124] *Denver Post*, April 27, 1901.

time was spent in trying to make each other believe that they intended leading.[125]

Johnson was learning. He was still more of a super-middleweight or light heavyweight in size, though Stift was no bigger. Jack claimed to have eaten nothing but bread and water while in jail, so he probably was not at his strongest or most fit. The Stift bout took place slightly over a month after his release from jail. Keep in mind also that Stift was the older and far more experienced fighter, and he had fought the better quality of opposition.

It is also likely that coming off a knockout loss, Johnson became more inclined to be cautious and focus on defense; not to take chances on getting stopped. Plus, losing meant that he would earn no money in a winner-take-all bout. Trying to win could lead to a loss, because taking risks left one exposed to punches and/or fatigue (at a high altitude). However, keeping it close and fighting to a draw meant that the two combatants would split the purse. Johnson was probably taking no chances of coming away with no money. Clearly, his skill managed to neutralize a strong and experienced fighter who had been expected to defeat him. Something about his ability and tactics kept Stift cautious as well. Hence, the bout was dull.[126]

The next big local bout would be Sharkey-Russell. Johnson continued sparring and training with Sharkey. On April 28, 1901, immense crowds came to the Sand Creek house to watch Sailor Tom train. "The sailor appeared in fine fettle. He was as lively as a kitten and as strong as a bull. When he punched the bag to the ceiling it could be heard a block away, and he boxed ten rounds with Kelly, Armstrong and Johnson without so much as drawing a long breath." Johnson was already sparring again a mere two days after boxing 10 rounds with 5-ounce gloves, perhaps a testament to his improving defense, as well as his toughness.

That same day, Fred Russell was training hard as well. He was a big man, weighing a rock-solid 210 pounds. The confident Russell said he would knock out Sharkey and then go after Ruhlin and Jeffries.[127]

On April 29, in the morning, Sharkey walked a mile, and then an hour later he ran 10 miles. At 2:30 p.m., Bob Armstrong, Spider Kelly and Jack Johnson all boxed Sharkey in turn. "This is the hardest exercise of the day and the men go at it so rough that one would almost think they were

---

[125] *Denver Times*, April 27, 1901.

[126] In January 1902, Marvin Hart would knock out Billy Stift in the 3rd round. In a rematch in August 1902, Hart would win a 6-round decision over Stift. In April 1902, Jack Root scored a KO2 over Stift. Billy would suffer 6-round decision losses to Philadelphia Jack O'Brien and George Gardner, and in 1903 Tommy Ryan would stop Stift in the 4th round, although Stift had lasted 10 rounds with Ryan in 1902. In 1904, Jack O'Brien would score a KO2 over Stift.

[127] *Denver Post*, April 29, 1901. Fred Russell's record included: 1899 L20 Joe Kennedy, 1900 L6 and L10 Frank Childs, KO9 Mexican Pete Everett, LDQ4 Joe Choynski (Russell disqualified for hitting Choynski after the bell and knocking him out), and 1901 KO1 Texas Jack/Jim McCormick (who was currently in jail for counterfeiting).

engaged in a real contest. The bout between Sharkey and Armstrong is especially interesting, and is a treat to witness."

After completing the rest of his exercises, which included bag punching for an hour, Tom skipped rope for 10 minutes. Sharkey said the work he did was harder than what most laborers and miners did. "Only the stoutest and strongest constitution can stand this work. Why, I have trained with fighters in the past who tried to keep up with me in my training and do as much as I do, and I have yet to find the first one who can stand the pace." Bob Armstrong sung Sharkey's praises in the loudest terms. "I have trained him for all his big fights and I'll swear I never saw the man in such splendid condition."

Fred Russell was surprised that Sharkey was the 2 to 1 favorite. He was bigger than Sharkey, younger, and had never been knocked off his feet. He did not see how Sharkey could knock him out. He noted that the underdog had won the last several main events.[128]

On Friday May 3, 1901 in Denver, before the Colorado Athletic Club, a 5'8 ½" 192-pound Tom Sharkey scored a KO4 over the 6'4" 205-pound Fred Russell of California. In Sharkey's corner were Spider Kelly, Tommy Ryan, New York Jack O'Brien (not the famous Philadelphia Jack O'Brien, who was overseas at the time) Bob Armstrong, and likely Johnson. Russell had Young Corbett, Abe Attell, and Mexican Pete Everett, who would later fight Johnson. Tom Sharkey could hit hard enough to knock out a big man like Russell, handing him his first knockout loss.[129]

The next day, on May 4, Sharkey's aggregation of fighters, which included New York Jack O'Brien, Spider Kelly, Bob Armstrong, Tommy Ryan, Dave Barry, Mexican Pete Everett, and Jack Johnson, left for Cripple Creek under the management of Jack McKenna and A. E. Charlton. Sharkey and crew were scheduled to give exhibitions there, opening the new Olympic Club on the 7th. Tom was set to box Mexican Pete Everett 6 rounds and attempt to stop him. Everett had been training with Fred Russell.[130]

On Tuesday May 7, 1901 at the Cripple Creek opera house, under the auspices of the Olympic Athletic Club, in the preliminary, first Tom Sharkey boxed lightweight Spider Kelly 4 rounds. Jack Byrom then scored a KO1 over Young Forbes.

Jack Johnson boxed 4 exhibition rounds with Bob Armstrong. No decision was rendered. The local *Cripple Creek Evening Star* said it was a very tame 4-round sparring exhibition. The *Denver Post* said Armstrong made a great hit by his clever exhibition.

The 6'3" or 6'4" nearly 200-pound Armstrong's results included: 1895 KO10 Frank Slavin; 1896 KO4 Slavin and KO19 Charley Strong; 1897

---

[128] *Denver Post*, April 30, 1901.

[129] *Denver Daily News*, May 3, 4, 1901.

[130] *Denver Daily News*, May 1, 5, 6, 1901; *Cripple Creek Evening Star*, May 6, 1901. Sharkey was also scheduled to exhibit at Leadville, Aspen, Colorado Springs, and Pueblo.

KO6 Joe Butler and L6 Frank Childs; 1898 LKOby2 Childs, KO5 Yank Kenny, KO3 Butler, L10 James J. Jeffries, DND6 Joe Goddard, D10 Ed Dunkhorst, and KO14 Pete Everett; 1899 LKOby6 Frank Childs, KO2 Denver Ed Martin, W20 Tom Conroy, L10 Dunkhorst, and KO3 Jim Jeffords; and 1900 ND6 Ed Martin. Armstrong would later that year be a sparring partner for James Jeffries, assisting the champion in his preparations for his title defense against Gus Ruhlin.

In the main event, Sharkey entered the ring again, this time in a serious bout against Mexican Pete Everett. In the 1st round, immediately they went at it hammer and tongs. Everett landed several solid blows. However, eventually, late in the round Sharkey decked Everett, either with a right to the body or a left hook to the head (or both, depending on the source). While he was on the mat on one knee, Sharkey struck Everett with a right to the jaw that knocked Pete out. Referee H. C. Johnson disqualified Sharkey. The round had lasted just over two and a half minutes.[131]

The next day, the crew returned to Denver. Sharkey was set to leave for New York that morning, ending the exhibition tour early. It was said that the rest of the party, except Barry, would remain. Sharkey indeed left on May 9.[132]

Bob Armstrong

Interestingly enough, a late-June issue of the *National Police Gazette* said that a true bill charging both Choynski and Jack Johnson with prize-fighting had been found by a Texas grand jury and that both men would either have to forfeit their large bail bonds or return to the Lone Star State to stand trial.[133] Johnson did not return to Texas.

On July 13, 1901, Peter Jackson died of tuberculosis, known at that time as "consumption."

---

[131] *Cripple Creek Evening Star, Denver Daily News, Denver Post*, May 8, 1901.
[132] *Denver Daily News*, May 9, 10, 1901. On May 24, 1901 in Louisville, Marvin Hart scored a KO6 over Dan Creedon.
[133] *National Police Gazette*, June 22, 1901.

Johnson claimed to have given exhibitions in Colorado for a while. Eventually, he was matched to fight a 20-round bout with Mexican Pete Everett, to be held in mid-August at the Gold Coin Club in Victor, Colorado.[134]

On August 1, 1901 in Baltimore, Maryland, the Democratic state convention that met there "declared that the purpose of the party, if successful in the election, is to eliminate the negro from politics in Maryland, if such a thing be possible under the constitution of the state." The Democratic party recognized that the "peace, good order, personal safety and proper development of our material interests depend upon the control of the commonwealth by its intelligent white residents. Without the aid of the 60,000 colored voters, the Republican party in Maryland would be a hopeless minority." They wanted to prevent the control of the government "from passing into the hands of those who have neither the ability nor the interest to manage public affairs wisely and well."[135]

A week later, the Western Negro Press Association met and made several resolutions. They wanted people to be judged not by their race or the color of their skin but by the right and wrong of their acts. Resolutions included,

> That the recent remarks made by one of South Carolina's representatives [Tillman] at a meeting held in the great state of Wisconsin, when he said that all men were not created free and equal gives the lie to the framers of the Constitution who said that all men were created free and equal ... Tillman further denounced the educational plans of the Hon. Booker T. Washington – the plan that has met the approval of the best and most educated people of the world. Tillman further said that the negro was not fit to vote. ... Democrats in Maryland in attempting to disfranchise the negro are unwise, unpatriotic and un-American.[136]

On August 10, 1901 in Victor, Colorado, Jack Johnson refereed a bout between Morgan Williams and Kid Rolly, won by Williams in the 1st round.

At that point, it was said that both Johnson and Everett were training hard. The Mexican was the betting favorite.[137]

Jerry Mahoney of Cripple Creek, who had arranged the bout, was selected to referee the Johnson-Everett fight. "Both men have been given to understand that they have got to fight, and those who attend are certain to see a slugging match, as the men are pretty evenly matched."[138]

26-year-old Pete Everett, who had been boxing professionally since 1894, had nearly a 40-bout career which included: 1896 KO7 Jim Williams

---

[134] *Denver Daily News*, August 4, 1901.
[135] *Colorado Springs Gazette*, August 2, 1901. Article entitled, "The Negro As An Issue."
[136] *Colorado Springs Gazette*, August 8, 1901.
[137] *Denver Daily News*, August 11, 1901.
[138] *Denver Daily News*, August 12, 1901.

and KO7 Mike Queenan; 1897 L4 Young Peter Jackson; 1898 KO6 Billy Woods, LKOby3 James J. Jeffries, and LKOby14 Bob Armstrong; 1899 KO10 Jim Williams, L6 Frank Childs, and LDQby7 Joe Choynski; 1900 LKOby9 Fred Russell, W20 Mike Rowan, and L10 Frank Childs; and 1901 WDQ1 Tom Sharkey and KO3 Ed McCoy. Everett was from Colorado, so he would be the popular local man. Since August 1899, all of Everett's bouts had been held in Colorado.

Before fighting Jeffries in 1898, Everett was listed as standing just over 6 feet tall and weighing a little over 190 pounds. The big and powerful Jeffries quickly overwhelmed and easily beat Everett, who put up such little competition that Jeff accused him of lacking gameness. His subsequent fights against less powerful punchers than Jeffries showed otherwise. Everett was at least durable, although big men such as Armstrong and Russell had stopped him late. At this point, Jack Johnson was more of a super-middleweight or light-heavyweight, so he was probably at least 20 pounds smaller than Everett.

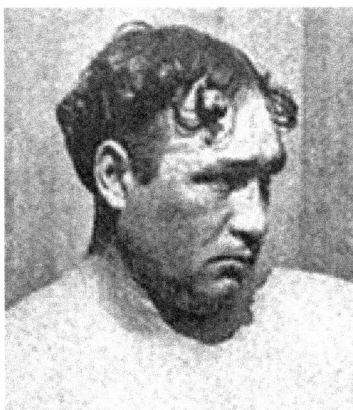

Mexican Pete Everett

On Wednesday August 14, 1901 in Victor, Colorado before the Gold Coin Club, 500 patrons of pugilism watched Jack Johnson of Texas and Cripple Creek's Mexican Pete Everett box the full 20 rounds. The *Denver Daily News* reported, "The contest was a very tame affair from beginning to end and could properly be called a hugging match. Jerry Mahoney, who refereed the match, called it a draw." This newspaper explicitly called it a 20-round hugging match. The *Denver Post* echoed that the fighters spent most of the time hugging each other and boxed 20 tame rounds to a draw.

Clearly, the bout was a dull 20-round draw that featured a great deal of clinching. One way of viewing matters is that at that point, the smaller Johnson likely did not have the power or finishing abilities of a Jim Jeffries,

Joe Choynski, Bob Armstrong, or Tom Sharkey, all of whom had decked Everett. Further, following the Choynski bout, Johnson had become fairly cautious, fighting two draws in a row, one of which featured a lot of posing and cautious feinting but little leading, and another that featured a great deal of clinching.[139]

However, there was another, entirely different perspective put forth about this bout. A special to the nearby *Colorado Springs Gazette* from Victor said,

> It was plainly evident that the match was fixed and it was very tame throughout. The house was worth about $500 to the fighters and management. Everett was very slow, while Johnson proved himself to be a good man and could at any stage of the game have put the Mexican out. The sports were disgusted and were not slow to let the fighters know that they were so.[140]

It is possible that the fight was a hippodrome in which Johnson, in order to earn a payday, had agreed to work with Everett and keep it even, or at least not try to stop him. Johnson might not have cared if it was a draw because he would still be paid and make much more than he would if he had not fought at all. Clearly, there were those who thought Johnson was carrying Everett.

However, it is also possible that because the fight was so dull and featured so much clinching, that the fans considered the bout to be a fix. Often, when the fighters were more concerned with their safety and clinched a great deal, and did not give their best efforts to take a chance to win by knockout, the fans or writers called the bout a fix. Regardless, this writer believed that Johnson was better and could have won by knockout if he had not held back.

Years later, when discussing all of his drawn bouts, Johnson said,

> In all those fights, I never once tried to win by knockout. I was studying boxing. I wanted to learn as much as I could and beat my opponents on points. I don't like to brag, but I could have knocked out my opponents and gotten things over with a whole lot quicker, if my great desire hadn't been to use those matches as a form of training.[141]

The question remains whether Johnson simply could not knock out his opponents, or could have done so had he not been inclined to be so cautious, fearing getting caught himself by opening up, or fearing fatigue if he opened up on a consistent basis and failed to stop his man, which could be very dangerous in a 20-round bout, or whether he was indeed carrying his foes so that he could earn money and obtain fights and experience.

---

[139] *Denver Daily News, Denver Post*, August 15, 1901.
[140] *Colorado Springs Gazette*, August 15, 1901.
[141] *My Life and Battles* at 36.

Johnson said that the day after the fight with Mexican Pete, his first wife, Mary Austin, a black woman whom he had married in 1898, left him. However, Johnson returned to Denver and reunited with her, for the time being. Later that year, in December 1901, they split permanently.[142]

On August 19, 1901, white residents of Peirce City, Missouri (spelling changed to "Pierce" in the early 1920s), a town 30 miles from Joplin, ignited a rampage. An approximately one-thousand-member white lynch mob assembled in response to the day-before discovery in the woods of a dead white woman, whose throat had been cut. The mob went to the jail where a black suspect was held, dragged him outside and hanged him. Although the evidence against him was circumstantial, early newspaper reports deemed the evidence "conclusive." Unsatisfied, the mob shot at the body swinging from the Lawrence Hotel, and a stray bullet hit and killed a white boy in the audience.

The mob next descended upon the town's colored section, where it engaged in a firefight with and shot and killed two black males. Their bodies were later burned.

There was then a call to "run the niggers out of town." The rioters broke into the Missouri National Guard armory, stole the weapons, and began shooting at the town's black community in general - men, women, and children. They also torched the houses in that area. Essentially, the mob violently banished the town's 200 - 300 black residents, who fled in fear for their lives.[143]

On August 23, 1901 in Denver, Jack Johnson allegedly seconded ex-world featherweight champion George Dixon in a 10-round draw against Abe Attell.[144]

On September 6, 1901 at the Pan-American Exhibition in Buffalo, New York, U.S. President William McKinley was shot by Leon Czolgoz. McKinley died of his wounds on September 14. The same day, Theodore Roosevelt was sworn in as president.

October 16, 1901 was the first time that a U.S. President, Theodore Roosevelt, dined in the White House with a black man, Booker T. Washington. The action aroused much criticism and indignation, especially in the South. The New Orleans *Times-Democrat* wrote, "The negro is not the

---

[142] Johnson, *In the Ring and Out,* at 45, 72. Later, in about 1902 or 1903, Johnson saw a colored woman named Clara Kerr, with whom he was infatuated, but Kerr eventually left him for another man. "The heartaches which Mary Austin and Clara Kerr had caused me, led me to forswear colored women and to determine that my lot henceforth would be cast only with white women."

[143] This incident later prompted Mark Twain to write the essay *The United States of Lyncherdom*. A 2007 PBS documentary, *Banished*, featured the incident. To this day, Pierce City is 96% white. In May 2003, a major tornado destroyed and damaged much of the city. *Encyclopedia of American Race Riots,* Edited by Walter Rucker, Jr. and James Nathaniel Upton, Greenwood Publishing Group, 2006; Kimberly Harper, *White Man's Heaven: The Lynching and Expulsions of Blacks in the Southern Ozarks, 1894 – 1909,* University of Arkansas Press, 2012.

[144] Ward at 38.

---

social equal of the white man. Mr. Roosevelt might as well attempt to rub the stars out of the firmament as to try to erase that conviction from the heart and brain of the American people." The New Orleans *Daily States* called his action an insult to the South. The Memphis *Scimitar* said it was a "damnable outrage" for the President to invite a "nigger" to dine with him. The Memphis *Commercial Appeal* said, "This is a white man's country. It will continue to be such as long as clean blood flows through the veins of white people. ... [R]ace supremacy precludes social equality." Another editorial said Roosevelt had committed a blunder worse than a crime. The *Augusta Chronicle* said the act would antagonize the South and "meet the disapproval of good Anglo-Saxon sentiment in all latitudes." Georgia Governor Allen Candler said, "No self-respecting white man can ally himself with the President after what has occurred. ... As a matter of fact, Northern people do not understand the negro. They see the best types and judge the remainder by them."[145]

When giving a lecture on the race question at a Presbyterian Church, the U.S. Senator from South Carolina, Ben Tillman, said, "Democracy means white people in the South. In my state the negroes are in subjection; we expect to keep them that way. Of course, you people in the North do not see the race matter in our light. We invite you to come down. ... You will feel this matter some day."[146]

---

[145] *Evening Times*, Washington, D.C., October 19, 1901.
[146] *Guthrie Daily Leader*, October 29, 1901. Senator Tillman also allegedly said, "The action of President Roosevelt in entertaining that nigger will necessitate our killing a thousand niggers in the South before they learn their place again."

CHAPTER 6

California Dreaming:
A Mixed Bag

In October 1901, Jack Johnson headed from Colorado to Los Angeles, California. He allegedly engaged in a tryout with the Dixie Kid, a black welterweight.[147]

In early November, the *Police Gazette* said that Jack Johnson, "the large black person who was tangled up with Joe Choynski in the Texas troubles, has arrived in California and is looking for fights."[148]

Johnson's first California fight was against a well-respected black fighter named Hank Griffin. Hank Griffin stood about 6'2' or 6'3", weighed in the 180-pound range, and had a very long reach of 81 ½ inches, amongst the longest in the business. Griffin was one of the best black fighters in the country, with about 30 known bouts to his name. His early record included: 1891 KO11 Happy Jack, 1892 KO4 Harris Martin (a.k.a. "the Black Pearl"), and 1893 D20 Frank Childs, the "colored cyclone." The 175-pound Childs would later become "colored heavyweight champion."[149]

Hank Griffin

Somewhere between 1893 and 1895, a young James J. Jeffries, in his pro debut, knocked out Griffin in the 14th or 15th round. However, prior to being knocked out, Griffin had been clearly winning on points, outboxing the much larger and stronger man.

---

[147] Ward at 39.

[148] *National Police Gazette*, November 9, 1901. The *Police Gazette* was usually 2-3 weeks or more behind in its reports.

[149] Boxrec.com cites the Apr. 4, 1900 *Oakland Tribune* as reporting at least five bouts for Griffin up to 1893. Some of these are unconfirmed. *San Francisco Evening Post*, July 21, 1902.

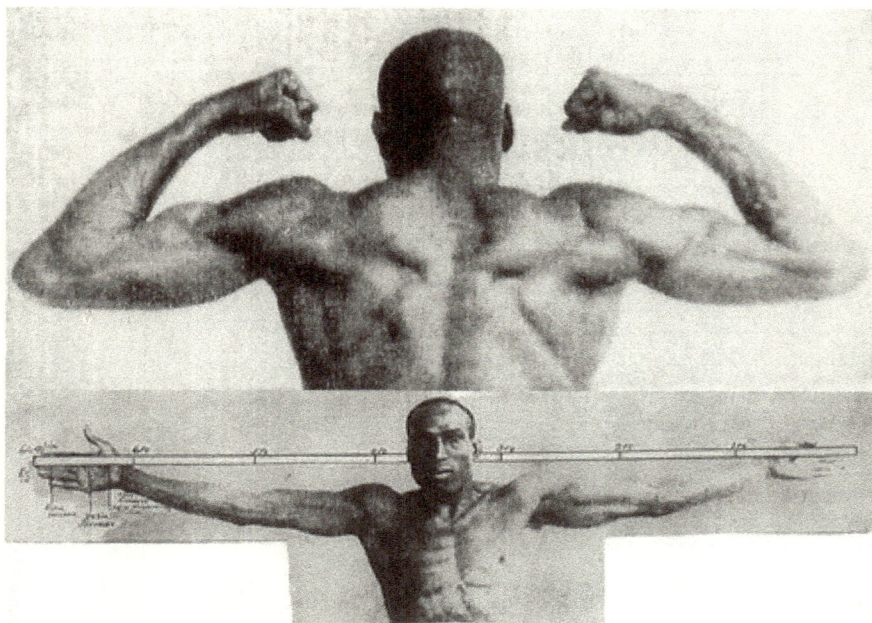

Hank Griffin shows off his powerful back muscles and long reach

Griffin fought often in the Los Angeles area, as well as throughout California. His later record included an 1896 KO4 Hank Lorraine; 1897 KO4 Dan Long, and 1900-1901 W20 (and possible D20) Jack Munroe, a husky fighter who weighed over 200 pounds. His only loss during that time was a 1900 LKOby11 to Bob Jones. In 1901, Griffin fought big Joe Kennedy to two 20-round draws. On July 30, 1901 in Los Angeles, Griffin won the Pacific Coast Heavyweight Title with a KO9 over Ben Tremble.[150]

On September 17, 1901 at Hazard's Pavilion in Los Angeles, Hank Griffin boxed a 4-round exhibition with heavyweight champion James Jeffries, who was in training for his upcoming title bout with Gus Ruhlin. Jeff offered to pay Griffin $100 if he could last 4 rounds. Before the exhibition, it was said, "There are many who believe that Jeffries has taken a big contract on his hands in attempting to stop Griffin in four rounds, for the husky heavyweight is very shifty and has a good defense." Griffin had defensive skill and a knockout blow. Therefore, many locals did not think that Jeffries could stop Griffin in only 4 rounds. Jeff was weighing around 220-230 pounds to Griffin's 180+ pounds. Hank was in good shape and looked good when boxing and wrestling with black middleweight Billy Woods.[151]

---

[150] Cyberboxingzone.com; Boxrec.com. *Los Angeles Express*, September 17, 1901; *National Police Gazette*, November 1, 1902.
[151] *Los Angeles Express*, September 12, 1901; *Los Angeles Times*, September 16, 1901.

Jeffries said of Griffin, "I guess I know about as much as anybody; I fought him once. He is a big fellow, and very strong…. If I cannot knock him out in four rounds I will not kill myself or tear my head off trying to." To another newsman, Jeff offered another, less gracious assessment of Griffin, saying, "They think a lot of Griffin here, I can see, but he did not succeed in whipping Joe Kennedy, and Jack Root used to do that every day when he was training for his fight with Kid Carter. Root is a light heavyweight, and if he could put it all over Kennedy, and Griffin could not whip him, it seems as if Griffin wasn't any wonder."[152]

Still, Griffin was the odds favorite to make it the full 4 rounds. The *Los Angeles Herald* said,

> Griffin has never disappointed an audience that assembled to see him fight, and while he has not always been proclaimed the winner he has never quit for a little punishment. The proposition in which Griffin is the favorite does not mean that he shall defeat Jeffries, but that he shall be on his feet at the end of four three-minute rounds, with the usual one-minute intermission.[153]

In the 1st round, Jeffries pursued Griffin and knocked him down with a "half-arm swipe on the side of the head." Griffin moved and clinched to survive.

In the 2nd round, Griffin continued moving and evading blows until Jeffries dropped him with a half-arm overhand blow or hook to the jaw. Hank tried to clinch, but received many hard punches. He mixed it, but Jeff smiled and responded with rib shots that made Hank run again. A Jeffries left counter to the ear dropped Griffin again for another nine-count. Hank rose and moved and held to survive.

In the 3rd round, Hank ran, ducked, and clinched. He occasionally landed some hard blows, but Jeff just laughed. The champion ripped in hard punches, but "Griffin's defense in the clinches was remarkably clever." They mixed it up a bit, and when they broke from a clinch, Jeff attacked and doubled his left to the head and jaw, dropping Griffin to a knee again for a nine-count. After rising, a Jeffries left dropped him for eight seconds. Another left decked Griffin for nine more seconds. The crowd hissed Griffin for not fighting, but seemingly voluntarily going down to avoid punishment and kill the clock. Hank ran to survive.

In the 4th round, Griffin survived by mostly clinching and running, only occasionally striking back and mixing it up.[154]

The *Los Angeles Times* concluded, "Griffin is a good man at his weight, but has no business, of course, with the champion. Had he stood up and

---

[152] *Los Angeles Daily Times, Los Angeles Express*, September 17, 1901.
[153] *Los Angeles Herald*, September 17, 1901.
[154] *Los Angeles Daily Times, Los Angeles Express, Los Angeles Herald, San Francisco Call*, September 18, 19, 1901.

fought he would not have lasted two rounds, but he did not go in the ring to fight, as the crowd knew."

However, the *Los Angeles Express* applauded Griffin as being clever for not leading, fighting a smart defensive fight, and utilizing good ring generalship.

The *Los Angeles Herald* reported that despite the fact that Jeff was from Los Angeles, the immense crowd rooted for Griffin to last. After all, most in the crowd had bet on him to survive the 4 rounds, and Hank actually had fought more often in Los Angeles than had Jeffries. The *Herald* was critical of Jeffries' failure to knock out Griffin.

> To be sure he went to his knees several times, but throughout the four rounds there was not a blow delivered which constituted a clean knock down. In the first and second rounds Jeffries had a seemingly good chance to put his opponent away, but he always hesitated with an apparent idea that the negro had something up his sleeve. ... Jeffries is far from being a Sullivan. He is more shifty, perhaps, and has learned the science of foot work and defense more thoroughly, but he is not the possessor of a decisive blow which made the name of Sullivan a terror to all aspirants to heavyweight honors.

However, the *National Police Gazette* reported that the result was not a surprise to Eastern followers of the game who had seen the champ in action. "Jeff is not a quick finisher. He has never won a fight in short order. That is not his style. He depends upon his wonderful endurance, and wins after having worn the other fellow out gradually."[155]

Quite a number of black patrons attended the match, many of whom were concerned about Griffin's welfare, and early on, they told Hank to stay down and forget the money, for Jeffries might kill him. However, at the end, they celebrated his ability to avoid being knocked out.

One week later, on September 24, 1901 in Oakland, James Jeffries knocked out Joe Kennedy in the 2nd round. Kennedy had twice gone 20 rounds with Hank Griffin to draw verdicts.

Two weeks after Griffin had boxed Jeffries, on October 2, 1901 in Los Angeles, Hank Griffin fought "Denver" Ed Martin, a big and tall 200-plus-pound black fighter who at that time was a sparring partner for Gus Ruhlin, who was preparing for his title shot against Jeffries. From the start, Martin was superior. He dropped Griffin four times in the 6th round and knocked him out in the 7th round with a right to the jaw. The victory catapulted Martin's career. The *Police Gazette* said, "There doesn't seem to be any real reason to question 'Denver Ed' Martin's claim to the title of colored heavyweight champion. The manner in which he disposed of Hank Griffin the other night at Los Angeles settled all controversy on the subject." After the victory, Martin resumed training with Ruhlin.[156]

---

[155] *National Police Gazette*, October 12, 1901.
[156] *National Police Gazette*, October 26, November 16, 1901.

Griffin returned to the ring one month later, against Johnson. At that point, Griffin was 31 years old to Johnson's 23 years of age. Griffin likely would have slight height, reach, and weight advantages.

In late October, it was announced that Joe Woods, the Bakersfield Athletic Club's matchmaker, had matched Jack Johnson "of Denver" with Hank Griffin of Los Angeles for a 20-round fight to be held in Bakersfield. "Johnson has gone into training for his fight already, as he expects a hard fight from the long, lean-looking fighter from the south. Johnson has secured Herrera's old training quarters to do his afternoon work."

It was said that if the respected Griffin had a good manager, he could make lots of money. "He is a willing fighter, and it is not everybody who can whip him. ... Griffin will meet all comers next week in four-round bouts."[157]

On Monday November 4, 1901 at the Bakersfield armory hall, under the auspices of the Bakersfield Athletic Club, Jack Johnson fought Hank Griffin. Both fighters wanted Aurelio Herrera to referee, but Frank Carillo/Carrillo, who either was or would become Johnson's manager, would not allow it. Eventually, they agreed upon Jack Wooley to be the referee.

The local newspaper said both boxers were in condition for a long, hard fight, and they needed it. They kept their hands busy throughout the entertaining bout. It was a clean fight, with both breaking nicely from the clinches. Towards the end of the fight, Griffin claimed a foul, but it was not allowed. At the conclusion of 20 rounds, Referee Wooley awarded the very close decision to Griffin. Some questioned the verdict, implying that it could or should have been a draw. The local *Bakersfield Daily Californian* said,

> Griffin landed many hard punches during the evening, but so did Johnson. That Griffin had a shade the best of it during the last few rounds is admitted but Johnson had the best of it for the first seven rounds, although no damaging blows were landed during that time.
>
> The Bakersfield Athletic Club will make friends and money provided it arranges in the future such matches as the Griffin-Johnson fight last night.

Clearly the entertaining bout had been a competitive and closely-contested one. Johnson had the edge early, but Griffin had finished well. Often, how a man finished a fight tended to count more with a referee's final verdict, so Griffin narrowly edged the bout. However, the local paper argued, "Owing to the willingness and fairness of both men a draw decision would have met with general favor." Once again, Johnson had fought a close and competitive bout with a respected veteran, in what many thought

[157] *Los Angeles Express*, October 24, 1901.

easily could have been a draw. The bout had been exciting enough such that the fans and promoters would want to see Jack in action again.[158]

On November 15, 1901 in San Francisco, James J. Jeffries successfully defended his world heavyweight championship when Gus Ruhlin retired after the 5th round. Jeffries had dominated and twice dropped a man who had once fought him to a 20-round draw, and had knocked out Tom Sharkey.

On November 20, 1901, the front page of the *Anadarko Daily Democrat*, based in Oklahoma, reported,

> Councilman Robinson took three shots at a nigger last night. The nigger had gone into the Cow Boy saloon and asked for a drink.
>
> Mr. Robinson informed him that niggers all drank at the end of the bar and that he would have to move down apience. The nigger answered with an oath and called Robinson a vile name. Robinson promptly reached for his revolver and as the nigger ran he fired three shots after him. At the second shot the nigger fell, but quickly rose again, so that Robinson could not tell whether he hit him or not. Robinson is a man of courage and action, and he voices the sentiments of a large percent of the citizens when he says: "There should not be a nigger in the city."

In December 1901, Jack Johnson was in the San Francisco area, acting as a sparring partner for the highly regarded, very experienced, tough, exciting veteran middleweight/light-heavyweight Edward "Kid" Carter, who was in training for another bout with George Gardner. On August 30, 1901 in San Francisco, Gardner had knocked out Carter in the 18th round. Subsequently, on October 15, 1901, Kid Carter knocked out Joe Walcott in the 7th round.[159]

On Sunday December 15, 1901, visitors to Kid Carter's training quarters saw him go 4 hard and fast rounds with Jack Johnson. The game

Eddie 'Kid' Carter

---

[158] *Bakersfield Daily Californian*, November 5, 1901.

[159] *San Francisco Evening Post*, December 14, 1901. Kid Carter's 50-bout career had included: 1898 D10 and L10 Jack O'Brien; 1899 L20 Matty Matthews; 1900 KO10 George Cole, KO7 Andy Walsh, LKOby12 Bill Hanrahan, LDQ19 George Gardner, KO10 Bill Hanrahan, D25 Andy Walsh, D20 Bill Hanrahan, and L6 Tommy Ryan; and 1901 WDQ19 Joe Walcott, LDQ4 Jimmy Handler, D20 and W20 Jack Bonner, LDQ15 Jack Root, LKOby18 George Gardner, and KO7 Joe Walcott.

pugilists hammered each other, neither holding back. "Carter is a vicious boxer. He can't exchange love taps when training. He must always be at it." Johnson was said to have ambitions, and was there to do his best.

> In the very first exchange of blows the colored man hit Carter low. It was accidental, but Carter lost his temper. He sailed in for Johnson, and within a minute there was the liveliest kind of a mixup. Johnson did some landing, judging by the way the Kid's head went back. Carter ripped in heavy body punches and crossed the negro on the jaw and head. Time and again Johnson saved himself by clinching. Every round was a repetition of the first. Carter did all the leading. His aggressiveness showed him to be in great shape. At the end of their bout Johnson went over into a corner, to commune with himself.[160]

Years later, famous sports-writer Tad Dorgan said that the first time he ever saw Johnson was in 1901, when he was acting as Kid Carter's sparring partner at Croll's Gardens in Alameda, across the bay from San Francisco. He said Johnson was a happy-go-lucky fellow who liked to tell jokes. Dorgan watched Johnson spar 4 hard rounds with Carter. "Carter did his best to knock Johnson stiff, but instead of showing the tall colored fellow up, he was shown up himself, and only for Promoter Coffroth, who stopped the bout when Carter was groggy and all in, the big card might have been a flop."[161]

On December 18, 1901 at Fort Erie, Ontario, Canada, Joe Walcott won the world welterweight championship when he knocked out James Rube Ferns in the 5th round. Walcott was only the second black world champion of the gloved era. He would defend the title against both blacks and whites.[162]

On December 20, 1901 in San Francisco, George Gardner defeated Kid Carter for the third time, knocking him out in the 8th round. Gardner demonstrated cleverness, great strength, and splendid courage in a desperate, thrilling battle that had almost all of the 6,000 in attendance standing on their feet, screaming with enthusiastic delight.[163]

Oakland's Reliance Athletic Club was set to host a show on Friday December 27, which would feature a main event between colored heavyweight Hank Griffin of Los Angeles and Jack Johnson, Kid Carter's sparring partner. "Johnson is also colored and is a fighter from way back. He has a California record as a chicken fiend, but his Eastern fighting record is better."

---

[160] *San Francisco Evening Post*, December 17, 1901. Carter then hit the bag, hammering the inflated bladder for eight minutes, and then he skipped rope.

[161] *Dorgan, Tad,* writing in Johnson, Jack, *In the Ring and Out* at 11.

[162] On December 17, 1901 in Louisville, Kentucky, Billy Hanrahan knocked out Marvin Hart in the 1st round. It was Hart's first loss.

[163] *San Francisco Evening Post*, December 21, 1901.

At Bakersfield a few weeks ago these men met in a twenty-round affair which proved a great fight. The decision went to Griffin, though many who saw the bout thought a draw would have been a far better ruling. Johnson is anxious to wipe the stain of defeat from his reputation before he returns to the East, and promises to make Hank get a big hustle on if the Los Angeles fighter expects to annex the winner's end of the purse.[164]

Another local paper said, "Carter has a good opinion of Johnson and predicts his success with Griffin."[165]

The *Oakland Tribune* said Hank Griffin had fought there before, and his ability was well known. He and Johnson fought at Bakersfield and Griffin got the decision, though it reported that the fight was very even and many thought a draw would have been popular and fair.

When Griffin had knocked out Con Sheehan in 7 rounds back on November 22, 1901 in Oakland, Johnson was at ringside and challenged the winner, wanting to avenge his loss. Jack claimed that he was in poor condition for their prior bout.

The local paper noted that when Kid Carter was preparing for the recent Gardner bout at Croll's Garden in Alameda, Johnson assisted him and was one of the hardest workers in the camp. "His clever work with Carter attracted attention, resulting in the return match with Griffin. He is now in splendid shape, and will have no excuses if again defeated."

A few days later, the local paper said that Johnson "nearly put Kid Carter out while boxing at Croll's Gardens."[166]

The *Oakland Enquirer* said the recent Griffin-Johnson bout was the most interesting ever seen in Bakersfield. "Johnson has a fine Eastern record and his work as sparring partner of Kid Carter has made him a lot of friends here." Griffin, who regularly fought in Los Angeles, was known to be a good man.[167]

Interest in the "important battle" between Griffin and Johnson continued to grow.

> Both men have made excellent impressions in various localities, and are aspirants for heavyweight honors.
>
> Everybody is familiar in one way or another with Griffin's style. He does not believe in procrastination, and roughs it like a madman from the start, at the same time exhibiting rare judgment and unmistakable

---

[164] *San Francisco Evening Post*, December 19, 1901. The *Evening Post* said Johnson had defeated Mexican Pete Everett in 20 rounds and had stopped Jim Scanlon at Galveston in 7 rounds (both incorrect assertions). He had also won a decision over George Lawler at Hot Springs. It was likely relying on Johnson as its source.
[165] *San Francisco Call*, December 21, 1901. It said Johnson also held a victory over Dan Murphy, and had fought Bob Armstrong to a 6-round no decision in Denver.
[166] *Oakland Tribune*, December 24, 27, 1901.
[167] *Oakland Enquirer*, December 26, 1901.

courage. He can hit a terrific blow and can take a great deal of punishment, and as much can be said of Johnson, whose ambition it is to whip the man from Los Angeles. It will be a red hot battle, and the Reliance Club will doubtless be crowded to the doors.[168]

The *San Francisco Call* echoed that in their previous fast bout, honors were about evenly divided, though Griffin got the decision. By humbling Con Sheehan, pride of the British navy, Griffin had proven himself to be a man of considerable account. Both Griffin and Johnson were in first-class condition.[169]

Johnson said that when he was in jail for a month with Choynski, they were fed bread and water. Ever since then, when he entered a new town, it was his habit to ask what the Sheriff fed his guests at the County jail.

The *San Francisco Bulletin* said Hank Griffin's record went all the way back to June 1891, when he knocked out Billy Manning in Los Angeles. It said his record included: 1891 KO11 Happy Jack; 1892 KO4 Black Pearl; 1893 D20 Frank Childs; 1895 KO11 Ed Woodworth; 1896 KO4 Hank Lorraine; December 1896 LKOby17 James Jeffries (bout likely took place years earlier); 1897 KO7 Tom Massey and KO2 Billy Kennedy; 1898 D15 Bob Jones; 1900 KO3 Charles Lawler, W20 Jack Morrow (actually Jack Munroe), and KO14 Jim Clark; and 1901 KO1 P. J. McGarrey, KO4 Jim Clark, KO2 Rufus Thompson, D20 Joe Kennedy (twice), KO8 Ben Tremble, ND4 James Jeffries, LKCby7 Ed Martin, W20 Jack Johnson, and KO7 Con Sheehan.

The *Bulletin* said Johnson had met such men as Bob Armstrong, Dan Murphy, Klondike, Jim Scanlan, Mexican Pete Everett, Billy Stift, and Joe Choynski.[170]

Hank Griffin.

[168] *San Francisco Evening Post*, December 26, 1901.
[169] *San Francisco Call*, December 26, 1901.
[170] *San Francisco Bulletin*, December 26, 1901.

The *San Francisco Examiner* said they were to meet in a 15-round bout, which was attracting an unusual amount of interest. "Johnson is supposed to be a wonder."[171]

The day of the fight, the *Bulletin* said that on account of his prior victory over Johnson, and his good showing in several fights, Griffin would be the betting favorite, though Johnson would not lack for support. Jack had a creditable record and was confident of reversing the decision that Griffin gained over him.[172]

On Friday December 27, 1901 at Oakland's Reliance Club, approximately 10 miles from San Francisco, the Jack Johnson vs. Hank Griffin rematch took place. A large crowd packed the gymnasium. Ed J. Smith refereed the main event, "and gave satisfaction as he always does." The judges were Jack Williamson and Dr. W. J. Smith. They would decide the contest if it went the full distance, with the referee becoming involved as a tiebreaker if the two judges did not agree. George Gross acted as timekeeper, and Walter Fawcett as announcer.[173]

The *Oakland Times* said Hank Griffin, heavyweight champion of the Pacific Coast, and Jack Johnson of Denver fought a hotly contested 15-round draw. "Hank Griffin found a match in Johnson." Griffin ran up against a good fighter who was also strong.

> For fifteen rounds the spectators were kept in the height of excitement, and although Hank tried his best to get at his man, Johnson proved to be too shifty, countering with telling effect. So evenly were the men matched that there was hardly a round in the whole fifteen that could be picked out as belonging to either. Johnson proved a wonder at in-fighting. He landed every time on Griffin, who is supposed to be an adept at that part of the game. When it came to leading, Hank had it all his own way, that being the only thing that kept him within the money.
>
> At the end of the fifteen rounds the judges, W. J. Smith and Jack Williamson, declared the go a draw, the decision meeting with general favor from those present. Ed Smith acted as referee.[174]

The impression given by this local account is that the only reason Griffin earned a draw was the result of the fact that he did more of the leading. Johnson was hard to hit and landed effective counterblows. Further, even when Hank got in close, Johnson did very well on the inside.

The semi-local San Francisco papers had a divergence of viewpoints. Some thought Johnson was the cleverer fighter, while others thought Griffin had the superior cleverness. The majority of accounts reported that the fans were satisfied with the draw.

---

[171] *San Francisco Examiner*, December 27, 1901.
[172] *San Francisco Bulletin*, December 27, 1901.
[173] *Oakland Tribune*, December 28, 1901 gave few details.
[174] *Oakland Times*, December 28, 1901.

Allegedly, according to the *Examiner* and *Evening Post*, Johnson weighed 168 pounds to Griffin's 165 pounds, though this seems a bit too low to be true, at least as it pertains to Griffin, who was listed as weighing 180 pounds when he boxed Jeffries fairly recently. Weights rarely were confirmed back then, for heavyweights did not have to weigh-in.

The *San Francisco Examiner* said it was 15 rounds of hard fighting. Griffin had done the leading throughout, but many of his leads went wild. On the other hand, "Johnson had countered well and landed more blows than did his opponent. Both men did fast and fierce infighting, Johnson being the more clever."[175]

These two accounts gave the impression that Johnson had the better defense, had landed more punches, was an effective counterpuncher, and was also good on the inside, but that Griffin evened up matters by being a bit more active and aggressive, and leading more often, something which counted back then.

The *San Francisco Evening Post* said it was impossible for either man to gain an advantage over the other. It had been 15 rounds of hammer and tongs fighting, and the draw decision "seemed to be a vastly popular one." It was a hot, fast fight from beginning to end, but the men were very evenly matched. Griffin had the advantage in the leading but Johnson did by far the best defensive work and thus evened up matters considerably.[176]

The *San Francisco Bulletin* offered a different perspective. It said the bout, which drew a large crowd, was declared a draw after 15 rounds of slow fighting. Throughout, Griffin was the aggressor and led more often than his "dusky rival," but Johnson was right there when it came to exchanging punches, and he also shone in the mix-ups. The first 4 rounds were very fast, with each man trying hard for a knockout. However, both slowed down in the 5th round, and thereafter, fought cautiously until the end of the bout.[177]

According to the *San Francisco Call*, both fighters were in splendid condition.

> Johnson proved himself a clever infighter. Both men did some hard hitting, but there was little of particular interest in the bout. As far as giving and taking punishment were concerned honors were about evenly divided, but Griffin did most of the leading and seemed to be the cleverer of the two. The judges' decision seemed to give general satisfaction.[178]

The *San Francisco Chronicle* said, "Griffin showed more cleverness and did more of the leading, while Johnson depended almost exclusively on occasional leads for the ribs and infighting. The majority of the spectators

---

[175] *San Francisco Examiner*, December 28, 1901.
[176] *San Francisco Evening Post*, December 28, 1901.
[177] *San Francisco Bulletin*, December 28, 1901.
[178] *San Francisco Call*, December 28, 1901.

seemed to think that Griffin had a shade the best of the fight from a scientific standpoint."[179]

Clearly, 1901 had been a challenging year for Johnson, though one of quality experience, having fought several lengthy bouts against reputable fighters with more experience and/or lengthier careers. He had lost to Choynski, drawn with Stift and Everett, and both lost to and drawn with Griffin. He was still growing and learning, both physically and in terms of his skills and experience as a fighter. He was constantly improving, and had shown his talent against a respected veteran in Griffin in two very close bouts. As time passed, the knowledge gained from such experiences would bear him fruit.

---

[179] *San Francisco Chronicle*, December 28, 1901.

CHAPTER 7

Jim Jeffries and the Color Line

Soon after successfully defending the title against Gus Ruhlin, heavyweight champion James Jeffries drew the color line against Ruhlin's sparring partner, Denver Ed Martin, who had knocked out Hank Griffin.

> When Jeff was asked the other day if he would fight Martin, if he beat Ruhlin, Delaney chimed in by saying, "No, we won't fight a negro for the championship … Suppose he were to fight Martin and be defeated, which does not seem possible. America would have to bow to a negro champion."[180]

Bill Delaney did not want to allow such a bout to take place, irrespective of whether or not it would be competitive, and even though he thought Jeff would likely win. His views were consistent with the time's existing beliefs about separation of the races, which often were mandated by law.

Furthermore, boxing was still struggling to gain full legal acceptance. It is more than likely that legislators would have been even more uncomfortable about legalizing or maintaining the legality of a sport which threatened the dominant racial hierarchy and social order maintained by racial separation.

Still, many boxing writers, particularly those from the *Police Gazette*, argued for equal opportunity to compete when it came to boxing, a sport which did not always honor the color line.

Since January 1901, Ed Martin had been a Ruhlin sparring partner. He weighed over 200 pounds and stood about 6'4". Like Ruhlin, he was managed by Billy Madden. In June 1899, Bob Armstrong, who had lost a 10-round decision to Jeffries, knocked out Martin in 2 rounds.[181] However, since then, Martin had gone undefeated in eleven straight bouts, with eight won by knockout.

When Martin had challenged Tom Sharkey in late 1900, Sharkey responded that he had "never barred nobody outside of a

DENVER ED MARTIN,
Gus Ruhlin's Sparring Partner.

---

[180] *National Police Gazette*, December 7, 1901.
[181] *Cincinnati Enquirer*, January 15, 1901; *San Francisco Chronicle*, June 7, 1899; *National Police Gazette*, June 24, 1899, January 5, 1901.

nigger. I will not fight no nigger. I did not get my reputation fighting niggers and I will not fight a nigger. Outside of niggers, I will fight any man living."

Gus Ruhlin's sparring sessions with Ed Martin were fierce. From September to November 1901, things said about their sparring included, "He and Martin are in the habit of mixing it up rather lively at times for the amusement of the spectators." Martin was "a likely man himself." He and Ruhlin "gave a pretty exhibition of hitting and stopping, which showed both off to advantage."[182] Of their 3 rounds of sparring on September 16, 1901,

> It was a display of science and it was also a display of strength and a capacity to give and take punishment. ... Blows were struck strong enough to fell a horse, and both the pugilists felt their effects, Martin going to his knees several times. Ruhlin, of course, was the more scientific of the two, but Martin was sufficiently skilled to make the contest a most interesting one.

They repeated their performance on the 17th, again boxing 3 rounds.

> Ruhlin is a magnificently-formed man and for a man of his weight is light and shifty on his feet and clever with his hands. He forced the play last night and dealt blows which were not intended to be taps. Martin is a boxer of considerable ability and helped to make the bout an entertaining one indeed.

Ruhlin and Martin continued sparring 3 rounds nightly.[183] Of the November 5 Ruhlin-Martin sparring, "They pummeled each other hard and often, and in this bout Gus exhibited a remarkable improvement."[184]

Ed Martin was a good-looking fighter and might have been a contender in his own right, but "white champions are more profitable as show cards than the colored variety, and goodness knows what might happen if Gus and Martin locked horns in a regulation Queensberry engagement."[185]

Martin said of Ruhlin,

> If anyone can lick Jeffries, it will be Ruhlin.... I have been with Gus a year now, and I know that he is faster, stronger and more clever by far than I have ever seen him. ... [S]hould Jeffries lick Gus he can then go down the line among the other big fellows like breaking sticks.[186]

On the day of the Jeffries-Ruhlin championship fight, November 15, 1901, Billy Madden said, "Ruhlin is faster now than he ever was in his life. That fellow, Denver Ed Martin, is a wonder for speeding a man up, and

[182] *National Police Gazette*, September 28, 1901; *San Francisco Call*, September 16, 1901.

[183] *Oakland Tribune*, September 17, 18, 20, 1901.

[184] *San Francisco Call*, November 6, 1901.

[185] *San Francisco Examiner*, November 7, 13, 1901; *San Francisco Evening Post*, November 6, 1901.

[186] *San Francisco Examiner*, November 11, 1901.

when a big man like Gus can cut out a pace with him I think he is pretty good, don't you?"[187]

Ruhlin's poor showing against Jeffries had astonished everyone, particularly those who had seen him looking good in sparring with Denver Ed Martin, or had observed him dismantle Sharkey. Either Ruhlin froze, left his fight in the gym, or Jeffries was just vastly superior and on an entirely different level. Opinions varied.

Ed Martin, Gus Ruhlin, George Siler, Billy Madden

The *Police Gazette* mentioned Martin as an up-and-coming fighter on the horizon who might be a possible title challenger. The *Gazette* said Martin's experience with Ruhlin was of considerable benefit to him.

> He is young, almost if not quite as clever as Ruhlin, can punch harder, is ambitious and thoroughly game. As I said several weeks ago, of all the men now looming up on the pugilistic horizon not one has better qualifications for usurping the title than he. ... The next champion will be a black man, mark the prediction.

Martin claimed that he could defeat Jeffries. He said that Ruhlin had left his fight in the gym, and was frozen with fear against Jeff.[188]

---

[187] *San Francisco Bulletin*, November 15, 1901.
[188] *San Francisco Evening Post*, November 27, 1901.

As the weeks passed, Jeffries said he would ignore Martin's challenges. "While Jeffries does not draw the color line strictly, yet he refuses to box a negro for the championship." Jeff drew the color line when it came to championship bouts. The heavyweight championship was a whites-only position, and therefore only whites could challenge for the title.[189]

Denver Ed Martin

Bill Delaney insisted that Jeff would not fight Martin. Besides, Bob Armstrong, a man whom Jeff had defeated with a broken hand, had knocked out Martin in 2 rounds in 1899. Still, the press noted that Martin had been undefeated since then, and had impressed many observers of his sparring with Ruhlin.

The color-line aside, the *Police Gazette* felt that although Denver Ed Martin was the only "comer" who looked to have an eventual chance to succeed to the title, he needed time to develop properly. It opined that Martin needed another year of development in order to be ready for Jeffries. "Martin hardly has class enough yet to go after Jeffries, and will do well to wait until he wears the scalps of a few minor factors in the heavyweight game at his belt before he aspires to the title." He needed more experience, and given that he was just recently being noticed, he required more time to be properly marketed, for at that point there was no public demand for his title challenge. Certainly though, this was the first time that the potential for a black challenger to Jeff's title had been mentioned, and it had been refused outright as a result of race.[190]

In the meantime, following his draw with Hank Griffin, in January 1902, Jack Johnson sparred and trained with Jack Root, helping Root to prepare for his upcoming late-January bout with George Gardner in San Francisco.

---

[189] *San Francisco Examiner*, December 28, 1901.
[190] *San Francisco Examiner*, December 28, 1901; *National Police Gazette*, February 1, 1902.

To that point, the undefeated Root had a known record of 38-0-1. Root was a fast and clever boxer-puncher.[191]

Johnson consistently proved that he was willing to spar with anyone, which likely helped develop his skills. It also made him some money, and kept his name in the minds of the local managers, promoters, and press.

On January 31, 1902 in San Francisco, Jack Root defeated George Gardner via DQ7.

Denver Ed Martin scheduled a bout with then colored heavyweight champion Frank Childs. Although some were calling Martin the champion, Childs had the superior claim. Frank was a tough fighter who "has defeated nearly every prominent colored boxer in the country, and also a number of white pugilists. He hits a very hard punch, is fairly clever, and some time ago [Jan. 1898] he knocked out Armstrong in two rounds."

Jack Root

On March 4, 1899, Childs scored a KO6 over Armstrong to win the "colored heavyweight championship of the world." His last loss was a September 1898 20-round decision to George Byers, but he avenged it with a March 1901 KO17 over Byers to gain undisputed recognition as the colored champion.[192]

On February 24, 1902 in Chicago, Denver Ed Martin won a 6-round decision over Frank Childs. As a result, many began calling Martin the colored heavyweight champion of the world. However, others said the bout

---

[191] Jack Root's record included: 1898 KO2 Jack Hammond, KO2 Jimmy Watts, and W6 Australian Jimmy Ryan; 1899 W6 Harry Peppers, WDQ7 Billy Stift, KO2 Dick Moore, W20 Jimmy Ryan, W6 Stift, W6 Frank Craig, and KO6 Alex Greggains; 1900 W6 Tom West, KO2 Jack Hammond, W6 Dick O'Brien, D6 Tommy Ryan, KO1 Dan Creedon, and KO3 Dick O'Brien; and 1901 KO9 George Byers, WDQ15 Kid Carter, and KO2 Jimmy Ryan.

[192] Frank Childs' record included: 1895 LKOby3 Joe Choynski; 1898 KO2 Bob Armstrong and L20 George Byers; 1899 KO6 Armstrong, W8 Ed Dunkhorst, W6 Mexican Pete Everett, W6 John "Klondike" Haines (who was coming off a TKO5 win over Jack Johnson), D6 Joe Kennedy, and KO3 Klondike Haines; 1900 W10 Everett and W10 Fred Russell; 1901 KO17 Byers (gaining the legitimate claim to the colored championship); and 1902 KO4 Bill Hanrahan (who held a recent KO1 over Marvin Hart). Boxrec.com; *National Police Gazette*, March 11, 25, 1899, September 2, 1899.

was too short to determine who the better man was. Martin had great advantages in height (at least five inches) and reach, and that, together with his cleverness, enabled him to easily outpoint Childs in a short bout. However, it was said that Childs was never known for his cleverness, but rather his ability to knock a man out, and he landed some hard, staggering blows in the bout. On the other hand, it was said that Martin was not a puncher, at least not to the extent that Childs was, for Frank took all his blows with a smile. Therefore, it was unclear regarding who ultimately would win in a lengthier battle.[193]

CHILDS AND MARTIN,

---

[193] *Chicago Tribune*, February 25, 1902.

CHAPTER 8

Starting To Recognize

Oakland's Reliance Club was sufficiently impressed with Jack Johnson's performance in his 15-round draw with Hank Griffin such that in early March 1902 they brought him, rather than Griffin, back for a scheduled 15-round bout against Joe Kennedy. Clearly, those who ran the club saw his potential, and perhaps thought he might have gotten the better of Griffin.

The 6'2" 220-225-pound Kennedy had been a sparring partner for Pete Everett (1898), Tom Sharkey (1898), and Jack Root (1901). Kennedy had some good quality experience and results, including an 1898 W20 Jack Stelzner; 1899 W20 Gus Ruhlin, LKOby2 Peter Maher, D6 Frank Childs, KO4 Soldier Walker and W20 Fred Russell; and 1900 KO1 Dan Long. In May and July 1901, Kennedy fought Hank Griffin to two 20-round draws. Victories over big, strong men like Ruhlin and Russell, and draws with Childs and Griffin demonstrated that Kennedy was a good heavyweight.[194]

On September 24, 1901 at the Reliance Club in Oakland, champion James J. Jeffries knocked out Joe Kennedy in the 2nd round with a short left hook to the jaw. The fight was fun,

Joe Kennedy

fast-paced, and competitive while it lasted. Jeffries called Kennedy big, strong, willing, and hard-hitting.[195]

---

[194] *National Police Gazette*, November 4, 1899; *Los Angeles Daily Times, Los Angeles Express*, September 24, 1901; *Louisville Courier-Journal*, June 25, 1899; *New York Clipper*, July 1, 1899: Boxrec.com.

[195] *Oakland Tribune, Oakland Enquirer, San Francisco Call*, September 25, 1901; *My Life and Battles* at 44.

The Johnson-Kennedy bout attracted an unusual amount of attention. It was looked upon as a very even and interesting match-up between two heavies willing to mix it up. Johnson was considered to be decidedly fast and clever, while Kennedy was thought to be strong, fast, very clever, and tough.

BILLY WOODS

Johnson was sparring every afternoon at the Reliance Club with sturdy and skillful black Los Angeles middleweight Billy Woods, and they made their bouts "warm" for one another. Woods previously had served as a Hank Griffin sparring partner. He had fought several 20-round bouts. A couple years later, in 1904, Woods would box Tommy Burns to a 15-round draw.

It was anticipated that Johnson would weigh in the neighborhood of 172 pounds when he entered the ring.

Although not underrating Kennedy, Johnson was confident of taking home the large-end of the purse. Jack did not think that Joe could assimilate his stiff body jabs. Johnson was so confident of success that he was "like a boy." He had a joke for everyone and usually wound-up his gym work by telling about his experience in the Galveston jail, where he spent a month with Choynski.

When Bill Delaney asked Johnson if he would meet Jeffries in a 4-round bout, Johnson quickly replied, "Yes, and I'll outpoint him, too." Delaney had watched him work, and the veteran trainer said he thought Johnson was good.

The confident Johnson said that if he was successful, he would go after Denver Ed Martin.

The *San Francisco Chronicle* said Johnson was "considered by many as a possible candidate for championship honors."

> By his work with Jack Root, Kid Carter and others, Johnson has demonstrated that he is a very levelheaded boxer. He has the height, weight, reach and speed requisite to the making of a first-rater, and thus far has not developed the 'yellow streak' which has stopped many a likely member of his race from becoming a top-notcher. ... His great setback is his inability to get anyone to don the mitts with him for a workout. For this reason his gymnasium work is confined for the most part to bag punching.

Apparently Johnson had a gym reputation. He was so good that few wanted to spar with him. The allusion to the "yellow streak" of blacks was one of the era's racial stereotypes; that blacks had no heart.

The *Oakland Enquirer* echoed that Johnson was "looked upon by many as a possible candidate for championship honors." He had demonstrated that he was a "very capable man. He is clever, has a good punch with either hand, and with height, weight and reach in his favor will, if properly handled, make his mark in the fistic world."

Hence, even coming off a draw, his good performance against Griffin, in conjunction with what observers had seen of him in sparring with top local pros like Carter and Root, had impressed experts sufficiently to talk of him as a potential top contender.

The 32-year-old Kennedy was expected to weigh at least 200 pounds, though likely much more, so he would have a clear weight advantage. He was training at Johnnie T. Collins' place at the corner of Tenth and Bryant streets in San Francisco, sparring with heavyweight Charles Post.

Kennedy felt confident that he would stop Johnson. He said he was in fine condition and would be able to fight all 15 rounds at a fast clip if necessary. He intended to make Johnson fight hard at all times. "Joe thinks he will be able to put an end to Johnson's aspirations in short order, but those who have seen both men at work seem to think he will have a contract on his hands." Surely, the way he went at Jeffries demonstrated that Joe was not afraid to mix it, "for while he suffered defeat he made it interesting for the champion while the bout lasted." The *Oakland Enquirer* said, "He will be in good shape Friday and the San Francisco people think he is a sure winner."[196]

Both men had a large following, so a full house was expected. This was somewhat of an Oakland vs. San Francisco battle. Johnson was the local favorite in Oakland, where the fight would take place, but Kennedy was the favorite in the larger town of San Francisco, across the bay. Plenty of Kennedy admirers would be willing to back their man with coin.

At that time, Oakland was a much smaller town than San Francisco, with a population of 75,400. The annual salary of a letter carrier was $850, though it was supposed to increase to $1,000 per year after the population exceeded 75,000, which it recently had. As of the 1900 census, San Francisco had a population of 342,782, making it the ninth most populous city in the U.S.[197]

The *Oakland Tribune* said,

> Kennedy is an exceedingly clever boxer and he figures that he will be able to stall off Johnson's rushes and wear him down with his left. Joe thinks he will be able to stop anything the colored man can give,

---

[196] *Oakland Tribune*, March 1, 1902; *San Francisco Chronicle, San Francisco Bulletin, Oakland Enquirer*, March 5, 1902.
[197] *Oakland Tribune*, March 4, 8, 1902.

figuring, no doubt, that as Johnson was unable to knock out Hank Griffin, he has no punch. In this he will find he is mistaken, for if any man was ever severely punished it was Griffin when he met Johnson. Seeing the mistake he made by making a defensive fight of that bout, Johnson has expressed his determination to make an aggressive fight from the tap of the gong. As Kennedy does not run away, this will mean a fast and furious encounter.[198]

Clearly, this local paper believed that Johnson had been able to administer plenty of severe punishment to Griffin, even while acting on the defensive. The irony of Kennedy's thinking that Johnson had no punch because he had not been able to stop Griffin was that Kennedy himself had been unable to stop Griffin in two fights, and Kennedy had a big weight advantage, unlike Johnson.

Kennedy had made himself solid with union men during the recent strike, "when his ability in the fistic line served the strikers well on more than one occasion." Thus, he would have their support, heart and soul.[199]

MR. JOHN JOHNSON, WHO WILL MEET MR. JOSEPH KENNEDY AT THE RELIANCE CLUB FUNCTION TO-MORROW EVENEING.

San Francisco Bulletin, March 6, 1902

The Reliance Club was known for putting on good fights, and the regular attendance had grown so steadily that recently the club was compelled to double the seating capacity. The club expected the largest audience it had ever handled. Regardless, every seat in the gymnasium offered a good view of the ring.[200]

---

[198] *Oakland Tribune,* March 5, 1902.
[199] *Oakland Tribune,* March 6, 1902.
[200] *San Francisco Bulletin,* March 6, 1902.

Johnson's final day of training on March 6, the day before the fight, impressed observers. "If confidence and condition are anything Johnson should win in a walk, for he is surely in fine fettle. That Jack is a hard worker all who have watched him know."

While watching him train, Bill Delaney said to Charlie Kohl, then Johnson's manager, "If that boy keeps it up like he is going now he'll do all right. I never saw a man aside from Jeff, who liked his work as he does."

Johnson, who was 23 years old (a month shy of 24), figured that while he was beating the third-raters and improving, the fellows at the top would be going back.[201]

The local papers said Kennedy had trained hard and was in fine fettle. He had the weight advantage by well over 20 pounds. Hence, he remained the favorite across the bay in San Francisco, but the Oakland people still saw but one man. They liked Johnson and were willing to bet almost anything on him.[202]

On Friday March 7, 1902 at Oakland's Reliance Athletic Club, Jack Johnson took on Joe Kennedy. The bout was scheduled for 15 rounds, and they were fighting for the Pacific Coast heavyweight championship. Ed J. Smith refereed.

All of the San Francisco and Oakland papers said that despite the previous reports of Kennedy's good training and appearance, he was fat and flabby, "clearly overburdened with superfluous flesh," and not in the best shape. He easily could have had a 50-pound or more weight advantage. A very large crowd was in attendance.

1 - Both men seemed very anxious. Kennedy did the leading and appeared to have the best of it. He landed his speedy left on the nose and mouth whenever he wished, but Johnson fought back hard and landed several good body blows.

2 - This round belonged to Kennedy. He landed his left to the eye and followed with several good wallops. Johnson fought back gamely but was not able to do any damage.

The *Chronicle* said that in the first 2 rounds, Johnson was just feeling him out and taking his measure.

3 - Early in the round, Johnson started in wickedly and dazed Kennedy. Joe saved himself by clinching. Johnson got Joe in the corner and gave him a good beating. He had him holding on when the gong sounded. Kennedy was very tired and groggy.

4 - Johnson sent in a hard left to the face and repeated it a second later. Kennedy then landed his most effective punch, a left uppercut which Johnson dodged into. However, it only seemed to spur Johnson on, for he went right after Kennedy and began sending in alternate rights and lefts into

---

[201] *Oakland Tribune,* March 7, 1902.
[202] *Oakland Enquirer, Oakland Times,* March 7, 1902.

Kennedy's head, face and ribs, landing almost at will. Johnson had a tendency to turn tiger when hit hard. However, Kennedy fought back gamely, and several times sent Johnson's head back with left jabs. Yet, the Johnson counters which invariably followed eventually dazed the big white man. Johnson went after him, rushing Kennedy into a corner and landing hard on the face and body, making Joe groggy.

Finally, in a fierce rally, Johnson landed a hard left to the jaw, and as Joe tried to steady himself, Jack landed a stiff straight right to the nose, knocking Kennedy down flat on his back. Joe took the full ten-count.

When assisted to his feet, Kennedy was too dazed to know where he was. His second helped him to his corner. Joe finally came to and said that he had been up against something worse than "booze." The fight had only lasted halfway into the 4th round.

The local papers all agreed that Kennedy was not in the best shape. The *Oakland Tribune* said, "Condition had much to do with the result. Johnson was trained to the minute, while Kennedy appeared fat and flabby and could not stand the pace cut out by his opponent." The *Examiner* said, "Kennedy was as fat as a porker and showed not a sign of having trained." The *Chronicle* also said Kennedy was willing, but flabby and out of shape.

The *Oakland Enquirer* and *Oakland Times* both said Kennedy went up against it hard. Despite being the smaller man by at least 20 pounds, Johnson did not have the least bit of difficulty in the mix-ups, and outclassed Kennedy, who was a "dead one."

The *Oakland Tribune* said Kennedy made a poor showing and was easy for Johnson, who turned loose a few jolts and uppercuts that sent Joe down for the count.

According to the *San Francisco Chronicle*, Kennedy went up against a "hard-hitting and scientific boxer." Overall, "Aside from a few jabs in the face and one left uppercut which Johnson ran against, Kennedy's punishing of his opponent was slight." Johnson had outclassed him.

The *San Francisco Examiner* said, "It was not a fight." Kennedy used straight lefts to keep Johnson away for a couple of rounds, but then became tired. Johnson had him all but out in the 3rd round, punching him in the wind and jaw until Joe's knees dragged and he clung tightly to save himself. The fatal punch in the 4th round was a short-arm wallop on the nose.

The *San Francisco Call* said the bout was lively, and Johnson showed himself to be a hard and fast hitter. "Johnson proved a fast man on his feet and wicked at infighting." In the 1st round, he landed repeatedly, for Joe tired noticeably as early as the opening round. On the other hand, Jack was in "fine fettle and hard as nails." During the next three rounds, Johnson hit the jaw and face. He turned loose in the 4th round and hit Kennedy so hard and often that he went down and out. The punches that laid Kennedy low were a succession of lefts and rights to the head which came so rapidly that Kennedy was dazed. It said the final swing that stretched the white boxer onto the mat was brought up against his left cheek and opened a large gash.

The *San Francisco Bulletin* noted that despite the fact that Kennedy looked as though he had not trained, Johnson was still the 10 to 7 underdog. The first 3 rounds were slow, but Kennedy exerted himself considerably to lift his left occasionally and land on Johnson's head. After the 3rd round, Kennedy's poor condition began to tell, and after receiving a few jolts on the jaw in the 4th, he dropped to the canvas. The crowd yelled, but Joe refused to rise. Many thought he "didn't want no more from Mr. Johnsing."[203]

The *Oakland Tribune* concluded,

> The big colored fellow has been a hard and willing worker in these parts all winter, but has had a little the worst of luck in his public contests. Now that he has gained a victory and proved his willingness to keep in condition and at all times perform to the best of his ability, he should be given a chance by the clubs across the bay as well as local clubs.

Jack Johnson was finally starting to obtain some real recognition and respect. He had easily knocked out a man who once defeated Gus Ruhlin and had twice drawn with Hank Griffin.

Joe Kennedy would later become a sparring partner for James Jeffries.

Charles Kohl, Johnson's current manager, said he would try to match Johnson with George Gardner. "He has good prospects for several big fights."

Johnson obtained his next match as the result of a fortuity. Manager Tom McCarey of the Century Athletic Club in Los Angeles had arranged a bout between Jack Jeffries, brother of world heavyweight champion James Jeffries, and Hank Griffin. However, Griffin was not happy about the proposed purse division, which gave Jeffries a little the best of it on account of his being the bigger drawing card, despite the fact that he had an inferior record to Griffin. The Jeffries name alone put bodies in seats. Hank did not post the required $100 forfeit.

McCarey offered Johnson the bout instead. Jack immediately accepted and wired the forfeit money from Bakersfield, where he was residing. The local press was satisfied with the opponent change, saying of Johnson, "He is much better than when he fought Griffin the first time, and should be at least an equally good drawing card."

Tom McCarey signed the Jack Jeffries vs. Jack Johnson fight on May 1, with the bout scheduled to take place on May 16, 1902 in the Jeffries' hometown of Los Angeles, California.[204]

---

[203] *Oakland Tribune, Oakland Enquirer, Oakland Times, San Francisco Chronicle, San Francisco Examiner, San Francisco Call, San Francisco Bulletin,* March 8, 1902.

[204] *Los Angeles Herald,* May 1, 1902; *San Francisco Call,* May 2, 1902. Tom McCarey would arrange most of the big fights in Los Angeles during the next several years, and brought Los Angeles boxing to new heights.

Jack Jeffries immediately began training with his champion brother, James J. Jeffries.

Jeffries' Training Quarters

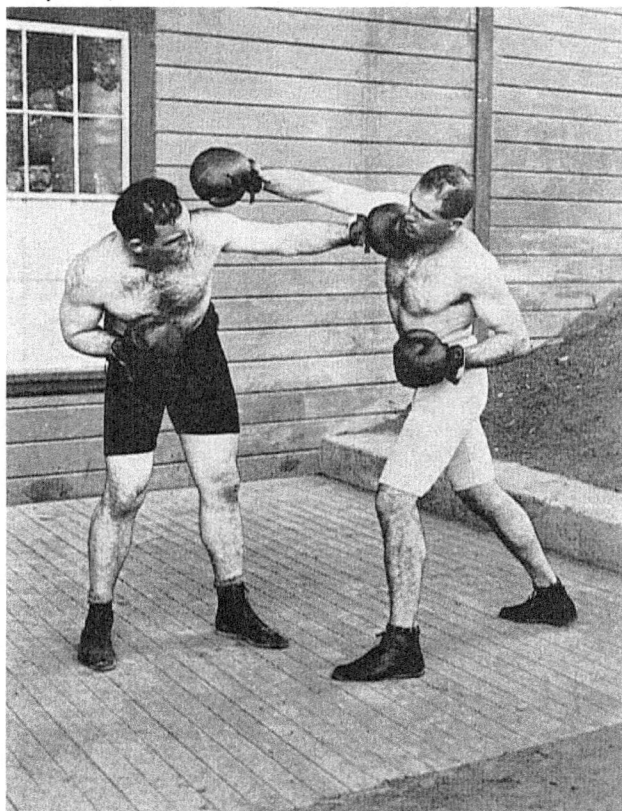

James Jeffries spars with his brother Jack Jeffries

25-year-old Jack Jeffries had neither the talent nor the fighting proclivity that his brother had. He primarily earned his living as his brother's sparring partner. He rarely engaged in pro fights, but the few that he had included: 1900 KO4 Jack Beauscholte, and L6 and D10 Billy Stift. The local papers also said he had a draw with Jack Stelzner. Regardless of his lack of experience, he had the Jeffries name, and justified or not, that name brought with it an aura of ability and credibility.

Jim Tremble sparring Jack Jeffries

Sparring many rounds with his brother was at least decent experience, though wise ones know that there is a big difference between sparring experience and actual fight experience.

On May 5 at the Chutes in Los Angeles, before a good-sized and enthusiastic audience, Jack Jeffries sparred 3 lively rounds with his brother James. One or two of the blows would have floored ordinary men.

At that time, Jack Jeffries, who appeared to be a greatly improved man, was in better shape than his champion brother. James was not as concerned with his own training as he was in helping his brother Jack prepare for his upcoming bout with Johnson. The champion was in negotiations for another bout with Bob Fitzsimmons.

In their daily sparring bouts, the champion was allowing his brother Jack to punch away at him to his heart's content. Jack hit him with some hard blows, but they utterly failed "to even disconcert the big fellow, who acts as if he liked playing punching bag for a change. Occasionally Jeffries gets shifty in his work and for a large man he shows amazing speed. The champion is a great deal faster now than when he won the world's title from Fitzsimmons."

A small majority favored Johnson over Jack Jeffries, although the local *Herald* said the fight was really an even-money proposition.[205]

Johnson had been working in a shack near First street and the river. Colored middleweight Billy Woods once again was Johnson's sparring partner. Woods weighed about 155 pounds, while Johnson was estimated to weigh between 170 and 175 pounds. They went at it so ferociously that

---

[205] *Los Angeles Herald*, May 6, 10, 12, 16, 1902.

Woods was called more of a fighting partner than a sparring partner. "The boxing feature is worth looking at, for neither man spares his strength. Each goes in and they rough it from the start, ripping out the vicious uppercuts, hooks and short swings in profusion, and with steam that means sore jaws and sore heads whenever the punches land." Observers believed that Jack Jeffries would have anything but a walkover with the "ebon-hued giant." Ordinarily, Johnson did road work, bag punching, and a few rounds of sparring with Woods.

Jack Johnson spars with Billy Woods

Johnson had never fought in Los Angeles before, but he was known for his two bouts with Hank Griffin, "who is one of the best known of the city's productions in the second rate division." Johnson was said to resemble Griffin, being of the same height, weighing about the same, and carrying similar muscular development, although Jack had the advantage in the latter area, having well-rounded shoulders that were heavily muscled, "as fine as any seen here."

It was said that like most colored gents, Johnson was a great admirer of fine clothing, and "he shows rather more taste than do most of his race in the selection of their apparel. He wears better clothing than three-fourths of the people on the streets, and is proud of his clothes."

Jack Jeffries was sparring with his brother and Jim Tremble, who was set to fight Johnson's sparring partner Billy Woods in the preliminary. Jeffries weighed between 180 and 185 pounds, so he would have the weight advantage over Johnson.[206]

Johnson did not expect a tough fight. "Johnson is supremely confident, and says the white man will never have a chance from the start."[207]

On May 12, 1902 at Fort Erie, Ontario, Canada, Joe Gans won the world lightweight championship when he knocked out Frank Erne in the 1st round. He became the third black fighter to win a world championship, joining George Dixon and Joe Walcott, though he was the first U.S.-born black fighter to become a champion. Dixon was Canadian and Walcott was from Guyana and Barbados.

Both Johnson and Jeffries had been training hard and were in condition. "Jim Jeffries has been indefatigable in his efforts to get Jack into winning form."

The day of their fight, the *Los Angeles Express* said Jack Jeffries would enter the ring at about 185 pounds, while Johnson would weigh about 182 pounds.

> Of Johnson much can be said about his ability as a pugilist. He is a glutton for punishment, and he can administer blows with both right and left which are terrific. He is a trifle slow in action, which will be a considerable advantage to his opponent, who is said to be a little faster on his feet. He makes up, however, for his slowness by taking punishment. …
>
> Two San Francisco men…who have seen the big negro do things in the Golden Gate city, said today that the backers of Johnson should give odds, as he has displayed the better form in his performances and has more fights to his credit than Jack Jeffries. There is considerable truth in this statement, but the betting hardly accords with this view. Even money seems quite general.[208]

The *Los Angeles Times* noted that the card featured white men fighting blacks. The Jeffries-Johnson bout was scheduled for 20 rounds. It said Jack Jeffries was best known as his brother James' sparring partner. Johnson was "a big negro, who has beaten several second-raters and is rated by many as a comer." The big fellows were called clever, willing, and evenly matched. The only scheduled local fistic attraction for months was greatly anticipated.

---

[206] *Los Angeles Herald*, May 10, 1902.
[207] *Los Angeles Herald*, May 11, 1902.
[208] *Los Angeles Express*, May 16, 1902.

Both Jeffries and Johnson express confidence in their ability to win, and each has quite a following among local ring patrons. But the great body of sports is undecided. ... The little betting done has been at 50 to 35 against the negro.

If there is a favorite, the white man is it. He certainly has a host of well-wishers here, and his would be a popular victory.[209]

JOHNSON JABS AND BLOCKS

"JEFF" SIDE STEPS A SWING

PHOTOS BY MOJONIER

JACK BEATS THE BAG

JACK LANDS A LEFT

The *Los Angeles Herald* said the sporting element was almost evenly divided on the merits of the men, but a small majority favored Johnson's chances. It opined that the contest was a 50-50 pick 'em. Both were in first-class condition, and both were willing to rough it. "Opinion is in favor of

---

[209] *Los Angeles Times*, May 16, 1902.

Jeffries if the bout be prolonged. There is a suspicion that the negro will not stand up to his work under punishment, though his record in the past has been that of a game man." The suspicion that blacks would not stand up to punishment was a typical claim based on racial bias.

It was reported that at first, champion James was against his brother Jack meeting a colored man, but eventually he relented.

James Jeffries and Joe Egan would corner Jack. The preliminary bouts were scheduled to start at 8 p.m. [210]

On Friday May 16, 1902 at Hazard's Pavilion in Los Angeles, Jack Johnson fought Jack Jeffries.

Both the *Los Angeles Herald* and *Los Angeles Times* said the crowd was the largest ever seen at a boxing contest in Los Angeles, with estimates ranging from 4,000 and up. Al Levy said the turnstile registered over 5,000 admissions. When the first preliminary was called, outside on the street there was a line of people 150 yards long, waiting to purchase tickets. The *Los Angeles Express* said Hazard's Pavilion was packed to the rafters with humanity. Many were turned away. The ground-floor seats were selling for $3. In the balcony, spectators were wedged in like sardines. It estimated there were 2,800 present, though the seating capacity was 2,200. The *Times* believed that the large attendance was due to the desire to see the champion, even though he wasn't fighting.

In the preliminary, Johnson sparring partner Billy Woods, whom the *Times* called a "saddle-colored darky," versus Jack Jeffries' sparring partner Jim Tremble, a white man, resulted in a dull 20-round draw that featured weak punches and a lot of clinching. The *Times* thought they were afraid of each other.

The main event was called at 10:30 p.m. Johnson was first into the ring, and when he entered he was greeted with a round of applause. He was wearing a most amazing pair of pink pajamas, which excited a fair amount of merriment and gasps of astonishment. The *Times* said, "It wasn't an ordinary, inoffensive kind of pink. It was one of those screaming, caterwauling, belligerent pinks." It called "Bold Mistah Johnsing's pajamas cruel." Johnson was the only one in the hall whose nerves were not affected. Taking the southeast corner, he sat back in his corner "half asleep and yawning like a big cat." With him was Frank Carrillo, who had bet $100 on Johnson.

Jack Jeffries was delayed for a while, but eventually he entered the pavilion with his brother James. When the champion approached the ring, there was a fever of excitement. The great cheers showed how dear the Jeffries brothers were to the hearts of the crowd.

Referee Harry Stuart wore a pink shirt. He introduced the champion of the world. The crowd yelled madly. Jeff had to jump through the ropes and bow. The crowd called for a speech. Acquiescing to their demands, Jeff said

---

[210] *Los Angeles Herald*, May 16, 1902.

he expected to meet Fitzsimmons in July, and was leaving the next day for San Francisco, where he would try to finalize the arrangements for the match. The crowd cheered his announcement.

The *Times* said that in his corner, Johnson looked at the champion, the great hulk of a man, "the way a little mangy dog with a lame leg stops in the road and looks up at a St. Bernard."

Each side examined the hands of the other. Jeff then climbed out of the ring to second his brother Jack.

Prior to the start of the fight, Hank Griffin said he wanted to meet the winner.

Referee Harry Stuart announced that a spectator's house had been burned, and that man hurried out. Then the fight began.

1 - Little was done by either. Johnson was the aggressor in a mild way. He opened with a light left to the head and they clinched and roughed it vigorously. Johnson landed a left to the nose, which started the blood. They sparred the rest of the way, feeling each other out. Jeff looked worried, while Johnson's face had a confident air. After the round, James swabbed off his brother Jack's nose and face with a sponge.

2 - Johnson started in aggressively, landing on the face. He struck a right to the jaw, and a minute later rocked Jeff's head with the same blow. Jeffries came back with a hard punch of his own, but Johnson was not rattled. He replied even more aggressively and put a stinger to the face. Johnson forced Jeffries to break ground constantly. Johnson finished the round with two stiff jabs to the nose and face.

The *Los Angeles Express* said that at the gong, Johnson had the advantage. The *Los Angeles Herald* observed, "The white man's finish seemed to be only a matter of time." The *Los Angeles Times* said that during the round, great anxiety was on the champion's face. After the round was over, in the corner, James told his brother to get in over Johnson's guard.

3 - Jeffries took the initiative and went at Johnson in vicious style, driving in a stiff left to the head. He landed a right to the face and repeated the blow. It was a hard, effective right, and Johnson showed that he felt it, for his eyes dilated and his head wobbled. However, he recovered himself, feinted, and then when Jeff attacked, Johnson clipped him with a resounding blow on the jaw that must have shaken Jeff a bit. Jeffries countered with a hook to the head. They clinched and both worked hard on the inside. On the break, Jeff ducked a vicious swing. At long range, Johnson shot in another left to the jaw. Jeff countered in kind, and they clinched, both working vigorous short-arm jolts. In rapid succession, Jeff landed four or five hot body blows.

The *Herald* thought that Jeff had a little the better of the infighting in this round, though it subsequently said this round was even. The *Express* felt that Jeffries got the better of the round.

4 - Johnson began aggressively, and kept it up throughout the round. As they were rushing to a clinch, Johnson landed a stiff right high on the jaw,

jolting the white man severely. The blow sounded like a battering ram. Jeff recovered in time to sting Johnson's ear with a long hook. Johnson swung a right to the back of the head. They clinched and worked. Johnson landed several effective body blows in rapid succession. Jeff ripped a left to the side of the jaw and a right on the cheek. Johnson hurled a vicious right to the ear. Jeff countered to the jaw. Jeff jabbed the face, but Johnson countered to the top of the head.

The *Express* said time was called with Johnson having a little the better of the round. The *Herald* said, "This was as much Johnson's round as the one before had been even."

5 - The men came up none the worse for wear. Jeffries was fresh and held his ground for a minute, and they went at it furiously. Jeff struck one to the face. However, Johnson's long hard right to the ribs started him back. They sparred. Jeff could not move back as fast as Johnson could move forward. They exchanged left jabs, and both landed. Johnson dove in and quickly drove three piston-rod rights to the jaw and face. A stiff left hook followed.

Suddenly Johnson crossed hard with a right to the jaw, putting all of his weight into the punch. Jeff's knees loosened and he collapsed to the floor, striking it with a thud.

Referee Harry Stuart counted to ten. The *Herald* said, "This was a useless formality, however, for half a minute would have done Jack Jeffries little good." The *Times* said Jack turned over with a half moan while counted out. After the count had concluded, Johnson lifted him up in his arms like a bag of wheat and handed him to his seconds.

The *Los Angeles Herald* was impressed. It took Johnson just 14 minutes to land the right cross that took all of the fight out of Jeffries. The clean blow came at the end of a great deal of infighting in which Johnson landed a series of punches. Jeffries was outclassed. "Johnson showed himself to be fully as good a man as his record would warrant. He is no showy boxer. He is a two hand fighter and a free hitter, and with these qualifications he couples fair ability to get out of the way of counters."

> [Jeffries] had been systematically beaten down, and the victory of Johnson was not all due to one punch as many had supposed. Johnson got to his man's head with regularity and dispatch, paying little attention to the less vulnerable body, except when an unusually tempting opening presented itself.

Afterwards, in Johnson's dressing room was a mob of colored gentlemen that swooped in, anxious to congratulate the winner. Grinning broadly with two rows of ivories that strongly contrasted with his black skin, Johnson said, "Dat was a bad punch, sure 'nuff. Huh, jes like findin' money."

When asked about potential future fights, including Hank Griffin, Johnson replied, "Now, dat feller Hank dun know sure nuff he ain't in mah class, an' I dun show Maher pretty soon something, dat's a fac'."

The *Herald* opined, "Johnson deserves a mill with big 'Denver Ed' Martin, with whose style he seems rather familiar."[211]

The *Los Angeles Times* said, "Jack Jeffries lasted just five rounds in front of a good-natured black animal named Johnsing." Early in the fight, which was fast and furious, Johnson took a rap to the nose and woke up to the fact that there was something doing. He came at Jeff with eyes "that glared like a wild beast's. After that it was all up with Brother Jack." During the 5th round, James J. turned his head away and looked down, as if watching the blows strike his brother hurt him more. The black arm shot up under Jack Jeffries' guard, and from the corner, champion Jim looked sad.

In somewhat contradictory fashion, the writer for this newspaper also said that Jeffries was doing nicely until a swat under the chin took him out.

The *Times* further said that by rights, from appearances, brother Jack ought to have won. He was a fine-looking fellow with a body like a Greek god, muscles glistening with health. Conversely, "Mistah Johnsing is a long, lean, bullet-headed, flat-chested 'coon.' Jack [Jeffries] stands up to it like the pictures in the *Police Gazette*. Mistah Johnsing straddles out like a sick chicken."

This newspaper did say that Johnson "goes into the ranks of the candidates for the first class of pugilism." He was "too much color" for "Brother Jack."

Speaking of James J. as a cornerman, the *Times* wrote,

> Ordinarily a second's job is not one to be ardently sought. You are to swab down the sweaty back of a prize fighter, and wave a towel and feed him water out of a bottle; when you try to get rid of a little valuable advice, he tells you to go to hell, that he is doing the best he can; when it is all over, he tells you you are a lobster for letting him lose.
>
> But it is different when you happen to be da champ. Brother Jack kept his eye peeled on Jim more than on Brother Johnsing; hence the swipe on the jaw.[212]

The *Los Angeles Express* said some of Jeff's friends claimed it was a lucky punch. However, it was a clear-cut and premeditated one. The *Express* called Johnson a clever fighter.

> While the colored fighter apparently was the better of the two men, and had it over Jeffries in rapidity of action and headwork, still the latter put up a better fight than was expected, showing indomitable courage, and in the knockout round his strength and staying powers by no means were spent.[213]

---

211 *Los Angeles Herald,* May 17, 1902.
212 *Los Angeles Times,* May 17, 1902.
213 *Los Angeles Express,* May 17, 1902.

Up north, the *San Francisco Call* reported that Jeff showed cleverness and footwork, but did not have a damaging punch. Johnson was stronger, and had an effective right and left. In the 5th round, Johnson forced Jeff to a corner, and, feinting with his left, sent in a hard right to the neck below the ear, and Jeff went down and out like a log.

The *National Police Gazette* reported, "The bout was very interesting while it lasted, but the champion's brother was no match for his opponent. Jeffries fought gamely, but his blows were not hard enough to make any impression on the negro, who dropped him with a right to the jaw just after they began the fifth round."[214]

After returning back north, Johnson urged Tom McCarey to try to arrange a match with him against Peter Maher. He was also willing to meet Choynski again.[215]

Los Angeles was being noticed as an emerging hotbed of boxing. The Johnson-Jeffries fight had drawn a big house. Still, Los Angeles had less than one-third the population of San Francisco, with a mere 102,479 people as of the 1900 census.

In mid-June 1902, fighter Ben Tremble, who had lost to Hank Griffin, said he would fight Johnson if Jack could make 165 pounds. However, "Johnson cannot do 165 without sawing off a leg." Johnson's frame had been filling out.

Century Club manager Tom McCarey arranged a third fight between Jack Johnson and Hank Griffin, to be held at Hazard's Pavilion in Los Angeles in late June.

In preparation, Johnson

HANK GRIFFIN

sparred with Bob Jones, whose record included 1898 and 1900 D15 and KO11 Hank Griffin.[216]

---

[214] *San Francisco Call*, May 17, 1902; *National Police Gazette*, June 7, 1902.

[215] *Los Angeles Express*, May 27, 1902.

[216] *Los Angeles Herald*, June 15, 1902. Bob Jones was matched to meet Billy Woods.

Both Johnson and Griffin were said to be in the pink of condition, had pride, and valued their reputations, so the bout would likely be a fast one. Johnson was "a determined fighter and has great confidence in his ability." He expected a hard fight, though. Johnson's backers were offering odds of 10 to 8, and there were few takers. Still, Griffin's supporters said Hank would show Johnson a trick or two.[217]

Tom McCarey said, "If Johnson disposes of Griffin in anything like short order, I will feel convinced that he is good enough for any of them, and will have no compunctions in putting him against the best of the light heavies I can find." This suggests that Johnson was still hovering in the 175-180-pound range.

Johnson was fully confident in his ability to defeat Griffin, but felt that he might have to do so via the decision route. He said,

> I knows dat Hank Griffin, and he cayn't hurt me. I know dat he cayn't knock me out in a punch, and dat's de only way he would have a ghost ob a chance. If I get a jaw broken, or a busted arm, de worst dat I could get would be a draw. How does I know he cayn't punch hard? Why, all I has to do is to look at de way he slammed it into Joe Kennedy and den didn't get him. Did'n he cross Joe just as hard as ever he could, and den not put Joe out? No, he cayn't hurt me and I'll hurt him plenty, but as to saying when I is going to get him, why, dat cayn't be done. Dat Hank Griffin's is an awkward man to cop, shore 'nuff. Why? Well, he's big as I am and shifty some. I don' known how soon I'll be able to get him; it may take pretty much all of the twenty rounds, and I may get him as quick as I did Jack Jeffries. 'Cose I admits dat he's a better man dan Jack.

When asked who the hardest man he had ever tackled was, Johnson replied, "Well, to tell de troof, day's all ben easy; dat is, all dat I got. I usually gets my man inside ten rounds if I gets him at all."

Hank Griffin argued that because he took the decision once and got a draw the other time they fought, he stood an equal chance with Johnson. Hank had a large following, and as the fight approached, they were betting at 10 to 8, with Johnson on the long end.[218]

The *Express* noted that the entire card featured all black fighters, something the club had never before offered. The *Herald* called the all-black competition "black night" and "dark night."

The *Express* did not necessarily think that Griffin should be the underdog.

> Griffin is a game fighter, and conservative sports are inclined to think that the latter is being underestimated. Hank Griffin must not be considered passé, because of the difference in ages [Griffin was 32

[217] *Los Angeles Express,* June 19, 1902.
[218] *Los Angeles Herald,* June 19, 1902.

years old to Johnson's 24] or by reason of the fact that Johnson has been exhibiting several hard punches of late. Griffin has a punch or two left which he can make quite effective if the opportunity presents itself. Los Angeles sports should recall a few of his victories and how he gained them. Griffin's stand against Champion Jeffries is no criterion upon which to base a prediction. There are other things to be considered. Even Griffin's staunchest friends seem to display a weakness for Johnson. Both men will enter the ring weighing about 182 pounds.[219]

The point was that just because the huge 220-plus-pound Jeffries easily handled Griffin did not mean Hank would not put up a very competitive fight against Johnson, who was similar in size. He was experienced, crafty, and clever, and had a few good punches himself.

Griffin had been sparring up north with Bob Fitzsimmons, who was preparing for his championship fight with James Jeffries. Sparring with a huge puncher such as Fitz showed that Griffin was durable.

The *Herald* said they were well-matched, and if a knockout came in the early rounds, it would have almost as much to do with luck as skill. Johnson was the general favorite.

The dope on the case is a little bad, however. In two previous meetings Johnson lost a decision and gained a draw once. He says he was in no condition the first time, which is fairly proved. The second mill resulted in a draw, but if Billy Delaney and William Lavigne are good authority, Johnson had all the best of the last rounds.

Johnson had stopped Kennedy in 4 rounds, while Griffin had not done so in two 20-round draws. The Jack Jeffries bout, "aside from showing that the black man has a punch, proved nothing." Both were in good condition.

Harry Stuart, the official Century Athletic Club referee, would handle the bouts. "Stuart's past performances in the fistic judging line have been of the very highest class, both as to good judgment and impartiality. He has yet to make that first mistake the best umpires of sports occasionally commit."[220]

On Friday June 20, 1902 at Hazard's Pavilion in Los Angeles, Jack Johnson fought Hank Griffin for the third time. Harry Stuart refereed.

In the preliminary, former Johnson sparring partner Billy Woods won a 10-round decision over recent Johnson sparring partner Bob Jones.

According to the *Los Angeles Times*, when the main-event boxers appeared, because he seemed heavier, Johnson loomed up better than Griffin. The betting line was even money that Johnson would knock out Griffin.

[219] *Los Angeles Express,* June 20, 1902.
[220] *Los Angeles Herald,* June 20, 1902.

1 - The *Times* said they went at it hammer and tongs and made it a stand-off. The *Herald* said Johnson split open Griffin's nose.

2 - Johnson got the best of the round.

3 - Griffin won this round.

The *Times* said that in the first few rounds, Johnson showed to good advantage. He was quick and active for a big man. Griffin's footwork was noticeable, and this enabled him to keep out of Johnson's way most of the time. The *Express* said Johnson landed frequently in the first 3 rounds, drawing blood.

4 - Griffin gained confidence and landed several hard body blows, having a slight lead in the round.

5 - The *Express* said Johnson landed a hard right on the jaw and clearly had the advantage of the round.

The *Times* said Johnson was the aggressor in the early part of the fight, and might have ended it within 5 rounds, but he waited too long to take action.

It also said Griffin's nose bled in almost every round after the 5th round. Johnson continued as the aggressor through the first 12 rounds, but Griffin generally countered on his leads and partially evened matters.

6 - Griffin did all the fighting.

7 - Honors were even in this round.

The *Express* said that for the first 7 rounds, Johnson was the aggressor, though he did not have the advantage all of the time.

8 - Griffin landed on the jaw and administered several hard body punches. In the clinches, Johnson's body blows were effective, but Griffin landed a few as well. Hank easily had the advantage in the round.

9 - The round was even.

10 - Griffin earned the round. He landed a hard body blow which made Johnson stagger a bit.

11 - Neither man had an advantage. Both landed freely on the body and face.

12 - Griffin had a bit of the advantage.

13 - The *Express* said Hank was quite aggressive and had Johnson side-stepping. The *Times* said Griffin began to shine in this round. He landed solidly five or six times, "and had much the best of the bargain at this stage." After this round, Griffin more than held his own, and had the best of matters.

14 - They were even in this round.

15 - Hank clearly had the advantage.

16 - Griffin worked fast, but failed to land anything that was effective. Hence this round was even.

17 - This round was also even.

18 - Johnson showed to better advantage, outpointing Griffin. The *Herald* said Johnson landed a succession of short-arm blows in a clinch which put Griffin on queer street for a minute.

19 – 20 - Hank did all the work.

Referee Harry Stuart ruled the fight a 20-round draw.

According to the *Los Angeles Express*, Griffin surprised the local patrons with a wonderful performance.

> [Griffin] put up a fight that entitled him to a draw if not the decision. Several old-time pugilists claim that Griffin had a little the advantage, but it was so slight that a decision in favor of either hardly could be rendered. A draw was the only alternative and Referee Stuart declared it such.

Taking its scoring round-by-round, the *Express* had it 9 rounds Griffin, 5 rounds Johnson, and 6 rounds even. Of course, if all or all but one of those even rounds had gone to Johnson, it could have been a draw or a Johnson victory. It had been a fierce, clever, and close battle.

> Griffin displayed more science, better generalship and a better eye than Johnson, while the latter had the advantage of strength and good fighting position. Hank displayed several excellent blocks and repeatedly checked Johnson's most effective swings.

When Referee Stuart ruled the fight a draw, Bakersfield's Frank Carrillo, Johnson's manager, protested quite fiercely. "You never will referee another fight for me. My man did all the fighting and you have robbed him." Stuart retorted, "You are lucky to get a draw, and Griffin was the aggressor."[221]

The *Los Angeles Times* called it one of the best fight-nights ever given in the city by the Century Athletic Club. "Griffen" and Johnson fought before one of the largest crowds that ever witnessed any of the club's events, for the house was packed. "The decisions in every instance met with universal approval, except in the main event, and about all the complaints on that came from those sports who had eagerly bet 3 to 1 and 10 to 8 on Johnson to win." The *Times* argued that the "showing between them on the whole fight was so even that the referee could do nothing else but call it a draw."[222]

The *Los Angeles Herald* said that before the fight started, Johnson talked big. When the 1st round began, Jack went in at Griffin like he thought he

---

[221] *Los Angeles Express*, June 21 1902.
[222] *Los Angeles Times* June 21, 1902.

was a sure winner. During the first few minutes of the fight, Johnson split open Griffin's nose.

However, Johnson found that Griffin was not likely to succumb to a single hard punch, so he modified his tactics a little and backed off. For the rest of the fight, Johnson was content to try to reopen the nose. Sometimes he did so with a jab, while at others it was an elbow that "scratched the battered nasal organ sufficiently to turn on the claret. Hank's nose emitted all the gore produced during the mill."

Regardless of the blood, Griffin proved to be a surprise to Johnson, for he put up a good fight, fighting neck-and-neck and back-and-forth throughout.

The only time Johnson came close to winning outright was in the 18th round. He landed a succession of short-arm blows in a clinch, and for a minute, Griffin was dazed and hurt. Jack had a decided but temporary advantage. After the round, Hank's second did good work in the corner and got him ready to mix it well for many more rounds.

The *Herald* agreed with Referee Harry Stuart's 20-round draw decision, saying that it was "the only possible one, for the progress of the rounds was see-saw. Griffin would have the shade in one, and a hard wallop by the other man would give him the best of the next round." It called it a satisfactory bout.

The meeting gave the Los Angeles fans the first real opportunity to get a line on Johnson's ability, "for his bout with Jack Jeffries is scarcely to be considered." The locals knew that Griffin was a tough fighter and real test.

Given the high quality of opponent, the *Herald* was impressed with Johnson. It appreciated the subtle effectiveness of his work.

> Johnson last night showed as good a punch as ever, but he was loth to cut loose and take a chance with it. His foot work was excellent; his blocking superb, and Griffin hurt him but little. On the other hand, he dealt a few to Hank in the clinches that came near settling the event and but for Griffin's level head and good generalship would have done so instanter. Johnson's infighting was effective, but not many in the house appreciated it at its true value. He uses few of the spectacular smacks over the kidney affected by some boxers, but continues his efforts to short uppercuts and piston rod jolts that sting wherever they strike.

Afterwards, Johnson said he wanted to fight Griffin again, feeling confident that he could stop him in another meeting, "but as he has failed to do it in three attempts, many doubt his ability to do so."

In his dressing room, "Johnsing" was gloomy. He and his seconds strongly disagreed with the referee's decision. "Ise jes been robbed," Jack said as he carefully folded his pink pajamas. "Everybody knows dat Hank was licked." Johnson explained some of the fine points that he felt the spectators and referee had overlooked. Clearly, the draw result did not affect Johnson's confidence or belief in himself.

Hank Griffin had little to say, and seemed a bit disappointed at not having been able to knock out his opponent.[223]

Despite Johnson and his manager's complaints, Stuart's decision was well received. In fact, in general, Stuart was considered to be a very good judge and arbiter of fights. "It is understood generally that the fair and able judging of ring sports done by the local man has not been unnoticed outside of Los Angeles, and many favorable comments are made on his work by boxers and their managers." James Jeffries had been "much impressed with the justice and accuracy of his decisions."

Regarding his decision in Johnson-Griffin III, the *Herald* insisted, "Stuart Friday night added to an already long list another absolutely fair verdict. Johnson was lucky to get a draw, for he slackened up decidedly in his work after the opening rounds. Nineteen men out of twenty were abundantly satisfied with Stuart's judgment."[224]

Johnson later said in his autobiography that he had two "severe" fights with Hank Griffin that were both draws – one 15 and one 20 rounder. "In summing up my fights, throughout my career, there were none, even in the championship bouts, which were harder than those with Griffen, and I believe that the greatest punishment I ever received in the ring was at the hands of Griffen." Johnson never did defeat Hank Griffin officially, having failed to do so in three attempts.[225]

Two days after the fight, Hank Griffin returned to Skagg's Springs in Northern California to resume the arduous task of being a Bob Fitzsimmons sparring partner. "Hank is authority for the statement that posing as the boxing aide to the Cornishman is anything but a sinecure." Griffin sparred with Fitz in late June and throughout July 1902, helping to prepare Fitzsimmons for his rematch with James Jeffries.[226]

Fitzsimmons typically sparred alternating rounds with heavyweights George Dawson, Soldier Tom Wilson, who stood over 6 feet tall and weighed over 200 pounds, and Hank Griffin, who was "there to take a punching, and it is safe to say that he gets all that is coming to him."[227]

Griffin was the snappiest and most earnest worker of the bunch. "He is a willing worker and exceedingly shifty." Fitzsimmons liked working with Hank the most, because he could mix it up more with him and not have to hold back as much. "It is give and take and he is right after Fitz all the time." Griffin made a good impression.

Hank was impressed with Bob's roadwork, saying,

> Well, Lord, you should see him go. He didn't know when he was going up the hill. It was all level to him. Why, I guess I must have lost

---

[223] *Los Angeles Herald* June 21, 1902.

[224] *Los Angeles Herald* June 23, 1902.

[225] Johnson, *In the Ring and Out*. at 47.

[226] *Los Angeles Herald*, June 22, 1902. On June 25, 1902 in London, England, Gus Ruhlin scored a KO11 over Tom Sharkey.

[227] *New York Clipper*, June 7, 1902; *National Police Gazette*, June 28, July 5, 19, August 23, 1902.

my wind before I had gone two miles…. When I came in I was all done up. While Mr. Fitzsimmons, he looked as if he had just done a cakewalk around the barn.

Bob Fitzsimmons jogs with Hank Griffin

On July 9, Fitz dropped Griffin with a short-arm blow. "Fitzsimmons is hitting as hard as ever."

In subsequent days, Griffin said there was nothing to the fight, for Bob would defeat Jeffries.

Jim Jeffries was sparring with his brother Jack, as well as Joe Kennedy.

Fitz's sparring with Griffin was kept up on a daily basis. On July 14, Fitzsimmons did his morning run with Griffin. In the afternoon, he hit the bag. Then he boxed his usual alternating rounds with George Dawson, Tom Wilson, and Hank Griffin. Bob banged Hank hard and often, but Griffin took it and fought back. The circuit of alternating rounds continued, with Fitz remaining in the ring for 8 rounds. In the final round, Fitzsimmons "hammered the colored boy good and plenty. … Bob sent a short jolt into his jaw that gave him a dizzy spell." Afterwards, Hank said, "Did you see him give me that jolt? … It was a dandy. What would it have been if he had meant it? Oh, Lordy!"

James Jeffries sparring Joe Kennedy

On the 16th, Fitzsimmons ran 10 miles. He boxed 8 fast rounds with Wilson and Griffin, dropping Wilson several times. Griffin was also knocked down. The following day, he banged them around for 6 rounds.

In Fitz's 6 rounds of sparring on the 18th, Wilson was dropped to the mat, while a blow to the jaw dazed Griffin and caused him to stop working for a few seconds. Both men worked hard and at a fast pace, giving Bob some pretty hard raps, but none of them had any effect.

Fitzsimmons commended Hank Griffin as an excellent sparring partner. Hank stood 6'2", weighed 180 pounds in top condition, and had a very long reach of 81 ½ inches. Fitz said it was no easy task to subdue Griffin, calling him a wonder.

On July 21 at the Olympic, Fitz took his morning run, boxed with each of his three trainers, and punched the bag. He mostly played defense against Griffin, for 4 rounds allowing him to slug away, while Bob blocked and eluded blows. In the last round, Fitz showed what he could do if he so desired, slugging Hank and keeping him trying to survive. He then wrestled for 30 minutes with Dawson and Griffin, and seemed fresh afterwards.

On the 23rd, with San Francisco Mayor Eugene Schmitz watching, Fitz boxed 4 fast rounds with Griffin. "He hammered Griffin hard and blocked all the heavy blows Hank sent in." The mayor was impressed.

Afterwards, speaking of Griffin, Bob said, "That fellow is one of the hardest men I have ever tried to hit; he has a way of smothering up that leaves nothing but bones in sight."

Griffin complimented Fitz as well. "When I first came to the camp Mr. Fitzsimmons had hard work getting at me, as I used the crouching position, but now it does not bother him in the least. … I have been up against Jeffries, and I know how he can hit, and I tell you I am pinning my money on Bob."[228]

On July 25, 1902 in San Francisco, Hank Griffin was amongst Bob Fitzsimmons' cornermen in Bob's attempt to regain the crown from James J. Jeffries. Despite Fitzsimmons' excellent performance, Jeffries took all that Fitz had to offer, and with his non-stop pressure and body punching, eventually wore down Fitz and knocked him out in the 8th round. It had been a wonderful championship contest. A crowd of 7,000 spectators paid $31,880 to witness the bout.

On August 18, 1902 in Salt Lake City, Utah, George Gardner stopped Jack Root in the 17th round. In Gardner's corner were Alex/Alec Greggains and Dave Barry.[229]

On September 13, 1902 at Hazard's Pavilion in Los Angeles, 185-pound Hank Griffin was slightly ahead on points against 6'3 ½" 210-pound white fighter Fred Russell, when in the 14th round, Griffin was hit in the head and went down. While he was on one knee and about to rise, Russell deliberately fouled Griffin by hitting him with an uppercut while he was still down. However, instead of disqualifying Russell as he should have done, Referee Tom Darmody counted out Griffin and gave the bout to the offender. The *Los Angeles Express* harshly criticized Darmody for failing to keep Russell back until Griffin had risen, and for not disqualifying Russell. It opined that Darmody was either ignorant or deliberately biased.

> To strike a man when he is down never has been considered anything but unfair, no matter in what grade of society it may be, and in boxing contests it is looked upon as more than a disgrace. It is a heinous offense and is punishable by the loss of the fight, according to the rules governing boxing contests.[230]

The *Herald* agreed that Russell should have been disqualified, as did the majority of the crowd, which raised its roar of protest at the decision.

Before the fight, Jack Johnson, who was present, announced that he wanted to meet the winner. A gentleman who represented Oxnard's Sam McVey expressed similar sentiments. Both would eventually fight Russell.[231]

---

[228] *Los Angeles Herald*, July 10, 1902; *San Francisco Bulletin*, July 3, 5, 9-11, 14, 15, 17, 19, 21, 24, 1902; *San Francisco Evening Post*, July 14, 17, 21, 22, 1902; *San Francisco Call*, July 22, 24, 1902.
[229] *National Police Gazette*, September 13, 1902; *Daily Inter Ocean*, August 19, 1902. On that same date, August 18, 1902 in Chicago, Marvin Hart won a 6-round decision over Billy Stift. Hart had previously scored a KO3 over Stift.
[230] *Los Angeles Express*, September 13, 1902.
[231] *Los Angeles Herald*, September 8, 13, 1902.

CHAPTER 9

Colored Champion and More

24-year-old Jack Johnson's next bout, set for late October 1902, was of great significance. It was for a claim to the colored heavyweight championship of the world. 35-year-old 5'9 ½" Frank Childs was a very experienced veteran, with over 50 career fights, including: 1892 KO3 and WDQ8 George LaBlanche; 1893 EX4 Peter Jackson, KO3 James "Soldier" Walker, KO12 Australian Billy Smith, and D20 Hank Griffin; 1894 LKOby3 Dan Creedon; 1895 LKOby3 Joe Choynski; 1897 W6 Bob Armstrong and KO1 George Grant; 1898 KO6 and KO4 Klondike Haines, KO2 Bob Armstrong, W6 George Grant,

FRANK CHILDS

WDQ3, D6, and W6 Charley Strong, L20 George Byers (colored championship), KO3 Henry Baker, and W6 Tom 'Stockings' Conroy; 1899 KO6 Bob Armstrong (claims the colored championship)(Armstrong had lost an 1898 10-round decision to Jeffries), W8 Ed Dunkhorst, W6 Pete Everett, D6 Jack Bonner, D6 Tom Conroy, W6 Klondike Haines (for Haines' claim to the colored title)(three months after the first Klondike-Jack Johnson bout), D6 Joe Kennedy, and KO3 Klondike Haines; 1900 W6 and D6 Bonner, D6 Byers, W6 (twice) and W10 Fred Russell, KO6 Joe Butler, and W10 Pete Everett; 1901 KO17 George Byers (undisputed colored heavyweight championship); 1902 KO4 Bill Hanrahan (who in 1901 had scored a KO1 Marvin Hart), L6 Denver Ed Martin (Martin claims the colored title, though some disputed the claim owing to the fact that it was only a short rounds victory), and KO3 Joe Walcott. The Walcott fight took place on October 9, twelve days before the Johnson fight.

Johnson had been a Childs sparring partner back in 1899 in Chicago, so they were somewhat familiar with one another. Upset at the poor treatment he received from Childs, Johnson was looking for revenge.

The bout was scheduled for 20 rounds at Hazard's Pavilion in Los Angeles.

The *Los Angeles Herald* called Childs the colored heavyweight champion. To prepare for the bout, Childs sparred with Hank Griffin.[232]

The betting odds stood at 10 to 7, with Childs as the favorite. After all, Childs was considered one of the best black fighters in the country, and had a long history of success. He was powerful and experienced.

Local sports took considerable interest in the mill. A great deal of money was wagered, perhaps more than any other fistic event that had taken place for some time. Every available reserved seat had been sold.

Despite the fact that Childs was the favorite, Harry Stuart, who refereed and decided the recent Johnson-Griffin bout a draw, wrote,

> [T]hose who saw the rapid-fire leads, jolts and counters that [Johnson] dealt out so promiscuously to the ever-willing and reliable trial horse, Hank Griffin, a few days ago, cannot help but admit that he has a swell chance. Frank Carillo has great confidence in his man's ability and will back up his opinion with a stack of your Uncle Sam's.[233]

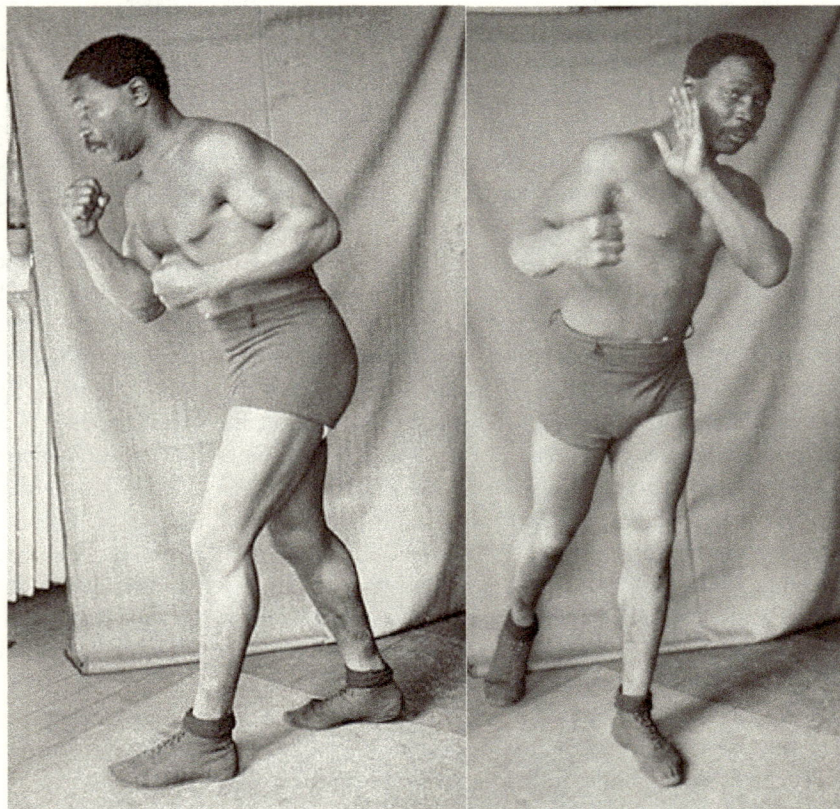

Frank Childs

[232] *Los Angeles Herald*, October 18, 1902.
[233] *Los Angeles Herald*, October 20, 1902.

H. C. Roussellot, Childs' manager, was complimented for his refreshing honesty, for unlike other managers who often fibbed about their man's record (upon which lies newsmen often relied), he admitted that Childs had suffered losses to George Byers (which was avenged), Dan Creedon, and Denver Ed Martin. Perhaps he was trying to obtain better odds. He could not make as much betting on his man if he was the strong favorite.

Local promoters wanted to develop a local man who would be able to test the emerging Denver Ed Martin, and give Martin a stronger claim to a title fight with Jeffries.

At that time, Sam McVey, Oxnard's pugilistic wonder, was being matched to fight Fred Russell. The winner of that contest would be matched with the winner of Childs-Johnson, and it was hoped that the victor of that battle would be a formidable opponent for Martin. "The latter's science or punching power none will question, the only doubt is, will he stand the gaff?"

It was Tom McCarey's plan to have the winner of Johnson-Childs meet Fred Russell, and the winner of that go to meet Denver Ed Martin. At that time, McCarey was negotiating to have Martin fight before his club. "There is little doubt in the minds of the local sports that Martin will win easily over any Pacific coast aspirant, and that he then will be ready to take on 'de champ.'"[234]

There was a fair amount of wrangling over the choice of referee for Johnson-Childs. Johnson's manager, Frank Carillo, objected to Harry Stuart, the club's choice, feeling that Stuart robbed Johnson of the recent Griffin decision by calling their fight a draw. The *Times* responded, "Johnson had the best of the go for six rounds and from that until the twentieth, Griffin had a shade the best of it. Referee Stuart could do nothing else but call it a draw, and Carillo always thought Johnson had been robbed. No one else thought so, though." The *Herald* said Carillo had interposed a "senseless objection" to Stuart. Carillo felt that Stuart had given his fighters several raw deals, but the newsmen did not back him up, feeling that Stuart's fighters had been fairly whipped. "In his showing against Griffin, Johnson was awarded a draw and many thought he was lucky to get off without losing the decision."

JACK JOHNSON, THE LOS ANGELES HEAVYWEIGHT.

[234] *Los Angeles Herald*, October 20, 1902; *Los Angeles Express*, October 21, 1902.

Tom Darmody, who had refereed Griffin-Russell and botched it, did not want the job, because he did not again want to be the target of criticism.

Ultimately, "Honest" John Brink consented to referee and judge the bout. Brink had a reputation for honesty and fairness. He was a former Los Angeles Athletic Club amateur heavyweight champion who became a referee and promoter, and had become the LAAC's president in 1895. He had once sparred with a young James J. Jeffries.

The day of the fight, the advance sale of tickets was very large, and indications were that the pavilion would be packed, "for Childs is a fighter of wide reputation." He was the 2 to 1 favorite, but there was plenty of Johnson money in sight.

According to the *Times*, both would weigh about 180 pounds.[235]

Some were saying that Childs was not in proper condition. However, the *Herald* said, "When Childs came here he was in good shape, and several days of work have not changed matters for the worse." Frank remained the favorite, and generally was expected to win.

Those who thought Johnson had a chance noted that Childs had lost to Martin. Frank also had a 6-round draw with Kennedy, while Johnson recently had knocked out Kennedy in 4 rounds. Childs and Johnson had the same results against Griffin (D20) and Choynski (LKOby3), though Childs had the better results against Haines and Everett than did Johnson. Childs held two decision victories over Pete Everett, whereas Johnson had fought him to a draw, though some felt that Johnson had carried Everett. Childs had a W6 and KO3 over Klondike Haines, whereas Johnson had a loss, draw, and recent TKO14 victory over Klondike. Frank also held a knockout victory over big Bob Armstrong. Childs was considered to be more of an aggressive puncher and finisher, and he definitely had more experience. It was an intriguing match-up.

> Johnson is in perfect condition. He has been doing a great deal of training. The big black realizes this is his chance to get into the stake horse class, and a number of friends report having secured as good as two to one for their money on the Johnson end. ...
>
> On form, there is nothing to the contest but Childs; but Johnson's known peculiarities warrant the statement that he may be returned the winner if he gets off right – that is, makes an effective start. If Childs adopts his usual two-handed aggressive tactics at the start, the fight will either be settled in quick order or will drag itself out to the limit on Johnson's playing for a draw. This, however, the big black says he will not do. He professes a desire to 'lick or be licked.' ...
>
> There will be little disparity in weights. Both will be over 185 and under 190. Johnson is taller and has more reach. He can punch, and it must be admitted he is fairly clever. The main claim Childs has on the

---

[235] *Los Angeles Express, Los Angeles Times, Los Angeles Herald,* October 21, 1902.

public money is his reputation as a fighter, and, be it added, a dead game one. There has been some question raised here about Johnson's willingness to take a beating. If there is anything wrong with the big fellow's heart Childs is the man to find it out.

The advance seat sale amounts to nearly $1,000, showing what interest the public takes in the mill. It is an unprecedented figure here.[236]

On Tuesday October 21, 1902 at the big Hazard's Pavilion on Fifth street in Los Angeles, Jack Johnson fought Frank Childs. John Brink refereed. The house was one of the largest ever seen there.

According to the *Los Angeles Times*, the main event was slow. The boxers cautiously fiddled around the ring. The crowd was so quiet that the reporters could be heard dictating to stenographers, and a small voice in the gallery occasionally could be heard urging the men to hurry things along. "Round after round went by and the crowd began getting weary. The air was full of hissing."

Childs kept stepping around Johnson. Some thought that Frank was not concerned with points, but simply awaiting a chance to get in a single knockout blow. However, in the meantime, Johnson was punching him, piling up points. His punches gradually had their effect. Regardless, the two often grinned at each other and conversed.

By the 11th round, Childs was spitting blood and had one eye closed. He kept looking out of the other eye for an opportunity that never came. After the round ended, his seconds put towels around him. They kept urging Frank to do something, but he only shook his head sadly.

In the 12th round, "they sallied around and gave each other love pats. Then it was noticed that Childs's right arm was hanging limp. Johnson saw it, too, and rushed him savagely to the ropes, beating him about the face." At that point, a Childs second rolled a little sponge into the middle of the ring to retire his man, and the bout was stopped.

Afterwards, Childs claimed that the reason the sponge was thrown up to retire him was because he had injured his right elbow the day before, sparring with Hank Griffin, and it had been aggravated during the bout.

In the dressing room, two physicians on behalf of the Century Athletic Club, doctors Hagedorn and Lanterman examined his right arm and found it to be in good condition with nothing wrong with it, in spite of Childs' claim. They said it appeared to be just as sound as the left arm.

Club manager Tom McCarey said Childs would not be paid unless he could bring proof within 24 hours that his arm was in bad condition. Otherwise, his share of the receipts would be donated to charity.

Summarizing, the *Times* said the "colored champion of the world," "a big, gobby coon named Frank Childs," was licked by "the Johnson Giant," "the new champion of coon pugs." While Childs was waiting for one big

[236] *Los Angeles Herald*, October 21, 1902.

punch, Johnson punched him all over the ring. "The new champion is a big, lean grinning negro named Jack Johnson. He was scared to death because the sporting men were betting 10 to 7 he would get his head punched off." Johnson was cautious, but Childs was even more so. As a result, the bout was a "bore" and tame. "It's more fun to see two little boys fighting over marbles." Clearly though, something about Johnson's punches made Childs cautious, and despite his vaunted punching power, Frank was not able to land an effective blow on Johnson, while Johnson landed most of what he threw, closing Frank's eye and drawing blood from his mouth, picking up the pace and doing better as the bout progressed.[237]

The *Los Angeles Herald* summarized,

> During the main event Johnson appeared to be falling short with his punches. He was playing it very safe with Childs and evidently would have been well pleased with a draw had the mill gone the limit. Toward the finish he began to cut loose with excellent effect, being just as good as Childs at the rough work and much more effective at long range. After the tenth Johnson looked much better thanks to his superb condition.

Another discussion of the bout by the same paper said,

> Childs had held his man too cheap. He was fat and looked to be fifteen pounds heavier than normal. Johnson put up a much stouter resistance than his friends had hoped; drove in a number of stiff body punches and succeeded in marking up Childs' physiognomy, put a big bunch under his left eye, and at all points had the best of the bout. Childs was not at all impressive, nor was he effective. He repeatedly missed openings to deliver the right swings which have made him famous and after the first few rounds showed plainly the effect of the pace Johnson was making him set. On two or three occasions he drove in good short rights to Johnson's face, ear and ribs, but the lanky black man as soon as he regained confidence adopted jabbing tactics with such effect that he stopped Childs and sent his head back every time the burly black rushed. Johnson's stock went up 100 per cent last night.

Childs, who "poses as the colored heavyweight champion," was there to cop a little easy money, but he ran up against a "snag of good sized-proportions." Johnson's showing was a surprise to many. He controlled the bout from start to finish.

Childs was a distinct disappointment, and his poor work led some to believe that his claim of an arm injury suffered the day before while boxing with Hank Griffin might be genuine.[238]

[237] *Los Angeles Times*, October 22, 1902.
[238] *Los Angeles Herald*, October 22, 1902.

The *Los Angeles Express* was even harsher. It said the sports were disgusted and called the bout a fake. They were convinced that Childs never tried to win, and demanded an investigation. Interspersed with hisses and catcalls were cries of "Fake! Take 'em away! How much money will be spent in coontown tonight?" It ended in the 12th round with a tame surrender on Childs' part. The "fight was the rankest ever held in this city." Some argued that Referee Brink should have declared all bets off. Instead, at least $20,000 changed hands as a result of the wagering. Even more money was bet in San Francisco.

Part of why some thought Childs threw the fight and that it was a prearranged affair was that he did not appear to train seriously or be at all concerned about the bout. Upon his arrival in Los Angeles from Chicago, he adopted a careless mode of living. Frank was seen on many occasions going around smoking strong cigars. He was found in saloons drinking beer. Childs was mysteriously noncommittal as to the location of his training quarters. He invited no members of the press to see him train. When a well-known cigar and tobacco dealer remarked to him that he didn't appear to be training much for the Johnson fight, Childs replied, "What's the use? I don't have to train any to lick him." That, combined with his lackluster, half-hearted effort, and questionable arm-injury claim, raised doubts.

Either Childs had no intention to win or he was overconfident, not thinking much of Johnson. Perhaps he didn't realize how much Johnson had improved since he had sparred with him back in 1899, and therefore underestimated him. Johnson was probably about 20 pounds bigger than he was in 1899, and he was much more experienced at that point. It is also possible that Childs went into the bout with an injury, which affected his performance.

Nevertheless, the *Express* said that due credit had to be accorded to Johnson for having trained faithfully for the mill. He was obviously fit. If the fix was in, he had nothing to do with it, for his preparations showed that he had taken the bout seriously.

The promotion wanted to have Johnson meet Ed Martin, and the winner of that contest meet Jeffries.[239]

Up north, the *San Francisco Examiner* reported that Childs claimed to have wrenched the elbow joint. The right arm had been injured in sparring with Hank Griffin, and the lame arm received rough usage and was twisted during one of the numerous clinches which occurred during the 11th round. He did not use it at all during the 12th round, and dangled it at his side.

Regardless, Jack Johnson obtained accolades. "Johnson is a clever boxer. He is light on his feet, maintains a perfect balance and is quicker than an adder's tongue with either hand." Every time Childs rushed, Johnson met

[239] *Los Angeles Express*, October 22, 1902.

him with a left, which he used frequently. Childs mostly missed his powerful blows and was "well drubbed."

Despite the claim of an injury, "The impression among the sports is that Childs deliberately quit when he found defeat staring him in the face and that he arranged the bad arm ruse and the sponge finish when he conferred with his seconds at the end of the eleventh round." It saw the bout less as a fix but a legitimate fight wherein Childs tried but realized that he could not win, so he found a way out of the fight and an excuse for the loss.[240]

The *National Police Gazette* offered its readers a different perspective, saying,

> The fight was terrific for every round it lasted. Both men waded right in to win in a punch, if possible, and they took all kinds of chances.
>
> The dislocation of Childs' elbow was caused by a terrific swing, which caught Johnson on the head. It was sent for the jaw, but missed, being too high. Childs tried to continue fighting, but being plainly in great pain his seconds ended things by throwing a sponge in the ring.[241]

The next-day *Herald* noted that careful investigation of the wagering on the bout did not show anything suspicious. Wagers on Johnson were relatively small.

The same doctors, Lanterman and Hagadorn, again examined Childs' arm the day after the fight and found that the right arm was a quarter of an inch larger in circumference at the elbow joint than when examined the night before. Therefore, Tom McCarey was satisfied that an injury indeed existed and decided to pay Childs the loser's end of the purse.

Frank's manager, H. C. Rousselot, said his man was fairly beaten and that Childs "now admits as much in a half-hearted way." The *Herald* opined, "It is a cowardly trick for a man after being whipped to attempt to rob his opponent of the credit of victory by feigning injury as excuse for inability to continue." The feeling was that Johnson was better, and though Childs had an injury, nevertheless, he could have continued, but decided not to do so because he was being thoroughly whipped.[242]

Regardless of the manner of victory, because of Childs' good results against top fighters, and because of his claim to the colored crown, Johnson's victory over him had some real significance. It can also be seen as the start of Johnson's real ascendance as a top fighter.

Years later, Johnson said the bout was personal to him. Childs had mistreated him when Jack was his sparring partner. "When I saw I had him I thought of all the mean things he had done to me and I gave him the slamming of his life."[243]

---

[240] *San Francisco Examiner,* October 22, 1902.
[241] *National Police Gazette,* November 15, 1902.
[242] *Los Angeles Herald,* October 23, 1902.
[243] *San Francisco Bulletin,* July 27, 1910.

On October 24, 1902, Johnson and his manager, Frank Carrillo, arrived in San Francisco. They were set to meet with Alec/Alex Greggains to sign articles for a 20-round match with George Gardner, to be held there on October 31, which would be a mere ten days after the Childs fight. Just imagine a fighter today going 12 rounds with 5-ounce gloves and then scheduling a 20-round bout, set to take place just over a week later.[244]

Top middleweight George Gardner was another elite fighter with a lot of quality experience. His nearly 40-bout record included: 1898 KO7 C. C. Smith; 1899 KO17 Harry Fisher, LKOby18 Jimmy Handler, and KO8 Jack Moffat; 1900 KO12 Fisher, D15 George Byers, KO3 Jimmy Handler, WDQ14 Byers, KO9 Bill Hanrahan, D15 Byers, WDQ19 Kid Carter, and WDQ4 Frank Craig; 1901 KO3 Jack Moffat, KO18 Kid Carter, L20 Joe Walcott, and KO8 Carter; and 1902 LDQby7 Jack Root, W20 Joe Walcott, and KO17 Root. He had at least 32 victories to his credit and only 3 losses, all avenged. He was 25 years of age, one year older than Johnson, and stood 5'11 ½".

George Gardner

The well-known referee, Harry Stuart, thought it was an even-money fight. Gardner had the advantage in experience, but Johnson had advantages in weight, height, and reach. Stuart said Johnson had a pretty good chance to win, but not enough to influence the betting. Stuart also had some criticism of Johnson, saying,

> Johnson has been fighting only about three years and lacks the generalship and ring tactics that come with long experience. His greatest failing is a disinclination to mix things. There is no reason why he shouldn't have knocked Frank Childs out in less than eight rounds the other night. Childs was not in condition to fight and was weak and puffing at the expiration of the third round.
>
> This lack of aggressiveness will prevent Johnson from ever reaching the top round of the pugilistic ladder. He is too slow to realize actual conditions confronting him.[245]

Gardner was training at Joe Millett's with his brother Billy Gardner, a lightweight, amongst others. They were boxing together on a daily basis.[246]

---

[244] *San Francisco Bulletin*, October 24, 1902.

[245] *San Francisco Bulletin*, October 27, 1902.

[246] *San Francisco Bulletin*, October 28, 1902. "Millett" was sometimes spelled "Millet," but in this book the more common "tt" spelling will be used.

As the fight approached, the oddsmakers had Johnson as the 2 to 1 *underdog*. Frank Carrillo was not concerned. He said Johnson was just as big an underdog going into the Childs bout, yet emerged victorious. Before the Childs fight, Carrillo had bet a few hundred on Johnson, and everyone told him he was crazy. He said he was going to bet another chunk of money on this fight too, for he was not as crazy as he looked. He thought Johnson was underrated.

GREGGAINS HAS TAUGHT
GARDNER THIS DEFENSE

On October 28, a large crowd watched Johnson train at Blanken's. He started off with 15 minutes on the bag, and then he boxed three men in succession. The first was named the "Black Muldoon," the next was an unknown heavyweight who weighed 245 pounds, and the final boxer was the Dixie Kid. After boxing them all, Johnson did not take one long breath.

Harry Corbett said, "I never saw a man in better condition. If Johnson loses it will not be for lack of condition." Billy Lavigne replied, "I agree with you, and I am one who looks for Johnson and Gardner to put up a slashing good fight. I am not picking winners, but if Jack won there might be some surprised people, but I would not be one of them. He is a strong, clever fellow, and he has a chance with any of them."

Johnson said he would enter the ring weighing 182 pounds, which would make him about 10 pounds heavier than Gardner (though others thought Jack would have a 20-pound advantage). Jack said he would have two young rabbits in his corner for luck, which some boys had given him the other day.[247]

---

[247] *San Francisco Bulletin*, October 29, 1902.

San Franciscans had seen six of Gardner's bouts and liked what they saw. Despite the fact that Gardner would be significantly lighter than Johnson and would have height and reach handicaps, George was the 4 to 10 odds favorite going into the fight. Johnson money was scarce. Still, they expected a good fight. The *San Francisco Chronicle* said,

> The colored giant does not figure to win, it is true, but his past performances show that he always made a fight, and concealed in either glove he carries a wallop that means trouble if it lands right. Again, Gardner is scientific in only a clumsy sort of way, while Johnson has the true boxer's cleverness and is said to be a vastly improved man. Another thing which lends uncertainty to the affair is the fact that Johnson will outweight and outreach his opponent. Fight followers figure, however, that Gardner will win and do it handily, without allowing the battle to go the full limit.[248]

The *San Francisco Examiner* thought it peculiar that the odds were so heavily in Gardner's favor, especially given the "ebony-hued battering ram's" recent decisive victory over Frank Childs, and his superior physical attributes. It feared that the fight might prove to be another fake. It was surprised that so few were betting on Johnson.[249]

It is possible that the fact that Johnson had never before fought in San Francisco might have affected the odds, though

George Gardner boxing with Jack Dunn at his training quarters at Baden

he had fought twice in nearby Oakland, so top San Francisco sports had seen him in action. However, Gardner was more familiar and he had beaten some elite fighters (Byers, Carter, Walcott, and Root), whereas Johnson was only starting to emerge. Gardner was coming off a very big KO victory over the highly regarded Jack Root. George had beaten fast, strong, and clever fighters.

---

[248] *San Francisco Chronicle*, October 31, 1902.
[249] *San Francisco Examiner*, October 31, 1902.

141

JOHNSON, WHO MEETS GARDNER, HAS A CREDITABLE RECORD

Jack Johnson Boxing With the Black Muldoon—The Photographer Caught Them Just as Johnson Landed a Right Jolt to the Jaw.

Jack Johnson, Who Meets George Gardner Friday Night.

The *San Francisco Bulletin* noted that Gardner's record was familiar to all those who followed the sport, while less was known of Johnson, who had done most of his fighting elsewhere. Jack was listed as weighing 182 pounds and standing 6'1 ½" tall. "He is not a terrible hitter, but when it comes to clever execution he is quite the equal of Gardner."

The *Bulletin* listed some previously unknown and unconfirmed bouts on Johnson's record, including a knockout over Charley Strong in 7 rounds at Trenton, N.J., Thunderbolt Smith in 3 rounds in Memphis, and a draw with Al Weinig in 20 rounds at Hot Springs, Arkansas, amongst others. No dates were provided, and some of the known results were inaccurately listed, so it might have been mistaken.

Jack Johnson, the Shortender in Tomorrow Night's Fight.

Sports often feared that a fight might be a fake. Given that the odds were so strong in Gardner's favor, they thought perhaps Johnson had agreed to throw the fight. Alec Greggains gave assurances that he had never been connected with a fake in his life, and if there was anything wrong with the fight, the boxers would not receive a cent. "I have every reason to believe that the fight will be honestly contested. Johnson has a great chance to make a reputation for himself by beating Gardner, who is the best man of his weight in the world, and he is not going to throw it away." Jack Kitchen, a former Olympic Club boxer who years earlier had sparred with Corbett, was selected to act as referee, and he was instructed to protect the public.[250]

On Friday October 31, 1902, the Jack Johnson vs. George Gardner fight took place at Woodward's Pavilion in San Francisco, under the sponsorship of the San Francisco Athletic Club. The bout was scheduled for 20 rounds. Jack Kitchen refereed.

---

[250] *San Francisco Bulletin*, October 31, 1902.

Before the fight started, Johnson was a 10 to 4 underdog. One reason offered for the depreciation of his stock was that for two days prior to the fight, Jack had been laid up in Mount Zion Hospital with gastritis, an inflammation of the stomach lining. Hence, it was thought that a Gardner body blow might do him in.

The main event fighters entered the ring at 10:15 p.m. Behind Gardner were Alec Greggains, Billy Gardner, Dave Barry, Joe Millett and Jack Dunne/Dunn.

Johnson had Tim McGrath, C. Ferry, Kid McFadden and Frank Carrillo looking after him.

After the men were introduced formally, Charley Goff on behalf of Denver Ed Martin challenged the winner.

1 - When the fight began, instead of going on the defensive and fighting carefully as was expected of him, Johnson surprised everyone by walking up to Gardner and opening hostilities. A stiff straight left on the face shook up Gardner. This caused George to rush him. Johnson showed his ability to cover, blocking any short-arm blows thrown at close quarters. Johnson was not at all rattled by Gardner's known ring prowess. He was as cool as if he was fighting an unknown. His ability to successfully guard his head and body confused Gardner.

Johnson began rapping Gardner on the sides of the head with short-arm jolts. However, he did not keep up the attack for any sustained length of time, fighting in spurts. Regardless, George was rattled. Early on, Gardner let up and clinched and hung on repeatedly to save himself, clearly affected by Johnson's blows.

2 - Gardner went after him, leading short with his left and swinging his right for the ribs. He repeated this a number of times, but the rights were either stopped by the elbow or they went around the back. Johnson landed his own right, and a stiff straight right to the ribs affected Gardner. Jack followed with a left flush on the cheek that sent George's head back.

At that point, Gardner started to hang on and clinch as often as he could, which he kept up throughout the fight. The *Bulletin* said Johnson was always ready to break quickly and resume fighting, but Gardner "clung to him like a long lost brother, and in this way much time was wasted."

Thereafter, the rounds all resembled each other, with little variety. Gardner did the swinging, but he could not land. His shifts were ineffective and he missed badly. Johnson did not use any swinging blows. He carried his arms close together, and was always in a position to move in quickly with a straight jab, or retreat when Gardner tried a rush.

3 - Gardner fought clumsily. He landed occasionally, but with no particular force, while in the meantime he received a number of left jabs between the eyes. Johnson continually planted straight left jabs to the face.

4 - According to the *San Francisco Bulletin*, Johnson ripped in a short-arm right which dropped Gardner to his knees.

5 - Gardner tried to rough it, but Johnson showed that he was decidedly stronger than his opponent, whom he easily shook off, jabbing him as they parted.

6 – 7 - As was the pattern for the fight, in general, Gardner was busy enough, but rarely landed. Johnson was able to jolt and jab the lighter man when he pleased, but was cautious in between. "The negro was either timid or else thinking of his patched-up stomach, for he hit snappy blows and only mixed it on rare occasions." Gardner clinched and worked but could not land, while Johnson played defense and opened up in spots, but effectively so.

8 - The gallery urged Johnson to get in and fight. "The negro seemed piqued by the uncomplimentary remarks and he cut loose in the eighth round." This was a lively round, both exchanging hot punches at short range, but Johnson again showed himself to be the stronger man in the mixup.

The *Call* said Johnson dazed Gardner and sent him to his knees. George hung on and was saved by the bell.

Neither the *Bulletin* nor the *Examiner* mentioned a knockdown. The *Examiner* said Johnson mixed it and outfought Gardner, whose head rolled from side to side. At times, Gardner laid his head against Johnson's breast to rest and recover. However, the blows were not forceful enough to distress Gardner for too long, and George struck at the ribs as often as he could, landing some and missing others. "Johnson's nimble manner of jerking himself out of range" caused most of the blows to land with little force.

9 – 10 - Johnson slowed up again. He liked to work, then rest. He would do damage in one round, then take one or two off and play defense.

11 - As a result of the crowd's urgings, Johnson quickened again. During the busy spells, Johnson landed repeatedly with both hands, but took some body punches in return. Still, the round was in his favor.

12 - The round was devoid of intensity.

13 - The crowd managed to spur Johnson to action again. A number of left jolts to the head put Gardner in some distress. Johnson delivered the two best blows of the fight, a left on the nose and a hard right on the jaw. Gardner appeared to be rattled, but he feinted, and the cautious Johnson hopped away and allowed him to recover. Jack did not follow up his advantage. Near the end of the round, Johnson landed a couple left jabs.

14 - The round was in Johnson's favor, though it appeared that the shower of blows he landed to the head had very little steam in them. Gardner landed a few lefts to the stomach and Johnson tilted his head with a long left.

The *Call* said Johnson sent Gardner to the mat again. The *Chronicle* said Gardner went down partly from a blow, but more from slipping out of a clinch. The *Examiner* said that while milling at close range, Gardner slipped to the floor a couple of times. The *Call* said that after decking Gardner, Johnson backed off again.

15 - Gardner landed his right to the ear and around the back. Johnson crouched and kept as far away as possible.

16 - Johnson acted in a listless manner.

17 - The gallery got after Johnson again. He hustled, but the blows were "only kitten taps, and the crowd hooted him when he showed an eagerness to keep as far away as possible."

18 - A damaging Johnson right and left to the head hurt Gardner, making him a little groggy again, but Johnson "put on the brakes as usual."

19 – 20 - The *Examiner* said that during the last few rounds, "Johnson boxed in a streaky fashion. He clearly outpointed Gardner, but his blows lacked steam." Johnson appeared to want to win the fight without taking any chances. The *Call* said there was some "bustling work" in the last couple rounds, but it was with open gloves and no damage was done. The *Chronicle* said Gardner was strong at the end of the fight and "could have continued indefinitely."

Referee Jack Kitchen awarded the clear 20-round decision to Johnson. Gardner had been down in the 4th, 8th, and 14th rounds.

Summarizing, the *Examiner* said that soon after the bout started, it could be seen that Gardner had a tough proposition to handle.

> Johnson was taller, heavier, broader shouldered and stronger than the white man. As a body fighter Gardner is a specialist, but he failed to land his most damaging smashes on the colored bruiser's frame.

> Johnson's poise was perfect. He held a low guard and he rocked rhythmically on his feet. At times he crouched – not the solid, stone-walling crouch which Jeffries assumes, but a position from which he could either spring like a tiger or skip backward out of danger.

From the start, Gardner bombarded the body, but Johnson was able to take care of himself. The punches glanced off his elbows and then Jack grappled Gardner and held him so that he could do no further damage at short range. Many of Gardner's rights went too far around and spent their force on Johnson's back. Either Gardner's judgment of distance was off or Johnson was too quick at stepping inside.

Johnson did just enough fighting during the bout to remain in the lead. When Referee Kitchen awarded him the 20-round decision, the "spectators wondered how much harder and faster Johnson could have fought had the occasion demanded it." The suggestion was that Johnson did just enough to win, but did not and would not push himself unless necessary. "The general impression seemed to be that Johnson could have defeated Gardner in a half dozen rounds if the negro had shown more fighting spirit."

Referee Kitchen said Johnson was too strong and clever for Gardner, and was his master at every point in the game. Both Kitchen and club manager Alex Greggains said that Gardner did the best he could against the odds.[251]

Jack Johnson was a winner, but he did not like to take chances, and was content to win a cautious points decision rather than let loose in order to secure the knockout, but risk leaving himself vulnerable as well, or potentially risk fatigue if he failed to secure the knockout. Hence, he fought in short spurts without opening up too much, too often, or for too long. Certainly, he had respect for Gardner. Plus, one cannot underestimate the potential for fatigue in a 20-round bout. Taking risks in a lengthy 5-ounce glove fight could have its drawbacks. Furthermore, the fact that Jack had a stomach ailment and had spent time at a hospital shortly before the bout probably indicates that he was not at his best physically. Regardless, during the fight, Gardner threw a number of body punches, but Johnson showed no symptoms of collapsing at any stage.

The *San Francisco Chronicle* said Gardner put up a very poor fight.

> At no time did the white lad look like a winner. It was not so much that Johnson was wonderfully clever but he was just good enough to stall off Gardner at all times and during the progress of the entire contest the latter scarcely laid a glove on the big black man. Always clumsy in his work, Gardner appeared to the worst possible advantage in front of a really shifty man. His swings were wild, his uppercut practically useless and his body punch ineffective.

> On the showing made by Gardner little praise can go to the winner. Johnson was much the better and was never in trouble, but he held his opponent's reputation in such regard that he failed to make use of his opportunities.

Neither fighter received a scratch. Johnson was never hit by a stinging blow. On the other hand, from start to finish, Gardner saved himself by clinching and holding. Johnson's lead in the fight was so long that the referee had no trouble in selecting him as the victor. "Nothing short of a knockout could have given the long end of the purse to Gardner at any point after the fifth round."[252]

The *San Francisco Call* said it was the most disappointing fight in years. Each boxer hit with open gloves for the greater part of the exhibition. The bout dragged along in weary fashion. Gardner rarely threw his allegedly powerful body punches, and the ones he tried were either thrown with open gloves or glanced off to one side without doing any damage. Gardner often clinched and hung on to save himself from being stopped. He seemed content to last without trying to win. "It was a case of too much Johnson."

[251] *San Francisco Examiner,* November 1, 1902.
[252] *San Francisco Chronicle,* November 1, 1902.

Johnson dropped Gardner in the 8th and 14th rounds, but Gardner saved himself by clinching, and Johnson backed off. It appeared that Johnson could have stopped Gardner at any time had he cut loose and followed up with some consistency. He was cleverer, a harder hitter, and outweighed Gardner by at least 25 pounds. Yet, Jack seemed happy and content to do what he was doing, laughing throughout. He only lost his temper on the occasions when Gardner hit in the clinches. Even when they seemed to be fighting desperately, those at ringside could see that neither man was inflicting any punishment. Whenever Johnson did have Gardner in distress, he "drew away and gave him ample time to recover. The spectators were quick to see all this and jeered and hooted the boxers round after round."

Johnson had an excellent defense and was able to land readily. Throughout, he jabbed with his left, sending Gardner's head back with a snap. George landed some blows, but there was little force behind them.[253]

The *San Francisco Bulletin* said Gardner's ring prowess was given a hard setback. His victory over Root had sent his stock sky high. He was the heavy favorite over Johnson, who was not given credit for being even a fair second-rater. Only a small audience turned out, owing to the fact that most thought it was going to be an uneven match in Gardner's favor.

However, Johnson had proven himself to be quick and nimble, and outpointed Gardner every step of the way. "It was the largest sized surprise that has been handed the sports of late." Gardner could not land at all. Johnson could move in quickly with a punch, usually a jab, or retreat when Gardner rushed.

The *Bulletin* said Johnson dropped Gardner in the 4th round. After the 8th round, there were few thrilling rounds. Johnson continued firing in straight jolts which were not hard enough to cut the flesh, but strong enough, and enough of them, to give him the decision by a safe majority.

Gardner's showing was a sad disappointment to those who had bet a lot to win a little. Afterwards, many wondered how it was that he had defeated a man as good as Jack Root. Perhaps Jack Johnson was much better than they had realized.

Gardner thought he had earned a draw, but "the decision was perfectly fair, and no other could have been given." George said, "I could not get going somehow or other. Don't know what the reason was, but I was not myself. I guess I did not train hard enough." Good fighters have a way of making others feel that way, though. Again, perhaps it was just too much Johnson.

---

[253] *San Francisco Call*, November 1, 1902. In the years to come, George Gardner would continue to figure prominently on the fight scene. Subsequent results would include: 1902 W6 Billy Stift and W6 Kid Carter; 1903 KO6 Al Weinig, KO1 Peter Maher, TKO12 Marvin Hart (retirement owing to broken hand), KO12 Jack Root (world light-heavyweight crown), and L20 Bob Fitzsimmons; 1904 D15 Marvin Hart (most considered Hart to have been superior), D6 and L6 Root, D6 John Willie, and D10 Jim Flynn; 1905 LKOby20 Mike Schreck and KO5 Stift; 1906 LKOby14 Al Kaufman; and 1907 LKOby18 Flynn.

JOHNSON OUTPOINTS GEORGE GARDNER IN EVERY ROUND

How the Fight Looked to One Who Was Near the Ring.

San Francisco Bulletin, **November 1, 1902**

Jack Johnson was jubilant over his victory. "I would have knocked him out sure, if I had not been under a doctor's care two days before the fight. That water down at Blanken's knocked my bowels out, and I was out at Mount Zion Hospital for two days. I was clever as I ever was, but my blows lacked steam. If I had been right I would have beaten him just as quickly as I did Childs."

Johnson said he was ready to fight Jeffries, Fitzsimmons, Root, McCoy, or any of the big guns. Frank Carrillo said he would back him for $2,000 against any man in the world.[254]

Alec Greggains was at a loss to account for Gardner's poor showing. George worked well while preparing for the contest, and Alec thought he would make short work of the colored man. He thought perhaps Gardner underrated Johnson, and after running up against it for a few rounds, and seeing that Johnson was there good and strong, George grew puzzled in his attack.[255]

A Chicago paper subsequently said it was a "bit of bad judgment" for Greggains to match Gardner with Johnson. There was very little money in the house, and Johnson won a decision over Gardner just when George was beginning to become a sure money maker. The loss would hurt Gardner's market value. Conversely, Johnson's reputation had surged.[256]

The following year, in 1903, George Gardner would win the world light-heavyweight crown by stopping Jack Root in the 12th round. Hence, Johnson's victory over Gardner was significant at the time, and it gained increasing significance given Gardner's subsequent success.

In an interesting incident at ringside on fight-night, Sergeant Wolf relieved Johnson's manager, Frank Carrillo of Bakersfield, of a revolver. He returned it to him after the fight. Later that evening, after leaving the fight, Carrillo was arrested on a charge of carrying a concealed pistol. He was released on bail.[257]

Carrillo said it was all the result of joking remarks he made in the afternoon. First he said that if Johnson didn't stand up to Gardner that he would see to it that he knew what lead felt like. He just wanted to make sure that Johnson would not take a dive. After all, given that the odds were so strong in Gardner's favor, some gamblers suspected it was because Johnson had agreed to lay down. Also, feeling that his fighters on occasion had not been given fair decisions, he jokingly said that he might shoot the referee if the decision was not fair.

> I said yesterday in a josh to some fellows that if that nigger tried to lay down I'd see that he stayed down with the weight of a little lead. I may have said the same thing about the referee if his decision wasn't on the square, but I didn't mean it. I had a wad of money up on Johnson because he looked good to me and I didn't want the double cross worked on me. It was all a josh and someone, I guess, took it the other way. ... All I had with me was a little thirty-two gun that I always carry and that wouldn't be worth a pinch of pepper if a man started out gunning for any one.

---

[254] *San Francisco Bulletin,* November 1, 1902.
[255] *San Francisco Bulletin,* November 2, 1902.
[256] *Daily Inter Ocean* November 9, 1902.
[257] *San Francisco Call,* November 1, 1902.

Shortly after the fight, Carrillo was found in a saloon near the pavilion, and the patrolman who searched him found the weapon and took him into custody, despite the fact that he had a permit from Bakersfield.

When he saw the judge in the morning, Carrillo said, "I'd like to go home and vote." Judge Conlan replied, "Case continued for a week, and say, Carillo, don't forget to put in a Democratic vote when you get the chance." The *Bulletin* believed that the charge likely would be dismissed, for under the statutes he was entitled to go armed without a local permit since he was a traveler.[258]

Carrillo and Greggains had a disagreement about the receipts. Carrillo claimed that Greggains took $250 from the fighters' share to pay for the preliminaries, in direct opposition to the articles signed. Greggains said the men originally agreed to box 75% winner/25% loser, and for the fighters' 50% of the gross to cover the preliminary bouts. But then Carrillo came to him and insisted on the money being split, so a new agreement was signed. Gardner and Johnson each took 50% of the 50% fighter's share of the gross receipts, evenly splitting the fighter's share, regardless of result. Gardner had made just as much as Johnson did. The new articles failed to address payment for the preliminary bouts. Carrillo believed this meant that the promoter was to make payment. Greggains felt that the original term regarding payment to the preliminary fighters remained in effect. Carrillo argued that Greggains had taken the two parts of the two agreements that best suited Greggains and combined them. Regardless, he took solace in the fact that he had the better fighter, and said he was willing to bet up to $5,000 on Johnson against anyone in the world.

The receipts from the fight yielded $1,667. After deducting the $250 for payment of the preliminaries, a balance of $1,417 remained, 50% of which was split evenly between the main-event fighters, with each boxer receiving $354.25, at least a solid payday by the time's standards.[259]

Tom McCarey offered a $10,000 purse for a James Corbett vs. Denver Ed Martin fight, with the winner potentially to meet Jeffries the following year. However, Corbett did not fight at all in 1901 or 1902, and eventually was able to obtain the Jeffries title fight without having any interim matches.[260]

On November 14, 1902 in Baltimore, Maryland, world lightweight champion Joe Gans knocked out white challenger Charles Seiger in the 15th round.

> Believing that the exhibition of the negro pugilist, Joe Gans, mauling and drawing the blood of a white fighter or boxer, has an unwholesome effect upon the rough negro element, tending to make it more disorderly, the police authorities are considering the

---

[258] *San Francisco Bulletin,* November 1, 1902.
[259] *San Francisco Bulletin,* November 2, 1902.
[260] *San Francisco Chronicle,* November 2, 1902.

possibility of refusing to issue permits for contests between white and colored boxers. ... For several years Baltimore has been a haven for pugilists and their exhibitions, but for the above reasons the authorities may decide to put a stop to such contests altogether.[261]

As this reveals, the long tradition of legal limitation and impediment upon the sport of boxing is in part based upon race. This remains the case today, even if only on a subconscious knee-jerk level; based on tradition. In 1902, writers, police, and politicians were fully cognizant of the racial implications that these fights had.

Fred Russell

On November 19, 1902 in Philadelphia, Marvin Hart and Jack O'Brien fought a 6-round no-decision. Most thought O'Brien technically outpointed Hart, but they still felt it was a draw because O'Brien was knocked down in the 6th round and was almost taken out.

Jack Johnson's next fight was back down south in Los Angeles, a month after defeating Gardner. It was against the white fighter who had defeated Hank Griffin controversially: Fred Russell. 24-year-old Russell's record contained at least 25 known pro bouts, including: 1899 WDQ5 Theodore Van Buskirk and L20 Joe Kennedy; 1900 KO9 Jack Curley, L6 (twice) and L10 Frank Childs, KO9 Mexican Pete Everett, and LDQby4 Joe Choynski (striking and knocking out Joe after the bell); 1901 KO1 Jack McCormick, LKOby4 Tom Sharkey (Sharkey sparring partner Johnson saw this fight), and LDQby10 Denver Ed Martin (Russell engaged in deliberate foul kicks to the shins after having taken a beating); 1902 KO3 Klondike, D6 Joe Walcott, LND6 Kid McCoy, LND6 Peter Maher, KO14 Hank Griffin (though most

261 *Philadelphia Record*, November 19, 1902.

thought Russell should have been disqualified for hitting Griffin while he was down)(Johnson was present at this fight), and November 1, 1902 LKOby5 to Sam McVey, an emerging large and powerful black fighter.

For the McVey fight, Russell was listed as standing 6'4" and weighing 215 pounds. Hence, against the 180-185-pound Johnson, he would have a three-inch height advantage and about a 30-pound weight advantage. Fred's friends did not think his recent loss one month earlier to McVey meant much. Fred claimed to be in fine trim for the Johnson fight.

Common opponents included [Russell's result versus Johnson's result]: Kennedy (L20 vs. KO4), Childs (L6, L6, L10 vs. TKO12), Everett (KO9 vs. D20), Choynski (LDQby4 vs. LKOby3), McCormick (KO1 vs. ND15 and WDQ6), Klondike (KO3 vs. LTKOby5, D20, and TKO14), and Griffin (KO14 vs. L20, D15, and D20).

The *Herald* said Johnson was the favorite. Fight fans were cognizant of the "careful, clever way that Jack fiddled and outpointed the hard hitting George Gardner." His showing was more appreciated in consideration of the fact that before that bout, Gardner had scored a knockout over Root, "the acknowledged kingpin of all light heavyweights." Just recently, Root had easily won a 6-round decision over Marvin Hart, who in turn almost knocked out the vaunted, skillful, experienced clever boxer Jack O'Brien. Form followers would be justified in picking Johnson.

Still, it was also noted that Johnson outweighed Gardner by fully 15 pounds. Russell would have the weight, height, and reach advantages over Johnson. The *Express* said, "Johnson is considered more clever than Russell in ring tactics and relies on this to overcome the advantage of Russell's height and weight." Jack Jeffries was training Russell.[262]

Up north in San Francisco, the contest was arousing more interest than any other given by the Century Club, in part because the winner was to

---

[262] *Los Angeles Herald*, December 1, 1902; *Los Angeles Express*, December 3, 1902.

meet Denver Ed Martin, whose manager Billy Madden was calling "the best there is to be had." Tom McCarey was making all of the arrangements.[263]

After arriving in Los Angeles from Bakersfield, over the course of ten days, Johnson changed his training quarters several times. First he trained at a police station on Third and Alameda streets with policeman Dan Long, who had once fought James Jeffries. However, the police did not appreciate the disruption, so Jack was forced to discontinue the use of Long. He also worked at a ball park, and then at the Lilly Club's quarters at 320 New High street. He looked fit and in perfect shape. Johnson said he was in the pink of condition and would put up the fight of his life.

Johnson's manager, Frank Carillo, thought the odds making Johnson nearly a 2 to 1 favorite were too sharp, so he was not betting on his man unless the odds became tighter. "Russell is bigger, strong and young; he can hit hard, and I cannot see any 100 to 60 on my man, though I expect him to win." Carillo had met Russell the night before at the Hoffman and had engaged in a debate with Fred about the relative merits of the two combatants, and apparently Russell more than held his own. Fred had seen Johnson fight, and was not afraid.[264]

As a result of the objections raised by the police authorities to Dan Long being his sparring partner, Johnson had ceased sparring several days before the fight. Jack found it difficult to find someone else, so he took longer runs, along with punching the bag. "He seems to be in perfect time and is as fast in his movements and actions as a man of his weight could well be. In fact it is asserted by many that there is not a more clever or faster man of his weight in the pugilistic ranks today. He will enter the ring weighing a little over 180 pounds."

Russell trained at the Jeffries ranch in East Los Angeles, where he boxed with Jack Jeffries every afternoon for two weeks. "Russell will weigh about 219 pounds when he enters the ring." If such was true, he would have nearly a 40-pound weight advantage. Fred said he should not be rated by the McVey fight, because he underestimated McVey and a chance blow caught him napping. "Indeed, most ring followers hereabouts take the same view of the matter and it is generally believed that in a return battle Russell would be the victor."

As the fight approached, more Russell money came into sight, tightening the odds and making Johnson the favorite at 7 to 10. Apparently, Carillo's refusal to bet on his own man unnerved some, and made Russell's supporters more eager to wager. The day before the fight, the odds were just about even. The *Los Angeles Express* prognosticated, "Russell should win the battle inside of six rounds if he rushes things from the start."

Despite Carillo's previous objections to him, Harry Stuart was set to referee. "Stuart is popular with ring followers in this section because of his

[263] *Los Angeles Express,* December 3, 1902.
[264] *Los Angeles Herald,* December 3, 1902.

unbiased decisions." Another said Stuart enjoyed the public's confidence. The preliminary would begin at 8 p.m.[265]

The fighters' relative merits were debated. Those who supported Johnson cited his victory over Gardner and his renewed confidence as a result. Those who supported Russell cited Johnson's failure to defeat Griffin in three attempts. They also said that Johnson did not like to get hit, that Russell could punch and so Jack would "stop like a clock if things do not go his way." Russell had been stopped by McVey, which some called a fluke, while others said no one knew just how good the Oxnard black was. Russell would be motivated, because if "he takes two successive beatings from negroes he will draw nothing but flies hereafter." There was another insightful perspective about Russell. "Then there are those who think Russell is likely to get foul, and lose that way if the battle goes against him." After all, Russell had been disqualified twice already, and most thought he should have been disqualified three times. Ultimately, the *Herald* opined,

[265] *Los Angeles Express, Los Angeles Herald,* December 4, 1902.

[I]t looks as if Russell's superior size and strength must win for him inside the ten rounds, if at all. ... If the battle lasts over ten rounds it is very likely to go the limit, in which case Johnson's superior skill as a boxer doubtless will win a decision for him. The contingency of a foul is always to be considered wherever Russell goes on.[266]

On Thursday December 4, 1902 at Hazard's Pavilion in Los Angeles, under the auspices of Tom McCarey's Century Club, the Jack Johnson vs. Fred Russell fight took place. There was an immense crowd in the pavilion.

For the main event, Referee Harry Stuart entered the ring and removed his coat. Johnson entered with a pack of pugs who swabbed his back with towels and squirted some water in his face. The *Times* said, "They were led by a fat Mexican with a frightful scar on his face," who was Frank Carrillo, Johnson's manager.

Fred Russell was boosted up tenderly into the ring. He was a big, hulking fellow, with chrysanthemum hair and blue eyes. He sat smiling sweetly to the crowd.

Before the bout, boxing celebrities were introduced, including Toothpick Kelly, Sam McVey, and Billy Woods.

Referee Stuart announced that if the fight went the full 20 rounds that he would award the contest to the most aggressive fighter. The fight was fought under straight rules, which meant that they could fight in the clinches with one arm free, and hit on the breaks. Hence, the fighters would have to protect themselves at all times.

When they got ready for the bout, "Johnson shone up with a gleaming black hide, but Russell had a big plaid plaster of artistic design spread across his chest, and another over his kidneys."

Johnson controlled the fight from start to finish. Although Russell in cowardly fashion had worn a large plaster which protected his body, during the fight, Johnson had a way of "staring with bulging eyes at a spot in the middle of that mustard plaster that was distinctly disturbing to the nerves of Miss Russell. Before the fight was over, that mustard plaster was a bedraggled rag."

In the 3rd round, Johnson landed a vicious jab or short left hook to Russell's right eye, cutting it badly. Blood spurted from the wound, and soon both fighters and the referee were covered in Fred's blood. Johnson landed a paralyzing blow that sent Russell reeling sideways along the ropes, half dazed. Then Johnson landed a short, sharp swing that sent Fred to his corner, streaming with blood.

At the start of the 4th round, Russell was a horrible spectacle, the dripping gore streaking down his cheek onto his breast and trickling down his body in a curling stream. His face was a ghastly picture. The referee's shirt was badly stained as he repeatedly wrenched the large, sweating bloody bodies apart. At the end of the fight, Stuart looked like a butcher.

---

[266] *Los Angeles Herald*, December 4, 1902.

The 5th through 7th rounds featured slow but terrible infighting – clinch and pound, clinch and pound, with an occasional wild flurry of fists. Once Johnson hurled Russell to his knees, but Fred immediately bounded to his feet and continued fighting. However, despite being the much larger man, Fred was growing weak. His face was bleeding from several places, and the flesh on his body was torn and raw in several places as well. The *Times* said,

> He was writhing under the awful beating. But the coon was as jolly and as good-natured as though it were just a little appetizer. He grinned like a china exhibit every time he was hit. He was generous in the clinches and many times raised his arms straight up in the air like a man in a hold-up to show it was not he who was doing the hugging.

In the 8th round, they were fighting in the middle of the ring when Johnson doubled up and bent over like a wounded animal, with an expression of excruciating agony on his face. He hopped like a rooster, unable to stand erect. He acted as if he had been hit low, though the reporter for the *Times* had not seen the blow. However, Jack showed his pluck by coming back to fight.

Soon thereafter, Russell stooped down and landed another low blow. Johnson fell over onto Russell's shoulder. Fred proceeded to land two more furious low blows to the same place. Each time Johnson jumped up, and then he dropped and rolled over and over on the floor in agony, holding his hands clasped frantically to the "unmentionable delicate part of the body."

The big crowd rose with a yell of rage and fury. "A man does not often hear that yell and live to tell of it." A riot was brewing. Dignified professional men sprang from their chairs, screaming with anger. Standing at ring center, Russell seemed worried.

Police entered the ring to prevent the crowd from tearing Russell to pieces. Johnson remained on the rosin-covered floor, groaning in agony. One man rushed through the ropes, wanting to shake Johnson's hand, but the police captain hurled him out of the ring. Another sport tried to get through, but a plain-clothes detective threw him with a dull thump onto the floor. The police captain told Russell to return to his corner.

Referee Harry Stuart waived his arms and asked for silence. The noise of the mob slowly died away. Stuart yelled aloud that three distinct fouls had been committed, and he awarded the contest to Johnson on a foul. A great cheer followed, and Russell managed to sneak out of the ring. Johnson was half carried to his dressing room.

Hank Griffin, whom Russell had fouled not long ago, stood at a corner, howling excitedly, "What did I tell you; what did I tell you?" He insisted that Russell was a foul fighter who should have been disqualified in their bout.

The *Los Angeles Express* said those who thought Russell would give Johnson all he could handle were sorely mistaken. "Johnson had his opponent at his mercy throughout the battle." The *Times* agreed that

Johnson had the fight all his way. "Johnson just waded into him and battered him into a pulp."

Russell's face was cut to ribbons of streaming blood. From the 3rd round on, copious amounts of blood ran from the cut over his right eye.

Throughout the contest, Russell's blows lacked steam, and he continually held and clung to Johnson when they clinched, refusing to break clean.

Johnson also utilized clinching tactics. The *Times* said, "That hunky coon Johnson would reach out and grasp the white man in a loving embrace and send a rain of frightful short-arm blows to his bleeding body. They didn't seem to be so very hard, but there was a crash and a groan to every one."

After badly cutting and dazing Russell, thereafter, Johnson confined his left to deepening the cut, and landed his right to the body with good effect whenever they came together. "The negro was a winner at all times."

During the 8 rounds of fighting, three times Russell "turned tail" and literally ran half-way around the ring to avoid punishment.

Overmatched, Russell decided to resort to foul tactics. The *Los Angeles Herald* said Russell was whipped and not game enough to take a beating, so he deliberately fouled. Fred was maddened and frustrated by his inability to hit Johnson with anything tangible. He was bleeding from a deep cut over his right eye. Therefore, by disgraceful and cowardly acts, he marred what was otherwise a pretty contest.

Russell's fouls were acts of "pitiable cowardice." Several times he fouled Johnson. Referee Stuart twice let it go in order to give the crowd a full run for its money. The *Herald* said Russell's first attempt to foul was with his knee, but it was not effective. He used his glove the next time and hit low, taking Jack off the floor. Johnson was game and tried to continue. The *Times* said, "Russell was getting terribly licked by a good-natured grinning coon…and [in the 8th round] committed three deliberate fouls of a particularly atrocious character to save himself." The third attempt was so effective that after restoring order, Referee Stuart immediately and properly awarded the contest to Johnson, the only decision possible under the circumstances.

It was a sporting axiom that a man may be defeated and still lose honorably. However, Russell not only lost, but lost in a way that would cause athletic clubs to think twice before using him again, or else they might be taking liberties with their licenses to do business and with the money of their patrons. Some said that Russell's career was finished.

Fred Russell had "clinched his title as a foul fighter and a coward." Fred had long been known as a dishonorable fighter. "He fouled Joe Walcott and he fouled Choynski. He will never be allowed to fight before this club again. He is a dub, anyhow. He is a first-rate thing to stick mustard plasters on."

Manager Tom McCarey said he had given Russell the contest on the promise that he would fight cleanly, but he had not been true to his word. Tom called Russell's tactics reprehensible and dirty. McCarey was considering holding back Fred's share of the purse. "If the Century club can prevent it Russell will never again enter the ring." The spectators went home disgusted with Russell, but satisfied with Stuart's decision.

Jack Johnson's performance had been impressive. He had fought a clean, scientific battle against a much larger man.

> Johnson appeared last night as a wonderfully improved fighter, reminding one very strongly of the grand old man of them all, Fitzsimmons. His head was level, his left was accurate and his right seldom failed to leave its imprint on Russell's much beplastered body. The white man entered the ring with two strips of adhesive cloth across his chest and kidneys. Johnson's wallops had the chest plaster torn almost free before the eight rounds were over.[267]

On December 10, 1902 in Philadelphia, Ed Martin and Bob Armstrong fought a 6-round no-decision bout. The bell saved a hurt Armstrong in the 3rd round, but in the 4th round, Armstrong dropped Martin six times. Martin recovered and nearly had Armstrong out in the 5th round. Both lasted the distance. Previous results between the two included: 1899 Armstrong KO2 Martin; 1900 ND6; and 1902 Martin W15 Armstrong.

On December 20, 1902 in Butte, Montana, James Jeffries, who was on a money-making sparring exhibition tour with Bob Fitzsimmons, boxed a 4-round exhibition with miner Jack Munroe. Munroe had been the Olympic Club's heavyweight champion back in 1900. He had sparred with Tom Sharkey, Joe Kennedy, and Jack O'Brien, and had lost a 20-round decision to Hank Griffin. He weighed around 200 pounds.

Press releases had varying facts and levels of veracity regarding what happened in the 4-round Jeffries-Munroe exhibition bout. However, many papers throughout the nation ran a story saying that Munroe did very well with Jeffries. Some even said that Munroe dropped the champion and outpointed him. This story was used to catapult his career, and Munroe and his press agent repeated it quite often. Jeffries continually disputed the truth of the stories, and was extremely irked by them. Jeff claimed to have carried Munroe for 2 rounds, slipped down when missing a punch, and decked Munroe several times. His version was closer to the truth.

However, subsequent Munroe bouts and exhibitions with men like Jack "Twin" Sullivan, Mose Lafontise, Ike Hayes (a black fighter), and Tommy West further bolstered Munroe's growing reputation as a good fighter. Over time, he was sold to the press and public as a legitimate threat to Jeffries.

In late December 1902, the *Butte Intermountain* reported, "Big Jack Johnson of San Francisco now wants to fight any of them. Johnson, himself as black as Erebus, says he bars no color. Mars Johnson is a humorist as well as a fighter."[268]

At that time, U.S. Senator John Morgan of Alabama, a former Confederate general and advocate for racial segregation and limitation of

---

[267] *Los Angeles Herald, Los Angeles Express, Los Angeles Times,* December 5, 1902.
[268] *Butte Intermountain,* December 23, 1902.

black rights, proposed a plan for colonizing the negroes of the United States in the Philippines and other foreign places. He said,

> When I first came to congress I introduced a resolution to recognize the Congo Free State as an independent nation, merely to afford the negroes of this country a place to which they might emigrate when their numbers increased to an extent that would make emigration necessary. The resolution passed the senate and house, and the colonization of the negroes in the Congo was well under way when the United States acquired the Philippines.

However, Senator Ben Tillman, who in theory liked the idea, responded that the plan was unfeasible because it would cost too much to transport so many people, to prepare temporary habitation until they were able to provide for themselves, and to feed them until they raised their first crops. The cost would be so enormous that it would require oppressive taxes.[269]

In the meantime, the *Butte Miner* declared that "the colored heavyweight championship lies between" Denver Ed Martin and Jack Johnson, "the black whirlwind of the coast," and "neither will have a clear title until he whips the other."[270]

Johnson briefly took a trip to Chicago, attempting to get a match there, but was unsuccessful, so he returned to Los Angeles.[271]

The Martin-Johnson fight had been building to a crescendo, and was eventually set to take place in early February 1903 in Los Angeles (two months after the Russell bout), to determine the undisputed colored heavyweight championship. Martin had been receiving the press build-up, and was being touted as a potential top contender to Jeffries.

Denver Ed Martin stood 6'4" tall and weighed "considerably over 200 pounds, not an ounce of it superfluous." "Being a colored man, it is needless to say he had sporting proclivities." He learned to box at the Denver Athletic Club, and while there showed "a remarkable aptitude for catching the blows of his opponent and getting in a few himself, together with a most commendable willingness to learn." Billy Madden saw him box and was sufficiently impressed to take him under his wing. "Since the start of his career, Martin's strongest card has been his cleverness. ... Endowed to an unusual extent by nature in respect to size and strength, he is also one of the most skilled men in the profession, big or little." He had defeated Hank Griffin, Bob Armstrong, and Frank Childs, which established him as the best black heavyweight. The Childs victory, although only a 6-rounder, was so decisive that "no cloud rests on his right to the title" of colored heavyweight champion.[272]

---

[269] *Billings Gazette*, December 23, 1902.
[270] *Butte Miner* December 26, 1902.
[271] *National Police Gazette*, February 7, 1903.
[272] *Los Angeles Herald*, January 28, 1903.

To that point, colored title claimant Ed Martin's known record contained at least 18 bouts, though he likely had more, including: 1899 LKOby2 Bob Armstrong (Martin's only loss), TKO14 Charley Stevenson, and KO2 Ike Hayes; 1900 WND6 Klondike, ND6 Armstrong, and KO1 Yank Kenny; 1901 WDQ10 Fred Russell and KO7 Hank Griffin; 1902 W6 Frank Childs (colored championship), KO5 Sandy Ferguson, W15 Bob Armstrong (avenging his only loss), KO3 and KO4 Frank Craig, "the Harlem Coffee Cooler," and ND6 Armstrong. Many reporters had gained a great deal of respect for Martin as a result of his sparring performances against Gus Ruhlin in 1901, and were even hyping him as a potential world title challenger, causing Bill Delaney and Jim Jeffries to state expressly that they would not allow a colored man to challenge for the championship.

The local paper also noted four additional victories, dates unknown, not currently listed on Martin's record, such as KO4 Mike Queenan, W6 Mexican Pete Everett, KO3 Tom Carey, and KO13 Mexican Pete Everett.[273]

Secondary sources list Martin as 21 years of age, though the local paper said he was 24 years old. Johnson was 24 years of age; approaching 25. Martin was never out of condition, and never went on sprees. He always looked fit.

Some speculated that Johnson was weak in the body, something often claimed about black fighters, but one reporter noted that such a notion was false. To prepare for the fight, Johnson had been sparring with Hank Griffin (whom Martin had defeated), and Hank well-tested Jack's body.

> The other day just to show a few of his admirers that he was sound as a drum amidships, Johnson bid Griffin go to his stomach full speed, and Hank obeyed perfectly. Of course Johnson set himself, but had there been any flaw there the terrific short-arm drives shoved in by the Griffin would have developed it promptly.[274]

Johnson and Martin engaged in debate regarding which of them was the colored heavyweight champion. Martin had first defeated Childs, though it was only via decision in a short 6-round bout. Johnson argued,

> Dey doesn' awahd championships in six-round goes, an' decisions ob-dat soht. Ah beat de waddin' out of dat Chicago coon right in dis town, an' made him quit in de twelft' round, an' ah, if anybody is de colored heavyweight champion. Ah fo't him a twenty-round go, which is supposed to be a finish, an' ah finished him. Ah did. Now, if ah ain't de champion, ah wants to be shown.

General opinion regarding who would win favored Martin. Most thought that Johnson's most important contest was his W20 over George Gardner, but some criticized that Johnson outweighed Gardner by about 15

[273] *Los Angeles Herald,* February 5, 1903.
[274] *Los Angeles Herald,* February 3, 1903.

pounds and had failed to put him away. Martin had defeated Griffin decisively, something Johnson had not done. Martin would have the physical advantages over Johnson in terms of height, reach, and weight. Ed was the one who had been receiving the big newspaper build-up, and had been highly touted by sportsmen as the next contender to Jeffries' crown.

"DENVER ED" MARTIN.

However, "Many sporting men like to back big Jack on account of the careful way he behaves in the ring. He takes no rash chances of losing the money of his followers." Wise gamblers liked Johnson because his cautious style meant he would not be caught with a chance blow, and typically either he won or earned no worse than a draw, in which case the gamblers' money was returned to them. Hence, from an economic standpoint, Johnson was not a bad bet.[275]

Tom McCarey's Century Club, as usual, would manage the program. As the fight approached, McCarey reported a big sale of seats.

It was expected that the fight would be of interest to boxing aficionados throughout the country, for the winner would be in line to fight top white boxers. "Martin has quite a reputation in the East, and will surely go into this fight a favorite over Johnson." Johnson, who was listed as a local fighter, "while not as experienced as Martin, has youth and ambition in his favor and has an idea he is as good as the best of them."[276]

On Thursday February 5, 1903 in Los Angeles, the scheduled 20-round Jack Johnson vs. Denver Ed Martin bout took place.

According to the *Los Angeles Herald*, 10,000 men were outside

[275] *Los Angeles Herald*, February 5, 1903.
[276] *Los Angeles Times*, February 2, 1903.

162

Hazard's Pavilion, eager to purchase tickets. The lone policeman stationed there had to send for reinforcements to handle the disorderly crowd. He ordered the prospective patrons to form a straight line, and had to use his club to enforce his command. The sidewalk and most of the street was filled with humanity anxious to get inside. "Men willingly paid the advance asked by ticket speculators who ran up and down the line."

The *Los Angeles Express* said that the fight was held before the largest crowd of spectators ever brought together by a local boxing contest. The *Los Angeles Times* said a crowd of 4,000 packed Hazard's Pavilion.

Johnson was handled by Hank Griffin, Mark Shaughnessy, and Kid Solomon.

Martin was at least 20 pounds heavier and half a head taller.

Harry Stuart refereed.

According to the *Herald*, from the start, realizing that Martin had every physical advantage, Johnson played a waiting game, looking to counter. He assumed a peculiar position, half crouched, and blocked the clever Martin's efforts in a way that repeatedly evoked cheers from the house. "A prettier exhibition of ring science has never been seen in the west." The gigantic pair made a wonderful showing.

> They mixed like bantams, fought in and out like middleweights, and were lightning fast on their feet. In covering ground rapidly Martin showed himself to be a wonder. His footwork was splendid, his boxing phenomenally stylish, and his appearance in the ring most impressive. Six feet four inches in height and of splendid physique, he might have posed as the model of a Greek sculptor engaged in fashioning the likeness of an Ethiopian prince. Trained to the minute, both men were as fit as they ever could be, and the record-breaking crowd had a splendid run for its money.

The wiser heads in the audience quickly appreciated Johnson's boxing.

> Not as showy as Martin, the smaller man did not block as far; did not attempt to parry a punch before it had well started on its mission, but contented himself with interposing an arm or a glove between his body and the blow of the giant, or perchance stepping a few inches in, or a few inches back, never making a pronounced move as did the other; never playing in the least to the gallery, but almost invariably slipping well meant body blows that were not to be blocked without uncovering possibly more vital points.

Throughout the contest, Johnson kept his right in reserve and exchanged lefts. It was mostly a jabbing fight, but it was pretty. They tried every punch in the book, and the skill shown by both evoked repeated cheers from the crowd.

According to the *Herald*, over the course of the first 10 rounds, Johnson had a shade the best of it with his counterpunching. Thereafter, his superior stamina began to assert itself.

According to the *Times*, in general, both fought very cautiously. Practically nothing was done for the first 10 rounds, which were relatively tame and unproductive. Some even yelled "fake," wanting to see more action. The men spent their time boxing in very clever fashion, and smothering rushes with clinches. Some hard blows were landed - Martin landed a solid right in the 1st and 8th rounds - but they seemed to be without effect. "Martin was always the aggressor, following Johnson continually, and feinting and leading in a very clever manner." The smaller and shorter Johnson moved away cautiously.

Martin's style was complimented. One said he was a polished boxer, with good footwork and side-stepping ability, and he forced the fighting, but was unable to mark Johnson in the least, for though Martin was aggressive, Johnson cleverly blocked his blows and rushes and occasionally landed a good stiff right either to the ribs or wind. Another said,

> [Martin] is one of the prettiest boxers that ever stepped into a prize ring here. He has a finely-moulded form, stands erect, feints, breaks ground, and side steps in an almost perfect manner. His footwork is all that could be asked for, but he don't seem to have the knock-out punch for a man like Johnson, who can block a blow about as well as the next one.

However, the 11th round proved to be sensational and the best of the bout. Martin was trying to open a path with his left, but left himself open as he rushed in. Johnson instantly countered with a lightning straight right flush on the chin. Martin plunged forward into Johnson's arms and hung on with the sheer desperation of a beaten man. It was only by clinching that he saved himself from going down. When the referee broke them apart, Martin fell to the floor, all but out. Referee Stuart pushed Johnson back and began counting.

The crowd yelled, cheered, screeched, and stood on their chairs with delight. The noise "would have made a boiler shop in full blast sound like a tin whistle." It was so overpowering that it was impossible to hear oneself speak. Ed rolled on the ring floor, trying to recover himself.

One of Martin's seconds dashed cold water over the prostrate giant to help revive him, which technically was a foul. Martin struggled to get to his knees at seven, and as he was getting up, he had not fully risen when his legs gave out again and he crashed backward onto his shoulders. Stuart again began to count, and Martin staggered to his feet just in time to avoid being called out. When he rose, he was groggy and all in.

Johnson rushed and partially landed a right, but Martin, still weak, went down again. He rolled over on his back, then slowly rose in bad shape at seven as Referee Stuart kept Johnson away. Martin staggered about the ring in a dazed condition, though he protected himself surprisingly well, ducking and clinching.

Johnson rushed him in a rather wild fashion. Martin, his legs all but gone, had a quasi-excuse to go down again without receiving a punch. As he went down to the floor, he grasped Johnson's legs. Stuart finally separated them.

Martin rose again, weak and staggering. In the face of Johnson's rush, Martin ducked and clinched to save himself. While holding, Ed wobbled, leaned forward and pushed Jack's back to the ropes. Holding Johnson tightly with his arms around him, Martin then grabbed onto the top rope with both hands, pinning Johnson's back against the ropes, holding on and smothering for dear life dazed, all but out and helpless. The gong sounded, saving him from a knockout.

One local paper said gameness, clinching, and the bell had saved Martin. Another said Martin lasted out the round by hanging on at every possible opportunity and committing at least two fouls in doing so, but he got away with them. The gong unquestionably saved Martin, who had been down five times.

During the minute's rest, Billy Madden did very good work in reviving Martin and giving him advice.

> Madden's management of affairs deserves special notice by that class of dub seconds who think the chief duty of such officials is to make themselves as noticeable as possible by rushing to the center of the ring after each round and spewing a mouthful of water into the face of their man, hustling him back roughly, and making him half crazy by a volley of conflicting commands during the progress of the round. Whatever Madden has to say he says in the intermission, and his man has everything done for him that is possible.

According to the *Times*, after that round, none of the spectators complained, for there was something doing all the time in the way of blows struck.

One opinion was that Johnson could have finished Martin in the 12th round, but he preferred to play it safe rather than attack and risk getting caught himself. "It is practically certain that he could have secured a knockout by forcing matters a little harder, and many censure him for not doing so, but as the black boy says, he was out to win without taking unnecessary chances with the money of his backers." Two other writers said Martin recovered and came back strong in the 12th round, which might explain Johnson's caution.

The *Herald* said Johnson preferred to coast to the end, fighting the same cautious but clever fight that he had up to the 11th round.

The *Times* said that for the remainder of the 20-round contest, Martin actually had a shade the best of it in the way of leading, for Johnson was careful all the way through. However, "What Johnson lacked in the way of aggressiveness he made up in his ability to block Martin's leads and rushes, and he gave the big man back as much as he handed out." Johnson was strong on defense and counterpunching.

Both were tired in the last three rounds, but the spectators were in good humor.

At the conclusion of the 20 rounds, Referee Harry Stuart awarded Johnson the decision, and the verdict was met with roaring audience approval, for it was "well-earned." The *Herald* believed that the work he did in the 11th round alone was enough to justify the victory, but it also said that Johnson's work overall was more effective, so the decision was merited. Jack Johnson was the undisputed "heavyweight colored champion of the world." The *Express* said, "Johnson so pronouncedly demonstrated his ability to reach his opponent that there were few dissenting voices when Referee Stuart gave him the decision." The men put up one of the best fights ever seen there and were applauded for their work.

Afterwards, Johnson was examined, and he had no marks.

Billy Madden said, "I want another fight with that man. Martin was the aggressor throughout, and had it not been for the eleventh round when he fought like a longshoreman, I believe he would have won. I want them to meet again, and will ask for a return match."[277]

The *National Police Gazette* summarized,

> Johnson showed remarkable cleverness, though he lacked the power to deliver a hard punch. Had he been endowed with that necessary there were times during his bout when he would have knocked out 'Denver Ed.' Martin was the harder hitter, but that did not help him any. Johnson's cleverness was something he could not solve. His left jabs sailed by Johnson's ear nearly every time.[278]

This criticism was a bit unfair. Clearly Johnson had a punch, given how badly he hurt a man who weighed over 20 pounds more than he did. He had taken out Joe Kennedy, who was even bigger, and made big Fred Russell de facto quit by fouling. What might be said was that Johnson had a punch, but his natural cautiousness made him not as much of a finisher as some might have liked.

Johnson later claimed that before the fight, Martin had said to him, "I do regret having to knock down such a cute and charming little thing as yourself." Jack made him eat his words.[279]

On the heels of this significant victory, and one that was financially lucrative, the Century Club quickly arranged to have Johnson make his first defense of the undisputed colored crown, to be held a mere three weeks after the Martin fight. Imagine a fighter today going 20 rounds and then fighting another scheduled 20-round bout a mere 21 days later! It would be unheard of, even if it were possible. Johnson's defense, conditioning, and relaxation had to be amazing to be able to go another 20 rounds so soon.

The next man Johnson took on was another very tough customer and emerging highly touted up-and-comer on the heavyweight scene: Sam McVey. He was managed by William A. Roche of Oxnard, who discovered

---

[277] *Los Angeles Herald, Los Angeles Times, Los Angeles Express,* February 6, 1903.
[278] *Police Gazette,* February 28, 1903.
[279] *My Life and Battles* at 37.

him at his livery stable. Oxnard was where they grew sugar beets. Hence, McVey was sometimes called the "pride of Beetville." Hank Griffin was his trainer. Sam was called clever, rugged, and a powerful puncher.[280]

As of early 1902, Oxnard's Sam McVey (later known as McVea) was already fighting in scheduled 20-round main-event bouts. He fought an April 12, 1902 main event against George Sullivan, winning by knockout in the 6th round. Both weighed around 200 pounds. At that time, the *Oxnard Courier* called Sam a "quick, handy boxer for a man of his tremendous size. McVey has been in eight contests, six out and out victories and two draws."

Harry Stuart, who refereed McVey's October 1902 KO5 over Jack Fogarty in Oxnard, said,

> The Ventura county sports have in their champion, Sam McVey, a boxer of whom they can well be proud and one who in the near future will make any heavy weight hustle. There is no one at present in the Queensberry game who is possessed of a better physique than McVey – six feet in height, weight 210 pounds and hard as nails, with no bad habits and his twenty-first birthday yet to greet him.

Before McVey fought Fred Russell in the main event at Oxnard, he was listed as standing 5'11" and weighing 210 pounds. Russell was listed as standing 6'4" and weighing 215 pounds. It was said that the winner would probably be matched against Johnson.

On November 1, 1902 in Oxnard, before a full house, Sam McVey knocked out Fred Russell in the 5th round with a right to the jaw. McVey was physically inferior to the taller and heavier Russell, but was the better fighter, being well-trained by Hank Griffin.

It was reported that McVey was a Texas native, 19 years old, and would be age 20 on February 24 (though secondary sources say he was 18). He had traveled around, having lived in California and even Australia. He did not smoke or drink. He had twice been in the ring before coming to Oxnard, once in Salinas and once in Australia, and had sparred good men.

One report said that when striking the punching machines that registered the force of a blow, McVey's punch registered 1,270 pounds of force, and he had done it more than once. Striking the same machine, Jeffries had registered 1,100 pounds and Fitzsimmons 1,070.[281]

McVey was then "regarded as a rival of Jack Johnson, another colored fighter of promise. … As a matter of fact… Johnson and McVey are looked upon as the most promising heavy-weight novices that have come to the front in a couple of years."[282]

On January 6, 1903 at Hazard's Pavilion in Los Angeles, McVey knocked out 240-pound Toothpick Kelly in the 4th round. The finishing touch was a right to the solar plexus. He previously had decked Kelly in the

---

[280] *Los Angeles Herald*, November 10, 1902.
[281] *Oxnard Courier*, March 29, 1902, October 25, 1902, November 8, 15, 1902.
[282] *Philadelphia Record*, November 18, 1902.

2nd round with a right to the jaw. The newsmen said Sam had a right wallop that would deliver the goods any time it connected properly. "Sam McVey, the Oxnard black, made good everything ever said about him and displayed a right that is legal tender for the goods any time it lands."[283]

After knocking out Jack Lavelle in the 1st round on February 1, 1903 in Oxnard, the press again said the colored lad was a terrific puncher.[284]

According to one source from the time, McVey was undefeated in 14 bouts, all won by knockout within 7 rounds.

Newsmen had taken notice of McVey after his defeat of Russell, considering him, along with Johnson, to be one of the two best emerging heavyweights. He was a big, strong, imposing figure, with a punch to back him up. Harry Stuart said that lovers of the game were eager to see McVey and Johnson hook up.[285]

McVey's manager, Billy Roche of Oxnard, agreed to a match with Johnson in order to see just how good McVey was.

The 24-year-old Johnson had the superior experience and maturity at that point. Still, going up against a 14-0 with 14 KOs fighter with talent and huge punching power; the bout had great intrigue. McVey would have a 25-pound weight advantage, and he definitely was known as a bigger puncher and better finisher.

The *Los Angeles Herald* said,

> There has been a saying that two black men do not make a good contest to look upon, but the Griffin-Martin and Johnson-Martin battles give ample guaranty that a meeting between McVey and Johnson will be worth watching. McVey has beaten all his opponents to date in less than seven rounds, and everybody who follows boxing locally knows Johnson. The strength of the Oxnard boy's right hand wallop is such that nobody of his weight will have much the best of him in a mixup, and it will be interesting to note what style of battle Johnson will assume against such a fighter. McVey is at one extreme of the boxing game and the clever, rangy Maddenite, Ed Martin, is at the other. Johnson seems to be one of those rare and favored individuals who combine with their cleverness an indisputably able punch for use at opportune times. Usually it is characteristic of the cleverest boxers that they are deficient in punching power.[286]

Clearly, the *Herald* felt that Johnson had both cleverness and power.

Johnson, wearing a new suit of black clothes, an overcoat, kid gloves, a new stiff hat, and carrying a cane, spoke of his recent match with Martin, and the upcoming one with McVey.

---

[283] *Los Angeles Herald*, January 7, 1903; *Oxnard Courier*, January 10, 1903.
[284] *Los Angeles Herald*, February 1, 20, 1903.
[285] *Oxnard Courier*, January 17, 1903.
[286] *Los Angeles Herald*, February 7, 1903.

Well, he wos hol'in he's guard low, comin' out of de clinches, and I waited until the time was right, an' sent in mah right good an' hahd. He's a game man, dat Martin — must give him all possible credit fo' dat. He's de mose gentlemanly man ah evah fo't — it's a pleasuah to ahgue with him. Yes, ah's goin' do mah best with Misser McVey. He's very strong young fellow, an' can wallop some; ah'll have to be cahful, but ah'll win all right.

Johnson would take a short little vacation of two or three days to hunt some rabbits before resuming his training.[287]

Six days after the Martin fight, on February 11, 1903, the colored champ resumed training at the New High street quarters. Jack was a cautious fellow, and did not intend to be caught unprepared by such a tough and powerful customer as McVey. "There is a general love for the punch among the public, and McVey is credited with it to a remarkable degree."

McVey was sparring with Hank Griffin, who could give him tips about Johnson, for Griffin had fought and sparred with Johnson as well.[288]

The *Oxnard Courier* said the bout promised to be one of the fastest goes ever seen, for McVey was a whirlwind. It quoted the *Los Angeles Times* as saying that the local sports could not pick the winner in advance of this one, although Johnson would probably be the favorite. Both men had beaten all of their foes of late, but McVey had knocked out his opponents, and quickly at that. "Johnson may be the better boxer of the two, but he has no harder punch than McVey." Sam was game, quickly carried the fight to his foes, and could give and take a punch.[289]

Johnson opened as a 10 to 7 betting favorite.

Johnson is in his usual splendid condition. He is working every afternoon with Jack Lavelle [a former McVey victim], Laplace and Tom Kingsley, going a round each with the boys in rotation without intermission. Yesterday Johnson went a dozen rounds without a rest and came out of it very far from tired. ...

Kingsley and Lavelle mix it up quite a little with Johnson, and the latter makes a clever showing against the big darkey. Kingsley is not nearly as clever as Lavelle, but he is a very willing chap and comes back for more right along. Occasionally one of the boys stings Johnson a little and then the hooks begin to fly.

From Oxnard, Hank Griffin reported that McVey was in splendid shape and looked like a winner. Paying McVey a very high compliment, Griffin said that he could not last 4 rounds before his own protégé, "which is fair dope in itself."[290]

[287] *Los Angeles Herald*, February 8, 1903.
[288] *Los Angeles Herald*, February 12, 1903.
[289] *Oxnard Courier*, February 14, 1903.
[290] *Los Angeles Herald*, February 20, 1903.

Sam McVey

The *Oxnard Courier* said the "wonder" McVey came from Melbourne, Australia a little over two years ago, having begun his pugilistic career there, defeating a fighter by the name of Peter Jackson in 2 rounds. He then fought in San Francisco, defeating his foe in 8 rounds. He defeated Lee Haley in Salinas in 7 rounds. Since then, his bouts had been managed by William A. Roche and held either in Oxnard or Los Angeles. He knocked out McCall in 3 rounds, Fogarty and Russell in 5, Kelly in 4, and Lavelle in 1.[291]

---

[291] *Oxnard Courier*, February 21, 1903.

The *Express* said Johnson was the favorite because he had defeated several top-notchers and had won the colored championship from "the most clever of them all. He is a scientific boxer, and his foot-work is good. He has a hard right punch that tells when it lands."

However, McVey would weigh 25 pounds more than Johnson. He had a knack for putting away his foes in short order. Those from Oxnard were willing to bet nearly $1,000 on him.[292]

Three days before the fight, on February 23, Johnson ran 15 miles. At his Lily Club training quarters, Jack worked for an hour with several machines. He also punched the bag for 4 rounds, and then sparred Tom Kingsley and Jack Lavelle, 8 rounds each. No love taps were given on either side. Johnson landed his corkscrew left uppercut with telling effect.[293]

The *Herald* said it was a tough fight to pick. Regardless of their difference in experience, the fight had the sports guessing. It was a question of whether or not McVey could land his powerful right. If he could, he would win, but if not, Johnson would likely take the money, "though he will probably require the full twenty rounds to annex it." McVey likely would be the aggressor, while Johnson would avoid his blows and counter.

Although the folks from Oxnard were betting wholeheartedly on the very strong McVey, Johnson had plenty of local backers. Both were in great shape. Johnson always took good care of himself and never was far from good condition. McVey was the knockout artist, but gamblers liked to bet on Johnson because they felt that his style was one that either would win or do no worse than a draw, in which case the bettors' money was returned.

> Whenever Johnson is satisfied he has not a swell chance to win, he will lay back and make a draw of it. He seldom takes the initiative in his contests, but usually prefers to 'lay for' the other fellow and after timing him, beat him to a punch. One big thing about the colored champ is his predilection to the short-arm blows, his ability in the hooking line being about his best card. This comes handy to Johnson in many ways, as he is a shifty blocker and likes to carry his mitts high.[294]

It was expected that the odds would even up when McVey's hometown Oxnard fans arrived by special train with their money. They already had put up $1,000 on McVey at the prevailing odds, "and do not see how he can lose." There had been a big advance sale of tickets.[295]

McVey arrived in Los Angeles from Oxnard on the 25th, with Hank Griffin and Frank Fields. Griffin said, "McVey is sure-enough a wonder,

---

[292] *Los Angeles Express*, February 23, 1903.
[293] *Los Angeles Express*, February 24, 1903.
[294] *Los Angeles Herald*, February 25, 1903.
[295] *Los Angeles Times, Los Angeles Herald*, February 26, 1903.

and will surprise the talent down here with his work." Sam would weigh about 205 pounds. The odds remained at 10 to 7.[296]

Years later, Johnson said he knew that McVey would be a tough foe. He had seen him sparring a number of times, and realized that Sam knew more about boxing than any other pugilist he had fought, with the exception of Choynski. Sam was heavier than Johnson and very quick on his feet.[297]

1—GRIFFIN. 2—M'VEY. 3—STUART. 4—JOHNSON. 5—SHAUGHNESSY.
JUST BEFORE TIME WAS CALLED FOR THE CONTEST.
—Flashlight Photograph Taken Especially for The Herald.

On Thursday February 26, 1903 at Hazard's Pavilion in Los Angeles, under the auspices of Tom McCarey's Century Athletic Club, the Jack Johnson vs. Sam McVey fight took place. Harry Stuart, the club's chief official, refereed and judged the main event. In his corner, Johnson had Mark Shaughnessy, while McVey had Hank Griffin. McVey said he weighed 203 pounds. Johnson owned up to 178 pounds. More than 3,000 spectators were in attendance.

According to the *Los Angeles Times*, for 20 rounds, Johnson easily handled the "Oxnard Wonder." McVey "was beaten and pounded and slammed around and punched and jabbed."

---

[296] *Los Angeles Express*, February 26, 1903.
[297] *My Life and Battles* at 39.

Johnson would lambast his head for a while, and then try his floating ribs. Sometimes McVey made a face, and it couldn't be said he liked it much, but it didn't seem to seriously affect him.

They don't arrange these coon fights right. The afternoon before the fight they ought to run the fighters through a steam carpet-cleaning machine, and set a pair of men pounding them a while with meat cleavers. A little thing like twenty rounds of punching can't worry a coon like McVey much. He could stand up for twenty rounds lashed to a post and let the other man take an ax.

Any man who can stand up twenty rounds before McVey's face, however, and not run howling through the ropes for help, deserves a great reputation for bravery. McVey has a countenance that would scare back the rising moon. When you see his face peeking over his two gigantic fists, and realize that it is you he is after, it's enough to throw a man into fits.

There was no gore and no shudders in this fight. It was hot, clever boxing, and Johnson had the best of it.[298]

Johnson easily won the 20-round decision. At the end of the bout, the crowd stood up and howled with joy until the roof shook. They appreciated Johnson's clever performance against such a big and powerful man.

The *Los Angeles Herald* said that contrary to expectations, Johnson proved himself to be McVey's master in every department, close in as well as at long range. McVey was supposed to be Johnson's most dangerous rival, but Johnson was the winner at all points in the contest. He took the initiative at the outset and crowded his heavier opponent from corner to corner, going around him "like the proverbial cooper around a barrel, driving in here and there an effective straight left, a hard right chop to the kidneys, or occasionally sending his right across to the ear with considerable force."

Whenever McVey would start to rough it in the mixups, Johnson made him stop with a shower of left and right hooks to the head that "made even the Oxnarder's bullet-like brain-box rattle like a dried walnut."

Johnson confused McVey by continually changing his tactics. First he played for the face with jabs and occasional hooks, and then, closing in, he would use the right over the kidneys. McVey repeatedly winced from the mauling, and his efforts to block were futile.

McVey began the fight with an intention to land his right, but whenever he cut loose, Johnson was not there, or he would block the blow with a glove, arm, or something other than unprotected flesh. "Johnson's blocking was splendid as it always is, and McVey did not land to exceed ten good blows during the fight, not over half of them at all effective."

---

[298] *Los Angeles Times*, February 27, 1903.

On the other hand, in every round, Johnson landed a dozen or two jabs, hooks, crosses, and chops. "It is not often that a fighter obtains a commanding lead over his adversary at the outset of a contest and retains it throughout without a single intermission in favor of that other, but last night's battle was such one." Johnson was dominant.

McVey displayed admirable courage and ability to absorb punishment "that would have whipped half a dozen ordinary men." However, he had less science and was outclassed. "There is no colored heavyweight in the world today who is likely to wrest the title from Johnson while he retains his present form."

Referee Harry Stuart declared the bout to be one of the finest he ever saw, and was much pleased with Johnson's showing. He declared Johnson to be an unusually brilliant boxer and the possessor of a knock-out blow with either hand from almost any position, despite the fact that the fight went the full 20 rounds. Stuart rendered the only possible decision, and even McVey's friends and backers agreed. The bout was clean and the men fought fairly.[299]

The *Los Angeles Express* said McVey stood up to blows that ordinarily would kill any other man. Yet Sam showed no evidence of being hurt, beyond making a grimace. McVey forced the fighting from the start, but after 5 or 6 rounds he dropped back to the defensive, and Johnson proceeded to give him a merry time in blocking the vicious blows showered in with both right and left. McVey cleverly blocked many blows and returned with some hard rib punches, but overall he was hit much more often. McVey could not keep clear at all times, and Johnson found his face, ribs, or kidneys. No blood was spilled. Johnson landed more often and harder, and avoided returns. The loss did not affect McVey's standing, but rather was a good lesson.[300]

McVey's hometown *Oxnard Courier* said both men were strong at the end, though McVey received the severest punishment of the two and lost on points. Johnson was undoubtedly the cleverest fighter in the ring at present. He was too active and managed to keep away from the terrible McVey right, at the same time jabbing in now and then. There was no soreness whatsoever over referee Harry Stuart's decision, although many in the big crowd felt that it should have been a draw because of the fact that McVey was the aggressor during the entire contest.[301]

Despite the setback, in the years to come, young McVey would be a top fighter. Folks would realize later that there was no shame in being outclassed by Johnson, for he would do it to a lot of good fighters.

Afterwards, the confident Johnson said,

[299] *Los Angeles Herald,* February 27, 1903.
[300] *Los Angeles Express* February 27, 1903.
[301] *Oxnard Courier,* February 28, 1903.

I will challenge Jeffries. I am going to Galveston to spend a month with my people and will return to Los Angeles and put it up to the champion. I am by rights the next man that Jeffries ought to meet, and if the mill comes off I will give the crowd plenty of fun for their money.[302]

At that point, Jim Jeffries was scheduled to engage in a lucrative payday against former champion James J. Corbett, who previously had given him a tough title defense. However, Corbett had not fought in 3 years.

Of course, even if the Corbett fight was not on the horizon for Jeffries, Johnson would have to deal with the color line, which Jeffries already had drawn unequivocally. Race was still a big factor and impediment.

Two days after the McVey-Johnson bout, it was reported that a local Methodist bishop declared that he was not opposed to interracial marriage and miscegenation. This "stirred up a violent controversy among the Methodists of the city." The bishop admitted he knew that most folks naturally would shudder at the idea. His "startling admissions" about his views drew expressions of surprise and wonder.[303]

Johnson said that while in Los Angeles, he met and trained with world featherweight champion Young Corbett II (a.k.a. William Rothwell), when Corbett was preparing for his fight with Terry McGovern, which took place in San Francisco on March 31, 1903, which Corbett won via KO11. Johnson liked to stay in the gym, remaining fit and active, sparring with whoever was willing to work with him.

[302] *Police Gazette*, March 21, 1903.
[303] *Los Angeles Herald*, February 28, 1903.

CHAPTER 10

An East-Coast Sampler

Owing to his burgeoning national reputation, Jack Johnson finally obtained a fight back East, this time in Boston, Massachusetts. At that point, with his recent string of big wins against Childs, Gardner, Russell, Martin, and McVey, he was more of a name, so the Easterners were willing to try him out. He was scheduled to fight the local John "Sandy" Ferguson, a 23-year-old white boxer from Chelsea (less than 4 miles from Boston) who took on all-comers and did not draw the color line. Ferguson was another big and tall heavyweight, typically weighing in the neighborhood of 220 to 225 pounds and standing 6'3". Hence, he would have significant height, reach, and weight advantages over Johnson.

Sandy Ferguson

In 1901, Ferguson had been a Bob Fitzsimmons sparring partner. He had over 30 fights under his belt. His record included: 1900 LDQby4 Dick O'Brien; 1901 L5 Ben Taylor; 1902 D4 Charlie McKeever, W10 Taylor, KO3 Yank Kenny, D6 Taylor, and LKOby5 Ed Martin; and 1903 D8 George Byers, KO4 Dick O'Brien, and W12 Byers. The victory over Byers came just eight days prior to the Johnson fight.

The *Boston Post* said the fact that Johnson was making his debut in the East was sufficient incentive to bring out the full attendance of club members. "Johnson is really a big attraction, for his defeats of Denver Ed Martin, George Gardner and other fistic celebrities within a few months have put him well to the fore in the boxing profession, and a real candidate for the world's championship." Ferguson was an ex-champion of England, having won several bouts while he was there.[304]

On Thursday April 16, 1903 at Boston's Essex Athletic Club, the scheduled 10-round Jack Johnson vs. Sandy Ferguson bout took place.

In the preliminary, Sam Langford fought Bob "Stonewall" Allen, both colored, in a 6-round bout. By agreement the bout was a draw, though Langford was superior.

Johnson made a big hit when he entered the ring just before 10 p.m., "gayly gowned and dolled in pink pajamas, and wearing a highly checked gold cap." As a result, the *Boston Herald* called him the "Pauline Chase" of the ring. Chase was a famous stage actress who had created a sensation as the Pink Pajama girl in the "Liberty Belles." With Jack was Joe Walcott, who on April 2 in Los Angeles had fought a punishing hurricane 20-round draw with Billy Woods, and locally in Boston the day before, on April 15, had won a 10-round decision over Mike Donovan.[305] Walcott was resplendent in diamonds and was smoking a long black cigar. Together, he and Johnson formed a visual combination hard to beat. Ferguson's attire was more modest and less attractive.

The *Boston Herald* and *Boston Globe* saw the fight similarly. In the first few rounds, Sandy did not land a clean blow. Johnson landed sinking lefts into the stomach and rights to the head, though they did not appear to hurt Ferguson. Still, Sandy refused to mix it up.

Johnson did all the forcing and leading. "Johnson was the aggressor all though the contest, and he landed many a hard left and right on Sandy's stomach and face." Ferguson received about all of the punches that were landed. Johnson's jabs worried Sandy, who appeared to be afraid for most of the bout.

Ferguson did little boxing, but mostly chose to stall and block. He was content to get into a clinch, and the referee had to work hard to separate them.

The *Globe* said the pace was fast, but the *Herald* said the contest was rather slow. It seemed as if Johnson and Ferguson were friends. Johnson's pajamas were a bigger hit than the work with the gloves.

Finally, in the 9th round, Sandy cut loose and landed on Jack's jaw several times. It was the only time in the bout that Sandy got angry and cut loose, swinging a few hard blows.

However, Sandy's work in the 9th round was not enough. Ultimately, Ferguson only landed perhaps a half dozen clean punches in the entire 10 rounds.

Johnson easily and clearly earned the 10-round decision.

---

[304] *Boston Post*, April 16, 1903.
[305] The following week in Boston, on April 20, 1903, Walcott would fight Jack O'Brien to a 10-round agreed-upon draw. Walcott was a dangerous puncher, but he could not land, owing to O'Brien's tremendously fast footwork. *Boston Post*, April 21, 1903.

The *Herald* said Johnson was content to do just enough to win a decision, while Ferguson was content to last the bout without getting hurt. Sandy was not fazed by Johnson's punches, and was comparatively fresh at the end, but he disappointed his followers with his performance. "Johnson, too, failed to show as well as was expected, and though he did all the work for the distance he was unable to phase 'Sandy,' and many are wondering how he earned his title of colored heavyweight champion."

Likewise, despite the bout description strongly in Johnson's favor, the *Globe* argued, "Johnson's showing last night was not that of a champion, and had Ferguson more heart he would have easily evened matters with Johnson." Of course, this overlooked the possibility that if Ferguson did more, he also might have gotten hit more as well.[306]

Regardless of these somewhat critical views, Johnson did what he had to do in order to win the clear 10-round decision over the larger local man without suffering any punishment. Despite the reporters saying that Ferguson was not phased, Sandy appeared to have enough respect for the much smaller Johnson's speed and power such that he fought very cautiously and defensively, seemingly content to last the distance without really trying to win. Johnson was content not to try too hard to hurt Sandy as long as Sandy was not trying too hard to win.

The *Boston Post* was much higher on Johnson, saying that he verified all that had been said about his ability as a boxer. "He was all over the Chelsea giant from the start." Throughout, Johnson jabbed him in the face, landed many effective body punches which made Sandy wince, and escaped without being hit. For the first 8 rounds, Sandy mostly stalled by breaking ground and clinching. To that point, the bout was one-sided.

Ferguson only showed well in the 9th round, when he finally mixed matters a little and landed some. However, he again returned to his stall tactics in the 10th round, breaking ground and clinching. Referee Dan Donnelly declared Johnson the winner.

Although the performance was consistent with his somewhat cautious style and general habit, Johnson was the aggressor in this bout.

It is possible that Johnson did not want to attempt a knockout for fear of legal repercussions. On April 6 in Boston, George Gardner had knocked out Peter Maher in the 1st round. Gardner was charged with assault, and on the morning of the Johnson-Ferguson bout, Gardner was found guilty and sentenced to a $100 fine. The judge was not persuaded by Gardner's argument that it was a consensual boxing bout and that they both took the same risk of injury that a football player takes. Perhaps Johnson did not want to risk losing his money or his liberty.[307]

The day before Johnson-Ferguson, on April 15, 1903 in Joplin, Missouri, a black man named Thomas Gilyard was taken into custody for the murder

---

[306] *Boston Herald, Boston Globe*, April 17, 1903.
[307] *Boston Post*, April 17, 1903.

of a policeman. Gilyard had been arrested for less than an hour before the Joplin streets had filled with around 2,000 angry white men. The mob soon demanded Gilyard be surrendered to "justice," which to them meant a lynching without a fair trial. The mob got its way and hung him.

Following its lynching, the mob drove all of the black citizens from the streets into the northern "colored" part of town. The mob then set fire to the houses there, and simultaneously endeavored to prevent the Fire Department from extinguishing the flames.

The Joplin lynching was national news not for the lynching, which was nothing out of the ordinary, but for the subsequent riot aimed to eliminate the town's black population.

The April 16, 1903 *Boston Evening Standard* headline read: "Lynching at Joplin, MO. Negroes then driven from the town."

This began the history of Joplin being all-white. Joplin was just 30 miles from Peirce City, another all-white town that used mob violence to force out all of the black people.[308]

On April 22, 1903 in Detroit, Jack Root won a 10-round decision over Kid McCoy, dropping him several times throughout. Root began claiming the world light-heavyweight championship, although George Gardner disputed his claim, given that he had scored a KO17 over Root in their August 1902 bout.

On April 27, 1903, W. E. B. Du Bois' book, *The Souls of Black Folk*, was published. Regarding the topic of blacks obtaining civil rights, Du Bois rejected Booker T. Washington's philosophy of gradualism, conciliation, and accommodation, and instead called for agitation, protestation, and insistence upon recognition of black rights. Years later, Jack Johnson also rejected Washington's philosophy, stating,

> White people often point to the writings of Booker T. Washington as the best example of a desirable attitude on the part of the colored population. I have never been able to agree with the point of view of Washington, because he has to my mind not been altogether frank in the statement of the problem or courageous in the formulation in his solutions to them.[309]

On May 3, 1903 in Philadelphia, 182-pound Marvin Hart fought 158-pound Philadelphia Jack O'Brien to another 6-round no-decision in which O'Brien outpointed Hart in the first 4 rounds, but then Hart dropped and badly hurt O'Brien in the final two rounds.

Just under a month after the Ferguson bout, the colored heavyweight champion was in Philadelphia to take on fellow black fighter Joe Butler in a scheduled 6-round bout, the longest distance allowed by law there. Although very experienced, with nearly 60 known bouts under his belt,

---

[308] To this day, Joplin is 87% white. Joplin was the city famously destroyed by a tornado in 2011.

[309] Johnson, *In the Ring and Out* at 239.

Butler was getting on in years at age 36, a week shy of 37. He stood about 6-feet tall. Butler's record included: 1892 KO3 C. C. Smith; 1893 KO2 Frank Craig, KO6 Jim Daly, and D4 George Godfrey; 1894 LND4 Peter Maher; 1895 ND4 Bobby Dobbs and ND4 Jack McCormick; 1896 W4 McCormick, LKOby1 Henry Baker, LKOby1 Frank Slavin, NC10 Walter Johnson, and LKOby1 Charley Strong; 1897 KO1 Henry Baker, LKOby6 Bob Armstrong, KO1 Frank Slavin, KO5 Tom Carey, LKOby2 and LDQ2 Jack Bonner; 1898 LKOby3 Bob Armstrong, KO1 Harry Peppers, and KO2 James Payne; 1899 LDQby2 Frank Childs and KO6 Ed Dunkhorst; 1900 LDQby2 Jack Stelzner and LKOby6 Frank Childs; 1902 LND6 George Cole; and 1903 ND6 Jack Butler.

The *Philadelphia Inquirer* called Joe Butler Philadelphia's local giant heavyweight, one of the city's most popular boxers. "It has been a long time since Butler has been seen in the ring with a man who is a match for him. In Johnson he meets one of the cleverest men today in the ring, not excepting Jim Corbett. Johnson has a remarkable record of victories and is a candidate for the crown of champion Jim Jeffries."

Joe Butler

The *Philadelphia Evening Bulletin* said Johnson had a first-class reputation and was credited with being second only to Jim Jeffries.[310]

On Monday May 11, 1903 in Philadelphia, at the Washington Sporting Club at 15th and Wood streets, Jack Johnson took on Joe Butler.

Johnson entered the ring first. He introduced a novelty into the business by wearing a pair of pink- or plum-colored pajamas, utterly devoid of anything that would remind anyone of the seriousness of the event. He seemed very confident. Young Mississippi acted as one of his seconds.

Butler was also attired in a lovely mauve bathing robe, though at the bottom it had "all the colors of all the clans that Scotia ever produced."

Johnson was taller, heavier, and longer in the reach than Butler. He would also prove to be faster and stronger.

[310] *Philadelphia Inquirer, Philadelphia Evening Bulletin*, May 11, 1903.

1 - Not much happened. Johnson landed several lefts in the face and a good right to the body, but took a left in the face and right to the body.

2 - The round opened with a fast mixup, with no advantage or damage done. There was a lot of shoving with both arms locked, but Butler snuck in a hard one to the face.

3 - Johnson pushed Butler all over the ring. With a glancing right, Jack started the blood from the corner of Joe's eye. The champ countered pretty hard on the face and then shoved Butler about the ring again.

Butler broke loose from a clinch and landed a hard left on the face, but when he tried to repeat it, Johnson let go his right to the jaw and Butler dropped. He rolled over onto his back. Even after Referee William Rocap concluded the ten-count, Butler laid motionless for several minutes.

Johnson came over and picked up Butler, with the aid of his seconds, and placed Joe on the stool in the ring center. It was some time before Butler got his bearings.

The *Philadelphia Record* reported that Johnson was a wonder at blocking, and had little trouble in stopping most of Butler's leads. Johnson was very fast, though sometimes Butler landed a stinging left to the face, which shook the big fellow two or three times. This made Joe's local followers happy. However, for the most part, Johnson just toyed with him as a cat does with a mouse. Sometimes he would stand up at his full height and hold off Joe with his long reach, and at other times he would crouch in the California style and counter on every blow.

There was a lot of hugging and pushing about the ring, and Johnson was the chief offender in this regard. He seemed to feel that he could do what he chose, and was in no hurry.

Up to the knockout, Butler was doing fairly well. However, it was evident that Johnson was playing a waiting game, and he did not cut loose until he had Butler just where he wanted him.

The *Philadelphia Inquirer* said that from the start, Butler was not in it, although he did his best.

> Mr. Johnsing fondled Joe in a patronizing manner in the first two rounds, and even went so far as to permit Joe to land his rather capacious gloves on his dial. But his good nature vanished in the third round, when, after considerable guying from the spectators, he concluded to cut loose. He thoughtlesslike dropped a few wallops into Joe's well-fed pantry, a right or two into his Aeolian attachment, and then, biff!

The *Philadelphia Press* agreed that the contest was a friendly bout for 2 rounds. The 3rd started out in brotherly fashion as well, until the crowd started to voice its disapproval. This cued Butler to cut loose. However, as soon as he did so, "Johnson showed just how good a fighter he is." There was a short mixup. One or two short jolts made Butler drop his arms, and a pretty, short right hook to the jaw knocked him down and out.

The *Philadelphia Evening Bulletin* said Butler was a mark. Johnson fooled around for a while, and the fight looked like a "barney." It was apparent to everyone that Johnson did not try at all during the first two and a half rounds. He blocked most of the leads without turning a hair, and made the experienced Butler look like an amateur.

However, in the 3rd round, Johnson suddenly cut loose and crossed his right over Butler's left lead and the local man sank to the ground, where he remained for several minutes. When Johnson had sent his first and last good punch across, it was done without any effort, and there was steam to spare behind the blow. Yet it was good enough to score a clean knockout.

As would be seen in his career, Johnson was often content to box cautiously, and at times would only really let loose with his power and offensive arsenal when his opponent nailed him with some good ones, or attacked and tried too hard to defeat him.

Just five minutes after earning his victory, Johnson had left the ring and was on his way back to the dressing room. A crowd gathered around him, wanting to greet him and give him accolades.

While Jack was shaking hands with his admirers, Harry Burke, a local white Philly featherweight/lightweight boxer, smashed Johnson with a bottle on the top of his shaved head. Johnson sank to his knees. A long gash was cut in Jack's scalp, from which he bled profusely. Burke was promptly arrested by the police and held in jail with a $600 bail. His friends took Jack to his dressing room, and then he was taken to the Hahnemann Hospital to have his wound dressed.

The trouble started in the dressing room before the fight. Burke asked Johnson for the use of a towel, but Jack refused to loan it to him, saying that he would never lend a white fighter a towel, for the reason that no white pugilist would do him the same favor.

Burke insisted and came at Johnson, who slapped him on the face, knocking Burke down. Burke grabbed a bottle, but was persuaded not to use it. He instead found his opportunity to do so in cowardly fashion after the fight.

Afterwards, Johnson said he did not know who hit him, for his back was turned, and he saw no reason for his being assaulted in a strange town. He said he would make no charge against anyone, for he intended to leave for Butte, Montana the following day.

One local paper reported a rumor that Johnson was told to carry Butler the full 6 rounds, and was warned that if he knocked out Butler that he would be assaulted.[311]

On May 13, 1903 in Louisville, Kentucky, 168-pound George Gardner won a furious fight with 178-pound Marvin Hart when Hart retired after the 12th round due to a broken right hand.

---

[311] *Philadelphia Record, Philadelphia Inquirer, Philadelphia Press, Philadelphia Evening Bulletin,* May 12, 1903.

On July 4, 1903 at Fort Erie, Ontario, Canada, George Gardner solidified his claim to the world light heavyweight championship with a KO12 over title-claimant Jack Root. The fight was filmed.

The Philadelphia folks were impressed sufficiently with the clever Jack Johnson such that they brought him back to fight a 6-round no-decision rematch with Sandy Ferguson, two and a half months after the Butler bout. Since Philadelphia only allowed 6-round no-decision bouts (no points verdicts were allowed), there would be no formal victor unless there was a knockout or disqualification, although the newsmen usually rendered their own decisions in the event of the bout lasting the full 6 rounds.

Ferguson was the New England heavyweight champion. Since losing a 10-round decision to Johnson, Ferguson had scored a KO6 over Dan O'Brien, but most importantly, on May 26, 1903 in Boston, Ferguson had fought Gus Ruhlin to a 15-round draw. This was significant because since losing to Jeffries, Ruhlin's results included: 1902 KO2 Peter Maher, KO11 Tom Sharkey, and KO2 Mexican Pete Everett. The *Police Gazette* reported that Ferguson, the "Chelsea Strong Boy," had "placed himself in the rank of prominent heavyweights." In fact, "To a majority of those who witnessed the contest, Ferguson

Sandy Ferguson

outpointed Ruhlin, but he was not on an equal footing in forcing the game. The Chelsea lad repeatedly jumped in and jabbed with his left, getting away or closing in before Ruhlin could return." Ruhlin never backed up, carrying the fight to Ferguson throughout, but had trouble landing on account of Sandy's cleverness at blocking. In the final round, Sandy landed several rights that gave him the advantage. Ferguson had outpointed Ruhlin, but it was ruled a draw because Ruhlin had forced matters more.[312]

The *Philadelphia Evening Bulletin* said Sandy's performance against Ruhlin put him in line to meet the winner of the upcoming Jeffries-Corbett fight.

---

[312] *Police Gazette*, June 13, 1903.

"Johnson is a fighting marvel and if Ferguson can get away with him he is indeed a wonder." Both were said to be in good shape.[313]

On Friday July 31, 1903 at Philadelphia's Penn Art Club at 20th street and Montgomery avenue, Jack Johnson fought Sandy Ferguson in a 6-round no-decision bout. For whatever reason, the bout failed to draw a paying crowd, for the attendance was rather slim. "The contest was promoted by ex-Councilman Leo Meyer, and despite the fact that he was compelled to dig deep down in his pocket he ran the show as advertised."

The *Philadelphia Record* called the bout 6 rather slow rounds. Neither fighter did the other any harm, for not a telling blow was landed. Most of the hard punches went wide of the mark, and the others did no damage. The bout was uninteresting. "Ferguson is not a hard hitter, and neither is Johnson noted as a knocker-out." However, both were fairly fast for big men.

Ferguson landed quite a number of left jabs to the face, perhaps a dozen or more, and also a few straight rights, but his blows lacked power and none of them shook Johnson much. Johnson directed most of his attack at the head, but failed to connect very often, missing quite a number of hard swings and landing only a few easy ones.

The fact that they had fought once before gave each man knowledge of the other's style, so they were able to offset one another. Both were good-natured. Johnson wore a particularly broad grin throughout the contest. "From appearances the two men could have continued at the same gait for an hour or two without doing each other any damage."[314]

The local press had varying views of the last two rounds. The *Record* said that in the 5th round, a light blow in the face and a trip sent Johnson down to a sitting position. The *Press* said that at the end of the round, Ferguson caught Johnson off his guard and sent him to the floor with a right hander. The *Inquirer* said that at the start of the 5th round, Johnson asked, "Where do you want this?" He then slammed a short right into Sandy's body. Ferguson returned with a left jab to the face. Johnson temporarily let himself out and landed hard drives with both hands to the body. In a clinch at the bell, Johnson lost his balance and went to the floor. He got up laughing.

In the 6th round, the *Inquirer* said Sandy was very tired, despite Johnson's "evident consideration for Ferguson." The *Record* said Ferguson went down to all fours when trying to avoid a punch. The *Press* said Johnson retaliated in this round and the battle wound up in a mix-up.

The local papers all reported that afterwards, Ferguson said his right hand was in bad shape, which handicapped him. During training, he had landed it accidentally on a beam while punching the bag. A small blood

---

[313] *Philadelphia Evening Bulletin*, July 31, 1903.
[314] *Philadelphia Record*, August 1, 1903.

vessel had been cut, and either four or six stitches (depending on the source) were necessary to put it into shape in order to box.

The *Philadelphia Inquirer* was the highest on Johnson. It said Ferguson stayed the 6 rounds, but Johnson at no stage of the game turned himself loose consistently. Sandy was obviously out of condition, appearing to have too much flesh in the abdomen and legs, and was breathing heavily.

Even granting Ferguson's subsequently reported hand impediment, "He gave no evidence of his ability to cope successfully with a boxer of Johnson's undoubted ability." That he stayed the full 6 rounds appeared to be due to Johnson's "gentlemanly forbearance. If he had turned himself loose for a continuous performance there was every reason for believing that there would have been nothing to the bout, for every time he did extend himself he had the Bostonian visibly worried."

Johnson appeared to be in good condition, and showed contempt for Sandy's punches. Sandy landed a stylish but ineffective left jab to the face time and again, but it did not bother Johnson at all. From the start of the bout, Johnson wore a "smile that would not come off."

Throughout, Ferguson showed a disposition to clinch, but particularly so in the last 3 rounds. Johnson did not seem to mind, and appeared to be carrying Sandy. "In fact the black seemed to content himself by suggesting to the spectators what he might do if he felt inclined that way, without actually trying to do it."[315]

It appears that Johnson liked to chill out his opponents, get them to back off, and then Jack would coast, doing just enough to remain in control, but not enough to thoroughly dominate a bout. If they tried harder or landed a good one, he spurted again to show them their place, and then he was content to box cautiously again. In this case, he did not need to fear an official points decision, given that there would be none.

The *Philadelphia Press* was not as high on Johnson. It said he had just a shade the better of the bout. "The spectators agreed that it was a draw."

> Johnson was by far the cleverer boxer, but Ferguson's style is awkward and dangerous and through the bout he bothered the colored champion a great deal. Ferguson was anxious to mix it up, but Johnson would not permit this style to figure. It was pretty even throughout with Johnson having a shade the better of the milling.[316]

The *Philadelphia Evening Bulletin* gave a different view of matters. It said they fought 6 rounds at an unusually fast pace for big men. There was plenty of action in each round. Ferguson continually landed his left jab. Johnson, however, did not mind the jabs, and working at close range, landed some telling body blows on Sandy. Ferguson was willing to mix matters at all times. When he started rushing, Johnson closed in, which usually resulted in a clinch. "On clean work Johnson had a shade the better

[315] *Philadelphia Inquirer*, August 1, 1903.
[316] *Philadelphia Press*, August 1, 1903.

of the bout, but as Ferguson was there at all times with the good and fighting strong at the finish a good draw was the consensus of opinion of the rather slim attendance." Ferguson received great credit for his showing, having entered the battle with two injured knuckles received during training.[317]

Hence, the overall perspectives were that Johnson either won or had a slight shade the better of it, but seemed to be holding back, or that it was a draw, the latter view particularly being held by the spectators.

If Johnson and Ferguson were being paid based on gate receipts, and the attendance was small, it might explain why they did not do much. Often fighters were not willing to give it their all for a paltry amount. Or it could have been that Johnson and Ferguson were simply content to box cautiously, or that their styles offset one another.

The Butler and Ferguson bouts in Philadelphia showed the good and bad of Johnson. Jack could be minimalist, defensive, and cautious, toying with and even carrying his foes, much to the chagrin of the crowd. However, when he cut loose, he often threw and landed hard and fast punches which made it obvious that he was the superior pugilist. He could knock someone out, or he could do just enough to remain in control. This puzzled some, and also led to many underestimating him.

---

[317] *Philadelphia Evening Bulletin*, August 1, 1903.

CHAPTER 11

The Case Is Made

In July 1903, Jim Nell, a San Francisco sporting man, offered $2,500 to bind a match between Jack Johnson, "the hard-hitting colored heavyweight champion, and Bob Fitzsimmons." However, Fitz said that he was drawing the color line. "Johnson is undoubtedly one of the best men in the game, as was shown when he beat George Gardiner on the coast. He is a second Peter Jackson in science and hitting power and fully as clever as the old Australian."

At that time, Fitzsimmons was with James Jeffries, helping to prepare him for Jeff's upcoming rematch with Corbett. Fitz and Jeff sparred with each other starting in August.[318]

Johnson had been unsuccessful at arranging matches with some of the best whites in his class. He reportedly would be heading for the West Coast, where he was to witness the Jeffries-Corbett battle.[319]

On August 14, 1903 in San Francisco, 28-year-old heavyweight champion James Jeffries defended his title in a rematch against 36-year-old James Corbett. Before the fight, announcer Billy Jordan read off challenges to the winner from Jack Munroe and Jack Johnson. Munroe's challenge received jeers, but the crowd applauded Johnson's challenge. Jeff told Delaney that he would not fight a colored man, but would meet Munroe.

Jeffries knocked out Corbett in the 10th round. Jeff hurt Jim in the 2nd round with a left body shot, dropped him in the 4th with a left hook to the body, again in the 6th with either a left hook or right to the jaw, and then twice in the 10th, the first time with a left hook to the body, and then finishing him with a right to the body. They fought before a crowd of 10,669 which generated $62,340 in gate receipts, breaking all of the state's attendance and gate receipt records.

Jeffries was being called the greatest heavyweight champion ever.

> Jeffries now fears there is no pugilist on earth capable of giving him a battle. He laughs at Jack Monroe and smiles when Jack Johnson is mentioned. The negro may be a good, clever fellow, but he would be outclassed worse than Corbett was. He has a soft punch, and could not hurt the big gladiator in a month.
>
> There is one man who might have a faint chance of success, and that is Sam McVey, the Oxnard giant. He weighs in excess of 200 pounds, and has a very hard wallop. He is the only kind of a man of whom the

---

[318] *National Police Gazette*, August 1, 1903.
[319] *National Police Gazette*, August 8, 1903.

champion would stand in the least bit of danger. Punchers like Gardner, Monroe, Sharkey and Ruhlin are easy game for the champion.[320]

Jack Johnson said,

> They say there's only two men left who have a chance [with Jeffries]; that's Sam McVey and myself. Well, I have beaten this Mr. McVey once and can do it again any time he gets a side bet ready. ... My man now is Jeffries. I'm big enough, weigh near 200, and I'll tell you the fight won't be one-sided. He can't touch a man with his right, and I'm sure I could take care of that left and slip him a few on the side.[321]

Many wanted to see a Johnson-McVey rematch. It was said that McVey had improved wonderfully since their prior bout, and possibly could reverse the outcome[322]

Sam McVey, the Oxnard Giant.
This is the dark gentleman who is looked upon as the only likely heavyweight with a chance at Jeffries. He meets Denver Ed Martin in Los Angeles next month.

[320] *San Francisco Evening Post*, August 17, 1903.
[321] *San Francisco Bulletin*, August 18, 1903.
[322] *Oxnard Courier*, July 4, 1903.

Hank Griffin wanted to fight Johnson, and disputed Jack's claim to being the best black fighter. He had a victory over Johnson and noted that the best that Jack could do against him was a draw. "According to that, I must be the [colored] champion and not Mr. Johnson." However, Griffin had been stopped by Ed Martin, whom Johnson had defeated.[323]

On August 20, 1903 in Boston, Sandy Ferguson knocked out Bob Armstrong in the 1st round. This was significant, given that in early June, Armstrong had scored a KO3 over "Denver" Ed Martin. Naturally, such results earned Johnson more credit for his victory over Ferguson.

Jim Jeffries said he would fight any white man on earth, but "there is no chance of his ever crawling through the ropes with a coon."

Johnson acknowledged that Jeff was right to draw the color line against any old colored fighter, but felt that after all of the colored fighters had faced one another and one emerged as the best, that Jeff would withdraw his objections and accept his challenge. Johnson said that he would challenge the winner of the upcoming Ed Martin–Sam McVey fight.[324]

THOSE DARK CLOUDS.

San Francisco Bulletin, **August 27, 1903, referring to Johnson, Martin, and McVey as "dark clouds."**

Obviously, race remained a factor in boxing for writers, fans, fighters, and promoters alike.

> It is amusing to note the way in which the crowd at a ringside receives the different nationalities of fighter. There is always a hearty cheer and earnest backing for the Irishman; grins and good-humored tolerance for the German, and virulent hostility to the Italian and the negro.[325]

Newsmen were asking who would be Jeffries' next challenger. Jeff was "pre-eminently supreme in the possession of his title," and was sighing for others to conquer. However, that challenger would have to be white. Jeffries said, "I will fight any white man in the world, but will not fight a

---

[323] *San Francisco Bulletin*, August 18, 1903.
[324] *San Francisco Bulletin*, August 24, 27, 1903.
[325] *Police Gazette*, August 22, September 5, 1903.

negro." He had said the same thing after being asked about fighting Ed Martin, who subsequently lost to Johnson.

The *Police Gazette* said the next title holder might be a black man. During 1903, sporting experts had noted the emergence of colored champion Jack Johnson as a potential test for Jeffries. Johnson had "huge muscles" and "threatens to provide a choice package of assorted trouble for the heavyweight champion at some time not distantly remote." The *Police Gazette* never supported the color line, so the champion's stance generated some criticism for Jeffries and instant support for Johnson.

> Jeff knows him, and has followed his career with no little interest ever since he burst upon the scene as an eligible opponent for titular honors. George Gardiner, the present light heavyweight champion, who believes he can whip Fitzsimmons, proved to be little more than a plaything for this burly black fellow, and the latter did awful things to 'Sandy' Ferguson, a second-rate heavyweight fighter who knocked out Bob Armstrong in one round the other night. Johnson likewise put a terrific crimp in the championship aspirations of Denver Ed Martin, the giant black whom we all thought a year or two ago was the legitimate successor to the title. Just because he happens to be black, Sharkey, Ruhlin, Corbett and Fitzsimmons can't see him when he assumes a fighting attitude, and now Jeffries has found his eyesight so acute that he can differentiate between colors, and draws the line, although he was, perhaps, afflicted with a peculiar sense of blindness when he fought Peter Jackson, Bob Armstrong and Hank Griffin.

> Notwithstanding the prevailing objection to color, just keep your eyes on this black fellow. He has all the qualifications needed to face Jeffries but experience – size, weight, strength and ability. Give him a chance to get ring-wise by facing him against the whole group of second-raters, and I am confident that in two years time he will give Mr. Jeffries a surprisingly good fight.[326]

In subsequent issues, the *Police Gazette* continued voicing its support for Johnson, who was campaigning for a shot at Jeffries.

> While Jeffries continues to reiterate that he will not fight a black man for the title of heavyweight champion of the world, the curtain-colored individual whom he believes to be the only menacing factor to his remaining in undisputed possession of that title, has started on a campaign of fistic engagements which he hopes will in time justify the support of public opinion in his demands upon Jeffries for a fight. That person is Jack Johnson, who is now the recognized colored champion heavyweight. Johnson is matched to fight Sandy Ferguson in the new fistic arena at Colma, Cal., on Oct. 16. Ferguson and Johnson have already fought a couple of draws in Massachusetts,

---

[326] *Police Gazette*, September 5, 1903.

where ten rounds is about as far as the authorities will allow fighters to go, but at Colma these big fellows will be privileged to scrap for twenty-five rounds if they can't settle their argument in less time....

Though not quite twenty-one years old Sandy weighs 226 pounds in condition and stands 6 feet 3 inches in his stocking feet. This makes him a bigger chunk of humanity than the present champion, who is no Lilliputian. Ferguson is no untried soldier in the arena. Aside from meeting Johnson twice he has a draw with Gus Ruhlin and two wins over Bob Armstrong, whom he defeated in a round each time. Tim McGrath, who is training him, says that Ferguson does not know his own strength. He has seen him play with 500-pound iron dumb-bells as if they were so much wood.[327]

However, the Ferguson bout would have to wait. In late September 1903, Johnson signed to box in a scheduled 20-round rematch with Sam McVey, to be held in Los Angeles in late October. It would be for the colored championship, for which "McVey is considered the most promising aspirant."

Subsequent to his decision loss to Johnson, McVey had impressed Los Angelinos with his performances there in two significant victories. In May 1903, McVey knocked out the game Kid Carter in the 11th round, dominating and decking him several times throughout. Carter held knockout victories over Choynski and Maher.

On September 15, 1903, Sam McVey knocked out Denver Ed Martin in the 1st round. McVey was powerful and improving.

Among sporting men here who have followed both, much doubt is expressed as to Johnson's ability to repeat the dose. McVey is now larger and stronger as well as faster, and he has improved considerably in ring skill since the previous meeting, as shown by his quick disposal of 'Denver Ed' Martin. The Oxnard man is not yet 20 years old and many ring followers think they see in him a black Jeffries.[328]

Back East, the *Detroit Free Press* wrote,

It really looks as if Jeffries will have to fight a black man or quit the game. McVey's easy victory over Ed Martin has boomed the first named's stock at the coast, and a battle between McVey and Jack Johnson should now be a big drawing card. With this over, there would be nothing further to consider but a match between the winner and Jeffries. The champion is doubtless right in his contention that a black champion would be repugnant to most sport followers. Still, we have a few of them now, with Gans at the top of the lightweight

---

[327] *Police Gazette*, September 26, 1903.
[328] *Los Angeles Times*, September 19, 1903.

division and Walcott the leader of the welters. Their accessions to their respective thrones did not result in civil war. Dixon was the boss of his class for years, and was popular, though never so great an idol as he would have been had his skin been white. It is possibly up to Jeffries to show us that in some of the divisions that white talent is better than black. And defeat of Jeffries would merely result in greater activity in the heavyweight class, in the effort to bring to light a white man capable of recovering the lost laurels.[329]

Johnson had been residing in the San Francisco area. Many club managers were trying to get him to fight there, and didn't want him to go to Los Angeles. His wife had been sick lately, so that also kept him up North. However, Tom McCarey had offered Johnson enough money to fight in Los Angeles again.

Jack began calling himself "J. Arthur Johnson." The *Los Angeles Times* said the local betting fraternity would always refer to "the big coon" lovingly as "Black Jack" Johnson. The colored champion was also called the "Black Fitzsimmons" and "Mistah Johnsing."

Johnson was scheduled to arrive in Los Angeles on September 30, and Tom McCarey would escort "the big dingy" up town. Johnson was expected to train at the Fourth street quarters.

McVey was being called a "black Sullivan." The humble Sam said, "Ah nevah expected to beat Mahtin in any one round. ... Ah expected to get him in about twelve to fifteen rounds."[330]

---

[329] *Detroit Free Press*, September 20, 1903.
[330] *Los Angeles Times*, September 30, 1903.

In mid-October 1903, Jim Jeffries said, "I am still in the game, and will fight any white man they can trot out, but I draw the line on colored men. Not that I am afraid of the dark skinned fighters, but if I am booked for a licking I want a white man to do the trick."[331]

Jeffries also said, "When there are no more white men to fight I shall quit the game." However, "There are no men for me to fight in America except negroes, and I don't intend to fight colored men."[332]

As the Johnson-McVey fight approached, the *Express* said both men were in good condition, and the bout promised to be one of the best contests ever witnessed.

Training in Oxnard, McVey was focusing on speed, and he was looking very fast. His development of speed was said to be a revelation to his friends. Denver Ed Martin had been assisting him in his training, acting as a sparring partner and coach. Sam had also been working on his footwork. Observers were impressed.

To that point, less than a week before the fight, the betting had been done at even money. Already nearly $6,000 had been wagered on the result. A very large crowd was anticipated, for McCarey had received ticket orders from as far as San Francisco and El Paso, Texas.

Although Johnson was saying he had a "cinch" on his hands, he was training very hard, revealing that he thought otherwise.[333]

McVey's manager, Billy Roche, was so confident in his fighter that he was paying $250 to have a diamond and gold belt made, which would be given to the winner of the colored championship fight. No one thought Roche would do so unless he was sure that his man would be victorious. "Besides, Jack has all the diamonds he can pay interest on right now. They keep him poor. If he should ever fall into the water with his entire collection of rocks on his person he would be sure to drown."

The championship belt was made of a heavy silk U.S. flag, with a large solid gold buckle, upon the center of which was enameled the figure of a colored man, in whose belt was a fine large diamond, and in one end of the buckle was an emerald, and in the other a ruby. It would bear the inscription "Colored Heavyweight Championship of the World. Presented by Billy Roche. October 27, 1903."[334]

Johnson did not care much about the belt, saying,

> Ah allus weahs suspenders. Nevah could get use' ter a belt. No swell dressers wears 'em, nohow. No, suh, Sam kin hev th' belt ef he wants it — jess' lemme win that fight an' Ah shorely meks a liberal prescription todes buyin' him all the belts he kin weah.

[331] *Chicago Tribune*, October 17, 18, 1903.
[332] *Los Angeles Times*, October 21, 22, 1903.
[333] *Los Angeles Express*, October 19, 21, 1903.
[334] *Los Angeles Herald*, October 21, 1903; *Oxnard Courier*, October 23, 1903.

Am I feelin' right? Well, don' Ah look lahk it? Ah kin wallop hardah than evah befo' in mah life an' that sugah beeter shore goin' ter think he been kicked by er mule.

The local *Los Angeles Herald* writer responded, "All right, Jack, but you'll have to show us first. At any rate, the coming mill will be the biggest drawing card ever pulled off in Los Angeles and the man who gets a pass to it had better take it home and frame it as a souvenir." "And whichever man wins, the public will see the fiercest argument ever pulled off inside the ropes."[335]

Despite having lost to Johnson the first time, the *Oxnard Courier* reported that McVey had become the betting *favorite*, and was even being discussed as a possible Jeffries opponent. Apparently, either Johnson was being overlooked and underestimated, or fans were extremely impressed by Sam's appearance in training, as well as his recent performances.[336]

Regardless of his underdog status, Johnson was totally confident. "If you look up Jack Johnson he will tell you that this Oxnard man will be like eating chicken for him – chicken and watermelon. Jack may go so far as to tell you that he is truly ashamed to take the money." When approached, Johnson, who was puzzled by the odds, said,

> Now, jes' yo' tell me huccome it Ah kain't repeat on disyere country coon? Huh? Didn' Ah jes' nachelly collaborate de soopreme whey outten him once afore? Huh? Didn' Ah mek him look lahk Canadian money? Huh? Didn' Ah walk eround disyere farmer des' lahk a weasel eroun' er bline hen? Huh? Huccome he ter hab a chance with me now? Ah'm a-tellin' you now, an' Ah'm a-tellin' you, right, dat Ah's GOT to win this time, suah! Lemme tell you, disyere brack chile ain' gwineter be one, two, seven! Ah'm no sebenth son ob a sebenth son, but Ah can fohtell dat Oxnard is gwine on de bum after dis match. An' you des' bettah git all ob dat beet sugah yo' kin corral, kase Ah'm gwineter bust up dat beet combine. Yassir![337]

Not only was Jack Johnson a lover of jewelry, but he also had a great appreciation for fine clothes. When he came to town, it was wise to get your own order in quickly, for he could keep tailors booked for many a day.

When Johnson was in town before, he mentioned to Tom McCarey that he was thinking of having a suit made. McCarey told him he knew of a good tailor, and directed him across the street. "Go over there and turn in your order. … If the man wants any references you tell him I will stand good." Jack went away, and ten minutes later, a fat tailor appeared in the doorway, cocking one eyebrow at McCarey. Tom nodded his head, and the tailor went away satisfied.

---

[335] *Los Angeles Herald*, October 21, 1903.
[336] *Oxnard Courier*, October 23, 1903.
[337] *Los Angeles Herald*, October 23, 1903.

Several moons later, the tailor appeared before McCarey, saying, "I've got that bill for Johnson's clothes here, and Jack says it will be all right after his next fight." McCarey replied, "Oh, that's all right. Just give it to me and I'll settle." Tom expected something large, like $30. Well, continuing the story, McCarey said,

> And what do you think that bill called for? Honest, you couldn't guess it in a thousand years! F-O-U-R H-U-N-D-R-E-D A-N-D E-I-G-H-T-Y D-O-L-L-A-R-S! Say, I nearly dropped dead! And what do you think that fellow had ordered? Three suits at about $80 a throw, a swell new top blanket, twenty-five waistcoats of every conceivable pattern and shade, and fifteen pairs of pants!

McCarey Learned the Extent of Jack Johnson's Wardrobe by Guaranteeing the Tailor's Bill

When interviewed about his present supply of clothes, Johnson said, "Yassir, Ah allus 'lowed to carry a few extra clothes. Ah has only twenty-two suits jus' now, but Ah'm thinkin' of fattenin' up mah wardrobe some – not much, jes' half a dozen suits or somefin' lahk dat." Johnson had a taste for the good life, but he had to win his fights in order to continue enjoying it.[338]

The *Express* said Johnson weighed around 190 pounds. McVey weighed about 206 pounds. It listed McVey as being 18-1 with 18 knockouts.

McVey wanted revenge against Johnson, who had handed him his only defeat. He traveled to Los Angeles on October 23.

Upon his arrival in Los Angeles that day, McVey sparred with Ed Martin at the Lily Club. Wearing 8-ounce gloves, McVey dropped Martin four times in 4 rounds, and completely out in the 5th. Martin was willing to take the pounding, because Roche offered him good money to work with McVey. Roche had offered Martin a flat fee of $100, or in the alternative, $50 if Sam lost or $150 if Sam won. Martin was so confident in McVey that he took the latter offer.

The horsemen, headed by Zeke Abrams, who was currently managing Johnson, were backing Johnson at even money, but most of the smaller bets were being placed on McVey.[339]

In order to secure the Johnson-McVey fight, Tom McCarey had guaranteed a $4,000 purse to the fighters, which was a great deal of money. Therefore, he needed to sell a lot of tickets to cover it. "The public demanded that the match take place here and Tom went ahead and arranged it. Now it is up to the lovers of the game to make good."

However, as the fight approached, it was said that although it was a fat wad to guarantee the fighters, McCarey had nothing to worry about, for there was a great public demand for tickets. McCarey already had a sold-out house. He had even made arrangements to expand the pavilion's seating capacity to add accommodations for 1,000 additional spectators, for "no house in Los Angeles will begin to hold the crowd that wants to get in." Oxnard residents would practically treat the day of the fight as a legal holiday and come to Los Angeles to see the fight.[340]

For several weeks, McVey's training had focused on speed, and Billy Roche was more than pleased with the result. Sam was already as "strong as an ox." He had developed a "good bit of cleverness," and he came in "with a punch lightning fast." No one had ever been able to hurt him. Johnson had landed on him several times in every round in their first fight, yet McVey only smiled and came on for more. The style of battle McVey was currently displaying "will make it almost necessary for Johnson to put him away to play it safe."

---

[338] *Los Angeles Herald*, October 24, 1903.
[339] *Los Angeles Express*, October 24, 1903.
[340] *Los Angeles Herald*, October 21, 25, 26, 1903.

Johnson is clever as a weasel, but Denver Ed Martin is clever, too, and it did not avail anything against such bull-like rushes as McVey makes. A clever man may be able to keep away for a time, but sooner or later the rushing boxer lands one; and with a man like McVey one is usually enough. McVey shows up as fast as a bullet and his wind is almost perfect. ... Denver Ed says it will be like stealing the money for McVey to put Johnson away.[341]

The *Detroit Free Press* reported that Johnson believed himself to be unbeatable by anyone in the second division. It said that if McVey was as good as his record made him appear to be, that Johnson should take him quite seriously and not be overconfident. "The man who wins this bout will be entitled to class himself very best of the second division of heavyweight fighters. Were he white he might demand a meeting with the champion."[342]

Regardless of boxing's popularity, it remained under the constant potential of legal attack. Delegations from ministerial and church societies were urging the Los Angeles City Council to take action against the sport. The City Attorney was drafting an ordinance to prohibit prize fights within the city, and it appeared that a majority of councilmen were inclined to vote for the bill. "Sports are sore over this attempt to stop fighting, as advance sales for the Johnson-McVey fight have been unprecedented. Manager McCarey expected a $10,000 house. Practically all the best seats have been sold. The betting is 10 to 8 in favor of McVey."

There was some fear that the City Council might try to interfere with the upcoming fight. In defense of boxing, noted was the fact that there had been no rowdyism associated with any of McCarey's cards. Fortunately, ultimately the Council left matters alone.[343]

The day of the fight, the *Los Angeles Times* reported that both McVey and Johnson were in splendid condition, fit to fight for their lives. The fight was drawing the attention of the sporting world from every area of the country. Whoever won "will be the next real aspirant for the world's heavyweight championship honors now held by James J. Jeffries of this city."

At that point, most of the betting was wagered at even money, though some of McVey's followers were willing to bet at 10 to 8 in his favor. The *Times* believed, "If there was a favorite in the fight it would have to be Johnson." McVey's fans alleged that their man had improved, though Johnson's fans said the same about him. The "McVeyites" cited the fact that Sam stopped Martin in 1 round, whereas Johnson had been unable to stop Martin in 20 rounds. However, "the Martin whom McVey fought was no more the same Martin that met Johnson than the Sullivan whom Corbett whipped was the same Sullivan who electrified the world when in

---

[341] *Los Angeles Herald*, October 26, 1903.
[342] *Detroit Free Press*, October 25, 1903.
[343] *Los Angeles Express*, October 24, 26, 1903; *Chicago Tribune*, October 26, 1903.

his prime." The *Times* also noted that Johnson previously gave McVey "one good beating, and ring history usually repeats itself."

> The colored champion in addition to being as hard a hitter as any of them, is a splendid ring general, shifty, clever to a degree, and a man who, if he cannot win, will certainly not lose through any rash chance. If Johnson cannot get better, he will get a draw. ...
>
> Johnson in his previous fight actually made the Oxnarder forget all about being rough, and displayed rare ability as a mixer himself, but the sports are carried away with Billy Roche's promising protégé, and have forgotten more than they ever knew about the previous performance of the pair.

There was considerable wagering on the fight's duration. Odds were even money that the fight went the limit; 1 to 3 that McVey won in 10 rounds, and 1 to 2 that McVey won in 15 rounds. Johnson was the favorite to win a decision if there was one.[344]

The *Los Angeles Express* said the sporting men were experiencing considerable difficulty in picking the winner. McVey had developed his speed to such a degree that the force in his blows was now so terrific that it seemed impossible for any man to stand up when hit. He had trained hard and had an abundance of confidence.

On the other hand, Johnson was also looking better than ever, "and this is saying a great deal," for he had always been one of the most clever and scientific boxers, and hit like a steam engine. He always kept himself in the best condition.[345]

C. E. Van Loan of the *Los Angeles Herald* said the fight looked like an even-money proposition. McVey had many admirers among the sporting fraternity. James Morley, a baseball magnate, said, "McVey has improved wonderfully, and if he has the stamina to rush Johnson from start to finish, he may win with a knockout." Henry Berry said, "It ought to go to a draw. McVey is too tough a man to be put out, and Johnson is too clever." Another man said, "This McVey has improved more than Jack thinks. He's too strong for Jack and sooner or later he will beat his guard down and land that one. One will be enough." Opinion seemed to be about evenly divided. Johnson investors would have no trouble in placing any amounts they wanted to wager, for there were plenty of McVey admirers who would cover their bets.

Johnson's manager at that time, Zick Abrams (also called Zeke), said,

> I regard Johnson as the most scientific heavyweight in the world today. You understand me? In the world. I look for him to outclass McVey and take a decision. Do you know what that big fellow did the other day? Went an hour and fifteen minutes at hard work and

---

[344] *Los Angeles Times*, October 27, 1903.
[345] *Los Angeles Express*, October 27, 1903.

never stopped once to draw breath. Finished up as fresh as a daisy. You understand me? Fresh as a daisy. I look for him to win this fight and win it by a city block. [346]

JACK JOHNSON, WHO WILL MEET WITH M'VEY TONIGHT.

On Tuesday October 27, 1903 at Hazard's Pavilion in Los Angeles, the Jack Johnson vs. Sam McVey rematch took place. The pavilion was packed with the biggest crowd in its history. Every seat was sold, and the hall was filled even to the doors.

Johnson was the first to appear at the pavilion. He watched the first preliminary, clad in a swell bobtailed top blanket, the latest creation in the shape of a cloth cap, as well as a four-pound diamond stud. He had an air of calm, unruffled dignity.

[346] *Los Angeles Herald*, October 27, 1903.

The *Police Gazette* later quoted one report as saying of Johnson's appearance before the McVey fight, "He wore his best smile and three of his finest diamonds." It humorously responded, "Positively indecent. Where was the police?"[347]

When it was time for the main event, McVey entered the ring first. He had in his corner Denver Ed Martin and Billy Roche. He took Johnson's lucky corner – the southeast – the one in which he had won the colored championship. In order to secure that corner, ordinarily Johnson would appear first, but a matter of pride and vanity prevented him from doing so this time.

Johnson wore a new bathrobe that had just come from the tailor. It was "the most amazing garment ever aired in public." It was covered with large red roses the size of young cabbages. He looked like a "colonial wall paper design." It took a great deal of time to arrange the Watteau pleat so as to give it the proper effect. It hung too much on the bias, or the line diagonal to the grain of a fabric. Johnson, being the model of fashion that he was, would not appear before a large audience in anything but the correct form. Therefore he waited while Zick Abrams filled his mouth with pins and proceeded to do his best imitation of a modiste, or maker of fashionable clothing. Hence, while Jack was being fixed up, McVey entered first and took Johnson's lucky corner.

When Johnson arrived in the ring, there was trouble. He wanted the southeast corner, and said so with emphasis. He had always sat there in his previous battles, and considered it lucky. However, McVey had arrived first and took it, and refused even to toss for the honor. McVey believed that possession was nine-tenths of the law and sat on his rights, and would not budge. Johnson temporarily went to the southwest corner, rather than the northwest corner diagonally across from the southeast corner as would be proper. He remained standing for a moment until he could find a towel to carefully wipe off the chair. He did not want to take any chances of dirtying his new bathrobe.

When Referee Charlie Eyton arrived on the scene, Johnson went over to the southeast corner and insisted that was his corner. Eyton suggested that they flip a coin to settle the matter. However, McVey announced that there was nothing doing, insisting that he had the corner and was going to stick to it. Seeing that the argument was useless, Johnson finally gave in and waived his claim. It was for him to show that the corner he used did not matter. His assortment of pails, towels and bottles were moved over to the north corner.

Both fighters appeared to be in magnificent shape. Johnson's body was a "splendid testimonial to the hard, but judicious work of his trainer, Australian Tim Murphy." Jack also had Mark Shaughnessy as one of his

[347] *Police Gazette*, December 12, 1903.

able seconds, directing the battle from the corner with his usual keen judgment.

1 - Johnson advanced and then circled confidently. He stood in his usual graceful and effective attitude, feet well apart, guard carried well up, his chest and left arm half extended. Johnson came after McVey, forcing him to give way before his rapid feints. Mac led first with some body shots, but Johnson easily avoided them and a moment later landed a stiff left jab to Sam's face. McVey rushed but Johnson side-stepped and launched a stiff uppercut to the face. McVey made another rush but was met with a right cross.

McVey came on and rushed in again, but Johnson stepped back, set himself, and then landed a terrific well-timed short straight right to the point of the chin, and McVey went down for the first time in his life.

At the count of four or five, Sam scrambled to his feet, looking dazed and surprised. He clinched to clear his head. Sam swung several haymaker rights, but Jack eluded them. Johnson was wary and took no chances of rushing in blindly to end it. Jack hooked his right on the ear and then crossed hard again with it on the mouth. Johnson ended the round with some lefts to the face. It was entirely his round and his partisans yelled for joy.

When Sam went to his corner, Roche shoved smelling salts under his fighter's nose.

2 - McVey covered his jaw with his right glove and stepped lively to avoid Johnson. Sam then rushed and tried to outmix Johnson, but met his master at infighting. McVey got inside Jack's guard and landed a hard left swing on

the ribs. McVey missed a right for the head and Johnson crossed him beautifully.

In a brilliant rally, Johnson landed three effective short-arm blows to the body, hooked to the head, and fought McVey all over the ring. Sam's left uppercut only grazed Jack's face. Johnson uppercut the ribs and neatly blocked a counter. They fought at close quarters until the referee separated them. Johnson landed a left on the ribs and McVey tried a left and right for the head but missed as Jack danced away with his customary smile. McVey rushed twice but his blows were smothered before they reached their mark. Both fighters were cautious, disposed to set themselves and wait for the other to lead.

3 - Johnson feinted, stepped in and landed a hard rap on the kidneys, and then blocked Sam's right swing for the head. McVey rushed and swung his right, but Johnson avoided it by drawing away and coming back quickly with a left hook to the face. Jack jabbed, McVey came on and mixed it, and they fought on the inside. In the clinches, Sam pounded Jack's kidneys with his right. Johnson made McVey quit being rough. He landed a hard left on the face, and as Sam came in again, Jack hooked a hard right to the head.

After the referee separated them, Johnson landed a straight left to the face that sent Mac back against the ropes. Another left in the same spot caused Sam to clinch. After recovering, McVey wanted to mix it, but Johnson kept away again. Johnson repeatedly feinted McVey into a knot and chopped him at his leisure. McVey missed a left swing but landed a short right on the ear that did no damage because Johnson was too close in and the blow lacked force.

4 - Johnson landed three hard left jabs in quick succession to the face, the final one staggering McVey, and then Jack sent a right uppercut to the nose. McVey badly missed an uppercut and Johnson laughed at him. Sam landed a straight left to the face but Johnson was going away from it so it did no damage. McVey rushed and swung both hands but missed. In the clinch that followed, Sam landed a right to the ribs and pounded the kidneys. Still, Jack drew in so close that the blows did no harm.

McVey started another rush, but was met with a straight left that stopped him. Sam tried to get in close enough to reach the body with a left hook. However, Johnson was always there with his own big hook. McVey tried desperately to reach the jaw with his vicious right and left swings, but without success. Johnson was able to step nimbly out of the way of Sam's rushes. McVey looked worried. Johnson landed a left, blocked a return, and closed the round with a right hook.

5 - McVey did a bit better in this round. After playing it cautiously for several rounds, he began to bore in viciously. However, every time he started anything damaging, Johnson would reach out about four feet and pick off the blow before it was ripe. "In fact, Johnson's exhibition of blocking was something to marvel at."

McVey opened with a rush and they came together in a fierce mix in which Johnson had the better of it. Sam could not land his right swing. In a hot mix, McVey reached the ribs and swung wildly. In the clinching, he was disposed to rough it. Johnson timed him coming in and caught him with a right uppercut that hurt.

Both waited for the other to lead. McVey tried a left hook but was met with a left jab and right uppercut to the body.

Sam's face began to show the effects of Johnson's left stabs. Johnson landed a left to the face and the blood started. As McVey advanced, Johnson landed a hard right hook. They were sparring at the gong.

6 - McVey rushed but Johnson shouldered into a clinch without a blow being struck. McVey rushed again, missed his left, and being partially off balance, took a stiff right uppercut to the chin that sent him down on his haunches, the second knockdown of the fight.

Sam was up in a flash, being down for no more than a second. However, his stock dropped again. After rising, McVey landed a light left, but as he tried to repeat it, Johnson beat him to the punch. Jack landed a left uppercut and hooked a left to the ear.

Johnson simply laid back, coolly waiting for Sam to rush or lead, and then beat him to the punch and timed him cleverly with his right uppercut as he came in. McVey barely missed a terrific right. Johnson was too foxy and got out of the way. He had the fight well in hand up to this point. Sam hit the stomach at the gong.

7 - Johnson forced matters, and with lightning feints, had McVey rattled. Sam lashed out with both hands for the head, but Johnson got inside the blows and sent a stiff right to the heart. He forced McVey to break ground, jabbing him on the sore nose twice in quick succession. Mac tried to fight him off but received two more lefts. Johnson cornered him and forced Sam to clinch.

After Referee Eyton pried them apart, Johnson quickly stepped in again and landed a stinging straight left to the nose which sent McVey's head back. They mixed it at close quarters and Johnson showed to better advantage. McVey struck his left to the chest, but did no damage. Johnson laughed at him.

McVey landed a hard left to the throat, the first clean blow he had landed in the bout up that point. Another perspective was that it was a straight left as fast as a bullet, which caught Jack under the chin.

8 - McVey rushed and swung his left but Jack got inside it and planted left and right hard on the face instead. Johnson rained in left jolts upon his face. A right hook to the ear also scored. McVey fought wildly for the body and took two stiff left jabs to the face. In close, Johnson blocked all of the blows sent his way. Johnson pounded McVey's kidneys with right chops.

McVey forced matters but was too slow for Johnson, who stepped in with a hard right on the ear. Mac tried all kinds of swings but only managed to land on the kidneys. Sam was short in his attempts to counter the jabs with a right cross. McVey seemed to be the fresher of the two at the end of the round, but clearly he was unable to solve Johnson's style.

9 - Like the other rounds, McVey started with a rush but ate a left jab before they clinched. They fought fiercely on the inside. McVey landed a left hook that made Jack angry. Sam missed a couple of follow-up blows for the face, so he turned to the kidneys and ribs, landing a few.

McVey was forcing matters, trying desperately to beat down Johnson's guard and land a knockout blow, but wherever he landed he found either elbows or a glove waiting for him. Jack had Sam guessing.

McVey had the better of it for the first two minutes of the round, for Johnson appeared rather tired. However, Johnson evened it up in the final minute, winding up the round rather strongly with a spurt in that last minute, scoring on the face several times. He tried hard to land a knockout punch with his right. McVey's face began to swell up considerably.

10 - Johnson stung McVey with his left to the sore mouth. A moment later he hooked his left to the jaw. Sam was rattled and fought wildly. He missed a left swing which turned him half-way around. Johnson came after him and chopped him on the back of the head with a hard right. Sam forced matters again and Johnson stopped him with a left on the sore mouth.

McVey started to bore in again, but Johnson "shooed" him off, cautioning him by saying, "Don't crowd me, Sam; don't crowd me." Another quoted him as saying, "See heah, Sam, don' yo' crowd me!" Jack followed that with three jabs on the nose and Mac badly missed a huge uppercut.

Johnson attacked and rained rights and lefts on his head and body, forcing McVey to break ground and clinch. At close quarters, Sam slammed away at the body with both hands, landing a good right on the ribs, but Jack responded with lefts to the mouth and swung a left on the kidneys. A series of straight lefts to the face cut up McVey a little more.

11 - Johnson set himself to receive Sam's rush, and as he came in, Jack straightened him up with a left on the face and ripping right on the ribs. Sam missed his blows and took another on the body which caused him to make a sour face.

Johnson fought fast, and in quick succession, planted his left on the face and right on the body. McVey was wild and repeatedly missed. Jack simply timed his swings and countered beautifully with his right uppercut to the body and head. Some said that Jack had Sam in a bad way.

McVey began to cover up and assume his old crouching style. He ended the round with an ineffective rush and took a stiff right on the body. Jack had all the advantage of the round.

12 - Johnson came up briskly and jabbed his left to the bruised mouth three times without a return. Sam lunged wildly and Johnson uppercut him three times with his right on the face.

McVey's lips showed the effects of the blows, for they had increased to three times their normal size. Jack twice landed a stiff right to the body, and the blows made Sam wince. Johnson blocked McVey's blows cleverly and sent right crosses to the jaw and straight lefts to the face which were well-timed and effective.

A Johnson left to the face staggered Sam against the ropes. For a moment he seemed dazed. When Johnson stepped in, McVey swung a vicious right that barely missed the jaw. The gong found them sparring cautiously. Jack maintained his advantage.

13 - Neither man wanted to give ground. They sparred for an opening. Johnson stepped in close and planted a right on the jaw. He repeated the blow by placing his left on Sam's glove and then swatting him on the ear. Sam rushed like a mad bull and swung with both hands for the jaw. Johnson stung him with a left on the sore mouth. Sam landed his right chop on the kidneys. They repeatedly came together and clinched without striking a blow.

Johnson sent his head back twice with straight lefts. Johnson landed a right to the head, ribs, and a hard left to the stomach. A left uppercut to the face and a jab on the mouth followed. Jack rushed his heavier opponent to the ropes, but did no damage with the flurry that followed.

McVey seemed worried, and during the minute's rest his seconds rubbed a sore spot on his stomach.

14 - When they began the round, Johnson jabbed and hooked his left to the face several times. McVey came back with a swing but missed and received a terrific right over the heart that caused him to double up and clinch. On the break, Johnson missed a right uppercut.

Jack rattled McVey with his fast feinting and stepping around, and for a moment Mac was undecided as to what to do. Johnson landed a straight left that caused Sam's face to swell a bit larger.

McVey got the worst of every rally, and in the in-fighting, which was supposed to be Sam's strength, Johnson made him give way every time they came together. Johnson landed jabs, uppercuts, body shots, and hooks.

The *Herald* said that from the 11th to the 14th rounds, not much of a "startling nature" had taken place.

15 - Sam's seconds encouraged him to go in and mix it, which he started to do, but he met Johnson's left glove squarely on the mouth. In the clinch which followed, Johnson shoved him against the ropes as if he were a lightweight, showing his strength. Johnson then stepped back and landed a hard right on the ear.

They fought fast at close quarters for a few moments. Jack landed hard rights to the stomach. McVey came out of a clinch with a rush that carried Johnson to the ropes, though no damage was done.

After another clinch, Johnson sent Sam's head back with a left jab that found the sore mouth. Jack got inside of some swings and ripped in a hard right smash to the ribs and a right cross to the nose. He repeated the right twice and landed on the ear with sufficient force to have knocked out an ordinary man. It was the same short right blow that dropped Ed Martin in their recent battle, but McVey absorbed the punishment.

Jack jabbed stiff lefts to the head. He landed a right, a hook, and a stiff right cross on the mouth.

The *Times* said, "Any one of three punches landed by Johnson in this round would have knocked out an ordinary man."

The *Herald* said that in this round, Sam's face began to take on the appearance of an "over-ripe tomato." It did not seem possible to make McVey appear any less beautiful than he already was before the contest began, but Jack landed to the face with great regularity, and every punch left a mark. McVey's face underwent a change, and "one side of his countenance soon showed up seven inches out of plumb."

16 – As McVey was coming in, Johnson caught him with a hard right over the heart. Sam clinched and sent his right to the kidneys. He wanted to mix it, but Johnson was satisfied to fight at long range and cleverly avoided the rushes. Mac missed a left swing and took a right uppercut on the body. Jack kept him at arms' length and stopped his rushes with well-timed lefts. He alternated with ripping right uppercuts to the ribs.

Jack relied almost entirely on his right, driving it to the ribs, the head, then using it as an uppercut, and another into the body. Both were still fresh and strong at the end of the round.

17 - As McVey rushed blindly, Jack stood his ground and met his bull-like antagonist with a series of hooks to the head with both hands. He fought Sam to the ropes with a series of rights and lefts on the body which forced Sam to clinch and hold on.

McVey was desperate and tried hard to land his swings, but it was no use. Johnson was always either out of reach or inside the blows. Mac covered his face with his right and crouched. This position did not puzzle Johnson, who landed his left stab with a smile. He was cool and satisfied that he had the battle well in hand. Jack landed a left to the face and right to the heart. He ripped a long uppercut into the ribs.

18 - From this round until the finish, McVey made wild attempts to stem the tide of certain defeat. He rushed over and over again, but he always ran into Johnson's gloved fists. Jack was too good, and try as McVey might, he could not land the one punch he needed to change the fight.

McVey landed a stiff right on the ribs which riled Johnson. Jack went after him and punished McVey severely with left jabs on the sore mouth, and had his nose and lips bleeding freely.

Johnson tried to end the fight, firing some fierce blows. Jack jammed the right into the ribs as they came to a clinch. After breaking, in a fierce mix, Johnson scored with the left to the head, hooked a stiff left and smashed a right to the jaw, knocking McVey down to the floor, the third knockdown of the fight.

McVey took no time to rest, but rose immediately and rushed. He was too wild to land on the wily Johnson, and instead ran into a left hook that stopped him abruptly. Johnson stepped in, whipping left and right hooks to the head, and winding up with a wicked right hook to the ear. "McVey was very tired and looked all but out. He was pounded to a pulp and had taken the worst of it again in trying to mix."

19 - Both came up strong and were willing to mix it. McVey forced the pace, but was not able to land his swings. In a clinch, Johnson lifted him up from the floor just to show Sam that he was still strong.

McVey got inside and landed a stiff right to the body and a left to the face. As soon as they were separated, he rushed Johnson again and landed left and right on the body.

Johnson kept away and used stiff lefts to the face. He repeated these blows at every rush and punished McVey severely on the nose and mouth. Johnson hooked a left to the head and repeated it in a clinch. Jack drove in a pile-driver left, staggering McVey. Three times in succession Johnson met McVey with straight lefts. At the close, Sam landed a stiff left to the head.

20 - They shook hands to start the final round. McVey was still willing to mix it and took chances in the hope of landing to the jaw just once. Johnson held him off however, and was content to jab and smother the wild swings. Jack landed both hands over the heart.

McVey rushed him to the ropes. He landed once or twice, and Johnson ripped in a right to the ribs, followed by another as the gong sounded with the men in a clinch.

Referee Charles Eyton promptly lifted Jack's arm in the air to signify his decision in Johnson's favor. The thousands of sports in the big crowd chirped their unanimous approval with the verdict, many climbing on their chairs to do so. All of the local papers agreed that Referee Eyton could do nothing but give the big end of the purse to Johnson, who had earned a decisive victory. The verdict was unanimously popular, and not a single hiss greeted it − "a remarkable thing in fistic annals." With the decision came McVey backer Billy Roche's presentation of the gift of the elaborate gold belt to Johnson.

Jack Johnson not only won the rematch; he dominated. He had scored knockdowns in the 1st, 5th, and 18th rounds, and was in control the entire way.

Summarizing, the *Herald* said that inside of the first two minutes of the fight, McVey showed that he believed that he could only win by making a whirlwind affair of it. He tried to do so, but Johnson put him down. That knockdown gave McVey something to think about, so he decided that the rushing game was not wise, and he tried to play it safe. McVey discarded his rushing tactics for a while, and for 4 - 5 rounds he contented himself with an occasional lead. His stock dropped lower and lower. In various rounds, Sam returned to rushing furiously, to no avail.

Johnson had to be given full credit for outclassing, outgeneraling, and outpunching McVey for 20 rounds. The only thing he could not do was outgame him. The Oxnard Wonder took a fearful amount of punishment, and though he was game and strong throughout, he clearly was outclassed.

The *Times* agreed that McVey was outfought at every point and hammered until his face looked as though a goat had chewed it. In the 1st round, Johnson landed a terrific right smash to the jaw, dropping the "Senegambian" for the first time in his life. Jack also scored flash knockdowns in the 6th and 18th rounds. Johnson assumed the advantage from the start and never relinquished it.

McVey's face was beaten to the consistency of a pounded beefsteak, with one eye closed and the other nearly so. He fought 20 hopeless rounds, over one hour and twenty minutes of the worst hell ever inflicted upon a heavyweight in Los Angeles. Johnson pounded him at will, wherever he pleased, though he might as well have "pounded a street car fender." McVey was a punching bag, "a foil for the shifty colored champion's art." Referee Eyton was completely exhausted from "wrenching apart the great dripping, struggling black carcasses."

Whenever McVey became too ambitious, Jack smashed his right over the left shoulder onto his jaw, and Sam "stopped like a shot clock." Any man other than McVey would have been knocked out half a dozen times. The punishment he absorbed spoke well of his endurance and gameness.

McVey was courageous and did his best, but it wasn't enough. Sam spasmodically cut loose and bore in like a bull, swinging wildly, but Johnson's anatomy was always well protected.

> Each time Johnson set himself for a telling blow, waited like a panther about to spring – crouched – his eyes flashing and both hands drawn up in perfect position to strike. As McVey would advance, Johnson's trusty left would shoot out from the shoulder like a piston rod, and the force of his whole weight would rend the

quivering frame of his opponent, creating a temporary opening for that deadliest of all punches, a straight right to the jaw.

Johnson's cleverness was ghastly; his defense was mechanically perfect; a peculiar intuition seemed to divine for him in advance just what blow his opponent was trying for, and not once did the shifty fellow miscall the turn. McVey was just as much puzzled by Johnson's style as he was the first time they met.

Jack Johnson was a finished boxer whom Sam McVey utterly was unable to solve. "Nothing so much discourages a fighter as being totally unable to hit his opponent." McVey only landed two effective blows in the entire 20 rounds, one to the jaw, and the other on the ribs. All of the other punches, Johnson either blocked before they were well started, or avoided by a well-timed side-step or duck. "His work was finished; as a boxer he displayed the very acme of the mitt art. Not only in defense was he superb; his lightning delivery of crushing blows with either hand wrested cheer after cheer from even McVey's backers, and they were by no means in the minority in the hall."

Johnson mostly relied on left jabs, but neglected no opportunity to swing, hook, uppercut, or shift. In no way did his actions give the slightest indication of what blow he would deliver. "Each came like a shot; clean-cut, decisive, effective. They were timed perfectly and caught McVey at the most dangerous time – when he was rushing."

Johnson was never in distress, though once in the 9th round he was a little tired, but in the final minute of that round he evened up the temporary advantage McVey had gained.

Afterwards, McVey was a pitiable spectacle. His mouth looked like a balloon. His left cheek was puffed out so badly that it had closed one eye, and a series of contusions on the other side put the other eye out of business. His whole body hurt to be touched. Conversely, Johnson came out of the bout without a scratch.

After the fight, Johnson said McVey was a good man, a terrific hitter, and one who would make his mark against anyone else. Jack was right.

The *Los Angeles Express* for the most part echoed the other local papers. After McVey defeated Martin, he seemed invincible, but Johnson clearly outclassed and decisively whipped him throughout. Sam could not connect with his hard blows. His terrible left hook missed by many inches, and the champ would counter with his right, which was stopped by Sam's face.

McVey lost heart in the 1st round, when Jack caught him on the jaw and dropped him. Although he was still strong and aggressive, McVey was at the same time wary and held back more than he had in the first few seconds of the contest. Clearly his battle plan had been to rush furiously, but when that strategy led to him getting decked, he became more cautious and sparred, but at that game Johnson just gave him a beating anyway. Sam's body blows fell short and he would walk into returns from Jack's right.

Referee Eyton had plenty of work to do with the big fellows, and at times had to use considerable force to make them break.

A few thought it should have been called a draw owing to the fact that McVey was the more aggressive, "but to those who were close enough to see the blows struck, and the magnificent way in which Johnson blocked his opponent, the decision appeared to be just and honest." Johnson was cleverer, more scientific, and a better ring general, and won beyond all doubt.

Sandy Ferguson challenged the winner, and was said to be Johnson's next opponent.

A dispatch from San Francisco said that experts there were not at all surprised by the result. Those experts "put Johnson in the championship class and say that he would whip Fitz and would give Jeff the battle of his life." Spider Kelly, considered to be one of the best judges of ringsters, declared, "Johnson would whip Jeff, as he would wear the champion out in futile rushes and then punish him as Corbett did John L." Johnson had a consummate guard which made hitting him quite difficult. It was said that Fitz would fight Johnson if the purse was big enough, but the sports there were confident that the "negro would whip the Cornishman."[348]

Regardless, both Fitzsimmons and Jeffries were on record as drawing the color line. Furthermore, George Gardner already had signed to fight Bob Fitzsimmons for the world light heavyweight championship at an agreed-upon catch-weight of 168 pounds. Gardner had become light-heavyweight champion after Johnson had defeated him decisively.

All local box-office records were smashed by the Johnson-McVey contest. They nearly doubled the largest previous amount ever recorded in Los Angeles. Around $7,600 was generated. The fighters' share was 60%, of which was split 60% to the winner, Johnson, and 40% to the loser, McVey. Johnson made $2,796, McVey $1,864, and the club earned $2,940.

Manager Tom McCarey said that all four of his biggest houses featured Johnson as a contestant, proving that he was a drawing card. The Jack Jeffries fight generated $4,000. That was then the record. The first Johnson-McVey bout generated $4,100. The Ed Martin fight set yet another record at $4,200, until this most recent McVey bout outdid them all.

The Johnson-McVey fight was also the greatest betting bout that was ever known to the city. It was estimated that at least $30,000 had been wagered. Johnson won a bet on himself, cashing in over $600. His managers, T. C. Lynch and Zick Abrams, each cleaned up handsomely as well. Will Tufts was so pleased with his winnings that he presented the champion with a fine shotgun. There was "nothing Little Arthur loves better to do than bowl over jackrabbits on the run near his place in Bakersfield." Johnson gathered up a number of handsome presents from a host of admirers who had earned money wagering on him.

---

[348] *Los Angeles Herald, Los Angeles Times, Los Angeles Express,* October 28, 1903.

Billy Roche, McVey's manager, said Johnson beat his man in magnificent style. "Johnson made such a grand fight that I can express only the greatest admiration for him as a boxer and a hard hitter. It was rather rough on me buying him a belt, but I hope he lives long to wear it, for I do not think it could be on a better man, or one more fit to have it."

Advocating for a Johnson title shot, the *Los Angeles Times* ran a headline, "It's 'Up to You,' Champion Jeffries." It said that Jack Johnson was now the logical opponent for the champion. He was easily the master of his race and possessed of undeniable ability, both in giving and escaping punishment. He was a black Fitzsimmons worthy of the champion, "for he is a better man than Jeffries has yet met, barring possibly Bob Fitzsimmons."

> The color line gag does not go now. It is 'pay or play' in the fighting business. Johnson has met all comers in his class; has defeated each and every one. Now he stands ready to box for the world's championship. He is a man who would wear that honor with decent grace if it fell on his shoulders, and Jeffries's solicitude for the future of the game is needless – that is safe in the hands and hearts of the sporting writers of the United States.
>
> Jeffries thus far has met all comers. Will he turn down this one? … The public, through the daily newspapers, demands a fight for the championship in behalf of Jack Johnson. Jeffries must heed the call. … Johnson is the man who will give him a chance to show the best that is in him. If he can beat the negro, Jeff need never fight again.
>
> When they meet, the world will see a battle before which the gladiatorial combats of ancient Rome pale into childish insignificance. And meet they some day will. It is up to Jeffries to say when.[349]

The *Los Angeles Herald* also signified its support for a Johnson title shot, saying, "It is now up to James J. Jeffries." Clearly, at this point, Johnson was seen as the best contender to the title.

Two days after the fight, on October 29, 1903, Zick Abrams, Johnson's current manager, was taken to court on a suit filed in order to collect on a $297.25 note held by Johnson's former manager, Frank Carrillo of Bakersfield. Carrillo had wanted to garnish Johnson's share of the receipts from the McVey fight, for he held a note that Johnson had given him. The debt was still owed. However, when a constable went to the Century Club on Tuesday night to collect, Al Levy, the Century Club's treasurer, told him that Johnson's share already had been paid over to Abrams. Abrams had demanded the share before the fight was pulled off, and Levy paid him around $2,000. So Carrillo took Abrams to court to get his share of Johnson's money, which was owed.

---

[349] *Los Angeles Times*, October 29, 1903.

On the witness stand, when asked if he had any of Johnson's money, Abrams coolly testified that Johnson received nothing from the fight. "Johnson didn't have a cent coming. That money I got from Levy was mine, not Johnson's." Attorney Dwyer responded, "What? Didn't Johnson get any money out of that fight at all?" "Nope. Not a bean." Abrams said he had been advancing money to Johnson to the extent of $4,000, so Johnson owed *him* money. He then pulled out of his wallet a note signed by Johnson for $3,500. The *Herald* writer jokingly commented, "Johnson's notes must be good. Everybody seems to have them." Johnson was tied up to Abrams for one year by an ironclad contract.

When asked what Johnson did with the money that was loaned to him, Abrams responded, "He bought his wife a nice sealskin cloak and that made the $4,000 look sick. Then he went up against other propositions with it." Dwyer asked, "How does he live?" Abrams replied, "Well, I'll tell you. He's a witty sort of fellow and he just lives by his wits." Dwyer: "But I understand that he rides about in a carriage." Abrams: "Does he? Well, that's more than his manager does. But, then, Jack's awfully clever on the touch. You ought to handle him for a week and see." Dwyer asked, "Johnson cannot have dissipated all the money he has made. What does he do with it?" Abrams responded, "Do with it? Why he shoots craps with it. You know how that is. Every nigger has to shoot craps." The attorney replied, "I used to shoot craps when I was young, but 15 cents was my limit." Abrams: "Oh you was just a piker, that's all." Trying to get in a final jab, Dwyer asked, "You've got a pretty good thing, haven't you?" Abrams: "A good thing? I know it. He's a puddin', that's what he is; a puddin'. I only wish I had four more like him. You understand?" Ultimately, the settlement of the Carrillo note was not going to be done through Abrams, who had the winning hand in this case, which was dismissed by Justice Young.[350]

The *Police Gazette* discussed Jeffries' conundrum, saying that he did not have a challenger before him who could give him a real fight, unless he took on a black fighter. "There are a few negroes in the game, who might do for a few rounds, but they will not be given an opportunity by the champion, who within the past year or so has drawn the color line." It appeared that Jeff would lay back for a while and await the emergence of a white contender, allowing the candidates to fight it out amongst themselves until hopefully one impressed the public enough to justify a title shot.[351]

Kidding around, Johnson said of Jeffries, "He says he won't fight me because my skin is black. I can't change the color of my skin, for it won't fade." Johnson said he would be willing to take on Jeff in a horse race instead. In Texas, Jack used to ride horses, and was adept at it.

Lou Houseman told about a young Jack Johnson and his rise to prominence. He said Johnson was loafing around Springfield, Illinois. He

[350] *Los Angeles Herald*, October 30, 1903; *Los Angeles Express*, October 29, 1903.
[351] *Police Gazette*, October 31, 1903.

fought and won a battle royal. Johnny Connors saw him and got Paddy Carroll to give him a match at the old Lyceum. "Johnson was starved." As a result, he was besting Klondike, but grew weak and faint. Connors subsequently abandoned him. Johnson went to Memphis and got enough to eat. He began whipping other black men, and grew a local reputation. He beat Klondike, who had spoiled his career in Chicago. "From this time on Mistah Johnson rose. He now has considerable money, ranks as the best black fighter in the world, and is probably the third best heavyweight on earth, granting Jeffries and Fitzsimmons to be his masters."[352]

Jeffries was consistent in his drawing of the color line against all black contenders. He even refused to box McVey, whom Johnson had just dominated. The Colma Athletic Club in the San Francisco area was offering a $20,000 purse for a Jeffries-McVey bout. Jeff replied, "I have made up my mind never to fight a negro again as long as there are white men in the field. Then again, McVey is not to be regarded as a championship possibility. His last fight resulted in defeat by Jack Johnson. The latter is a little fellow, compared to McVey, so I don't see where the latter figures at all."[353]

Some wanted to see Jeff fight McVey more than they wanted to see him fight Johnson. This had to do with style and perception regarding how entertaining the bout would likely be, and therefore the amount of money potentially generated. Johnson was considered to have somewhat of a cautious, defensive, at times minimalist or boring style. McVey had more of an entertaining, hard-punching, aggressive style. He was a big, strong dude with a punch who usually won by knockout. So a Jeffries-McVey fight would likely be much more fun to watch than Jeffries-Johnson, even though Jack was the more effective and had beaten McVey. A McVey bout might generate more excitement and ticket sales. Regardless, Jeff wasn't fighting Martin, McVey, or Johnson. It came down to color, not economics, ability, or style.

Johnson was determined to get a match with Jeffries. Not lacking in confidence, he figured that he could beat him. On November 7, he told a reporter in San Francisco,

> What I have to say is this: I feel that Jeffries will fight me. He has been advised by certain of his friends to withdraw the color line and I think he will accept my challenge just as soon as he convinces himself that the public believes I am the proper man to oppose him.
>
> I would like to box Jeffries twenty rounds…. If it becomes necessary to meet him in a fight to a finish, I will not dodge the issue. I will fight him under any conditions he imposes. He can dictate all the terms. The only thing I will insist upon is that the contest shall be for the championship of the world.

[352] *San Francisco Bulletin,* November 5, 1903.
[353] *San Francisco Call,* November 5, 1903.

Now, I want to tell you why I believe I can defeat Jeffries. ... I do not think the men Jeffries has been meeting are my equals in the ring. I am tall, I weigh over 180 pounds and I have plenty of strength. I know Jeffries is a wonderfully strong man, but so is Sam McVey, whom I defeated recently at Los Angeles. McVey is a marvel of strength and he expected to rough me in the clinches. I met him at his own game and fought him all over the ring. I believe I will be able to take just as good care of myself with Jeffries as I did with McVey. There is a wrong idea around in regard to my style of fighting. I hear men talking of me as a great fellow at long range, and all that kind of thing, but the real truth of the matter is that infighting is my long suit. I know I can punch hard, and I am sure that I will hurt Jeffries if ever we get together. I suppose whoever suggested that I meet him in a finish fight thought to scare me off, but while I don't care for a finish fight, because you can't have an affair of that kind in a big city where the money is, I believe my chances of becoming champion of the world would be better in a finish fight than in any other kind. The longer I go the better I get.[354]

However, Jeffries and Delaney were firm in their insistence that he would not defend against a black man. Yet, the press and Johnson seemed to think or hope that eventually Jeff could be convinced or compelled to change his mind.

On November 7, 1903 in Philadelphia, Jack Munroe stopped Peter Maher in the 4th round.

During November 1903, Jack McCormick began training Marvin Hart. On November 16, 1903 in Philadelphia, Hart fought Joe Choynski to a fierce and entertaining 6-round no-decision which most deemed to be a draw.

---

[354] *Detroit Free Press*, November 8, 1903, from a San Francisco dispatch.

CHAPTER 12

Victories Misunderstood

In addition to his desire to fight James J. Jeffries, Jack Johnson also wanted to fight the winner of the upcoming late-November 1903 Bob Fitzsimmons vs. George Gardner light-heavyweight championship bout. His manager, Zeke Abrams, posted $1,000 with the *San Francisco Bulletin* to bind a match. Abrams called attention to the fact that Johnson had defeated Gardner already, so he did not think George would be too anxious to meet Johnson again. Champion Jeffries had knocked out Fitz in the 8th round the previous year.

Jack Johnson, Who Has Challenged the Winner of the Gardner-Fitzsimmons Fight for a $1,000 Side Bet.

Abrams had negotiated another match for Johnson with Sandy Ferguson, to be held in the San Francisco area, at Colma, in December 1903. Abrams said,

> Ferguson is not going to beat Johnson. Now, listen to me. There isn't a man living who can get a decision over that coon, and this doesn't bar Jeffries. I guess you think I am kidding you, but I ain't. Jack can beat Jeff as sure as you are sitting in that chair, or I am no judge. I'll tell you, he is another Peter Jackson.[355]

Johnson was training in West Oakland, doing some light work to keep himself in condition.

Jack sent a letter to the *Police Gazette* saying, "I feel that notwithstanding the heroic efforts of Mr. Jeffries to erect the color barricade, I will yet get in the square with him, in the event of which I promise a good account of myself." The *Gazette* said quite a few people agreed. Johnson was a comer.

> It is to be regretted that Jeffries, just at this time, when a huge, black cloud comes to obscure the pugilistic sky, found it convenient to draw the color line. If he had not previously fought Peter Jackson and Bob Armstrong and established a convincing precedent that he felt no race prejudice, it would have been quite consistent for him to decline the opportunity to meet the big, sturdy black man who now menaces his championship glory; but having engaged in contests with the two men above named, it seems as if he can hardly evade a meeting with Johnson, especially in view of what the latter has done to establish his prestige as a fighter.

> Nobody can honestly believe that Jeff has anything to fear in the outcome of a meeting, but a lot of unthinking people will jump to the conclusion that he fears he will be beaten and offer that as a reason for his declining to fight. As Jeffries himself says: ...

> "I am ready to meet any fighter in the world, if he is a white man, and as far as a licking is concerned, I don't fear any black man, but if such a thing should happen that I was to be beaten, I would rather give up my title to a white man."

> Of course he would, but if, as he says, there are no white men left to fight him, why he has only one alternative left, and that is to become color blind.[356]

However, there were other alternatives for Jeffries. He could either wait until a marketable white fighter emerged, or he could retire.

Regarding the upcoming light-heavyweight championship bout, Sandy Ferguson, who had once been a Fitz sparring partner, picked Gardner to

[355] *San Francisco Bulletin*, November 18, 1903.
[356] *Police Gazette*, November 21, 1903.

defeat Bob. Sandy recently had sparred with Gardner, so he was in a position to compare the two.[357]

Those picking Gardner also included Jim Corbett, Spider Kelly, DeWitt Van Court, Eddie Hanlon, and Aurelio Herrera. Alex Greggains, Gardner's trainer and sparring partner, said Fitz was past his best, a shell of himself, and that George would defeat him in a few rounds.

Sam Berger, Bob's heavyweight sparring partner, said, "You may think him old but watch Gardner when Fitz lands either hand. It's the worst wallop in the ring still." Jim Jeffries picked Fitz, saying he was a wonderful hitter and ring general combined.[358]

On November 25, 1903 in San Francisco, at age 40, former world middleweight and heavyweight champion Bob Fitzsimmons won the world light-heavyweight championship with a 20-round decision victory over 26-year-old George Gardner. Both men weighed in at 168 pounds. Fitz dropped Gardner in the 4th, 5th, 13th, and 14th rounds. Fitzsimmons alternated between boxing cautiously from a distance and keeping the pace slow, using his jab, doing very little, playing defense and allowing Gardner to work, and then occasionally suddenly exploding with hard punches. Fearful of Bob's power, Gardner was loath to take too many chances, and fought cautiously despite being the aggressor. Overall, the bout was dull. Jack Johnson was in attendance.

Afterwards, Fitz said his hands had gone bad on him, that he was old and sick and his ring days were over. The reporters complimented the victory, but agreed that Bob's best days were past, and felt that he should retire. He was slower, grew fatigued more quickly, did not punch quite as hard or as often as he once did, and could no longer finish a man. Age and a lengthy career were clearly telling on the war-worn veteran.

The *Chronicle* opined that this version of Fitzsimmons would never land on Jack Johnson. Still, it was a very big victory over a well-respected, much younger champion whom many had thought would defeat Fitz, and it was a very lucrative bout. The total gate receipts were $16,435.[359]

Johnson noted that neither Gardner nor Fitzsimmons appeared interested in a match with him, so his manager Zick Abrams drew down the money that he had posted with the *Bulletin*. Johnson intended to continue on Jeffries' track.[360]

Speaking of Jeff's refusal to fight Johnson, Bill Delaney, Jeffries' trainer/manager said, "If ever a colored man should happen to win the championship the white people would have to move out of San Francisco."

[357] *San Francisco Call*, November 24, 1903.
[358] *San Francisco Bulletin*, November 10-25, 1903; *San Francisco Examiner*, November 17-25, 1903; *San Francisco Chronicle*, November 24, 25, 1903; *San Francisco Call*, November 25, 1903.
[359] *San Francisco Chronicle, Examiner, Bulletin, Call*, November 26, 27, 1903.
[360] *San Francisco Bulletin*, November 27, 1903.

The *Police Gazette* responded sarcastically, "Please, Mister Johnsing, don't do anything that would lead up to such an awful calamity!"[361]

Jack Johnson.

Johnson finished 1903 with a third match against Sandy Ferguson. Since boxing Johnson in July 1903 in a relatively tame 6-round no-decision, Ferguson had knocked out Bob Armstrong in the 1st round, won a 12-round decision over Tom Carey, and won a 15-round decision over welterweight champion Joe Walcott, who was skillful and strong enough to box men of all sizes.[362] Ferguson's victory over Armstrong was significant, given that Armstrong was coming off a KO3 over Ed Martin. Walcott was coming off two 15-round decisions over Kid Carter. Plus, Ferguson had the past W12 George Byers and the D15 Gus Ruhlin on his resume, and he was a big white man who looked the part of coming contender, all of which made him marketable.

John H. "Sandy" Ferguson was born in Moncton, New Brunswick, Canada, though as a fighter he resided in Chelsea, Massachusetts. He was 24 years old. He stood 6'3" and weighed anywhere from 210 - 225 pounds. Secondary sources say Ferguson had about 40 fights to that point.

---

[361] *Police Gazette*, November 28, 1903. On December 1, 1903 in Boston, Marvin Hart scored a KO15 over Kid Carter in a brutal and highly entertaining bout.

[362] One local writer felt that Walcott had been robbed against Ferguson, having won every round, despite the 60-pound weight disadvantage. Even John L. Sullivan said, "I never like to see a nigger beat a white man, but they could have been half decent and made it a draw without going further." Dan Donnelly refereed. *Boston Post*, November 11, 1903. However, *Police Gazette* reports, which were usually based on local dispatches, wholeheartedly supported the decision, saying that Ferguson had boxed well with his fast jab and had hurt Walcott on several occasions. *Police Gazette*, November 28, 1903.

Ferguson trained hard for the fight. He looked well and was boxing cleverly in his sparring sessions. Sandy said, "I have fought Johnson before and know his style. During the past few months I have studied upon how to meet him in battle and have succeeded in outlining a course which will be as mysterious to him as his was to me when we put on the gloves before."

However, most ring followers thought Johnson was too clever for Ferguson. Johnson claimed that he would not only win, but was willing to bet that Sandy would not be able to hit him on the nose even once.[363]

San Francisco's James Coffroth was going to try to get Jim Jeffries to sign for a bout with Johnson.

> In the sporting world the opinion prevails that Johnson is the best man who has not yet fought Jeffries for the championship. He is big, young, strong, exceedingly clever and in the full flush of youth. He will be able to put up more of a fight against the big fellow than has any man since Bob Fitzsimmons engaged him in contest for the first time in New York.

> In San Francisco Johnson has many friends. They pin their faith to him, and declare that he will not, if he enters the ring, prove a George Gardner or a Gus Ruhlin. He will be on the spot, and will not be afraid to hand out a punch when the opportunity offers. He claims he can beat the big fellow, and has talked this idea into the heads of many wise judges of arenic events.[364]

---

[363] *San Francisco Evening Post,* December 1, 1903.
[364] *San Francisco Evening Post,* December 3, 1903.

JACK JOHNSON, THE "COLORED WONDER," IN TRAINING FOR HIS "GO" WITH SANDY FERGUSON.

Ferguson was training at Millett's in Colma, San Mateo county. He knew the majority of local sports did not believe he could win, but promised to surprise them with his speed and cleverness when they saw him in action. He had twice met Johnson. "On each occasion I learned something about his style and methods. I pride myself that I have him down fine, and promise you that I will put him out when I go against him."

Johnson was confident that he would win. "I don't think I am going to let Ferguson get away with this mill when upon it hinges a meeting with Jeffries for the world's championship."

The *Evening Post* estimated that Johnson would weigh around 190 pounds, while Ferguson would weigh at least 210, if not more. "The white man is considerably the larger of the two, but size is at a discount in a battle with so clever an opponent as Johnson, who proved the fact in the battle he fought a few weeks ago at Los Angeles with McVey."[365]

The *Police Gazette* felt that Johnson might be growing overconfident, recently displaying symptoms of a swelled head, particularly so since his defeat of McVey. "This suggests a characteristic weakness of the negro race."[366]

---

[365] *San Francisco Evening Post*, December 5, 1903.
[366] *Police Gazette*, December 5, 1903.

Ferguson and his trainers on the road

The Colma Athletic Club was having a tough time selling tickets, because most thought that Johnson would be an easy winner. "He is clever, big and strong, and should make a chopping block of the comparatively slow fellow from the Hub." Still, Ferguson had a good record and at least a 20-30-pound weight advantage. Furthermore, Sandy could take a punch.

The Colma Club did not seem overly concerned about the ticket sales. In fact, it was making special preparations for the fight in anticipation of a large gate. A new floor was being put in and the seating capacity was being enlarged. Two special trains would take spectators from San Francisco to the fight at Colma, leaving from Third and Townsend streets at 7:30 and 8:00 p.m., arriving at Valencia street.

Training in West Oakland, Johnson was feeling good. It was expected that a large number of his friends from Los Angeles would be up to see the fight.[367]

Ferguson was training as if his life depended upon it. Each morning he did 8 to 10 miles of road work, running and walking, jumping fences, and sprinting over a route through Golden Gate Park to the Cliff House and back. In the afternoon, he was boxing with Joe Millett and Walter Marino at Millett's gymnasium, going from 10 to 15 rounds each day without a rest. He was light on his feet for a 220-pound man and had a particularly hard left. Sandy was confident and said he never felt better.

---

[367] *San Francisco Evening Post, San Francisco Examiner,* December 8, 1903.

SANDY FERGUSON'S METHOD OF DELIVERING A
RIGHT SWING FOR THE BODY.

Regardless of Sandy's hard training, gamblers liked Johnson so much that he was a 3 to 10 favorite. His defeat of the much touted McVey had placed him high in their estimation. His known speed and cleverness made him a legitimate favorite. They would fight in a 20-foot ring, which would favor Johnson, for he was a hard man to work into a corner. "Local sports have come to the conclusion that if the negro cannot win he certainly cannot lose, and for that reason they argue that the worst they can possibly get is a draw."[368]

From his training quarters at Link Dennis' gymnasium in West Oakland, while being rubbed down by Australian Tim Murphy, Johnson said,

> I have an ambition to meet James J. Jeffries for the championship. I have fought myself into a position where he can't avoid a meeting with me. When Jeffries and I have signed articles then my ambition will have been satisfied.
>
> Jeffries is willing to fight me. I am sure of it, but it's those around him who won't let him get in the ring with me. But immediately after my fight with Ferguson – which I feel sure I'm going to win – then I'll send a challenge to Jeffries and keep after him until he either says 'Yes' or 'No.' If he won't meet me, then I am open to fight with any other heavy-weight in the world. I'll agree to stop Gardner in ten rounds.

Despite his confidence in himself, Johnson was not taking Ferguson lightly. Jack felt that the public was underestimating Sandy, but he was not. He had a lot of respect for Ferguson, whom he thought was dangerous. Johnson said of Sandy,

> He is about the fastest man on his feet for a heavy-weight since Corbett. He is quick, too, and is there with the punch. He is being underestimated by the public here and if I should happen to lose then it will be said that I am no good. My plan is to make him fight all the time. I will keep him going from bell to bell. Of course I can't tell, but I believe that the fight will go well toward twenty rounds.[369]

On December 8, 1903 in Boston, a young colored pugilist from Cambridge named Sam Langford clearly won a 15-round decision over world lightweight champion Joe Gans. He did not win the championship because it was an over-the-weight-limit non-title fight. At that time, the lightweight limit was 133 pounds. Gans weighed 135 ½ pounds, while Langford weighed 140 pounds. In the years to come, the strong and talented Langford would be an elite fighter in several different weight divisions, including heavyweight.

---

[368] *San Francisco Call, San Francisco Evening Post, San Francisco Examiner,* December 9, 1903.
[369] *San Francisco Examiner,* December 9, 1903.

(Photo by Green.)
SAM LANGFORD,

(Photo by Bushnell.)
JOE GANS.

That same day, in Norfolk, Virginia, there was a small riot when Democrats forcibly opposed the voter registration of negro voters. The streets filled with a mob of 300 white men armed with shotguns, rifles, and clubs. A company of militiamen eventually dispersed the crowd.[370]

Boston, Ferguson's home area, boosted Sandy and said he was being groomed for a shot at the championship. The *Boston Globe* said Ferguson was afraid of Johnson in their first meeting because of Jack's reputation. Johnson won, but he did not hurt Sandy. Ferguson had more courage in their 6-round rematch, which was close. "Ferguson has one of the best left hands of any pugilist in the country, and when he lets his right go over in earnest it generally proves to be a haymaker."

After Sandy's 1st round knockout victory over Bob Armstrong, some colored sports began calling Ferguson the colored champion, having so read in a newspaper. They later learned that "Sandy" was white.[371]

After his training at Link Dennis' gymnasium, Johnson said,

> I am in grand shape now and if I lose I will have no excuse to offer.
> My hands are in perfect condition and when I meet Ferguson I
> expect to win. I don't mean to say I think I have a 'cinch,' for this
> man is just a little better than the people out here give him credit for.
> I fought him in the East and I know he is a game fighter and has a
> dangerous punch. Mark what I say, he will put up a good fight, but I
> expect to win. I think I shall get him in from twelve to sixteen
> rounds.

[370] *San Francisco Call, Boston Post*, December 9, 1903.
[371] *Boston Globe*, December 10, 1903.

I shall enter the ring Friday night at about 180 pounds. I am nearly down to that weight now and I have not begun to dry out yet. What I want to do is to beat Ferguson and then get a chance at 'Jeff.'[372]

Johnson engaged in the practice of 'drying out' as fights approached, which meant that he would drink little or no water. Back then, they erroneously thought it helped performance, though today we know it does the opposite.

Two days before the fight, on December 9, Ferguson ran 10 miles in the morning. In the afternoon, he boxed 4 rounds each with Joe Millett and Walter Marino. The bout with Marino was fierce, and showed Sandy at his best, "as he seems unwieldy unless when boxing at a high rate of speed." After the day's workout was over, he weighed 207 pounds. Sandy remarked that his condition could not be improved upon. In addition to his sparring partners, he would also have Spider Kelly and Tim McGrath in his corner.

Ferguson did not understand why he was the 10 to 3 underdog. He had twice boxed Johnson, and while admitting that Jack was a very clever boxer, he said Johnson could not punch, and therefore he had no fear of his blows. Sandy believed that he could outpunch Johnson and rely on his superior hitting force to win. "I will ask Jeffries for a match if I defeat Johnson. I will have a better chance of getting on with Jeffries as he won't object to my color."

A headline in the *Examiner* that day said, "Ferguson Says 'Nigger' Don't Hit Hard Enough To Hurt."

While Jeffries was in Massachusetts, a Harvard doctor examined him and found that his weight had increased from 228 pounds three years ago to 247 pounds. The doctor said that Jeff was a wonder who had ten years of fighting ahead of him, if he wanted. "His only danger is a tendency to obesity." Jeff was known to gain a lot of weight between fights.[373]

[372] *San Francisco Call*, December 10, 1903.
[373] *San Francisco Examiner*, December 10, 1903.

Johnson said he had a high regard for Ferguson's right. He would outbox him, but would be as wary as a fox in avoiding punches that might mean destruction.

> I cannot afford to lose my position in the fistic game by doing anything foolish. … The bout may go the limit – probably will – and if I get what is coming to me you can start up town and cash your tickets. Close to 180 is my weight. The other fellow has over thirty pounds the best of me. He is a good boy, too, but I know I am better. I will beat him sure.

The *Chronicle* said Johnson liked to use a careful, scientific style that might get slow at times, but was clean-cut and effective. "While Johnson will not evade any opportunities to put his man away, his record shows that he is not a student of the knockout school unless the other fellow presses him too hard." Therefore, Ferguson might "avoid some unpleasantness by being 'lady-like' and not trying to force a pace that will rile the Southern scrapper."[374]

Jack Welch, the Colma Athletic Club's official referee, was selected to referee the bout. Zick Abrams had wanted him, though Alex/Alec McLean, Ferguson's manager, had wanted Eddie Graney. They put the two names into a hat and McLean drew Welch. Regardless, Welch was called competent, capable, and popular.

Another version of the story was that Johnson had wanted Eddie Smith to referee, while Ferguson wanted Eddie Graney. Welch was the Colma Club's official referee, and the articles provided that the club referee would be used if the two sides could not agree upon one. Ultimately, both principals were satisfied with Welch.

Johnson's muscles were firm and pliant and he looked like a well-trained athlete. He said his training had gone well; he had no complaints, and was in perfect shape. If he lost, it would be because Ferguson was the better man. "If I win, as I think I will, I hope I will get a chance to box Jeffries for the championship."

Ferguson's friends claimed that Johnson did not take kindly to punishment and that Sandy would surely land on him. Manager McLean said, "I have seen them fight twice and have a good line on Johnson's ability. The colored champion will have to be 50 per cent better than he was on the previous meetings, or he will not have a chance with Sandy."[375]

Scouting the bout, the *Evening Post* said,

> Johnson should win. He has superior cleverness and in his mill with Sam McVey he showed that he has the ability to take on a slow though much heavier man than himself and whip him through the

---

[374] *San Francisco Chronicle*, December 11, 1903.
[375] *San Francisco Call*, December 11, 1903.

exercise of science and the employment of evasive tactics. The negro is without doubt a wonder with the gloves.[376]

As the fight approached, one paper said the sporting population had not gone wild over the event and therefore it was anticipated that the crowd would be relatively small, for ticket sales had been light. Conversely, another paper said the advance sale of seats had been much heavier than expected.

The odds had shortened up slightly, from 10 to 3 to 10 to 4, with Johnson still the heavy favorite.

Ferguson said he was never so well trained for any previous contest. He was confident that a surprise awaited the sporting world.

Johnson also insisted that the local sports had held Ferguson too cheaply. Perhaps he was trying to sell tickets, or perhaps he wanted full credit when he won. He was looking forward to a hard fight, but expected to win and then make a businesslike challenge to Jeffries.[377]

On Friday December 11, 1903 at Colma, California, under the auspices of the Colma Athletic Club in the San Mateo County pavilion, Jack Johnson fought Sandy Ferguson for the third time.

The *Examiner* said the attendance was large, but the *Call* said attendance was light, there being less than $2,000 in the house. The *Chronicle* said around 2,000 people were present. Small boys scampered over the roof and tore off shingles in the hope of seeing the fight. They probably would have been allowed to remain had they not dropped shingles and debris on the heads of the spectators. A deputy sheriff climbed on the roof and scattered the daring youths.

Ferguson entered the ring first, to the tune of a waltz played by the Colma band. Sandy's seconds included Tim McGrath, Joe Millett and Walter Marino. Ferguson wore black trunks and a sash of red, white and blue. His skin was pink, and he looked a trifle fat, despite all his hard work.

Johnson entered somewhat later, owing to the fact that he wanted to come down the middle aisle in step with a ragtime melody. His appearance created a sensation. He looked like a "colored Santa Claus." His bathrobe would "make any member of his race turn green with envy. It was a creation. Pink and blue roses on a black background, and a pink girdle set off the robe. Johnson's black face and gold teeth shone beneath the big hood that covered his shiny head." He was so proud of it that upon entering the ring he walked around and displayed his robe to the spectators, "amid great laughter."

Both principals were in the ring by 9:15 p.m.

When Johnson discarded his robe, it could be seen that he wore a purple breech-clout and purple stockings. He appeared to be in splendid shape. Attending him were Mark Shaughnessy, Australian Tim Murphy, Harry Foley, and Muldoon McDonald.

---

[376] *San Francisco Evening Post*, December 11, 1903.
[377] *San Francisco Examiner*, December 11, 1903.

1 - Ferguson extended his hand to shake, but Johnson refused. Perhaps Jack had taken offense at Sandy's comment that the "nigger don't hit hard enough to hurt." Sandy started in a business-like manner, but Johnson blocked his blows neatly. After feinting for a while, Ferguson blocked a Johnson jab. Jack landed a left lightly to the face. He neatly blocked a left swing. Ferguson landed a heavy right on the back. Jack feinted and landed a left on the nose. They exchanged lefts and both landed.

Johnson ripped a solid left into the stomach. Ferguson rushed Johnson across the ring using both hands, but Johnson blocked and moved away. Johnson rushed and Ferguson ducked out of danger. Sandy became wild and Johnson forced his head back with a left. Jack blocked a right for the head. Toward the end of the round, Sandy landed with both hands, but Johnson's head rolled with the punches, so he was not harmed.

2 - Johnson started the round with several piston-rod lefts to the face that sent Ferguson's head back and appeared to sting him. Sandy ducked and grabbed Johnson around the hip. The referee had some trouble in breaking them. Shortly after that, Sandy heeded the call from his corner to use his left, and he caught Johnson with a solid jab on the mouth. The blow was hard enough to rile Johnson, who made an effort to even up matters with a right at the jaw, but Sandy got under it. Jack planted a left into the body but missed a hook to the head. Sandy blocked body shots with his elbows. Johnson landed a hard left to the body and Ferguson smiled. Johnson missed a right to the head and they clinched.

3 - Johnson hooked and swung on Ferguson, who in turn clubbed his right and smashed "the dusky-skinned fellow" over the kidneys. Johnson was "on his mettle at this point and wanted to get to close quarters, but Sandy lumbered around the ring in an awkward fashion and contrived to keep out of range."

When Johnson led with his left, Ferguson met him with a right swing for the head which made Johnson cautious. Sandy missed a right for the jaw. He landed a left jab on the stomach. Johnson put both arms in front of his face and moved side to side, trying to draw Ferguson. Sandy missed a left for the stomach. They clinched. Johnson landed a left and right on the head and body and they clinched. Sandy landed a left jab on the mouth and the crowd cheered. Both missed swings. Sandy slapped Johnson's kidneys. At the bell, when he went to his corner, it was seen that Ferguson's glove was loosened.

According to the *Chronicle*, in the early rounds, there was "hardly a leaf stirring," with the undoing of Ferguson's right glove being the only happening worth mentioning. The fighters were cautious and neither landed anything of real significance.

4 - Sandy's glove was still loose. They sparred for a while. The crowd called for Sandy to go in, but he held back.

Johnson rushed, landing left and right to the head and body. The *Call* said, "He sent Ferguson against the ropes and the force of the blows and the shove sent Ferguson out among the newspaper men." Ferguson had gone through the ropes and was resting for a moment on a ringsider's shoulders. The *Chronicle* version said, "In the fourth Johnson rushed the giant across the ring and shoved him out into the audience with a light left."

Sandy part hauled himself back into the ring, and in part was hoisted back again by Johnson, who helped him. Both men laughed hilariously.

Ferguson was a bit dazed from the fall, and the referee cautioned him for subsequent holding. Johnson pecked at Sandy's face in a half-hearted way. Sandy came back fighting and landed on the head. Johnson rushed and staggered Ferguson with left and right to the jaw and body.

Sandy ducked and shouldered into Johnson, picked him up onto his shoulders, and swung him around playfully in midair. Johnson grinned and remonstrated until Sandy placed him back onto his feet. Jack landed a hard left jab to the jaw and again staggered Sandy. Jack tried a vicious right uppercut that missed. Johnson went to his corner laughing.

5 - Sandy was perspiring profusely. Johnson continued using his left, frequently sending Ferguson's head back. In a clinch, Sandy clung to Jack's shoulders, swinging Johnson round and round while the crowd hooted. Johnson then picked him up and did the same. This was an example of more "burlesque."

Johnson landed his left and caught Ferguson a hard right on the kidneys. He followed up by knocking his head back with a straight left. Ferguson said with a grin, "You can't whip me." Johnson sent his head back again with a jab between the eyes and they clinched.

The spectators' jeers at the slow pace incited Johnson to temporary action, and he went after Sandy. Ferguson missed a wild right. Johnson took advantage of the opening and landed a heavy right on the body. He also planted his left on the body.

As Johnson was landing body shots, Sandy made a face and claimed that he had been fouled, but the blow was fair, so Referee Welch did not recognize the claim. Another local version said a glancing low blow brought a claim of foul, but Welch motioned Ferguson to continue.

6 - Ferguson began the round smiling, but Johnson removed it by knocking his head back with a left jab. Sandy missed a left and slapped Johnson on the back. Ferguson was not able to land his right. He broke ground and blocked some swings and hooks. During this round, at times while they were clinched, Sandy whispered in Johnson's ear.

Both mixed it for a few seconds and then clinched. "Johnson did a lot of showy work, rushing Sandy to the ropes and dealing him lefts in the stomach which did not seem to carry much force. The negro appeared to overlook lots of openings and the round became tedious."

They landed heavily on the body. Ferguson appealed to the referee and claimed low blows, but the claim had no foundation. "To many it looked as if Ferguson did not like the gaff and was willing to quit."

7 - According to the *Examiner*, while Johnson was feinting and fooling around in a fanciful manner, giving color to the belief that he was withholding his best punches, Sandy fired one good, solid, snappy right crack on the chin that brought Johnson down to the ground.

The *Call* saw matters differently. It said Johnson assumed the aggressive and tried to finish Ferguson, but without success. Johnson tried a left shift that missed, and the momentum of the blow caused Johnson to fling himself to the floor.

The *Chronicle* said Ferguson caught Johnson napping and landed a hard right to the back of the head, which dropped Johnson. Perhaps he caught Johnson as Jack was in the process of throwing and missing his left. However, Jack rose in a moment and Ferguson failed to follow up his advantage. It said this was the only time that Ferguson appeared to have a chance to win. "Johnson then increased his lead in every round until the end."

The *Examiner* said that when he arose, Johnson "attended strictly to business for a while." Jack was okay, and Ferguson did not follow up.

The *Call* said Johnson rose in an instant. Ferguson thought he had sent Jack down and tried to win. He rushed and sent in heavy blows, some of which were blocked, but others landed on the head and body. Johnson seemed concerned and broke ground. The crowd yelled at Ferguson to go in and win.

However, when Sandy rushed again he was met with lefts and rights that sent him back. Johnson fought hard, rushed him to the ropes, and planted a heavy right to the body.

8 - Johnson sent his left to the face. They fought a bit in the clinches. The crowd tried to get them to continue fast fighting, but both held back for a while.

Johnson pressed forward and Ferguson poised himself as if he was about to deliver a right. Johnson landed his left on the sore nose. Sandy fell short with his left. He rushed and slapped Jack's back. Johnson landed a left on the body and they clinched. Johnson sent his left to the face. Ferguson missed a left swing. Johnson missed a right.

They posed at ring center, and the crowd yelled for them to fight. Ferguson landed a heavy right on the head. Johnson retaliated with a left to the face, sending his head back. Ferguson tried another right and grazed the jaw. Sandy feigned grogginess to bring Johnson in. Jack laughed and stepped away. Sandy laughed and straightened up and they resumed the game of "dare and dassent."

9 - Johnson landed to the body and sent Sandy's head back with a jab. Ferguson set himself and did nothing. Jack played for the body and landed

two good lefts to the stomach. Sandy fell short with his jabs. Johnson rushed him to the ropes and landed with his open glove. Ferguson came back with a left jab on the mouth.

Johnson staggered him with a heavy left on the jaw. Ferguson went against the ropes and looked surprised. Johnson jabbed him on the body. He missed a right for the jaw.

10 - At the bell, Ferguson made a wild dash and Johnson side-stepped out of the way and laughed. Sandy rushed again and went against the ropes as the matador eluded him. Jack took advantage and landed a left and right to the body. He caught him a little bit low and Ferguson appealed to the referee. It was accidental and the referee told him to go on and fight. Johnson jabbed the mouth. He rushed and Sandy clinched.

Johnson landed to the head repeatedly. He followed Ferguson around the ring and the crowd jeered the white man because he would not mix things. As the round closed, Johnson sent a heavy right to the head.

The *Chronicle* said that during this round, after rushing away from a vicious swing, Sandy turned to the crowd and sung out, "Not a nigger in the world can beat me." The unwise remark cost Sandy many wallops.

According to the *Examiner*, rounds 8 through 14 were all Johnson's.

According to the *Call*, in rounds 11 through 15, Johnson played with Ferguson. He landed his left repeatedly on Sandy's head. Ferguson took terrific punishment. Still, Jack could not land his right to the jaw, for Ferguson was always moving away from him.

Perhaps unfairly, the *Call* also said, "Johnson did not show championship form." Jack feinted and tried to obtain an opening, but Sandy held his jaw behind his massive shoulder.

Once in a while, Ferguson unlimbered himself and sometimes landed his left, but did no damage. He rarely used his right. Sandy was tired but game.

14 - While being rushed from pillar to post, Ferguson shouted, "You see this fellow can't hit." He was greeted with more hoots.

15 - The two were hanging together and laughing, while the onlookers hooted. As they went to their corners, the crowd jeered them.

16 - As the round began, it seemed as if every man in the crowd was shouting, "Fight! Fight!" Johnson took the hint and tried to reach Ferguson's jaw with his right, but Sandy's height helped him, and with a little twist of his body he stopped the colored champion's blow with his shoulder.

The *Call* said Johnson sent Ferguson's head back. Jack crossed him with the right and Sandy went down to his knee.

The timekeeper counted to two and Sandy arose somewhat worried. He clinched and assumed the defensive. Johnson followed him all over the ring, trying to land another right, but Ferguson blocked the blows. The *Examiner* failed to mention the knockdown.

17 - Johnson staggered Ferguson with a left on the jaw. He sent him against the ropes. Ferguson came back with a vicious right that missed. Johnson kept sending his head back with lefts. He rushed him to the ropes and landed three hard lefts to the body. Ferguson landed a heavy left to the stomach. Johnson rushed him to the corner, and as Ferguson was pressed against the ropes he raised his knee and nearly fouled his colored opponent.

The *Chronicle* said that during this round, Ferguson took another trip though the ropes.

18 - Ferguson began to fight, trying some swings that missed. "He made such a poor showing that the crowd hissed him." When Johnson would swing the left for the body, Ferguson would duck low in the hope of saving himself punishment. Sandy slapped Johnson with his open glove and the crowd hooted.

According to the *Examiner*, in the 17th and 18th rounds, not much happened. It said the fight was dull.

19 - Ferguson landed a heavy right to the head. Johnson rushed him to the ropes and landed left and right to the head and body. Johnson staggered him with a hard right to the jaw. He used his left and kept sending Sandy's head back, landing several straight lefts.

20 - They shook hands to start the final round. Ferguson caught him with a left on the nose. Johnson lashed out with his left. Sandy clinched to smother the blows. They fiddled around the ring. Johnson shot his left, right, and left to the head and body and Ferguson saved himself by clinching. Johnson landed a heavy right on the jaw. They clinched.

Johnson tried desperately to knock him out, but failed. He worked hard and did all of the aggressive work.

Tim McGrath frantically appealed to Ferguson to use his right and fight back, "for old Boston's sake." However, Ferguson shook his head and intimated it was hurt.

Ferguson was thoroughly listless, apparently waiting for the end. At that point, Johnson seemed about equally as anxious to take things easy. Just before the end, Johnson landed a left on the face and right on the ear.

According to the *Call*, after the bell rang, Ferguson walked straight to his corner, seeming to realize that he had lost, so he did not wait to be informed of the fact officially. Referee Jack Welch tapped Johnson on the back and declared him the winner. "Ferguson retired to his corner and said the coon had to fight to win."

The *Examiner* said Referee Welch pointed his finger at Johnson and there was renewed hooting. "It was acknowledged, of course, the negro had made the better showing of the two, but no one seemed to think he had done himself proud by any means."

The *Chronicle* said no real fighting took place in the 18th through 20th rounds. The last few rounds were "slow, slower, slowest."

All of the local newspapers were fairly hard on both Johnson and Ferguson for this one. Although Johnson had won clearly and had beaten a large man considered to be in line for contention to Jeff's crown, the local writers were not impressed with the performance.

Summarizing the bout, the *Call* said Johnson easily outpointed Ferguson, but his cleverness was offset throughout by the burly man's clumsy and awkward style. It called the bout 20 rounds of "variegated milling. It was more comedy than fight at times." Ferguson was big and awkward, "without ability as a boxer and without any knowledge of ringcraft." Yet, he was so big and clumsy that it threw off Johnson. Sandy leaned so far back and kept his left so far out that Johnson's blows seldom landed. When Jack did land, he rarely was effective.

Ferguson was no more effective. Sandy's stinging left, which against others had the bite of a viper in it, proved harmless. His right was seldom used. Ferguson claimed to have injured it in the 3rd round. He often swung it like a flail and struck with his open glove. There was no force in it, or in any of his punches.

Early on, the spectators felt that neither man was doing the fighting expected of them. The crowd jeered repeatedly and urged them on sarcastically whenever they got busy, although the boxers were doing no damage. The fans were with Ferguson from the start, and joined his seconds in their calls for Sandy to go in and do something. He either did not know how to or was not willing to take a chance, for invariably he was on the receiving end of a punch when he did try.

Johnson did what he had to in order to remain ahead on points and win, but he did not do as much as he needed to in order to win impressively. "Johnson was the aggressor, in a mild sort of way, at all times, but there was something lacking. He could not make the spectators believe he was in earnest." It did not seem as if he was doing his best. He could outfeint Sandy at any time, and Ferguson seemed all at sea when Johnson made a few passes in front of his face.

For a while, Ferguson seemed anxious for an excuse to stop, claiming several blows were foul, even though they were palpably fair. Referee Welch ordered him to continue fighting.

The majority of the blows struck landed on Ferguson, but they seemed to have no effect on him.

Ferguson's only bright moment came in the 7th round. "In the seventh round Johnson stumbled down and the spectators thought Ferguson had him. Johnson was up in an instant, but for the time being he had all the fight taken out of him."

Johnson only commenced using his right in the 16th round, which made some spectators believe that he had bet on the number of rounds and had been carrying Ferguson. He knocked Ferguson down, though Sandy rose at two. Ferguson showed the first trace of blood in the 17th round.

Another *Call* summary said that in every round, Johnson sent Ferguson's head back with straight lefts. He knocked him through the ropes on two occasions and had him down for a two-count. Johnson did not begin fighting hard until the 15th round, when he tried to win. Regardless, Jack was the aggressor throughout.

Unfortunately, Ferguson's style did not match up well with Johnson's. Ferguson had a style that was not always easy to look good against. He had fought more to neutralize Johnson and survive rather than to take chances to beat him. He was what we might call a spoiler.

Johnson was not loathe to take victory however it came, and did not worry about how he looked in winning. Like Ferguson, he did not care to take too many chances. This led to a dull bout.

However, style and manner of victory left an impression, and mattered when it came to press and public opinion of a man's ability. Despite the clear victory over a big, strong, awkward, and defensive-minded opponent, the victory made the colored champion's stock drop.

> One point the spectators were agreed upon. That was that both men should keep as far away as possible from Jeffries. From the showing they made last night the big champion could have whipped both of them without turning a hair.[378]

W. W. Naughton of the *Examiner* called it 20 rounds of "burlesque boxing." Despite the fact that Johnson clearly had defeated a man with a solid record, Naughton was critical.

> No two heavyweights ever furnished a more spiritless display of fisticuffs. Johnson's showing was far from being in line with his fight with George Gardner. As a possible opponent of Jim Jeffries, Johnson has receded in the opinion of San Francisco fight patrons.
>
> The only fair knock-down of the match occurred in the seventh round, and it was Ferguson who scored. ...
>
> In some of the rounds after that Ferguson was on the floor, and he was also pushed through the ropes a couple of times. He was not felled with a clean punch, however. It was his clumsy way of bearing himself that caused him to flop and flounder around.
>
> It is seldom that a fight crowd shows such palpable feelings of disgust as the gathering at Colma did last night. In many of the rounds the negro and the white man stepped to the scratch amid a chorus of hooting and jeering, while the yell "Fight! Fight! Why don't you fight?" became monotonous.
>
> For a while the opinion prevailed that Johnson was under a wrap, his purpose being to allow Ferguson to stand before him the full twenty rounds. It was known that a good deal of money was bet on Ferguson's chances of lasting eighteen rounds, and some of the

---

[378] *San Francisco Call*, December 12, 1903.

disgusted spectators were quick to connect Johnson's disappointing work with this phase of the wagering.

There were many among the ringsiders who believed that it was simply Ferguson's natural awkwardness that bothered the negro and kept him from showing to advantage. In his affair in this city with Gardner Johnson boxed perfectly. He judged distances to a nicety and knew how to stop Gardner's punches with a little catlike wave of his hand. He baffled Gardner at every point and at the same time gave him a good drubbing.

The difference in size between Ferguson and Gardner may have had all to do with it. In last night's affair Johnson rarely landed a clean right cross, and this was one of his most telling blows in his fight with Gardner and in his later fight with big McVey at Los Angeles. They say he ripped out a half dozen of McVey's teeth with a crack of the right in the southern country. Last night his right would not have mashed a house fly.

As a matter of fact, all of Johnson's blows were lamentably deficient in force. He rapped Ferguson under the heart several times, but the big Bostonian appears to be as impervious to the effect of body-punching as is Champion Jeffries.

In the early rounds Johnson used a stinging straight left. He made a specialty of this punch again in the nineteenth and twentieth rounds, and when it was noticed how easily he reached Ferguson's face the crowd wondered why he had not pegged away with the left clear through the contest.

Ferguson's best effort was a kidney punch with the right. He resorted to it about a dozen times altogether ... and, as far as could be judged, this peculiar visitation hurt the colored man considerably.

In the later rounds, under frantic urging from his corner, Ferguson cut loose with a straight left. He tilted Johnson's head with it many times, but it was hard to hold Sandy to this particular style of boxing.

It was one of the humors of the contest to watch Tim McGrath bending in through the ropes and crying in a beseeching voice; "For my sake, Sandy, hit him with the left, do, Sandy, please."

The two heavies seemed to know that they were the josh of the spectators, and they laughed derisively in many of the rounds. Ferguson, too, acted in a thoroughly irresponsible way, standing with his back to the ropes and his hands down many times when Johnson was only a foot or two distant. It looked as though all Johnson required last night was a small amount of fighting blood to encompass Ferguson's downfall a dozen times.

Naughton also said that after the 7th round, the rounds were all Johnson's.

> From that point on the rounds were much alike, Ferguson varying the monotony at times by spreading his legs and going to the floor or by projecting himself half-way through the ropes. He shouted to one of the newspaper men, "Wait till the last five rounds," and those who heard it imagined that Sandy was saving himself for a whirlwind finish.

However, that fast finish never came.

Naughton argued that although Johnson won the decision, "Jack Johnson's showing at Colma last night did anything but entitle him to a match with Jeffries for the championship." He said the performance served to show that the colored champion would be no match for Jeffries.[379]

Other local papers agreed that Johnson's victory actually reduced the opinion of him. The *San Francisco Evening Post* said it was a poor contest that disgusted the spectators. It went so far as to say that the Colma Athletic Club probably had conducted its last fight. The contest was both unpleasant and unprofitable. Johnson was called a finished boxer but a poor fighter. He won the decision after 20 harmless rounds of sparring.

> From the beginning of the mill to its finish the African was in the lead. He parried Sandy's punches and countered lightly with both hands.

> At no time, however, did he strike hard enough to break an egg. Occasionally his target slipped to the mat, but he quickly regained his feet and roughly pressed in, knowing that the negro was considerate enough not to hurt him.

It said the bout was reminiscent of the Johnson-Gardner fight, in which, according to the *Evening Post*, "Johnson was given the decision, but he hardly deserved it, for he simply dodged about and avoided receiving any of the clumsy leads the Lowell man aimed at him. He did not counter with effect and simply received the long end of the purse on account of his dancing tactics." The next-day accounts did not agree, though.

Like the *Call* and *Examiner*, the *Evening Post* also felt that Johnson would have zero chance with Jeffries.

> Last night's bout showed conclusively that Johnson is no match for Jeffries. A mill between the negro and the champion would not draw. ... In the first place, Johnson is too soft a tapper to make an impression on Jeffries. The past has shown that the man who will defeat the big fellow must be a man of extreme speed, size and cleverness.

---

[379] *San Francisco Examiner*, December 12, 1903.

He must in addition have a hard punch and the ability to send it home with rapidity and effect.

Johnson has only one of the high qualities to be found in the coming champion and that is cleverness. He is too small, however, to cope with Jeffries and in punching power he hardly compares to Young Corbett or Frankie Neil. He will have to retire to the woods and look for bouts with dubs or men of his own race. He does not show the quality to entitle him to a battle with the champion of the world.[380]

Young Corbett was a featherweight and Frankie Neil was a bantamweight, so saying that Johnson's punching power hardly compared with them was a pretty big insult.

The *San Francisco Chronicle* called the bout a "roaring farce" and a poor exhibition. It seemed to realize that it was a bad style matchup. Johnson was the only one to show any knowledge of the game. "One clever big black, who couldn't hit hard enough to put his man away, and one awkward, big, alleged fighter who wouldn't fight tells the whole story of the unpleasantness." Johnson tried, but never took an unnecessary chance. "The absolute badness of the Scotchman put Johnson at a disadvantage." Johnson could not exhibit his fancy footwork because Ferguson rarely made an advance. Johnson's pretty blocking was rarely in evidence because Ferguson rarely did any leading. Sandy appeared to be happy to have stood up for the 20 rounds. Ferguson's style was "so miserably bad as to completely overshadow all of Jack Johnson's cleverness."

Ferguson appeared to treat the bout as a joke. He tried some tricks such as feigning grogginess and allowing his knees to give way after a light tap. He even shouted some "comedy stuff" at the audience, but they were not amused, and yelled at him to go in and fight. Ferguson's methods were "very bad." He repeatedly made low blow claims to the "obdurate Welch, who always motioned for him to go on." Sandy started his blows from too far back and with his weight on his rear foot. In that position he saved himself from the repeated jabs, but did no good from an offensive standpoint.

Johnson was always set and ready to attack, but the necessary steam was lacking. At intervals Sandy straightened up and seemed about ready to use his superior strength, but a jab sent his head back, which invariably caused him to return to the "old, unnatural position."

Despite the criticisms of Johnson's power, clearly he hit hard enough to make Sandy very cautious, and this was a man who had done well with big strong men like Ruhlin and Armstrong. Yet the locals seemed to overlook this.

Ferguson was a great disappointment, given that he had looked good in training. This reminded sports of George Gardner, who had looked great in training before the Fitzsimmons fight, only to disappoint when in action.

---

[380] *San Francisco Evening Post*, December 12, 1903.

Of course, gym work is a lot different than the actual fight, and the opponent has something to say about how a fighter looks. The local writers failed to give Johnson the credit for making Sandy look bad. Perhaps it was a bit of a backlash to all the good publicity that Johnson had been receiving.

Only a couple thousand people saw the bout, and they felt like they were suckers and gullible for having paid to see it, believing the men to be more than they were.

The *Chronicle* agreed that neither combatant would be a contest for Jeffries.

> "To the woods" with the talk about either of them meeting Jeffries after what happened in the Colma arena last night. It would be nothing short of a slaughter, with Jeffries wielding the cleaver. Johnson is a clever boxer, and that lets him out. Ferguson is nothing at all that can be commended in a fighting way.[381]

Regardless of their potential lack of fairness, the opinion of the San Francisco press and public mattered, because San Francisco was one of the few places in the country at that time that was allowing fights of the length required for championship bouts, and it had the population necessary to make them lucrative. From 1901 to 1904, all of James J. Jeffries' championship fights were and would be held in San Francisco.

What the critics failed to acknowledge or realize was that Jack Johnson did not fight to impress, nor to win by knockout, nor to entertain the fans. He fought to win. Throwing a lot of punches, or trying to knock out an opponent meant that Johnson might leave himself exposed to being hit, hurt, or stopped himself, and it also might leave him fatigued. A fatigued fighter is more vulnerable to being hit, to having slower reactions to punches, and not taking them as well. Johnson was a very cautious and careful fighter. Fighting hard on a consistent basis over 20 rounds is not easy. Johnson knew himself, knew the dangers and risks involved in a lengthy bout with small gloves, and did what he had to do to secure victory against a clever, cagey, much larger, and potentially dangerous big man. The fans and critics did not have to absorb the punches from five-ounce gloves, nor did they have to suffer the potential consequences of a loss. Given how hard the press was on him in a victory, imagine what they would have said had he lost. Plus, styles make fights. Ferguson's style did not lend itself to an entertaining affair. Very few writers realized or chose to recognize this.

Regardless, Johnson's style and methodology often brought him expert criticism and fan loathing. A cautious style could mean less ticket sales and demand to see Johnson fight, which meant that a potential championship bout would be less lucrative to a promoter or to a champion, who not only might be taking a competitive risk but a financial one. Champions typically want more money for a riskier fight, not less. However, risky fights were

---

[381] *San Francisco Chronicle*, December 12, 1903.

only worth big money if fans demanded to see them. Hence, there would be consequences to Johnson for using such a style, even with a victory.

A couple days after the bout, Naughton said that sports were now laughing at the idea of Jeffries and Johnson meeting. The opinion was that if Jack was not under contract to let Ferguson stay 20 rounds, then Johnson was frightened of him. Ferguson did his best, but "his best was worse than mediocre."

> Johnson is a horse of another color. He has made several good fights in this city and Los Angeles and we began to figure on him as the man destined to batter and bewilder herculean Jim Jeffries and relieve him of the championship.

> As matters are now, to remind a man that he boosted Johnson as a fit opponent for Jeffries is to invite a quarrel.

> There are few who argue that Johnson did not lose caste by his fight with Ferguson. Some of these have suggested, rather naively, that Johnson might have held back a bit in order to encourage Jeffries to withdraw the color bar.

> This is far fetched. Johnson's best hope of gaining recognition from Jeffries was by standing well with the sport-loving public. From the turn things have taken the negro will find no one to champion his cause if he tries to draw Jeffries into a match.

> Johnson says that Ferguson is a dangerous, awkward man to handle. So was big Joe McAuliffe, who Peter Jackson trimmed so neatly and completely at the old California Club fifteen years ago. ...

> It was purely on the strength of Johnson's supposed knowledge of neat ringmanship that he was talked of as an opponent for Jeffries. If his talents in the direction named are insufficient to enable him to defeat Ferguson in a clean-cut manner he must perforce admit that he stands a mighty poor show of subduing Jeffries.

> Johnson will be heard from again, but not as a world's championship candidate. ... [H]e would do well to engage in work calculated to increase his punching force.[382]

What this analysis failed to consider was that Johnson won, and was a consistent winner at that point in his career. Regardless of his knockout or finishing power, he hit hard enough to make a big man cautious against him. He had gone undefeated in seven fights in 1903.

The gate receipts from the fight allegedly were $1,732. The boxers received 50%, which was then evenly divided. Therefore, each fighter earned $433, not bad at all by normal societal standards at that time, but not

---

[382] *San Francisco Examiner,* December 13, 1903.

so great for elite fighters either. Ferguson was set to travel to Chicago, where he was to box Klondike.

The *Examiner* printed a poem about the fight, which certainly gave the impression that racial animus had at least something to do with the criticism of Johnson:

Sing a song o' Colma, pockets full o' "rhi,"
Four an' twenty uppercuts, wouldn't hurt a fly.
When the round was over, nigger outer breff - -
Isn't he a gally coon to talk o' fightin' Jeff?
"Club" was in the box office countin' up the money,
Gods were in the gallery bawlin' "Soak him, honey,"
Two big dubs a-gigglin', everybody sore,
Crowd hotfootin' to the train yellin' "Nevermore."[383]

The *Police Gazette's* report called the Johnson-Ferguson fight uninteresting. Johnson was the aggressor, landing his left often. Ferguson occasionally landed his jab, but without effect. Sandy was hooted and hissed because he was not willing. Johnson's performance was called disappointing.

If his fight the other night was the best evidence of his ability that Jack Johnson can give then he had better chloroform his ambition to ever become heavyweight champion of the world and content himself with occupying a less exalted sphere. Incidentally, Jim Jeffries is to be pitied for so hastily drawing the color line, and by so doing cheating himself out of a chance to add many thousands of dollars to his already plethoric bank roll by doing up the negro with neatness and celerity. It is plainly evident now that Jack Johnson, the huge Texan Black, has no pugilistic claims to justify his classification with the champion. He is all right in his own division and is probably the best negro fighter in the world today, but that isn't saying very much, for since the days of Peter Jackson there hasn't been a black-skinned fighter who merited serious consideration as an aspirant for championship honors. Johnson fought twenty rounds with Sandy Ferguson...[and it] it was about as uninteresting an affair as heavyweights could furnish. Neither man showed enough form to try conclusions with the champion. Jeffries, without extending himself, could defeat both men in the same ring.

What might be called the only clean knockdown occurred in the seventh round, and it was Ferguson's. Johnson, at the same time, was fooling near the ropes and creating the belief that he was under a pull. Later it was thought by many of the ringsiders that it was Ferguson's awkwardness that bothered the negro. At this point Ferguson saw an

[383] *San Francisco Examiner,* December 13, 1903.

opening and whipped his right across on the chin, dropping Johnson to the mat.

Ferguson was on the floor in some of the rounds that followed and was also pushed through the ropes a couple of times, but was never knocked to the mat with a punch. It was his manner of floundering when hard pressed that put him off his balance.

The contest created universal disgust. For a while the impression prevailed that Johnson was under a wrap, so that his friends could get a bet down on him. Ferguson was badly battered and took a lot of punishment, but Johnson's showing was a great disappointment to those who imagined that he might be pitted against Jeffries.[384]

Because he was black, even if Johnson had looked good, Jim Jeffries was not going to fight him. However, Johnson's showing gave Jeffries another excuse and justification for not doing so, and he would not have to take as much heat for refusing to fight Johnson. Jeffries said,

If the public demands that I should fight Johnson I will surely have to decline. … If I am defeated, the championship will go to a white man, for I will not fight a colored one. Now mind you, I am not shirking from this match because I am afraid of Johnson, for I think I could lick him as easily as I have the rest, but I simply will not fight a colored man for the championship. The only regret I feel is that Sandy Ferguson did not whip Johnson. I would have willingly given Ferguson a match – I was anxious that he should win in order that I might do so.[385]

Jim Corbett told a reporter that a Jeffries-Johnson championship fight "would be no attraction, and there would be nothing but Jeffries to it." Corbett "did not blame Jeffries for drawing the color line, and thought that Johnson should meet such men as Ruhlin, Munroe, Hart and one or two others before going after the world's champion." However, those men all drew the color line on Johnson.[386]

On December 15, 1903 in Boston, 200-pound Jack Munroe stopped 6'4" 220-pound Al Limerick in the 4th round. Limerick's claim to fame was that he had knocked out Jack O'Brien in the 3rd round of a sparring bout. Against Limerick, Munroe showed aggressiveness and punching power. One reporter said, "Munroe was cheered to the echo and he deserved it. He has gone up another rung of the pugilistic ladder, and has stronger claims than ever for a match with Jeffries." In preparation for the bout, Munroe had been sparring with Bob Armstrong and Jack "Twin" Sullivan, and observers had called Munroe quick, clever, and strong, with a superb physique.

---

[384] *Police Gazette*, December 26, 1903.
[385] *Boston Globe*, December 14 1903.
[386] *Boston Herald*, December 15, 1903.

The next day, Jeffries "admitted that Jack [Munroe] has a stronger claim for a match for the title than he had a week ago. Jeff says that if Munroe will fight a couple more of the big fellows and beat them he will give him a match." The *Boston Post*'s Rob Roy said, "Munroe stands today before the sporting world the one and only legitimate rival that Champion Jim Jeffries has. ... As a puncher he is one of the most tremendous I ever saw." He believed that no one but Jeffries could defeat Munroe. Many in the press were boosting the white Munroe as much as they could.[387]

On December 17, 1903 at Kitty Hawk, North Carolina, Wilbur and Orville Wright became the first persons to invent and successfully fly a motorized airplane.

1903 was also the year that Henry Ford started his auto company, which by October 1908 began mass-producing automobiles (the Model T) and making them more affordable to those who were not rich. Jack Johnson would become a huge fan of the automobile, purchasing many during his lifetime.

On December 26, 1903 in Chicago, Sandy Ferguson won a 6-round decision over Klondike Haines. Defeating such a well-respected boxer showed that Ferguson was better than some had believed after the Johnson bout.

Some thought that Jack Johnson's relatively poor showing in the Ferguson fight might do him some good, because it might make more fighters willing to take him on. Denver Ed Martin, who had stopped Ferguson in 5 rounds, was particularly critical of Jack, saying, "Johnson should have effectually whipped that fellow Ferguson inside of ten rounds. I think he was afraid of Ferguson, and I should like to have a return match with him.... I am certain I can beat him and hope he will give me a show." Eventually, Martin would earn his chance at a rematch with Johnson.[388]

The only white boxer to take on Johnson in the past year, since Fred Russell in December 1902, was Sandy Ferguson. Regardless of Jack's most recent performance against Ferguson, no white fighter other than Ferguson would step into the ring with Johnson until 1905. Hence, despite the criticisms, the white heavyweights were none too eager to enter the ring with Jack Johnson.

On January 5, 1904 in Boston, in their rematch, 175-pound Marvin Hart fought 167-pound George Gardner to a 15-round draw. However, the spectators and the press agreed that the aggressive and hard-punching Hart, who had scored a knockdown in the 2nd round and hurt Gardner on several other occasions, had clearly won and deserved the decision.

On January 18, 1904 in Boston, Sandy Ferguson scored a KO2 over Jim Galvin.

[387] *Boston Post, Boston Globe, Boston Herald*, December 16, 17, 1903.
[388] *Police Gazette*, January 9, 1904.

In his early 1904 inaugural address, Mississippi Governor James K. Vardaman, a Democrat, said that education had no deterrent influence upon the black race in the commission of crime, and that the Negro grew more criminal as he became more intelligent. He felt that education harmed the black race more than it helped it. Vardaman was a pro-slavery advocate who believed that negroes were less than human, unworthy of consideration, and had no rights which whites need respect. It was opined that by obtaining his goal of limiting educational opportunity for blacks, the governor would not only limit them economically but could also limit their right to vote.[389]

CAN HE MAKE IT?

Freeman, January 2, 1904

---

[389] *Colored American*, January 30, 1904; *Seattle Republican*, April 8, 1904; *Muskogee Cimeter*, August 11, 1904.

In late January, 1904, Jim Jeffries said, "As for Jack Johnson, I will pass him up. There would be no money in it for me to fight him. He failed to put out Ferguson, and there is where the public would draw the line."[390]

Jack Munroe scheduled a fight with Tom Sharkey. Jeffries said, "Munroe has done the proper thing by taking on Sharkey, whom I consider a hard proposition. If he whips him he will be in line for heavyweight honors."[391]

As of February 1904, from New York, Jeffries said, "I don't think the public wants me to defend my title against any one but a white man. Don't think I am afraid of a negro. I'm not. They can be licked just as easily as anybody else." Bill Delaney said Jeff would fight neither Johnson nor any other colored man, if he had any say in the matter and could prevent it.[392]

At that time, Jack Johnson was in Philadelphia. His next bout came about in an unusual manner. Jack McGuigan, manager of Philadelphia's National Athletic Club, had arranged a main event between Kid Carter and Billy Stift, to be held on Saturday, February 6, 1904. However, he made the bout via a third party who might have been less than on the up-and-up. It turned out that Stift had never even heard of the match. So McGuigan wired to Sandy Ferguson to come quickly from Boston as a last-minute substitute. Sandy arrived. However, the night of the bout, Carter refused to meet Ferguson. He argued that he had agreed to meet Stift, and it was up to the club to produce him.

Desperate for a main event, McGuigan saw that Jack Johnson was in the house as a spectator. McGuigan asked Johnson to go on with Ferguson, and vice versa. Johnson and Ferguson got together in the lobby and talked it over. "Such easy money! How could they help it?" Jack and Sandy agreed to do the 6-round bout.

Manager McGuigan then informed the spectators about what had transpired. He offered to refund the money to those who were dissatisfied. Only two persons took him up on his offer.

Johnson and Ferguson proceeded to box in their impromptu bout. However, the *Philadelphia Inquirer* called it a "raw fake." Neither man tried at all. They just went through the motions so they could make some money. "After warning and threatening them, and there being no improvement in their work, Manager McGuigan jumped out of the ring, leaving them there." McGuigan, who had been acting as referee, decided that the men were trying to obtain money without actually doing much, so he terminated the bout early, in the 5th round, and left the ring. Essentially, doing so was his way of ruling it a no contest. The *Inquirer* harshly declared,

> This should be the last of Johnson and Ferguson in this city or anywhere else. There is not the slightest doubt that Johnson was bound to not hurt or stop Ferguson; there would have been no way

[390] *Detroit Free Press*, January 31, 1904.
[391] *Police Gazette*, February 6, 1904.
[392] *Philadelphia Inquirer*, February 6, 1904; *Philadelphia Press*, February 7, 1904.

of pulling the latter into the ring with the big black if the bout had been on the level.

In explanation of his showing Ferguson said that he had come on to box Carter and that he was in no condition to box so big a fellow as Johnson. He should not have gone on with Johnson. ... For the sake of a little easy money he has killed himself in this town and knocked the game out of which he could earn a good living if he only had the courage. As for Mr. Johnson, the quicker he turns himself loose from Philadelphia the better it will be for the boxing game. He has all the earmarks of a great fighter, but he has passed up his usefulness in this town.[393]

Basically, either Ferguson had gotten Johnson to agree to take it easy, or they fought cautiously owing to mutual respect. Their perspective was that they were doing the management a big favor by going on at all. Without them agreeing to box, the show would have been canceled. Ferguson was a last-minute substitute to fight Carter, and Johnson had just been a spectator.

Johnson was hurt by the accusations. He called the *Philadelphia Record* office to defend himself. He said that he did the best he could under the circumstances. He claimed not to have faked or stalled, and should not be called a faker, given that he did all of the leading and forcing of the pace from start to finish.

I had no idea of boxing when I went to the National Club on Saturday night. I had just gotten back from a trip to Baltimore and had eaten a big supper, and during the day I had drank quite a lot of water. ... I was in no condition to box a hard contest, and did not want to go on, but merely did so to oblige the club manager, Mr. McGuigan. I never faked a fight in my life, and have no cause to do so here, as I have had lots of chances to fake in California, where I was a 10 to 4 favorite, and where I could have made a lot of money by throwing a fight for the gamblers, who will offer lots of inducements out there to men who can be bought. I was willing to continue to the end of the six rounds, but the referee left the ring and did not give me a chance to finish the bout. Ferguson is a big, husky fellow and Gus Ruhlin could not stop him in 15 rounds, and I have previously tried to stop him...but failed to do so.[394]

The *Police Gazette's* report on this substitute bout said,

It was evident the pair had an understanding, for neither did any real fighting until after the third round, in which the referee announced that he would stop the bout if there was no improvement in the work

---

[393] *Philadelphia Inquirer*, February 8, 1904.
[394] *Philadelphia Record, Philadelphia Evening Bulletin*, February 8, 1904.

of the men. This had little effect and Referee McGuigan left the ring disgusted with the farce.[395]

At that time, the National Boxing Association, consisting of 15 clubs throughout the nation, was organized to regulate the sport and promote its interests. Weight classifications included, 105, 110, 116, 122, 127, 133, 140, 148, 158, 175, and 175+.[396]

Johnson continued lobbying for a title shot, saying, "Unless Jeffries consents to withdraw his color-line declaration and fight me, I shall claim the world's championship. It was not my fault that I was born black, and Jeffries will have to meet me in three months or drop the championship title."[397]

On February 9 in Boston, in a wrestling match, Jack Munroe and Gus Ruhlin wrestled to a draw. Neither man could secure a fall after 1 hour and 15 minutes of wrestling. Some boxers made additional money in wrestling bouts.[398]

Black Bill

Despite the criticism about the recent Ferguson bout, Johnson was still in demand in Philadelphia. Nine days later, on Monday February 15, 1904 in Philadelphia, for the Lenox Athletic Club, Johnson fought Black Bill, whose real name was Claude Brooks. Bill was then listed as fighting out of Merchantville, New Jersey. He stood six-feet tall and was 26 years old, one year older than Johnson. He had been fighting since 1897. Secondary sources say he had at least 20 bouts of experience. Bill held 6-round no-decision newspaper victories over Charley Stevenson (three times), Bob Long, and the very experienced Young Peter Jackson (who had fought welterweight champ Joe Walcott to a 20-round draw). In 1903, Bill "lost" 6-round no-decision bouts to Stevenson and George Cole, and Larry Temple stopped Bill in the 3rd round, his only official loss. Bill had won five bouts since then.

They fought for a crowded house. Johnson had the height and reach advantages, and a little bit of an advantage in weight, but not much.

In the first 2 rounds, Bill was quite aggressive, going at Jack and doing most of the leading.

---

[395] *Police Gazette*, February 27, 1904.
[396] *Philadelphia Evening Bulletin*, February 8, 1904.
[397] *Philadelphia Record, Detroit Free Press*, February 8, 1904.
[398] *Police Gazette*, February 27, 1904.

1 - Bill landed a hard left to the nose. However, Johnson came back with a quick left and right to the jaw. Bill again landed his left to the face, and Jack caught him with a vicious left to the nose, which caused Bill to clinch.

2 - In quick succession, Bill twice landed his left to the nose. Johnson then cut loose and hammered him with right and left to the face and body. He ended the mix-up with a hard right to Bill's ear.

3 - Johnson started in as though he wanted to finish Bill. He went at him and hammered Bill with right and left. Bill had to hang on to save himself.

4 - Johnson continually jabbed his man. Near the end of the round, he started using his right, and sent Bill to his knees with a hard right behind the ear.

Bill rose in an instant, but went down again from a right to the jaw. This time he remained down for 8 seconds.

In the 5th and 6th rounds, Johnson was always after him, but Bill clinched and hugged often enough to save himself.

5 - Johnson fought himself out of a clinch and rushed Bill across the ring, putting him to his knees.

6 - Throughout the round, Bill continued using his hanging-on tactics to survive and stay the limit.

The *Philadelphia Record* and *Philadelphia Evening Bulletin* agreed that Johnson had the advantage in the hot and fast 6-round bout. Bill had been down twice in the 4th round and once in the 5th. He was hurt from the 3rd round on, and only his incessant clinching and hugging tactics saved him from being stopped. Johnson could not land the decisive blow, so it lasted the distance.[399]

The *Police Gazette* reported,

> Johnson gave Black Bill a severe drubbing for six rounds, but was unable to land the blow soporific.

> Johnson used his left effectively and soon had Bill bleeding from the mouth. He then brought his right into play and smashed Bill's jaw hard. The latter took the punishment gamely, but seemed afraid to lead. There were several hot mixups, but Johnson easily held his opponent safe throughout.

> In the last round he made a desperate effort to bring the bout to an end before the gong, and although he hit Bill hard and often the Merchantville man was on hand at the gong.[400]

Despite the dominant performance against Black Bill, some Philadelphians still were not sold on Johnson, and remained begrudging in

---

[399] *Philadelphia Record, Philadelphia Evening Bulletin*, February 16, 1904.
[400] *Police Gazette*, March 5, 1904.

their praise of the black man. Over a week later, the *Philadelphia Record* wrote,

> If any of the lovers of boxing were really worried over the idea that the championship of the world was likely to fall to a colored man they can cease their lamentations for a while at least. ... One thing is an almost absolute certainty. If the championship ever goes to a colored man his name is not Jack Johnson. Johnson's performances in this city have not been anything like that of a champion or of a boxer who ever had any chance of disputing the honor with a man of either the calibre of James Jeffries or Bob Fitzsimmons.

The *Record* went on to say that previously, Johnson had made a good impression with his neat and workmanlike dispatch of Joe Butler. However, his subsequent work had wiped out the good impression left by that contest. His recent Ferguson bout suggested a "lack of form," and its tameness did not please the spectators, who thought Jack was faking. Johnson was not happy about that.

He was given a chance to prove himself against Black Bill. When they fought, Johnson appeared to be trying as hard as he could to stop him, but could not do so. "When it is considered that Larry Temple put Black Bill away in two rounds, and that George Cole beat him badly in six rounds and really knocked him out, it is hard to see why any one should worry over any possibility of Johnson ever becoming heavy-weight champion of the world."[401]

This criticism was harsh and unfair, given that Johnson dominated Bill and had almost taken him out in a short bout, dropping him three times in only 6 rounds. Bill survived by clinching often. Plus, he had been stopped only once before. Still, many writers were not overly impressed with Johnson, and were looking for ways to criticize or belittle him, even when he won clearly. It seems that this was a recent theme that writers had caught onto and perpetuated.

Perhaps it was all a backlash to the positive publicity that Johnson had been receiving, in order to curtail the momentum for his challenge to Jeffries. After all, there were those who did not like the idea of a black man challenging for what they felt a white man should own. Obviously, at the very least, these critics were not satisfied easily, wanting an exciting dominant performance terminating with a knockout before they would give any credit. That was not always easily done against solid experienced pros, particularly ones who knew how to survive. The ironic catch-22 is that sometimes when Johnson did knock out his foe, instead of giving him full credit, the press chose to denigrate his opponent.

On February 26, 1904 at Chicago's Battery D, Jack Johnson was in attendance to watch a Canadian-born fighter named Tommy Burns, formerly known as Noah Brusso, knock out George Shrosbree in the 5th

---

[401] *Philadelphia Record*, February 28, 1904.

round of their 158-pound middleweight bout. In the main event, top 170-pound light-heavyweights Jack Root and George Gardner fought to a 6-round draw.[402]

On February 27, 1904 in Philadelphia, 196-pound 27-year-old Jack Munroe "won" a 6-round no-decision bout against 182-pound 30-year-old Tom Sharkey. The *Police Gazette* reported that Munroe had both outboxed and outslugged Sharkey. Both were down in the 1st round, first Sharkey, then Munroe, who rose and dominated thereafter. The performance made believers out of many skeptics.

The *Police Gazette* agreed that Munroe had earned his right to a title shot. He had defeated strong punchers in Maher, Limerick, and Sharkey, which supported his claims that he could compete with Jeffries, and his claim that his performance in the Jeffries exhibition was no fluke. A bout between the two would give Jeffries the opportunity for revenge; to prove false Munroe's claims to have bested and dropped him in their 4-round exhibition. Plus, he was white, so he was perfect. The pair accepted San Francisco's Yosemite Athletic Club's offer of a $25,000 purse for a fight between them.[403]

Jack Munroe did not have anywhere near the experience against tough opposition that Johnson did, and primarily had built his record on nobodies or has-beens in short bouts. Yet, his challenge was being boosted. He did not have to endure the level of criticism that Jack Johnson did.

Johnson had a bout scheduled with John Willie in Chicago, set to be held March 11. Jack agreed to forfeit his share of the purse if he failed to stop Willie within 6 rounds. This was a tall task, because Willie was coming off a late-January 6-round draw with the hard-punching Marvin Hart.

However, someone tried to change the bout's terms, which would make it more of a hippodrome/fake. Johnson would not agree to such terms. Hence, the Willie bout was called off.

> It was learned yesterday that each man was to receive a stated amount for his services, which was satisfactory, but Johnson says he was asked to permit Willie to stay the limit and also to accept a knockdown, which he refused, so the management declared the match off. Johnson is without doubt the most scientific colored heavyweight in the world. He is making Chicago his home, and says he does not care to get mixed up in any shady fight transactions. He might have failed in stopping Willie, as the latter is a tough proposition to down for the count, but he showed his willingness to try at the expense of his reputation.[404]

---

[402] *Chicago Daily News*, February 27, 1904.
[403] *Police Gazette*, March 12. 1904; *Boston Post*, February 28, 1904. The Jeffries-Munroe championship fight originally was scheduled for June, but shortly before it was scheduled to take place, Jeffries suffered swelling on his knee, necessitating a postponement until August.
[404] *Chicago Daily Tribune*, March 11, 1904.

On March 16, 1904 in Hot Springs, Arkansas, 185-pound Marvin Hart narrowly won a 20-round decision over an alleged 197-pound Sandy Ferguson. Most thought Sandy had at least earned a draw, and some even thought Ferguson had won. Ferguson used his laid-back outside style, boxing with his effective jab, and occasionally landing a hard right, demonstrating his skill. He even dropped and hurt Hart. However, Hart was the active aggressor throughout, throwing vicious blows to the head and body, punishing the tough Ferguson. It was a very close bout, but Hart's power, aggression, and activity gave him the slight edge with the referee.

Regardless of the decision, the bout proved that Sandy Ferguson was an underrated quality fighter, and explains why Jack Johnson did not have such an easy time with him.

In April 1904, Johnson would return to the West Coast for a third bout with Sam McVey, whom he had defeated clearly twice already.

They were set to fight on April 22 at San Francisco's Mechanics' Pavilion, for the newly formed Shasta Club. McVey had been quietly training for the past month in his hometown of Oxnard. Johnson was set to leave Chicago and arrive in San Francisco some time during the second week of April.

The bout was expected to attract an unusual amount of interest, owing to the fact that it would be a meeting of "the two greatest colored men." "It is now generally thought that if Jeffries defeats Monroe he will withdraw his refusal to meet a colored man and take on the winner of this month's bout." Of course, that might have been wishful thinking, or just a way to promote and hype the upcoming bout.[405]

---

[405] *San Francisco Chronicle*, April 8, 1904.

Jim Coffroth, the Shasta Club's matchmaker, noted how the two boxers had filled the house in Los Angeles, drawing the largest crowd ever known in that town. Dollars make sense to promoters, which explains why he made the match. Coffroth said Johnson had defeated McVey, but had to go some to do it, for Sam gave him a hard, exciting battle. However, the knowing ones were expecting Johnson to win by a fairly wide margin, as he had done on the two previous occasions they had met.

JACK JOHNSON

SAM McVEY

Despite Jeff's staunch refusal to do so, Coffroth was hoping to convince Jeffries to remove the color line and fight the winner "for the sake of the money, if nothing else." The *Chronicle's* writer, Waldemar Young, opined, "But if [Jeffries] does agree to meet the winner of this month's fight, it will be 'Goodbye, Mistah Johnson; curtains for you.' All that's left of the aspirant will be gathered together and sent to his folks."[406]

---

[406] *San Francisco Chronicle*, April 10, 1904.

On April 12, McVey arrived from Oxnard and took up training quarters at Millett's roadhouse at Colma. Johnson was due to arrive that night. They had agreed to Eddie Graney to referee their bout.

After having been in New York for about six months, Jeffries arrived in San Francisco as well. He was set to start training at Harbin Springs for the upcoming Munroe bout.[407]

The *San Francisco Bulletin* described Johnson as a "showy colored man," who wore good clothes and "makes some pretensions to being a beau among the gentle sex of Colordom."

Johnson was anxious to wipe out the memory of the bad showing he had made with Sandy Ferguson the previous December at Colma. The *Bulletin* said that his performance on that occasion was lamentably poor. Jack had a variety of excuses to explain it away, including either a sore arm or that he was over-cautious owing to his anxiety to get on with Jeffries, not wanting to risk a loss. He said Ferguson would not have a chance with him if he cut loose. Johnson also said,

> Come ovah and see me. I'm training at Link Dennis' in Oakland. Ah'll be there from now till next Friday night. Ah want to show you Ah've got a punch.

> I am awful glad I got this match. I want to have the people here in San Francisco see me right. I boxed George Gardner twenty rounds heer a year and a half ago and got the decision. Every one wondered why I didn't put him out. Why, I was fortunate to be able to stand up. They drove me in a carriage from the hospital to the ringside.

> I know the Ferguson bout was not any too good, but I have already explained about that. Here's my chance to show what I can do and I want to, as I'm anxious to get on with Jeffries or the winner of the Jeff-Monroe fight.

---

[407] *San Francisco Chronicle*, April 13, 1904.

McVey is a tough customer – the toughest, I think, in the country. Although I twice got a decision over him in twenty rounds, I knew I was in a fight after each occasion. He is the hardest hitter in the business, in my opinion, but I shall see that he don't hit me.[408]

A week before the fight, on April 15, Johnson weighed 199 pounds. He said he would box McVey at about 190. McVey would "no doubt weigh close to 215."

Betting opened on the 19th with Johnson the 10 to 8 favorite. The city's colored population was divided in its opinion, but a slight majority thought Johnson would win. The entire Oxnard sporting population was expected to come up to San Francisco to watch the fight, and it was anticipated that the odds would shift once they arrived and bet on McVey.

McVey was training for the contest "as though his life depended upon it." His manager, Billy Roche, expected him to win, saying,

McVey will win Friday night. I base my opinion on the fact that he is faster by far than he was before. Furthermore, he never should have gone on on that occasion. He was suffering from gastritis and did not want to disappoint the club and its members. Despite that, I put Johnson's victory down to pure good luck. I don't think any man in the world can go through twenty rounds of fighting with McVey without getting hit hard and often. Johnson managed to escape throughout. The ring will be much smaller on this occasion and my champion will get him sure. To show my faith in his chances I have today left with Harry Corbett $2,000 to bet on his chances.[409]

From his training quarters, Johnson said,

I am good as I ever was and will put McVey out in short order. I know he is big and strong, but he will find when we next come together that I have learned something in the past few months. This next bout will be a fast one. There will be no time wasted in fancy sparring, for I shall go right in, set a rapid pace and establish the fact that I am a fighter as well as a clever boxer.

However, Harry Corbett thought that McVey was a physical wonder.

He is about the strongest made and the most wiry man I have ever seen. If he is half as good as he looks he should give Johnson a beating. If he wins on Friday night I shall never quit trying until I succeed in matching him with the winner of the Jeffries-Munroe battle.[410]

A physician on behalf of the Shasta Club examined McVey and said that he was in perfect condition, and that except for height, he was the biggest

[408] *San Francisco Bulletin,* April 16, 1904.
[409] *San Francisco Bulletin,* April 19, 1904.
[410] *San Francisco Evening Post,* April 20, 1904.

pugilist he had ever examined. "He is the biggest man for his inches in the world." The doctor claimed that although Jeffries was taller, McVey was bigger in every way. In fact, Jeffries, who was currently weighting 250 and generally fought between 220 and 230, weighed more than McVey did. Regardless, clearly McVey was a wonderfully muscular, impressive-looking fighter.

Spider Kelly, who was training Sam, said that McVey would defeat Johnson. The Spider had once been behind Toothpick Kelly, whom he thought was a future champion, until McVey knocked him out. It took them an hour to restore the Toothpick to consciousness. Harry Stuart, the famous Los Angeles referee, had seen the two prior fights between Johnson and McVey, and yet he still felt that McVey would win this time.[411]

The local press reported that except for height, McVey was larger and bigger than Johnson in every way. He even had a longer reach by one inch. According to the measurements of the hosting Shasta Club, Sam weighed 208 pounds and stood 6 feet tall. Johnson weighed 190 and stood 6'1 ½".

MEASUREMENTS OF M'VEY.		JOHNSON'S MEASUREMENTS.	
Weight	208 pounds	Weight	190 pounds
Height	6 feet	Height	6 ft. 1½ inches
Neck	18 inches	Neck	16 inches
Chest (normal)	41½ inches	Chest (normal)	40 inches
Chest (expanded)	44½ inches	Chest (expanded)	43 inches
Reach	77 inches	Reach	76 inches
Biceps	16 inches	Biceps	16 inches
Forearm	13 inches	Forearm	12½ inches
Waist	34 inches	Waist	32 inches
Wrist	7½ inches	Wrist	7 inches
Hips	41½ inches	Hips	40 inches
Thigh	25 inches	Thigh	22½ inches
Calf	16½ inches	Calf	15½ inches
Ankle	10 inches	Ankle	9½ inches

Both fighters were well motivated. McVey wanted to avenge his losses to the only man to have defeated him. Sam was confident of victory, and already was talking about fighting Jeffries for the championship.

Johnson wanted to make up for his previous poor showing in the local area against Ferguson. Jack said,

> I know I didn't make a great showing then, but what's the use of talking about that? I will make up for all the bad things Friday night. I hear every one saying what a 'wonder' this McVey is. Didn't I trim him twice? That's just the way it was in Los Angeles the last time we fought. Every one picked McVey, although I had a decision over him. I fooled them then and will fool them again. I want to fool them, as it looks like most of the club managers around want McVey to win, thinking they can get him on with Jeffries easier than me. I will win from McVey in such good style that the public will demand that Jeffries must fight me.

---

[411] *San Francisco Evening Post, San Francisco Bulletin*, April 15, 20, 1904.

Johnson had been training in West Oakland with Joe Walcott, who was training for a fight with the Dixie Kid. Jack appeared to be in perfect condition.[412]

Regarding their previous two bouts, the *Call* said, "It has always been a case of a marvelous boxer against a man with great strength and considerable cleverness." Of McVey, it said, "With all his size he is quick as a cat on his feet and moves about in a lithe, graceful way." Both pugilists felt that if either won decisively that Jeffries might wipe out the color line and fight the successful man. "With this as an incentive the colored giants are expected to put up a fast pace."

Regardless of the hype, at that point, the bettors had made Johnson a 6 to 10 favorite over the nearly 20-year-old "Herculean" Oxnard boxer.[413]

The burly McVey was said to be in good shape at all times. Still, he had put in the hardest sort of training at Colma. He was working on speed and skill, for he had plenty of strength and stamina. On the 20th, he sparred with Walter Marino, the clever amateur heavyweight, and with Frank Fields.

That same day, Johnson did some gymnasium work at Link Dennis' "colored hangout in West Oakland, without any boxing."[414]

On April 20, 1904 in Philadelphia, Marvin Hart clearly "won" a 6-round no-decision bout against Gus Ruhlin, dropping and hurting Gus in the 4th round en route to the bout's conclusion. It was said that Hart would soon be amongst the challengers to Jim Jeffries.

The day of the colored championship fight, the *San Francisco Examiner* called them the "two most famous colored heavyweights in the world."

> The colored boxers are of entirely different types. Johnson is tall, lithe and flat muscled: His build suggests speed and freedom of motion, while McVey has muscles like Sandow and has all the attributes of a professional strong man. For all that McVey is not muscle-bound or slow in his actions. He is sure-footed and uses his fists in a businesslike way. Those who have watched his career think he has improved wonderfully, but as the betting indicates he is still supposed to be much inferior to Johnson, who is regarded as one of the most talented boxers at present before the public.[415]

McVey supporters encouraged him to be aggressive and to bustle his opponent about, in order to neutralize Johnson's cleverness and effective boxing style. McVey was looked upon as a championship possibility, but for Johnson's wonderful dexterity with the gloves, which had proved a stumbling block. The *San Francisco Call* said,

> An impression has gained ground that if Jeffries ever wipes out the color line he would rather fight Johnson than McVey. While Johnson

[412] *San Francisco Bulletin, San Francisco Evening Post*, April 21, 1904.
[413] *San Francisco Call*, April 21, 1904.
[414] *San Francisco Chronicle*, April 21, 1904.
[415] *San Francisco Examiner*, April 22, 1904.

might outpoint him for a part of the journey, the big fellow knows he would land on the colored man sooner or later and that the fight would end right there. With McVey he would be fighting a man of equal strength, who can hit hard and who might be able to land a damaging blow.[416]

Of course, if Johnson could defeat in McVey a man of size, strength, and power, then it stood to reason that he had a chance with Jeffries too.

Explaining the odds making Johnson the 10 to 6 favorite, the *San Francisco Chronicle* said Johnson was conceded to be the far cleverer of the two. However, there was plenty of short-end wagering by those who believed that McVey was a dangerous man who was bigger than Johnson and had more strength and stamina. "Where Johnson is fairly fast and clever, McVey is bull-like and a fighter." Those who had seen his workouts were enthusiastic over Sam's chances. Most fans and experts preferred McVey's puncher's style, and that affected their judgment.

> There is no disguising the fact that nine-tenths of the sporting population hope to see the Oxnard giant the victor by the knockout route. J. Arthur, although the pride and the terror of Pacific street and a favorite with his colored confreres, is not as popular as he might be with the talent that studies the game and recognizes worth wherever it lies. Johnson's lamentable showing against Sandy Ferguson in the Colma Club's amphitheater left a bitter taste in the mouths of the many who made the cross-country trip in cattle cars.

It was said that Johnson won the decision over Ferguson "not because he was good but because Ferguson was so awfully, woefully poor."

Johnson realized that he had hurt his reputation. He wanted to set himself right, claiming that he was not in condition to fight Ferguson. He had trained faithfully for McVey. Given that he had fought a number of good fights during his career, the sports were inclined to afford him another chance.[417]

The *San Francisco Bulletin* believed that both fighters would be motivated not only by the fact that the colored championship was on the line, but by the possibility of a meeting with Jeffries, despite the fact that the probability was a slender one, given Jeff's repeated statements that he would not defend the title against a colored man.

> There does not appear to be a ringman in all the wide area where pugilism holds sway with sufficient inches and heft to meet the world's champion after Munroe than one of tonight's fighters.

> Many of the sports who desire to see Jeffries withdraw his objection to boxing a negro are divided in their choice of a winner tonight.

[416] *San Francisco Call*, April 22, 1904.
[417] *San Francisco Chronicle*, April 22, 1904.

Those who want to see Jeff opposed by the clever article long for Johnson, while the others pine for McVey on the theory that if Jeffries is to be defeated it will be by a man of his own size and bulk with a modicum of science thrown in.

Johnson is the cleverest big man now before the public. He simply toys with all his opponents and he wins his fights through their inability to hit him, rather than the punishment he administers. McVey, on the other hand, is the ideal fighter. He is strong and fast, and never once from the tap of the gong does he let up a moment in his consistent rushing and desire to get to close quarters. No amount of punishment can keep him off, and from the word 'go' he is going all the time.[418]

On Friday April 22, 1904, before the recently organized Shasta Club at the Mechanics' Pavilion in San Francisco, Jack Johnson fought Sam McVey for the third time. Behind McVey were Spider Kelly, his chief adviser, as well as Walter Marino, Frank Fields, and Joe Millett. Johnson had Tim McGrath as his chief second, as well as Joe Walcott. Surprisingly, allegedly the attendance was very small, with only $850 in the house, although the photos strongly suggest otherwise. Prior to the main event, announcer Billy Jordan introduced Joe Walcott and the Dixie Kid. Eddie Graney refereed.

---

[418] *San Francisco Bulletin*, April 22, 1904.

1 - Early on, it looked as if the fight would not last long. Both men were willing to mix it up. Johnson started in as though he wanted to score a knockout. He began with his jab, attempting to use it to get "the Oxnard sugar handler" to open his guard. He went after McVey with right and left to the head. Then McVey began to make the pace and forced Johnson to protect himself.

According to the *Call*, near the end of the round, as McVey was coming in and slightly off his balance, Johnson knocked him down with a clean left to the jaw. The *Examiner* said it was a straight left that sent him down to his haunches. Describing this sequence, the *Chronicle* said Johnson led with his left for the face and as McVey stepped back, he slipped and went to the floor. The *Bulletin* said Johnson caught McVey off balance and sent him flying to the mat with a hard right jolt.

McVey was up as quickly as he was down. Johnson was too surprised to follow up in the few seconds left in the round.

2 - McVey opened with a left lead for the ribs and followed with a right to the jaw which "raised his stock but did not damage." Johnson then rushed and uppercut him, but was stopped by a rib-roaster. One writer said Johnson landed right and left with great regularity. Another said the round was mostly slow. Jack closed the round with a series of jabs.

3 - According to the *Call*, early in the round, McVey shook Johnson with a right to the body, but he missed some wild swings to the head.

The *Chronicle* said Johnson threw a wicked straight left at the short ribs, but it was blocked. Jack tried a right to the jaw but McVey responded with a rib punch followed by a right to the jaw that started the blood from Jack's mouth and jarred "Mr. Johnsing" a bit. Johnson became more cautious of potential danger. A moment later, a McVey left jab to the bleeding mouth ended the round, which was decidedly McVey's.

4 - Johnson opened with a series of jabs, but ceased jabbing after he received an ugly right cross on the jaw. Johnson landed two hard rights to the body. Both men looked happy at the close.

5 - Johnson fought better in this round, and made his jabs tell. McVey began to slow up, and he gave Jack a chance to land several wicked uppercuts. At first, Johnson worked the head, but then he shifted to the body.

6 - McVey still had plenty of force in his blows, but he followed each punch with a hug, and slowed up a great deal. Johnson's uppercuts did some damage. Johnson staggered McVey with a right to the head, but the bell prevented further damage.

7 - The round was largely a wrestling match, and the fight had slowed to a snail's pace. At the close, a right and left Johnson rally was followed by McVey's cornerman, Spider Kelly, yelling, "Now, you do that, Sam." However, he was unable to do so. He kept trying to bore in, but Johnson danced nimbly out of his way at will.

8 - The round was almost a fight. McVey landed a right and left swing on the sides of the head, and he followed with straight rights for the body. However, overall, the fight was so slow at that point such that the crowd yelled to "throw them out." Both men appeared tired.

9 - This was an exciting round. The *Call* said, "Most of the fighting done during the evening was in this round." Johnson livened things up, deciding to force the pace and attack, trying for a knockout. Johnson staggered McVey with a right to the head. Jack jabbed and swung repeatedly, and landed so often that McVey was groggy at the close of the round. The round was all Johnson's.

10 - The *Chronicle* said Johnson followed up his advantage and scored a knockdown with a left cross that followed a right swing.

The "Oxnard Zulu" rose in a groggy state. However, "then the original cautious man showed his weakness. With all his cleverness and heavy hitting ability he lacks the fighter's instinct, and, as usual, he held back just when he had his man going." It felt that Johnson was a puncher but not a finisher.

The *Call* did not confirm the knockdown, saying that Johnson wrestled McVey down. Thereafter, Jack kept up his piston-rod left. The *Examiner* and *Bulletin*, which did not offer detailed round-by-round accounts, but rather general summaries, did not mention a knockdown in this round either.

11 - Johnson was busy, but did little damage.

12 - Johnson had McVey groggy again, but failed to follow up and allowed Sam to recover.

13 – 18 - According to the *Call*, there was almost no fighting at all worth mentioning in these rounds.

11 – 19 - The *Chronicle* said that these rounds were all the same. The fight had left McVey, and Johnson simply sparred. Several times, Johnson rushed and showed plenty of strength, but then held back whenever he had a chance to get his man. Perhaps he did not want to overextend himself and risk punching himself out, or leave himself vulnerable too long, lest he might get caught by a powerful blow. Regardless, Johnson landed enough punches to knock the sense out of McVey, who kept growing weaker.

19 - The *Call* said Johnson finally took a chance and staggered McVey with rights and lefts to the head. McVey was nearly out from a hard left to the body.

20 - McVey's head was hardly cleared, and Johnson went after him again. Throughout the round, he landed repeatedly to the head.

Near the end of the round, with only about 20 seconds left, according to the *Call*, Johnson landed a right and left to the jaw that turned McVey completely around, and he fell in a huge limp mass, face downward on the paddock floor. He laid there breathing heavily until counted out.

The *Chronicle's* description of the knockout sequence said that after a break, McVey turned to avoid Johnson, and quick as a flash, Jack caught him with a right and left swing and McVey went down with a thump. He rolled over onto his stomach and Referee Eddie Graney counted him out. McVey's two glassy eyes stared vacantly across the ring. The sleeping crowd woke up with a start and it was all over.

McVey's seconds assisted him to his corner. The sudden knockout ending proved a surprise, for most had thought the bout would go to a points decision.

When he woke up, Sam, or "Mr. Sambo McVey" as the *Bulletin* phrased it, asked Spider Kelly, "Was it a draw?" Spider amusingly answered, "It should have been, but they robbed you." Another quoted him as saying, "Yes, and they robbed us."

McVey was so thoroughly out that it wasn't until he was on his way to the dressing room before he realized that he had been "caught napping on the mat."

The *San Francisco Examiner* summarized the bout. After being decked in the 1st round, McVey became cautious and respectful of Johnson's power. McVey covered up and Johnson feinted continually in the hope of drawing fire so that he could counter with a right cross.

For several rounds, Johnson used his left jab, which messed up McVey's features. Then Johnson switched to using a left stomach punch, which disagreed with McVey. Sam mostly confined his efforts to a left swing and follow-up right, and nine times out of ten, neither blow landed.

McVey did a bit of willing work in the 8th round, and the crowd cheered his efforts. As a result, Johnson let himself out a bit more. In the 9th and 10th rounds, Johnson hammered McVey incessantly, prodding his face with left jabs, sending his left into the midsection, and at times landing a heavy right under the heart. Jack's occasional rights for the jaw were blocked by McVey's shoulder.

At no time after the start of the 11th round did it appear as though McVey had any lingering hopes of winning. The crowd began to boo Johnson for holding back. They felt that McVey had zero chance to win, and that Johnson should go ahead and finish him. Even Tim McGrath, Johnson's principal handler, beseeched him to get in close and wind up matters. "Johnson was quite satisfied with the way things were progressing, however. He busied himself in spots only, but finally restored himself to favor with the gallery in a measure by polishing off McVey in style."

According to the *San Francisco Bulletin*, for the first six or seven rounds, McVey showed a great deal of pluck. "Then, until the ninth and tenth, he tried to avoid punishment. In the rounds mentioned there was some hot slugging and McVey was in such a condition that at the sound of the gong he reeled along the ropes to his corner." His left eye was closed and his naturally large lips were puffed out prominently.

From the 11th round on, the pace slackened, and there was little variation. Johnson kept slamming in his right and an occasional hard left, mostly to McVey's face. Sam took the blows bravely. The crowd called for Johnson to hit the body, but Jack did not seem too anxious to go there. Perhaps he feared a counter if he reached down.

In the 17th and 18th rounds, the pace was so slow that some suspected that the men were not giving their best efforts. Some in the crowd began crying, "Fake." That woke up Johnson a bit, but it did not appear as though he could knock out McVey, and was just coasting to a decision victory.

However, halfway into the 20th round, Johnson opened up with a terrific fusillade and beat McVey to the ropes. Just 30 seconds before the end, he caught the staggering giant with a right swing on the jaw that sent him down and out cold. Sam was carried to his corner.

The *San Francisco Call* harshly called it the poorest fight seen in San Francisco in many years. Although the bout started with some promise, eventually it became quite boring, so much so that at first, spectators satirically applauded the boxers' feeble efforts. Then they jeered the "alleged gladiators," making several comments. Someone at ringside sarcastically remarked, "Cease this brutality." This brought down the house with laughter. "As hardly a good blow had been struck for ten rounds the humor of the remark pleased the weary spectators."

The bout became so slow and dull that many spectators simply left the building while the bout was in progress, leaving a small proportion of the already small attendance to sit it out and endure each tiresome round. When the bout concluded, despite the knockout, there was no cheering, but instead the patrons quietly retired from the scene.

McVey could not land effectively at any time during the contest. What he could do was take a lot of punishment without flinching. "Beyond this he did nothing. For round after round he did not land a blow on the elusive Johnson." His mighty right was useless, and he hardly threw it. "With all his strength and ruggedness, he showed no signs of aggressiveness, and will never make a fighter."

Johnson showed all of his known cleverness, landing an incredible number of blows to the head, but he did not follow up his advantages. He was very cautious, and even on the occasions when he hurt McVey, he was content to land and then play defense and not let himself out too much. "He had his opponent in distress several times, but he refused to take a chance and backed away out of danger."[419]

Jack Johnson was content to win in a careful, safe, and therefore somewhat uninteresting manner. He gradually broke down his foe. Instead of lauding his brilliant skill, his eventual 20th round knockout victory proved anticlimactic and garnered no appreciation from the press or the paying spectators, despite the fact that McVey was a big, strong, dangerous puncher who had never before been knocked out. McVey would not be stopped again until 1909, five years later, and even then, it was only via retirement after 49 rounds of fighting against Joe Jeannette. Johnson proved not only his skill and condition in this bout, but also his punching power, stopping a man that was not easily knocked out, and one who had been highly touted. Jack Johnson was a winner, but ironically once again managed to have the opinion of his fighting ability diminish, even in a dominant victory over a man whom, up to that point, no one else could defeat. Quite simply, Jack Johnson was an underappreciated winner.

The *Examiner's* W. W. Naughton was not quite as harsh, but also called it an unsatisfactory contest. Johnson simply was McVey's master at the game. For most of the bout, though severely pummeled, McVey managed to keep his chin tucked behind his raised left shoulder. However, in the last half-minute of the bout, the demoralized McVey's guard was beaten down by Johnson's savage attack, and a right to the jaw sent Sam down and out. Johnson had been cautious for several rounds, but finally cut loose with all manner of punches. As McVey tottered towards the ropes, Johnson sprung after him and brought him down.

The bout was unsatisfactory because McVey could not cope with Johnson in either strength or fighting talents. After just a few rounds, he started to act like a man who knew that he was up against his master at the game. His showing was so poor that some found it hard to imagine that Sam had defeated Ed Martin and Kid Carter. Perhaps it was great Johnson.

---

[419] *San Francisco Call*, April 23, 1904.

After all, he had dominated McVey in three separate bouts. Yet, the press seemed to overlook this.

McVey thought more of protecting his chin than anything else. The way he crouched and covered prevented the use of his right without giving Johnson warning that it was coming. McVey landed a few times with his left, but the blows lacked sting, and Johnson never blinked. The best that could be said for Sam was that he was game. "He stood to be pecked to pieces last night and by the time shifty Mr. Johnson got through with him his right eye resembled a buttonhole, and his lips were badly puffed."

> Johnson improved to some extent on his showing with Sandy Ferguson at Colma, but still left the crowd wondering what was the matter with him. He is cleverness personified, but the fighting spirit seems to flare in flashes with him. He loafs along grinning and at peace with himself and the other fellow while his seconds are bawling themselves red in the face in their attempts to get him to go in and mix it.

> He showed before last night's fight was ten minutes old that he had McVey thoroughly at his mercy, yet he played with the beet field warrior as a cat plays with a mouse. His tactics were such that the gallery became frantic with chagrin and disgust. It hooted the fighters at the finish of every round from the thirteenth to the nineteenth, and, in the belief that it was to be deprived of the privilege of witnessing a knockout, it became insulting and sarcastic.[420]

Essentially, Johnson gave the impression of a fighter who never gave it his all, but one who held a lot in reserve and did the bare minimum to win in the safest, most risk-averse manner possible. He only showed his full offensive ability and arsenal in flashes, and often only when forced to do so, or when angered as a result of his opponent landing a blow, or when he felt completely safe to do so.

The *San Francisco Evening Post* said the city's sports were tired of Johnson. He was a clever pugilist, but the spectators were compelled to work so hard at encouraging him to keep active that they did not appreciate his game. "The contest is hardly worth a description."

Despite his awesome appearance, McVey was no match in strength for Johnson, who was built like Fitzsimmons, but "more graceful in motion and less rugged in conformation." Johnson owned him from start to finish.

> The victor stood off at arm's length and punched his opponent to the head or body at pleasure. It was noticeable, however, that he put no ginger in his punches, but drove in soft taps. Occasionally, when spurred on by the hoots of the gallery, he put force behind his delivery, and on such occasions demonstrated that he has a knockout

---

420 *San Francisco Examiner*, April 23, 1904.

punch, but is afraid to use it, apparently fearing that his rival would come back with as good as was sent.

After 10 rounds, the spectators were "jeering the tappers with shouts of fake." As a result, Johnson finally did some fighting. His spasmodic efforts soon had McVey staggering. However, he backed off again. The crowd increased its hooting. Near the end of the contest, the jeers finally once again spurred on Johnson to renewed efforts. He increased the rapidity of his gait and decisiveness of his punches, and brought the unequal contest to a close with 20 seconds remaining in the 20th and final round, sending McVey down and out with a punch on the jaw.[421]

The *San Francisco Chronicle* said Johnson had made a poor showing for most of the 20 rounds, choosing to side-step, feint, and box in pretty fashion until he finally redeemed himself by turning a decision into a knockout. "This was the only thing that saved the king of the colored heavies from unmerciful excoriation."

It was Johnson's fight all the way, for his superiority was apparent from the start. McVey won no more than one section of the fight. Sam was momentarily encouraged when he drew blood from Johnson's mouth in the 4th round. McVey was faster than in previous fights, but not fast enough to reach a vital location with his punishing blows. The longer and lankier J. Arthur fought all around McVey, but did not do much mixing, nor did he seem too anxious for clashes. Instead of wading in with his considerable strength, Johnson did not attempt to finish his slower and clumsier opponent, but rather preferred to exhibit his boxing skill and remain on the outside and use his cleverness. He appeared to be operating upon the theory that a fight was a "parlor entertainment."

Johnson's style made him no friends. The crowd appealed in unison, "Fight! Fight!" Towards the end of the bout, they changed their indignant yells to cries of "Fake! Fake!" From the 10th to the 20th rounds there were hisses and hoots and all sorts of catcalls. Once again, it appeared that Johnson was content to win a careful, boring decision, until he finally nailed McVey with 20 seconds left and took him out.[422]

In fairer and perhaps more insightful fashion, the *San Francisco Bulletin* offered other reasons for why Johnson had taken so long to finish McVey. It said Johnson had beaten McVey throughout the contest, "but it was like hammering a carcass of beef hung in a butcher shop." The tough McVey could absorb punishment. "McVey stood a horrible walloping, and it was only his great strength and endurance that kept him from meeting his fate earlier in the fight. When pressed too hard, McVey found his way into clinches and wrestled around in Johnson's arms, waiting for a return of his wind." McVey was just plain tough, and he knew how to clinch and survive

[421] *San Francisco Evening Post*, April 23, 1904.
[422] *San Francisco Chronicle*, April 23, 1904.

when hurt. It was not easy to stop a man who could take it and knew how to grab and recover when hurt.[423]

Jeffries' manager, Bill Delaney, had attended the Johnson-McVey fight. During the fight, when asked whether there was a chance for Jeff to fight the winner, Delaney said,

> Not the least. Jeff recognizes that Johnson, who looks like the winner, is a good man, and may be the best heavyweight aspiring to be champion, but he has thoroughly made up his mind never to fight a colored man again. He is determined upon this, and no argument or persuasion can change his course. When Jeff has his mind set once, you don't know how hard it is to change it. Yes, my advice to him will be to fight a couple more battles and then retire, the undefeated champion of the world, and I think the greatest champion in the history of the prize-ring. Jeff has enough money whereby he doesn't have to stay at the game.

Delaney also said that any man who remained in the fight game long enough eventually would get licked. He hated to see once-great ex-champions, like George Dixon, who were past-it but continuing to fight for money, travelling around getting beaten by second-class men, losing prestige. He did not want that for Jeffries, but preferred to see him retire while still in his prime.[424]

The *Police Gazette* said that by defeating McVey, Johnson, "the dusky hero of a score of fights, has placed himself in a position to legitimately claim a fight with Jim Jeffries for the championship of the world." Jack Johnson was the undisputed best black fighter in the world and also the best black fighter since Peter Jackson.[425]

However, in San Francisco, the calls for Jeffries to face Johnson were dying out. The problem for Johnson was that he most needed to convince the San Francisco press and paying public of his merit in order to garner sufficient interest and demand for a title fight with Jeffries, even assuming Jeff could be persuaded by public and press pressure and financial incentives to withdraw his color-line objection. San Francisco was the only place at that time that could both host a proper lengthy championship fight and generate enough money to make the fight worth Jeffries' while. Los Angeles was trying to compete, but at that time it simply was not on the level of San Francisco in terms of the finances that could be generated. However, San Francisco was fairly hard on Johnson, who put up some of his least entertaining and least appreciated performances in that area against Gardner, Ferguson, and McVey, even though he won those bouts clearly.

The *Chronicle* said,

---

423 *San Francisco Bulletin,* April 23, 1904.
424 *San Francisco Bulletin,* April 23, 1904.
425 *Police Gazette,* May 14, 1904.

Both Jack Johnson and Sam McVey conclusively settled any championship aspirations which they may have by their poor showing on Friday night. With the possible exception of the Fitzsimmons-Gardner contest, it was the tamest excuse for a fight foisted upon an indulgent public in many months. When Johnson clamors again for Jeffries to drop the color line his desire should be granted, and he should be allowed to meet the big fellow, if for nothing else than to get his block knocked off. Judging from his cautiousness with the clumsy and ignorant McVey, Johnson would die of fright before the first gong were he to meet Jeffries. It is a safe gamble, too, that the champion could take the pair of them in one night and send them both to sleep in ten rounds.[426]

The *Evening Post* said San Francisco wanted negro boxers and their style of fighting to move on. Johnson had "furnished all of this sort of sport this metropolis can stand for months to come." It said that another bout with him as a principal would not draw money enough into the box office to pay the rent for the building.

When speaking with promoter James Coffroth, who had wanted to match Jeffries with Johnson, Jeff said,

I suppose I will now be relieved of any further talk of a match with Johnson, after the miserable showing the colored champion made with Sam McVey. That battle proves one thing decisively and that is that a pugilist must have the willingness to fight as well as the ability.[427]

Jeffries was thinking about retiring soon. The 29-year-old had been married the same day as the Johnson-McVey fight, in Oakland on the evening of the 22nd. Manager Bill Delaney said it was his intention to have Jeff do all his fighting within a year and then to retire as champion and the greatest fighter of the age.[428]

In late April, the *Police Gazette* reported that Johnson had offered to beat both Jack Root and George Gardner on the same night.[429] Apparently, there were no takers.

On May 20, 1904 in Baltimore, Marvin Hart fought Gus Ruhlin to a 12-round draw. Despite being badly cut and bloodied, Hart viciously attacked throughout, and even dropped Ruhlin once in the contest. Most agreed with the draw decision.

In May 1904, Jack Johnson returned to Chicago for a scheduled 6-round bout there in a rematch with former colored heavyweight champion Frank Childs, who resided in Chicago. Since his 1902 12th round retirement against Johnson, Childs' record included 1902 L6 Joe Choynski and 1904 KO2

[426] *San Francisco Chronicle*, April 24, 1904.
[427] *San Francisco Evening Post*, April 25, 1904.
[428] *San Francisco Bulletin*, April 24, 1904; *Police Gazette*, May 7, 1904.
[429] *Police Gazette*, April 30, 1904.

Chicago Jack Johnson, a different Johnson. Childs had over 50 bouts of experience. They would be fighting for the colored heavyweight title. It was estimated that they would weigh about the same.

FRANK CHILDS.

It would be the first time that Johnson fought in Chicago in several years, for he had not fought there since losing to Klondike.

Both men knew that the other was a tough proposition, so they trained hard. Plus, at age 36, Childs had the additional motivation of knowing this was perhaps his last chance at the big time. If he won, he would get back into the highest ranks, but if he lost, he would be called a member of the has-beens.

Johnson was focusing on his speed, and was supremely confident that he would bewilder Childs. "In fact, he thinks there is no man in the world, not even excepting Champion Jeffries, that can beat him." Still, Johnson knew that Childs had a terrific punch that had laid low many scrappers.[430]

[430] *Chicago Chronicle*, May 29, 1904; *Daily Inter Ocean*, June 1, 1904.

George Siler said, "Johnson is easily the cleverest black the ring has seen since Peter Jackson's day. He will have it on Frank in youth, height, reach and every detail except one – the hitting department. Childs has always carried a mighty punch." Childs had knocked out several fellows who had height and reach advantages, and he would try to do the same to Johnson. "He thinks he can 'bull' into Johnson, escaping any serious damage from the numerous but gentle jabs of the tall man, and finally send one across to win."[431]

On Thursday June 2, 1904 in Chicago, before the newly formed Empire Athletic Club, inside Apollo Hall, located at Blue Island Avenue and 12th street, the Jack Johnson vs. Frank Childs rematch took place. Abe Pollock refereed.

There was an extreme diversity of perspective regarding what happened. The next-day *Chicago Record-Herald* said that in the 1st round, Johnson boxed cautiously, seeing what Childs had. In the 2nd round, Johnson cut loose and hammered Childs all over. A right to the jaw dropped Childs. Frank came back quickly and fought gamely, but received a shower of head and body blows. The rest of the bout was a repetition of the 2nd round. Childs was willing to mix matters, but was so far outclassed that he rarely could land a blow or block any of Johnson's punches, and occasionally he went down.

Johnson won easily, doing whatever he pleased, throughout the contest landing hard blows to the face and body that were intended for knockouts. He pounded Childs about the ring at will, with scarcely any opposition. Childs was sent to the mat five times in all, but gamely lasted to the end. He was chopped up terribly at the bout's conclusion. The 6-round decision for Johnson was quite clear.[432]

The *Freeman*, based in Indianapolis, Indiana, which was one of the most popular and well-respected weekly colored newspapers in the country, with a national distribution, reported that Johnson outclassed Childs in a decidedly one-sided match. Childs was dropped in the 2nd and 3rd rounds for nine-counts, with only the gong in each instance saving him from a knockout. Johnson had things his own way during the final 3 rounds. He had Childs in a very bad way at the finish, although Frank survived.[433]

However, the local *Daily Inter Ocean* saw matters in an entirely different way, saying, "It was a slow battle, with Johnson the aggressor and Childs fighting on the defensive. Two knockdowns were scored, but as a general proposition the fight had a bad odor." Saying it had a "bad odor" was this paper's way of saying it thought Johnson had carried Childs.[434]

The *Chicago Tribune's* version, written by famous referee and respected boxing expert George Siler, agreed, saying that Johnson had won a slow fight that was a poor and unsatisfactory exhibition. He called the bout 6

---

[431] *Chicago Daily News, Chicago Tribune,* June 2, 1904.
[432] *Chicago Record-Herald,* June 3, 1904.
[433] *Freeman,* June 11, 1904.
[434] *Daily Inter Ocean,* June 3, 1904.

rounds of slow and indifferent boxing that was "too much on the brotherly love order to satisfy the spectators. Johnson did not come up to expectations, and Frank, although he tried, could do nothing with the champion." Johnson finally cut loose in the last 30 seconds, showing "some symptoms of his knowledge of the game. Johnson has been a long time trying to cut into the local game, and he bungled the job when given the opportunity."[435]

The *Police Gazette* printed the version of the bout that described it as dull, calling it the "slowest fighting imaginable."

> This was Johnson's first appearance in a Chicago ring since he was beaten at the Lyceum, and the crowd who came to see him put out old man Childs and get a line on his chances against James Jeffries left the hall sadly disappointed and at the same time wondering why Jeff is overlooking the chance to make the easiest kind of money. It took Johnson nearly a year to convince Chicago matchmakers that he has learned to fight and he was at last given a chance to show his prowess, but after his showing he could never command a $50 purse in the Windy City. The fight, if such it can be called, went the limit of six rounds. During the entire time four light blows were landed, and as Johnson landed them the referee was forced to give him the decision.[436]

Once again, Johnson had won clearly against an experienced hard-punching veteran, dropping him in the process anywhere from two to five times (depending on the version) in only six rounds, and yet he found it difficult to find respect and accolades. It seems as though much of the press would not give him credit for anything less than a dominant, exciting, fast-paced bout that terminated in an early knockout.

One has to wonder whether race played a part in some of these tough perspectives. Or perhaps it was simply lack of appreciation for Johnson's style. One thing that does emerge from the accounts is that often for Johnson's bouts, there could be several different perspectives.

Regardless of perspective, for whatever reason, Johnson either had failed to impress or failed to entertain the press or the spectators to their satisfaction. He never again fought in Chicago. Johnson would not fight again for four months, which was actually quite a while for him.

In order to challenge the winner, Klondike John Haynes/Haines was at ringside for the Johnson-Childs fight. Since Klondike's loss to Johnson (in 1900, retiring after the 13th round), he had losses such as 1902 LKOby3 Fred Russell, 1903 L6 Sandy Ferguson, and recent 1904 LDQ5 George Lawlor, all of whom Johnson had defeated, so Klondike didn't have the strongest argument to compel a match with Johnson. Yet, the *Police Gazette* reported, "Klondike was at the ringside to challenge the winner of the bout

---

[435] *Chicago Tribune*, June 3, 1904.
[436] *Police Gazette*, June 18, 1904.

and on his showing against Childs, Johnson cannot be conceded a chance with even a second-rater like 'Klondike.'" However, in his next fight, in July 1904, Frank Childs would score a KO8 over Klondike. Clearly, the press continued to underestimate Johnson and failed to give his victories due credit.[437]

The black-owned *Freeman* hoped that colored fighters would be exemplars of character and education, so that they could obtain something more than simply prominence as sparring partners to white fighters whom they could whip. Many blacks were relegated to sparring-partner status in order to make money. "Bob Armstrong is a man who occupies just such a position. He roves around like a big lost child simply for the want of a real manager." It urged that the "Negro race must soon develop qualified managers." It gave this advice because several colored fighters had become prominent before the public.

It also noted that "the history of important colored men, of a race very meanly represented to this country by newspapers, is kept very shady." Hence, it highlighted the differences in perspectives between black-owned newspapers and white-owned newspapers, even when it came to boxing.[438]

The *Freeman* claimed to have 500,000 readers and subscribers, calling itself "America's greatest colored newspaper." It was sold as far west as San Francisco, where boxing was hot. Even some whites read the paper, in order to learn about black perspectives on matters.

Regarding the color-line in boxing, the *Freeman* opined,

> All prize fighters who draw the color line are curs and cowards. All white heavyweight champions of the past, including John L. Sullivan and James J. Jeffries, can not go down in history as fighters with honorable records. They were cowards who were afraid of a black fighter, for good reasons. They dishonor the country and indicate the cowardice of white men in all other walks of life. For instance, no white man's newspaper will dare to be brave enough to publish my assertions. ... What kind of men do Edgren, Naughton and other sporting writers call themselves, to stand for a 'bluff' that the public does not like.... What do respectable people care about whether fighting champions are red or green since they have no social standing. What we need next is a good heavyweight champion who is not a coward or afraid of a colored man. Every time the 'white feather' cry goes up, the Negro race is flattered.[439]

Apparently, some folks on the West Coast were under the impression that Marvin Hart was black. Correcting the error, Jack McCormick, Hart's

[437] *Chicago Daily News*, June 1, 1904; *Daily Inter Ocean*, June 2, 1904; *Police Gazette*, June 18, 1904.

[438] *Freeman*, July 9, 1904. A one-year subscription to the weekly *Freeman*, sent to any address in the U.S., cost only $1. *Freeman*, December 19, 1908.

[439] *Freeman*, July 16, 1904.

manager, wrote the *San Francisco Evening Post*, "Hart is a white man who does not fight negroes, and has drawn the color line on two different occasions when challenged. He refused Joe Walcott and Jack Johnson for this reason. … Hoping you will let the people know that Hart is white." Marvin wanted to fight Jeffries after Jeff was through with Munroe.[440]

The *Freeman* noted that Jimmy Britt, James Jeffries, and Marvin Hart had promised not to take any chances of being whipped by a Negro. It believed that if they fought Joe Gans, Joe Walcott, or Jack Johnson, "they will surely go home in deep disgrace."

Bob Armstrong, who had been sparring with Bob Fitzsimmons, announced that he was disputing Johnson's claim to the colored title. He noted that Johnson had only won a 20-round decision over Ed Martin in February 1903, while Armstrong had scored a KO3 over Martin in June 1903. Armstrong claimed that Johnson was afraid of him and refused to fight him.[441] However, Armstrong had suffered knockout losses to Frank Childs and Sandy Ferguson, both of whom Johnson had defeated more than once. Ferguson had stopped Armstrong in 1 round, while Childs had stopped him in 2 and 6 rounds. Ed Martin had won a 15-round decision over Armstrong as well. Johnson appears to have been willing to fight anyone, so it remains unclear as to why an Armstrong bout was not made. Most likely, no promoters were interested in such a fight.[442]

On July 23, 1904 in Philadelphia, eight months after he won the world light-heavyweight championship, Bob Fitzsimmons fought "Philadelphia" Jack O'Brien before a crowd of up to 7,000 spectators. O'Brien outboxed him for the first few rounds, but Fitz owned the last three, even dropping O'Brien in the 6th round with a left hook, causing the police to step in and terminate the bout early

[440] *San Francisco Evening Post*, July 18, 1904.
[441] *San Francisco Evening Post*, July 22, 1904; *Freeman*, July 30, 1904.
[442] *Freeman*, July 23, 1904.

CHAPTER 13

Giving Them What They Want

Jack Johnson said he would be on hand at the Jeffries-Munroe championship fight to challenge the winner, notwithstanding the fact that Jeffries had said that he would not defend his title against a colored fighter. Jack said, "I've been taking on a chunk of weight, and I now weigh 200 pounds. That puts me in the champion's class, and I think I'm entitled to a fight with him. I believe he would have given me a chance before this, but Billy Delaney stands in the way." Johnson picked Jeff to defeat Munroe.

The *Bulletin* said, "Mistah Johnson can go some himself, and many look upon him as the only pugilist in the game who would stand a good chance to wrest the title from Jeffries. He is young, strong and willing, and has a punch that kicks in like a mule with his mad up."[443]

Jack Munroe on left shakes hands with James J. Jeffries

On August 26, 1904 in San Francisco, 29-year-old James J. Jeffries successfully defended his world heavyweight championship by knocking out Jack Munroe in the 2nd round. Munroe weighed anywhere from 210 to 220 pounds. Jeffries weighed about 225 to 230 pounds. Jeffries easily blew through him, dropping Munroe three times in the 1st round before finishing him early in the 2nd. Some said the gate receipts were $21,800, while others said $31,800 had been generated.

---

[443] *San Francisco Bulletin, San Francisco Examiner, San Francisco Call*, August 25, 26, 1904.

Reporters and observers agreed that Jeffries was the wonder of the age whom no one could defeat. They called him the best fighter in the world by far, and said he would remain champion until he was an old man. The *Police Gazette* said Jeffries was the greatest fighter who ever lived, and stood alone. Munroe, the man who had gone 20 rounds with Hank Griffin and had defeated Peter Maher and Tom Sharkey, could not even last 2 rounds with Jeffries.[444]

Referee Eddie Graney said Jeff could be champion for another ten years.

> Jeffries is bigger, faster and better than ever. He improves in each fight. Nature has been kind to the champion. He is too strong and hits too hard for any man. ... Munroe should not take his defeat to heart, as he was beaten by a champion of champions. ...
>
> He was always a fairly hard puncher, a clever boxer and a monument of endurance. He has increased in cleverness and punishing force and he is a marvel of speed. Above all things he has learned to economize so far as energy is concerned. He wastes no power and misplaces no blows. A twist of his forearm and a turn of his wrist speeds a punch that causes as much damage as a crack from a bludgeon.

Bill Delaney felt that Jeffries should retire. He had no equal, and there were no marketable challengers for him on the horizon. Delaney said, "This may be Jeff's last fight. He has met and beaten them all, and now I do not see whom they can bring to the front. . ... I would like him to retire on his laurels. If he has to wait for a couple of years he may not be in such good form." He also said, "I can't think of a soul who is entitled to a match, but somebody may spring up." Delaney preferred Jeff to retire rather than go stale waiting for a challenger to emerge. He meant a white challenger.

The *Call* agreed that there were no more men for Jeffries to meet, and that he might as well retire. "In the condition he showed last night he could defeat a whole ring full of aspirants for the championship." There was no true top contender in sight, whom the public really wanted to see Jeff fight. Promoters were not interested in digging up a man to put against him, for no one was good enough to draw a big gate.[445]

The *Bulletin* said Jeffries was too good for his own good. The public would not be overly enthusiastic about seeing him in the ring with anyone, because he was simply in another league. Jeff was "the greatest champion the world has ever seen. That is just the trouble with him – he is too confoundedly great for his own good."

The *Bulletin* felt that the only fighter with a ghost of a chance to make even a respectable fight of it was Jack Johnson. Jack was of a fair size and

---

[444] *San Francisco Call, Evening Post, Bulletin, Examiner*, and *Chronicle*, all August 27, 1904; and *National Police Gazette*, September 3, 10, 1904.
[445] *San Francisco Call*, August 31, 1904.

possessed an unusual amount of cleverness. Therefore he at least had a remote chance against Jeffries.

Jack Johnson was present at the Munroe fight, and tried to get through the ropes to challenge Jeff, but according to the *Bulletin*, the management would not allow him to do so. The *Call* told a different story, claiming, "Jack Johnson had announced his intention of challenging the winner, but one glance at Jeffries caused him to change his mind. He maintained a discreet silence."

Regardless of which story was true, the next day, Johnson's manager, Zick Abrams, was out with a challenge on Jack Johnson's behalf, saying that Johnson would make an immeasurably better showing than did Munroe. He gave the *Bulletin* a check for $2,500 as a guarantee of good faith in the challenge. He said that they were willing to bet $10,000, and would make the fight winner-take-all. The *Bulletin* said, "Johnson is the only heavyweight in sight who has the size, cleverness and punching ability to make the champion get busy in order to win."

A Black Cloud In Sight.

Jeffries had said that he was not willing to enter the ring with a negro when the title was on the line. However, the *Bulletin* thought that he did not seem as determined on this point as he was six months ago, for Jeff offered economic rather than merely racial reasons, saying, "We wouldn't draw. ... Johnson hasn't any reputation. What's he ever done, and besides he has a shady record aside from being shady in color." It opined that if the public demanded the fight, and no white challenger loomed up in the near future, that Jeff would brush aside the color line. The public might demand the fight if Johnson sufficiently proved himself, because the general boxing public had no prejudice about mixed-race boxing matches. "It matters little to the average ring-goer whether the fighters be white or black as long as the sport is of a high order and the best man wins. And Jeffries' popularity would not suffer a particle if he fought Johnson, for some of the best liked pugilists the world knows never drew the color line." It was up to Johnson to give strong enough performances to garner public momentum on his behalf.[446]

[446] *San Francisco Bulletin*, August 28, 1904.

Still, a couple days after the fight, Jeffries said he would hold firm regarding the color line, regardless of economics. When Tim McGrath told Jeff that he would have to fight Jack Johnson, Jeffries responded, "Well, you might as well forget that, because I'll never fight a nigger. I could put him away in less time than I did Munroe, but I'll never fight a nigger."[447]

The *Police Gazette* quoted Jeffries as saying, "I have no desire to see a colored man even get a chance to win the world's championship, and I will never meet one."[448] Jeff also said,

> All that Sandy Ferguson has to base a demand for a fight on is the fact that he has beaten Gus Ruhlin and a few third and fourth raters. He doesn't class, and a fight with him wouldn't draw flies. I do not think he is game, and would be willing to meet six men of his capacity in an evening.
>
> Jack Johnson is a fair fighter, but he is black, and for that reason I will never fight him. If I were not the champion I would as soon meet a negro as any other man, but the title will never go to a black man if I can help it. I do not think this fellow has anything on a lot of heavies that I have licked. He's a good man, but not as good as Fitz and Sharkey. He is an in-and-outer, and has some queer fights in his record. But the only thing that makes a fight with him impossible is that he is a negro.[449]

Jeffries was referring to some of the mixed results in Johnson's early career, as well as some of the more recent victories that the press and spectators perceived as less than impressive or entertaining performances.

However, Johnson had not lost a fight since his last loss in November 1901, and though he had drawn since then, he had won every bout since October 1902. He had done no worse than a draw in any fight for almost three years, over the course of at least eighteen bouts. He had fought a high caliber of opponent, particularly from the black community, and he fought often and ducked no one, whereas most top white fighters drew the color line against him. Given the frequency and great number of lengthy bouts fought against solid opponents, and given his style, it wasn't always easy to look good every time out.

Jim Jeffries was only fighting once or twice a year at most since 1899, including some semi-serious 4-round exhibitions thrown in, whereas Johnson had fought at least six times in 1900, five times in 1901, six times in 1902, seven times in 1903, and would fight five times in 1904. In his career, Johnson had fought in at least ten bouts that went 20 rounds, so that is 200 rounds of boxing in those fights alone. Johnson's style was not to engage in a war, and given the number of 20-round bouts in which he was

---

[447] *San Francisco Evening Post*, August 29, 1904.
[448] *Police Gazette*, September 17, 1904.
[449] *Police Gazette*, October 8, 1904.

participating, a defensive and cautious style might have been wiser for his health and career longevity. Jim Jeffries was often cut or injured during or in between his bouts. Furthermore, Jeffries had fought only 12 total career pro bouts before fighting for the championship.

On September 16, 1904 in Seattle, 158-pound middleweight Tommy Burns fought top black middleweight (and former Jack Johnson sparring partner) Billy Woods to a 15-round draw, although the majority of spectators thought that Burns deserved the verdict.

During September 1904 in Los Angeles, Jack Johnson was a sparring partner for experienced middleweight Jack "Twin" Sullivan, who was preparing for a bout with Kid McCoy. Both McCoy and Sullivan had been Munroe sparring partners. Johnson was one of Sullivan's seconds for the Sullivan-McCoy bout, held on September 27, 1904 in Los Angeles, won by McCoy via 20-round decision.[450]

Next up for Johnson was a rematch with Denver Ed Martin, set for October 18, 1904 in Los Angeles before Tom McCarey's Century Athletic Club. Ever since losing his colored title to Johnson in a February 1903 20-round decision, Ed Martin had wanted a rematch. Since that loss, Martin had mixed results, such as 1903 LKOby3 Bob Armstrong and LKOby1 Sam McVey. Denver Ed had shown chin issues.

However, Martin re-dedicated himself, and in August 1904 at Hazard's Pavilion in Los Angeles, in a card promoted by McCarey's Century Club, Ed Martin defeated Sam McVey in their rematch, winning a 10-round decision. Martin outpointed the hard-punching McVey at all stages of the game, demonstrating all of his cleverness and speed. After the victory, the locals called Martin's prior loss to McVey a fluke. The Los Angelinos liked the 23-year-old Martin, and wanted to see him in with Johnson again.

The Johnson-Martin rematch would be the last major bout held at Hazard's Pavilion, which McCarey's Century Athletic Club had used successfully for its promotions. Apparently, a Baptist church had obtained an exclusive lease that was soon to go into effect, and at that time religious folk were opponents of the sport and refused to allow further boxing programs to take place there.

Tom McCarey was not down and out, though. He already was looking into alternative locations to host boxing shows. He said,

> Since I have had charge of boxing in Los Angeles no city has had cleaner, better managed sport. There has never been a scandal connected with the game here and the people who have been good enough to patronize us have had their money's worth. The best men in the city – the solid business men – are regular patrons. ... We will soon have a place of our own, where we shall not annoy anybody and for the matter of that, people who are not in favor of boxing are not forced to attend our shows. On the other hand, since they do not

---

[450] *Freeman*, October 1, 1904.

enjoy them, they should be liberal enough to refrain from depriving others who do like them. You may say that not a single boxing date in sight will be canceled on account of this change in our plans.

At the Lily Club, where he was training, when Jack Johnson heard the news that the Baptist Church was taking over Hazard's Pavilion and would no longer allow boxing shows to be held there, he said,

Ah nevah would have thought it, nevah, nevah. An' him a Baptis', too. Yassir, dat's what hu'ts de worst, 'kase Ah'm a Baptis' mahse'l. Dat old buildin' where Ah whipped Jack Jeffries and Sam McVey and this Martin man what Ah'm to whip again on de 18th − dat old buildin' where de gate receipts is always so big − dat ole building turned plum 'round inter a Baptis' Church! ... Say, Bo, you wouldn't think one Baptis' oughter treat 'nother Baptis' like dat, would you?

Boxing was not dead, though. "There are many influential citizens who favor this kind of sport and who patronize it liberally." A substitute location likely would be found. McCarey said, "There is room enough here for all of us to get along peaceably and without conflict."[451]

On October 7, 1904 in Milwaukee, in a middleweight bout, "Philadelphia" Jack O'Brien won a 6-round decision over Tommy Burns.

The *Los Angeles Examiner* said Jack Johnson was not a tough interview. He usually was full of talk, and it was no trouble at all to learn his opinions. A reporter did not "have to arm himself with a corkscrew in order to extract answers. Jack always has a great deal of surplus language." Johnson said,

Ah reckon youalls wants to know how Ah'm feelin'? Well, if Ah felt jess de leas' mite better, Ah'd have to call in a doctor! Couldn't possibly stan' it! In course, Ah looks bigger − Ah IS bigger! Ain' no trouble foh me to tell about mah weight − Ah'm no Jeffries. Yesterday Ah weighs 185, an' Ah reckons as how Ah'm gwine be bigger yit! ...

Nevah felt mo' like winning in mah life! Youall knows Ah ain't been fightin' much East. Gotter win something so's Ah kin pervide mahse'f with that new fall wardrobe. Gotter have some of them brown weskits an' some of them tan suits. When Jack Johnson gits trimmed down so's he's only got 'leven suits what he kin allow himse'f to wear, something's got to be doing right presently.

Ah sees that Kid McCoy says that Cohenski...hits him de hardes' wallop he evah remembahs. Say, bo, you alls write me down 'long side McCoy. That Cohenski he suttinly is a earnest an' a tremejous hitter! Bo, a gover'mint mule is a spring lamb to that Cohenski! An' a left hand − m-m-m, he's jess outrageous with it! Ah oughter know,

---

[451] *Los Angeles Examiner*, October 8, 1904.

'cause Ah's fought lots of these punishin' hitters an' this Cohenski party, he sure is the leadin' man when it comes to handin' out a little sufferin' on the end of a four-ounce glove! White man, feel de lump on top of dis haid. ... Well, dat's a triflin' present from Cohenski. Suah, he pounds mah haid clean outen its usual contour...an' ef dey hadn't stop de fight Ah'm tellin' yo' he'd ha' done wuss things to me than that. Cohenski is the onliest man what knows me down in a fight. See that scar on top of mah dome of thought? Ah wins it in Philadelphia. Ah wins it out with a quart bottle. Ah'm coming outen de ring afteh fightin' six rounds when wham! Some gen'leman what Ah nevah even been presented to busts his bottle on mah crust! Nevah even staggers me, but Cohenski he hits me er general wallop alongside mah lef' eye an' Ah hits dat floor like Ah's 'lectrocuted! Well, they stops the fight, an' ef they hadn't Ah'd hey stopped it mahse'f. ...

Suah, there's a fat chance fo' me to fight Jeff. Afteh this fight Ah'm going' afteh him an' deman' a scrap. How kin he be champion of the worl' if he don' meet all comers? Britt's goin' wipe up de color line an' tackle Gans, an' the public will expec' Jeff to meet me. Guess Ah'm de onliest heavyweight what wants a chance an' if Ah cain't stall along longer than Munroe Ah don' want a cent fo' mah services.

The *Examiner* agreed that Johnson was the only man in the ring at present who really deserved a fight with Jeffries. Johnson hoped to dispose of Martin in such quick time as to enable him to use the fight as a means of forcing Jeffries to pay attention to him. Johnson weighed 185 pounds and was growing larger all the time.[452]

Ed Martin was training hard at the Onyx Club on Alameda street. The "giant mulatto" was very satisfied with his progress. His long morning runs had improved his wind, and he could box 10 rounds in the gym without showing even the first signs of weariness or shortness of wind. Ed had a piano playing at the ringside while he trained.

Martin's chief sparring partner was a black fighter named Edward Whitesides, who was the "color of an old boot" and looked something like Joe Walcott. Whitesides was called a black Joe Grim, for like Grim, he could absorb a lot of punishment. He was aggressive and went in to knock Martin's head off. Martin hit Whitesides with a right uppercut under the chin that lifted his feet a foot off the floor and sent him down to the mat onto the back of his head. "It was a punch which would have stopped a rhinoceros, but Whitesides only shook his head like a bull and came boring in again." Martin also boxed 3 rounds with Frank Fields, and then a few more with "Muscogee," a "handsome young negro" who Martin played with and hammered at will.

Martin said,

---

[452] *Los Angeles Examiner*, October 11, 1904.

Ah sees Johnson says he's going to get a fight with Jeff on the strength of what he's going to do with me. Better tell Mistah Johnson to wait a lil' while - wait a week anyway. Mebbe Ah'm the feller who's going to challenge. Ah'm faster than evah befo' and if you watch me work, you'll see mah wind is right. Ah cain't see where Johnson has got it on me foh clevahness, on me whatevah, and Ah guess Ah can git away from that punch. Mebbe Ah can punch mahse'f. Ask Joe Grim over there![453]

MARTIN ADVISES JOHNSON TO DELAY CHALLENGE TO JEFF

"DENVER ED" MARTIN AND HIS POWERFUL RIGHT, WITH WHICH HE EXPECTS TO PUT A STOP TO JACK JOHNSON'S ASPIRATIONS FOR CHAMPIONSHIP HONORS

Zeke Abrams, Johnson's manager, came into town with a fat roll of bills, and he was willing to bet all of it on Johnson. Each fighter had put up $250 forfeits with Century Club Manager McCarey.

---

[453] *Los Angeles Examiner*, October 12, 1904.

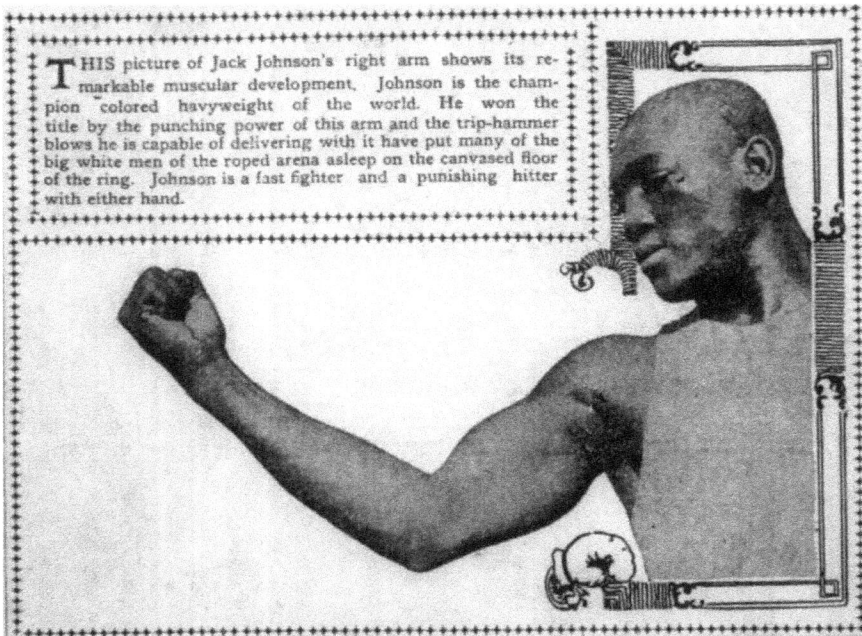

THIS picture of Jack Johnson's right arm shows its remarkable muscular development. Johnson is the champion colored heavyweight of the world. He won the title by the punching power of this arm and the trip-hammer blows he is capable of delivering with it have put many of the big white men of the roped arena asleep on the canvased floor of the ring. Johnson is a fast fighter and a punishing hitter with either hand.

Both participants were in top condition. Martin had been sparring with Frank Fields, Dixie Kid, and Edward Whitesides. The *Herald* said Martin was "just as speedy as he ever was and with a punch in either hand is confident that he will be the dingy heavyweight champion before another week has passed." The motivated Martin was working hard, realizing that defeat would make him a back number.[454]

At that time, the *Seattle Republican* printed an article by Clifton Johnson that was written for the *Springfield Republican* (in Massachusetts), which offered some insights regarding the feelings of whites towards blacks, particularly in the South.

> One of the oddest impressions that a northern person gets in the South is that there are no colored people or Negroes there, but only "niggers." The term is recognized as opprobrious. It is like calling an Irishman a "paddy," an Italian a "dago," or a farmer a "hayseed." It is equivalent to a kick, yet there is a superstition that it is not only the Negroes' due, but that it is necessary to administer these verbal kicks in order to avoid the possibility of their forgetting their inferiority. Besides, it is affirmed that the Negroes will not work unless one is rough and vigorous with them. "If you want anything done, you must say, 'Come here, nigger!' Why, if you was to say, 'Come here, Mr. Jones,' they wouldn't do nothin' for you."
>
> "A nigger is all right in his place," the whites explain, but add emphatically that his place is very lowly and that he must not step out

---

[454] *Los Angeles Herald*, October 14, 1904.

of it. If he fails to keep "his place" of his own volition, they will go to any length of force or subterfuge to compel him to do so. ...

The intolerance with which the Negro is regarded is a natural outcome of the former relations of master and slave; but it is depressing to find that in all the years since the war, so little progress has been made. Men of intelligence will soberly argue with you that "niggers" are not wholly human, that they are more akin to beasts and should be dealt with accordingly. "If anything would make me kill my children," declared one woman, "it would be the possibility that niggers might sometime eat at the same table and associate with them as equals. That's the way we feel about it, and you might as well root up that big tree in front of the house and stand it the other way up and expect it to grow, as to think we can feel any different."

I was solemnly assured that for a southern white man to invite a Negro, however accomplished, into his house as his guest, would mean that white man's social ruin. "It's like this," one informant remarked — "equality ain't safe. Now I've got a servant that was raised with me. He loves me and I love him. He'd do anything for me, and I've remembered him in my will. But if I was to take him into my family and treat him like a white man, he'd murder me in three days. They always do jus' thataway when you go to favoring 'em."

"And yet the president of the United States has had a nigger to dine with him! The South never got a worse shock than that. Up to then we'd thought a heap of Roosevelt down hyar. Why, we'd named all our dogs after him and members of his family; but we've changed those dogs' names since that dinner."

In one town I heard a tale of a colored army officer who attempted to attend a white folks' church and sit in a pew among his white skinned brethren. To them this was intolerable. They compelled him to get out, and he barely escaped the worst scouring he ever had in his life. ...

Whatever tends to lift the Negro out of a position of servility is regarded with suspicion and irritation. ... "You northern people don't understand this matter. If you would come down here and live six months you'd see it just as we do."

Their view is that a Negro must constantly in word and action acknowledge the whites' superiority. He must be respectful to them on all occasions, while it is optional with them whether they shall be respectful in return. Hence they have a decided preference for the older Negroes who began life as slaves and have had the right sort of training to make them humble. ...

The sentiments of the whites being such as they are and their pride in their superiority so keen and belligerent, it is no wonder that the lynch spirit is often aroused. Unquestionably there are Negroes who are to be feared, and they are a good deal of a nightmare to the southern household. The whites all have guns in their houses ready, for black depredators. ... Very little provocation is required from a Negro to make a white man get out his gun, and bullets and lynch law are not by any means reserved for the more serious crimes. ...

I do not wish to infer that sympathy is entirely lacking between southern whites and blacks. In most ways there is no friction, and as a rule the whites are considerate and kindly. ...

But after the war there was chaos. "The niggers were turned loose just like a herd of cattle," an Alabamian enlightened me. "There never was a more fatal mistake. Not one in a thousand knew beef from a side of sole leather. We've got an ole nigger still living in this town who come clost to getting into the United States Senate, and he's only a common brick mason. I bet he couldn't tell in three guesses how much seven and six is."

The situation was intolerable, and the whites felt they must by fair means or foul disfranchise the blacks. ...

It is recognized that the colored people must feel chafed by southern conditions, and yet it is argued that they are better off than they would be in the North. A story told for my benefit was that, "There was a Mississippi nigger who had been sent to the penitentiary, and the governor of the state give him his choice between bein' set free and goin' to Massachusetts, and he said he'd rather go back to the penitentiary."

The joke perhaps travesties Massachusetts, yet our treatment of the Negroes is scarcely angelic. We have the same feeling of superiority that exists in the South. This is characteristic of the Anglo-Saxon race in its relations with all other races, and very likely the North would discriminate against the blacks more if they were with us in greater numbers. Nor is the southern antipathy without any reasonable foundation. A colored preacher recently declared: "The only way to get rid of the 'Jim Crow' car is to get rid of the 'Jim Crow' Negro. If I could use 200 bars of soap on the unwashed Negroes that travel on trains and hang around depots I would solve the Negro problem about 20 per cent."

There is a vast deal of slovenly poverty and thriftlessness, easy morals and lack of ideals among the Negroes, and the leaven that works for better things is entirely inadequate. The chance of their being vouchsafed any but the most meager political rights for a long time to come is very small; and it would seem as if their especial need was to strive quietly and steadily for better homes, for better and more general education, and for the ownership of property. They are a race apart, and must learn self-reliance and build up a worthy social life in their own ranks.

It is often claimed by southern men that the Negroes were better off as slaves than they are now, with regard to physical comfort and all essential needs, but this view finds no indorsement among the Negroes themselves; and even the whites are agreed that for the owners and the South itself slavery was a curse.[455]

Efforts would be made to convince Jim Jeffries to fight the winner of Johnson-Martin II, despite the fact that Jeff clearly said that he would never give a black man a chance to fight for the championship. Abrams would never stop urging Johnson's claim. Others hoped that Jeff might be persuaded to waive his objection if the public demanded the fight and there was enough money in it. However, the question was, when push came to shove, whether the public, press, or promoters actually would demand or back a mixed-race heavyweight championship fight.[456]

Johnson was a strong 2 to 1 favorite, but Martin was full of confidence. He boxed with four or five "dark gentlemen" each afternoon, pounding away on them. The consensus of opinion at the Onyx Club was that Martin would surprise Johnson. Ed said, "Ah jess been a loanin' dat champeenship to Jack, and now Ah wants it back. … Ah'm shorely going at him hard to git it back."

Johnson was training at Ernie's gymnasium on the Downey block. He heard about how Martin had been pounding on Ed Whitesides, who could take it like Joe Grim. Pleasantly grinning, Johnson said,

Bettah tell Mistah Martin mebbe it would go good fo' him to stan' some of that Joe Grim business. Fo' Ah shorely am a goin' to hit him an' Ah'm goin' to hit him right hard. Mebbe he better condition himse'f to stan' de beating an' not dat Whitesides man. … Youalls remember as how we put up one rattling great fight heah onet? Bo', Ah've heerd noises some in mah time and Ah'se been present at a right smart heap of disturbances, but lemme say, Ah nevah in mah life heahs nothing like dat noise when Ah has Martin on de floor dat time! Every man in the place is up on he hin' legs yellin' like loonatics! Yassir! Can't nobody say he didn't get his money's worth dat night! An' Ah'm jess as right now as Ah was then, and Ah hope Martin will be as good, too![457]

Martin responded to the odds making him a 2 to 1 underdog, which he took as an insult to his abilities.

---

[455] *Seattle Republican*, October 14, 1904.
[456] *Los Angeles Examiner*, October 15, 1904.
[457] *Los Angeles Examiner*, October 16, 1904.

Jess 'kase Johnson soaks me one wallop in dat las' fight is no criterion as to why he's a 2-to-1 favorite on me now! Ain't Ah favorite over him dat las' fight? Ain't Ah goin' some in de las' five rounds? Huccome dis man from Galveston a 2-to-1 shot? Dat's what Ah wants to know! In course Ah's glad dat mah frien's kin git a good price on me – Ah's tickled to death dat they gits a chance to mek money an' all dat, but mah professional feelin's is ruffled, sah, badly ruffled! Ah ought to be even money wid dis man, bo, even money! Mighty seldom they's any real legitimate two-to-one shots in de fighting business. Man's always got a grand chance so long as he kin stan' up an' pump 'em in, aint't he? Well, run 'long an' git some of dat 2-to-1 money – all mah frien's will be spendin' it on Wednesday!

HOW MARTIN IN TRAINING LOOKS TO THE CARTOONIST

Los Angeles Examiner, **October 16, 1904**

On October 16, Whitesides refused to box any more with Martin. He was angered by the beating that Ed was putting on him every day. "Martin was unusually rough in the clinches and the fat negro was knocked down so many times in quick succession that he finally lost his temper." Whitesides, said,

Look yar, yo' blame big gorilla! Whuffor you' all de time a soakin' me on de one spot? Whut mek yo' never hit me nowhar but on disyear side of my jaw? Doggone yo', Ed Martin, ah ain't been a eatin' nothin' on de lef' side of mah face foh a week already an' yo' still a soakin' me on de point! Scatter yo' blows, man! Scatter yo' blows! Ain't nuffin' scientific about dat – always a hittin' an' a slammin' on de same ol' spot! ... Dis' years de las time, Ed Martin! De LAS' time! Think 'kase yore a yaller niggah and ah'm brack, dat ah kain't FEEL nothin'? Yo' done pasted his coon a plenty an' now Mistah Whitesides is done gone on a strike! Yo' go git a cigah sto' Injun an' beat HIM up!

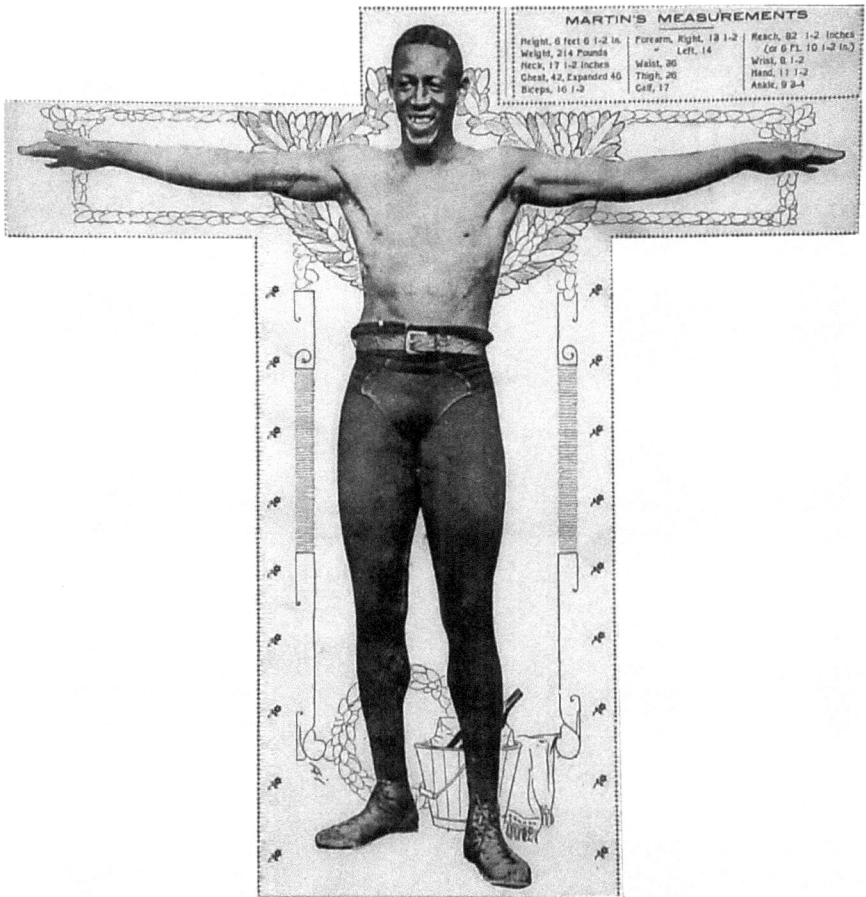

MARTIN'S MEASUREMENTS

Height, 6 feet 6 1-2 in.	Forearm, Right, 13 1-2	Reach, 82 1-2 inches
Weight, 214 Pounds	" Left, 14	(or 6 ft. 10 1-2 in.)
Neck, 17 1-2 inches	Waist, 36	Wrist, 8, 1-2
Chest, 42, Expanded 46	Thigh, 26	Hand, 11 1-2
Biceps, 16 1-2	Calf, 17	Ankle, 9 3-4

Martin was in great shape, and "never before has he showed the conditioning that he does now." His muscles were like steel, his wind perfect, his speed remarkable for a man so large, and his eye for distance was as good as it ever was.

However, Martin was the underdog, in part because the sense was that he had what was known as a "paper jaw." "Martin can be knocked out and knocked out with one punch if it happens to land on a vital point." In Johnson, Ed was boxing against a man whose cleverness was "not second to that of Jim Corbett at his best. He is as showy as Corbett in his manner of fighting and his blocking is a revelation in itself." Johnson had been dropped and stopped only once in his career, by the "man-killer Choynski," when he was a much smaller and less experienced fighter than at present. Jack had a punch, the cleverness to land it, and the defense. Hence, he was the favorite. That said, Martin had gone 10 rounds recently with McVey, a man known for his punch, and had defeated him.[458]

---

[458] *Los Angeles Examiner*, October 17, 1904.

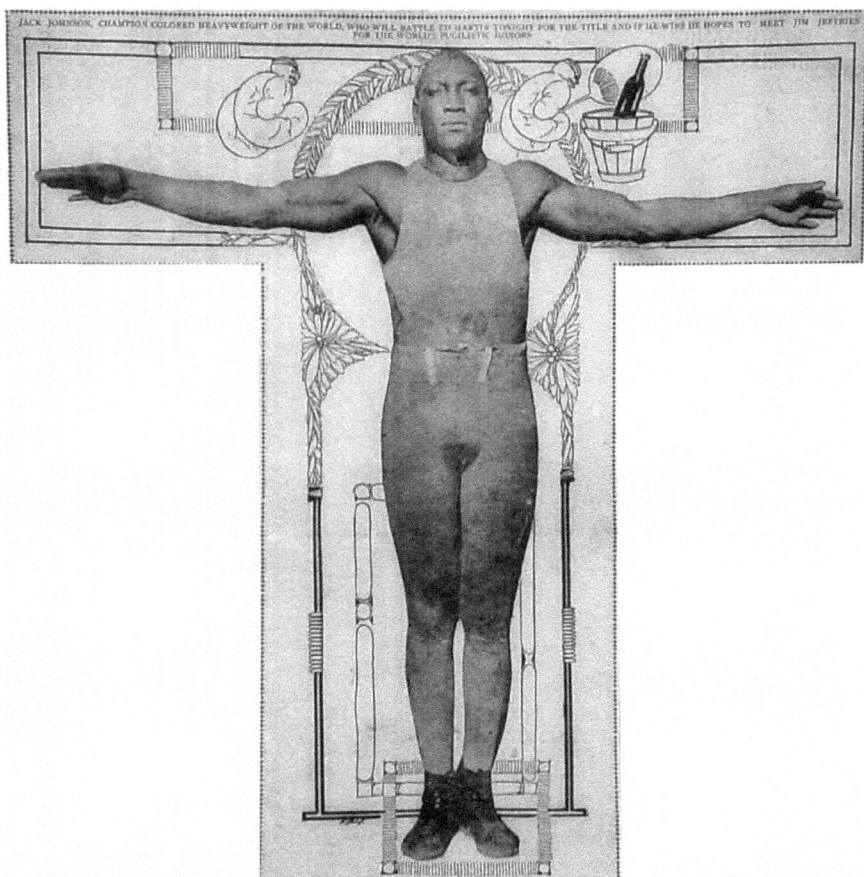

The *Los Angeles Herald* said Martin would have the crowd on his side. He generally was better liked than Johnson, both in terms of his style and even on a personal level.

> Denver Ed always conducts himself in a most fitting manner and has won the ring patrons by the way in which he fights, always clean and aboveboard. Johnson, on the other hand, is but a slight personal favorite even with those who support him with their money, and if Denver Ed whips him tonight but few tears of sorrow will be shed.

Much of the betting was wagered on whether the fight would terminate within 10 rounds or go longer than that. The over/under was at even money.

Martin would have the best of the weight by 22 pounds. He allegedly weighed in the day before the bout at 205 pounds (though some said he was closer to 214), while Johnson allegedly scaled 183 pounds. Both men felt that they were at the proper weight for themselves.

Manager McCarey promised the combatants that if their fight was up to expectations that he would do all in his power to match the winner with Champion Jeffries. The *Los Angeles Herald* said,

As Johnson has been hollering for a go with the champ for some time it is expected that he will make a rushing fight of it from the tap of the gong tonight, and as a result of this fact the betting contingent is playing the go to be of short duration. Just why they should look at it this way is an open question, for Martin is known to be some of a mixer himself.[459]

The *Los Angeles Times* said,

> Considering the form of the men, it looks anything but probable that Johnson will finish his man before the fight has half gone its scheduled course The colored heavyweight champion has never won any medals as a "knocker out," owing to his cautious style of fighting. He has announced an intention to break away from his old habit and tear in tonight, hoping to make so decisive a battle that Jeffries will be forced to concede him a chance at the title, but fighters have promised that before, and if Johnson keeps his word there will be more than one man surprised in this town tonight. For verily it is easier for a leopard to change his spots than for a fighter to change his style. Johnson has the endurance, the strength; he carries the guns and has the armor to make a splendid battle at close quarters, but always has been content with punching his men at long range and winning decisions.

However, it conceded that both fighters knew that a fight with Jeffries might be made if they performed well, in an exciting fashion, and that such might motivate them to make a hot fight of it rather than fight cautiously.

> The men have every incentive to tear in from the gong, and should they make a rough mix-up of it, all predictions are worthless. Neither is an adept at that style of milling, both being lovers of the long-range game, though on occasion Johnson has shown that he could infight with strength and skill.

Martin was considered the most showy in style, while Johnson was quite as effective while using less expenditure of energy. Martin had weight, height, and reach advantages. Johnson was favored in terms of endurance and rugged strength. He was also the harder puncher. In the final analysis, the *Times* opined that it was hard to pick anyone but Johnson, though it felt that it likely would require him to go the distance to win.

> He has never been a sprinter; going the route has got his purses. So the prediction would be Johnson in twenty rounds, assuming the men fight as they always have fought. If they mix from the first somebody is liable to drop early. Johnson's capacity for assimilating punishment is better surmised than established, as he never yet had to take a beating from anybody. Martin is game enough, but his physical make-

---

459 *Los Angeles Herald*, October 18, 1904.

287

up is not such that he can take the gaff, and a good punch may get him any time he becomes careless. Roche has trained him carefully, and if need be, Martin can prove hard to catch. The advance sale of seats indicates that most of the town wants to see how it is for itself.[460]

The *Los Angeles Examiner* echoed that Johnson had never evinced a desire to "tear in," which caused many to like the betting proposition that the fight would go over 10 rounds. However, it agreed that there was an incentive for Johnson to throw caution to the winds, to make the kind of showing that would enable him to point to it as entitling him to a championship match.

Regardless of the bout's potential length, Jack remained a 2 to 1 betting favorite to win. "People in the South hate to bet against Johnson. He has won a barrel of money for his backers and they know him to be careful, extremely clever and a protector of the money from first to last."

Johnson was fit and ready. He was larger than ever before, and since he was young, at age 26 he still had a certain measure of natural growth coming. "His arms appear more powerful than ever before and he wallops the black punching bag unceasingly and seemingly without fatigue."

More and more sportsmen wanted to see world champions be willing to meet all comers. Such continual insistence had forced Jimmy Britt into making the upcoming fight with Joe Gans. It was hoped that the same would be the case with Jeffries.[461]

On Tuesday October 18, 1904 at Hazard's Pavilion in Los Angeles, under the auspices of Tom McCarey's Century Athletic Club, the Jack Johnson vs. Denver Ed Martin rematch took place.

After the preliminaries, Johnson came to the ring first, wearing a suit of pink pajamas which put the crowd in good humor. Upon seeing Jack's apparel, a black man in the audience who was wearing a black check suit arose and exclaimed, "My King! Looka dat niggah!" The *Examiner* said, "We have seen Kid McCoy's fighting trousers and Twin Sullivan's green belt; we have seen Jim Jeffries and his red, white and blue sash, and we have seen S. McVey and his face, but Jack Johnson's pink pajamas win by miles and miles."

The "dream of pink splendor" leaped into the ring like "a barber hurrying to catch the customer with the money." The crowd cheered the "champion mandolin player and colored pugilist of the world." Jack sat in a corner.

After some time passed, the next "dark cloud" to enter was Martin. He was attired neatly in a passé dressing gown and a big gray sweater. The *Herald* said that although Ed was given a cordial reception, Jack's pink pajamas had won the noise. However, the *Examiner* said Martin was cheered

[460] *Los Angeles Times*, October 18, 1904.
[461] *Los Angeles Examiner* October 18, 1904.

more loudly than his opponent. With Martin were a troop of "black-face minstrels." They put him in a chair and fanned him with towels.

Not to be outdone, Johnson whistled, and several of his colored supporters entered the ring. Under their strict supervision, Martin arranged bandages on his hands.

Fat Albert, the announcer, introduced Norman Selby, better known as Kid McCoy. McCoy wore a Tuxedo, a ruffled shirt, and a bow tie. Referee Charles Eyton wore a soft white shirt, and he was freshly shaven.

Observing Johnson, Eyton, and Martin together, James Morely, who managed the local Los Angeles baseball team, said the color scheme of the three men looked like a checker board.

COLORED HEAVYWEIGHTS AT THE BEGINNING OF THEIR FIGHT AT HAZARD'S PAVILION LAST NIGHT, FLASHLIGHT PHOTOGRAPH TAKEN BY AN "EXAMINER" PHOTOGRAPHER

JACK JOHNSON   "DENVER" ED. MARTIN

1 - Johnson adopted new tactics and pursued his opponent from the start. He threw vicious body blows, paying little attention to the jaw. It was obviously his intention to focus on the belly. Johnson's "thick, muscular arms like the legs of a horse in their sleek but massive symmetry, shot in and out as the rods of some great steam engine."

Both men feinted rapidly for an opening, and then started to mix it up. In the first tangle, Martin went to his knees. Several observers thought Martin had slipped to the floor in the clinch. However, the *Times* insisted that a short right to the heart had dropped Martin to his knees. Many did not see the punch, it was so short and fast.

Martin arose, but was weak on his legs and never again himself. Martin rushed into a clinch again. Johnson rapidly worked his right into the midsection.

Martin broke away and moved about, but then in another clinch, he again went to the floor. Folks were not sure whether he was being knocked down or was just slipping down without being hit. His footwork seemed awkward. One black spectator asked, "Whaffo that coon up dar? Dem feet uh his am better adapted foh restauran' wuk dan foh sprintin' roun' dis enclosure."

Martin rose and courageously made a rush, but his knees were unloosed, and coming into a clinch he slipped to the floor without a blow being struck, and Johnson in his anxiety swung off his balance and sat down suddenly as well. Another source describing this sequence said Martin showed none of his cleverness, and in a pull-and-drag about the ring, both men went to the canvas.

Jack jumped up smiling. As they came together again, Martin led with his left for the face and they clinched. Johnson worked his free right arm, hammering the kidneys and midsection with terrific force, doubling up the giant. As they broke, Johnson uppercut hard with a short but very stiff blow. In another clinch, Johnson landed his stiff piledriver right to the kidneys, belly, and heart, and again Martin winced.

At the end of the round, Martin rushed and planted a straight left to the face, his only good blow of the fight. Ed then blocked a hard right for the jaw. The gong sounded with both in Martin's corner.

Some said Martin had gone down several times in the round as the result of slipping without being hit. He seemed off balance a great deal, and his feet gave him trouble throughout. Others said it was the crushing force of body punches that had lifted Martin from the floor, and by the end of the round the finish was near.

2 - The tall fellow started in to mix it, trying to take a chance to change the tide. However, Martin slipped down, taking a three-count.

After rising and resuming, Martin clinched, and Johnson's right landed to the ribs. The "big mulatto" Martin landed a light left to the face. Johnson uppercut the jaw. Johnson charged and drove in left and right to the ribs with great force and Martin's body wobbled. Johnson forced the fighting, seeing that he had his man going.

The *Times* said Martin collapsed from a right to the ribs. The *Examiner* version said Johnson shot his right towards the jaw, and though the punch was partially blocked, he immediately followed it up with a whipping pile-driver left shift to the heart, and Martin went down as if struck by lightning.

Martin did not move for four seconds, and then slowly, one limb at a time, he got himself together and found his feet again at the count of nine. Martin raised his hands and awkwardly shuffled toward Johnson. His gloves waved uncertainly before him and his eyes were rolling in his head. Johnson immediately rushed and in a whirlwind mix-up fired his right heavily into the pit of the stomach and Martin toppled again, as if he was shot.

Martin rose at seven and went at it, but was all-in. Jack was careful for a few seconds, awaiting an opening. The yells of the house urged him to end it quickly. An opening came and again Jack landed his right to the body, dropping Martin for a nine-count.

Martin rose, and once more Johnson's piston-rod right crashed into the body between the stomach and heart – a solar plexus blow, and Martin's wobbly knees loosened. Jack immediately followed up and caught him with a vicious, clean, tearing left hook flush on the point of the jaw and the six feet, six and one half inches of Martin shivered, then toppled like a tree struck by lightning, falling face forward onto the canvas floor with a crash.

As Referee Charley Eyton counted, Martin tried to respond, at the count of six drawing up his knees under him, but it was as if his head was tied to the floor, and he could not raise it. He again went limp and fell forward onto the canvas, out cold. After the count concluded, his seconds had to carry his body to the corner. It was ten minutes before he recovered full consciousness and was able to leave the ring.

This time, Johnson gave the fans an exciting, quick knockout. He hurt Martin in the 1st, possibly dropping him one or more times, and dropped him four or five times in the 2nd round en route to a decisive knockout victory. The question was whether the critics would give him credit this time.

Instead of lauding Johnson's dominant performance, the *Los Angeles Herald* instead chose to denigrate his opponent. It harshly said that Martin was a disappointment, was finished as a fighter, and would no longer be a drawing card. Many spectators hissed him. It said that all the talk about Martin being in the pink of condition was simply "con" talk.[462]

Unlike the *Herald*, which focused on Martin's poor performance, the *Los Angeles Times* praised Johnson, who had shown class, using effective body punching to defeat Martin quickly and decisively. Burly "Black Jack" was bigger, stronger, and faster than ever before. He was determined to force the pace, as was warranted by his magnificent physique. The victory was quite impressive, short and sweet. Johnson was called a truly wonderful man; another Peter Jackson.

This Johnson was a "different man from the cautious, fearsome fellow who tentatively drew his opponent out" when he last fought Martin in Los Angeles, when he had won practically with one punch, but then allowed Martin to recuperate.

> The Johnson who beat down Martin's clever guard; who tore in for the body with uppercuts that lifted the giant's bulk from the floor; whose blows sounded as falling lumber – was a finished artist; a past master of the new school which says not "hit and get away," but "punch and punch again." Nor would a match between Martin's conqueror and the White King be any Jeffries-Munroe affair. In Johnson, the champion will meet the toughest game of his career – a man who not only can box with the best, but whose blows travel with

[462] *Los Angeles Herald*, October 19, 1904.

the speed of a shot and the smash of a pile-driver. No fool is this man; instead he is a cool, level-headed ring general equal to any, and up to all the veteran's tricks.

True, Martin was a "has been," but there was no fluke about the defeat. Ed had met a better man, and "one that other heavyweights had best sidestep from now on, always the White King excepted."

The *Times* fully supported Johnson's right to fight Jeffries. "No longer can Champion Jeffries urge lack of class in answer to Johnson's insistent demands for a chance at the title." Johnson's performance showed just how mighty he was. Until Jeffries abandoned his "untenable position on the color line and sets himself right with the world that loves fair play, Johnson's admirers will be just as incessant in their nagging as the black fellow himself has been."

Johnson said, "I want Mr. Jeffries next. I think I am entitled to a fight with him and it was to prove that I am right that I went in this way tonight. I am faster than ever and bigger, and stronger. I'll be no Jack Munroe and I guess everybody knows it."

After the fight, Tom McCarey announced his offer of $15,000 for a Johnson-Jeffries fight.[463]

The *Los Angeles Examiner* said it took only a trifle over five minutes for Johnson to batter Martin with rights and lefts over the heart and drop him time after time with terrific body blows, until a left clip to the point of Martin's "paper jaw" sent him down and out for the final time. The fight was short and fierce, and "Martin never had one chance in a hundred to win. He was fighting a different Jack Johnson than we have ever seen before."

The suddenness of it all had surprised the crowd. One moment they had seen Martin dancing in and out like a shadow, full of fight, and then next he was staggering uncertainly on his legs, his hands moving aimlessly in front of him, and his strength turned into weakness. "Johnson's blows had been delivered so quickly and at such close range that not half the people in the house saw them go home, but the effect was plain to all." Martin was awkward on his feet and clinched frequently to avoid punishment. To break them, Referee Eyton rushed between the "two Black Diamond express trains" in a dashing manner.

The net gate receipts, generated by patrons both black and white, were $3,885. Johnson received $1,165.50 and Martin earned $777, on a division of 60/40% winner/loser.[464]

The *Police Gazette* reported that Martin was out cold for so long that the police briefly detained Johnson until assured that Martin was not seriously injured.[465]

---

[463] *Los Angeles Times*, October 19, 1904.
[464] *Los Angeles Examiner*, October 19, 1904.
[465] *Police Gazette*, November 5, 1904.

The day after the fight, Ed Martin was interviewed. He said,

Ya-a-assir, he done done it ter me all right, mek no mistake erbout dat! ... Yo' tells 'em Denver Ed done receive HIS las' night – yo' tell 'em he got it GOOD. Tell 'em dat Johnsing pahty is one gran' fighting man – aw, tell 'em any ole thing you wanter – ah knows yo' will anyhow!

How does it happen? Sufferin' Moses in de bullrushers! How yo' 'spect dat ah'm gwineter know? Sposin' yo' backs inter a buzz saw, yo' gwine say 'Dis yere's de tooth whut cotch me? All ah knows an' all ah kin say is dat it happens kinder toomultaneous like – sorter simulchoose all ter onct an' ah never will know des whut he git me with but oh; bo, he done gits me RIGHT – mek no mistake erbout it. ...

Dat Johnsing pahty done rise one awful disturbance inside dis niggah! Youall sees him – ain't a hittin' me anywhere else but des' bam! Bam! Inter de stomach all dat fu'st round. Ah thinks mebbe ah kin git to him wit' a wallop or two an' git him leary, but he's right there des' like a butcher snippin' off pork chops an' des' as regular. Every time ah comes erlong, wham! In de clinches, an' ah sees dat if ah gits anything ah has to hurry.

Dat secon' round is kinder obscure like in mah recollections. Ah'm all right up to dat time when Johnsing meks a pass fo' mah jaw. Mah guard goes up in plenty of time, but de nex' thing ah knows ah's slowly and thoughtfully a removin' mah self from de floor. Ah hears aftehwu'd – an' de way mah ribs an' stomach a feelin' dis mawnin' ah reckons ah heahs right – dat Johnsing done sink somethin' inter mah stomach when mah hands done busy elsewhere. Done knock all de fight outten me right there. Ever git one of them wallops in de pit er de stomach? Hey? Med yo' feel like a orphan child for erwhile, all right, don' hit?

Well, dat's pinteely all ah knows. Ah'm listenin' to de little birds a singin', ah sees de green fields a wavin' and de cows in de runnin' brook an' all them other knockout dreams comes to me, an' when ah gits back to earth again ah finds ah been a long time daid, an' they done meks me de respperent of de information dat ah done been knocked stiff es a board.[466]

Johnson said Jeffries "was sidestepping behind the color line, and that Jeffries knew that he was the only fighter that could make the champion extend himself." Johnson also said, "I will not rest until public opinion forces Jeffries to recognize my claim for a fight with him. His drawing the color line is all bosh." Jack said Jeff was not entitled to draw the color line,

---

[466] *Los Angeles Examiner*, October 20, 1904.

for he had fought negroes before, including Griffin, Jackson, and Armstrong. Johnson called the color-line a time-worn, old, cowardly, four-flusher's means to side-step a top opponent.[467]

The *Los Angeles Examiner* said that as a result of his rapid defeat of Martin, Johnson was "a very much tickled coon" and was "crazy about himself," saying that he would give Jeffries no rest until he consented to a meeting. "There are many who believe that Jeff will make the Galveston gentleman jump out of the ring, but Johnson is not among them." Johnson said,

> Jess what Ah tol' you – jess what Ah tol' yo'. Ain' Ah good, bo? See me soakin' dat yaller man in de stomach las' night? Ah knowed he couldn't stan' no bombardment to de porch, so Ah nevah plays anywhere else. Dat jaw punch was jess a love tap, nuffin' else. Dat heart wallop done settled de fight an' now Ah'm after dat man Jeffries. Huccome he got er right to claim any championship when Ah wants a fight an' can't git it? Ain' he des nachelly 'bleeged to meet all comers? Yo' kin say foh Jack Johnson dat he's goin' to git er fight wit' Jeff one way or another, an' when he does, yo' string a pinch of change on dat short end, yo' hyar me, bo?

Zick Abrams, Johnson's manager, said,

> I believe this big black chap of mine has shown championship timber. … I think public opinion will force this fight on Jeff. You remember how it used to be with John L., don't you? Every time he appeared on the stage somebody in the gallery was sure to yell, "Why don't you fight Peter Jackson?" … I feel that he has earned it, earned it twice over, you understand me? … I see that the Eastern sporting papers are all for it strong. The Munroe business left a bad taste. Let Jeff fight a real man. I'll guarantee that Johnson will make a good showing and the champion won't have any cinch with him.[468]

Jack Johnson had fought five times in 1904, having gone undefeated. He had not lost in three years, not since his close decision loss to Hank Griffin in late 1901. He had won at least 14 consecutive bouts, many against tough customers with quality experience and solid reputations. He was coming off an impressive, dominant, quick knockout performance. Clearly, he was deserving of a title shot.

However, once again Jeffries declined to consider a Johnson match. It did not matter how good he looked in the ring, nor what style he used to win, for Jack was black. Between acts at the theater in San Francisco where he was playing Davy Crockett in a play of the same name, Jeffries said,

[467] *National Police Gazette*, November 5, 1904; *Utica-Herald Dispatch*, October 19, 1904.
[468] *Los Angeles Examiner*, October 20, 1904.

I do not care whether Johnson licks the Japanese army. I have repeatedly declared that as long as I am in the fighting business I will never make a match with a black man. The negroes may come and the negroes may go, and some of the negroes may be excellent fighters. Just tell the public that James J. Jeffries has made up his mind that he will never put on boxing gloves to give battle to an Ethiopian.

I might have admired Jack Johnson's prowess as a pugilist had I been at the ringside Tuesday night. I will even go so far as to state that I think he would be able to give a pretty good account of himself were he in the ring with a man many points better than the fellow he whipped last night. But when Johnson applies to me for an engagement I will tell him in direct language to look for some one of his own color and class to give him a fight.

I am against boxing black men first, last and all the time.[469]

Los Angeles Examiner, **October 23, 1904**

On October 29, 1904, the *St. Paul Appeal* reported that South Carolina Senator "Pitchfork" Ben Tillman, upon hearing the statement of someone who suggested that the race question could be settled by education, replied,

"Educate niggers?" repeated the senator, and then he laughed. "Say, there is only one nigger in 100 that can stand an education. The first thing that an educated nigger wants to do is to preach the gospel. If not that he wants to practice law or teach school. Somebody has got to pound it into their heads that they were put on earth to pick cotton and that's what they'll have to do in the South. You certainly have

[469] *Los Angeles Examiner,* October 21, 1904.

made a mess of the nigger in the North. It's mighty seldom that a nigger becomes educated. He gets a sort of veneering and wants to associate with white people, and when he learns that he can't he drops the veneering and becomes just a plain nigger. A nigger is a nigger and you can't make anything else out of him. It will come mighty near being war if the fifteenth amendment is not repealed."

The 15th amendment granted all citizens, regardless of race, color, or previous servitude, the right to vote.

What Credit Is It For An Elephant To Crush An Infant.

Cartoon that appeared in the *Freeman*

Jack Johnson was hoping that public pressure and economics would cause Jeffries to withdraw the color line. Such had influenced Jimmy Britt to withdraw the color line and fight world lightweight champion Joe Gans.

On October 31, 1904 in San Francisco, Johnson was present and introduced at the Britt-Gans lightweight championship. Britt thoroughly beat up Gans, but when Gans went down in the 5th round and Britt clearly struck him while he was down, Referee Eddie Graney disqualified Britt. Angry at the decision, Britt proceeded to attack and strike Graney before they clinched and went to the ground. The police entered the ring and intervened. The fight generated a whopping $31,790, of which the fighters had agreed to split evenly the 70% fighters' share, so each came away with about $11,123. Mixed-race bouts could generate a lot of money.[470]

---

[470] *San Francisco Call*, November 1, 1904.

Some, like the *Police Gazette* in New York, criticized Jeffries' drawing the color line, given that he had fought blacks prior to winning the title. Hence, they saw his decision as inconsistent and selective. However, Jeffries and Delaney saw a difference between fighting a black man in a championship bout and one in which the championship was not involved. The symbolic racial and social impact was much different. Jeffries was refusing to defend the world title against a black fighter, for he did not want to give a black man even the chance to win the title. Still, the *Police Gazette* said, "Many people say Armstrong was the cause of Jeff's drawing the color line, because he broke his arm on Armstrong's head."[471]

The *Police Gazette* said that Jeffries' lament over not being able to find an opponent worthy of his consideration would be silenced quickly if he would sidestep his prejudices and agree to fight a black man. The manner which Johnson whipped Martin, showing wonderful class, qualified him for a title shot. "Private advices say that Johnson looked every bit a whirlwind heavy of the kind that would make Jeffries fight for his life."[472]

In several of its issues, the *Police Gazette* continued supporting Johnson's challenges to Jeffries. It enjoyed trying to make good fights.

> Jeff does not seem to care one bit how many people may knock him and even accuse him of cowardice in warding off Johnson with the old-time color line dodge. He won't budge from his position, notwithstanding the public clamor that he fight the negro champion.

> Jack Johnson's record entitles him to a match with Jeffries and he is the only man now in sight who would seem to have a chance with the hitherto invincible rivet driver. Jeff will not add any to his popularity by sticking to his lately adopted color line....

> Ordinarily fighters don't make much of a hit when they draw the color line. The fighting game is not a calling that permits of such finely drawn social distinctions. The public does not care whether the champion in a certain class is black or white or green as long as he's a good, game fighter and willing to fight any deserving aspirant for his title without surrounding his championship pedestal with a lot of impossible and unreasonable conditions.

> When a fighter draws the color line it is usually not far to seek for the "nigger in the woodpile." A few years back many a first-class featherweight drew the color line on George Dixon. It's pretty safe to say that Tommy Ryan's principal reason for the color line was Joe Walcott. Even old John L. Sullivan had a bad case of the color line bugaboo. Peter Jackson was in his prime in those days. ...

---

[471] *Police Gazette*, December 3, 1904.
[472] *Police Gazette*, November 5, 1904.

So, taken on the whole, the color line is looked upon as a pretty shallow excuse for a good fighter to use in side-tracking a good match. There are but few who think Jeffries has any fear of Jack Johnson, but he, nevertheless, lays himself open to an accusation of cowardice in refusing to meet the husky negro.

Jeffries has a strong hold on the American people. He is a most popular champion. But a fighter is expected to fight, not rest on his laurels, while there is a man in sight who has a possible chance for the title. Jeff's most partisan admirer must admit that Johnson has a chance. His record certainly gives him a stronger title to fight for the world's heavyweight championship than Jack Munroe had. Denver Ed Martin is rated a better man than Jack Munroe. Yet Johnson put him out in exactly the same time and method in which Jeff finished the miner.

The fight loving public wants to see Jeffries fight and fight soon. Jack Johnson stands ready. It's up to Jeffries to forget the color line until he has rubbed this big black speck off his title.[473]

Providing a black perspective, the *Freeman* wrote that Jeffries was a coward who had disgraced the country.

The color line, as everybody knows, is out of date but comes in session only in social circles and is there only because the newspapers and the second degree of rich remind us of the fact. ... This is not a social question; no, it's a cowardly slugger's cry and yet some reporters don't seem to have sense enough to know that this nuisance has come to a place where the laugh is on the white man. ... Any fighter who is small enough to incite race prejudice in this new age simply to evade a Negro fighter for fear of defeat should retire from the business as quick as possible and so prevent a general white skin disgrace.

It believed that Johnson should keep after Jeffries and continually practice his craft.

Many big, strong fighters like Johnson would resent Jeffries' continual insults by publicly slapping his face and make him fight any how or shut his mouth forever. But I would not advise Johnson to slap Jeffries' face while he has his pants on for fear that the big coward would draw his revolver and shoot him dead. In such a case Jeffries could call it an accident and poor Johnson would be out of the way.[474]

If Jeffries was not going to fight Johnson or any other black man, then the question was what white contender had a chance to garner sufficient

---

[473] *Police Gazette*, December 3, 1904.
[474] *Freeman*, December 3, 1904.

public interest to justify a title defense. Promoters were trying to discover an eligible white opponent, but no one stood out as deserving. Since the public thought Jeff would blow through all white contenders, there was no match that would be financially lucrative or justifiable. The champion did not want another Munroe blowout. Hence, Jeffries was "in a peculiar position. He is a pugilist who wants to fight but cannot secure a logical opponent to meet him. ... Rather than swap punches with a negro Jeffries says he will go without an engagement and retire from the ring."[475]

Jeffries said that he would fight any white man that the sports-writers chose for him to fight. If the demand was present, he would fight again within a few months. If not, he would retire.

Omaha sports-writer Sandy Griswold criticized Jeff's color-line stance, though he did not believe it had anything to do with fear of Johnson.

> Not that I think for a moment that Jeff has the slightest apprehension as to the outcome with Johnson, for I believe he would be as easy as Jack Munroe, but his lofty stand is ridiculous to the extreme. ... He took down $12,000 for making a holy show out of that big Montana booby, and owing to the peculiar condition of things just now, I think he would double this sum by showing up the coon.[476]

On December 24 in Denver, Jeff performed in *Davy Crockett*. While there, he said,

> I have nothing against the colored fighter himself, but his followers. ... I have seen times, and from what Delaney tells me, when [Peter] Jackson was in his prime in San Francisco the colored element were almost unbearable. They were insulting and insolent and every time an argument came up about fighting they would insult all the white people within their hearing. I therefore came to the conclusion that I would not be instrumental in any manner, no matter how remote, of reviving that state of affairs on the coast.[477]

The *Examiner* said Jeffries was a dominant champion, and the men who wanted to fight him were only hoping for a big fat loser's end.

> The one man who is regarded by some people – not by all – as a suitable vis-à-vis for the colossal champion is a black man, and, as Jeffries never wavers in his declaration that he will retire from the ring before he will change blows with a negro, the prospect for a meeting between Jeffries and Johnson is particularly slim.[478]

W. W. Naughton said Jeffries would slaughter the present crop of young heavyweights. The scarcity of championship timber was marked in the

[475] *Police Gazette*, December 10 1904.
[476] *Police Gazette*, December 17 1904.
[477] *Pittsburgh Press*, December 24, 1904.
[478] *San Francisco Examiner*, January 1, 1905.

heavyweight division. Jeffries had a wonderful physique that enabled him to retain his fighting powers all these years, even though he had not exactly lived carefully. He had absorbed the punishing blows of men like Fitzsimmons, Ruhlin, and Sharkey, all of whom had good knockout punches. He intentionally had allowed the 200-plus-pound Ruhlin to hit him so that he could counter. However, "his massive jaw and his powerful frame seem to be as little susceptible of injury as the metal he used to hammer at in his 'prentice days at the boiler-making." He had even outboxed and outfooted Corbett, much to the surprise of many, proving that he was a complete fighter.

> Some fighters who are rock-ribbed, large limbed and heavily muscled are not able to impart speed to their movements or use their strength to the best advantage. Not so with Jeffries. He is quick on his feet and is both fast and sure with his punches. … Now it is admitted that the great big champion combines all the qualifications necessary to constitute him a world beater.

Given Jeff's determination to bar colored men, as of early 1905, the sporting public had about come to the conclusion that Jeffries likely had fought his last championship battle. Like Sullivan vs. Jackson, it appeared that the public would not be able to see Jeffries vs. Johnson.[479]

JAMES J. JEFFRIES.

Careful Study of the Prize-Ring Horizon Shows No Opponent For Jeffries

---

[479] *San Francisco Examiner*, January 4, 1905.

CHAPTER 14

The Road to Hart

Some said that Jim Jeffries was so superior to all others that it would be in boxing's best interests for him to retire and give others a chance to fight it out in competitive matches. As long as he was champion, he would be without an opponent who could give him a challenge, particularly if he would not withdraw his color-line objection. Hence, "Jeffries is so good that he is a bad thing to have around." In Fitzsimmons, Corbett, and Sharkey, Jeffries had defeated three of the greatest men known to ring history. "Jim Jeffries is the champion of all champions and the greatest wonder known to the world of sport."

In late 1904, another rising heavyweight contender, Marvin Hart, came to San Francisco and proclaimed that he wanted to fight any man in the world, including Jeffries.

> It seems rather presumptuous on the part of Marvin Hart to imagine he has a chance to beat Jim Jeffries but the Louisville former middleweight has grown into a smashing big fellow. ... [Hart] says he intends to tackle Kid McCoy and Jack Johnson...before fighting the big boilermaker. Hart may dispose of McCoy, who has seen his best days, and he may even put it all over Johnson, but he hardly has a chance to beat Jeffries. Hart weighs about 180 pounds when fit, and would be meeting Jeffries at probably forty pounds the worst of the weight. He is slow, awkward and not a marvel in point of science, although he has a pile driving wallop that can do a heap of damage if it lands.

Hart recently had fought the respected Gus Ruhlin to a bloody and entertaining 12-round draw. "The Louisville fighter is game, ambitious and knows how to take care of himself."[480]

Despite the recent report, in fact, Hart was reluctant to fight Johnson or any other black man. Johnson's manager, Zick Abrams, had accepted Hart's alleged challenge to fight anyone. Apparently, Alex Greggains of the San Francisco Club agreed to stage a bout between Hart and Johnson. However, Hart was from the South. He previously had drawn the color line on Joe Walcott and had refused to fight Johnson. He likely did not authorize the statement that he was willing to fight Johnson, but rather either his manager, Greggains, or a press agent had done so.

Regardless, the *Police Gazette* argued,

---

[480] *Police Gazette*, December 24, 1904.

If Hart expects to succeed Jeffries as champion when the boilermaker retires, he can show his prowess in no better way than by tackling Johnson. By whipping the black man he would at one bound take second place in the line, with no one ahead of him but the unbeatable champion. It is up to Hart to make good his challenge or class himself as a bluffer who wants easy game or none at all.[481]

MARVIN HART, OF LOUISVILLE.

Anyone who had followed his career knew that Marvin Hart was afraid of no one. As "Marvelous" Marvin was a Southerner from Louisville, Kentucky, he was concerned about taking heat from his hometown fans if he crossed the color line. Hence, he had never fought a black man. However, he knew that beating Johnson would quickly put him in line to fight Jeffries, or for a vacant title if Jeff retired. He also knew it was a potential money-making bout. A typically active fighter, Marvin had not been able to obtain a fight for several months, since May 1904, and diminishing funds have a way of motivating fighters to take fights that ordinarily they would not.

Like Johnson, fewer and fewer white fighters had been willing to take him on, making it tougher for Hart to obtain bouts. Fighters knew they would likely lose a decision to Johnson, but with Hart, they knew that they might get knocked out, or at least have to go through hell. Marvin had the reputation for hurting and punishing his foes.

Eventually, despite his concern about violating the color line, Hart was convinced to agree to fight Johnson. However, the question was whether Alex Greggains actually wanted to host the match. Both Johnson and Hart expressed themselves as willing, "but Greggains has not satisfied himself as to how the pair will draw." Despite his entertaining reputation, San Franciscans had never seen Hart box in an actual fight. Johnson's recent San Francisco-area bouts had been considered to be amongst his most dull and uninteresting, so he was not necessarily going to be a gate draw, despite his winning reputation.[482]

---

[481] *Police Gazette*, December 31, 1904.
[482] *San Francisco Call*, December 26, 1904.

Regardless, after some negotiations, on December 27, the 20-round Johnson-Hart fight was signed, initially set to be held on January 27, 1905 at Woodward's Pavilion under the auspices of the San Francisco Athletic Club. The winner would receive 65% and the loser 35% of one-half of the gate receipts. The combatants agreed to use Greggains as the referee. Johnson signed for himself, while manager Jack McCormick signed for Hart.

> Both men weigh over 200 pounds, but Johnson will probably tip the beam a bit heavier than his opponent. ...
>
> The match should create much interest, as the winner is almost sure to be pitted against Jeffries for the championship of the world. Johnson has boxed many times in this city, but never with a man who was able to give him a hard fight. For this reason, he has lacked popularity to a certain extent.
>
> In Hart, Johnson will meet a strong young fellow who is willing and able to take and return a punch. ... Hart has been an in and outer since his advent into pugilistic circles some years ago, but he has shown his best form lately and his friends say he is Johnson's master in the ring.[483]

Johnson immediately started training in Oakland. "Johnson is anxious to win quickly from Hart, as he thinks public opinion will then force Jeffries into the ring with him."

Hart trained about 16 miles north of San Francisco in Larkspur, where he had been boxing for some time. "From present appearances Jack Johnson and Marvin Hart will be two of the best trained heavyweight boxers which have stepped into the ring here in years."[484]

Marvin Hart was a very strong, active, and exciting fighter who could take any amount of punishment and always come forward throwing nonstop power punches with both hands. He had excellent conditioning and recuperative powers. He generally won his bouts by knockout, and even when his fights went the distance, Marvin usually managed to hurt or deck his opponent at some point in the bout. He was known to have all-out wars, forcing his opponents to duke it out with him. This made him a fan favorite.

The 5'11 ½" Hart had begun his career in 1900 as a large middleweight and small light heavyweight, but gradually grew into a heavyweight, weighing in the 180-pound range, though like Johnson, he was continuing to put on weight. Significant bouts included: 1900 KO6 Kid Hubert and KO17 Pete Traynor; 1901 KO11 Al Weinig, KO7 Australian Jimmy Ryan, KO16 Tommy West, KO6 Dan Creedon, KO10 Jack Beauscholte, and LKOby1 Billy Hanrahan (his only true knockout loss); 1902 KO3 Billy Stift,

---

[483] *San Francisco Call*, December 28, 1904.
[484] *San Francisco Call*, December 29, 1904.

KO3 Dick O'Brien, KO9 Kid Carter, W6 Stift, L6 Jack Root, and DND6 Jack O'Brien; 1903 DND6 Jack O'Brien (although outpointed early, Hart decked and badly hurt O'Brien late in both no-decision bouts), LTKOby12 George Gardner (retirement owing to broken right hand), DND6 Joe Choynski, and KO15 Kid Carter; 1904 D15 George Gardner (vast majority felt that Hart won), D6 John Willie, W20 Sandy Ferguson (most felt Sandy deserved a draw), and WND6 and D12 Gus Ruhlin. While in San Francisco, Hart had been sparring with a 19-year-old amateur named Al Kaufman, who soon would become a rising contender. Kaufman stood 6'1" and weighed 190 pounds, and was growing still. To that point, Hart's record consisted of at least 35 fights: 24 wins, 3 losses, 3 draws, and 5 no-decision bouts, with 19 knockouts.

Against common opponents with Hart, Johnson had a 1901 LKOby3 Choynski and D10 Stift; 1902 W20 Gardner; 1903 W10, ND6, and W20 Ferguson; and 1904 NC5 Ferguson. Hart had done better with Choynski and Stift, having fought Choynski to an entertaining no-decision draw in a war, and having knocked out Stift in 3 and winning a decision against him. However, Johnson had done better with Gardner and Ferguson. Johnson toyed with Gardner to win an easy decision, whereas Gardner and Hart had duked it out in competitive fashion, though most thought Hart clearly had won the rematch. Johnson's bouts with Ferguson were fairly dull, but Jack obviously won. Hart's battle with Ferguson was an entertaining bloody war, and though Hart won, many thought Sandy had earned a draw. Johnson had fought Hart's trainer/manager/sparring partner Jack McCormick to a 1900 ND15 and WDQ6.

On the East Coast, the *Police Gazette* reported that Johnson had agreed to stop Hart within 20 rounds or lose the fight, which perhaps explains why Hart took the fight. Hence, Johnson may well have handicapped himself. He was not known as a knockout artist, but rather an expert at winning points decisions, or at least not losing them.

> Johnson has agreed to stop the Southern man within twenty rounds, and Alex Greggains of the Yosemite Club has arranged everything. The two big men are to divide the proceeds on a sixty and forty per cent basis, and if Johnson does not put Hart away before the end of the bout he is to get the short end, regardless of what he shows as a clever boxer. In agreeing to knockout so tough a fellow as Marvin Hart Johnson has undertaken no easy task. Hart has been hailed as a comer by Eastern sporting critics for the past year or more. He is a big, tough boy, not overly clever, but with more than an ordinary amount of endurance. While he may not be able to reach Johnson with a knockout punch, it is certain that the colored champion will have to go some to put him away.[485]

---

[485] *Police Gazette*, January 14, 1905.

Whether or not Johnson actually had contracted to stop Hart is unclear. There could have been such an understanding, the report might have been in error, the terms could have later changed, or it is possible that advertising this was just a marketing ploy, a way to get fans to show up by assuring them that Johnson would put up a more entertaining bout than he had in the past, given the incentive. Perhaps it was the promoter's way to get Johnson to fight hard, and Johnson, feeling confident, and likely underestimating Hart, agreed. Local talk did not mention such terms. Such a feat, if attempted, would be quite difficult. Hart had been stopped only once, on a fluke in the 1st round when he was caught cold by a known puncher. He once retired with a broken hand. Other than that, no one had been able to stop Marvin Hart. The odds were not in Johnson's favor to do so.

The fact that the bout was taking place in San Francisco was no coincidence. "At present 'Frisco is the only centre where championship contests of at least twenty rounds can be had with the assurance of a large crowd." Only eighteen states allowed boxing, though most had many restrictions. California could host big fights because it allowed 20-round bouts.[486]

However, boxing was coming under attack even in California, as it intermittently did. State Senator William Ralston intended to introduce a bill to stop prize fighting. He said the state had attained a dignity equal to the East, but that California still had the reputation of being the "wild and wooly West" because prize fighting was allowed. The only way to destroy that impression was to destroy the game. He also said boxing needed to be banned because of all the crookedness and fakes that had been perpetrated. "The last fight I saw was the Sharkey-Fitzsimmons affair about six or seven years ago. It was the rankest fake ever put up on the public and I have never seen a fight since then. I have read, however, in the newspapers of many fakes since then and it is time the game is closed up."

The proposed bill created a panic amongst boxing lovers. The two legislative houses appeared to be about evenly divided. However, even those in favor of boxing were reluctant to speak up in its defense too much, for fear of incurring the wrath of their church-going constituents.[487]

Apparently, Alex Greggains was not sure what fight he wanted to host in January. He was making changes to his cards daily, discussing a myriad of bouts with various boxers. It was not all that clear that the Johnson-Hart fight would take place in January.

When Jack Johnson appeared at the San Francisco Club, as he passed heavyweight fighter and longshoreman Jim Casey, Casey whispered to a bystander, "I'd like to get the big nayger." Someone told Jack what he said. Johnson responded, "I'll fight him for $4. Clear away the chairs in the back

---

[486] *Police Gazette*, January 21, 1905.
[487] *San Francisco Examiner*, January 5, 6, 1905.

room." However, there were no hostilities. "This was a matchmaking party."[488]

Since the proposal of the anti-boxing bill, a deluge of fighters were expressing themselves as willing to fight. As was the case with the expiration of the Horton law in 1900 in New York, many fighters feared that their days of good paydays might be coming to an end, so they became more willing to fight. This gave promoters more options, and they wanted to select the bouts which they thought would be the most lucrative, before they no longer would be able to host boxing cards. Johnson-Hart was not necessarily at the top of the list.[489]

For whatever reason, the Johnson-Hart bout was derailed temporarily. Various theories circulated. There appears to have been some suggestion that McCormick's mouth may have caused him to fall into some temporary disfavor. On January 15, the *Chronicle* reported, "Marvin Hart has been barred from San Francisco fight arenas because his manager has been criticizing fights held in that city." The next day, it reported, "Marvin Hart and Jack Johnson are undoubtedly of championship caliber. Both talked themselves into nervous prostration as soon as they reached the Coast, and now they are unable to meet in the ring."[490]

In support of the theory about Hart's manager coming into disfavor, when the bout eventually was rescheduled, it was said, "Hart's manager, it seems was in bad odor on the coast, but Marvin, it is said, has renounced him, which placed the Kentuckian in good standing."[491]

On the East Coast, the *Police Gazette* offered an interesting theory regarding why the Johnson-Hart fight was called off, saying,

> The limelight of publicity has been turned upon an inside view of boxing affairs as they exist in San Francisco and the disclosures are of such a manifestly rotten character that an announcement from the authorities that no more contests would be permitted would not be surprising. Jealousy among the managers, brutal rivalry between the fighters, fakes, frame ups and crooked decisions have brought matters to a crisis. One of the first suspicious events was the cancelling of the supposedly on the level Marvin Hart-Jack Johnson fight, that was to have been held on Jan. 27. Rumors at once flew in all directions as to the cause of the cancelling.
>
> It is now asserted that the affair was booked as a frame up for Hart to win under all circumstances, so that he would be a logical opponent for Jeffries in March, because it was feared that if Johnson won, Jeff would still refuse to withdraw the color line.

---

[488] *San Francisco Chronicle*, January 7, 1905. On February 17, 1905, Sam Berger would knock out Jim Casey in 1 round.
[489] *San Francisco Examiner* January 15, 1905.
[490] *San Francisco Chronicle*, January 15, 16, 1905.
[491] *Freeman*, February 25, 1905.

So strong did this rumor become that the management called the fight off altogether.[492]

This rumor lent credence to the prior report that Johnson could not win in any way other than via a knockout. The feeling was that all Hart had to do was last the distance and he would win, so that a Jeffries-Hart bout could be arranged. There was no money in it for promoters if Johnson won, because Jeff was not going to fight him, no matter what. Hence, unless Johnson knocked out Hart, he was going to lose. Or so the rumor went.

Another perspective was that promoter Greggains was more interested in making some other, more lucrative bouts, before putting on Johnson-Hart, which caused it to be put on the back burner.

However, if the fix rumor was true, then it might make sense to call off the bout temporarily, until the legal issues surrounding the sport were first handled. A fight with any form of crookedness taking place before the vote on the anti-prize-fight bill would hurt boxing's chances to remain afloat.

One writer later opined that the reason why boxing was under attack by politicians like Ralston was because the sport's members brought it on themselves with their own big mouths and comments. The club-managers, the fighters, and their managers were the ones who stirred up the stench that finally filtered to certain persons who would have glove bouts banned. "Not knowing all the ins and outs of these pugilistic matters and forming an opinion by reading some of the caustic remarks of the men and managers as published, they come to the conclusion that all fighters are fakers."[493]

The *Freeman* later reported that Greggains practically had Hart and Johnson matched in January, "but as one of the Frisco publications refused to mention it in its columns he called it off and substituted Frankie Neil and Dick Hyland." Perhaps Greggains was concerned about a lack of promotion of the bout by the newspapers. But the question remains: why did the newspaper refuse to publicize the bout? Was it because of some suspicion regarding its legitimacy?[494]

On January 17, Mexican Pete Everett and Tom Tracy were released from federal prison, having served one year for engaging in a prize fight at Ponca, in the Oklahoma Territory, in violation of federal law. Boxers were not the especial favorites of the legal community.[495]

On January 31, 1905, Greggains promoted and refereed the Frankie Neil vs. Dick Hyland bout, won by bantamweight champion Neil via a 15th round knockout.

There was some discussion of Johnson possibly traveling to Australia to fight Australian black Peter Felix, although Felix had been knocked out by Bill Squires, a rising contender.[496]

---

[492] *Police Gazette*, February 11, 1905.
[493] *Oakland Tribune*, March 22, 1905.
[494] *Freeman*, February 25, 1905.
[495] *San Francisco Chronicle*, January 18, 1905.
[496] *Police Gazette*, February 25, 1905.

Regardless, as of mid-February, in San Francisco it was reported that negotiations for a rescheduled Johnson-Hart fight were ongoing. Greggains still wanted to make the match. Hart had been prepared to leave town, but Manager Greggains prevailed upon him to remain. It appeared at that point that the parties all wanted the fight. However, the Board of Supervisors had not yet granted a March permit, which was the reason given that the bout had been held up at that time.[497]

In response to Jeffries' declaration that it would lower the pugilistic game should a black man become champion, former colored pugilist Allen Johnson said Jeffries had to be slightly afraid of losing to Johnson. He disagreed that having a black champion would ruin the game. "The American public is fair minded enough to give fair play to any champion, no matter what his color or creed may be." Allen also had heard that Jeff declared that he did not want to fight a black man because their heads were too hard. "I can say that it does not take a harder blow to knock out a Negro than a white man."[498]

With the Ralston bill vote on the horizon, there had been an unprecedented scramble for the March boxing permit, with five clubs clamoring for it. Apparently, only one permit was given out per month. However, Greggains had filed his request first.[499]

Eventually, as of February 27, the Police Committee of the Board of Supervisors awarded the March fight permit to Greggains, manager of the San Francisco Athletic Club. He then announced the Hart-Johnson fight, to be held in late March. The fight was back on. "Greggains figures that the winner of this bout will be pitted against Jeffries, but the sporting public in general is rather doubtful of this fact."[500]

On March 1, 1905 in Grand Rapids, Michigan, 46-year-old 273-pound former heavyweight champion John L. Sullivan knocked out Marvin Hart's manager, 218-pound Jack McCormick, in the 2nd round, with a straight right to the jaw.[501]

On March 3, Jack Johnson arrived at Link Dennis' gymnasium in West Oakland to start training.

The *Oakland Tribune* said his name was John James Arthur Johnson. "He stands over six feet tall, rather well built, with a heavy pair of shoulders set beneath a shiny head that is shaped like a chocolate drop. When he smiles he shows a clean set of ivories and a lot of good nature." Jack had long arms and legs. He had big feet, and a size-15 shoe would not be too roomy for him. "In his manners he is quite gentlemanly, like Peter Jackson, and he knows that his color entitles him to a back seat when everything shows

---

[497] *San Francisco Call*, February 15, 1905.
[498] *Freeman*, February 18, 1905.
[499] *San Francisco Chronicle*, February 19, 1905.
[500] *San Francisco Call*, February 28, 1905.
[501] Even fat and at an advanced age, Sullivan still had serious punching power. *St. Louis Republic*, March 2, 1905.

white in front of him. He never fights outside the ring. He likes money, and spends much of it for clothes." He also liked jewelry and adornments, such as a watch, cane, diamonds on his shirt and tie, and a diamond ring on his finger. "That's Jack Johnson as he is today. What would he look like should he become the champion of both the white and black class?"[502]

On March 7, 1905 in Tacoma, Washington, 158-pound middleweight Tommy Burns fought Jack "Twin" Sullivan to a 20-round draw, though most ringside patrons felt that Burns deserved the victory.

On March 9, 1905 at Sacramento, the Ralston anti-prize-fight bill was narrowly defeated in the assembly by a vote of 35 Noes to 33 Ayes.[503]

Colored boxers J. Arthur Johnson and Joe Gans were scheduled to be the judges at an amateur boxing show on March 10 at Woodward's Pavilion.[504]

During early March 1905, both Marvin Hart and Al Kaufman were sparring every day with 1904 Olympic heavyweight gold medalist Sam Berger, who was preparing for a March 15 bout. Berger complimented Marvin. "Hart is rounding into grand fix, and I declare myself right here that I think he'll beat Johnson. I've boxed enough with him to get a better line than most people, and, believe me, he's the goods."[505]

Apparently, a man named Thomas Ryan was taking up a collection, trying to offer $10,000 as a bonus on top of any purse, to convince Jeffries to fight Johnson. He figured that some club would offer about $25,000 for the fight. Hence, Jeff could make a lot of money. He contributed $100 to the fund. When hearing about this, Johnson said,

> Well, well, I'll give a few dollars toward that fund myself. ... It is my one ambition to face the champion, and I believe that upon the showing I make with Hart there will be a public demand that he meet me inside the ropes.
>
> Public opinion is being gradually turned into the channel leading to the making of a match with Jeffries. He can not always refuse to meet me because I am not white, for he has fought colored men before.

Johnson would do some sparring with colored middleweight champion Billy Woods, who was preparing for his own bout.[506]

Every morning, wearing caps, sweaters, and heavy outer garments, Marvin Hart and trainer Jim McCormick were seen running along the park roads at a pace that would be hard to follow. They left from Sheehan's, on Ocean Beach, where Hart was training, and covered no less than 8 miles. "The big Kentuckian seems to enjoy his work, and the more difficult the task the more he smiles."

---

[502] *Oakland Tribune*, March 3, 1905.
[503] *Oakland Tribune*, March 9, 1905.
[504] *Oakland Tribune*, March 7, 1905.
[505] *San Francisco Bulletin*, March 10, 11, 1905.
[506] *Oakland Tribune*, March 14, 1905.

In the afternoon, Hart was sparring with McCormick, the hard-punching Dave Barry (who in May 1905 would lose a 20-round decision to Tommy Burns), and lightweight champion Jimmy Britt, 4 rounds with each. Britt's speed was great preparation for Johnson, whose speed was being compared with Corbett's.

Hart held back in sparring, never turning loose with his full power, although he still packed power. "He is essentially an infighter, and such a vicious one that even pneumatic body protectors were of little service to his sparring partners. It is claimed for him by Jack McCormick that Johnson's extreme cleverness will avail him naught."

By mid-month, Jack Johnson was running 12 miles every morning at Joe Millett's training facility near Colma, California. In the afternoon at Millett's, Johnson sparred with Denver Ed Martin and New York heavyweight Jim Haywards, 6 rounds with each for a total of 12 rounds. Johnson was in excellent condition.[507]

Various top boxers were asked to make their predictions for the Hart-Johnson fight. James J. Corbett said,

> Best fight the Pacific Coast has had for some time in the heavyweight line. ... The colored man is the cleverest of the two and should jab his man to pieces. I fancy Johnson's chances, but he will have to take care that he doesn't run up against Hart's handy right. Don't look to see the colored fellow win on a knockout – it will be points.

Bob Fitzsimmons said,

> Well, I don't know very much about this man Hart, but I understand that he is a big, strong fellow and I feel certain that his bout with the negro, Johnson, will be the best 'Frisco has seen for some time – years in fact. I venture to say that Johnson will win. From what I know of the two, I believe that he figures the best. Yes, Johnson should win after a hard fight.

James J. Jeffries said,

> Well, I should say that it's a pretty hard meeting to pick the winner. But on form Johnson should gain the decision on points. I will say, however, that Hart can deliver a blow capable of laying Johnson to the mat.
>
> Will I fight the winner? Well, no, not if it comes out the way I anticipate. My ideas are too well known.[508]

On March 17, Hart ran 10 miles. "Nothing seems to tire the big man from Kentucky; He is a glutton for work, and is always reluctant to quit, whatever exercise he may be indulging in, when his trainer commands him to stop." Marvin wanted all of the local talent to come spar with him, so he

---

[507] *San Francisco Bulletin*, March 17, 1905.
[508] *Oakland Tribune*, March 18, 1905.

could show them that he was the real deal, unlike Jack Munroe. Big heavyweight Al Kaufman joined his sparring crew.

McCormick wanted the soft surgical bandages to be put on inside the ring to ensure that there would be no application of plaster of Paris. He also wanted to make sure that straight Queensberry rules would govern.

McCormick said Johnson had been in the habit of wearing an elastic bandage which covered a portion of his abdomen. He would object to it. He wanted Johnson to wear the regulation ring costume.[509]

In his sparring, Johnson instructed Denver Ed Martin to bore in all the time, as he expected Hart to do. Martin obeyed his instructions, continually coming after Johnson. Occasionally Johnson cut loose with a hard wallop that ordinarily might spell a knockout, but the heavily padded gloves only made Martin stagger across the ring, and then he would come back for more.

Johnson was working harder in his preparations for this bout than for any of his previous ring affairs. A 10-mile run per day was the minimum road work. He never boxed less than 12 rounds. After the gymnasium work, Jack would take a six-mile walk before eating. Top conditioning for 20 rounds was no easy task.

Johnson ate well and tried to put on weight in the evening, given that he burned off pounds during the day. He was the picture of rugged health at 194 pounds.[510]

On March 18, wet roads kept the boxers indoors. Hart skipped rope for over an hour, an activity in which he was "in a class by himself, his skill and agility at the work being truly wonderful for a man of his size and weight." Marvin worked for another half-hour at other exercises. Trainer Jack McCormick was pleased with Marvin's condition. "There is no difficulty in training as willing a worker as Hart."

Having heard that Hart was a great body puncher, Johnson was devoting a considerable amount of time to developing his stomach muscles. Neither fighter was leaving anything to chance. The possibility of being matched with Jeffries was causing both principals to show a great deal of earnestness in their daily work.[511]

One local writer believed that it was an evenly matched bout, and agreed that the winner would be considered the logical opponent for the world championship. Hart was weighing 194 pounds, just 1.5 pounds more than Johnson. Hart was said to be the stronger and more rugged of the two. However, Johnson's admirers claimed that he was the cleverest big man ever to don the mitts, not excepting Jim Corbett.

A good fight was expected not only because of the even match-up and possibility of fighting Jeffries, but because Hart "has as much regard for a colored man as most Southerners have." The implication was that racial

[509] *San Francisco Bulletin*, March 18, 1905.
[510] *San Francisco Evening Post*, March 18, 1905.
[511] *San Francisco Bulletin*, March 19, 1905.

animus and the desire not to lose to a black man would be additional motivation for Hart.[512]

On the 19th, Johnson spent 20 minutes at the punching bag, 20 more skipping rope, 10 minutes with the medicine ball, and then 6 rounds apiece sparring with Denver Ed Martin and Jim Gallagher, showing his delightful condition. "He was never idle for a moment, and even during the minute rest between rounds he gave as neat an exhibition of shadow boxing as any one would care to see. The spectators went away well satisfied with the shifty smoke's condition."

Johnson's sparring bouts with Ed Martin came as near to a real fight as anyone could hope to see without paying admission. Jack was just as full of ginger at the end of the day as when he started.

While being rubbed down, Johnson said, "I never felt better in my life. I've been working hard for nearly three weeks now, and I could fight tomorrow. They tell me that this Hart is a pretty tough proposition, but he ain't worrying me none. I'm looking right over his head at Mr. Jeffries."

That same day, Hart impressed spectators with his business-like approach to gym-work at Sheehan's beach resort. Observers gave him little outbursts of applause as they watched him train. He showed considerable speed in sparring 4 rounds with big Jack McCormick and 4 more with shifty featherweight Dave Sullivan. Hart had a tendency to bore in continually. "In fact it is claimed for Hart that he has yet to break ground for an opponent." Hart always came forward. He delighted spectators with his exhibition of strength and endurance over two hours of work that would be hard to equal. Hart's wind seemed unaffected by his strenuous work.[513]

The *Oakland Enquirer* said that although the men would weigh about the same, they were different physically. Johnson was tall, with a long reach, while Hart was chunky and solid, like Tom Sharkey. He liked to rough it just like Tom did. Marvin relied more upon infighting.[514]

Having heard that Hart would rely on infighting to win the battle, Johnson responded by saying that he intended to show the public that he could change tactics and prove that he was just as much at home in the rough going as he was at long-range fighting. Johnson said,

> They tell me that Hart has yet to break ground for an opponent. Well, if that's the case, spectators will see something unusual, for I am going to make him back up some. I have been conditioning myself for close-range milling, and the Kentuckian cannot set too warm a pace for me. I am going to bet a little of my own money that Hart does not stay the limit.[515]

---

[512] *San Francisco Call*, March 19, 1905.
[513] *San Francisco Bulletin, San Francisco Evening Post*, March 20, 1905.
[514] *Oakland Enquirer*, March 21, 1905.
[515] *San Francisco Chronicle*, March 21, 1905.

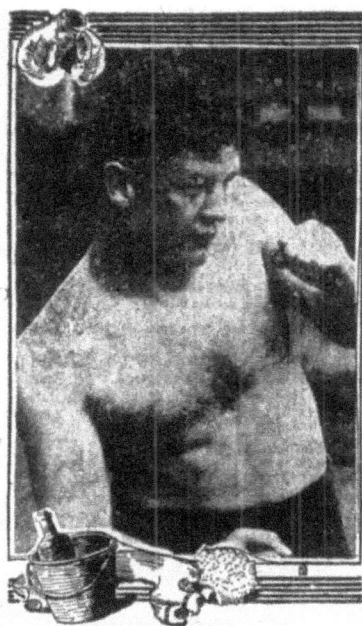

JACK JOHNSON.

JACK JOHNSON, THE COLORED BOXER, WHO WILL MEET
MARVIN HART.

In spite of the rain and slush, on March 20, Hart took to the roads, running his usual 10 miles. Marvin was a glutton for road work, and kept a fast pace throughout, always finishing strong. He had no superfluous flesh on his body. Although practically a stranger in California, those who had seen Hart at work were impressed with his ever-aggressive style and the ease with which he hustled about big men such as Jack McCormick and Al Kaufman. Hart boxed 20 rounds that day.

One newspaper said Hart had been assured of a match with Jeffries if he was successful against Johnson.

San Francisco Bulletin, **March 21, 1905**

Marvin's record was good enough to demonstrate that he was a high-class fighter. "He has met and defeated the best in the business." When Hart hit someone solidly, they usually went to the mat. He had been a full-fledged heavyweight for only about a year, but was strong enough to compete with anyone.

Likewise, Johnson was looking better than ever, and the amount of work he was doing each day was proof that he would be in condition to go 20 rounds on fight-night, March 28. "Johnson is well known in this city, where he has done his best work." Jack had won all of his local bouts, and had made himself conspicuous by challenging Jeffries at every opportunity. Furthermore, "He can take a wallop without flinching, and usually hands out as good as he receives." Another said, "Unlike most colored boxers, Johnson can take a beating if it comes his way, and has yet to show one trait of cowardice."

Both men were in first-class condition. "Two more rugged, big athletes would be hard to locate." At that time, Hart was weighing 194 pounds, while Johnson was weighing 192 ½ pounds. Johnson expected to weigh in the neighborhood of 195 pounds on fight-night.[516]

---

[516] *San Francisco Call, Evening Post, Bulletin*, March 21, 1905.

Originally, Hart had come to California with the understanding that Kid McCoy was to be his opponent, but when things didn't work out, he was convinced to take on Johnson.

> He is a Kentuckian, born and bred, and has the Kentuckian's race prejudice. It took an even two months to convince him that it was to his best interests to meet a colored boxer, even though Johnson was colored heavyweight champion of the world. Nothing short of his desire to get at Jeffries by using Jack as a stepping stone brought about the change of sentiment. The fact that he does not care to be put on an equality with a negro will only add fuel to the flame next Tuesday night. A Kentuckian is going to take a world of beating before he will succumb to a man of Johnson's color.[517]

On March 21, Johnson did not spar. Instead, he spent 10 rounds punching the bag and 10 more shadow boxing. He finished the day with a 15-minute wrestling bout with Ed Martin. Johnson was looking faster, stronger, bigger and better than ever. He also did a prodigious amount of roadwork that day, in part owing to the fact that he got lost on his run.

Hart was still sparring, but had cut the length of the rounds down to 2 minutes apiece. At 195 pounds, Marvin was looking as rugged and fit as any specimen of athletic manhood. "To say that Hart looks fit would be to put it mildly."[518]

W. W. Naughton said Hart had a world of confidence and feared no man. He long ago had established his reputation for grit. His punishing encounters with Kid Carter, another human bulldog, were sufficient to earn Marvin a name for courage. "He boxes in a free-handed, willing way with Kaufman and McCormick." The sound of the punching bag when he struck it gave ample evidence of his power. Naughton further said,

> Johnson has been seen in action many times by the sports of San Francisco, and the opinion prevails here that he is the only fighter in the lists at present capable of making Jim Jeffries extend himself. Hart is a stranger in these parts. He has nothing to commend him but his record and the work he is doing at present. Truth to tell, the record is not an imposing one. He has never overlooked a chance to fight. He has hooked up with some of the hardest men among the second-rate heavies. He has won and he has lost, but, taken by and large, his past has been a bloody rather than a brilliant one. ... [A]ccording to Trainer Jack McCormick, he will enter the ring weighing 196 pounds. This is quite a gain for a fellow who fought at 170 a couple of years ago.

Hart knew that performing well against a first-class heavyweight like Johnson could mean a heavyweight title shot. Marvin said, "I am a bigger

---

[517] *San Francisco Bulletin*, March 22, 1905.
[518] *San Francisco Evening Post*, March 22, 1905.

man, or I might say, a bigger fighter, than I was. I feel that I have increased in strength as well as in weight. I am certainly big enough for Jeffries, and I know, of course, that my chances of getting a whack at the world's championship hinge upon what happens next Tuesday night."[519]

The *Oakland Tribune* argued that the most important feature to the fight was the fact that the bout would determine whether or not Johnson had the right to demand a fight with Jeffries. If he "handily defeats Hart and shows 'class' in so doing, he should not be overlooked by the white fighter." However, if "Johnson does not in a few rounds show that he is superior to Hart, or if he resorts to his old tactics and breaks ground every time his

JACK JOHNSON SILENT

JACK JOHNSON, the fighter who is champion heavyweight of the division the color of this type, is working hard for his meeting with Marvin Hart next Tuesday and is saying nothing except—

"It's Jeffries next"

Oakland Tribune, March 22, 1905

opponent makes a rush, he should not be 'touted' as a championship possibility." The fight would "either make or break the colored man in so far as he can be considered as an opponent for Jeffries."

Requiring him to win in a certain way was not exactly fair to Johnson. Regardless, public opinion was necessary to get Jeffries to consent to rub out the color line, which Jeff had insisted he would not do, even in the face of Johnson's most entertaining performances (first McVey fight and second Martin fight), so it didn't really matter how Johnson performed. Yet, "win impressively" was a press mantra.

Hart was a bore-in-with-swings and take-a-punch-to-give-one kind of fighter. Johnson was "beyond any doubt the cleverest of all the heavyweights of today, and is regarded by many as showing more boxing cleverness than did Jim Corbett." He also had a good punch and a cool head. Against Gardner, Jack showed that he could put up as good a display of fistic knowledge as did Fitzsimmons. Gardner could not land a clean punch on Johnson.[520]

On the 22nd, Johnson played handball, an important part of his indoor exercise. He boxed 5 rounds with Ed Martin, doing little leading, being

[519] *San Francisco Examiner*, March 22, 1905.
[520] *Oakland Tribune*, March 22, 1905.

careful not to injure his hands. Johnson ran a 100-yard dash and showed his remarkable speed. It was said that he might have been a 10-second man had he devoted himself to sprinting instead of pugilism. Jack was weighing 193 pounds, and claimed to be in finer fix than he had been in for the past two years.

Jack was overflowing with good nature, smiling all the time. He entertained no thoughts of defeat. Johnson told his camp members that Charles M. Schwab had the best private rail car in the world, for he had been in it as an invited guest.[521]

As of the 23rd, Johnson was the heavy 1 to 2 odds favorite. Jack McCormick felt that if more San Franciscans had seen Hart fight, Marvin would be the favorite. "If this fight was coming off in the East in any town where both Hart and Johnson have been seen in action, Marvin would be a one to two shot over the colored man." The confident McCormick was happy that Hart was the odds underdog, because he wanted to bet on him and make even more money. Johnson was clever, but Hart had fought clever men and beaten them. "I tell you these wise guys out here don't know how good a fighter Hart is. He is not a boxer, but he is a natural fighter, and when he lands one of his body wallops, it's curtains."

As McCormick was being interviewed, the building started to tremble, as if there was an earthquake. Someone asked, "What's that?" Mac replied, "That's Hart starting to punch the bag." The reporters went down the stairs to watch Marvin.

Hart's exhibition of endurance made the crowd of spectators open their mouths in amazement. He showed an immense capacity for work. "He is, beyond any question, the most earnest and the most nearly tireless of any fighter that has trained around San Francisco in the present generation."

Marvin worked the pulley weights, wrist machine, and punching bag for 15 minutes each. He caused the entire building to shake from the tremendous power as the bag struck the platform. The heavy bag came next, and then shadow boxing with heavy dumbbells. Marvin hit the punching bag so hard that the rope broke twice. "At the same time he showed that he was shifty on his feet and that he has the speed of a lightweight." Skipping rope and work with Indian clubs were next. Finally, Hart bounced a tennis ball on the floor using his hands, moving about for 10 minutes. "He makes a neat piece of work out of the exercise, which keeps him constantly on the move and quickens his eye." Al Kaufman entered and the two big fellows tugged each other around until Kaufman was tired out. "Hart's breathing apparatus seemed absolutely unaffected by the hour and a half's work." Marvin then took a dip in the surf and got a rubdown. After all of his work, he weighed 192 pounds.[522]

When interviewed, Marvin said,

---

[521] *San Francisco Call, Evening Post, Chronicle,* March 23, 1905.
[522] *San Francisco Evening Post, Bulletin, Chronicle,* March 24, 1905.

I don't see how I can lose. Mind you, I'll grant that Johnson is as clever as there is in the business, but his cleverness won't get him nothing with me. I broke up Joe Choynski's cleverness and did the same to Jack O'Brien, and Johnson cannot be any faster than these men. One punch is all I want to land on the nigger, and I'll do that before the fight is half over. I don't care how fast the man is, he'll go down for the count if I land on him, and I'm not afraid to take a few to get mine in.[523]

Another reporter quoted Hart as saying,

I tell you right here that this coon will have to go some to beat me. He won't beat me. ... I realize that this coon Johnson is a clever fellow. I am not a clever fellow except in my own peculiar way, but I have got the wallop that will win. What has the coon ever done that should make him a favorite over me? I knocked out Billy Stift in three rounds. The coon was lucky to get a draw at the end of ten rounds. I fought Philadelphia Jack O'Brien six rounds in Philadelphia, and the papers agreed that if a decision had been rendered it would have gone to me by a mile. Has the coon done anything as good as that? I am a knockout fighter. He is a clever boxer. One punch will be all that's necessary for him.

That same day, on March 23, Johnson boxed a few rounds with Denver Ed Martin and he also did some light gymnasium exercise and roadwork.[524]

All of the newsmen and experts were intrigued by the matchup, and analysis proliferated. Philadelphia's Frank Crowhurst, who had seen both men in action in their bouts, said,

The fight should prove one of the most important fistic encounters of the year, as either of the principals may be, in the near future, the world's heavyweight champion. Both men are in line for this honor, and while neither is likely to defeat Jeffries for the championship, the mantle would assuredly fall upon the shoulder of one of them should Jeffries resign. Until a year ago Hart was practically classed as a middleweight. ... Nature has now supplied this want. ...

No one will gainsay the fact that Hart is one of the cleverest, pluckiest and coolest ring generals over the middleweight limit, and the important question is, will his additional weight enable him to withstand the punishment which he is almost sure to get from his dusky opponent during the first few rounds. ...

Fortunately for him, his increase in bulk and strength has come perfectly natural, whereas to some it might prove a handicap, to him

[523] *San Francisco Bulletin*, March 24, 1905.
[524] *San Francisco Chronicle*, March 24, 1905.

it is a decided advantage. He is as agile now as he ever was, while his endurance is nothing short of remarkable.

On the other hand, Johnson is a natural fighter, beautifully built for strength and agility, and a past master of the school of hit and get away. Unfortunately this dusky marvel has had few opportunities to show his real worth, and although such men as Frank Childs, Denver Ed Martin and Sam McVey have in the past fallen easy victims to his skill, he has never tackled such a tough proposition as he will face on Tuesday.

Judging of the past performances of the two men, Johnson appears to have a shade the best of it, but this may be more than offset by the additional weight and strength Hart will have at his command. ... Should both be fortunate enough to survive the earlier rounds the contest will be one of endurance. Therein Hart will have an advantage. If Johnson secures a victory it will be in the first few rounds, after which the betting should be strongly in favor of Hart.[525]

Crowhurst said the fight looked so even to him that he could not make a pre-fight selection.

Both of the principals' respective managers, McCormick and Abrams, wanted Alex Greggains, a former fighter himself, to officiate the bout. However, initially, Greggains was reluctant to do so, feeling that as manager of the hosting San Francisco Athletic Club, he did not want to expose himself to criticism as the fight's arbiter and judge. He hoped that they would agree upon someone else.[526]

However, as the fight approached, McCormick/Hart would not agree to any referee other than Greggains. Johnson suggested Ed Graney or Jack Welch, who had sterling reputations. McCormick insisted that there would be no fight unless Greggains agreed to referee. He felt that Alec would insure an impartial deal for both sides, although he did not say why the other named referees, who had more experience, would not do so. Johnson's manager, Zick/Zeke Abrams, was comfortable with Greggains as a fair man. Therefore, Greggains eventually gave in and agreed to referee the bout.[527]

The newsmen were happy with Greggains' selection as the bout's arbiter. "Greggains has handed down the verdict in many important battles, and has yet to incur the disfavor of the fight fans. His name was the only one mentioned that was agreeable to both principals." Another paper said it was doubtful if the fighters could have made a better selection. "Greggains has always made good with the public when acting in the capacity of referee... [and] the local fight fans can depend on the ex-scrapper for an

---

[525] *San Francisco Bulletin*, March 25, 1905.
[526] *San Francisco Call, Evening Post, Chronicle,* March 23, 1905.
[527] *Oakland Tribune*, March 25, 1905.

honest decision, based on a thorough knowledge of the game. Neither of the principals would stand for anybody but Greggains."

Still, the *San Francisco Evening Post* predicted that Greggains would have a tough job on his hands if the bout went the distance and he had to render a decision.

> If the fight is to be decided on cleverness, Johnson has a good chance, should the contest go twenty rounds. If aggressiveness will gain the verdict, Hart's chance looks to be the better.
>
> If the mill happens to go the limit the galleryites will no doubt be divided in their opinions, and will shout themselves hoarse for their favorite, so the referee's job will be no sinecure. Greggains, however…can be depended on to pick the best man, when all is said and done.
>
> Greggains will decide what looks to be the most nearly even heavyweight battle that has been contested in San Francisco in many a month.

Hart was 192 pounds of solid muscle and bone. "He is fit to go the distance at a terrific pace, and in shape to take every punch which comes his way without flinching. He has absolutely no fear of his opponent." Although a heavyweight, Marvin "moves around with the agility of a bantam." As he gradually increased his weight, his speed and shiftiness kept pace with his increase in bulk. He was as fast as he was when the newspapers first touted him as a "speed marvel" in the lower weight classes.

> His opponent, Jack Johnson, is conceded to be the fastest big man who ever stepped into the ring. Unlike most clever fighters, the colored boxer is also there with a punch. … He depends mostly, however, on his ability to hit and get away, and in this respect compares favorably with James J. Corbett in his best days.
>
> Whether Hart can hit the black fighter or whether Johnson can elude the vicious onslaughts of the Louisville lad is a question that can only be decided after the two have settled their argument.[528]

The bout was a big deal, and received plenty of hype and newspaper ink. "Although neither has yet proved the right to be considered in the class of the unapproachable Jeffries, the unquestioned fact that they are among the best of the other heavies makes the card attractive."

Johnson had been training for a month, and appeared to be in better condition than he had been for the past two years. "His workouts with 'Denver' Ed Martin have shown him shiftier than ever before and he is thoroughly satisfied with himself and confident of beating the Kentucky boy." Johnson was a masterful boxer.

---

[528] *San Francisco Evening Post*, March 25, 1905.

Still, "In Marvin Hart Johnson will meet the toughest proposition of his career. … Hart is continually after his man, willing to take any amount of punishment if he can only land his wallop once in a while." Hart was a "natural fighter of the slashing type."[529]

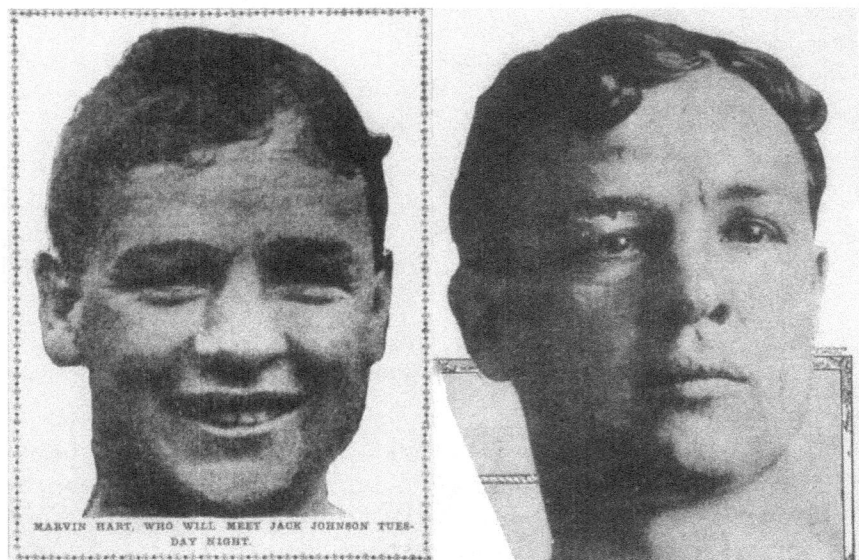

MARVIN HART, WHO WILL MEET JACK JOHNSON TUES-
DAY NIGHT.

San Francisco Chronicle, **March 26, 1905**

[529] *San Francisco Call*, *San Francisco Chronicle*, March 26, 1905.

Despite the betting odds which made Johnson the strong favorite at 1 to 2, most sporting experts felt that the odds should be even, and many were picking Hart to win. Harry Corbett said the contest was too close to wager. Jimmy Britt said, "I can't see anybody but Hart. The coon might make him look cheap for the first few rounds, but Hart has the stamina and will finish strong." Tom Dillon said, "I like the coon to get the decision." San Berger said, "Nothing short of a death in the family could keep me from seeing that fight. It will be a case of a boxer against a fighter. I can't express a preference." Dave Barry said, "Hart for mine. Any man that puts Jack O'Brien to the floor six times in a six-round bout will have no trouble in reaching Johnson." Spider Kelly said, "I look to see the closest heavyweight fight of my life." Billy Wilson said Hart was "in grand shape and ought to win. He'll have a task on his hands with the clever smoke, but he's beaten fast fighters before." Tom Davis said he would bet on Johnson.[530]

There was some discussion and concern regarding Johnson's tendency to give dull performances, which could hurt ticket sales. No one wanted to pay to see a boring bout. The press raised this concern with Greggains. "It was suggested to him that the public should be assured that Johnson intends to fight from the first gong, and not to loaf along through…twenty rounds to a decision." Greggains responded to this concern by saying,

> I have notified Johnson that he must fight all the time or the fight will be called 'no contest.' I don't expect any difficulty on that score. Johnson's manager, Zick Abrams, has also told him that he must win in a hurry. "If you stay twenty rounds for a decision," Abrams told him, "we will run you out of town."[531]

Hence, both the promoter (who was the referee) and Johnson's own manager were putting a great deal of pressure on Johnson to alter his style and try to win by knockout rather than simply attempt to win a decision by cautiously outboxing his opponent. When a boxer's own manager tells him "we will run you out of town" if it goes the distance, one has to question that manager's allegiances.

The following day, the *San Francisco Chronicle* said,

> Johnson's predilection for loafing during an engagement is well-known, but in meeting Hart he goes against a ripping, smashing fighter who will mix things from the first gong. Hart is not clever, except in a way that is peculiarly his own, but he has worlds of steam and willingness. His reputation is that of a short finisher, with a wallop that Jeff himself might well fear, and any hopes Johnson may have of easily getting away with something may be rudely shattered.

> There is a possibility, however, that the dusky J. Arthur will be clever enough to keep out of the Kentuckian's way.

---

[530] *San Francisco Bulletin*, March 26, 1905.
[531] *San Francisco Chronicle*, March 25, 1905.

There was concern that Johnson would attempt to do what he did against Sam McVey in San Francisco the previous year, which was considered a clever but boring sparring exhibition for 20 rounds, "with not enough vim and dash to it to keep the wildest enthusiast awake. In that battle he kept out of harm's way for nineteen draggy rounds, and in the twentieth dropped the Oxnard sugar squeezer with a punch that he could have delivered at any time during the fight."

San Francisco fight fans did not quickly forget a poor exhibition, and, "They will recall for some time, too, that sorry affair between Johnson and McVey." Fight fans were willing to spend their money only if they were assured that they would get their money's worth. They wanted the referee to ensure that they got it.

> Alex Greggains matched the two with the idea of giving the public what it wanted, and he is to be thanked for that. Now if he will give 'Mistah' Johnson to understand that no money will be forthcoming if the big 'dinge' does not get busy, he will have the eternal gratitude of those who intend to occupy chairs.

> Of course, there may be no need for any suggestions of the sort. Johnson may have decided that the only way he can win back the regard he lost last year is to go in and make a brilliant fight of it. He realizes as well as anybody else that his stock has been below par ever since that affair. Nobody is questioning his ability to fight, but the jeers hurled at him through nineteen slow rounds were sufficient indication that no repetition of that sort of milling will be allowed. Hart will undoubtedly have something to say about this too. He will rush into the fray at the beginning, and will be plunging in from then until the finish.

The expectation was that Johnson would not be allowed to fight in that cautious manner again. "If he attempts to loaf Tuesday night it is the duty of the referee to warn him, and then, if he still refuses to mingle with the gentleman from Kentucky, to stop the fight and declare it 'no contest.'"

A prejudice existed against Johnson not only because of race, but because of his less than entertaining (albeit effective) style. The prejudice towards him based on prior performances and manner of victory was on the minds of the press, public, and referee going into the bout. Indeed, Johnson was being pre-judged.[532]

Still, there was excitement surrounding the bout. Tickets had gone on sale at Greggains' café at 112 Ellis street, and they were selling like hotcakes.

W. W. Naughton said Jeffries would need to be reminded on the day after the bout that he needed to return to the ring again. "Each individual admirer of the fistic game rebels at the notion of the big fellow retiring undefeated. A thing of that kind would leave an aching void. It is like being

---

[532] *San Francisco Chronicle*, March 26, 1905.

asked a conundrum and then told there is no answer." Naughton correctly identified the trouble and frustration with determining a new champion to a vacated title. "If Hart should down Johnson in a fair fight the rest will be easy. Marvin will be the sensation of the hour." Jeffries would then be open to a match with him, because Jeff was out to make as much money as possible, as long as the opponent was white. "The champion has already said that he will not hesitate about giving Hart a match, if Hart disposes of the colored heavyweight."

But first, Hart needed an impressive and decisive victory in order to garner sufficient public and press clamor for a Jeffries-Hart bout, which was necessary for the fight to be financially lucrative for Jeffries. Jeff was ready to retire, and was only willing to box again if the bout would yield a big payday. Jeff said he hoped that Hart would win decisively so that he could draw fans and a big gate.

However, if Johnson won, it was not clear whether Jeff ever would withdraw his color line objection. "Up to date neither criticism nor cajolery has caused Jeffries to waver in his determination never to fight a negro." Still, if Johnson won, the agitation for the match would be revived. It was hoped that a very large financial incentive could change Jeff's mind.

Jeffries insisted that he would not withdraw the color-line bar. From New York, when asked if he would meet Johnson if he defeated Hart, Jeff said:

> No; I'm not fighting skunks as yet, not while there are white men in the field. I'm not going to discuss Johnson's abilities as a boxer. He may be a wonder and all that, but if any one is to take my title I want that man to be of my own color.

> If Hart wins I will cheerfully give him a fight. I suppose it will be up to me to do so. He's a young fellow, and they say he has physique, too. I hope he will draw, though, for I'm not going to be drawn into another Jack Munroe farce. That affair did not yield me a penny. In fact, I lost money on it, and I don't like the idea of fighting for the love of it.[533]

However, W. W. Naughton felt that Jeffries eventually might give in to the public pressure that might mount if Johnson defeated Hart in a convincing fashion. Hence, there was pressure on both Johnson and Hart either to score a knockout or win clearly. That was not going to be easy, given that both were expert at their respective styles of boxing and in tremendous shape.[534]

Two days before the fight, on March 26, before a packed crowd of spectators, Hart proved conclusively his ability to go 20 rounds at the fastest kind of pace. Marvin was absolutely tireless, and he entertained them

---

[533] *Oakland Tribune*, March 27, 1905.
[534] *San Francisco Examiner*, March 26, 1905; *San Francisco Chronicle*, March 27, 1905.

with "as fast an exhibition of indoor work as they will ever see in their lives." Even Billy Jordan, who had seen thousands of fighters, said Hart was the hardest worker and hardest-hitting fighter he had ever seen.

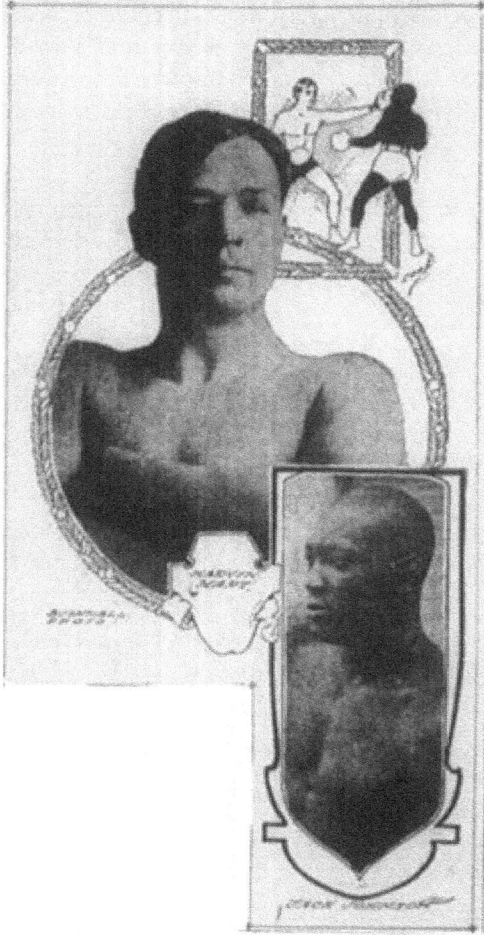

Hart sparred 6 rounds with Jack McCormick, roughed it for a few minutes with Sammy Brooks, and boxed and wrestled with Al Kaufman for a half hour. He did his usual hour and a half of work. Marvin "proved beyond all doubt that he has an awful wallop." The way that Marvin hustled each of them around "bodes no good for the dusky Mr. Johnson. Hart cannot box. He is essentially a fighter and even when trying to restrain himself his blows carry a sting." Marvin finished the day with a plunge in the ocean.

One local reporter said that if more of the public had seen Hart's secret boxing bouts, the gold brick would have been discovered long before this fight. It would not take a good judge of fighting material long "to come to the conclusion that Marvin is there with the class." Veteran fight fans marveled at Hart's strength and speed. "He appears to be as fast as any lightweight, and the old-timers were unanimous in declaring him a wonder."

Hart said that he was in perfect shape and had never before trained as hard as he had for this fight. He knew that it was his one chance to justify a match with Jeffries.

That same day, Johnson boxed with Ed Martin and Jim Haywards. Like Hart, Johnson was a perfectly trained athlete. "He is faster than ever and the amount of work he goes through without even breathing hard proves him to be stronger."

Johnson said, "I'm stronger and heavier than ever before in my life, and if we were going to fight a hundred rounds I'd be prepared to go the distance."

For several reasons, the *Evening Post* expected the bout to be a grand contest. Neither had a weight advantage, both were in the best of form, victory meant a potential match with Jeffries, and the fact that one was a white southerner and the other colored would mean that no friendly feeling existed between the two, so the bout was bound to be rough.

It was again noted that the selection of Greggains as referee was as pleasing to the fighters as it was to the fight fans. "Greggains has refereed important contests before. He decides a fight on his own judgment, and has never been influenced by the shouting of the gallery gods."[535]

On the 27th, the day before the fight, Hart covered 4 miles by running and walking, mostly doing the latter. He spent 5 minutes on the wrist machine and 3 rounds on the punching bag. Marvin then weighed himself and scaled 192 pounds.

Johnson only took a 6-mile walk. He was weighing about 191 pounds.[536]

In the days leading up to the fight, Johnson had been a 10-7 favorite. The night before and day of the fight, the odds were 2-1 for Johnson. Even on the East Coast, it was reported that Johnson was the favorite at odds ranging from 6 or 8 to 10.[537]

Regarding the feelings towards blacks at that time, in the local news the day before the fight, a Boston correspondent said that Liberia was never without tribal wars, and slavery was in full swing there. Conditions were bad in Haiti, but not as bad as in Liberia, the reason being because of the infusion of white blood in Haiti.

> Our great duty toward the negro is in protecting him against himself. We must govern him according to what he needs, and not according to what we think he needs. There isn't a negro who is fit to legislate for a cat. It is a degradation of white citizenship to elect one to office, and nobody knows that better than a negro.[538]

The day of the fight, each local paper offered its final analysis and comparisons of the two fighters. The *San Francisco Evening Post* noted that the two men scaled within a pound of each other. Hart was a stranger in San Francisco, while Johnson had won all of his San Francisco bouts, making Jack the favorite. However, the *Evening Post* said, "Hart's record appears to be even a little better than Johnson's, and why the black man should be installed favorite is hard to guess."

When interviewed on the day of the fight, Hart said, "I'll not give Johnson a chance to use his cleverness. I'll not give him a minute's rest, and if he lasts more than ten rounds I'll be surprised. The betting looked exceptionally tempting to me, and I bet every cent I possess that I win."

[535] *San Francisco Evening Post, Bulletin, Examiner*, March 27, 1905.
[536] *San Francisco Bulletin*, March 28, 1905.
[537] *San Francisco Examiner*, March 26, 27, 1905; *Trenton Times*, March 28, 1905.
[538] *San Francisco Call*, March 27, 1905.

Johnson said, "I don't see how I can lose. My condition was never better, and I think I am stronger than ever. Hart may be a big strong boy, but I've met and defeated his kind before. It's up to 'Jeff' to cut out that color line for I'm the man he will have to meet."[539]

The *Evening Post* prophetically discussed how the bout might be scored, based on the time's understood scoring style for closely contested fights and given that the fighters were trying to justify a Jeffries bout.

> Johnson, although having won most of his success by his extreme cleverness, has declared his intention of roughing matters with Mr. Hart. … In fact, Johnson realizes that he will have to equalize the aggressiveness of this match if he expects the verdict to come his way. It will be necessary for him to exchange blow for blow with the southerner, for by merely showing his ability to avoid a punch he would not be much of a drawing card if matched with Jeffries. The public much prefers seeing a man take a punch and making an attempt to return it than sidestep it cleverly without striking a blow.

> Hart…is one of those never-say-die scrappers, willing to mix from the first tap of the gong, never stopping until something drops. He is never beaten until counted out.[540]

The *San Francisco Examiner* said that in Hart, "Johnson meets the strongest opponent that has yet been matched against him."

> The Kentuckian has gone through a long and arduous training and has shown that he can go at a rattling fast pace and still breathe with ease. … People who have seen him work think very highly of his chances with the cleverest colored pugilist in the world.

> Hart is a 'Battling' Nelson on an enlarged scale. He loves to root in and to carry the fight to his opponent. Nothing can daunt him. He will mix it as long and as furiously as the rules of the game permit.

> Johnson likes a different kind of game. The shifty big fellow prefers to hit and run away, winning his contests by the decision route. This sort of milling has made the dusky giant rather unpopular with the sports in this city and if Johnson wants to reinstate himself in popular favor he will have to try for a clean knockout.

> Tonight's fight looks to be the first good heavyweight match that has been carded for two years. Aside from this, general interest is being manifested because of the probability of a match with Jeffries, should Hart be returned the winner. Jeffries has, of course, persistently declared his determination to draw the color line. If Johnson, however, would give incontestable proof that he is a knockout fighter

[539] *San Francisco Evening Post*, March 28, 1905.
[540] *San Francisco Evening Post*, March 28, 1905.

as well as a boxer there is no telling what popular clamor might do to disabuse the world's champion of his prejudices.[541]

However, the night before the fight, from New York, Bill Delaney again insisted that Jeffries would not fight Johnson, saying,

> Should Hart beat Johnson tomorrow night Jeffries will fight Hart, but if the negro wins there is nothing doing. In June 1905, Jeff will arrive in California, and by that time, if there is no white man ready to make a match with him, Jeffries will forever retire from the ring. I understand Jeffries thoroughly, and know that in order to fight well he must fight often. I do not propose to have Jeffries make the mistake that all former champions have made, that is, of fighting once too often.[542]

The *San Francisco Chronicle* reported that Alex Greggains again confirmed that Johnson would be required to fight rather than just defend. It also assessed the bout.

> Greggains stated last night that he will allow no loafing from Johnson, and that both men must fight all the time they are on their feet. With this assurance the public will be inclined to give the show liberal patronage.
>
> Both men have trained hard and faithfully for the battle, and the outlook is that it will be one of the best between heavy-weights that has taken place for a long time. Hart is a slashing fighter, with wonderful powers of endurance, and if he follows the plan of campaign which has been his in other battles he will give the colored man plenty to do. He isn't clever, as cleverness is judged in fighters, but he has plenty of speed and will be mixing things all the time.
>
> As a matter of cold fact, Hart's ability as a fighter is being underestimated here in San Francisco. The fact that he gave 'Philadelphia' Jack O'Brien the hardest fight that careful Quaker ever had, knocking him down five times during six rounds, is overlooked by the local dopesters. Johnson's pronounced cleverness is the only thing which many are taking account of, not realizing that a fighter of Hart's style may connect from the cleverest man in the world and win with a punch. That is what Hart is liable to do to-night. He has a terrific wallop, and if he succeeds in reaching a vulnerable part of the colored man's anatomy it will be 'curtains.'
>
> As a special inducement to the two men to go in and make a rattling fight of it, Greggains has practically promised a match with Jeffries to the winner – in case the winner should be Hart. If Johnson wins, matters will not be altered so far as an opponent for Jeff is

---

[541] *San Francisco Examiner*, March 28, 1905.
[542] *Washington Post*, March 28, 1905.

concerned, since the Hairy One has not withdrawn the color line and has no intention of doing so. If Hart wins, however, and brings about his victory in a way that looks good to the sporting public, he will be next in line for the champion of champions.[543]

The *San Francisco Call* said,

> Johnson will in all probability use his cleverness and ring generalship on his husky opponent. Johnson is one of the cleverest big men who ever pulled on a mitt, and he can hold an opponent at bay in grand style. ...
>
> If Hart wins the battle and makes any kind of a showing it is about settled he will be matched with Jeffries. ... He is anxious to get after the big fellow and for that reason he will probably put up the fight of his life when he steps into the ring to-night.
>
> Johnson is also after the champ, and should he beat Hart quickly and decisively there is a possible chance that Jeff may take him on, though he vows and declares he will not. Johnson figures on winning quickly and showing beyond a doubt that he is Hart's master.[544]

The *San Francisco Bulletin* said the time-honored custom of shaking hands would be eliminated from the proceedings, owing to race. "A natural hatred seems to exist between the two, and every blow struck, besides bringing the smiter that much nearer the long end of the purse, will carry more than the ordinary sting on account of the clashing of the two ever warring races."

As both were the same size, the loser would not have the usual excuse used in heavyweight bouts, that the opponent was too big. Both were in the best possible condition, so that could not be an excuse either.

Regarding the scoring criteria, the *Bulletin* said,

> Johnson realizes that he will have to stand his ground and mix with his husky opponent, for by depending entirely upon his cleverness the decision would certainly go to Hart for his aggressiveness. He will have to prove that he is a fighter as well as a boxer, if he expects to meet Jeffries in the future. On the other hand, Hart can be depended on to mix matters from the start. He knows no other style, but to bore in and fight from gong to gong. This characteristic explains his having so many knockouts in his record. He is game to the core, and if he is beaten, his seconds will have to pack him out of the ring.[545]

The problem for Johnson was that he was the best boxer, not the best attacker, and he was fighting the most aggressive man in the business. Hence, if the fight was going to be decided on aggressiveness alone, unless

---

[543] *San Francisco Chronicle*, March 28, 1905.
[544] *San Francisco Call*, March 28, 1905.
[545] *San Francisco Bulletin*, March 28, 1905.

Johnson scored a knockout, the fight was already in the bag for Hart in its inception, because there was no man alive more aggressive than Marvin Hart.

The *Philadelphia Press* said Hart's best chance of winning would depend upon his ability to force the fighting without exposing himself too much to Johnson's terrific swings. Johnson was the 10 to 8 favorite because he had the advantages in height and reach. However, it felt that Johnson's record was no better than Hart's. Several second-rate fighters had gone the distance with Johnson "because of his cautious methods of fighting."

> Unless Hart is too careless he appears to have a good chance against Johnson. For a big man, Johnson is a timid fighter. He is not cowardly and perhaps would stand the 'gaff' if he had to, but he has never been put to the test. He is not a mixer. He uses his long arms with marked skill to keep an opponent away and no excitement, no virtual certainty of victory will beguile him into wading into knockout.
>
> Hart is not a clever fighter. … [A]ny moderately good man can land on him hard and often. But he is at his best when the going is most furious. He can land a knockout blow with either hand, and the man he is fighting never gets much rest.[546]

Those on the East Coast wondered whether the fight or its decision would be on the level. Some thought the fight was fixed for Hart, given that Jeffries would not fight Johnson, no matter what. The *Trenton Times* wrote,

> The bout has a peculiar looking angle to it, for the reason that Hart has repeatedly declared that he would not enter the ring with a negro. He once announced in Boston after winning a bout from Kid Carter that he was a Southerner and would not insult his friends by fighting a colored man. For this reason sporting men are somewhat skeptical about the genuineness of the fight, some hinting that Johnson is certain to lose in order that Hart may force Jeffries to a meeting, the latter having refused many times to fight Johnson.
>
> The negro on physical points, is Hart's superior. He has longer arms, is taller and stronger than the Louisville man and has shown himself to be very scientific. Hart affects the rushing style and is considered a slugger pure and simple. Many good judges say that Johnson would give Jeffries the hardest fight of his life.[547]

The fear was that a points decision surely would go to Hart no matter what, so that a lucrative Hart-Jeffries bout could be made. A Johnson-Jeffries fight probably would be even more lucrative, but because of Jeffries' color-line stance, it appeared that fight could not be made even if

---

[546] *Philadelphia Press*, March 29, 1905.
[547] *Trenton Times*, March 28, 1905.

Johnson won. Hence, the sense was that Greggains might be more inclined to award the bout to Hart if he wanted to promote a heavyweight championship fight. There was no real future money in it for Greggains if he awarded the bout to Johnson.

Further, the fact that previously Hart had drawn the color line consistently, but now was willing to fight Johnson, made some think that he had been told that he would be given the decision if it went the distance, and hence he withdrew his objection. Perhaps this is why the Hart side had insisted on Greggains as the referee and would not accept anyone else, including reputable men like Graney and Welch. Plus, there had been some pre-fight news reports on the East Coast that Johnson could only win via knockout.

However, Hart explained that he was fighting Johnson because no other fighter was willing to fight him. Hence, out of frustration and inability to obtain a fight during the second half of 1904 and the first part of 1905, he was forced to withdraw the color line. He had not fought in ten months, since late May 1904. Johnson himself had not fought in five months. Marvin said,

> This is the first colored man I ever fought and it will be the last, win or lose. Fighting is my business, and I am just forced to fight Johnson, as he is the only man that will fight me. I have been idle for the past year and have tried to get Gardner, Root, McCoy, O'Brien, Willie and others to fight me, but they all passed me up. I have been out here four months trying to get on a fight.[548]

Oddly enough, though, back in Hart's hometown of Louisville, it was reported that "Johnson must knock Hart out to win." The *Louisville Times* quoted Hart as saying, "Johnson has to knock me out in twenty rounds to get the big end of the money, and this fact will work to my advantage, as it will cause him to attempt to carry the fight to me." This comports with what originally was said about the fight's terms, back when the bout was first announced.[549]

Was there an agreement that Johnson had to knock him out? Was it understood that Johnson could not win a decision? Had Johnson agreed to handicap himself? Had Greggains promised Hart the decision if it went the distance; in order to induce him to accept the fight? No one said so immediately after the bout, including Hart and Johnson, but there appears to be some evidence for the assertion.

---

[548] *Louisville Courier-Journal*, March 30, 1905.
[549] *Louisville Times*, March 28, 1905.

CHAPTER 15

A Matter of Perspective

On Tuesday March 28, 1905 at Woodward's Pavilion in San Francisco, 26-year-old (just three days shy of 27) Jack Johnson fought 28-year-old Marvin Hart. Because it was a heavyweight bout, no official weigh-in was required, but it was generally estimated that on fight-night the two pugilists weighed somewhere between 193 and 198 pounds.

MARVIN HART   JACK JOHNSON

AS JOHNSON AND HART WILL LOOK IN THE RING TONIGHT.

Both men appeared to be in superb physical condition. Present in the crowd were Battling Nelson and famous English boxers Jabez White and Charley Mitchell.

Johnson examined Hart's hand bandages carefully, and initially objected to their thickness, but finally retired to his corner and had some light bandages fixed upon his own hands.

The local *Examiner*, *Chronicle*, and *Call* each gave round-by-round accounts, in addition to global summaries, while the other local papers simply offered overall analysis.

1 - Hart crouched low and jumped at Johnson with his left. They clinched and attempted blows while holding on. It seemed that it would be a rough and tumble fight. Both worked the body and head. Johnson particularly worked his right at the body. They exchanged blows and clinches. Johnson liked to block and hold between punches, and laughed at Hart's efforts to land. Hart was much busier. Johnson landed a vicious right to the cheek at the bell.

The *Examiner's* W. W. Naughton said it was Johnson's round. The *Call* said there was very light fighting in this round and no damage was done. Johnson was the much cleverer man. The *Chronicle* said, "Hart led time and time again before Johnson woke up to the fact that he was there to fight. When he did mix it he had the better of the argument."

2 - Johnson clinched, landed rights to the kidney and jaw, and smothered Hart on the inside. When Marvin rushed in, he landed his right to the heart

a couple times. Hart tried to get close, but Johnson landed a left hook to the stomach that hurt, and he also landed some right uppercuts, getting the better of the mix-up. Marvin liked to focus his right on the body. Jack cleverly blocked some rights and lefts to the jaw, and blocked body shots with his elbows. In the breakaway, Jack landed heavily on the jaw. Hart landed a stiff left to the head but Johnson retaliated with a right and left hook to the nose that drew blood. At the bell, Hart landed a corker to the ribs and an overhand right to the neck that sent Jack back.

The *Call* said the honors of the round were in Johnson's favor. Hart bled from the nostrils as he took his seat.

3 - Johnson feinted rapidly. He mostly made Marvin miss, but Hart exhibited some good defense as well. They sparred and clinched. In the infighting, Hart tried uppercuts and swings, but Johnson was too shifty. Jack sent his right hook to Marvin's face and drove his left into the stomach. Hart landed a right to the jaw. Johnson hit the body but Hart landed two telling blows to the "bread basket." Marvin followed with a left lead, "and the coon swung a left uppercut that raised Hart to his tiptoes." Hart landed a right to the ribs. Both were inclined to rough it. Johnson sent in a right uppercut. Hart landed a right to the body and received a right to the head in return. Near the end of the round, both seemed afraid to lead, content to feint at long range. They were clinched at the gong.

The *Call* said, "Practically it was an even round."

4 - Johnson attacked and forced Hart back to the ropes with lefts and rights, proving his assertion that he would make Hart retreat. Hart came back and hit the ribs with both hands. "It hurt, and the negro grew vicious for a minute." To the surprise of the spectators, the angered Johnson swung like an amateur, while Hart eluded the blows. Hart landed a left to the face and right to the wind. Johnson retaliated with his uppercut. There was a good deal of clinching and their leads were smothered. The spectators jeered Johnson for some rough work on the ropes. A lively mix-up followed, with Hart landing overhand punches and Johnson landing rights to the ribs. Near the end of the round, each landed a right uppercut. They were clinching at the bell.

The *Call* said Hart had a slight advantage in the round.

5 - Johnson jabbed and landed repeatedly, but "there was not an ounce of strength in his blows." As Hart would step in, Johnson would land straight lefts and then clinch. Hart landed a right before a clinch. Jack landed right uppercuts. Johnson eluded and blocked some blows to the body and head. They sparred for a bit, and both exhibited some clever blocking. Hart landed a right to the body and they clinched. They fought at close quarters again, both missing several body shots. Hart swung his hard right on Johnson's ear but then Johnson uppercut him with his right to the jaw.

The *Chronicle* said Hart forced the fighting, but

[T]he coon was intent on being clever, and sparred lightly. It was not until Marvin reached his jaw with a corking half right swing and doubled him up with a left to the digestive organ that Black Jack really began to fight. He threw right and left into the Louisville man's bleeding face almost without a return. Hart came back just at the end with strong wallops to the coon's kidneys.

The *Call* said Hart landed a vicious left to the head as the gong rang. It said Hart had a shade the better of the round.

6 - Johnson kept up his jabbing tactics, paying particular attention to Hart's left eye, which was troubling him. A Johnson left jarred Hart's head back. Johnson shot in another straight left, "the most telling punch of the fight." Jack threw a left hook to the stomach before a clinch. Both used rights to the body and head on the inside, mixing it viciously. Johnson wrestled Hart to the ropes. Jack landed a right to the jaw and a right to the body, but they had no effect on Marvin, who seemed possessed of remarkable vitality. After the referee separated them from the usual clinch, they went right back to a clinch. Johnson hooked his right to the jaw and also landed a right uppercut. They clinched, and as they broke, Hart hooked a vicious right to the jaw.

After clinching and breaking again, as Hart was trying to get close and his lead fell short, Johnson struck him with a hard right. Jack followed up with a shower of blows. However, Hart kept coming and landed a right on Jack's jaw. Marvin blocked several Johnson right uppercuts with a crossed forearm. Hart landed the customary right swing to the head at the bell.

Despite the descriptions of others indicating an entertaining round, the *Call* said that overall, it was a tame and even round, and most of the blows that landed lacked force.

7 - They clinched constantly and fought at close quarters, neither landing much. Johnson hooked and jabbed several times, and used the occasional straight right to the jaw, but there was a great deal of clinching in between. As they broke out of a clinch, Hart landed a hard left to the head. He followed with a left to the body but received a right in return. Hart swung a right to the ribs but Johnson hit him twice on the jaw with his right. Hart went at him, but Johnson caught him with a left hook to the body.

Overall, they did more clinching than actual fighting, and the crowd constantly yelled for them to fight. Hart tried several rights, but Johnson blocked them. At close quarters, Johnson hooked a left to the body.

According to the *Chronicle*, after Jack jabbed, a wild swing from Hart jolted Johnson. "With this prodding Johnson set to work and rushed his man all around the ring." Johnson had a tendency to fire back hard when his opponent landed a good one. However, Hart got inside several of Johnson's hardest punches. Marvin then landed a left to the ribs that hurt.

The *Chronicle* concluded, "At the end of the round Hart was bleeding badly and weakening. His left eye was beginning to show signs of distress."

However, the *Call* said the fighting in this round was very tame and the fight dragged on in a monotonous manner. It said there was no advantage in the round.

8 - Johnson landed straight lefts and left hooks, and blocked Hart's swings. Hart landed a chopping left to the face and right to the heart. They fought at a brisk pace at close quarters, but the blows were ineffectual, for they mostly smothered each other's punches in the clinches. Johnson landed a right to the stomach, and on the break, a right uppercut. Hart landed a good right to the neck that caused several of his sympathizers to jump to their feet and yell. Johnson laughed and landed his right to the temple. Hart landed a right to the body and left to the jaw. Johnson landed a straight left to the face. Hart shot in a vicious left to the stomach and Johnson winced.

Hart was strong. He landed a left uppercut and followed with a right to the head. He also scored with a left to the body, but received a right uppercut in return. Johnson resorted to jabbing tactics, hitting the nose and bad eye. Hart got inside and rocked Johnson's head with right and left hooks before being held. Marvin roughed it with Johnson, forcing him around the ring. Hart walked into a right to the body which shook him up. Still, near the end of the round, Johnson was holding on to escape punishment. Hart landed a right to the body that made Johnson wince, and he followed with a right to the head. Johnson landed a heavy right cross at the bell.

The *Call* said they fought at a faster clip in this round, stimulated by the numerous calls from the spectators. If anything, Hart had a shade the better of the round.

9 - According to the *Examiner*,

> Johnson loosened up in this round and did some fast two-handed punching, reaching Hart's face repeatedly. Hart stood to his guns. He drove Johnson back with swinging blows, but Jack came at him again. Johnson reached the face repeatedly with both gloves and Hart bled freely. Johnson's straight lefts were particularly punishing. It was very evident by his exhibition in this round that he was either ultra careful or else was holding himself in reserve in the previous rounds.

The *Chronicle* said of the round that Hart went right at him, landing right and left to the stomach, "satisfied to take a wallop on the jaw in return. The fighting was terrific. Hart was beaten here had the negro followed up his advantage. He was bleeding badly and his eye was all but closed. Johnson let up, however, and Hart's trouble was over."

The *Call* said Johnson sent in a right and left to Hart's head that did not stop his onrush in the slightest degree. Hart's long range right connected with Johnson's jaw. Hart landed a left jab, but Johnson chopped him with rights to the jaw. Johnson attacked and backed Hart against the ropes, but Marvin drove his right to the face and swung his right to the kidneys. Jack retaliated with a vicious right over the eye.

Near the end of the round, they mixed it in the center of the ring and Johnson landed right and left to the face, bringing the blood in a stream from Hart's nostrils. Johnson punished Hart severely, making him bleed profusely from the nose and mouth. Johnson hooked his right to the stomach. Hart bore in close to escape punishment. Marvin bled freely as he went to his corner.

It was "Mistah Johnson's round by a wide margin."

10 - Hart rushed continually but Johnson kept administering punishment. Johnson jarred Hart with jabs, and in the clinches, pressed Marvin to the ropes. Jack went after Marvin's sore eye. Johnson also struck him with a number of left hooks and right uppercuts. However, there was no finishing power in his blows. Hart kept rushing, trying all the time. He kept sending in rights and lefts, some of which landed and had the effect of making Johnson still more cautious. Hart had Johnson in a corner at the end of the round.

The *Call* said the very cool Johnson again had the advantage in this round, and at this stage appeared to hold a safe lead.

11 - It was give-and-take slugging for most of the round. Johnson landed a staggering right, but Hart landed a left to the body. Hart started to improve. When Marvin landed overhand wallops, Johnson rolled his head with the blows. Johnson landed a right uppercut and a number of rights, puffing Hart's left eye.

Hart landed a right to the stomach and short-arm rights to the head, but Johnson retaliated with two forceful blows to the ribs. Hart was forced to cover up quickly to avoid the onslaughts that pushed him back to the ropes. Leaning against the ropes, Hart drove his right to the head and then shot two lefts to the stomach. Johnson countered with a left hook to the jaw and fast infighting followed.

They swung rights simultaneously. Hart was the first to land to the jaw and Jack reeled back. Hart drove his stiff right to the body and the bell rang. It was a good rally for Hart, and one local source believed it gave him the honors of the round by a margin.

12 - The *Chronicle* said there were fast and furious exchanges. Hart hit the stomach and Johnson hit the face.

The *Examiner* said the round was a series of clinches, and in between, Hart's face was battered. Hart continued pressing and landed lefts and rights, but did little damage. He finished the round by landing a right to Johnson's jaw.

The *Call* said Hart continued on the aggressive, the most effective blows being his right to the body followed by a right to the head. Marvin rushed in, attempting to land, but was met with a right hook to the jaw that shook him up a bit. In some infighting, Hart worked his right to the stomach. He blocked Johnson's attempts to dislodge him. They each cleverly blocked some blows. Several clinches followed, and finally, Hart planted his hard right on Johnson's jaw. Jack fought back, but Hart kept his head and sent Jack's head back with a straight right to the jaw. Johnson did some stalling, but never appeared to be in distress. It said it was Hart's round by a slight margin.

13 - The *Call* said Johnson devoted most of his energies to uppercutting, but he could not keep the aggressive Hart off of him. Still, Johnson had the better of the round.

The *Chronicle* said Johnson grew cautious and tried to evade Hart's left to the stomach. Johnson only liked to punch hard and show some aggression when Hart landed a good one. Marvin was constantly after him, "and it was not until the coon was riled that he got to fighting hard. He landed time and time again on Hart's bad face, but the Louisville gent seemed satisfied to take all that was coming."

According to the *Examiner*, Johnson looked serious.

> There was a deal of clinching and scuffling and Johnson in every breakaway managed to shoot right uppercuts in on Hart's chin. Hart did not clinch. He was continually trying to free an arm and get in a punch while they were grappling. Johnson set himself repeatedly and drove in right crosses. Hart's face swelled up, but he did not stagger nor fall.

14 - Hart landed a right to the ribs and a hard overhand right that removed Johnson's broad grin. Johnson landed jabs. Hart swung a left and right to the face but Johnson landed a crushing left to the mouth and nose. Hart led wildly and was met with a right and left. Hart landed his right a couple times and smothered Johnson's uppercuts. Near the end of the round, Jack ripped his left into the body hard.

There was a divergence of opinion regarding their respective merits. The *Call* said the round closed with honors even and both apparently strong. The *Examiner* said Johnson was slower in this round than in preceding ones. The *Chronicle* said, "The coon had all the better of the infighting, landing short arm hooks on Marvin's face at will. Hart kept plowing into the stomach, but with very little effect."

15 - Hart was the aggressor throughout the round and landed some hard right swings to the head. He charged and rushed Johnson to the ropes. Johnson landed left jabs, while Hart relied on his right. Marvin landed a few times to the neck and sent Jack's head back with a left.

On the inside, Johnson repeatedly landed uppercuts. Although the blows had to hurt, they did not slow Hart down. They fought at close quarters and Hart put his right to the body twice, but received a right to the jaw that partially turned him around. Undaunted, Hart waded in and hooked his left to the jaw. After a clinch and break, Hart landed his right to the ear. Johnson landed a vicious left uppercut on the jaw and Hart clinched. Johnson again landed his left uppercut to the jaw. A hooking right found Hart's face as well.

The *Chronicle* said Johnson got Hart on the ropes and hit him at will, but Marvin came back with right and left swings that "caused the coon to show a little of the yellow. Hart landed low and Johnson looked appealingly at the referee. When no notice was taken, he went at Hart hammer and tongs and the bell saved the man from the Whisky State." Hart was bleeding from the nose.

Despite Marvin's aggression, the *Call* said Hart took considerable punishment in this round. Johnson had the honors.

16 - They exchanged lefts. Hart began using a straight left and "tilted Johnson's head a couple of times." Both landed lefts to the face. Marvin landed a hard one before they came together in a clinch. Hart landed rights to the ribs and Johnson landed lefts to the side of the head. A wallop to Johnson's ribs made him grunt.

Johnson landed a wicked left uppercut to the jaw, and then repeated it. Jack rushed in but failed to connect. He missed a left jab and Hart sent his head back with a straight left to the jaw. They clinched repeatedly and fought at close quarters without result. Johnson did some clever blocking. No damage was done. Hart stepped back and drove his left straight to the jaw and Jack's head went back. The bell rang with Hart having somewhat the better of the round, which, on the whole, was tame.

17 - The *Chronicle* said, "Johnson put it all over his adversary from the very beginning. He jabbed his left into Marvin's bleeding nose and swung over his right on Hart's eye time and time again, but Hart was there asking for more at the end."

The *Examiner* said Hart jarred Johnson's head with a straight left. Johnson pressed him to the ropes and landed a right uppercut. Hart forced him back and landed a right to the body. Johnson landed another right uppercut. After Hart landed a left and right to the face, the crowd cheered. However, Johnson backed Marvin to the ropes and smashed his face with punishing lefts and rights. Hart rushed and rammed in a right to the ribs. Marvin was "well hammered in this round and appeared to be tired."

The *Call* said that early in the round, Johnson rushed in, missed a right to the body but landed his left to the head. Johnson fought Hart to the ropes and landed right and left to the head as Hart tripped over the ropes. For a moment, Marvin's head and shoulders were outside the upper rope. Johnson landed a hard right and left to the body but received a hard right to the body that hurt. Hart got inside quickly and sent a stiff right to the jaw. He also landed a vicious left hook that made Johnson wince. Hart landed a straight left, but Johnson drove him against the ropes with right and left hooks to the jaw and face. Hart fought back with great gameness and drove a straight right to the jaw. The fighting was desperate, both administering and receiving severe punishment. Hart showed the effects; the blood starting again from his lacerated nostrils. Unlike its two counterparts, who saw the round for Johnson, it said the round was about even.

18 - The *Examiner* said Hart landed a right to the heart and rushed and landed a right to the jaw. Johnson loosened up and landed lefts and rights to the face. Hart hit the kidneys with rights. They exchanged rights and mixed it up, but Johnson landed the greater number of blows. Hart did not falter though, and drove a right to the ribs and was pressing Johnson into a corner at the bell.

The *Chronicle* said Hart was stronger than ever and rushed Johnson, receiving some lefts and rights as he was "endeavoring to cave in the coon's ribs. When Hart would stop rushing Johnson would let up also."

The *Call* said Hart was the aggressor all through the round. He missed a right to the body and Johnson smashed him with a right to the face. They roughed it and Johnson hooked a wicked left to the stomach that caused Marvin to clinch. Hart fought back but ran into a jab. Marvin landed his right to the body. He jabbed the face and Johnson retaliated with left and right swings to the jaw, forcing Hart to the ropes. Hart got in a straight right to the face and then left to the head. Johnson put a left to the stomach and missed some swings to the head. It said the honors were even.

19 - According to the *Examiner*, Hart landed a left to the mouth, and in a clinch, a right to the ribs. Johnson landed two jabs and Hart again landed a right to the ribs. Hart continually hit the ribs, while Johnson countered to the face. Johnson appeared tired, but met a Hart rush with lefts and rights. Hart landed a right on the jaw to the cheers of the crowd. Johnson's cornerman shouted to Jack, "Will you please hit." Hart was outworking him, as Johnson played defense. The crowd chanted Hart's name.

The *Chronicle* said Hart rocked Johnson with vicious jabs, and followed with left hooks to the ribs. Johnson looked weak. It was Hart's round.

The *Call* said Hart was again the aggressor throughout the round. He waded in with blows, but Johnson eluded or blocked them and hit Marvin with jabs. Hart swung his right to the body and then made another series of failed attempts. Johnson drove a jab to the jaw that sent Marvin's head back. Johnson was very cool. However, Hart did most of the leading. Near the end of the round, Johnson landed a right and left that rocked Hart's head. Hart came back fighting and landed a hard right swing to the jaw, which took a lot of fight out of Johnson. The bell rang, with honors even.

20 - This was a vicious round, with Hart on top of Johnson all the time. After shaking hands, they rushed to a clinch, fighting desperately at close quarters. They grappled and punched, with the referee separating them several times in between exchanges of blows. Johnson landed several short-arm rights over the kidneys. They continued fighting hard at close range. Hart landed a stiff right to the jaw. Johnson uppercut with his right to the jaw and they again clinched. Johnson held on. Hart hooked his left to the jaw, but in a clinch, Johnson planted his left to the stomach. Hart landed a clean, straight left. Johnson used some footwork to evade Hart when he could.

They fought all over the ring, but Johnson would not take a chance with the nervy Kentuckian. He hung on for a time and the house was in a wild uproar, the spectators on their feet cheering for Hart and yelling for him to knock out Johnson. Hart seemed as fresh as when he started, and although he was no beauty to look at, he kept up a fusillade on any part of Johnson's anatomy within reach.

Just before time was up, a sudden flash of light from a photographer in the balcony made them think the round had ended. The referee told them to continue, and Hart quickly rushed at Johnson, who had stopped, and landed a right to the jaw. The bell then rang. The *Call* said the round was all in Hart's favor.

Referee Greggains immediately pointed to Hart and declared him the winner of the 20-round decision. The applause which greeted the decision lasted for several minutes. The white crowd overwhelmingly agreed with the decision.

In explaining his verdict, various local newspapers quoted Referee Alex Greggains as saying,

> I gave the decision to Hart because he was the aggressor throughout and carried the fighting all the way. The damage done to Hart's face was done by a few jabs. Hart blocked the majority of the colored man's blows. I always give the gamest and most aggressive man the decision. Johnson, in my opinion, dogged it. He held at all times in the clinches.

> Before the men entered the ring I warned them that if the fight went the limit the aggressor would get the decision. This was in order to make Johnson fight. Hart forced the fighting every step of the way, and, in view of my warning to them, no other decision was possible. I believe Hart won and I believe that he won all the way. It was a good fight to look at, but Hart did the work, and he properly received the decision. Under the same circumstances I would give the same decision at any time.

Of the contest, Hart said,

> Johnson is a big, clever nigger with a long left arm, and that is why I wear this battered face. Outside of his straight left jabs he had no punch. I nearly broke his ribs with the blows I sent in with both hands. If I hadn't injured my right in the second round I could have knocked Johnson out.

Marvin was also quoted as saying,

> The coon is big and clever and has a good left hand, and I think that lets him out. I nearly broke his ribs with right and left punches. I hurt my right in the second on the coon's hip. It was the hand I broke in my fight with Gardner and it was of little use to me in the balance of the fight. I did all the leading and wasn't blowing a bit at the finish.

He didn't hurt me any, although, of course his jabs bothered me. He has eight inches longer reach and that counted. Now I want a chance at the big fellow, but I want to wait long enough for my hand to heal.

Conversely, Johnson strongly denounced the decision, although he gave Hart some credit. "Hart is a big, tough fellow, very awkward and hard to hit. I will leave the verdict to those who saw the mill, and let them form their own opinions. All I can say is that I was robbed. After fighting until I reached the top, I have been thrown down by an unfair ruling." He was also quoted as saying,

> I was robbed. That is all there is to it. I fought a good fight and am satisfied with the showing I made. I got the worst of it. Had I had my way I would never have stood for Greggains at any stage, but it was all Abrams' say and I have to suffer.... I put up the best fight I knew how and was satisfied that I was a winner at every stage.

Hart was the visibly marked one and looked like the loser, but his advocates argued that the wounds were all superficial and external. "Hart showed no distress after the fight, in spite of the fact that his face was very much warped on the left side. His left cheek and the left side of his lips were badly puffed."

The sports-writers had mixed opinions. Some felt that Johnson either deserved the victory or no worse than a draw. Some explicitly stated that race prejudice probably influenced the crowd and the referee's decision. Certainly a prejudice in favor of Hart's more aggressive style disposed referee Greggains in his favor. Most agreed that Johnson was the more scientific, having shown better defense, landing more blows, and leaving the ring without a scratch, while Hart's face was puffy and bleeding. Still, several others wholeheartedly applauded the decision. Of course, the writers were all white, and some of them had their own biases, as reflected by some liberal use of the word "coon." If that was what they were willing to put in print, just imagine what they were saying and thinking outside of the newspapers. Writers and fans are only human, and they are in part a product of their times. The decision garnered a great deal of subsequent discussion and debate.

In explaining the decision, the local *San Francisco Examiner's* W. W. Naughton entitled his article, "PLUCK AND AWKWARDNESS BETTER THAN MIXTURE OF CLEVERNESS AND COWARDICE."

> [Hart won the decision by being] persistently aggressive and steadfastly game. Though his face was prodded into a condition of puffiness by Johnson's straight lefts he never faltered for an instant. Except when carried back by the force of blows he was constantly pressing towards his opponent.
>
> Johnson simply fought when he felt like it. He gave an admirable imitation of his Colma affair with Sandy Ferguson. He held himself

in reserve until the ninth round was reached and then he cut loose as though bent on finishing his man in double quick time.

He kept up his lick for a couple of rounds and then slowed up. With nothing else to guide him but the yells of disgust from Johnson's corner a tyro would have no difficulty in determining that Johnson's confidence had deserted him. The indifference to punishment and great pluck displayed by the white man seemed to discourage the negro. Johnson beyond a doubt showed that he lacks that essential fighting qualification – grit.

It would be ridiculous to say that Hart is a better ringster than Johnson. If Johnson were only as stout-hearted as the man from Louisville the chances are the negro would dispose of his opponent of last night in ten rounds.

Johnson did his best work with a straight left. He also bruised the side of Hart's face with right crosses. Hart, although anything but a neat boxer, had an awkwardly clever way of stopping Johnson's uppercuts.

Hart scored his biggest successes with a heart punch. He reached Johnson's ribs with this blow a number of times in every round. He also clouted Johnson on the temple and jaw with right swings.

There was a sameness between the rounds from the tenth onward. Johnson spurted occasionally and hammered Hart to the ropes. Then Marvin would pull himself together and force the big negro back across the ring. Johnson's seconds seemed to be in despair. They leaned in through the ropes and railed at the weak-hearted colored champion.

Johnson's second, Tim McGrath, several times cried to him, "Please hit him. You can't win unless you hit him." Jack's manager Abrams was also perturbed, saying, "For goodness sake go after him." However, "All this time the man from Louisville kept up a fast and even gait, hurling himself against the negro and bringing yelps of satisfaction from the watchers every time he planted what appeared to be a telling blow." The 20th round saw Johnson, as usual, "inclined to clinch," and Hart the usual aggressor.

Still, even Naughton said the decision was possibly in doubt for Hart. "From the manner in which the Louisville heavyweight skipped around it almost seemed as if he had not expected more than a draw." Naughton also agreed that Johnson was a "better ringster." However, another *Examiner* writer said, "Hart was the aggressor all the way and the referee could do nothing but give him all the glory."[550]

Like the *Examiner*, the *San Francisco Call* agreed with the decision. It said that although Johnson's muscles showed to better physical advantage, Hart

---

[550] *San Francisco Examiner*, March 29, 1905.

was stronger and the harder worker. "Hart was ready for a severe contest, as the farther it went the better he seemed to get. He began to show a slight lead when half the route had been traversed, and did much the best work in the last ten rounds."

The *Call* said the spectators had a chance to cheer throughout, as Hart outgamed his clever opponent in a hard battle, matching his gameness with Johnson's cleverness. Both were busy throughout the bout, but Hart was busier. Johnson had the superior cleverness, but he did not take any chances.

> Referee Alex Greggains gave an entirely just decision in favor of Hart. He was the aggressor throughout, and there was never an instant that he was not trying in an awkward style to land on the elusive negro.

> When the men shaped up for the first round, Hart's position seemed only a caricature of the way a fighter should shape up, while Johnson was the beau ideal of the boxer. It seemed the fight would last but a few rounds but Johnson showed his usual lack of aggressiveness and would not take advantage of the many openings his less skilled opponent left for him. At the beginning of each round Hart would make a dash at Johnson and invariably landed. Johnson would then get into action with right and left, but he was then satisfied to let well enough alone and would not follow up his man.

> While Johnson is fairly sheathed with muscle, the majority of his blows did not seem to have an ounce of strength behind them. It was astonishing the little damage done by the two powerful men, considering the apparent effort they put forth. Had Johnson a small part of the aggressiveness shown by Hart there would have been nothing to the fight.[551]

British lightweight champion Jabez White said,

> The only difference I saw between fighting here and in England is the holding that seems to be indulged in a great deal in San Francisco. ... I have not been accustomed to the tugging and holding that I saw to-night. ... I enjoyed the evening's entertainment very much and Hart was certainly entitled to the decision. We were somewhat disappointed in Johnson.

White was also quoted as saying, "Hart was the aggressor all the way and the referee could do nothing but give him all the glory. The big fellows clinch too much, something you very seldom see across the pond."

The *Oakland Times* and *Oakland Enquirer* also agreed with the decision, feeling that Hart beat the "coon," though they noted that there were plenty of those who thought it should have been a draw. Hart had earned the

---

[551] *San Francisco Call*, March 29, 1905.

decision after 20 rounds of sluggish milling. Both newspapers printed a nearly identical story, though the *Enquirer* left out a few statements that were favorable to Johnson. This is the more complete version:

> To a critical observer the decision was eminently a just one, but there were plenty of fight fans who thought that Greggains' verdict should have been a draw.
>
> Hart saw early in the fight that his only chance to win the scrap was to rush in, land a punch or two and clinch, and he carried out this program to the end. It more than proved his salvation and his ultimate victory, for at various times the dusky hued boxer showed that he was a veritable master of the fistic game at long range. Thus the fight took on a very sluggish aspect, with long clinches and rough work by Johnson in the break aways, and he was roundly hissed for some of his work.
>
> The fight started with Johnson in a slow attitude, but he quickly showed his white rival that he is a fast, clever hand with his mitts. Hart had a bad habit of clinching with his arm clear around the colored man's neck.
>
> Although fighting a trifle wild in the fourth, Johnson got in some good stiff ones to Hart's stomach and a fierce rally near the ropes was to the latter's disadvantage.
>
> Hart fought a good, steady, cool scrap and during the clinches and breakaways he got in his deadly work, landing repeated lefts straight to the colored man's jaw. The vulnerable spot in the negro was his stomach and many a distressing blow was received in that quarter.
>
> Things took on a rough turn in the seventh, the negro landing several punches while Hart was on the outside of the ropes.
>
> The eighth and ninth and tenth were very much the same, a series of rights and lefts being exchanged by both boxers.
>
> Only once did Hart succeed in getting Johnson anywhere near the knockout route and that was in the eleventh round. Both scrappers opened the round by calling each other names and Hart instantly landed a right and left in the coon's face, following these by two straights to the jaw. Then two more followed to the negro's stomach and Johnson came back with a right and left to Hart's jaw, but his blows lacked steam to do any material damage. Hart swung hard for the coon's jaw and landed, repeated the performance and then the bell rang.

From this round on it was all Hart's fight. His favorite punch was a left straight to the coon's jaw, this mode of attack being the prelude to his life-saving clinch.[552]

The *Oakland Tribune* gave a short report, saying that the decision was based on the fact that Hart was the aggressor nearly all the time, while Johnson was clever but unwilling, and failed to carry the fight to his opponent, being content to do most of his punishing with a stabbing left. Johnson was strong on points, but lacked Hart's grit and aggressiveness, which lost him the fight. Prior to entering the ring, the referee had warned the big fellows that should the battle go the distance that he would give the verdict to the fighter who was the most aggressive and made the fight.

> And on this line Hart fully earned the long end of the purse. He was after the black man at all times except when sent back by the colored champion's hooks and jabs. Had the decision been given on points scored by clean hitting, blocking and punishment administered, then Johnson would have won by a country mile.

Thus, the *Tribune* explicitly stated that Johnson clearly deserved the victory by a country mile if the decision was based on points scored by clean hitting, superior defense, and punishment administered. Essentially, it was saying that Johnson won by any standard other than pure aggressiveness and work rate.[553]

Despite frequently calling Johnson a "coon," the *San Francisco Chronicle* did not really agree with the verdict, though it explained and understood the justification for the decision. It said that both men were strong at the end. Johnson was strong on points, but not as active as Hart, and that cost him. One of its headlines announced, "Colored Man Not Aggressive, Hence He Lost the Fight, as the Contestants Had Been So Forewarned." It explained, "Greggains had warned the men in advance that the fighter who forced the battle, who rushed in and gave the crowd something to see, would be accorded the decision." Johnson was "clever but unwilling." The fight had been decided on style, entertainment value, gameness and toughness rather than upon number of scoring blows, defense, ring generalship, or effectiveness.

The decision was "immensely popular" with the local crowd. During the fight, the crowd yelled Hart's name, cheered when he landed, but remained silent when Johnson did so. The white crowd was inclined to pull for the game, aggressive, active white underdog rather than the more skillful, effective, and defensive black favorite.

> In all this enthusiasm there was doubtless a great deal of racial prejudice. There was also admiration for the under dog in the fight – for the short-ender. Throughout the entire battle the spirit was

---

[552] *Oakland Times, Oakland Enquirer*, March 29, 1905.
[553] *Oakland Tribune*, March 29, 1905.

manifest. Johnson's clean hitting, his cleverness at blocking and his work all through was allowed to pass with scarcely a murmur, while every blow landed by the white man was cheered to the echo. This blinded the judgment of many, beyond a doubt. But, even then, casting aside all favoritism, a big majority of the people present felt that Hart had won and was justly entitled to the decision. The minority cursed their luck and said under their breaths: "Robbery."

Few decisions have been given in the history of pugilism that have not had their dissenters. Those who did not agree with Greggains last night based their argument on the assertion that Johnson had shown pronounced superiority over Hart at all stages: that, if there was nothing else, his clean hitting should have entitled him to the verdict. The Hart faction answered this with the statement that Hart had forced the fighting all the way, and that if he had not done this there would have been no fighting to speak of.

While admitting that Johnson was far the cleverer of the two, it still seems that there is a deal of justice in this view. Johnson did more actual fighting last night than he has done in all his other fights in San Francisco put together. When he went against Sandy Ferguson, he did not fight – would not fight. When he met Sam McVey here a year ago, the jeers of the crowd could not taunt him into making a fight of it. Last night, Marvin Hart rushed him all the time, kept lunging at him, kept on top of him all the time, and Johnson was forced to retaliate. When he did retaliate it was much to Hart's discomfort, for the black man had everything in the way of cleverness, and the white man had little or nothing beyond his indomitable grit and his infinite willingness.

To put the thing briefly the way it appeared to a man who had no interest one way or the other – only a desire to see fair play and to have the better fighter win – on the score of aggressiveness Hart was entitled to the verdict. On any other score Johnson should have been the favored one. This is a thing that will be argued on the street corners for days.[554]

Essentially, this writer was saying that Johnson had won. The only area where Hart was superior was in aggressiveness. He had forced and made the fight. However, Johnson was superior in every other department. He landed more cleanly, had the better defense, and was far more clever. Hart's aggressiveness forced Jack to fight back, and he did a good job of it, too, fighting harder in this fight than in all his other local bouts combined, landing well when he did unload. However, he would then play defense and allow Hart to work.

---

[554] *San Francisco Chronicle*, March 29, 1905.

The *San Francisco Evening Post* had mixed feelings. It said Hart put up a gritty fight against Johnson, who lost "because he would not fight." Still, it also said that Hart's only redeeming quality as a fighter was that he was a glutton for punishment, coming on for more no matter how hard he was walloped. Hart fought hard all the time, whereas Johnson only opened up in spots, showing flashes of offensive brilliance, followed by long periods of defensiveness, cautiousness, and clinching.

> Johnson had the fight well in hand all the time, but failed to carry home the victory just because he would not fight. At times when Hart did land and it stirred up the black fellow the latter would open up and make things so lively that it was thought that the white man would not last, but these were only flashes, and Johnson would settle back in his old jabbing tactics and clinching.
>
> As a fight on ability, the fight belonged to Johnson, but when it is taken into consideration that Alex Greggains warned both men that they must keep fighting and aggressiveness would decide the fight it can be seen how the verdict could be given to Hart.
>
> One point in favor of such a proposition is that it will keep men fighting all the time they are in the ring.[555]

Hence, Johnson was content to jab at long range, but when hit, he turned up the heat, landed more blows, and backed up Hart. However, Marvin would continue coming forward again, and Jack would return to jabbing and blocking punches and only open up again when stung by something.

The *San Francisco Bulletin* strongly disagreed with the decision, feeling that Johnson won, or should have at least received no worse than a draw. It said Johnson had a decided lead on points and cleverness. In the first two or three rounds, it looked like Johnson would win easily. However, Hart's remarkable recuperative powers made the battle interesting.

> He was so aggressive and bored in with such determination that Johnson could never set himself for a punch, and the colored man's shifty left couldn't be brought into action with such telling effect as in his former local battles. At that he landed so often on the face of the Blue Grass State's aspirant for championship honors that the right side wouldn't recognize the left side if they should perchance gaze upon each other in a looking glass. Hart's left eye was put very much to the bad in the early stage of the contest, and his face began to puff out like a toy balloon. … However, this was the only damage suffered by either man, both being strong on their feet when the final gong sounded. …

[555] *San Francisco Evening Post*, March 29, 1905.

Naturally, the house was with Hart, not only because he was the short-ender, but also owing to racial prejudices. Whenever the Kentuckian landed a blow, no matter whether it was a love tap or a hard body punch, the gallery would howl with delight, and long before the final rounds cries of "Hart! Hart! Hart!" rang through the pavilion. So, when Referee Greggains pointed to Hart as the winner at the end of the contest, pandemonium reigned supreme throughout the auditorium, but if a person looked at the contest from an unbiased standpoint and carefully weighed everything in the balance, he would be compelled to acknowledge that the worst Johnson should have received was a draw. Looking at it from a scientific angle, the colored man should have been declared the victor. It is true that Hart did all the forcing and was ever on the aggressive, but his blows rarely landed on a vulnerable spot, and he never had his opponent in distress. On the other hand, Johnson outpointed and outboxed him from start to finish, and on several occasions forced the white man to break ground with such alacrity that the ropes alone saved him from going into the audience.

It too felt that except for overall aggressiveness, Johnson was the superior boxer. He was the more scientific, had the better defense, and was never in distress. Johnson outboxed and outpointed Hart throughout the entire contest, and several times backed him up.

The *Bulletin* felt that race prejudice was not only behind the fan support for Hart, but the referee's decision. It contrasted the decision to the Battling Nelson vs. Jimmy Britt fight, which was similar to this one. There, although Nelson was clearly the aggressor like Hart, and Britt was content to block and retaliate with jabs and uppercuts like Johnson, Britt still won the decision, although with a different referee – Billy Roche. Plus, Britt was white. In that instance, in a bout between two white men, superior cleverness won the day.

Of course, Greggains took the stand that he told both men that he would give the fight to the man who did the fighting, and on this score gave the decision to Hart. But this was not justice to the betting public who wagered their money on the merits of the two men as fighters and not simply on a man's bulldog tenacity and ability to assimilate punishment. What Johnson should have done was to have waded in and forced his adversary, as he was sufficiently clever and had such a decided advantage in reach to enable him to beat Hart to the punch, but like all clever men, he deemed discretion was the better part of valor and laid back with the expectation of getting the decision. This proved to be a fatal mistake. ... The general public was extremely pleased over the decision, but if Johnson was a few shades lighter and had no trace of negro blood in his veins there would have been a different story to tell.[556]

Hence, this writer believed that if Johnson was white, he would have been awarded the decision.

In conclusion, those who disagreed with the decision believed that Jack Johnson had outboxed and outpointed Marvin Hart. However, because Hart was the harder-punching aggressor, took the blows and constantly came back for more, and remained the more active fighter, and because Johnson often played defense and clinched in between hitting Hart cleanly and momentarily backing him up, Hart got the decision.

Regardless, the *Bulletin* also said that there had been 20 rounds of mediocre fighting in which neither man had particularly distinguished himself. Of course, this overlooked the possibility that because they were both good in their own way, they might have neutralized each other's effectiveness to a certain extent.

The ticket sales yielded $6,200, of which the club retained 40%, or $2,480, with $3,720 to be divided equally between Hart and Johnson, or $1,860 each. Apparently they had agreed to divide the fighters' share evenly, regardless of result. The *Evening Post* felt that it was a rough and tough fight in which the fighters had earned their money. "Few that saw the mill would go through the same mill for ten times $1,860."[557]

Wire dispatches allowed newspapers throughout the country to report on the fight. The *Los Angeles Daily Times* reported, "From appearances, Hart was the beaten man from a physical point of view." Hart's face was swollen and his left eye closed, and his face resembled a "large raw steak," while Johnson did not have a mark. Interestingly, this report said that Johnson "did not even appear to be tired, and yet he had fought as nobody had ever seen him fight before in California."

> Hart's gameness was what won the fight. He appeared to be awkward, and to know little of the art of boxing, but he carried the fight to his opponent all the time, and did his share of the leading. It was his forcing and fighting at all times throughout the fight upon which Greggains based his verdict. In point of cleverness and point of blows landed, Johnson led all the way. At times, he placed as many as a half a dozen short-arm uppercuts upon his opponent without return. In the mixing, he also landed oftenest; but Referee Greggains made up his mind that the Kentuckian's work was most effective. From the ninth round on, Hart was bleeding from the nose continuously, and it seemed at many times during the rough infighting that he could not see his opponent at all. But he lasted out, and fought and tugged like a demon all the time. Often during the

[556] *San Francisco Bulletin*, March 29, 1905.
[557] *San Francisco Evening Post*, March 29, 1905.

twenty rounds he was borne to the ropes and received full-arm uppercuts. Throughout the last five rounds he had the crowd shouting wildly for him. The Kentuckian's gameness won nearly every man in the house. Color certainly figured to some extent in this support of a practical stranger.

Johnson was a badly disappointed man. He considered he had landed two blows to every one that his opponent gave him, and he believed that he had led fully as often as the Kentuckian. Referee Greggains, however, figured that Hart's work was the best, and his decision went.[558]

The Associated Press report in that same newspaper had a similar version.

Hart was far from demonstrating that he is qualified to meet Jim Jeffries. Hart was as badly punished a man as has been seen in the ring for a long time, but he was game to the core, and kept boring into the big colored man all through the fight.

Johnson's much-vaunted cleverness did not count for much. While he was able to hit Hart frequently, his blows did not seem to damage the white man. ... The sympathies of the large crowd present were openly with Hart...and every lead he made at Johnson, whether he landed or not, was greeted with yells of joy. Hart did manage to deal the only effective blow in the eleventh round, when he landed a right swing on Johnson's jaw that staggered the black man and nearly knocked him over.

Referee Greggains stated that he gave the decision to Hart because, all through the fight, Hart did all the forcing and leading. According to Greggains, if Hart had not pursued his tactics, there would have been no fight, as Johnson merely contented himself with countering.

Hart's face was battered to a pulp, but Johnson's blows did not seem to have much sting to them. Johnson did a great deal of uppercutting, but Hart covered up, and the blows did not seem to hurt him.

The AP's round by round description gave the impression that it was a fairly close and competitive fight throughout. Its description saw the 1st round as dull, the 2nd for Johnson, the 3rd even, 4th and 5th slightly for Hart, 6th and 7th as dull with clinching, 8th for Hart, 9th and 10th for Johnson, 11th for Hart, 12th - 14th as even, 15th for Johnson, 16th for Hart, and 17th - 20th as even.[559]

On the East coast, the *Newark Evening News* and the *Trenton Times* presented exactly the same reports. They said "neither pugilist showed any championship form."

558 *Los Angeles Daily Times*, March 29, 1905.
559 *Los Angeles Daily Times*, March 29, 1905.

Hart was the worst punished of the two, and had the negro fought a fight which he showed himself at times capable of he would have won handily. Referee Greggains gave the decision to Hart because of his gameness and aggressiveness. The spectators were wholly of the opinion that Johnson was suffering from a streak of bright yellow. Whenever he did fight, he made Hart look like an amateur. The Louisville man's aggressiveness seemed to rattle Johnson and his courage would ooze. ...

The last ten rounds resembled each other. Johnson pegged away with straight lefts and rights, which cut Hart's face, while the Kentucky colonel walloped away with right swings to the body and head.

Overall, this account said Johnson did very well when he was active, particularly through the first half of the bout, landing solid blows, cutting Hart and outboxing him. However, Johnson chose to be active only in spots, often in retaliatory fashion after he was hit, or when forced to fight. He took every opportunity to clinch. Greggains explained that Hart was aggressive throughout and wanted to fight continually, while Johnson "dogged it."[560]

The *Philadelphia Evening Bulletin* said:

Hart's victory puts him in line for a fight with Jeffries, the champion sending a wire to the club last night to the effect that he would meet the winner, provided it was Hart. The latter's form was not good enough to warrant him being dangerous against Jeffries, but as he is the best man in sight local clubs will try to land the match.

The size of the crowd was disappointing, the general impression being that the fight was fixed for Hart to win and thus secure a match with Jeffries. As the contest progressed, however, it was apparent that both men were trying, although their efforts were slow. Although the general sympathy was with Hart and a majority of the sports wanted to see him carry off the honors, Johnson remained a strong favorite all during the day and was a hot choice at 2 to 1.

Before the fight, Johnson had said, "I am going to put Hart out long before the limit. I am in great shape for the fight. ... After I have disposed of Hart I will be just as anxious to fight Jeffries as ever. He is the one man that might make me extend myself, but I know what the result would be - a victory for me sure."[561]

The *Police Gazette*, which generally had been a Johnson advocate, said the referee gave the decision to Hart because he had been the aggressor, trying to fight all the time, while Johnson had been guilty of holding.

---

[560] *Newark Evening News*, March 29, 1905; *Trenton Times*, March 29, 1905.
[561] *Philadelphia Evening Bulletin*, March 29, 1905.

It noted that Hart was badly puffed and bruised, while Johnson was unmarked. Johnson "believed himself entitled to the decision by reason of his clean-cut and terrific punching." In fairness though, it recognized that Johnson held considerably and did not have as much power. "His blows, though, did not have as much steam behind them as did Hart's. The Southerner, when he landed, hurt his man."

Johnson was superior in the first 10 rounds, but after that, Hart made a better showing. Hart "showed far more gameness than Johnson, who fought cautiously after Hart began to force things. In the closing rounds Hart carried the fighting to Johnson so frequently that the black repeatedly clinched and held."

Still, the *Gazette* questioned the legitimacy of Hart's victory. "He did not have the better of the going and a draw would have been a present to him. Johnson undoubtedly prejudiced the referee by holding until he was ready to break." Johnson had the edge in cleverness and blows landed, but Hart "fought doggedly and like a man who would not be beaten." The crowd liked Hart, and the incessant shouts of support for him at least had a subconscious influence. "There is no doubt that Greggains' opinion was affected by the tremendous shouting of the crowd for Hart."[562]

The excellent conditioning, hard-punching, ferocious, busy aggressiveness that Marvin Hart had exhibited throughout his career once again came through for him. His exciting style had won him several close bouts, or gained him draws in bouts in which he was behind in terms of number of blows landed, even prior to Johnson, even against white fighters. Many thought he had not deserved the decision against Sandy Ferguson, but his aggressiveness had won it for him that time. Gus Ruhlin cut Hart to ribbons, yet Marvin's gameness secured him a draw.

It appears that most fair-minded writers felt that Johnson deserved the verdict, or no worse than a draw, though several writers agreed that the decision was justified. A draw might have been the more appropriate decision, even giving Hart the benefit of the doubt as a result of his gameness. This was one of those fights that probably should have been scheduled to a finish in order to determine who the better man truly was. But that would have required the bout to have been held in the less populated state of Nevada.

Alex Greggains was not the most neutral unbiased arbiter. Greggains was a promoter. Promoters needed to fill seats in order to make money, and therefore Greggains was concerned with fan opinion, for the fans generated dollars. Fans typically liked an aggressive, hard-punching, busy fighter like Hart, particularly when he was white and fighting a black man. The white fans cheered everything Hart did, but remained silent when Johnson did well. Being black didn't help Johnson, and the writers clearly admitted and

---

[562] *Police Gazette*, April 15, 1905.

agreed that race played a part in the analysis and the lack of fan support for Johnson. Greggains had to be influenced by the fans at least on a subconscious level.

If referee Greggains had said that if there was no knockout, then he was going to award the fight to the man who was the most aggressive, that gave Hart a distinct advantage in the scoring because there wasn't a fighter alive who was more aggressive than him. Everyone knew going into the fight that Hart was more aggressive than Johnson. Hence, Greggains was biased against Johnson's style even before the bout began, essentially formulating his scoring criteria in a way that assured Hart of victory in the event of a points decision. This also showed his promoter's bias, specifically saying that his scoring criterion was specifically designed "to make Johnson fight."

In fact, most of the pre-fight talk from Greggains centered on his statement that if Johnson did not fight he would declare it a no-contest. Everyone agreed that Johnson fought hard, harder than he had in his previous local bouts. Yet, there appears to have been a form of backlash against Johnson owing to his prior history of victories that were clear and effective, yet not very exciting or entertaining.

Also, even if only on a subconscious level, Greggains had to be influenced and biased by economics. Awarding Johnson the decision did nothing for Greggains, because Jeffries would refuse to fight Johnson. A Hart victory would be more popular with the white paying public and might lead to a big payday with a Jeffries-Hart promotion. Hence, Greggains, a promoter and referee, had a clear interest in having Hart win. He wanted to promote a Jeffries-Hart fight, the only one that Jeff might accept. Therefore, he naturally would have more of an inclination and incentive to award the bout to Hart. All these factors combined probably helped give Hart, with his more entertaining style, the edge, though not by much.

One has to consider all of the pre-fight talk that either the fight was fixed for Hart to win if it went the distance, or that Johnson had agreed to knock him out or lose. Even Hart said so, being quoted accordingly by his hometown newspapers. This, combined with the fact that the Hart faction insisted on Greggains and would accept no other referee put forth by Johnson, even ones considered wise and fair, must give one a moment of pause.

Ultimately, several writers seemed to agree that if Johnson was white, he would have won a close decision or at least have been awarded a draw. This viewpoint gained more momentum as time passed. The only ones who said Hart won said he won because he was more aggressive. However, none said his aggressiveness was more effective. It clearly was considered a decision that was open for debate, and was considered to have the stamp of controversy attached to it.

A day after the bout, Alex Greggains put forth an additional explanation for his decision.

When the men met to discuss the rules under which they were to fight I warned them both. ... They decided on straight Queensberry. I know, of course, that Johnson was unpopular with the sports over the way he held off in his fights with Ferguson and McVey, and I was determined that he should extend himself this time, if it was possible to make him. I said: "Now, you fellows have agreed to straight Queensberry rules, and you know what that means. If there is no knockout I will decide this fight on aggressiveness; so you know what to expect." Well, any man with half an eye could tell who was the aggressor. Hart wanted to fight all the time. Johnson just loosened up in spots, especially after he got a stomach punch in the tenth. He kept holding in the clinches and asking me to come and break them. I told him to fight himself loose, as the other man was trying to do. I think that if every referee would let it be known that aggressiveness would weigh the most when there was no knockout, he would have better contests.[563]

However, some writers noted that Hart did his fair share of clinching as well.

A couple days after the bout, Jack Johnson left for Philadelphia, while Hart returned to Kentucky. Johnson was broken up over the decision, and disputed Greggains' claim that he told the boxers before the fight that he would give the decision to the most aggressive fighter. Greggains might have told the newsmen that in order to justify his decision, but Johnson said he never told the fighters. "I want to say that he never did any such thing. All that he said before the gong sounded was, 'You fellows know the rules, don't you?' We said we did, and went at it. I did not want Alec to referee, but Hart would not take Welch or Graney, whom I mentioned. Hart said it was Greggains or nobody." Johnson said he hurt his hands in the 6th round, which prevented him from carrying out his intention of a knockout within 10 rounds.[564]

Perhaps it is telling that Greggains would not referee a big bout for the next five years. Greggains had refereed Jeffries-Sharkey I, and several other lesser bouts. After this decision, though, he fell off the map as an official.

James J. Jeffries was happy that the white man won.

I am glad Marvin Hart won over Johnson last night. Not that it means a prospective candidate for my title, but it places the negro out of the running. If Johnson had won he would never have fought me. My decision never to meet a negro while I am champion would have been faithfully kept.

I don't want the public to think that I'm looking for easy game, and if the press and public decide that Hart is a suitable opponent for me I

[563] *San Francisco Examiner*, March 30, 1905.
[564] *San Francisco Bulletin*, March 31, 1905.

will gladly meet him this Fall. I have defended the title against all white aspirants and stand ready to meet the popular choice, whoever he may be. If Hart is considered out of my class, I will retire from the ring this year forever.[565]

Jeff said he would fight Hart only if the public demanded that they fight. He was sorry that Hart had not knocked out Johnson.[566]

Regardless of who won, in many ways the bout served to lower the stock of both fighters. Because Hart had neither clearly nor impressively defeated Johnson (and many questioned whether he really had won), nor showed the qualifications to defeat Jeffries, there would not be a great demand for Jeffries to fight him.

Jeffries was not going to fight Johnson anyhow owing to race, but because Johnson had not been able to hurt or stop Hart, and at least had to struggle somewhat with a man who was not on Jeff's level in terms of size, strength, skill, or power, he too was not seen as good enough to handle Jeffries. They reasoned that if Johnson could not dominate and stop Hart, then he could not deal with Jeffries. Hence, there would not be further immediate demand from the press for Jeff to fight Johnson either.

Some tried to hype Hart's victory and attempted to build momentum for a Jeffries contest. They argued that Hart looked as good as possible given Johnson's very difficult style.

Hart wanted to fight Jeffries. "I am the only man in the world who would have a chance to beat him. I have beaten Jack Johnson, a man Jeffries has been side-stepping for months, and I can put it on the boilermaker, too."

> Hart and his friends are so jubilant over the way he polished off the colored man. … They say that to outfight Johnson as he did, giving the negro many pounds and a beating, shows that Hart is the best heavyweight in the world, outside of Jeffries. … Every man who saw the fight gave Hart credit for the battle he put up, and there were many who said the Kentucky man would make Jeff extend himself to the limit to win.[567]

However, there was a mix of opinion regarding Marvin's relative merits, and whether Hart was a viable contender to challenge Jeffries. On one hand, many who saw the Johnson fight said, "I tell you this fellow Hart is a tough customer and likely to give Jeffries a whole lot of trouble." That was "a common remark among fellows usually credited with judgment and discrimination in matters pertaining to pugilism."

However, W. W. Naughton said, "Hart would be candy for Jeff," and that it would be inhuman to put him in the ring with the champion.

---

[565] *Trenton Times*, March 29, 1905; *Philadelphia Press*, March 30, 1905.
[566] *Washington Post*, March 30, 1905.
[567] *Trenton Times, Newark Evening News*, March 30, 1905.

Just at present, Hart's principal fighting qualifications – pluck and endurance – are the very things that would place him in a serious predicament were he left alone in a Queensberry enclosure with the modern pine-bender, big Jim Jeffries.

Jeffries has all that Hart has in the matter of strength and ruggedness. He is heavier, more forceful and more durable than Hart. He is as fast as a feather weight and he would have little difficulty in landing on Hart. The Kentuckian's grit and powers of assimilation would only serve to prolong the agony. … For Hart and Jeffries the time is not yet. Hart may develop into a suitable adversary for Jeffries some day, but for a year at least he should devote his time to improving his knowledge of glove work.[568]

In fact, all of the local San Francisco writers who had seen the Johnson-Hart bout said in their next-day post-fight reports that Jeffries would defeat either Johnson or Hart easily. Hence, the fight actually served to diminish the press' opinion of both men.

The *Oakland Tribune* said, "Upon their showing made last evening neither Johnson or Hart is entitled to meet Champion Jeffries, for judging by form he could dispose of both in the same ring without perspiring." The *Oakland Times* and *Oakland Enquirer* said Jim Jeffries' troubles about the color line were over, for he would no longer have to scheme to dodge Johnson.

The *Los Angeles Times* reported, "The general opinion of those who witnessed the fight was that neither man would stand any chance with Jeffries. The champion would probably beat them both in the same night."

The *San Francisco Call* said, "It was the consensus of opinion that if either of them ever decides to fight Jeffries there will be another death in the ring." The *San Francisco Evening Post* said, "From what was seen last night in the ring, what a joke either fighter would be before Champion Jeffries. They would go down about as fast as Munroe passed away."

The *San Francisco Bulletin* said it was the unanimous opinion of the spectators that neither man would have a chance with Jeffries. "There is no doubt that Jeffries could take the two men on the same evening fighting each man alternate rounds and put them both away inside of ten rounds." Hart was criticized as not possessing the terrible punch he had been credited with (perhaps overlooking Johnson's defensive brilliance), and was in Jack Munroe's class in terms of cleverness. "The only redeeming qualities he possesses is rare gameness and a willingness to force matters. But if he should run into one of Jeffries' pile-driving solar plexus punches with the frequency that he displayed last evening in stopping Johnson's wallops it would be 'curtains' for the Kentuckian in short order."

The hope that either man would be matched with Jeffries was eliminated when "they demonstrated that the necessary qualification for a

[568] *San Francisco Examiner*, March 30, 1905.

champion was lacking, namely – a knockout wallop." Both men had incentives to fight hard due to the fact that they wanted to legitimize their challenges to Jeffries. However, "Johnson was not willing to mix matters with a vengeance, while Hart lacked the necessary cleverness and punch to decisively defeat the negro."

The local analysis probably was not fair to either Hart or Johnson, but such was the case. The local writers overlooked the fact that both men were tough customers and not easy for anyone to handle or knock out. In Tom Sharkey, Jeffries himself had failed to knock out a man like Hart. Marvin Hart was just plain tough to stop. Anyone who closely followed Hart's career was fully cognizant of the fact that he was extremely aggressive, well-conditioned, tough and durable, and had only truly been stopped once on a fluke when he was caught cold back in 1901. No one was ever able to keep Marvin from rushing.

In Hart's defense, it is not always easy to appear like a big puncher when you go up against a cautious, fast, defensive specialist with height and reach, who knows how to duck, block, move and clinch. Johnson had not been stopped since 1901, his only true knockout loss. It was a tall order to stop Johnson, for it was quite difficult to hit him. Johnson's blows were not easily avoided either, because he was fast.

Both fighters had gained up to 20 pounds since being stopped, and had become more durable as they grew larger. Two good, tough, strong, well-conditioned fighters often have a way of offsetting each other's strengths and weaknesses. Not everyone was easy to knock out, and quite frankly, even Johnson's supporters conceded that he was not a knockout artist. He could punch, but was not always a finisher, owing to his natural inclination towards cautiousness, not wanting to get hit with something in return or wear himself out in the attempt to finish a man.

Regardless, as a result of how the press interpreted the bout, there would not be any great immediate demand or pressure, and hence no great financial incentive for Jeffries to fight either Hart or Johnson at that time.

Two weeks after the fight, the *Police Gazette* was also tough on Hart, and questioned the decision, saying,

> As the critical public was not favorably impressed by the manner in which Hart won from Jack Johnson...there will hardly be any crying demand for such an unequal match [with Jeffries]. ... Hart did not prove himself a first-class pugilist. The only thing that he showed in the scrap was that he was capable of taking a lot of punishment. Johnson's defeat was as big a surprise to Hart as it was to the negro, and although the crowd as a body upheld Referee Greggains, he could only find one favorable thing to say in Hart's favor, and that was that he forced the fighting.

At the end of the bout Hart was the worse scarred of the two. His face was so puffed and bruised that one could hardly recognize him. On the other hand Johnson was unmarked.[569]

A week later, the *Police Gazette* said,

> Marvin Hart has not exhibited any frantic eagerness to force Jim Jeffries into a match. ... Hart has a Chinaman's chance. He will be the softest proposition that ever crossed the path of the Herculean Californian. ... Had Jack Johnson fought up to his standard he would have beaten Hart. ... When he did mix it up, Hart looked like a handful of nondescript change, which only goes to show that the Southerner was lucky in getting away with what he did.[570]

Bob Fitzsimmons said of Hart, "It looks like Johnson received a bad deal, but I'm willing to fight him if he wants to make the match. I do not know much about him, but from what I've heard I guess he is a comer."[571]

Yet, another week later, another reporter from the same periodical was giving Hart more of a chance against Jeffries, or at least to make a good showing. This balanced analysis said,

> It is true that Hart's victory over Johnson was not a decisive one. Many supporters of boxing would have been better satisfied had Hart succeeded in knocking the negro out. But he won, just the same, and a win by a close margin is as good as a win by mile. Hart...scales over 190 pounds, and at this weight he is quick and agile in his movements. In point of physique, strength for strength, blow for blow, Hart cannot be compared to the boilermaker. There are many who think that Hart will be just as easy for Jeffries as were the Californian's other opponents. ... Hart is a fighter who keeps coming all the time, and these tactics enabled him to predispose Referee Greggains in his favor. He had got by Johnson's long reach once in a while, kept boring in, and if he failed to do any damage to the negro, as Johnson at the finish was unmarked, he at least succeeded in cutting out the pace that counted in the end. As to Hart's gameness there is not the shadow of doubt. He took all that any man of his physique could stand in his mill with Johnson and never faltered. It is true that Johnson is not one-third the hitter that Jeffries is, but it must be admitted that the champion is not as clever as Johnson. The deduction is, it seems at this stage, that Hart has a fair chance of making a good fight.[572]

[569] *Police Gazette*, April 15, 1905.
[570] *Police Gazette*, April 22, 1905.
[571] *Police Gazette*, April 22, 1905.
[572] *Police Gazette*, April 29, 1905.

However, another reporter said, "Marvin Hart is now considered the next best man to Jeffries, but to borrow an expression from another game, there is a broad streak of daylight between Jeffries and Hart."[573]

With Jack Johnson's image tarnished by the Hart bout, he attempted to get Hart back into the ring for a rematch. "Johnson has been saying some sassy things about the Louisville idol." However, Hart insisted that he would never again fight a colored man. "The referee of the Hart-Johnson fight may have given a strictly fair decision, but it must have been very close when it took a column to explain it."[574]

Years later, Johnson said of the bout,

> I was overjoyed at the idea of finally fighting a man in my league. ...
> I must say up front that the man in no way disappointed me; from the opening bell of the fight, his performance never failed for a moment to be interesting for all concerned. I nonetheless never doubted for a second that I could bring him down. I knew that I was completely dominating him and so did everyone in the crowd. I was so sure of my victory on points that I didn't think for an instant that I wouldn't get it. Imagine my surprise and disgust when the judge...gave the win to Marvin Hart.

Johnson felt that he had been robbed; that the bettors had fixed the referee. "I was so outraged that I swore never to fight again on the West Coast until the system in place had been changed."[575]

---

[573] *Police Gazette*, April 29, 1905.
[574] *Police Gazette*, May 13, 1905.
[575] *My Life and Battles* at 44.

CHAPTER 16

Convincing the East
While Passed Over for the
Vacancy in the West

Following his controversial decision loss to Marvin Hart, which he hotly disputed, Jack Johnson got away from the West Coast, and for the rest of 1905 and all of 1906, primarily fought in the East.

Jim Jeffords

Just under a month after the Hart fight, on Tuesday April 25, 1905 in Philadelphia, before the Knickerbocker Athletic Club, Jack Johnson took on 24-year-old Jim Jeffords, a very large 6'4" white fighter who weighed over 200 pounds and had over 30 fights of experience. Despite his size advantages, Jeffords was more of a third tier heavyweight. In 1898, Jeffords had boxed a 4-round exhibition with James Jeffries. He scored an 1899 KO4 over a shot Peter Jackson in Pete's last fight. Jeffords had several knockout losses since then, including: 1899 LKOby5 Gus Ruhlin and LKOby3 Bob Armstrong; 1900 LKOby2 Tom Sharkey, LKOby8 Al Weinig, and LKOby2 Peter Maher; 1901 LKOby2 Maher; 1902 LKOby3 Weinig and LKOby1 Maher; 1903 LKOby5 Fred Cooley; and 1904 LKOby2 Maher, LKOby3 George Gardner, and LKOby3 Jack O'Brien.

Jeffords did have some respectable results mixed in, such as: 1899 KO1 Nick Burley; 1900 W20 Walter Johnson; 1901 WND6 Joe Goddard, DND6 Peter Maher, and W10 Jack McCormick; 1902 WND6 McCormick; 1903 L10 and LND6 (twice) Jack O'Brien, and KO2 Fred Cooley; 1904 LND6

Mike Schreck, KO1 Yank Kenny, WND6 Joe Grim, WND6 and LND6 Gus Ruhlin, and KO5 Cooley; and 1905 KO2 Cooley, KO2 Joe Butler, DND6 Larry Temple, LND6 Morris Harris, WND10 Jack Butler, and DND10 Jack Bonner. When he was on his game, he could beat quality fighters. Jeffords was 5-1-2 in his last eight bouts, which took place from November 1904 to April 1905. So at that time, he was sharp.

The bout was a scheduled 6-round contest with no decision to be rendered if it went the full route.

1 - They lost little time in sparring, but settled down to hard work from the start. Johnson kept trying for the jaw and Jeffords for the stomach. After an exchange, Johnson rushed Jeffords into a corner and punched him right and left.

After they broke from a clinch, Jeffords got out of the corner and landed his jab and right swing to the head. Jack tapped him on the jaw with his right, but not hard enough to hurt. He followed with a right uppercut to Jeff's chin or upper chest and then ripped a left hook into the stomach that made Jeffords wince. Both played for the body, each landing several hard blows. Jeffords landed a left to the face and right to the body.

Near the end of the round, Johnson sent Jeffords to the ropes with a left swing on the jaw and then pounded him with left and right swings on the face.

The *Philadelphia Press* said honors were slightly in Johnson's favor.

2 - Early in the round, Jeffords did fair work with right-hand leads for the body. Jeffords landed a left to the face. Johnson landed a hard one to the body and in a mix-up that followed, honors were about even.

Johnson got busy and landed fully a dozen blows without a return. He started jabbing Jeffords, landing three jabs without a return, one of which was particularly hard, full in the face, which started Jeff's nose bleeding, and possibly his mouth.

Jack followed up with three swings for the body which made Jeffords wince. Several times Johnson reached the body with hard left swings.

Despite his size, Jeffords could not break down Johnson's guard at long-range work, nor was he strong enough to cope with Johnson at close-range either.

3 - The round was a hot one, each landing hard several times. Johnson rushed Jeffords back to his own corner. Feinting with his left for the body, Johnson fired his right across the jaw and the white man went down to the floor.

At the count of nine, Jeffords rose, ran into a clinch, and hugged until the referee separated them. He then came back gamely, making a terrific rush at the advancing Johnson, raining a half dozen blows on his "dusky opponent." However, a stiff counter caught Jeffords flush on the mouth and kept him at bay again. Johnson was somewhat cautious as a result of three hard rights Jeffords had landed under his heart. Still, it was Johnson's fight from that moment onwards. Jack played with him for the remainder of the round. He was just awaiting his opportunity to land a decisive blow.

Jeffords' nose was bleeding. Jack landed his left to the face and right to the body. After a clinch, Jack landed left and right and Jim returned with a right to the face. Jack jabbed his left and missed his right, after which he smiled. Johnson managed to reach the body and face with jabs and swings, and Jim was tired at the bell.

4 - Early in the round, Jeffords seemed determined to make one supreme effort. He swung his right, which landed around Johnson's "capacious jaw." The smile that had illuminated Johnson's face throughout the bout suddenly disappeared. Trying too hard would soon prove to be Jeff's undoing.

Johnson discarded his "phony tactics," got serious, and finally extended himself. He swung his hefty left viciously into Jeff's body, and Jeffords hugged Johnson like his brother. After the breakaway, it appeared that Jeffords regretted getting too frisky and was "willing to apologize for his indiscretion." He boxed in a coy manner. However, he had raised Johnson's ire.

Johnson rushed Jeffords across the ring and landed some light punches. Jeffords landed one in return. A good mix-up followed, with Johnson having the best of it. Jeffords landed three hard rights to the body, while Johnson kept swinging for the face, landing frequently.

Each local Philadelphia paper described the sequence that ended the bout:

The *Inquirer* said Johnson quickly waded in, shifted and planted his left into the body, and Jeffords went down and out.

The *Public Ledger* said that while Johnson was endeavoring to shake off Jeffords from a clinch, Jim stepped away. Before Jeffords could place himself on guard, Johnson landed a short right swing into the solar plexus and Jeffords fell flat on his back. He was counted out, though he recovered quickly after being led to his corner.

The *Record* said that after they broke from a clinch, Jeffords landed a light punch. Johnson stepped back, and as Jeffords came to him, Johnson feinted with his right and then drove his left full into Jeffords' stomach. The Jerseyman dropped like an ox hit with an ax. Jeffords was on his back several seconds until he tried to get up, but he was unable to do so.

The *Press* said that suddenly, Johnson gave a little jump forward and his left arm swung in a long upward curve with the full weight of his body behind it, and his glove planted squarely into Jeffords' solar plexus. The big boxer went down and out with only 30 seconds remaining in the 4th round. Jeffords rolled over onto his back. Referee Hyland, seeing that it was not necessary to count, helped carry Jim to his corner, where it was several minutes before he had revived sufficiently to leave the ring.

The *Evening Bulletin* said Jeffords rushed in to swing a left, but Johnson got there first. His left sank deeply into the pit of the stomach and Jeffords went down and out. Johnson was unmarked.

In conclusion, Johnson had drawn first blood from the nose in the 2nd round, dropped Jeffords with a right to the jaw in the 3rd, and decked him with a left uppercut to the body in the 4th to finish off the larger man.

Summarizing, the *Philadelphia Inquirer* said that for the most part, Johnson had stalled and did not do much. He appeared to be carrying Jeffords, playing around with him, not taking the bout very seriously. Jack was a "joker." "Johnson made it clear that there is nobody in this vicinity who has any business with him. He simply stalled with Jeffords, and but for the latter's thoughtless punch in the last round the chances are that Johnson would have permitted the bout to have gone the limit."

Johnson was happy to box carefully and not try to hurt his opponents too much, just as long as they allowed him to be in control and didn't try to hurt him. However, once they tried too hard or landed a good one, he was prepared to make them regret it.

The *Philadelphia Public Ledger* said Johnson outboxed and outclassed Jeffords, giving the sports just a glimpse of his true form.

The *Philadelphia Record* said Johnson's performance "strengthened the belief of the spectators that he was robbed of the decision in his recent battle with Marvin Hart in San Francisco or that the latter battle was not on the level."

It was a good bout, but Johnson was Jeffords' master after the 1st round. There was little to choose between them as far as size and weight were concerned, though Johnson had a trifle advantage in reach and appeared more rugged. "Johnson showed that he is a clever boxer, and also that he can hit hard." He stopped Jeffords with a left full in the stomach, "and it was hard enough to stop any man living."

The *Philadelphia Press* agreed that Johnson made a splendid impression before the large crowd. He stood over six feet and was the picture of the perfect athlete. "Cool and clever, without any fancy movements, Johnson calmly followed Jeffords around the ring and made nearly every one of his leads count." On the other hand, Jeffords seemed scared and was wild with his blows, which Johnson had little difficulty in escaping. Johnson knocked him down at the start of the 3rd round with a right to the jaw and finished him in the 4th round with the left to the body.

The *Philadelphia Evening Bulletin* said Johnson showed his true form, completely outclassing Jim Jeffords. "A large crowd was present to see the man who claimed to have beaten Marvin Hart and his work convinced them that there might be foundation for the claim." For a heavyweight bout, it was surprisingly fast, though one-sided. From the start, Johnson was cool and collected, and easily the better man.[576]

---

[576] *Philadelphia Inquirer, Public Ledger, Record, Press, Evening Bulletin*, April 26, 1905.

The *Police Gazette* reported that some were suggesting that Johnson, who lost to Hart by a close margin, "purposely lost to Hart to facilitate the latter getting on a match with Jeffries," and that Johnson was trying to encourage that idea rather than cover it up.

However, the facts did not support that Johnson threw the Hart bout, given how strongly he disputed the decision immediately after it was rendered, and the fact that it was a close and debatable decision. If anything was not entirely on the level, it was the referee's decision. Johnson fought to win.

Johnson said he could lick Hart every morning before breakfast. Jack was willing to fight a rematch, but Marvin was not interested in fighting him again. Hart's reluctance to fight a rematch helped bolster Jack's position and make some suspect that Johnson was correct in his assertions that he was robbed.

Hart responded to Johnson's allegations that he was robbed by saying, "That coon has enough yellow in him to paint the City Hall. It cropped out in his fight with me so plainly that his own seconds noticed it. ... Johnson is a fancy boxer, but when he gets stung he is strictly a 'tin-canner and staller.' I'll never fight another negro."[577]

Johnson remained in Philadelphia. Just one week after the Jeffords bout, he returned to the ring again, boxing a rematch with Black Bill (Claude Brooks) of Merchantville, New Jersey, in yet another 6-round no-decision bout. Johnson had dominated and nearly stopped Bill in a February 1904 6-round no-decision bout. Since then, Bill had boxed Joe Walcott in a 6-round no-decision which some said Bill had won, while others said it was a draw. Other results included: 1904 D15 Young Peter Jackson, WND6 George Cole, LND6 Jack O'Brien, WND6 Charley Stevenson, and LKOby5 Morris Harris; and 1905 WND6 (twice) Morris Harris, WND6 Larry Temple, and KO2 Joe Jeannette (with a right to the jaw).

On Tuesday May 2, 1905 before Philadelphia's Knickerbocker Athletic Club on Broad and Snyder avenue, Jack Johnson and Black Bill fought their rematch. The *Philadelphia Press* said the biggest crowd of the season turned out to see Johnson.

Johnson was taller, but there did not seem to be much difference in weight. They agreed to box clean and break when ordered to do so, and both complied, for there was no rough work at any time.

1 - Johnson took it rather easy in the opening round. At the start, Black Bill did a little better than Jeffords did, managing to reach Johnson's face and body a few times, scoring some points. However, Johnson always came back good and hard, particularly to the stomach, though he missed several swings.

That same evening, April 25, 1905 in Indianapolis, Hugo Kelly won a 10-round decision over Philadelphia Jack O'Brien.
[577] *Police Gazette*, May 13, 1905.

2 - Early in the round, Bill landed a hard lead left hook that drew a little blood from Johnson's mouth. The crowd cheered. The blow angered Johnson, who in response landed hard right swings to the body and left jabs to the face. A fast mix-up ensued in Bill's corner. Bill avoided a left hook to the body, but "nearly turned white from fright." Each landed lefts to the face. At the bell, a little blood showed on Johnson's lips.

According to the *Philadelphia Inquirer*, Johnson took this bout seriously. He nearly put Bill out of commission during the first 2 rounds with his vicious swings to the body. Whenever the body blows landed, Bill obviously was hurt by them. Johnson varied his attack by ripping in a few uppercuts, which also jarred Bill badly.

3 - Johnson really cut loose, forcing the fight, trying to end matters. Initially Bill stood his ground and tried to mix it up. Jack landed a hard left swing to the stomach. It was hard enough such that Bill was afraid to get hit anymore.

The *Press* said that thereafter, every time Bill saw a blow coming his way he promptly dropped to the floor. The *Record* said that when Johnson rushed, Bill went to knees. He appeared to try to get his shoulders between Johnson's legs to throw him over his head. However, Johnson stepped over Bill and got away.

Jack aimed a blow at Bill's head, but drew it back and laughingly stepped to one side as Bill went down and took what seemed to be a very long count. The *Inquirer* said Bill had remained down for over 12 seconds, but Referee Hyland, wanting to give the public its money's worth, improperly ignored the time limit and indulged Bill, giving him a slow count and allowing him to continue.

Johnson rushed again and Bill went down without being hit. Bill rose and reached Jack's face, but it was only a slap. A light blow sent Bill down again.

The *Press* said Bill went down four times in the round without being hit. The *Inquirer* said Bill went to the floor five times, twice from punches.

4 - Johnson feinted and Bill dropped to the floor without being hit. Soon thereafter, Bill went down again without being hit.

Johnson feinted several times and on each occasion it seemed as if Bill was preparing to drop to the floor. However, seeing that Johnson was inclined to take it easy on him, Bill generated some courage and swung his left to the face. Johnson seemed pleased, for he thought it would cause Bill to mix it up a little. However, Bill refused to mix.

Instead, in the middle of the round, Johnson cut loose and rushed him around the ring and into a corner. Jack struck him three body blows in succession, which caused Bill to drop to the floor. Another local source said it was a left hook to the jaw and right to the body.

Bill declined to rise, despite the fact that the referee clocked off the seconds rather slowly and deliberately, seeming intent on giving him every opportunity to continue. Despite Referee Hyland's appeals and the long-count, Bill refused to rise until after he was counted out.

The *Inquirer* said Bill's refusal to continue was understandable, for he had endured a fierce grueling and realized that "Jack Johnsing" was too much for him. The *Press* said that when Bill quit, his lips were puffed to twice their size and his nose was swollen. He refused to continue and just be a punching bag.

The *Philadelphia Record* said Johnson punched Black Bill of Merchantville so hard that he quit in the 4th round.

Several times during the bout, Bill complained that his shoulder hurt him, and he said that it was on account of this that he was forced to quit. He indeed had complained about his bad shoulder for several days, and wanted the bout postponed. He only consented to box Johnson so as not to disappoint the big crowd which had gathered to witness the bout.

The *Philadelphia Evening Bulletin* said Black Bill was outclassed badly. Bill was leery of Johnson throughout, and covered up in such a way that Johnson had considerable difficulty in finding an opening. At no time did Bill have the best of matters. He was not willing to open up and fight.

The *Philadelphia Press* said Johnson did not have to extend himself or work any harder than he did to stop Jeffords the previous week.[578]

That same day, it was reported that James Jeffries would be retiring. He made the announcement from Cincinnati, Ohio, where he was on the stage performing in his play. Jeff said he was honoring his wife's request.[579]

Jeffries also said he was retiring because there was no big money fight on the horizon that the public demanded. Jeffries even went so far as to say that pugilism did not pay. However, if he had remained a boilermaker, his first profession, "he would probably have still been working 10 hours or more a day for the munificent sum of about $18 or $20 a week." Jeffries was rich, and no longer needed to box. He had married recently, and his wife wanted him to quit fighting.[580]

At that time, Marvin Hart arrived in Philadelphia to box John Willie. He and Johnson were both in the same town at the same time. Marvin refused to box Johnson again, although Johnson was willing to box Hart. This caused the local *Philadelphia Record* to suspect that something more nefarious was at work behind the Hart-Johnson decision, saying,

> The heavy-weights are not apt to figure in pugilistic history in the near future. The match between Jack Johnson and Marvin Hart, as well as the result of the same, seems to have been cleverly planned, but, according to the old Scotch saying, "the best-laid plans of mice

---

[578] *Philadelphia Inquirer, Philadelphia Press, Philadelphia Record, Philadelphia Evening Bulletin*, May 3, 1905.
[579] *Philadelphia Record*, May 3, 1905. Also that day, on May 2, 1905 in Tacoma, Washington, Tommy Burns won a 20-round decision over Dave Barry.
[580] *Seattle Post Intelligencer*, May 3, 1902; *Philadelphia Record*, May 7, 1905.

and men aft gang aglee," the public appears to have gotten wise, and there is little demand for a fight between Hart and Jeffries, for which all the fine work was done. It may be easy to fool some of the people, but you can't fool them all the time.

Johnson is still in Philadelphia, and he has shown by the way in which he so quickly disposed of Jeffords and Black Bill that he can punch considerably. Hart is still of the notion that he will not fight a colored man again. Hence, there is no chance to see Johnson and Marvin in a bout in this city, although such a contest would draw a big house. Hart probably knows his own business best, but a demonstration of the way he says he made a punching-bag and a foot racer of Johnson in California would be more convincing to the sporting men of this city than any mere recitation of his recollection of what took place in the ring in San Francisco. ...

A match for six rounds had been suggested between Jack O'Brien and Jack Johnson. ... Johnson would have considerable advantage in weight and height, but O'Brien would probably overcome this in cleverness and speed. Such a bout would be an exhibition of boxing which would be relished by Philadelphians and one which would give a pretty good line on Johnson, and set at rest some of the many rumors which came East almost as fast as he did regarding the recent battle with Hart in San Francisco.[581]

Clearly, the sense was growing that Hart had not truly earned the decision over Johnson.

On May 8 at the Washington Sporting Club in Philadelphia, Marvin Hart unofficially won a 6-round no-decision bout against John Willie. The *Philadelphia Inquirer* said, "Marvin is not clever. He is a big, strong, husky chap, willing to give and take."[582]

The next night, continuing his weekly fighting clip in Philadelphia, on Tuesday May 9, 1905, once again at the Knickerbocker Athletic Club, Jack Johnson took on Joe Jeannette and Walter Johnson, both black, each in scheduled 3-round bouts. He was going to attempt to stop each man on the same evening. Jeannette, who allegedly hailed from New York (he may have been from New Jersey), went on first.

To that point, Joe Jeannette (a.k.a. Jeanette) had a KO2 Johnny Carroll and had boxed in couple 6-round no-decision bouts with fellow black Morris Harris, but recently was stopped in 2 rounds by Black Bill. He had been boxing professionally only since late 1904, but the 25-year-old had talent.

---

[581] *Philadelphia Record*, May 7, 1905.
[582] *Philadelphia Inquirer*, May 9, 1905.

Johnson was told that Philadelphia Jack O'Brien was in the crowd. Given that Johnson wanted to fight him, some thought that he would not do his best, in order to induce O'Brien's willingness to fight him.

Joe Jeannette

One paper said Jeannette was handicapped in weight, height, and experience. Another said Johnson towered over Joe and was considerably heavier than him.

1 - Jeannette kept Johnson very busy. He was well-coached to rush in aggressively and keep close so as to neutralize Johnson's long arms. Joe was somewhat successful, although after every blow he landed, Jack rushed him at once. Joe covered up to avoid punishment. Johnson alternated his punches from the face to the body, using his left more than his right. He mostly missed his rights.

Although for the most part, Jeannette covered well, according to the *Record*, one of Johnson's rushes resulted in Jeannette going down. Still, Joe landed several blows in the round, one right making Johnson blink.

2 - A hot mix ended in a clinch. Joe kept rushing in. Johnson landed three lefts to the stomach in quick succession. Joe stood up gamely and landed several hard blows, including a right to the face.

However, both the *Record* and *Press* said Johnson dropped Jeannette, one saying it was the result of a head punch, while the other offered no detail. Joe rose and clinched considerably to survive and recover. Jack pounded his kidneys, which the crowd did not like, and hooted him for it.

3 - During this round, Jeannette caught Johnson on the jaw three times with left and right swings. They mixed it up well. Johnson landed several body punches. Joe slipped to the floor. Johnson rushed him and Joe was forced to cover up. Joe landed a good one to the body.

Johnson rushed him again and Jeannette went to his knees, the *Press* saying he was knocked down. Just as Joe rose, the bell rang. The crowd vigorously applauded Jeannette's game performance.

Jeannette had proven to be a surprise, for he had given Johnson a hard 3-round scuffle, despite being down several times. The *Inquirer* summarized,

> Jeanette not only held his own, but actually forced the milling in two of the rounds. He repeatedly got home to Johnson's body and face with a good left jab and landed a few right-hand wallops which caused the crowd to yell its approval. Jeanette was not any too gallus,

however, by his success and he invariably cleverly covered up whenever the big fellow came rushing in after being stung by some of Joe's punches. Johnson seemed unable to get to Jeanette with any of his blows effectively, although the New Yorker took the count more than once to gather his wits about him when the milling got a bit warm. Johnson did not seem to try very hard in the first round, but after Jeanette had made himself solid with the crowd Johnson sailed in for the second round like a hurricane. For a time things went badly for Joe, but before the round was over he was giving just as good as he received. The third he easily held his own, despite Johnson's desperate efforts to land the "ender" punch. The crowd went wild when the bell ended the bout with Jeanette fighting Johnson savagely.

Joe Jeannette had shown what he would demonstrate for the majority of his career. Although he went down a few times in the 3-round bout, he covered up fairly well, recuperated, showed gameness, and fought back hard. He was fast and landed some good blows. Jeannette would wind up becoming one of the era's toughest and best heavyweights.

After a minute of rest, next up that same evening was 28-year-old Walter Johnson, another black fighter, who had far more experience than Jeannette, including: 1895 D10 Bob Armstrong; 1896 KO17 Willie Lewis, WND4 Steve O'Donnell, and D4 Frank Slavin; 1898 LKOby3 Charley Stevenson and LKOby2 Charley Strong; 1899 LKOby7 Ed Martin; 1900 L20 Jim Jeffords; 1902 L6 Frank Childs, L6 Fred Russell, and D6 Klondike; 1904 ND8 Steve O'Donnell, LKOby2 and KO4 Bob Armstrong; and 1905 LND6 George Cole. The knockout victory over Armstrong probably was his best result.

1 - According to the *Inquirer*, the colored champion did not allow Walter Johnson a chance to do the same kind of boxing accomplished by Jeannette. From the start, Jack plunged in and hammered Walter unmercifully. A terrific right to the body seemed to take all of Walter's steam out of him.

The *Press* saw things a bit differently. It said Walter Johnson tried to be aggressive, and made a good showing in the opening round.

2 - The *Inquirer* said not much happened. The *Press* said Jack drew blood from Walter's mouth with a left hook, and he also punished his body.

The *Record* said that for the first two rounds, Walter Johnson did not do well. He seldom landed a blow. He spent most of the time "tin-canning and clinching."

3 - Immediately after shaking hands to start the round, Jack went right at him. Walter tried to get away, to no avail. Jack feinted with his left to draw out his opponent, and then sprang forward with a right to the jaw that sent Walter down. He tried hard to rise but could not, and was counted out.

The *Philadelphia Inquirer* summarized that Jeanette had been a "tartar," while Walter Johnson had been a "mark."

JACK JOHNSON.

The *Philadelphia Record* said Johnson "added a couple more scalps to his collection" by beating two colored men, each in 3-round bouts. He defeated Joe Jeanette of New York and Walter Johnson of Boston. While Jeanette lasted the full 3 rounds and made quite a good showing by rushing at Johnson, "yet it was easily seen that Johnson was his master as a boxer."

The *Philadelphia Press* said Jeannette put up a splendid battle and deserved a draw. Walter Johnson was knocked out by a right-hand swing.

The *Philadelphia Evening Bulletin* said Johnson defeated two men, continuing his winning career. Joe Jeanette of New York was first to appear, and he made a good showing, but Johnson hit him where and when he pleased. It was only Jeanette's good defensive tactics and fact that he covered up well that saved him.

Walter Johnson then entered, and for 2 rounds he stalled and managed to keep clear of Jack's swings. In the 3rd round, Johnson whipped a hard right to the jaw that dropped him. After counting five, the referee waved Johnson to his corner and stopped the bout. "Johnson appeared to be in rare trim and he looked as though he had only been out for a breezer when the bout was stopped."[583]

On May 13, 1905, James J. Jeffries officially retired at age 30. He said there was no one in sight to give the public a run for its money against him. Apparently, there was insufficient public demand and therefore insufficient financial incentive for Jeffries to fight Marvin Hart. Therefore, Jeff decided to retire. The *Police Gazette* said Jeffries was the greatest pugilist who ever lived and was without rival.[584]

Regarding which contenders were most viable or deserving to fight for the vacant title, the *Police Gazette* said, "Hart looms up as the most eligible because of his victory over Jack Johnson, a win that has been questioned in many quarters." Despite the questionable victory over Johnson, no black

<hr/>

[583] *Philadelphia Inquirer, Philadelphia Press, Philadelphia Record, Philadelphia Evening Bulletin*, May 10, 1905.

[584] *Chicago Tribune*, May 14, 1905; *Police Gazette*, May 20, 1905.

fighter was mentioned as amongst the strongest aspirants for the title, for it was understood that only two white men would or could fight for Jeff's vacant crown.[585]

Race excepted, Johnson and Hart should have fought a rematch in a fight to the finish to determine who was the most deserving of the vacant crown. However, Jack Johnson lived at a time when racial barriers prevented or at least strongly limited his consideration.

NATIONAL PLAY GROUND.

WILL DISCRINATING LAWS KEEP HIM OUT?

Freeman, June 10, 1905

Ultimately, as of May 27, promoters Al Livingston and Dan Egan matched Hart to fight Jack Root in a fight to the finish, to be held in Reno, Nevada on July 2 for a guaranteed purse of $5,000. Root had twice been knocked out by George Gardner, a man whom Johnson had defeated. However, Root had won a more recent 6-round decision over Gardner, had knocked out Billy Sift, held a 6-round decision victory over Hart, and had suffered only two defeats in his career, which included 46 victories. Plus, he

---

[585] *Police Gazette,* June 10, 1905.

was white, which meant that Hart would be willing to fight him. Eventually, the promoters paid Jeffries a hefty sum to convince him to referee the bout and name the winner the new champion.

Regardless of the color line, Jack Johnson wanted to fight the winner of Hart-Root. "Jack Johnson threatens to retire from the roped arena if he does not succeed in getting a match with the winner of the Jack Root and Marvin Hart battle."[586]

Obviously, Johnson was hurt and frustrated by the fact that he was not one of the combatants in the title bout. He felt that he had defeated Hart, who then drew the color line and would not rematch him. Johnson had sparred with Root, who refused to fight him. Root had been knocked out by Gardner, whom Johnson had handled easily. So Jack had to wait while others obtained an opportunity which he felt that he had earned, but for his race.

On June 7, 1905 in Detroit, in a middleweight bout, Tommy Burns fought Hugo Kelly to a 10-round draw.

Jack Munroe

Jack Johnson scheduled a late-June 6-round no-decision bout in Philadelphia against Jeffries' last opponent: Jack Munroe (sometimes called Monroe). Significant bouts in Munroe's career included: 1900 L20 Hank Griffin; 1902 EX4 James Jeffries; 1903 W4 Jack Sullivan, KO4 Peter Maher and KO4 Al Limerick; 1904 WND6 Tom Sharkey and LKOby2 James Jeffries; and 1905 D6 and KO6 James "Doc" Payne (Payne unconscious for several minutes afterwards), and KO5 Hank Pardello. Munroe was a muscular and thickly built fighter who weighed 210-220 pounds, though likely on the higher end for the Johnson fight. He stood 5'11 ½" and was 28 years old.

The *Philadelphia Public Ledger* said Hart and Johnson

[586] *Police Gazette*, July 1, 1905; *Philadelphia Record*, May 28, June 21, 1905.

were the only apparent candidates to the vacant crown. Hart was scheduled to fight Root, while Johnson could prove himself against Munroe.

> If Johnson wants to be considered as a worthy heavyweight, the public will expect him to make a good showing against Munroe and to beat the miner in a decisive fashion. Munroe is a big, strong young fellow and can punch hard at short range, as was shown in his bout with Sharkey before he met his fate with Jeffries.[587]

On Monday June 26, 1905, Jack Johnson fought Jack Munroe at Philadelphia's National Athletic Club, which was located at Eleventh and Catharine streets.

According to the *Philadelphia Record*, Johnson looked to be in good shape, though not trained very fine. Munroe's ponderous body and legs did not appear like those of a trained athlete. The *Philadelphia Public Ledger* said he appeared fat and out of shape. The *Philadelphia Press* said that when they removed their bathrobes, it could be seen that Munroe was the heavier man, though Johnson had height and reach advantages. Johnson looked to be trained to the hour, while Munroe appeared to be carrying considerable surplus flesh.

The men agreed to box until ordered to break by Referee McGuigan, and then to break clean.

1 - The *Record* said Johnson appeared confident, while Munroe seemed nervous. Johnson had an easy and graceful attitude, while Munroe covered up his jaw, fearful of a hard blow. Johnson stepped around to feel him out, leading lightly to the face with the left, stepping in and around. Johnson varied his work by sending the left to the face and right to the body. He was not too concerned by what the miner did. Munroe went for the body, and landed several punches there during the round.

However, Munroe's skills were criticized. His blows were not clean and half of them were hit with his arm only partly extended. Whenever he threw, he left himself open for a counter.

The *Public Ledger* said Munroe tried to rough it and work at close quarters, but Johnson jabbed him and sent the right across under the heart. The body blows made the miner wince.

The *Evening Bulletin* said Johnson's swings and jabs made life miserable for Munroe.

The *Press* said they exchanged back and forth, each landing some good blows to the body and head. "The men kept up their fast work, alternating in leading until just before the gong, when Johnson landed a left swing on Munroe's jaw. Johnson had a little the advantage of the round."

2 - Johnson's cleverness bewildered Munroe. Quite often, the miner walked right into a punch. Munroe realized that at long range, Johnson was his master, so he tried to mix it up in close. However, "This was his undoing, as

---

[587] *Philadelphia Public Ledger,* June 26, 1905.

the negro simply poised, waited for the rush and met him with a stinging blow before the miner could clinch." Munroe ducked under Johnson's vicious blows and hit the body.

Johnson became enraged at Munroe's presumption to force the contest. Therefore, he sailed in and dropped the miner to his knees with a right jolt to the chin. Most of the local sources noted this knockdown, though the *Press* did not.

Munroe quickly rose to his feet. He took generous punishment and was there for more. Johnson rushed and twice landed his right to the body, though Munroe landed his hard right to the eye in response.

Johnson rushed and landed another jolt on the jaw that made Munroe's knees kink. Had he not held onto Johnson he might have fallen to the floor again. He clinched and grabbed on to survive until the bell rang.

3 - The *Press* said Johnson came out of the corner with a lump under his left eye. He landed a right uppercut that drew blood from Munroe's mouth. He frequently missed swings for the face, though he landed several hard body blows.

The *Evening Bulletin* said Johnson owned the round and handed it to Monroe good and plenty, until the miner took the defensive to protect himself from the volley of wallops.

The *Public Ledger* said the bout became "tiresome." Johnson seemed able to hit Munroe when and where he pleased, but at times it was only too apparent to the critical observer that he was holding back.

Munroe realized that he was outclassed, so he endeavored to last the 6 rounds. "In this Johnson gave him all the assistance he could without making the bout look too queer." The *Ledger* believed that if Johnson had tried, the bout would not have lasted past this round. Munroe backed off, and therefore so too did Johnson, who only got fired up when Munroe pressed him or tried too hard.

4 - The *Press* said Johnson continued missing the head but landing to the body. The *Evening Bulletin* said Munroe did better and landed a couple of swings to the stomach, but Johnson did not notice the blows, and whipped his swings to the head with terrific force. He had the miner a trifle unsteady on his feet at the bell.

The *Public Ledger* said this was an especially tame round. The crowd began hissing its disapproval and yelled, "Take them off." Manager H. C. Crowhurst began to grow nervous, for he had deposited a $300 forfeit to insure the public that the bout would be "on the level." If the contest was stopped due to lack of genuine effort, the money would be forfeited and the spectators would have their gate fees returned.

5 - In the first part of the round, Johnson let out a link, showing a bit more effort. He swung his left into the stomach. The blow hurt and Johnson sailed in, trying for a knockout. He punched Munroe almost at will, alternating the blows for the body and face. Munroe took a hard lacing.

Twice Johnson staggered him with right hooks to the head. Munroe covered up well, bore in close and sent short punches to the stomach, but they lacked force.

Johnson slowed up a bit and lapsed into his posing style, waiting for a lead. However, Munroe was afraid to lead very often, concerned about Johnson's ability to counter attack. Hence, it was again dull. Johnson's punches had less steam than in the early rounds. Still, he opened a small cut over Munroe's left eye with a right uppercut, and the blood trickled down the miner's chest. By the end of the round, Munroe was tired.

The *Record* summarized that from the 3rd to 5th rounds, Johnson had battered Munroe around the ring as he pleased. Several times, Munroe was weak and held on so hard that the referee had difficulty breaking them apart. Johnson often backed off and boxed and fiddled around without hitting him, apparently not wanting to try to stop him. Johnson's tactics caused the impatient crowd to hoot after the bell ended the 5th round.

6 - Knowing that it was the last round, Munroe made a rally. However, for his impudence, Johnson landed left and right to the face, head, and body. Munroe tried to clinch as often as he could. However, a vicious right opened up an ugly gash on the miner's cheek-bone near the eye. Another blow further opened the small cut over his left eye, turning it into a large gash. The cuts bled freely and almost blinded him. Munroe fought back clumsily.

Johnson hammered away and rained in fierce blows. He had him wobbly, but none of the punches dropped Munroe, who at every opportunity got to close quarters, clinched and wrestled in order to survive and stay the limit. Munroe did his best to avoid the bombardment being dealt out. His legs were none too steady, and he was glad to hear the final bell.

Although Johnson failed to stop Munroe as Jeffries did, clearly he had dominated the bout. He dropped Munroe in the 2nd round, pummeled him at will throughout, cut up his face, and had him about ready to go out in the final round.

The *Philadelphia Record* said Johnson made a punching bag of Munroe for 6 rounds. Munroe dropped down once and almost went down on other occasions, but saved himself by clinching. Johnson appeared to be satisfied to outbox him rather than try to knock him out. For the last three rounds, Munroe was at Johnson's mercy. Some thought Johnson was under a pull, for he did not cut loose when several times it appeared that he had a chance to stop him.

The *Philadelphia Public Ledger* said Johnson lost yet another opportunity to make himself popular. Except for one minute of the 2nd round, he outclassed Munroe in every round. However, he did not put forth his best effort to stop Munroe, and the crowd knew it.

It appears that Johnson was the master of the silent agreement. If his opponent didn't try too hard, Jack was content to box cautiously to a decision, or no-decision victory in this case. If his foe forced him to open up, then Johnson would do so, and he would try to make him regret it. He would chill out his opponents, make them afraid to do much, and then he would back off. This line of thinking appears to have been in effect in several of Johnson's bouts.

The *Philadelphia Inquirer* said the fact that Munroe had once lasted 4 rounds with Jeffries and had outpointed Sharkey caused some to believe that he at least had a look-in with the world's best. However, the Johnson bout exploded that thinking. At no point in the 6 rounds did Munroe show anything to justify the belief that he was more than an ordinary husky fighter, endowed by nature with a large physique, but lacking the essentials which would make him even a second rater. Munroe was entirely too bulky, and his own feet were in his way.

Rather than laud Johnson's dominant performance, the press denigrated Munroe, and once again criticized Johnson as not being dominant enough, having failed to stop Munroe.

> Johnson himself did not by his performance demonstrate that he was the finished article that he has been cracked up to be. He won all the way to be sure, and at the finish had Munroe looking always for rest, but at that there were times when, had he been as good as his touters maintain, he would have saved a great deal of valuable time for those present. His punches lacked steam, although Munroe can bear cheerful evidence of the fact that they rarely lacked direction. In the fifth round Munroe's left lamp went out of commission, but outside of that there was nothing to suggest anything particularly sanguinary about the affair. It was Johnson first and Munroe nowhere.

The *Philadelphia Press* said the bout was a poor one, that Johnson was not able to land his boasted knockout blow, and his punches lacked power.

> Jack Johnson, who styles himself the heavy-weight colored champion, failed miserably last night to impress any one of his ability to ever get the title now held by Jim Jeffries. ... Johnson won the bout without much trouble but in the points which make a champion he proved to be lacking. This was especially so with the ability to deliver punishment.

> Not once did he succeed in sending Munroe to the floor, although he several times landed his famous solar plexus punch with all his power against the white man's stomach. Then, too, he managed to reach Munroe's jaw with swings in every round and yet he could not take the miner off his feet. Johnson, although clever, was not ring general enough to keep Munroe off.

> The miner evidently figured that the point of safety for him was at very close quarters and he got inside Johnson's guard as much as possible, occasionally taking advantage of the opportunity to work short arm punches against the colored man's ribs.

Johnson did his best work in the last minute of the 5th round and in the first two minutes of the 6th round. At those points, he cut loose, working at top speed, landing viciously on the body and face. One of his swings cut a gash over Munroe's eye, from which the blood flowed freely. Then Johnson appeared to tire and Munroe rushed to close quarters and clinched to survive.

The *Press* said Johnson had failed to meet expectations before one of the biggest crowds of the year. It did not think him likely to succeed Jeffries as champion. "If there is any championship material in Johnson, however, white heavy-weights must be of a poor quality if he succeeds in getting it."

The *Philadelphia Evening Bulletin* said Johnson outpointed and outfought Munroe "in a manner that will give several actorically inclined pugilists something to dream about of nights." The Butte miner was never dangerous. Johnson easily defeated Munroe and nearly ended him in the 2nd round.[588]

According to the *Police Gazette*, "Munroe lasted the 6 rounds, but for the last three he was at Johnson's mercy, and it seemed at times that the big black was under a pull, for he did not cut loose several times when he had splendid chances to stop his opponent."

Another *Police Gazette* writer said that although Johnson failed to stop Munroe, he licked him without much effort, and the miner was left "in such a disreputable battered up condition as to be almost unrecognizable by his friends."

Still, Johnson was criticized for failing to stop a man who was as "agile as an ice wagon." Jeffries had so easily blown through Munroe that it was like taking candy from a baby. This writer argued that by comparison, Johnson's performance did not add to his reputation.

The white press never seemed to overlook an opportunity to criticize the black Johnson's dominant performances as not being dominant enough.

> [T]he "Coon" must have left his alleged knowledge of the scientific art of scrapping in his dressing room. It was a roughhouse battle, devoid of science on one side and almost everything else on the other. Jeff need not have drawn the color line, for he could have met both of these men in the same ring simultaneously, so far as their ability to do him is concerned.[589]

One week later, on July 3, 1905 under the hot, over 100-degree Reno, Nevada sun, in a fight to the finish refereed by retired champion Jim Jeffries, 28-year-old 195-pound Marvin Hart knocked out 29-year-old 170-pound Jack Root in the 12th round to win the vacant world's heavyweight championship. Root outboxed Hart early, and even dropped him with a right at the end of the 7th round. However, Hart showed his usual ability to

---

[588] *Philadelphia Record, Philadelphia Public Ledger, Philadelphia Inquirer, Philadelphia Press, Philadelphia Evening Bulletin,* June 27, 1905.
[589] *Police Gazette,* July 15, 1905.

absorb punishment, his indomitable will, condition, and power, and eventually stopped Root with a single right to the body.

Referee James Jeffries, Marvin Hart, Jack Root

The *San Francisco Bulletin* said Hart "fought better than he did when he met Jack Johnson. He was less slovenly, less awkward, and used fewer wild swings. His style of fighting was the same. He relied on his strength and ability to absorb punishment to carry the day, and he carried the fighting to Root right from the start." The *Chronicle* said Hart showed better judgment of distance than when he fought Johnson. Many others said he had improved wonderfully since the Johnson fight, and showed science as well as toughness and strength. Perhaps the different opponent had something to do with it.[590]

There was some debate about whether Hart should be recognized as champion. Some thought that Hart was indeed the new champion; some considered him to be the tentative champion until Jeffries came out of retirement; others thought he needed to defeat more contenders to prove his right to the championship; and yet others thought that Jeffries was champion for as long as he was alive.

---

[590] *San Francisco Call, Examiner, Evening Post, Bulletin, Chronicle,* July 4-5, 1905.

Jeffries had been paid to announce that the winner of Hart-Root would be the new champion. However, afterwards, he said that only the press and the public could confer the title. "I hope the victor will fight his way to that point where no one can dispute his title." Jeff said Hart was champion "pro tem," and that a number of battles would establish his right to championship honors beyond a doubt.

W. W. Naughton noted that Hart had dubbed himself the champion, "and the conditions are such that he is perfectly justified in doing so." However, he also said that Hart was on probation as a result of the fact that he had not licked the linear champion. Therefore, it potentially would require some "sifting and shifting before a heavyweight looms up who will command the respect that a world's championship should command." Even if Hart came to be hailed as champion or someone was to defeat him and establish a better right to the distinction, "what will it all amount to anyhow, as long as Jeff is alive and enjoys good health?" Essentially, no one would be accorded the type of respect that Jeffries had earned, unless and until they defeated Jeffries.[591]

The *Los Angeles Herald* said,

> Hart will probably become the acknowledged champion despite his numerous shortcomings. Tom Sharkey is out of it. Jack Monroe was never in it. Jack Johnson has demonstrated that he won't do and Bob Fitzsimmons has about passed the century mark. Not for many years has there been such a dearth of heavyweight material in the prize ring.[592]

Jack Johnson and George Gardiner both challenged Hart. However, Hart openly drew the color line as champion. Hart was quoted as saying, "I will fight any heavy-weight in the world except niggers."[593] He also said,

> I am now ready to meet anybody in the world, except a negro. I fought Johnson because he was said to be the next best man to Jeffries. I will not fight another negro. When I fought Johnson it was very much against my will, but as I had defeated all the big ones outside of Jeffries I was obliged to take on Johnson.

The *San Francisco Evening Post* criticized Hart for drawing the color line, especially given that he had obtained a questionable decision over Johnson.

> At the end of the twenty rounds, with rings boxed all around him, the referee practically made him a present of the contest. A draw would not have been giving Johnson the best of it.

> With Root's scalp hanging to his belt the first statement uttered by Hart was to the effect that he was ready to fight any man in the

[591] *Los Angeles Examiner,* July 16, 1905.
[592] *Los Angeles Herald,* July 19, 1905.
[593] *Reno Evening Gazette,* July 3, 1905; *San Francisco Chronicle,* July 4, 5, 1905.

world, barring a colored man (meaning, of course, Johnson). In other words, Hart is not particularly anxious for Arthur's game, and the only way to side step is to draw the color line.[594]

Bat Masterson felt that most heavyweights were afraid of Hart, with the exception of Johnson. However, he thought that Hart would defeat Johnson in a fight to the finish.

There is no other heavyweight in sight willing to try conclusions with the recently made champion, with the possible exception of the negro, Johnson…[who] would not be likely to score a victory in a battle scheduled to go to a finish.[595]

Famed referee George Siler saw things differently. Although he recognized Hart as the new champion, he said,

Undoubtedly the best big man in the business at present is Jack Johnson, the colored heavyweight champion, and Hart shows excellent judgment in drawing the color line.

It is the opinion of all fair-minded witnesses that Johnson beat Hart in their recent fight at San Francisco, and undoubtedly can repeat the trick, so it probably is better for the game that Hart drew the color line. We have never had a colored heavyweight champion and it is too late to change the order of things.[596]

Some were even speculating that Jack Johnson gave Hart their fight.

Although the fighting critics throughout the country are inclined to believe that Johnson considerably helped to string his own scalp on the Louisvillian's girdle by laying down, Johnson so easily and neatly trimmed Jack Munroe in the recent meeting, that he must be reckoned with as a decided factor.[597]

The *Police Gazette* again said that Hart's fight with Johnson was an "alleged fake fight," that Hart could not lick Johnson "on the level," and that is why he drew the color line; to avoid another meeting. Perhaps it meant that it was the decision that was not on the level.[598]

The *San Francisco Evening Post* said the title would be clearer if Hart could knock out Johnson.

The memory of the recent Hart-Johnson fight, when nearly every report was that Hart was rushing and was being cut to pieces with jabs and hooks…does not linger pleasantly. … Nobody is especially anxious to see Johnson beat Hart. At the same time, the fact that

---

[594] *San Francisco Evening Post,* July 5, 1905.
[595] *Louisville Courier-Journal,* July 9, 1905; *Reno Evening Gazette,* July 13, 1905.
[596] *Philadelphia Inquirer,* July 9, 1905; *Police Gazette,* July 29, 1905.
[597] *Police Gazette,* July 22, 1905.
[598] *Police Gazette,* July 29, 1905.

Hart has drawn the color line will certainly not boost him. Johnson is one of the cleverest big men that ever stepped into a ring. Jeffries would probably beat him, as the big fellow apparently has most of his opponents bluffed so badly they are beaten before they enter the ring.

For the others, however, the chances are that Johnson will be the 'yellow peril' to be avoided for a long time. He showed this by the way he pranced around 'Miner' Jack Munroe, outclassing him and punching him at will.

Hart is the heavyweight champion as long as Jeffries is out of the ring. ... The best way for Hart to try to earn Jeffries' crown is to wipe out the smudge left on his record by Jack Johnson, for, though Hart did receive the decision it was anything but a clean one.[599]

Gus Ruhlin also wanted to fight Hart. He admitted that Hart beat him in their first bout, but claimed to have defeated Hart easily in their rematch, which was called a draw.

Ruhlin said Hart should fight himself or Jack Johnson. Gus had never fought a colored man, and did not intend to start now (though he didn't mind using blacks as sparring partners). However, he admired Johnson.

Don't think that I'm underrating this man Johnson. Outside of Jeffries, I think that this fellow Johnson can trim the world. Yes, Fitzsimmons and the whole bunch of them. I only saw him in one fight, but he's a marvel. He's a black McCoy, but I think he's even better than the Kid. The way he handles himself is great, surely. Why, he has a chance even with Jeff, in my mind. Jeff was a bit leary of him, too. I'm not saying that Jim was afraid of him, you know, but he didn't want any of it if he could get out of it. You know he drew the color line on Johnson, and he had met four coons before that time. I guess he knew a little about Johnson.

Gus thought Jeffries might come back eventually, but would suffer from a long layoff. "Oh, Jeff will get his, you know." Ruhlin said inactivity hurt any fighter. "If you stop awhile you lose your knack. ... When a fellow fights every month or so he's right in and fights his best, but a fight every six months or so is bad. ... A man can't be good forever and ever. He must fall some day."[600]

On Thursday July 13, 1905 in Philadelphia, at the Broadway Athletic Club, just seventeen days after the Munroe bout, Jack Johnson again took on two black men in one night in separate scheduled 3-round bouts. His opponents were Morris Harris and Black Bill.

---

[599] *San Francisco Evening Post*, July 13, 1905.
[600] *Philadelphia Inquirer*, July 5, 1905; *Louisville Courier-Journal*, July 11, 1905; *San Francisco Evening Post*, July 17, 1905.

Morris Harris' record contained at least 19 known bouts that dated back to 1903. His significant results included: 1904 LND6 Charley Stevenson, WND6 Joe Jeannette, KO5 Black Bill, and LND6 Jack O'Brien; and 1905 LND6 Black Bill, WND6 Joe Jeannette, LND6 Jim Jeffords, and LND6 Black Bill.

Morris Harris

Johnson entered the ring first. Black Bill and Morris Harris followed. They tossed a coin for choice of who would box Johnson first. Bill won the toss and said to Morris, "After you, Gaston."

The hand-shaking was not very cordial, for Harris barely extended the end of his glove to shake. Jack went at the local man like a whirlwind, slamming him hard. He punched him with both hands and soon had Harris sprawling on the floor.

As soon as Harris would rise, Johnson would knock him down again. Morris was quickly and immediately finding "a soft spot to escape the bombardment."

When Harris went down for the fourth time from a right to the jaw, Referee Baily stopped the bout. One reporter said Harris could not have risen within the required ten seconds, while another said the referee stopped it because Harris wanted none of it.

Despite Harris' having shown durability against fighters like Jeannette, O'Brien, Jeffords, and Black Bill, Jack Johnson stopped Morris Harris in the 1st round. It was Harris' first knockout loss.

The *Record* was impressed. "In his bout with Harris, Johnson gave the best exhibition of his skill as a boxer which he has shown since he came to this city. Harris was a mere plaything in his hands and it showed clearly that there was something wrong with the victory of Marvin Hart over Johnson in California."

Next up for Johnson that evening was Black Bill, who had boxed Johnson twice before, in a 1904 6-round no-decision, and a May 1905 bout in which Johnson stopped Bill in the 4th round. Since then, Bill had boxed Joe Jeannette to a 6-round no-decision loss.

The *Philadelphia Press* said Black Bill was a tougher proposition and stayed the 3 rounds, although he was beaten badly. During the 1st round, Johnson landed freely, but his blows seemed to lack steam. Bill did very little fighting in the 2nd and 3rd rounds, hanging on to save himself from being put to sleep. He was very tired at the end.

According to the *Philadelphia Record*, it appeared that Johnson could have stopped Black Bill just as quickly as Morris Harris if he had desired or tried, but he allowed the Merchantville boxer to last. Johnson obviously was holding back. Plus, Bill also survived the 3 rounds by clinching and holding.

Johnson "faked" all through the 3 rounds, laughing at Bill's clumsy efforts to hit him. Jack feinted a lot, never intended to land the blows that he did throw, nor did he land on a vital spot.

The *Philadelphia Evening Bulletin* agreed with the *Record*, saying that Black Bill was Johnson's "old friend," so he "just missed him" for old times' sake. After one round, it was obvious that it would not be a fight. Bill was there only to stay, and he accomplished it in part thanks to Johnson's generosity, for Jack suddenly became kind-hearted, or as this reporter called him, "chicken," at the sight of his old friend and second.

Afterwards, Johnson said the reason he did not stop Bill was because he had a sore hand.[601]

Johnson would fight again a mere five days later. He traveled to Chelsea, Massachusetts, just four miles from Boston, for yet another bout with Sandy Ferguson. Ferguson resided in Chelsea, so it was anticipated that the bout would be marketable to his hometown fans. In fact, the fight was so attractive and Ferguson such a fan favorite that he was actually the betting favorite.

This would be their fifth meeting. Since their last bout in February 1904 (an impromptu NC5), Ferguson's results included: 1904 L20 Marvin Hart (many thought Ferguson won or at least earned a draw), D10 Joe Walcott (draw pursuant to agreement if neither knocked out, though referee said he would have awarded decision to Walcott if authorized), and KO1 Charlie Haghey; and 1905 WDQ5 Jack McCormick. Sandy had nearly 50 fights of experience to that point.

Ferguson had trained for the bout "as he never did before." The *Boston Post* lamented that if only he had been possessed of common sense in the past, Sandy would be worth a lot more money. Instead, he was a "stubborn child" who refused to train properly, and was constantly getting into street brawls.

Sandy never felt so confident in his life. He would use a new line of both defense and attack against Johnson. Instead of holding back and driving in

SANDY FERGUSON.   JACK JOHNSON.

---

[601] *Philadelphia Press, Philadelphia Record, Philadelphia Evening Bulletin*, July 14, 1905.

counters, Ferguson planned to attack and score a knockout within the scheduled 15 rounds. Sandy said of Johnson, who thought he was good enough for Jeffries, "If he's good enough for Jeffries, he's good enough for me."

Johnson was a "wise baby," having trained hard, as usual, and was in his typically good condition. From experience, he knew that Ferguson was no slouch, and was "robbed" of the decision against Hart. Still, Johnson was confident and cheerful as always.

Ferguson wanted to force Hart into another match, and defeating Johnson would make that possible. The *Boston Globe* said if Ferguson beat Johnson, he would be first in line to fight Hart for the title. Hence, he was highly motivated.

Hart had questionable victories over both men. The majority of spectators maintained that Sandy was cheated out of the decision against Marvin. Like Ferguson, Johnson also felt that he was robbed against Hart. "Hart won the decision. Some say he deserved it; others say that Johnson beat the white man. But whatever the result and whatever the merits of the award, Hart again fortified himself by drawing the color line."

Ferguson's admirers claimed that Sandy would make Jack appear slow. However, "Joe Walcott says Johnson is the fastest big man in the ring today." Hence, it was a good matchup.[602]

Photo by Chickering.)
SANDY FERGUSON,
The Chelsea heavyweight, who will battle with Jack Johnson at the Douglas Club tonight.

The *Boston Post* said Ferguson would weigh 210 pounds, while Johnson would weigh 190 pounds. Sandy was 25 years old, one week shy of his 26th birthday. Johnson was 27. Ferguson's manager was Alec McLean. Bill Crowley of Hartford would referee.

Johnson would have Joe Walcott behind him. Walcott believed that Johnson would win handily. However, the local sports were inclined to think that Ferguson would win. On the coast, where Johnson became famous, "they say that Johnson is the most scientific big man the ring has ever known." Both men were fast and clever, had years of ring experience, and

---

[602] *Boston Post,* July 17, 1905.; *Boston Globe,* July 18, 1905.

could punch hard with both hands.

The day of the fight, both fighters remained confident. Johnson said,

> Ferguson, they tell me, is in grand condition. So am I. I know Ferguson is a hard man to beat and I know that he can hit a hard blow. At the same time I have no fear of the outcome. I feel that I was robbed of the decision in my recent fight with Marvin Hart.
>
> By winning tonight in quick time, I think my claim for another fight with Hart will be just. I am not afraid of any of them.
>
> I am willing even to fight Jeffries, and feel that I would stand a fair chance of beating Jeffries. When I enter the ring tonight I will be at my best.
>
> If I win I will be happy. If I lose I will bow to the winner and will have no excuses to make as to being out of condition.
>
> Ferguson will have something on me as to weight, but I am faster than he is, and speed will count.

Ferguson said,

> I am ready for Johnson. I feel great. I realize what a victory means for me, and I was never so confident before, and I will fight harder tonight than at any time during my career.
>
> I was robbed of the decision when I met Marvin Hart. He has an awful nerve to claim the heavyweight championship after the beating I gave him in Hot Springs a year ago.
>
> I will go after Johnson from the start. He is a dangerous man and I respect his ability. At the same time, when the decision is made it will go to me.
>
> By winning tonight I will be in line for the top of the class, and I will make Hart fight me whether he wants to or not.[603]

On Tuesday July 18, 1905 in Chelsea, Massachusetts, fighting before the Douglas Athletic Club inside the Pythian rink, in a scheduled 15-round bout, Jack Johnson took on Sandy Ferguson.

A corps of police officers struggled to keep the crowd outside in check. A huge crowd stormed through the entrance at 7 p.m. There was great demand to see the fight, but insufficient space inside the venue to accommodate the demand, so most attempts to enter after that first wave were futile. Thousands vainly attempted to enter. Holders of reserved seats who came late went home disgusted, because much to their chagrin, their seats were gone. As high as $10 was offered for admission tickets.

The *Boston Globe* said the rink was packed with a big crowd of between 2,500 and 3,000 people. The *Boston Post* said 4,000 people tried to crowd

---

[603] *Boston Post,* July 18, 1905.

into a place where 2,000 could not have been comfortably accommodated. It was the largest gathering that ever attended a boxing match in Chelsea.

Ventilation inside the rink was poor, which made the environment even hotter on this already hot summer day. The closely-wedged-together mob sweltered and perspired freely, the beads of sweat rolling off in large drops to the floor. It was the heat of the weather combined with the heat of the humanity crammed inside the poorly ventilated building which made the environment so oppressive. Hundreds smoked cigars, adding to the heat. Desperate to get a better view, crowds in the back surged forward. Chairs were broken. It was so hot that hundreds left before the main event started, unable to stand the intense heat. No one got their money returned.

In the boxers' corners, handkerchiefs were soaked in pails of water, and fans were used to cool the fighters.

Ferguson had to fight his way through the crowd just to get to the ring. He smashed right and left at men who blocked his way, for no one wanted to give ground for fear that he would lose his position. Johnson soon followed.

Earlier in the evening, Sandy had demanded a $100 advance so he could bet it on himself. As he sat in his corner, awaiting the start of the bout, he expressed the utmost confidence. Because he was the local man from Chelsea, naturally Sandy was the crowd favorite.

Ferguson looked good, but Johnson looked better. However, Sandy had the weight advantage. Referee Bill Crowley called them to the ring center, and after a few minutes of discussion, the boxers took their corners.

Behind Johnson were Billy Pierce, Joe Walcott, and Ed Keevin. Ferguson had manager Alec McLean and Bob Armstrong. At 9:30 p.m., the fight was on.

1 - All through the round, Ferguson used his left jab to the face beautifully. He also hit the body. Sandy landed his left to the mouth followed by a right to the side of the head. He also drove his right to the body. Sandy threw many jabs and rights to the body and was fighting furiously. Johnson did some hugging and bore into clinches. Jack mostly jabbed, but landed a hard left swing to the body as well as a fine right smash into the body.

Ferguson landed a couple of rights to the jaw and they clinched. Ferguson landed a savage left to the body and they clinched. Ferguson ducked a wicked left. A savage exchange of blows resulted in a clinch. Both men landed rights and lefts. Johnson landed a left to the jaw.

The *Boston Globe*, *Herald*, and *Post* all said it was Ferguson's round.

2 - Again Ferguson was the aggressor. They were about even in a fast mixup. Sandy drove his right to the ear and followed up with body blows. Johnson missed a bit but landed his jab to the mouth. He feinted prettily, but Ferguson blocked his punches. Johnson rushed him to the ropes and crossed left and right to the head and body. Sandy drove his right to the heart and snapped a left to the mouth. Jack missed a right counter. Sandy landed to the jaw and Johnson half-tripped back against the ropes. Jack

struck a hard left to the jaw. Sandy jabbed his left to the face three times. Johnson replied with a hard left jab to the nose that drew blood. Sandy went away laughing. It had been a very fast round.

The local reports agreed that Ferguson had a little the best of it.

3 - This round was fast. Johnson began cutting loose. Ferguson started showing the effects of the heat and pace that he had set. During a clinch, when Johnson banged him in the stomach, Sandy appealed to the referee. When Johnson drove him back with a left jab to the mouth, Ferguson longingly looked toward his seconds. Sandy fought back madly, but missed.

In an exchange, Johnson landed a hard right on the ear, but when he tried it again, Sandy landed a right and followed with jabs to the nose. Jack came back with a couple rights to the ribs and hooked his left to the stomach. He followed with both hands on the stomach in combination. Ducking Sandy's jab, Jack again hit the body. Ferguson landed a right on the jaw, but missed another, then ducked awkwardly away, with Johnson in pursuit. Sandy slipped and fell through the ropes to the mat, helped by Johnson's push. Jack helped him back to his feet and the crowd cheered.

Johnson led with his blows, but Ferguson was smiling. Sandy's corner shouted off more advice than ten men could hear.

The *Herald* said it had been an even round, with the two exchanging blows to the body and head. The *Post* said Ferguson again had a little the best of it, though Johnson was beginning to look good.

4 - They again mixed it up, firing blows to the body and head. Ferguson jabbed, and Johnson landed his left to the stomach. After Sandy blocked a left for the body, Jack followed with a right to the neck. Sandy tried a right to the body and was repaid with a left to the body. Ferguson blocked some lefts for the body but Johnson whipped in two lefts and a right. Jack landed a left wallop in the stomach. Sandy partially blocked a left hook to the ear but Johnson followed with a left hook to the kidneys. They exchanged several hard blows to the body.

Ferguson feinted his left. Johnson swung a right to the body and Sandy chased him around the ring. Jack landed a hard left to the body. They clinched savagely, then sparred for openings. Johnson blocked a right and landed a left to the jaw. At the bell, Sandy landed a hard punch to the stomach.

The *Herald* said the round was slightly Johnson's.

5 - This was a rapid round, with both mixing freely. Ferguson went through the ropes again, falling among the spectators. Each local source had its version of how it happened. The *Globe* said Ferguson missed a right and tumbled through the ropes. The *Herald* said Sandy jabbed and landed a right to the side of the head. As he went away Johnson swung at him and Sandy slipped and rolled out of the ring. The *Post* said Johnson jumped at Ferguson and again Sandy got his legs mixed up and he fell through the ropes.

After Ferguson got back into the ring, Johnson forced the action. Sandy jabbed and blocked. Johnson rushed him to a neutral corner and hooked a hard left to the body. Johnson smashed left and right to the body.

When Sandy again lost his balance, Johnson forced Ferguson to the opposite side of the ring onto the ropes, hooking left and right to the jaw while he was there. Sandy became more careful and jabbed lightly. Johnson went after him and planted three hard left hooks to the body. He was picking off Sandy's jabs.

Johnson chopped Ferguson with rights and lefts and Sandy clinched. In the clinches, Johnson had it all his own way, and Ferguson appeared bewildered. Johnson was looking better. His second yelled, "Go after him," and Jack obeyed. Sandy broke ground. At the bell, Jack was still chasing Sandy.

All of the local papers agreed that it was Johnson's round. Both seemed a bit tired, but Ferguson appeared even more fatigued. Overall, they were standing the pace fairly well and did not seem to mind the heat.

6 - There was a diversity of opinion regarding this round. One had it for Ferguson, one for Johnson, while a third said it was even.

The *Globe* said Ferguson was eager, but Johnson was cool. Sandy blocked a number of body blows and landed his own right to the ribs. He worked hard. They exchanged several blows, but Ferguson landed more often than did Johnson, particularly to the body. It was Sandy's round.

The *Herald* said Johnson continued forcing matters, landing stiff body punches. Ferguson jabbed and fired his right to the body. Sandy landed some good shots, but Johnson forced Sandy to the ropes with left and right to the body. Johnson's round.

The *Post* said Ferguson looked refreshed and got his bearings again. Johnson was fighting very cautiously. His judgment of distance was better than Ferguson's. He landed several lefts and rights, but they were weak, and Sandy did not seem to mind the punches. Sandy landed a good left to the jaw.

Johnson again cut loose and chased Sandy around the ring. Ferguson began clinching and holding on to Johnson, and every time that he did, Jack shot in wicked lefts and rights. Sandy was beginning to look quite tired. The round ended with honors about even.

7 - Sandy jabbed his left and landed a right on the ear. Johnson was cool and stepped out of danger. Sandy rushed fiercely. Jack jumped in with a right to the stomach.

They clinched savagely and started roughing it. The crowd began to hoot. After breaking, Ferguson landed some stinging left jabs. Johnson closed in and smashed both hands to the body.

Johnson landed hard lefts and rights. Ferguson seemed amazed, as well as tired out. Johnson realized that Sandy was tired, so he kept after him. "Go and get him," yelled Joe Walcott. Johnson kept attacking, while Ferguson broke ground. After another savage clinch, Referee Crowley tore them apart. Again they clinched. Johnson punched Ferguson in the stomach.

While clinched, Ferguson disabled Johnson by crashing both his knees into the lower stomach and groin area, one at a time, left, then right, then left again. Johnson fell back to the ground. Scores of spectators witnessed the breach of the rules. The fight was over. Ultimately, Ferguson was disqualified, but there was some initial confusion regarding the decision.

The *Boston Herald* said the pair had fought a rattling contest full of action, but Ferguson spoiled it with a deliberate foul. When Jack went down, a groan from the crowd could be heard, and many hissed Ferguson's action. Many fair-minded men jumped upon their seats, expressing their disgust. Referee Crowley tried to quiet the yelling thousands. While Johnson was suffering on the floor, Sandy walked up close to the referee. It appeared that Sandy tried to intimidate Referee Crowley.

The *Herald* said Crowley originally hesitated for a while before making any announcement, and when he finally pointed toward Ferguson's corner the crowd began condemning him in harsh terms. They incorrectly thought he had awarded Ferguson the decision. Others thought the referee was telling Ferguson to return to his corner, to get away from him.

Some in the crowd believed Ferguson had won, and they yelled "fake," "robbery," and the like.

The *Boston Post* said that in the 7th round, frenzied by the punches that Johnson sent in while clinched, Ferguson lost his head completely and in the "rawest manner ever seen in New England," three times struck his knee into Johnson's groin with great force. Johnson went to the floor in Ferguson's corner, writhing in pain, amid the howls and shouts of the immense gathering. "Referee Bill Crowley of Hartford did the only thing he could do – gave the decision to Johnson."

Ferguson rushed at Crowley, who then "waved toward Ferguson's corner, denoting that Johnson won, but in his jubilation over what he thought was a knockout, Ferguson took Crowleys' wave of his hand as meaning that he, Ferguson, had won, and with a wild whoop Ferguson jumped over the ropes." Ferguson's admirers seized him, and the building rang with cheers for Sandy. However, really, Crowley was ordering Ferguson back to his own corner.

The *Globe's* perspective was that Ferguson stood over Johnson, gloating over what he thought was victory. When referee Bill Crowley waived him to his corner, where Johnson was lying, many in the crowd broke out into cheers for Ferguson. However, he was pointing towards Johnson as the winner. Jack happened to by lying in Ferguson's corner, so it caused some confusion.

Several minutes later, Ferguson realized something was wrong. What the referee told him could not be heard, but Sandy threw his hands up high above his head and with a yell made a dash for his corner and vaulted over the ropes, landing among the spectators. Then he rushed out of the building.

The *Post* version was that Referee Crowley looked dazed amidst the extreme noise that the crowd made. He just stood there. "What's your decision?" yelled the crowd. He waved towards Ferguson's corner, but lying on the canvas floor in that corner was Johnson, so it was confusing regarding what he meant, whether he was pointing at Ferguson or Johnson as the winner. Ferguson rushed at Crowley. Again the referee seemed to wave towards Ferguson's corner. It was not clear whether he meant Ferguson or Johnson was the winner, or if he was telling Ferguson to go to his corner. Ferguson flew out of the ring, in either joy or disgust. No one was sure. Apparently, all the time Crowley meant that Johnson had won. The *Post* writer jumped into the ring and asked the referee, "What's your decision?" Crowley responded, "Why, there's nothing to it. Ferguson lost on a foul."

After many had left the building, the uproar subsided and order was restored. Referee Crowley once more made it known that Johnson had won on a foul. Initially, he had pointed toward Ferguson's corner, feeling that Sandy would have struck him had he known his real decision. He also said that he told Johnson's seconds that their man was the one who really had won. Few of the 3,000 in attendance nor hundreds more in the street realized it until later that night.

Johnson's seconds finally carried him to his corner. It took 15 minutes for Jack to be ready to leave the ring. His seconds helped him to the dressing room.

A club doctor examined Johnson and verified the foul, saying he had been struck hard and injured in the left groin. He was in pain for nearly an hour afterward.

Johnson said, "You can say for me that I will fight Ferguson at any time or place he may want to meet me. I was hit low and put out of the game, but I am confident that I can whip him."

The *Herald* said that up until the unsatisfactory ending, it had been a good contest, all that anyone had hoped for. From the outset, Sandy had forced the battle, smashing in stiff left jabs and crossing rights whenever the opportunity offered, to both the head and body. Johnson started off by blocking as well as he could and smashing the body in the clinches. They displayed wonderful skill and the speed of lightweights. Sandy did the forcing, while Johnson was somewhat the cleverer man.

Ferguson opened up a lead in the first two rounds, but in the 3rd round, Johnson got an even break. In the 4th, Johnson had a slight lead, but then he increased his lead as the rounds progressed.

Johnson was wearing Ferguson down in the 6th round with terrific body punches. All the while, though, Sandy fought gamely and wonderfully fast. Johnson's lead was increasing, though he was not hitting as hard as the

Chelsea man. Still, he was blocking many of Sandy's leads and outpointing the local man in fine style.

In the 7th round, Sandy rushed at Johnson, and for a while they went at it. Finally Johnson closed in on him in Ferguson's corner, and Ferguson deliberately brought up both knees, first left, then right, and Johnson went to the mat.

The *Herald* said Ferguson lost many friends and probably all prospects of ever fighting there again, or of getting his desired match with Hart. It said that up until a late hour, Sandy had not been made aware of the real facts of the case; meaning that he had lost.

According to the *Boston Globe*, the first couple of rounds were easily in Ferguson's favor. Sandy began the battle like a champion, going after Johnson. He fired lefts and rights, sometimes landing, though Johnson was never phased and grinned confidently, carefully pacing himself and allowing Sandy to work. In the 3rd round, Johnson began showing his form, and he held off his man. He did the same in the 4th round. In the 5th round, Johnson easily outpointed Ferguson, who was beginning to tire. In the 6th round, Sandy sailed in, and it was obvious that he wanted the battle to end quickly, but Johnson cleverly evaded his smashes.

The *Globe* said Johnson was fresh when the gong sounded to start the 7th round. Ferguson was still intent on making the fight a brief one if possible, but despite his aggression, he was wild and outgeneraled. After about a minute, Jack went into a clinch, driving his hard right to the stomach as he did so.

The red-headed Ferguson then decided to rough matters. He forced Johnson back by sheer strength, and while still entangled in each other's grasp, Sandy lifted his left knee and struck Johnson with it inches below the belt. His right knee followed rapidly, striking Jack in the left groin. Down he went in a heap, writhing in pain, unable to rise.

Up to the end, the fighting had been about evenly divided, with Ferguson doing most of the showy work, while Johnson was cool and collected at all times. He waited for Sandy to tire from his own efforts and the excessive heat.

It called the bout a mediocre exhibition. The crowd was disappointed by their performance, having hoped for a better contest.

The *Globe* said Ferguson's championship aspirations had been exploded by his deliberate and wicked foul tactics.

The *Boston Post* said 4,000 excited spectators saw a fierce contest. It speculated that Ferguson possibly wanted to lose on a foul, because he made his foul evident to all. "Never in the history of local fighting has such a deliberate foul been committed." Either Johnson was hurt badly or he was an exceptionally clever actor. He hardly was able to speak, and groaned aloud. Ferguson celebrated, thinking he had won.

When later in the evening Ferguson was told of the official decision, he raved and stormed about. "He claimed that he had been robbed, but not one man in 20 who was within sight of the ring had any doubt but that Ferguson fouled Johnson and fouled him raw."

Up to the end, the men fought in sizzling heat "with a determination that cannot be described." When the bout began, the crowd was silent and leaning forward in anticipation. They weren't disappointed. There was action in every round, with hard blows and clever footwork and even better head work. "They saw Johnson elude the bull-like rushes of Ferguson, and they saw Ferguson duck as Johnson would chop over his right and then his left."

During the fight, Bob Armstrong could not get near Ferguson to give advice, but instead his other seconds kept telling Sandy how good he was.

Twice in the earlier rounds, Ferguson crashed through the ropes, not from blows, but because in the clinches he tripped and went back through the ropes. As the bout progressed, Ferguson threw some really terrific swings that would have sent Johnson to the floor had they landed.

> Fighting at times as fast as lightweights, the men rushed back and forth, first one leading and then the other. For four rounds it was all Ferguson. He hit the colored man at will. Johnson stalled and did his best work in the clinches.
>
> Johnson began to come in the fifth. He chased Ferguson around the ring; he sent in rights and lefts. Chelsea's big man winced with pain, but he came back. Johnson had all the best of the fifth round. Both men were getting tired. The pace was beginning to tell.
>
> Ferguson carried 25 pounds more than Johnson, and had done the most leading. As the men squared off for the sixth round it was seen that Johnson was in a little better shape. He was cool as an ice box. The sweat rolled down his face in streams. Off Ferguson the sweat rolled down in torrents.
>
> It was a Ferguson crowd. "Get him, Sandy," yelled the mob in the sixth, and Sandy again began to force the fighting.
>
> Exchange followed exchange. Johnson was sending in wicked, cutting blows with both hands, while Ferguson was swinging wildly with both hands.
>
> As the sixth round drew to a close Ferguson was beginning to clinch and wrestle, although as the bell sounded the round was about even. Four of the rounds had been all Ferguson. The fifth belonged to Johnson and the sixth was about an even break.

In the 7th round, the men clinched savagely. Johnson, being a master at infighting, smashed blow after blow on Ferguson's chest and kidneys. Ferguson called to the referee, "Make him stop." The *Post* asked, "Was Sandy beginning to quit? He was yelling for no good reason." After they broke, Johnson followed Ferguson around the ring, stalking him. They again clinched. Ferguson had both of his hands around Johnson, who had one hand free and was using it to keep hammering away at Ferguson. The referee said, "Break away."

Then came the end. Ferguson's left knee went up into Johnson's stomach. Jack went back, but Sandy was still holding onto him. Ferguson's right knee then came up and Jack went back again, in a maddened state. Ferguson still held him, and once more his left knee was buried into Johnson's stomach, and Jack reeled to the floor.

The *Post* writer agreed with the decision. "Crowley was right. There was nothing to it. The writer saw the foul, or better, he saw three fouls. He was within two feet of the ring in the very front row. Johnson had been fouled and fouled in a most vicious manner." The writer had seen Ferguson's face turn purple with rage from the last punch that Johnson struck him. Then his knees went up. He had lost his head "as no heavyweight fighter ever did before." Of course, both before and since then, we have seen plenty of fighters lose their cool and foul under the extreme duress, stress, fatigue, and pain of a fight. Fred Russell had done the same thing to Johnson.

Before the fight started, Ferguson was a betting favorite at 3 to 1 odds. However, there was no speculation that he had thrown the fight for gamblers. "No one dared to say that the fight wasn't fought on its merits for the first six rounds, for if two men ever fought; Ferguson and Johnson did last night." Some thought that Ferguson possibly was afraid of losing on the merits, sensed that the tide of the fight was shifting, regardless of his best efforts, and therefore he grew frustrated. "One thing is sure; Johnson was beginning to look better and stronger. He wasn't carrying the great weight that Ferguson was. Not that Ferguson was not in shape, but Johnson was harder than nails while Ferguson is such a giant that it is impossible to get his flesh hard without weakening him." Plus, that fast pace in the heat would have a wearing effect on any big man.

Contrary to the modern thinking by many today who like to place too much credence upon weight when analyzing fights, analysts at that time saw both a positive and a negative to weight. Greater weight could assist a fighter's strength, power, and ability to absorb blows, but it could also slow a fighter down, make him less busy, and grow fatigued faster when the pace is kept at a high rate over many rounds. Smaller fighters often were perceived as more efficient and effective overall, though with exceptions, such as with Jeffries. As a general rule, huge fighters today would struggle badly to last 15 or 20 rounds, while fighters of yesteryear easily could enter the ring at higher weights if they knew they only had to go 12 rounds.

Despite having enjoyed the fight, the *Boston Post* writer opined that neither man had a chance to defeat Jeffries. "Jeffries could lick both men in one ring at the same time, yes, and with one hand. Both were fast, but Jeffries is like Lou Dillon and Ferguson and Johnson like truck horses."[604]

---

[604] *Boston Globe, Boston Herald, Boston Post,* July 19, 1905. Lou Dillon was a famous, very fast trotting horse, the first to run a mile in under 2 minutes. A truck horse was a strong, heavily built draft horse designed for hauling heavy loads.

On the West Coast, the *San Francisco Evening Post* said Ferguson had shown his true self - "a coward and a quitter." His deliberate and atrocious foul was called "a plain case of quit." It believed his career as a pugilist was over. "He hadn't received enough punishment to make a bantamweight go under, and the only reason that can be ascribed for his foul method of ending the fight is his yellow instincts."

A couple days later, the same paper speculated that Johnson was under a pull and took it easy on Ferguson, stalling and allowing Ferguson to tire himself out. Johnson did very little fighting, only showing his true form in flashes. Still, his body shots made Sandy want to quit.[605]

Joe Grim, the Mavel of the Ring.

On Monday July 24, 1905, just six days after the Ferguson bout, returning to Philadelphia again, Johnson took on Italian Joe Grim in a scheduled 6-round bout. Born Saverio Giannone, the 24-year-old Grim was a game and very experienced boxer who mostly lost his bouts. He was willing to fight anyone, and was quite durable, being famous for his ability to take a beating. He could be dropped, but usually he rose and finished the bout. Hence, when a fighter was called a "Joe Grim," it meant he could take a licking and keep on ticking. His record included: 1900 DND6 Dave Holly; 1902 LND6 and DND6 Holly, and LND6 George Cole (twice); 1903 LND6 Jack O'Brien, LND6 Jack Bennett, LND6 Charlie McKeever, LND6 Cole, LND6 Kid Carter, LDQ3 Peter Maher, LND6 Joe Walcott, WND6 Fred Cooley, LND6 Bob Fitzsimmons (Grim dropped several times in nearly every round), LND6 Joe Gans, and L6 Hugo Kelly; 1904 L10 Gans, LND6 Jim Jeffords, WND6 Owen Ziegler, LND6 Holly, WND6 Matty Matthews, LND6 Maher, LND6 Holly, LND6 Bennett, LND6 Billy Stift, L10 Dixie Kid, LND6 Larry Temple, L6 Dixie Kid, LND6 Jack Blackburn (twice), and DND6 Cooley; and 1905 LND6 Blackburn, ND6 Dixie Kid, LND6, L6, and DND6 Billy Burke, and LND6 Buddy Ryan, amongst many others.

[605] *San Francisco Evening Post,* July 24, 26, 1905.

A great crowd jammed the National A.C. to the doors, crowding the club-house to a point of suffocation. Every seat in the big arena was taken. Hundreds were turned away, unable to gain admission, while thousands of Italians blocked Eleventh street eagerly waiting to hear the result.

When the men came to ring center, the referee told them that they were to break when ordered to do so, and to break clean. Johnson was taller by several inches, had a longer reach, and was many pounds heavier. The *Evening Bulletin* believed that Johnson weighed at least 25 pounds more, and was about 8 inches taller.

The *Press* said that over the next 6 rounds, Grim would be dropped nine times. Each knockdown weakened him a bit more, for his legs grew wobblier and his eyes glassier.

The *Public Ledger* said Grim's awkward defense puzzled Johnson, just as it had scores of others. Still, Grim was down twice in the 2nd round, once in the 4th, five times in the 5th round, and eight times in the 6th round.

During the 5th round, when Grim dropped down with little provocation, at the count of eight he jumped up and leaped at Johnson like a lion. This aroused the Italians in the crowd to a point of wild enthusiasm. He was on the floor when the bell rang ending the 5th round, but "ambled to his corner like a two-year-old."

In the 6th round, when timekeeper Lew Duriacker yelled, "Only fifteen seconds to go," Johnson went after Grim like a demon and twice knocked him down. The final knockdown came within a few seconds of the bell. Jack dropped him with a clean straight right. Grim was out cold, but at the count of two, the referee stopped counting, for Grim was saved by the bell.

All of the local accounts and those at ringside agreed that only the bell saved Grim from officially being recorded as a knockout victim. There was no chance for him to rise from that blow, and would have been counted out, but Referee McGuigan had only reached the count of one or two when the gong sounded and Grim technically was saved from a knockout. At that time, fighters could be saved by the bell, and Grim was.

Grim was beaten badly. He was lying prostrate on his back, and his seconds had to assist him to his corner. Three minutes after the bout was over, Grim, "whose recuperative powers are the puzzle of medical men as well as ring followers," walked across the ring to Johnson and shook hands. Joe was first out of the ring, but he was very weak.

The local press said Grim came within a few seconds of losing his reputation of never having been knocked out, or at least officially counted out. Johnson nearly performed the feat which many of the biggest and hardest-punching fighters in the country had failed. In reality, though, indeed he had knocked out Grim.

The *Philadelphia Evening Bulletin* said that as usual, Grim stayed the 6 rounds. Johnson fought the Italian all over the ring. Grim made no worthy effort to fight whatsoever, but covered up or ran away to escape the punches rained upon him. He went to the floor eighteen times in order to evade punishment, and three times he hit Johnson with weak blows rather below the belt. Johnson tried to punch Grim off the map, but Joe was there with a blood-bespattered face grinning at him in the last round.

Fitzsimmons beat Grim more than Johnson did, but Johnson nearly ended Grim's career in the last nine seconds of the bout, when he jolted Grim's head with a left hook and quickly sent a straight right to the chin. Joe floundered on the floor. This writer said that when the referee reached eight, Grim had made no effort to rise, and his eyes had a glassy stare that made it appear that he was out. However, the bell sounded, saving him, and his seconds carried him to his corner. The only time a knockout seemed imminent was in the last few seconds.

The *Philadelphia Public Ledger* said Grim was no match for Johnson. Although Johnson did not administer the overall punishment that Fitzsimmons, Gans, and Blackburn dealt out, the few blows landed in the last two rounds seemed more effective, and for the first time in his career Grim had to be carried to his corner at the end of the contest.

The *Philadelphia Record* was harsh and perhaps unfair towards Johnson, despite the dominant performance. It said Johnson not only failed to stop him, but did not punish Grim as much as Jack Blackburn and other much lighter men had done in the same amount of time. Grim bled during the bout, though afterwards he showed few marks.

It also said that Johnson was fortunate to get Grim out of condition. Joe had not been taking good care of himself, and was fat and slow on his feet. He did not do any of the dancing around or show the activity level that was typical for him. Of course, that wasn't Johnson's fault.[606]

Whenever Johnson's performances drew some criticism from the white press, to whatever degree, one has to wonder and consider to what extent those criticisms were influenced by the general society's displeasure at a black man's success. It doesn't seem fair to criticize in any way a performance that featured so many knockdowns in a mere 6 rounds, with the opponent lying out cold on the ground at the bout's conclusion. Certainly, one has to bear in mind the social context of the times.

The *Police Gazette* reported that Grim was unable to land his punches, and Johnson beat the human punching bag to a pulp from the start. Grim bled so much that the ring was slippery. Johnson "did not show the slightest pity for his helpless opponent." Most every top heavyweight had attempted to knock him out and failed, and Jack barely missed the feat.

5,000 watched Johnson knock down Grim twice in the 1st round, once in the 4th, five times in the 5th, and from six to nine times in the 6th round.

The last knockdown was from a right hook to the jaw just four seconds before the end of the round. Grim was totally out cold, but saved by the bell, so Johnson did not get credit for a knockout. It was five minutes before Grim woke up.[607]

---

[606] *Philadelphia Press, Philadelphia Public Ledger, Philadelphia Inquirer, Philadelphia Evening Bulletin, Philadelphia Record,* July 25, 1905.
[607] *Police Gazette,* August 12, 19, 1905.

On July 28, 1905 in Los Angeles, before a huge crowd of 4,000-5,000 spectators, top middleweights Tommy Burns and Hugo Kelly fought to a 20-round draw. Everyone, including the referee, agreed that Burns would have been entitled to the verdict had the boxers not agreed to a draw decision if both were on their feet at the bout's conclusion.

At that time, the black-owned *Topeka Plaindealer* asked whether the white man was civilized, and answered the question in the negative. As soon as a white man learned that someone had colored blood, he looked about with dread, uneasiness, and hysteria. The white man tried in every way to close all avenues for negro livelihood, even importing foreigners to take his place in all classes of labor. Then, as a result, "because his castaway sits idle, he is called immoral, unfit for society of a white man, worthless."

Often, when a white woman had a consensual relationship with a black man, if she feared detection, "the old cry of rape or assault goes out from the lips of this virtuous white lady, and a poor Negro is lynched for daring to be near the premises of one of the best families of the South. Then come the yellow journals with a photo of a maiden of brave and pure blood, exonerated of all guilt." When blacks were lynched, the perpetrators of the lynching were never found or prosecuted.

> The white man's histories are false, even their holy book, teaching only the servility of the darker races and the superiority of the whites, from time 'immemorial' – base lies. His Christianity has long since failed as the above conditions show. He is more dishonest than any other race. His declaration of independence is a farce. His municipal governments are a fraud. He is the most envious, egotistic and jealous of human beings and has really grown to believe that this world was made for him to govern and for white men only.[608]

In August 1905, the *Police Gazette* reported, "Marvin Hart says positively that he will never meet Jack Johnson in the ring again." As champion, he was drawing the color line, refusing to allow the top contender to the throne the opportunity to win the title. The *Police Gazette* felt that such a declaration put Hart's title claims on the ropes. Certainly, not all white writers were unfair towards Johnson.

> A black man, in my esteem, is entitled to just the same rights and prerogatives, as long as he is cleanly and decent, upright, capable and honest. Both Jeffries and Hart have fought niggers, as they style their colored rivals, before, and why not fight again? .... [W]hen he barred colored men he was thinking of no one on earth but Mr. Johnson.... Mr. Hart knows, as well as he knows that he is alive, that Jack Johnson was entitled to that fight out in San Francisco, and he also knows, I'll bet my boots, that Mr. Johnson can lick him every day in the week, not even barring Sunday.

---

[608] *Topeka Plaindealer*, July 28, 1905.

I must say, however, in this connection, that I do not believe Mr. Jeffries barred Mr. Johnson for the same reason Mr. Hart has. Jim couldn't see any honor or dough in a win over Jack…. Again, I have always thought that Mr. Jeffries' virulent jealousy of Mr. Johnson's superior sartorial predilections had much to do with his denying him a chance.[609]

The *Police Gazette* continually criticized Hart's stance on the color line, even though no heavyweight champion before him had defended against a black fighter either.

Marvin Hart…will probably never know what a peaceful moment is until he fights Jack Johnson, the negro premier, again…

Johnson is a slugger and boxer of no mean ability; in fact, he is one of the best big men in the ring. But Johnson is colored, and the color line has been drawn by Hart, who, following in the footsteps of his predecessor, Jeffries, who so graciously donated the heavyweight championship to the Kentuckian, declares that as long as he is on top, no negro will get the chance of becoming the star of the fistic firmament. This was to be expected. Hart being a Southerner, he would be inviting trouble to fight a negro, so he says. Association between colored men and whites is not countenanced in the South, which fact is well established, and while Hart, for this reason, may have a good excuse for not fighting Johnson, he is not consistent. He once fought him and beat him. That was when Johnson was not what he is today, and no one can blame the negro for pressing his claims for another fight. Hart will find less worthy opponents than the colored man, but, then, race prejudice is a barrier to one of the best boxing cards that could be arranged. It's an unsatisfactory state of affairs that exists in the heavyweight and lightweight classes.[610]

---

609 *Police Gazette*, August 12, September 23, 1905.
610 *Police Gazette*, August 19, 1905.

CHAPTER 17

A Brief Western Return
Finds the Color-Line Awaiting

Following his no-decision victory over Joe Grim, Jack Johnson returned to San Francisco. He was hoping to get some of the big fellows to do battle with him there, but was unsuccessful. No one wanted to fight him. Several drew the color line to avoid him.[611]

On August 31, 1905 in San Francisco, in a middleweight bout, Tommy Burns scored a knockout victory over Dave Barry in the 20th round. Burns used his footwork to stick and move and cautiously outbox Barry for most of the bout. He dropped the hard-punching Barry in the 15th round, but then continued carefully outboxing him, rather than try to finish him. The spectators jeered and whistled. The *San Francisco Bulletin* compared Burns to Jack Johnson, saying that like Johnson, Burns "was content to jab and prance around and await the termination of the bout in order to receive the verdict." In the 20th round, when Burns had Barry helpless, he landed a right that sent Barry down and out cold with only 30 seconds left in the fight. It was somewhat reminiscent of Johnson-McVey III. Local papers criticized the bout as tame and uninteresting. Like Jack Johnson, Burns took heat for fighting cautiously, being unwilling to take chances with a man whom the press felt Burns could have knocked out much sooner. Perhaps they simply did not appreciate careful scientific boxing, regardless of race.[612]

Although not coming out of retirement, Jim Jeffries said,

> I am not bragging when I say that I could beat all four of them in one night. I mean Hart, Johnson, Ruhlin and McCormick. That Hart-Johnson mill was one of the saddest sketches ever perpetrated on an unsuspecting public. ... Not one of these men is better than a third-rate heavyweight.

Despite Jeff's claims that the aforementioned fighters were all big chumps, George Siler disagreed, and noted how Jeff had been quick to draw the color line on Johnson. "To my mind Jeffries is today really more afraid of Johnson than any other man in the ring."[613]

In early September 1905, the Russo-Japanese War ended with Japan having defeated Russia. This unexpected victory shocked the West, for it

[611] *Police Gazette*, September 9, 1905.
[612] *San Francisco Bulletin*, September 1, 1905.
[613] *Freeman*, September 9, 1905; *Police Gazette*, September 16, 1905.

was the first modern-era major military victory by a non-white Asian power over a white European nation. It challenged racial beliefs about white superiority.

The *Topeka Plaindealer* said the recent brutal burning of another Texas Negro in broad daylight by a mob of over 500 white barbarians who took the law into their own hands for the "old 'chestnut' charge of outraging a white woman," the second time in two months, should be the keynote for blacks of that state to fight back. It said that more often than not, the white woman was having a consensual relationship with a black man, and to save herself, she squealed on him and claimed rape, or to save her black sweetheart and herself, raised the alarm, and the first Negro that was brought to her, she laid the crime on him. "I for one, knowing the condition in the South as I do, do not believe the threadbare lies coming from that or any other section when it is charged that Negroes commit assaults upon the person of white women unwillingly. It is a lie, and a barefaced one at that."

Many newspapers fostered race prejudice. "The reporters of the Associated Press herald their falsehoods to the world and the world becomes prejudiced against the most humble and pathetic people on earth." It asked whether Negroes would forever submit to such indignities. The passing of resolutions would do no good. The Negro needed to fight back, defend themselves, and apply the torch in lawless communities that permitted innocent persons to be burned at the stake to satisfy the mob's mad bloodlust. "The Italian way of taking revenge must be the Negro's watchword."[614]

Those same Associated Press reporters were often the ones writing about boxing too. Hence, their critiques about black fighters sometimes needed to be taken with a grain of salt.

Marvin Hart again said that he would fight anyone in the world, except for a black fighter.

> What I have said heretofore about fighting negroes goes for all time. I am a Southerner, and do not like them. I was forced to fight Jack Johnson in San Francisco, and I beat him. Had the fight been to a finish I would have knocked him out. Toward the last he quit like a cur, and I demonstrated that I am a better fighter than he is – I say fighter – boxers seldom win fights.[615]

The *Police Gazette* again addressed Hart's inconsistency regarding the color line, given that he had fought Johnson once before. "Like all Southerners he has inherited a prejudice against the colored race." After defeating Kid Carter, Marvin had refused to fight Joe Walcott, saying, "I am a Southerner and my folks would disown me if I fought you…. I could not go back to Kentucky again."

---

[614] *Topeka Plaindealer*, September 15, 1905.
[615] *San Francisco Evening Post*, September 13, 1905.

Yet, Hart had fought Johnson. Initially, Hart had refused to fight Johnson, but he was heavily in debt, white fighters were refusing to fight him, and Johnson and others were taunting him as being afraid; plus he knew that defeating the top contender possibly could get him a title shot. Hence, he took the Johnson fight. So his moral stance was not as fixed as he claimed.

The *Police Gazette* writers went back and forth in their support of Johnson. Jack was both complimented and criticized, for the periodical provided several perspectives. One writer said, "Jack Johnson is the best heavyweight now before the public." Yet, another said of the Hart-Johnson fight,

> Hart, however, forced the fight all the time and the good judges who figured it out that he would make Johnson hold back, afraid of being hurt, had the right end.

> Johnson had repeatedly challenged Jeffries, but after Hart beat him that put an end to his claims for the championship. It proved also that Johnson never was in Jeffries' class.

Also said was, "The fact that Johnson lost to Hart stamps him as a faker or as a boxer with a yellow streak in his make-up, and either defect would kill his chances for first honors if pitted against such men as Jeffries or Fitzsimmons."

However, Fitz and Jeff appeared to be retired. "That leaves Johnson to fight such men as Hart and Ruhlin, either of whom he should defeat handily. But there is no reason why any such contests should be classed as championship fights, for they are only second rate fights at the best." Regardless, both Hart and Ruhlin drew the color line.

Eventually, the *Police Gazette* and others begrudgingly recognized Hart as the present champion. "Hart has more claim upon [the championship] than anyone else just now."[616]

The *Freeman* noted that some sporting editors of various papers had tried to drum up support for the idea that the "long forgotten" Bob Armstrong was the man that Johnson should battle instead of Jeffries. The question was whether any club would put up a sufficient purse for the bout, for "every one knows that poor old Bob would stand no show at all with even the likes of Johnson. It would certainly be a shame for Jack to take the money." After all, Armstrong had been stopped quickly by Ferguson, a man who had to foul to get himself out of a contest with Johnson.[617]

On October 2, 1905, in Harrison, Arkansas, a white mob stormed the jail and took two black prisoners, one of whom had been charged two days earlier with breaking into a doctor's residence, and transported them outside city limits. After whipping their captives, they ordered them to leave town.

---

[616] *Police Gazette*, September 16, 1905.
[617] *Freeman*, September 16, 1905.

Not fully satisfied, the thirty-member mob returned to town and expanded their rampage through Harrison's black community. They burned down homes, shot out windows, and ordered all black folk to vacate the town that night. Many did, fleeing to places such as Fayetteville and Eureka Springs, or to Missouri. In subsequent days, those blacks who remained were attacked and harassed.

19-year-old heavyweight "wonder" Al Kaufman, who showed promise, said that he too would draw the color line, no matter how long or short his career may be.[618]

JACK "TWIN" SULLIVAN

During October 1905, Jack Johnson traveled from San Francisco to Los Angeles and did some sparring with top middleweight Jack "Twin" Sullivan, who was preparing for a rematch bout against Tommy Burns. In March 1905, Sullivan and Burns had fought to a 20-round draw. Johnson had sparred with Sullivan previously, back in September 1904.

While in Los Angeles, Johnson allegedly proposed an interesting challenge to Jeffries, which kept his name in the news. The *Los Angeles Times* said,

The defi of Jack Johnson to go into a real dark room with Jeffries and let the first one who comes out be declared the winner, should contribute largely to the joyfulness of the summer hours. While he is a good fighter he would probably be on the short end of a 4 to 1 bet on the winner. Johnson is probably making his talk because he knows that Jeffries has retired from the game and wouldn't fight him if he was still in it.[619]

By mid-October 1905, Marvin Hart was still looking to make a heavyweight championship title defense. He said,

I am willing, and what is more, anxious to meet any man in the world in the ring in a finish fight. I mean just what I say. This challenge doesn't apply to colored people. …

---

[618] *Los Angeles Herald*, October 11, 1905.
[619] *Los Angeles Times*, October 13, 1905. This report is interesting because Jeffries later claimed that *he* made this proposal to Johnson, who turned him down.

I do not mind what Johnson says. I was forced into fighting him once, but I will not do so again. I am not side-stepping him, but it is against my principles to fight a negro.[620]

On October 17, 1905 in Los Angeles, before a crowd of 4,000 spectators, in a middleweight bout, Jack "Twin" Sullivan won a 20-round decision over Tommy Burns. Although Burns lost, it had been a fan-friendly fight that generated a great deal of revenue for promoter Tom McCarey, who therefore wanted to have either fighter box for him again.

On October 27, 1905 in San Francisco, a 165-pound Philadelphia Jack O'Brien scored a KO17 over 190-pound Al Kaufman, the highly touted up-and-comer.

The *Topeka Plaindealer* lamented the fact that the white man's policy to belittle the black man stood as a barrier against his progress. "There is a disposition in this country to undervalue all that the Negro has done since and before the war to increase the wealth of the nation, and it seems to be the policy of the white man to count for naught the labor of the Negro in bearing the white man's burden for 240 years." Blacks had cleared the forests, built homes, churches, and school houses, and had fought in every war. Yet, he was denied the most common rights of a free man, and the same government "now absolutely refuses to protect him" in the exercise of what rights he did have, for "thousands and thousands of black men have been murdered in this country." Because "God made them black the Negroes are condemned by the whites, and no doubt many have condemned God for making a black man." Despite all the obstacles and condemnation blacks had to endure, "the Negro is not allowed to hold office in many parts of this country for fear of political domination. ... and all manner of hellish schemes are devised and practiced by the whites to check and retard the progress of the Negro."[621]

George Siler said colored boxers were in poor circumstances. At times, the colored boxer was considered the king of the ring. However, at present, black fighters were not being given the chance to prove themselves, for white fighters were "greedy" and fearful that they would not get all of the money were they to fight black boxers. Hence they drew the color line. "It is not a case of qualification but it is greed. For if any thing the colored 'pug' is altogether too powerful in science and muscle – his ability to stand punishment and his knowledge of delivering punishment is too great." Men like Marvin Hart "should be laughed at whenever they speak of barring colored fighters." Instead, black boxers had to accept uneven challenges and give white fighters much the best of the financial arrangements in order to obtain a bout.[622]

---

[620] *Los Angeles Examiner*, October 15, 1905.
[621] *Topeka Plaindealer*, October 27, 1905.
[622] *Freeman*, November 25, 1905.

Jack Johnson said he would gladly allow Marvin Hart to dictate the terms of a match between them, for he only wanted to get him into the ring again. He was even willing to allow Hart to keep the entire fighter's end of the receipts if he didn't knock him out within 20 rounds.

Police Gazette writer Sam Austin opined, "Johnson is probably the best fighter among the heavyweights today, excepting Jeffries." Given what had happened in their controversial fight, Austin wanted another battle to take place between Hart and Johnson to "prove the black man to be all that I have claimed for him."[623]

---

[623] *Police Gazette*, December 2, 1905.

CHAPTER 18

Another Colorful Eastern Tour

Having been unsuccessful at obtaining any bouts during the few months that he was out West, Jack Johnson returned to the East Coast, where he would fight mostly other black boxers.

On Saturday November 25, 1905 in Philadelphia, at the National Athletic Club on Eleventh and Catharine streets, Jack Johnson took on Joe Jeannette in a scheduled 6-round no-decision bout. Johnson had boxed Jeannette previously in a 3-round bout in May 1905. Since then, Jeannette's record included: WND6 Black Bill, LND6 George Cole, KO7 Black Bill, WND6 Jim Jeffords, WND6 George Cole, and D6 Black Bill. It had been four months since Johnson last fought anyone.

The local press gave the bout little attention. Several did not even bother to print a post-fight report.

The *Philadelphia Public Ledger* said Johnson was beating Jeannette, but lost via disqualification in the 2nd round. Johnson had been outclassing Jeannette for a round and a half, but then lost as the result of an "alleged foul."

> Jeannette, after being thumped in lively fashion in the first round, assumed a crouching pose in the second round. He undertook to run in and clinch, ducking a vicious left-hand swing. Johnson ripped a right-hand hook up for Jeannette's jaw. The latter dropped to the floor, writhing in apparent agony. He claimed to have been struck a foul blow.
>
> He was removed to the dressing room and the club physician substantiated his claim. Johnson was promptly disqualified. Jeannette professed to be in great pain and lay in his dressing room in apparent agony. It is understood that the police proposed to keep Johnson, Jeannette and the club official under surveillance.[624]

Apparently, there was some suspicion that there was something fishy about the bout and its result. Clearly, based on the words this local writer used, he suspected that Johnson had not fouled. The local writer who actually saw the fight questioned whether Jeannette had fooled the referee into thinking it was a foul. The police wondered whether the fight had been fixed. Hence, their surveillance of the parties involved. Perhaps though, they had not seen the accidental low blow.

Contrary to the local paper, the non-local New York-based *Police Gazette*, which usually relied upon a local dispatch, reported that it was an exciting

---

[624] *Philadelphia Public Ledger,* November 26, 1905.

bout from the start, but Jeannette had the best of it. In the 2nd round, Jeannette grew even more aggressive and they exchanged blows to the body and head. Joe landed several good jabs, and the worried Johnson "rushed madly at Joe and swinging a wicked left it landed low on the New Yorker, who dropped to the floor, where he lay writhing in agony for some time, until he was carried to his dressing room." Johnson was disqualified.[625]

CJOHNSON FOULED CJANNETTE AT THE NAT·A·C·

Philadelphia Inquirer, **November 27, 1905**

Ultimately, the foul, if there was one, was regarded as an accident, and the bout did not tarnish Johnson's status as the world's elite colored heavyweight. In fact, the fight did not garner a great deal of attention. Besides, Johnson and Jeannette would fight again a mere week later to settle matters.

Some children had sued the Asheville, North Carolina Board of Education for refusing to allow them into a white public school. The children contended that they had no negro blood in their veins, but instead that their ancestor was of Portuguese ancestry. A jury found in the children's' favor, so they could attend the white schools.[626]

Just six days after the second Jeannette bout, Johnson returned to the ring again, in nearby Baltimore, Maryland, about 100 miles away from Philadelphia.

On Friday December 1, 1905, in a bout sponsored by the Eureka Athletic Club and held at Baltimore's Germania Maennerchor Hall, Jack Johnson took on Young Peter Jackson in a scheduled 12-round bout.

Although much smaller than Johnson, the sturdily built 5'6" middleweight Jackson had over 100 fights of experience under his belt, and still was only 28 years old. He was a very well-respected cagey veteran of the game, who had victories against several top welterweight and middleweight fighters, and even some heavyweights. His record included: 1897 W4 Mexican Pete Everett; 1898 LDQ4 Young Griffo; 1899 W20 Australian Jimmy Ryan, KO20 Jim Tremble, and KO2 Harris Martin (the Black Pearl); 1900 WDQ7 Tom Tracey, KO13 Jack O'Brien, L10 Otto Sieloff, W6 Fred

---

[625] *Police Gazette,* December 9, 1905.
[626] *Baltimore Sun,* November 26, 1905.

Thornton, L6 Tom McCune, LKOby18 Mysterious Billy Smith, and LND6 Jimmy Handler; 1901 L25 and D20 Bobby Dobbs, KO2 Mysterious Billy Smith, KO9 Jimmy Handler, KO8 Scaldy Bill Quinn, KO4 Harry Peppers, and L20 Joe Walcott; 1902 KO3 Handler, LND6 Walcott, WND6 Jack Bonner, KO2 Tommy West, D10 Walcott, WND6 Quinn, LND6 Charlie Haghey, KO5 Dan Creedon, LND6 Jack O'Brien, W20 Mike Donovan, L6 John Willie, and D15 Haghey; 1903 D12 Haghey, LND6 George Cole, D20 Joe Walcott (world welterweight title), LND6 Black Bill, L6 Willie, DND6 George Cole, and ND6 Cyclone Kelly; 1904 W15 Mike Donovan, D15 Black Bill, KO5 Joe Butler, KO4 Joe Walcott, KO4 Jack Scales, and D15 Dixie Kid; and 1905 LDQ2 and L10 Jack O'Brien, L15 (twice) and D15 Sam Langford. Victories of any kind over Jack O'Brien (KO13) and Joe Walcott (KO4) and a draw with Sam Langford (D15) stamped Jackson as a solid fighter, at the very least. He had been stopped only twice in over 100 fights, and not since 1900, five years earlier. He had far greater experience than Johnson.

Jackson was listed as being from Baltimore, the fight's location. Hence, if there was any bias or favoritism, it would be for the local man, Jackson.

Because Jackson was only a middleweight, and because Johnson was anxious to obtain a match, Jack agreed to a handicap. He agreed to stop Jackson in 12 rounds or accept the small end of the boxers' share of the receipts. The very durable and experienced Jackson laughed at the idea of Johnson stopping him in 12 rounds.[627]

Jackson's incentive was not to win the bout, but rather to survive the 12 rounds. He only needed to remain standing to earn the winner's end of the purse. Hence his financial incentive had nothing to do with his merits, but rather his ability to last.

Young Peter Jackson

---

[627] *Baltimore Sun*, November 25, 1905.

Jack Johnson was the "acknowledged peer of all the colored heavyweights, and conceded to be among the best of the big men of the ring." The local *Baltimore American* said many were doubtful that Jackson would be able to withstand the fusillade of blows that Johnson would rain upon him, for Johnson was a "vicious slugger." However, others noted that Jackson had won many fights by knockout and had a fairly enviable career himself, so they gave him a chance to turn the trick against Johnson.[628]

Club members filled the hall. The attendance was surprisingly large. A local paper said Johnson was 40 or more pounds heavier, and head and shoulders taller. A non-local source said Johnson announced his weight as 182 pounds, while Jackson confessed to 165 pounds.

1 - Johnson worked while Jackson covered. Johnson finally was able to land one solid punch. Jackson landed a couple of short punches.

2 - Johnson boxed fairly and hard. Jackson worked in the clinches. Still, cries of "Fake!" were heard. The crowd was anxious.

3 - Johnson beat Jackson about the ring. Peter didn't do much but defend and survive. After the bell ended the round, Jackson rushed in and began fighting Johnson, who fought back. The referee said, "If such fouling occurs again I shall disqualify both men."

4 - Peter covered as usual. Jack pounded him on the back.

5 - Jackson ducked and covered. Johnson worked for an opening, but had to be content with hitting Jackson on the back. Johnson told Jackson that he was a quitter.

6 - Early in the round, Jackson slipped down. Johnson was careful, for fear of committing the foul of striking his man while he was down. Near the end of the round, Peter slipped down again, and when he rose, he held on continually and would not break, despite the referee's commands. The gong ended the round.

7 - Johnson asked Jackson, "Who ever told you you were game?" Peter smiled and kept away. Jackson twice tried but failed to land his fierce short right over the top. He kept moving around rapidly. Johnson announced to the crowd, "I would like to show you people a fight, but I can't catch Jackson."

8 - Johnson sent Jackson through the ropes with a body blow. Peter stood up and fought back for some seconds. Then he returned to his survival tactics. Late in the round, Jackson threw a right intended for the jaw, and though it landed, it just missed the vulnerable point. Johnson smiled and continued punishing Jackson on the head and body.

9 - Jackson was forced through the ropes twice. As a result, he tried harder to land than before.

---

[628] *Baltimore American*, December 1, 1905.

10 - A right to the jaw sent Jackson to the floor. He was up in a moment, but went down again quickly from another punch to the head. At the gong, they were in a clinch, butting each other.

11 - Johnson fought Peter around the ring and was pounding him on the back when the round ended.

12 - In a clinch, Johnson did the punching. When they broke, Johnson taunted Peter and tried to hit him. Jackson ran around until Johnson cornered him, but then Jackson held. Johnson was pounding him at the end of the round.

The *Baltimore Sun* said Johnson was by far the more expert boxer; as clever as the reports said. Those who had seen Jackson fight to win in the past were fascinated with his style. However, that was not how he fought this time. From the start, Johnson went at Jackson and made an earnest effort to stop him, but Peter survived by using his crouch, covering up, dancing and sprinting away, and hugging in the clinches.

In the early rounds, Jackson hung on in the clinches and fought a bit foully, but Referee Jim O'Hara would not disqualify him. It seemed though, that Jackson was willing to be disqualified, because he continued such tactics despite the warnings.

It was not a pretty exhibition, and the only thing it showed was how a small man could keep away and avoid punishment when going up against a bigger and cleverer man. Johnson did all the fighting.

By surviving, Jackson had won 75% of the fighter's share of the purse and Johnson 25%, amounts which Manager Al Herford would not state. No formal decision was announced, as it appears to have been a no-decision bout. Clearly though, Johnson was the better fighter, having been in control all the way, and having dropped Jackson several times.

Afterwards, Johnson said, "I tried to give you gentlemen a fight, but it takes two to make a battle, and I was not fast enough to catch Jackson." Johnson jeered Jackson's pure survival tactics.[629]

According to the *Baltimore American*, for 12 rounds Johnson pecked away at Jackson, but could not put him out. The bout was unsatisfactory, for the crowd did not care at all for Jackson's tactics. He did not fight to win or be competitive in any way, but rather merely to survive. Hence, the bout was less than entertaining.

> Johnson did all of the fighting, while Jackson ran around the ring, and kept covered up to keep out of harm's way.

> Johnson fought cleverly, but could not penetrate through Jackson's iron-clad defense often enough to do the local colored man any harm. Jackson gave away many pounds, as he is but a practical welterweight, while Johnson is a full-fledged heavyweight. Jackson

---

[629] *Baltimore Sun*, December 2, 1905.

was only off his feet once as the result of a short right punch to the jaw in the tenth round. The blow did not affect him, as he was up in an instant to stand the gaff. Jackson showed no ill effects of the battle whatever, as Johnson did all the fighting.

At the start of the bout, they began roughing it. Some thought it would end early. In the 3rd round, Jackson went at Johnson, and they had a lively mix up. Thereafter, Jackson fought purely to survive, either running around or covering up. In the 10th round, Jackson attempted to butt Johnson. There was a lot of clinching, and Referee Jim O'Hara warned them that if there were any more rough tactics, he would disqualify the offender. However, he did not do so.[630]

The *Police Gazette* reported that Johnson contracted to stop him before the limit, but failed to do so only because Jackson would not stand up and fight. "The result was a draw, according to agreement, but on points Johnson won with much to spare."[631]

Joe Jeannette

On Saturday December 2, 1905, the very next day after going 12 rounds against Jackson, Jack Johnson was back in Philadelphia to again face Joe Jeannette in a 6-round no-decision bout that night. Imagine a fighter today going 12 rounds and then fighting a 6-round bout the next day. This was only seven days after Johnson had been disqualified for an accidental low blow against Jeannette. They boxed at the National Athletic Club on Eleventh and Catharine streets.

The *Philadelphia Public Ledger* reported that Johnson defeated Jeannette in 6 fast rounds. Johnson's judgment of distance was faulty when it came to leading, but he managed to catch Jeannette repeatedly with counters. Jeannette was plucky and always ready to mix it up. He surprised the crowd with his aggressiveness

Johnson dropped Jeannette once in the 5th round and three times in the 6th round. However, he could not stop Joe, who was still full of fight at the finish. Hence, despite scoring four knockdowns, Jack's punching power was questioned. What they did not realize was that Joe Jeannette was not easy to put away, as his subsequent career would prove.[632]

---

[630] *Baltimore American*, December 2, 1905.
[631] *Police Gazette*, December 16, 1905.
[632] *Philadelphia Public Ledger* December 3, 1905.

A couple days later, the *Philadelphia Inquirer* wrote that the bout between "Jack Johnsing" and Joe Jeannette of New York was in the nature of a vindication for Johnson. "He proved that although on the preceding Saturday night he may have put Jeannette out of commission by hitting him below the protected line, he is the New Yorker's master." Jeannette looked pretty good for the first two rounds, but after that, Johnson began to pull away.

Regardless, fight followers still were not sure about Johnson's real ability. He was well-built, and "uses his left like a mechanic." However, "his hitting ability and his gameness are yet to be demonstrated here." He had failed to stop Grim, Jackson, or Jeannette, as well as several other fighters. Yet, he had decked and clearly defeated all of them. "Taking him all in all, he is the hardest fighter to get a straight line on that has appeared in this section of the country for years." They were not quite sure what to make of Johnson, or how to assess his ability.[633]

According to a subsequent *Police Gazette* report, Johnson attacked Jeannette from the start, though Joe covered well. The 4th was Joe's best. He mixed it and let his fists go, and Jack smiled, but it was Joe's round. Joe kept coming in the 5th, but a right to the jaw dropped him. In the 6th, Johnson dropped him twice, but Joe managed to survive.[634]

Another *Police Gazette* report said Johnson was on the attack from the beginning, in the 1st round landing several hard lefts that staggered Jeannette. In the next three rounds though, Joe landed a jab that "rattled the gold-filled tombstones which were displayed when Johnson smiled." Johnson threw science out and rushed in, but Joe either clinched or stopped him with his left. The 4th was uninteresting, as Joe kept away. Jack was desperate in the 5th, and as Jeannette grew fatigued, Johnson battered and dropped him. In the 6th, Jack attacked like a mad bull and gave him no rest, dropping Joe twice. Jeannette was tired but used his generalship to smother Johnson and survive to the end.

This critical article said, "Johnson bested his man, but that is not anything for him to brag about."

> Somebody ought to tell Jack Johnson that being fancy and 'gallus' don't get a 'coon' anything in the fighting game. ... With every natural advantage at his command — height, reach and weight - he failed to put Jeannette away, and the latter must still be considered a novice, having only figured in the game for a little over a year.[635]

This writer was overly critical. Jeannette was very tough, talented, and underrated at that point. He consistently would prove to be one of the best, most durable, and talented fighters in the business. Within the same month, he would stop Sam Langford. Plus, it wasn't easy to stop a motivated, in-

[633] *Philadelphia Inquirer,* December 4, 1905.
[634] *Police Gazette*, December 16, 1905.
[635] *Police Gazette*, December 23, 1905.

shape man who had survival skills. Johnson still had managed to deck him three or four times in each of two bouts, with the third ending early as the result of an accidental low blow, which some questioned.

Jack Johnson had fought thirteen times in 1905.

The *Philadelphia Record* said modern patrons of the game were after slugging and action, and were willing to pay to see it, more than science. Unfortunately for Johnson, although he could hit, he was more a scientist than slugger, so he was never going to be wildly popular. He was a gambler's fighter because he was a safe bet, but gamblers were no longer the predominant or sole patrons of boxing, particularly in Philadelphia.

> A few years ago and in fact up to very recently there were certain qualities which every boxer needed in order to win favor in the eyes of the sporting fraternity. A man was expected to know how to hit straight and clean and be quick on his feet. He must have a good defense and be able to take care of himself in dangerous company in order not to sacrifice the money which his friends and backers had bet on him – in other words, the man who was considered to be best able to acquire preferment was the scientific boxer who could hit hard.

However, with reduced wagering, things had changed. Gamblers were no longer the main source of backing or income for fighters. The boxers were paid according to their ability to draw spectators, rather than their ability to win, and the boxers who drew the best crowds were the action fighters, those who could hit fast and keep on hitting, regardless of their quality or skill levels. Some fighters who drew well did not strike decisive blows to vital areas or have good judgment of distance, balance, or defense. These fighters were able to utilize action-packed styles effectively in short 6-round bouts, whereas if the bouts were longer they might grow fatigued or be struck by enough telling blows that eventually might knock them out. Regardless, as long as the public kept paying to see such bouts, the managers would give it to them. Jack Johnson was not that type of fighter.

The local Philadelphia lovers of skilled generalship wanted to see longer bouts, but the politicians would not allow it. "In spite of the crooked politicians who attempt to make capital out of the suppression of boxing, as if the sport was criminal in its every aspect, the game of fisticuffs seems to get stronger in popularity with the American people."

Illinois had a tough anti-prize-fight law which allowed boxing to be stopped at the pleasure of police officials. It too only allowed 6-round bouts, though with a decision. The present Chicago mayor had been elected by promising the city's sporting fraternity that he would allow the utmost liberality in interpreting the laws relating to boxing. However, after the election, he forgot his promises and clamped down on boxing. As a result, in the most recent election, the Chicago sporting men turned against the mayor's friends who were running for office and helped defeat them. A recent petition secured over 40,000 signatures asking that boxing be allowed.[636]

On December 20, 1905 in San Francisco, the winter's biggest fight took place before a crowd of 8,000 fans. 28-year-old Philadelphia Jack O'Brien won the world light-heavyweight championship by defeating 42-year-old Bob Fitzsimmons, when Bob retired following the conclusion the 13th round. O'Brien had dropped Fitz in the 3rd and 8th rounds en route to the victory.

The victory made O'Brien a big star, although he was already a big name in boxing. Some even said that O'Brien should be considered the heavyweight champion, because when Jeffries retired the title reverted back to the previous title-holder, which was Fitz, so O'Brien's victory over Bob made him champion. Others recognized Marvin Hart. Still others felt that James Jeffries would be champion for as long as he was alive. Eventually, when O'Brien refused to fight Hart, fewer recognized O'Brien.

Jack Johnson wanted to fight Jack O'Brien. His manager, Zeke Abrams, put up $2,500 as a side bet. He noted that Young Peter Jackson had defeated O'Brien once, and Johnson had handled Jackson easily. He was certain that Johnson

Philadelphia Jack O'Brien

could whip O'Brien. The *Los Angeles Times* opined, "A contest between O'Brien and Johnson would be an exhibition of boxing well worth seeing, as both are scientific fighters of the highest class."

However, even O'Brien refused to fight Johnson, and drew the color line. "O'Brien refuses absolutely to fight Jack Johnson at any time. He says Johnson would not be a drawing card, and besides he has drawn the color line." Yet, O'Brien had fought other black boxers.

Johnson paid a visit to the *Police Gazette* office in New York. "Jack doesn't understand why O'Brien should draw the color line since he whipped Fitzsimmons seeing that he fought George Cole, Black Bill and many other colored aspirants within the past five years."[637]

[636] *Philadelphia Record*, December 3, 1905.
[637] *Los Angeles Times*, January 3, 1906; *Los Angeles Herald*, January 7, 1906; *Police Gazette*, January 27, 1906.

415

O'Brien's color-line stance was inconsistent and selective. He once had drawn the color-line against Joe Walcott. The *Police Gazette* had then said, "The Philadelphian bases his refusal on Walcott's color, but he probably has another reason."[638] O'Brien eventually fought Walcott in a 1902 6-round no-decision bout.

Race politics were alive and well. In Kansas, the Wichita Board of Education had passed unanimously a regulation to take steps to establish separate schools for negroes and whites. There were over 300 negroes enrolled in the schools there.[639]

THE WAYS OF THE HEATHERN.

"WHATSOEVER YE WOULD THAT MEN DO UNTO YOU, DO YE EVEN SO UNTO THEM."

Is this the way for Christian Nations to aid in bringing---"Peace on Earth, Good Will to Men?"

Freeman, December 23, 1905

---

[638] *National Police Gazette,* October 19, 1901.
[639] *Topeka State Journal,* January 3, 1906.

At that time, a 1905 popular novel called *The Clansman: An Historical Romance of the Ku Klux Klan*, by Thomas Dixon, Jr., a Baptist minister and former North Carolina state legislator, had been converted into a play, and was set to start performances in New York on January 9, 1906. *The Clansman* was influential in putting forth the ideology that helped support the Klan. It portrayed blacks as inferior to whites, and advocated to Northerners to maintain racial segregation; the point being that when blacks were freed, they turned savage, robbed and plundered from whites, and when allowed to hold public office, over-taxed the people and enacted laws that encouraged interracial marriage. The Klan needed to be organized to overthrow the Republicans, restore white supremacy, and ensure that blacks be kept separate from whites. It was predicated upon the theory that the Negro was unfit for citizenship. The book and play were so popular that they later inspired D. W. Griffith's 1915 film, *The Birth of a Nation*. Many whites declared the play to be a true epic of the South. However, it aroused a storm of protests from blacks, who attacked it as ridiculously false.

KEEPING HIM PLUMP.

Freeman, December 2, 1905

The *Freeman* concluded that Dixon, Jr. was using the play to argue that "neither religion or education, or both combined, can make men of that part of the human family which God made black instead of white." Although Dixon was a minister who preached the gospel, his play was inflaming "the passions of the white race to murder the black people." It called him a dangerous character who was rousing up the blood of both races with his work.[640]

After color-line advocate Marvin Hart had been dropped in the 1st round en route to scoring a KO2 over Pat Callahan on January 15, 1906 in Butte, Montana, the local press said,

> After last night's exhibition Hart will have to show the Butte fans before he can pose as a champion. They no longer doubt but that Jack Johnson and Jack Root both had him jabbed to death as was reported when he fought those men, and that it was only his ability to stand punishment that enabled him to defeat them.[641]

Hart was scheduled to defend his heavyweight crown against Tommy Burns, whose original name was Noah Brusso. *Police Gazette* writer Sam Austin called Burns the "dago with the Irish patronymic." Burns was coming off a decision loss to Jack Sullivan at middleweight, but claimed that the reason for the loss was that he was weight drained. He claimed that he would be much stronger and have better condition at a higher weight. Some thought that Hart would have his work cut out for him when he met Burns. "In fact had it not been for his bout with Twin Sullivan, in which he was outboxed and outfought, Brusso's chances would look pretty fair, at that." However, others thought that the former middleweight simply would be too small for Hart. Burns had demonstrated skill and toughness in his Los Angeles bouts, and perhaps more importantly, he was a gate draw, so promoter Tom McCarey made a title fight with him as the challenger. Hart probably took the fight because he figured that a man whose last bout was fought at 158 pounds was too small to defeat him.[642]

So, once again, instead of being given an opportunity at the crown, Jack Johnson had to sit by as a former middleweight who was coming off a loss in a 158-pound bout was granted a world heavyweight title shot. Imagine the frustration.

The day after Hart-Callahan, on Tuesday January 16, 1906 in New York, before the Sharkey Athletic Club on West 65th street, Jack Johnson again met Joe Jeannette, this time in a 3-round no-decision bout. At that time, New York was only allowing very short 3- or 4-round no-decision bouts. To market the bout, it was said that they recently had fought two hard battles in Philadelphia, and as both bouts were hard-fought, this one should be exciting as well.

[640] *Freeman*, January 6, 1906; *Topeka Plaindealer*, March 2, 1906.
[641] *Butte Intermountain*, January 16, 1906.
[642] *Police Gazette*, February 3, 1906.

After their last fight in December, that same month, Joe Jeannette had scored a KO2 over Walter Johnson and stopped 22-year-old black middleweight Sam Langford, who retired after the 8th round. To that point, Langford had nearly 50 bouts of experience, so it was a quality victory for Jeannette.[643]

The *New York World* reported that Johnson vs. Jeannette was a very close 3-round main event bout, but Johnson seemed to have the better of it towards the end. It was interesting from the tap of the gong until the end. Honors were even in the first two rounds. Jeannette was the aggressor, and landed many stiff jabs in Johnson's face, and also banged him hard in the body. Johnson returned those blows by countering hard with left swings to the face and stiff uppercuts on the body. In the last round, Johnson had the best of the fighting, landing many hard smashes to the face and wind at close quarters.[644]

According to the New York-based *Police Gazette*, Johnson had a 30-pound weight advantage and stood a head taller than the middleweight-sized Jeannette. Therefore, Jeannette surprised the spectators with his good showing. Its report mirrored the *World's* account.[645]

The *Day*, a New London, Connecticut-based newspaper, said Johnson was too fast for Jeannette, and easily outpointed him. From the standpoint of cleverness, it was one of the prettiest bouts ever seen between big fellows. Both did exceptionally clever blocking and hitting. Several times in the 1st round Johnson landed clean jabs without receiving a return. Club members cheered. In the 2nd round, Johnson danced in and out with great rapidity, and each time landed jabs and swings to the head and face. Joe came back with a strong rally and landed two lefts to the face. Jack had the better of it for the rest of the round. In the 3rd, both landed hard wallops to the body, but Jeannette experienced difficulty in reaching his shifty opponent, who seemed to have wings on his shoes. At the bell, they were boxing fast and hard. "Johnson had a big lead."[646]

On January 25, 1906 in San Diego, Sam McVey scored a KO4 over Denver Ed Martin.

---

[643] *Police Gazette*, January 13, 1906.
[644] *New York World,* January 16, 17, 1906.
[645] *Police Gazette*, February 3, 1906.
[646] *Day*, January 17, 1906.

CHAPTER 19

A New Champion

Jack Johnson continually was looking for respect as the legitimate top contender to the crown, but he had to deal with the color-line drawn by champion Marvin Hart. Also, many reporters did not think he had done enough to earn a title shot. The *Los Angeles Examiner* said, "Jack Johnson might have forced a fight had he been willing to do his best against other heavyweights, but by his fights with Sandy Ferguson and Marvin Hart he lost all chance to be considered a coming champion in his class."[647] Regardless, on paper, he was far more qualified to fight for the title than the man against whom Hart was about to defend.

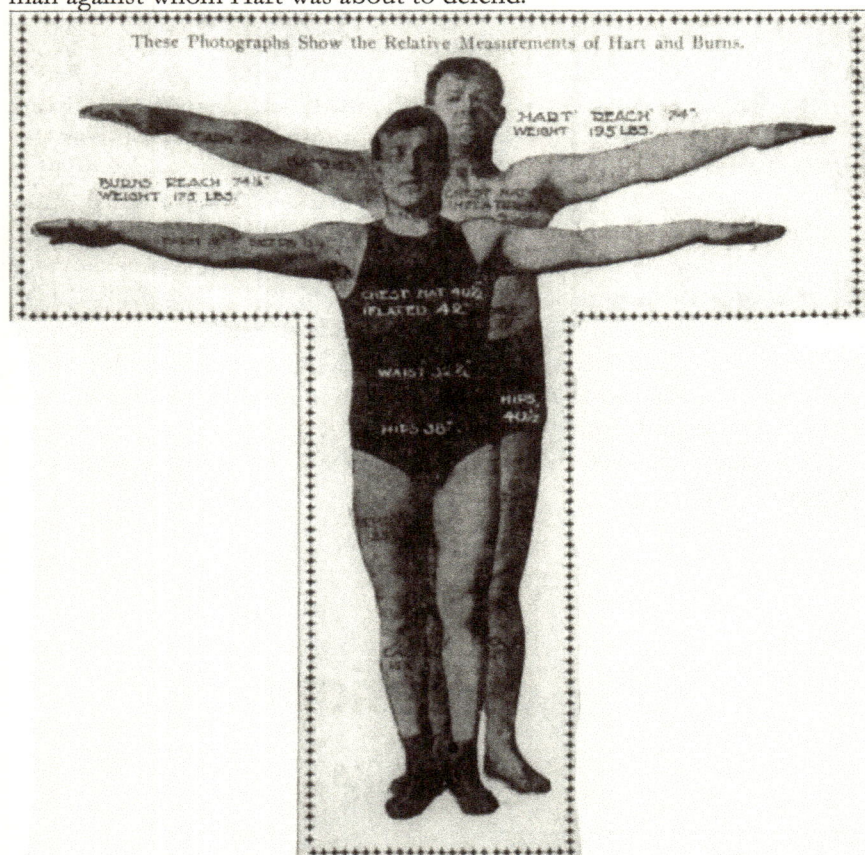

These Photographs Show the Relative Measurements of Hart and Burns.

---

[647] *Los Angeles Examiner*, February 7, 1906.

On February 23, 1906 in Los Angeles, before a crowd of 5,000 people, 175-pound Tommy Burns won the world heavyweight championship when he won a clear 20-round decision over 195-pound Marvin Hart.

According to the *Los Angeles Express*, Hart, the "so called heavyweight champion," made a "wretched showing." Burns used straight lefts to the face and then bore into repeated clinches. He "stepped in and out at will, sending lefts to the big fellow's nose, eyes and jaw and he hugged his way into the clinches, danced tantalizingly before the helpless bulk in front of him and grinned at his seconds." Burns suffered little to no damage, whereas Hart had a cut, swollen, and bleeding face, and "he spit blood from the bruises on his lips." At the end of the fight, it was obvious that Burns had won, and there was no doubt about the decision even before the referee raised his arm.[648]

The *Los Angeles Times* harshly called Hart a "monumental dub" and a "big stiff." On the other hand, Burns was "quick, active, strong, confident and courageous." Before the fight, it was even money that Burns would not last 15 rounds. However, "if they saw the fight…it was even money that Hart would not last twenty rounds from the beating the little man gave him from the third round to the finish." It was "practically Burns all the way," and it was "like a fox fighting a dog. It was a battle of a big man against a little one who jumped in and jabbed and then jumped away or hugged himself safe into a clinch."[649]

The *Los Angeles Examiner* said,

> Burns is a quick, shifty fellow, who can hit and go away or hit and go in as suits his pleasure. … He could hit Hart wherever and whenever he pleased. But aside from bringing the superficial blood from a cut eye and a bruised nose, he made no impression on the mistaken Kentuckian. Hart was merely tired at the end of the twenty rounds of futile efforts. He wasn't hurt, notwithstanding the blood that flowed from his skin-deep wounds. One could not help thinking as he watched the one-sided contest that if a less aggressive man than Burns were in the ring with Hart there would be no battle at all. It would be a walking argument, with Hart looking vicious and doing nothing at all.

Burns was both game and smart. "He went in and fought, and when fighting seemed to him too hazardous, he grappled and ducked. … It was hit and hug with Burns through the long, dreary twenty rounds." Because Burns was so much smaller, the crowd supported him even though he clinched a great deal. "Plainly, too, it was because whatever else he did he would fight some."

Another *Examiner* reporter harshly said that a "second-rate" middleweight had made the heavyweight title-claimant look like an amateur.

---

[648] *Los Angeles Express*, February 24, 1906.
[649] *Los Angeles Daily Times*, February 24, 1906.

"The reign of the Pretender is over. If Marvin Hart ever had the slightest claim on the heavyweight title, he lost it last night."

> For twenty rounds Tommy Burns made Hart look like the rawest kind of an amateur, feinting him into knots, jabbing him dizzy with straight lefts and wrestling him fairly off his feet the rest of the time. Burns fought a great defensive fight. He took no chances. It was jab and clinch, jab and clinch, and Referee Eyton wore himself out tearing Burns away from his victim. ...
>
> There was only one spot in the whole affair which closely resembled a real fight. It came in the fourteenth round. Burns stood up and began to slug and for fifteen seconds he rocked the big fellow with rights and lefts to the jaw. It was plain fighting, but Hart seemed unable to block any of the blows and Burns battered him dizzy before he backed away.

W. W. Naughton said,

> Burns didn't prove that he was a fighter. He simply proved that the other man was no fighter. He prevented Hart from fighting. ... Mr. Hart of Kentucky didn't place one good wallop.
>
> Burns had a trick of rasping his forearm against Hart's nose before diving into a clinch, and he made the clinches so frequent that the bout resembled a wrestling match more than a scrap with gloves.
>
> At no time was there a good, honest exchange of blows. Burns acted like a man who was there to stay the twenty rounds and to do just enough to keep in favor with the referee. ... Hart...was very willing. He slugged and cuffed, but he failed to accomplish anything. There was never a time when there was an air of despondency about the big Kentuckian. He seemed to be thoroughly imbued with pride and self-reliance; but his failure to accomplish things was piteous. ...
>
> As a rule, the winner of any kind of athletic event is cheered and his victory carries with it a certain degree of credit and glory. About the only thing accomplished was to show that Marvin Hart is a poor apology as a world's champion. ...
>
> Burns is built on the Sharkey order. ... He is very quick on his feet and very tricky. As shown by his fight with Hart, his aim appears to be to prevent himself being hurt rather than to hurt his opponent. ...
>
> The contest exploits the hopelessness of the heavyweight situation. ... Hart has little to commend him apart from his willingness, while Burns is simply a catch-as-can artist.
>
> Jack O'Brien is easily the master of either of the participants in last night's battle. As for Jim Jeffries, it would be downright cruelty to send him into the ring with either man.

The gist of the whole story is that the only heavyweights in sight are Jack O'Brien, Al Kauffmann and Sam Berger. O'Brien has already won from Kauffmann, but if the San Francisco promoters can bring about a match between Kauffmann and Berger the winner will be a worthy opponent of the gentleman from Philadelphia.[650]

The *Los Angeles Herald* was extremely high on Burns' performance. It said Burns outpointed, outfought, and outgeneraled Hart in every round to earn a decisive victory and the heavyweight championship of the world. Burns "won all the way, having a distinct advantage in every round." Tommy's footwork was a "revelation," and he gave the "prettiest exhibition ever seen in Los Angeles." What Burns lacked in weight and height he made up for in footwork, speed, gameness, and skill.[651]

Some did not want to accept Burns as the new champion. The *San Francisco Bulletin* said Jack O'Brien came closest to having the right to being called champion.[652]

However, in the days subsequent to the bout, the *Los Angeles Herald* fully supported Tommy, saying,

> Some disappointed fans are prone to scoff at the new heavyweight champion, Tommy Burns, and belittle his claims upon the title, yet his claim is ten times stronger than was that of Marvin Hart. ... If Hart was entitled to make the claim, Burns has demonstrated that he is more entitled to the honor, as he clearly outfought, outpointed and outgeneraled Hart at every point of their battle Friday night, unmercifully whipped the Kentuckian and emerged from the battle with not a scar or bruise. ... Burns was a revelation to the fans who have made the same mistake all along that the former champion made, that of holding him too cheaply and belittling his abilities as a battler. ...

> Burns fought Hart in much the same manner that Jack O'Brien fought Bob Fitzsimmons. Criticism of Burns' tactics is, therefore, criticism of O'Brien's methods. O'Brien, however, was much sung about for his speedy footwork and cleverness in avoiding punishment, while Burns is roundly criticized by a few who are, probably, incited by the pangs of disappointment.

> Hart was made to look like an amateur overgrown boy fighter because Burns clearly outclassed him at every point. Because Hart

---

[650] *Los Angeles Examiner*, February 24, 1906. Comparing Burns with a catch-as-can artist meant that Burns simply was concerned with winning the fight, regardless of the style employed.
[651] *Los Angeles Herald*, February 24, 1906.
[652] *San Francisco Bulletin*, February 25, 1906.

was so greatly outclassed, it cheapened the victory of Burns in some minds and robs him of much of the glory of the battle.[653]

The *Herald* argued, "Those who accepted Hart as champion must also accept Burns as the new champion." It noted that both Fitzsimmons and O'Brien, believed to be the top contenders to the title, had sidestepped Hart. Burns had met and defeated him in a one-sided affair when others had been reluctant to enter the ring with Marvin after he had knocked out the respected Root. "By defeating Hart, Burns becomes champion of the world in the heavyweight division, and none can gainsay his claim upon the title since Jeffries has retired and refuses to further defend his claim."

Few had given Burns a chance to defeat Hart, "just as they now hoot at his claims and scout the ability of the new champion to defend his title. Burns announces that he will defend the title against all comers." Tom said he was willing to fight Al Kaufman or Sam Berger, "both of whom have been suggested by the wiseacres of the game as more entitled to fight for the title than Burns, and Burns says he will fight both of them ten rounds on the same night if allowed thirty minutes between battles." Burns was also confident that he could defeat Jack O'Brien.[654]

Johnson was irked by the denial of an opportunity to win the championship. He felt that he had defeated Hart, yet Hart obtained the title shot, and then refused to face Johnson again owing to his color. Then a former middleweight who had lost his previous bout at middleweight secured a heavyweight title shot and now was world champion.

It also had to be very frustrating for Johnson to hear about Burns using a defensive style and strategy similar in many respects to his own, yet Burns won the decision against Hart, whereas he did not. Burns had used defensive footwork and clinching tactics to neutralize Hart. Tom also had outlanded the champion, primarily using the jab. Similar things were said about Johnson's performance against Hart, yet Johnson took some heat for his methods, whereas Burns' performance received much greater plaudits, and the referee's decision. Race likely played a factor in the varying perceptions. Regardless, several analysts said Burns had defeated Hart more convincingly and thoroughly than had Johnson.

The *San Francisco Bulletin* said the San Francisco public had been unable to forget Hart's bout with Jack Johnson, who "outpointed him," despite the referee's decision. "That one fight cooked Hart's goose with local fight fans as far as taking him seriously as a champion." Still, it was said that Burns had made Marvin look even worse.

Initially, Tommy Burns did not draw the color line. He said,

> I am willing to fight any man in the world, bar Jim Jeffries, and just say for me I think Jeff is a class by himself. I do not draw the color line. If Jack Johnson, Jack O'Brien or any other fighter in the world

[653] *Los Angeles Herald*, February 25, 1906.
[654] *Los Angeles Herald*, February 25, 1906.

wants to meet me I will be ready to talk business in a couple weeks. Heretofore I have gone out of my class and weakened myself fighting at the middleweight limit. I was twenty pounds heavier tonight and fought stronger than ever before.[655]

However, despite what he said, Burns did not make a match with Johnson.

In subsequent days and weeks, Johnson vainly attempted to obtain matches with white heavyweights, including Jack O'Brien. None would fight him. Again, the decision in the Hart bout was acknowledged to have been a "raw bit of work. Johnson won a block."

At that time, the fight that the white press and public most wanted to see, and which would generate the most revenue, was Burns-O'Brien. "If Burns meets and defeats O'Brien he will have a clear and undisputed right to the title." The fight had the feel of a unification match. Negotiations would be ongoing for several months.[656]

The new world heavyweight champion, Tommy Burns

[655] *San Francisco Bulletin*, February 24, 1906.
[656] *Los Angeles Herald*, March 25, 27, 1906.

CHAPTER 20

Status Quo –
Staying Busy in the East

Frozen out of the heavyweight championship title picture, instead, Jack Johnson arranged a scheduled 15-round bout to be held in mid-March 1906 in Baltimore against Joe Jeannette, who was "conceded to be the best of the colored boxers in the light-heavyweight division." Jeannette had been having the same trouble in obtaining matches. "The old cry of the color line has been the howl raised every time." Jeannette instilled enough fear into white heavyweights such that they had to use the color line to avoid meeting him. Hence, he and Johnson were fighting each other again.

The *Baltimore Sun* said, "Everything that Johnson does in the ring is noted all over the country, because he is believed by many to be the only possible successor to Champion James Jeffries at this stage of affairs." Promoting the upcoming fight, it noted that in short-rounds bouts, Johnson had not been able to defeat Jeannette decisively, meaning knock him out. This bout of longer length would be a better measure of their relative merits.

Both were conceded to be the best colored boxers.

> Johnson is well known the country over as one of the best colored heavyweights who ever stepped between the ropes. His color has been a serious handicap against him, and he has had great trouble in arranging matches. ... Jeffries would not grant Johnson a match, although the followers of the sport were anxious for it.

They were well matched. Johnson had a little advantage in weight, though their height and reach were said to be practically on even terms. A "little weight in men of that size makes but little difference."

Johnson was listed as 28 years old, 205 pounds, and 6'1" tall, with a reach of 74 ¾". His neck was 18 inches, chest 44 inches, waist 34.5 inches, thigh 25, and calf 17.5 inches. Jeannette was listed as 24 years old (he was actually 26), 185 pounds, 6-feet tall, with a 79-inch reach (giving Joe the 4-inch reach advantage over Johnson), 18 ¼-inch neck, 45-inch chest, 33 ¼-inch waist, 24-inch thigh, and 17-inch calf.[657]

On Wednesday March 14, 1906 in Baltimore, before the Eureka Athletic Club at the Germania Maennerchor Hall, Jack Johnson and Joe Jeannette

---

[657] *Baltimore American, Baltimore Sun*, March 12 - 14, 1906. Johnson had been training in New York.

boxed for the fifth time. Johnson appeared to have advantages of height, reach, and weight. He was seconded by Kid Sullivan, Sammy Harris, "Snowball," and Walter Bryan, while Jeannette was looked after by Billy Armstrong, Draggs Watkins and Harry Lyons. A big crowd was present. They agreed to break at the referee's order, and to break clean.

The *Baltimore American* said Johnson won the 15-round decision, but only by a small margin, as Jeannette was there at all stages of the game. No harm was done by either, and neither showed any marks. Fred Swigert refereed and rendered the decision after a close contest.

Johnson was the cleverer and landed more often, outpointing Jeannette, who was eager to mix it. They mixed at a fast clip throughout, but neither had a punch that would cause the other any worry. Johnson landed to the face and body, but did not make Jeannette uneasy in the least. Joe fought back in the same manner and gave Johnson a stiff argument. They were just as fresh at the end as they were at the start. There was no particularly exciting feature to the bout.[658]

The *Baltimore Sun* said Johnson boxed with Jeannette but did no fighting. Johnson had the reputation, while Jeannette was trying to earn one for himself. Before a packed house, Johnson did not add to his reputation, and Jeannette made none. It was mostly a boxing exhibition.

> There was not a really hard round fought, though there were many grand-stand plays and slappings of open gloves, which called for and received applause. Neither man was hurt or took a chance of being hurt unless he was crossed, and there was an absence of crossing.
>
> The exhibition of boxing was, however, a good one. Jeannette is at least 25 pounds the smaller man. He is not clever, though he is a well built light heavyweight.
>
> It looked as if Johnson should have stopped or put out his man in quick order. He looked to be able to do this, but there was no occasion for him to do it. He got the decision at the end of the fifteenth round and had not distressed his man. Johnson was considerate. Jeannette has to make a living and Johnson and he can double up and give nice exhibitions, such as they gave last night.[659]

Hence, this account felt that Johnson carried Jeannette and had done just enough to remain in the lead and earn the decision without taking any risks.

The non-local *Police Gazette* offered a totally different perspective. It said the men fought like demons. Jeannette, although outclassed, kept up in wonderful style and stood toe-to-toe with Johnson, exchanging wallops. Johnson's most effective attack was a short right uppercut to the jaw. He used this time and time again until he had Jeannette groggy. Jeannette was cut to ribbons at the end of the fight, and opinion was that it was doubtful

[658] *Baltimore American*, March 15, 1906.
[659] *Baltimore Sun*, March 15, 1906.

if he could have lasted another round. Several times, Johnson claimed that Jeannette was fouling by striking low, but the referee refused to do anything except caution the offender. Jeannette disputed the decision and wanted another crack at Johnson in a 20-round bout.[660]

Two weeks later, on March 28, 1906 in San Diego, California, heavyweight champion Tommy Burns fought two men in one night, scoring 1st round knockouts over both 190-pound Jim O'Brien and 180-pound James Walker. The Canadian native Burns, a "Detroit Italian," was called game, willing, and powerful, for weighing only 175 pounds, he had defeated a 205-pound Hart, as well as two other bigger men.[661]

As It Appears.

The People of Danville, Va. Took the Matter in Hand and Found that the. "Transgressors Were but a Handful of Young Men Who Took it Upon Themselves to Regulate the Community."—Indianapolis News.

Freeman, **April 21, 1906**

[660] *Police Gazette*, March 31, 1906.
[661] *Police Gazette*, May 12, 1906.

The *Topeka Plaindealer* was advising blacks to leave Texas, where Jack Johnson grew up, for it was no place for decent people to reside. "The Negro must go to places where he will be recognized as a man, but as Texas is so close to hell, we advise the Negro to stay away."[662]

Texas was not the only place where it was difficult for blacks to live. Lynchings were frequent throughout the South. During Easter weekend, on April 14, 1906 in Springfield, Missouri, a white mob broke into the jail, seized three black men and lynched them in the public square. It all began when a white woman and her male friend alleged that they had been assaulted and the woman raped by two black men on the night of Good Friday.

Despite the fact that the men allegedly wore masks, so there wasn't much of a description, the police found two black men and arrested them. Their foreman gave them an alibi and vouched for them, saying they had been loading freight all night long and had been with him, so it could not have been them. They were released.

However, a few hours later, the men were re-arrested, supposedly for their own protection, as rumors grew that a lynch mob was forming. Eventually, the mob descended upon and broke into the jail, took the suspects, and hung them from the Gottfried Tower in the Park Central Square, which ironically had a replica of the Statue of Liberty atop it. The men were then burned, and then dismembered by members of the mob, who took body parts as souvenirs.

The mob later also took a third black man who was in the jail being held as a suspect on a murder charge (who claimed he was innocent and named the man who actually committed the crime), and did the same to him.

Ironically, in the process, owing to the fact that the mob so badly wrecked the jail, 14 prisoners escaped.

The next day was Easter Sunday. The Missouri governor sent in troops from the state militia to prevent further violence.[663]

On April 21, 1906, the Missouri-based *Sedalia Weekly Conservator* quoted the *Kansas City Journal*, discussing what was called the "Bad Nigger."

> "Bad niggers," are only children in morals and intellect, but all that is brutal and cruel development to adult standard. It is the "bad nigger" that is responsible for most of the prejudice against the race. He is usually addicted to cocaine or whiskey, or both. He insists upon taking advantage of every opportunity to annoy a white man or woman if he thinks he can do so safely. ... [T]he "bad nigger" has not ordinary sense. ... The "bad nigger" is more of an enemy to the Negroes than the whites, as intolerable as he is to the latter. Race wars are started by the "bad nigger," and many innocent colored men and women are made to suffer through the conduct of one such

662 *Topeka Plaindealer*, March 30, 1906.
663 *New York Times*, April 16, 1906.

specimen. The three men lynched by the Springfield mob were probably innocent of the specific crime for which they paid the penalty, yet they were all known as "bad niggers," and it was apparently the mob's conclusion that if they were not guilty of the specified crime they should be killed on general principles. ... The Negroes themselves should take every reasonable precaution to allay feeling against them. They should do every thing possible to subdue the "bad nigger" who seeks to stir up strife. If the "bad nigger" were eliminated from the race problem there would be few lynchings and far less prejudice against the blacks.

The white-owned *Kansas City Journal*, in another one of its editorials, did not blame the white mob for its lawlessness, but instead blamed the officers of the law for failing to do their duty, as well as the town's Negro residents.

The Negroes, as a race, must shoulder their share of the responsibility for the crimes that led to the Springfield riot, because they are too tender with the lawless element of their own race. ... If they wish to win the respect of the white race they must show they are worthy by frowning down crime and ostracizing the criminals who disgrace them. Instead, too often the tendency is to defend the bad Negro, and to shield them from punishment.

In its scathing response, the black-owned *Topeka Plaindealer* said the *Kansas City Journal* was not only unfair, but created prejudice instead of quieting it. It blamed the one-sided views of white newspapers for the deaths of many blacks. It noted the utter failure to blame the vigilante white offenders who broke the law in several ways. Law-abiding Negroes were not responsible for the alleged crimes committed by low Negroes any more than the respectable class of whites was responsible for the crimes committed by their worthless class.

In reference to the colored people wishing to win the respect of the white race, we wish to inform you that if the respect of that class of white people that lynched these men of Springfield, is the standard to which you wish the black people to rise, you may as well stop wishing, for we are far superior to them and do not wish respect or anything else from such a class of thugs and hoodlums. Respectability is due any man who respects himself and the rights of others. ... It is an injustice to charge every crime that is committed to the bad colored people, and have it go down in history as sanctioned by the whole race. ...

This lynching and burning is due, to a certain extent, to the white newspapers, who aid and abet this class of lawless white men who commit these offenses, as well as give encouragement to the officers who are lax in their duties. The white newspapers are responsible for the majority of the lynching and burning in this country, and until they change their attitude toward those who are only accused of committing these offenses, the colored people must get their Winchesters, put them in their homes and be prepared for the emergency in all cases as they arise.[664]

About a month later, a special grand jury found that the victims of the Springfield mob had not been guilty of any crimes. The Negroes that were hung were innocent; and no assault upon the white woman was ever committed. Further, it found that the sheriff, his deputies, and the police department were negligent in the performance of their duties. There was even testimony that the police officers and the city marshal stood on the corner of the street and square, laughing and talking while the mob was conducting its final lynching.[665]

APPARENT CO-OPERATION.

The Most Lynchings Occur After the Accused Is Under the "Protection" of the Law.

Freeman, September 1, 1906

---

[664] *Topeka Plaindealer*, April 27, 1906.
[665] *Topeka Plaindealer*, May 25, 1906.

Eventually, 18 men were indicted for the lynchings, but none were convicted.

Fearing for their safety, blacks left the town in droves, dropping the black population of Springfield, Missouri from 20% to 2%. The desired effect was achieved. To this day, even over a century later, there are relatively few blacks in Springfield, Missouri, at about 4% of the population.

Jack Johnson's relative merits were constantly debated. Some lauded him, while others criticized him, particularly on the West Coast. The *Los Angeles Herald* said,

> Jack Johnson, the negro heavyweight champion, would have a greater chance with Jeff than any of the white battlers now in sight, but Johnson has never shown anything that would entitle him to the slightest consideration as an opponent of Jeff. Jeff would make him jump out of the ring inside of two rounds.[666]

One month after the Jeannette bout, and two days after the Springfield, Missouri lynchings, on Monday April 16, 1906, near Pittston, Pennsylvania, just outside of Wilkes-Barre, Jack Johnson took on Philadelphia's Black Bill for the fourth time. Since last boxing Johnson, Bill's career had included: 1905 LKOby7 and D6 Joe Jeannette; and 1906 LND6 Morris Harris.

The *Wilkes-Barre Times* reported that it was a scheduled 10-round bout. Only Philadelphia had the 6-round limitation, for each city was free to set its own limit. It said Johnson clearly outclassed Black Bill until Jack knocked Bill down for the full count in the 7th round. Buck Kelly of Pittston refereed.

The nearby *Scranton Republican* provided a more detailed account, and it said Bill was knocked out in the 6th round. From the first tap of the gong in the 1st round, Johnson mercilessly hammered and pounded on Bill, continuing to do so throughout. However, Bill gave one of the best exhibitions of pluck and endurance ever seen, suffering gamely until he was just about out in the 5th round. "Black Bill would have been counted out in the fifth round had not the bell saved him."

When the bell rang to start the 6th round, it was evident that Bill had not recovered from the terrible 5th round beating. 20 seconds into the 6th round, Bill sank to the floor "as helpless as a babe," for he could no longer stand up under the punishment. He was knocked out.

This local newspaper argued that Johnson had "proved his right to the title" of colored heavyweight champion, for he was "in a class entirely by himself." Bill did not land 10 blows during the whole fight. He was outclassed and could do nothing with Johnson, although he fought the best that he could. This writer said Bill had nothing to be ashamed of, for with the exception of Jeffries, Johnson could do the same thing to any man. "Johnson showed himself to be one of the cleverest men in the ring today

---

[666] *Los Angeles Herald*, April 2, 1906.

and has a punch in either hand that will bring home the money almost every time."[667]

On April 18, 1906, a huge, approximately 7.9 earthquake rocked San Francisco, and that, along with the resulting fires, destroyed nearly two-thirds of the city and left it in ruins. At least 3,000 people were killed, and 300,000 were left homeless. The losses were estimated to be 500 million dollars.

Jack Johnson was scheduled to box Sam Langford 15 rounds at Chelsea, Massachusetts, the bout to be held a mere nine days after Johnson's victory over McCormick. "Sam Langford, who has shown his willingness to box anyone in the world, and is now boxing in great form, has another tough match on for April 26 at the Lincoln club."

Langford was well-liked as a fighter, but most of the elite white boxers had drawn the color line on him. "As there are no colored boxers of his weight worthy of a chance against him, he was asked if he would meet Johnson." Langford replied, "You go and get Johnson and I'll meet him."

Johnson, who was in Scranton, accepted the offer to fight in Chelsea, just outside of Boston, which was Langford's residence. Hence, Sam would be the hometown favorite. "It is a big contract for Langford, for Johnson showed here twice that he was a very clever boxer, and besides he will have at least 20 pounds advantage over Langford." Yet, the very game Langford was confident that he would win.[668]

Sam Langford was a very talented 23-year-old fighter. He claimed to have been boxing since the age of 16, and had been boxing as a professional since 1902. To that point, Langford had over 50 known pro bouts of experience under his belt. The 5'7" Langford started his career as a lightweight, but consistently put on solid muscle-mass over the next several years. Like Burns, although he was relatively short, Langford had long arms.

In 1903, a 140-pound Langford won a 15-round decision over then world lightweight champion Joe Gans in a non-title bout. This was significant, because Gans was considered the best or one of the world's best fighters, regardless of weight, or what we would call today the pound-for-pound best. Gans had over 120 victories to his credit to that point, and would be lightweight champion for many years, from 1902 to 1908.

Other Langford results included: 1903 D12 Jack Blackburn (who years later would become Joe Louis' trainer); and 1904 L10 Dave Holly (a top tier lightweight) and KO2 George McFadden (who had over 70 fights of experience).

In 1904, Langford fought a 15-round draw with then world welterweight champion Joe Walcott, a fighter who himself was good enough to defeat

---

[667] *Wilkes-Barre Times, Scranton Republican*, April 17, 1906. The *Philadelphia Record*, April 19, 1906, said that on April 16 at Wilkes-Barre, PA, Johnson knocked out Black Bill in 6 rounds. Hence, some said it was a KO6, while others said KO7. In the preliminary, Johnson's white sparring partner, Jack Murray, boxed colored fighter Billy Clark to a 6-round draw.
[668] *Boston Globe*, April 16, 1906.

heavyweights and had 88 known victories to his credit. Some said Langford actually outpointed Walcott, but it was called a draw owing to Walcott's aggressiveness.

Langford followed that bout with a 1904 D15 Dave Holly and D15 Jack Blackburn (Langford weighed less than 150 pounds); 1905 D15 Holly (agreed-upon draw if both standing at the finish, though Langford was superior. Langford weighed 154 pounds to Holly's 137), W15 (twice) Young Peter Jackson (the elite middleweight who had over 100 fights of experience. Langford weighed 155 pounds), L15 Larry Temple, ND15 Jack Blackburn, D15 Temple, D10 Blackburn, and D15 Jackson.

In December 1905, against heavyweight Joe Jeannette, Langford retired after the conclusion of the 8th round. Sam followed that with a 1906 KO15 Larry Temple.

On April 5, 1906 in Chelsea, Sam Langford avenged his loss to Joe Jeannette by winning a 15-round decision over him, just a few weeks prior to taking on Johnson. Despite

Sam Langford

the fact that Jeannette had about a 30-pound weight advantage, Langford punished him. In the 7th round, Sam dropped Jeannette with a right. Joe stalled and recovered, and then attacked in the 8th, and Langford had to use his cleverness and footwork to elude Jeannette's swings. However, thereafter, Langford pummeled Jeannette. Joe showed a good flash of fighting in the 14th round, scoring heavily, but Langford made a punching-bag of him in the 15th round, and the verdict for Sam was well received.

Certainly, that victory had to embolden Langford and give him the belief that he could do well with Johnson.[669]

Langford probably weighed around 156 - 160 pounds. Johnson likely outweighed Langford anywhere from 25 - 35 pounds. Some secondary sources report that Johnson was 185 pounds, though he could have been even heavier. Regardless of the weight, Sam was an aggressive, strong, powerful, well-schooled, talented fighter with high-quality experience in the lighter weight divisions, and had just shown that he could compete with and defeat a larger, solid, respected heavyweight.

An April 19, 1906 bout in Chelsea, Massachusetts at the Lincoln Club between Mike Schreck and George Gardner was stopped in the 2nd round under suspicions that it was a fake, because Gardner did not fight and Schreck put little force into his blows, appearing to be taking it easy on him. Both Jack Johnson and Sam Langford, who were present in the audience, offered to step in and fight Schreck, but the club refused to put them on. Schreck claimed to be nursing a hurt hand.[670]

The *Boston Herald* said the upcoming Johnson-Langford bout was intriguing because Johnson was a claimant for the heavyweight title and Langford was one of the best middleweights in the business. The size difference made Johnson the favorite, but the fact that Langford had made a good showing against Jeannette, a much bigger man who had fought competitively with Johnson, made many feel that Sam had a shot with Johnson. Langford also had whipped the highly regarded Walcott. "The bout, in spite of the difference in the size of the pair, should be good. In the past when two colored boxers have been the main attraction, they have not drawn very well, but the chances are that there will be a large crowd present at this bout."[671]

As the fight approached, Johnson was so confident in his ability to defeat Langford that it was opined that extra police might be needed in the West End if he did not refrain from parading his views. The "giant Ethiopian" proclaimed his ability to stop Langford. Such statements nearly caused a riot on Cambridge street, for Langford was the local star and big fan favorite, and they did not care for Johnson's or his admirers' talk. The local Langford fans were sensitive about their man. Arguments regarding the relative merits of the two black fighters were exciting the local colored population. Several sports "had their hands full quieting the Darktown brigade, and yet the interest in the show is at fever heat owing to these clashes."

Johnny Mooney, a local expert who was called one of the best judges in the game, thought that Langford would win the battle. "He thinks that Sam

---

[669] *Police Gazette*, April 21, 1906.
[670] *Boston Globe, Boston Herald*, April 20, 1906. Schreck previously had stopped Gardner in the 20th round in their April 1905 bout.
[671] *Boston Herald*, April 23, 1906.

will win by body blows, and that Johnson is too confident and will consequently be careless."

However, Johnson's training gave no indication of overconfidence. He was not underrating Langford. "Jack is working as hard as if he had a match with Jeffries on."

Joe Walcott, who had fought Langford, and lightweight Jimmy "Kid" Murray, who was scheduled to box on the undercard, were both acting as trainers and sparring partners for Johnson.

A rapid, fierce battle was expected. "Johnson will have fully 20 pounds advantage in weight, but Langford believes he is capable of winning and expresses confidence in his ability to do so." Both men were training hard.[672]

The *Boston Globe* thought that Johnson would have a 40-pound advantage. Still, the bout had the sports guessing. Both pugilists were ready to put up a tough battle. However, ultimately it opined that Langford was due to lose.[673]

The day of the fight, the *Globe* anticipated a large turnout, for the locals believed it to be a good match-up. Both boxers were strong, rushing, hard-hitting, and clever men. The 15-round main event had stirred up an unusual amount of interest.

> A great many sports affect to believe that Johnson will stop Langford before 10 rounds have passed, but Johnson never takes a chance, depending upon his speed and skill to outpoint an opponent. In fact, he is regarded as the best money carrier now in the ring, and he should, by reason of his size and natural advantages, win a verdict over Sam.

Hence, there was some sense that Johnson's natural cautiousness might lead to a decision verdict.

Still, Langford believed that he had the harder punch, and since they would be able to fight at all times under straight Queensberry rules, he felt that he would clout Johnson with a knockout blow at some point.[674]

On Thursday April 26, 1906 before the Lincoln Athletic Club at Chelsea, Massachusetts, the Jack Johnson vs. Sam Langford bout took place.

The *Boston Post* reported that with his cleverness, Langford held his own in the first 3 rounds. Still, Johnson had a slight advantage in the 1st round, and the 2nd was even, but in the 3rd through 5th rounds, Johnson increased his lead.

The contest, for all intents and purposes, was decided in the 6th round, when Johnson twice put Langford to the mat. He decked him for the first time with a right to the heart, and the second time with a right uppercut to

---

[672] *Boston Post*, April 24, 25, 1906.
[673] *Boston Globe*, April 25, 1906.
[674] *Boston Globe*, April 26, 1906.

the chin. Both times, Langford barely beat the count, struggling to his feet at the count of nine. It did not seem possible for him to last out the round, but he stalled and managed to survive.

Thereafter, it became just a question of how long Sam could stay, and how much punishment he could stand. "After the sixth it ceased to be a contest. Langford merely stalled it out, clinching and holding on at every opportunity. ... He let Johnson do all the forcing, countering with a straight left occasionally, and then closing in and hanging on." At times, Johnson looked tired, but it was only from his own exertions.

Summarizing, the *Post* said Langford, the Cambridge lad, went the full 15 rounds, but was beaten badly. It called the bout the most one-sided ever seen at Chelsea. Johnson left the ring without a mark, while Langford's face showed that he had been through a war. Maffitt Flaherty refereed and awarded the 15-round decision to Johnson.

Despite being beaten thoroughly, Langford did manage to impress many with his extraordinary defensive work and his remarkable ability to take punishment.

> It was a wonder that he could stand the beating that Johnson handed him. He was game to the core, and won the cheers of the crowd by his courage and his defensive cleverness. But when that is said nothing more in praise of the bout can be added.
>
> It was too one-sided to be interesting. Johnson outweighed Langford by fully 30 pounds, was a head taller and had six inches more reach.
>
> Johnson didn't try very hard. His superiority was evident from the outset, and he didn't have to.[675]

Offering its version of the fight, the *Boston Globe* said that when Denny Murphy rang the gong to start the bout, the boxers lost no time. They exchanged lefts. Despite the size difference, Langford could reach his taller opponent, and did not back away. He shot his left to the mouth. This caused Johnson to rush to close quarters, sending short rights and lefts to the face. Sam landed some good body blows before they broke.

To start the 2nd round, Johnson rushed at Langford. After he landed two lefts to the face, they mixed it up.

In the 3rd round, Langford landed more often than Johnson did.

It was in the 6th round that it looked to be all over for Langford. After exchanging some lefts, Johnson got mad and rushed at Sam like a tiger. In the mixup, Langford was sent to the floor with a right jolt on the jaw. It looked as though the prediction that Johnson would knock him out had been correct. Sam rose before ten and Johnson tried hard to finish him. Langford recovered and fought back some, and when they broke out of a clinch, Johnson appeared to be about as badly off as Langford. He might have gassed himself trying to finish him.

---

[675] *Boston Post*, April 27, 1906.

Johnson began the 10th round by rushing and sending the left to the face, and in the clinch he landed a couple of rights on the kidneys. Langford returned some hard ones.

In the 15th round, Johnson looked disappointed at not having put Langford away. Referee Maffitt Flaherty declared him the winner, though.

Sandy Ferguson was at ringside, sitting near Johnson's corner. Several times during the bout, by his remarks, it appeared that he was trying to divert Langford's attention from Johnson and rattle him so that Jack could sneak in a blow. Furthermore, the day before, Sandy had gotten into an argument at a hotel with an ex-pugilist and knocked the fellow out. The local paper adversely commented on his conduct.

George Dixon was at ringside as well, and wanted Johnson to win, but conducted himself in a more quiet and sportsmanlike manner. When Ferguson and Joe Walcott, who was in Johnson's corner, got to shouting and hollering too much, Dixon told them both to shut up, as it did not help Johnson gain anything. At first they did not listen, but eventually their shouting subsided when they saw that Dixon meant it.

The overarching theme of the *Globe* article was its belief that with all of his physical advantages, Johnson should have stopped Langford. It said Langford surprised some by lasting so long and going the limit. Johnson won the decision, but it did not add any lustre to his record, whereas Langford earned a lot of credit. He was outweighed by at least 40 pounds and was a head shorter; yet he was good and strong when the bout ended.

Disagreeing with the *Post*, the *Globe* said that in order to stay the limit, Langford did not do a lot of clinching or stalling, but was willing to fight back almost all the time.

In an early round, Langford received a bad wallop on the left eye, which closed it, and that bothered him considerably for the rest of the bout.

Johnson did almost everything he could to put Langford away. He mugged him and held with one hand and hit him with the other. In the clinches, Johnson threw all his weight down onto Sam to tire him out.

> There were times when there was a scared look on Johnson's face, while Langford never once showed signs of flinching, even though blows were being handed to him hot and fast.
>
> Johnson's left hand is his better one. He hooked it over to Sam's face and jaw quite often, and shot it straight to the face or swung it onto the body. Owing to Langford's bad eye Johnson did not have much trouble putting the right on the face and jaw, but there did not seem to be much force behind them.

Langford did not just receive blows all the time, for he jabbed Johnson in the face a number of times and smashed into his body. He also did some good countering and blocking.

Regardless, there was "no question about the decision being a just one, for Johnson certainly outpointed Sam." The spectators had rooted hard for

Langford, and though he left the ring the loser, he was cheered loudly for his gameness.

The *Globe* further opined,

> Though Sam Langford was beaten by Jack Johnson he is held in higher regard by the fans. He proved beyond doubt that he is one of the gamest fighters that ever stepped in the ring. Badly handicapped as he was, he put up a good battle against the odds against him and he gave the fans a big bump by staying the limit.

> Johnson gained no credit by getting the decision, for a man as big as he is and having all the advantages he had, would not have let Langford stay 15 rounds if he was made of championship timber.[676]

Basically it agreed that Johnson had won clearly, but criticized him for not stopping Langford. However, as the future would show, Sam Langford was one tough cookie and not easy for anyone to stop, regardless of size.

The *Boston Herald* said Johnson tried with might to stop the Cambridge middleweight within the 15 rounds, but could not do so. Still, agreeing with the *Post*, the *Herald* also said that Langford took an awful beating. "Langford was hammered as no fighter ever has been hammered in the same number of rounds."

It was not clear whether Johnson had been unable to knock him out because of Langford's ability to take punishment, or because of Johnson's absence of a knockout punch. It said the fact that he went the distance might make it even harder for Langford to obtain matches than it was already. Fighters would know that Langford was tough enough to absorb the punches of even much bigger men.

Regardless, Johnson endured criticism for weighing 195 pounds and not being able to stop a middleweight. "Considering the fact that Langford was nearly 40 pounds lighter and fully a foot shorter this does not add to the credit of Johnson."

The battle itself was "wicked" and "too one-sided to be of interest." The only point of enthusiasm was the fact that Langford was game and tough enough to stay the distance. The betting was all about whether or not Langford could last. No one bet on him to win.

> For a while in the early rounds Langford showed beautifully, using his left in a wonderful manner, but after about the fourth round Johnson began hooking his left to the body and swinging right and left wickedly to the head. In the sixth round Johnson rushed Langford to the ropes, smashed him about the body and wound up with a terrific left hook to the jaw, and Langford went to the mat for the count, laying on his face and apparently all out. But he regained his feet and hugged through the round, but Johnson, with his superior weight and

---

[676] *Boston Globe*, April 27, 1906.

strength, shook Langford off and whaled him viciously and dropped him to the mat again for a few seconds.

From then on the fight was too one sided to be interesting. Johnson closed Langford's left eye and gave him the worst licking a man ever took in the Chelsea ring, and there was never a chance for Langford, though he was game to the finish and flashed occasionally. Langford's face was a sight at the end of the contest, and it is a question as to just how the licking he received last night will affect him in the future.[677]

The local *Boston Journal* echoed that Langford clearly lost, but put up a game fight.

Sam Langford was beaten badly by Jack Johnson at Chelsea last night, but earned the cheers of his admirers and many more besides by a superb exhibition of grit and courage that makes other local exhibitions of gameness in the ring fade almost into insignificance.

He was there all through the fifteen rounds, and saved a lot of money for his friends who had bet that he would last ten rounds, twelve rounds or stay the limit. But it is a question if he were wise, for the beating he took is enough to seriously impair his strength and health.

Most of the punishment was on the head, and so may not have the injurious effect that a severe drubbing on the body would have. Sam didn't have a chance on earth to win, for he was outweighed about thirty-five pounds, and Johnson was too clever, too fast, too heavy, too strong and too powerful in punching for him.

Sam went down three times. On the first occasion it looked as if he slipped or stumbled to his knees, as the accompanying punch was not heavy. He was knocked down with a powerful left hook in the middle of the sixth round and lay on his face. He was down just nine seconds, according to Timekeeper Murphy, a thoroughly honest man, and the referee, Maffit Flaherty, who says he was on his feet at the call of nine, and according to several watches in the hands of men around the ring.

Later on in the same round he was down again for nine seconds. On the first knockdown it looked as if he couldn't continue. But he arose within the specified ten seconds. The second time he went to the floor from a right hand smash on the jaw. He wasn't in such a bad way and arose all right. Johnson tried his best to give him his quietus, but was exhausted and weak from punching and couldn't land the knockout.

[677] *Boston Herald*, April 27, 1906. In the preliminary, Rudolph Unholz, the champion of South Africa, whipped Jimmy Murray, Johnson's sparring partner, in a 6-round battle.

It was a one-sided fight. It was all Johnson all the way. Sam did well on his left stabs and showed at times an inclination to shoot the right over for Jack's jaw. But he was outclassed too much naturally to make it any kind of an even fight.

Johnson's showing was commented on by everybody who declared that his challenges to Jeffries were preposterous. He would have been an easy mark for the champion had he been taken on.

Johnson was esquired by Joe Walcott, Kid Murray, Jack McCloskey and Sandy Ferguson and George Dixon gave advice from the corner. George Byers, Andy Watson and other friends were in Sam's corner.[678]

Years later, when attempting to secure a rematch, Langford and/or his representatives claimed that Sam had dropped Johnson, but those claims are not substantiated by any of the local reports for this bout and appear to be false. Given that Langford was the local man, the newsmen would have been more likely to mention something positive that the local favorite did, particularly since it would also make for good copy and a more compelling and interesting fight story.

Although Johnson initially, and for many years, called the story a fabrication, years later, perhaps when he wanted to help garner financial momentum for a rematch, he backed the false story. However, later, he again disputed it. "If Mr. Langford really gave this interview, all that I can say is that, in the language of the prize ring, he is punch-crazy, for no such knocking down of me occurred. The fact is that I dropped him a few times during the encounter." Johnson offered the names of Joe Walcott, Mike and Jack "Twin" Sullivan, noted Boston sport writer Stephen Mahoney, and promoter Alec McLean to attest to the truth of his remarks.[679]

The local primary sources confirm that Johnson beat Langford easily, despite what subsequent myths have claimed. Langford was given credit for gameness, being able to absorb a lot of punishment and keep trying without getting knocked out, but that is all. Overall, it was a one-sided fight. Given that Langford was the popular local man, it is highly likely that if there was any way to spin it in his favor, or to have written something favorable for him, the local writers would have done so. The best they could say for him was that he was game and could take a beating. Except for failing to stop him, Johnson utterly dominated Langford and easily defeated him.

According to the *Police Gazette*, Langford only weighed about 155 pounds, but showed "gameness and capacity for punishment that seemed beyond the powers of a human being." With at least a 30-pound weight advantage, Johnson "gave Langford a terrible beating." After the

---

[678] *Boston Journal*, April 27, 1906.
[679] Johnson, *In the Ring and Out*, at 173-174; *My Life and Battles* at 45; Nat Fleischer, *50 Years at Ringside* (N.Y.: Fleet Publishing Co., 1958), 78-80.

knockdowns, "From that time on Langford showed wonderful blocking and stalling, combined with remarkable gameness."[680]

Two days later, on Saturday April 28, 1906, a vaudeville entertainment and boxing exhibition was given at Boston's Hub Theatre for the benefit of the San Francisco earthquake sufferers. Between $500 and $600 was raised for the relief fund. Each bout consisted of 3 rounds of sparring, and there was no slugging, though the fighters could not resist the temptation to mix it up a little bit.

Jack Johnson's friends presented him with a gold watch. He boxed 3 rounds with Langford. The *Boston Post* said, "On Thursday Johnson closed Langford's eye, and last night he was very careful not to open it up."[681]

In April 1906, it was announced that after a hiatus of several years, and after recently only allowing 3- and 4-round bouts, New York would soon allow up to a maximum of 10 rounds in no-decision boxing bouts.[682]

On May 3, 1906 in New York, 175-pound Mike Schreck fought 195-pound Marvin Hart to a 4-round no-decision in a slugfest that was considered a victory for Schreck.[683]

On May 28, 1906 in New York, Gus Ruhlin and Sandy Ferguson pummeled each other over the course of a 6-round no-decision bout. Both men scored knockdowns, with Sandy dropping Gus in the 2nd, and Ruhlin dropping Ferguson twice in the 3rd round.[684]

Despite the earthquakes and fires, boxing was not dead in San Francisco. On May 31, 1906 at San Francisco's Woodward's Pavilion, Al Kaufman scored an impressive KO1 over Jack "Twin" Sullivan. This was significant, given that Sullivan held 20-round decision victories over Burns and Schreck. This victory served to boost Kaufman, but it boomed Jack O'Brien even further, given that he held a dominant knockout victory over Kaufman.

On Monday June 18, 1906 at Gloucester, Massachusetts, before the Gloucester Athletic Club, in a scheduled 12-round bout, Jack Johnson took on Charles Haghey of Lowell, MA, another veteran of the game with over 40 fights of experience. Haghey's record dated back to 1900, and included: 1902 LND6 George Cole, WND6 Young Peter Jackson, D15 Jim Jeffords, KO2 Dick Moore, LND6 Jack Bonner, L10 George Byers, KO4 Dick O'Brien, and D15 Young Peter Jackson; 1903 D12 Jackson, D12 Byers, LKOby5 Joe Walcott, W10 Jack McCormick, LKOby7 Larry Temple, W6 Gunner Moir, W20 Ben Taylor, LKOby3 Jack O'Brien, and LND6 Hank Griffin; 1904 LKOby3 Walcott, D10 Byers, KO3 Jimmy Handler, and LKOby1 Sandy Ferguson; and 1906 LKOby4 Bob Fitzsimmons.

[680] *Police Gazette*, May 12, 1906.
[681] *Boston Herald, Boston Post*, April 29, 1906. Others on the card included Rudolph Unholz, Eddie Toy, Jack and Mike 'Twin' Sullivan, George Dixon, and Joe Lannon, amongst others.
[682] *Wilkes-Barre Record*, April 19, 1906.
[683] *New York Sun, New York World*, May 4, 1906; *National Police Gazette*, May 19, 1906.
[684] *Police Gazette*, June 16, 1906.

The local *Gloucester Daily Times* reported that a good-sized audience watched the bouts. Johnson, who claimed the heavyweight championship of the world, towered a head over his opponent.

In the 1st round, several times Haghey led for the head, but each time Johnson cleverly blocked. Then Johnson turned and went after him. He got Haghey into a neutral corner and sent a series of rapid blows to his head and body, winding up with a left swing to the wind which sent Haghey through the ropes. He laid there while he was counted out in the very 1st round.

Non-local sources said the bout terminated in one minute. Haghey claimed that he had been struck low, but the referee and others who saw the blow were positive that it was a fair left hook to the body. Johnson had put it on him, landing at will, whereas Charley never landed.

Owing to the shortness of the bout, in order to give the fans their money's worth, the considerate Johnson boxed a 5-round exhibition with his lightweight sparring partner, Jimmy Murray of Cincinnati. Murray was much lighter, but they went at it in a lively manner, giving a fine exhibition, for Johnson made no effort to use his immense strength when striking his smaller opponent.[685]

On August 13, 1906, near Brownsville, Texas, whites who were upset at the placement of black troops at a fort in their area decided to blame the troops for a melee that led to the death of a bartender and a seriously wounded police officer. Commanding officers insisted that the soldiers had been in the barracks the entire night. When the soldiers refused to confess or point their fingers at fellow soldiers, asserting that they had no idea who committed the shootings, every member of the troop, including the 12 originally arrested and temporarily held on suspicion of participating, were recommended for discharge without honor on the basis of lack of cooperation and insubordination. No formal charges were brought, and no trial was held. The soldiers received no due process.

Cleverly waiting to make the final decision until after the Congressional election, so the black vote would not be lost, on November 9, 1906, President Theodore Roosevelt signed all 167 discharges. Many blacks were very upset at Roosevelt and the Republican party, for the general belief was that the soldiers were framed and that evidence of empty Army shell casings were planted to implicate the soldiers. Many soldiers had been in the military for over 20 years, had sterling records, were close to retirement, and lost their pensions as a result. In 1972, after a renewed investigation exonerated the soldiers, President Richard Nixon signed a bill correcting the soldiers' records to read "honorable discharge."

In September 1906, the *Freeman* called U.S. Senator Benjamin Tillman a "self-confessed murderer" who without provocation had assailed the country's Negroes. In his August address, Tillman said, "There are enough

[685] *Gloucester Daily Times,, New York World,* June 19, 1906; *Police Gazette,* July 7, 1906.

Negroes in the South to outvote the whites on any question if they were allowed to vote." However, he declared that there were enough shotguns in the South to carry the election for the Democrats. Tillman also said that although blacks were in the majority in some areas, "In behalf of the white people of the South I say to you that as long as I live, we will see them (referring to the Negroes) in hell before we will let them have their way." He further said, "I am glad that slavery was dead and gone, but I wish that the Negroes in this country were also dead and gone."

It was the "shot-gun policy" of folks like Tillman which demonstrated that the constitutional amendments written to protect blacks and ensure their voting rights in fact were not worth the paper upon which they were printed. "The history of the South since the Civil War has been an epoch of unremitting terrorism. Lynching, Whitecapism, incendiarism, kukluxing, intimidation and various other forms of outrage and crime have so permeated that section of the United States that it seems to be are established institution for the depraved." The *Freeman* called men such as Tillman and Thomas Dixon, Jr. satanic devils who supported the killing of Negroes.[686] However, Tillman was popular enough to be elected and re-elected several times, and Dixon's book and play, *The Clansman*, were hits.

Industrialist steel magnate and philanthropist Andrew Carnegie of New York wrote an article in which he made the case that the Anglo-Saxon race was destined to rule and monopolize the entire earth.

However, the *Bangor News*, in discussing race traits, said there were different kinds of Anglo Saxons.

> The men who settled at Jamestown were as thoroughly English as were the Puritans who landed at Plymouth. But the one made money and converted heathens and built colleges and equipped railroads and constructed factories, while the other owned slaves, went to cock fights on Sunday and fought duels and burned negroes at the stake.[687]

---

[686] *Freeman*, September 1, 1906.
[687] *Bangor News*, September 4, 1906.

CHAPTER 21

Going Through the Motions to Remain Active

Joe Gans

On September 3, 1906 in Goldfield, Nevada, in a world lightweight championship fight to the finish promoted by Tex Rickard, Joe Gans defeated Battling Nelson in the 42nd round, when referee George Siler disqualified Nelson for low blows. Gans was winning the bout and punishing Nelson at the time. U.S. President Theodore Roosevelt's son Kermit was in the audience. Champion Gans earned $11,000, while white challenger Nelson earned $22,500, the amount negotiated for the fight, win or lose. The bout once again demonstrated boxing's popularity and ability to generate huge revenue, as well as the superior negotiating power of top white fighters. The mixed-race championship fight was filmed, and the films would generate a great deal of additional revenue.

That same day, which was Labor Day, Monday September 3, 1906, in Millinocket, Maine, Jack Johnson boxed Billy Dunning to a 10-round draw. Not much is known about Dunning, but he had at least a few known wins and a couple of draws. Most notably, he held a 1904 KO1 over Patsy Corrigan, though that same year, Black Fitzsimmons stopped Dunning in the 1st round.

The semi-local *Bangor Daily News* said,

> The Johnson-Dunning mill took place in the pavilion. The exhibition was a good one and many expressions of satisfaction were heard. Up to about the 6th round it was decidedly interesting, and then, even, the interest did not die out, though some thought there was a spark of

tender heartedness in the burley darkey. At the end of ten rounds it was declared a draw.[688]

It sounds as if Johnson carried Dunning, the local white fighter.

The bout garnered little to no attention or discussion, in part because it was held on the same day as the very big Nelson-Gans fight, and probably also because Dunning was not a known quantity and folks likely knew or strongly suspected that Johnson took it easy on him in order to earn some money.

Secondary sources report that Dunning was a local firefighter for the town company, the Great Northern Paper Co. He was called the "Sawmill Champ."

Johnson later told a reporter that the police had warned him not to knock out the local man. Hence, he carried him.

W. M. DUNNING, of Millinocket.

Johnson probably didn't care, as long as he got paid. In 1910, Dunning would die after being knocked out in the 5th round by Jack Leon.[689]

Tommy Burns was trying to make a lucrative title defense, but several negotiations fell through. Burns said,

> I will defend my title as heavyweight champion of the world against all comers, none barred. By this I mean white, black, Mexican, Indian or any other nationality without regard to color, size or nativity. I propose to be the champion of the world, not the white or the Canadian or the American or any other limited degree of champion. If I am not the best man in the heavyweight division I don't want to hold the title.

The *National Police Gazette* began recognizing him as champion. It said,

> It has been the custom in the past…for the big fellows who have no shadow of a claim upon the title, among them Berger, Kaufman and O'Brien, to sneer at the claims of Burns, but it is notably true that Tommy has offered this trio every reasonable inducement to get them in a ring for a fight and has signally failed. Now Burns proposes to put it up to them in such a manner that they must fight or take off their hats to him as their master. Talk will not go with the public any longer, especially since Burns has issued this remarkable defi to the world. It is a case of fight or shut up.[690]

---

[688] *Bangor Daily News*, September 4, 1906.
[689] *Bangor Daily News*, November 27, 2010.
[690] *National Police Gazette*, September 22, 1906.

Of course, the men that Burns specifically challenged were all white.

On Thursday September 20, 1906 in Philadelphia, before the Broadway Athletic Club, just seventeen days after the Dunning bout, Jack Johnson yet again took on old nemesis (and possibly friend, given that they made so many paydays together) Joe Jeannette (sometimes spelled Jeanette) for 6 rounds. Since last boxing Johnson in a 15-round decision loss, Jeannette had also lost a 15-round decision to Sam Langford, but came back with a KO4 over Black Bill on September 6.

JACK JOHNSON,

World Famous Heavyweight Who Meets Jeannette Tonight.

1 - Jeannette assumed a crouch and shot his left to the face. He advanced and was met by a hard right to the heart. He retaliated by landing on Jack's head. When they clinched, Johnson worked on the body. He played for the heart and body continuously. Overall, Joe was the aggressor. They exchanged lefts and rights, but with little damage done.

2 - Johnson landed his left to the face and rushed, landing left and right to the body. The *Record* said Jeannette covered up and butted Johnson in the face, opening a big gash over his left eye. The *Inquirer* said Joe opened up an ugly cut over Jack's eye and this flow of gore rather blinded Johnson. Joe landed several jabs without a return. Neither was in any apparent danger during the bout, though.

3 - Johnson improved and they mixed it in good style. Joe clinched to evade blows. Johnson's close-range work was effective, and he also landed on Joe's jaw in a rush. Johnson sent both hands to the face as the round ended, partly closing Joe's left eye.

4 - Johnson kept meeting the advancing Jeannette with punches.

5 - At first, Jack broke ground and missed a left swing for the jaw. Joe tried for the body, and in missing, fell to the floor. When Joe came in again, Jack landed his left to the stomach.

Johnson's best blow of the fight was a terrific well-timed left to the nose as Jeannette rushed in. It knocked Joe back and caused him to swing wildly. Jack then landed a hard right to the jaw as they clinched.

6 - Jeannette began to lead with blows again and made Johnson retreat. However, the round was a continuation of clinches, with neither man able to do any damage. The crowd began hooting. They clinched often, though Jeanette seemed to be weakening as the bell rang.

The *Philadelphia Inquirer* said Johnson had met a tough customer, but "had a shade" on him, meaning that he was slightly better and had narrowly defeated Jeannette. Jeannette's clever covering up and ability to stand punishment enabled him to almost even up matters.

The *Philadelphia Record* said it was an easy bout. Jeannette held his own for the full 6 rounds. Johnson failed to do much, and "disappointed the big crowd by his poor exhibition." Jack had height and weight in his favor, but was slow in forcing matters, and many of his punches missed when he attempted to get to Joe, who covered up in close quarters.

The *Philadelphia Evening Bulletin* said Johnson made a poor showing, for Jeannette experienced no difficulty in lasting 6 rounds. Johnson was wild in his judgment of distance, and, outside of a left to the nose in the 5th round, his blows seemed to lack strength. The spectators hissed him in the 6th round for refusing to mix it up. However, Johnson was taking no chances in the no-decision bout.[691]

According to the *Police Gazette*, Jack had a 20-pound weight advantage and was taller. Jeannette held his own, though Johnson brought all his skill into play. "Jeanette's good work surprised the crowd, and judging by the way he fought Johnson he would make it warm for any of the big fellows."

Another *Gazette* article said Johnson was not trying hard to win by a wide margin, and delayed forcing matters. He was looking for an "easy ride." "Johnson, however, earned the decision, but without displaying too much of his real fighting quality." Of course, the decision was unofficial, for no points decisions were allowed there.[692]

The *Freeman* reported that although it was a very tame affair, Johnson was "a great deal too much for Jeannette. In the second round Jeannette drew blood from Johnson's eye, but after that Johnson knocked him at will."

The *Freeman* opined that Johnson was the only man who had a chance to defeat Jeffries, should Jeff be induced to come back by the ever-increasingly-large purse offers.

> It is evidently a fact that Jack Johnson is more of an equal of Jim Jeffries than any other man in the business today. Johnson has long ago demonstrated that fact. He has a terrific power in both arms and can deliver a very stiff punch. There is no doubt that he will certainly have a good time outdoing big Jim, but if he holds out any length of

---

[691] *Philadelphia Inquirer, Philadelphia Record, Philadelphia Evening Bulletin*, September 21, 1906.
[692] *Police Gazette*, October 6, 13, 1906.

time there is a great chance of him laying his opponent low because of his methods of science in ring work.[693]

Two days after Johnson boxed Jeannette, Atlanta, Georgia was home to one of the worst race riots since the Civil War. During the summer of 1906, white fears regarding increasing negro economic and political power, heightened by sensationalized rhetoric from unscrupulous white politicians who advocated the disfranchisement of blacks, combined with unsubstantiated and inflammatory news stories claiming several rumored assaults and rapes by black men upon white women, created a powder keg of racial tension in Atlanta. It exploded on the night of Saturday, September 22, 1906, later known as "Blood Saturday."

White mobs numbering in the thousands, which included law enforcement and military members, attacked, injured, and murdered blacks, and looted and destroyed their homes and businesses. Many yelled, "Kill the Niggers!" In response, blacks fought back and killed and injured many whites. One police officer was killed and another wounded. Many blacks were arrested merely for arming themselves in self-defense.

THE ATLANTA MASSACRE.

The Criminal Class, whether Black or White, should be Punished according to the law, but the Innocent should be protected if not Allowed to Protect Themselves.

Freeman, October 6, 1906

---

[693] *Freeman*, September 29, 1906.

The race war continued for at least four days, not ending until September 25, although minor skirmishes continued for a couple days after that. Hundreds were injured on both sides. Reports of the number of deaths widely vary, but supposedly anywhere from 10 to 25 blacks were killed (though some say 25 - 40) and allegedly only 1 or 2 whites were killed. However, some said many more whites than that were actually killed, closer to the numbers of blacks, but the real numbers were suppressed so as not to give blacks any ideas that their fighting back was or could be successful. Hundreds of blacks were arrested and thousands more fled the city.

It was later said that false newspaper reports about an alleged "carnival of rapes" had started the riots. The *Atlanta Evening News* was blamed for seeking to precipitate a race war. Its editor had championed the reorganization of the Ku Klux Klan and allegedly had offered a reward to lynchers of alleged black rapists. The editor of the *Georgian* was also blamed for stirring racial passions with race-baiting and inflammatory editorials.

The local *Voice of the Negro*'s attempt to expose the true causes of the riot led to its editor, Jesse Max Barber, being forced to leave the city, which caused the previously successful black newspaper's demise. Barber charged that if the Atlanta mobs were a pyramid, "we would find hoodlums at the base, but white politicians and newspaper editors at the apex."

The *Freeman* published a letter from a Georgia reverend who said,

> Various reasons have been given as being the cause leading up to the trouble, but people here on the ground know. ... Georgia had been swept from side to side with a flood of oratory defaming the Negro and demanding the election of Hoke Smith for Governor on the proposition to disfranchise the Negro. The vices and imagined and trumped-up vices of the Negro had been held up on every cross-road. ... Daily, weekly and monthly newspapers, ministers...and heads of families at their firesides had cursed and abused the Negro...to such an extent that the whole state was in a foment of excitement.

> Negroes were pictured as being hideous monsters, lying in wait to catch, ravish and kill white women and children. Just two days before the state primary, trumped-up charges of rape were announced as having been committed in great numbers.

> The *Atlanta News*, an evening daily, had been openly demanding the lynching of Negroes and the reorganization of the Ku-Klux-Klan.

Hoke Smith, on his campaign trail for governor, had fanned the flames of racial hatred. Smith was a lawyer, former Secretary of the Interior under President Grover Cleveland's second administration, and the former publisher of the *Atlanta Journal*. He overwhelmingly won the governorship on a platform advocating black disfranchisement.

White women were so worked up to a state of excitement, fear, and nervousness that even upon encountering a black man, the women would become frightened and make an outcry that he intended to assault her, or that he had raped her. Having read flaming headlines in the local papers, white mobs formed, swearing vengeance. Blacks were chased, shot, and clubbed like beasts.

> [T]here were as many wounded and bleeding white men as there were Negroes. The papers and news distributors would not say so, for fear that it would both embolden the Negroes and inflame the whites. I have learned from the most truthful and conservative sources that what is said above about the wounded is true about the dead. The number was very nearly equal between the two races. ... I personally conversed with a doctor who examined nine dead white men. ... The grand jury, in session, condemned the *Atlanta News* for its incendiary editorials, and held it responsible in a large measure for the mob that swept over Atlanta.[694]

Around that time, in October 1906, Mississippi Governor James K. Vardaman gave a speech in which he argued that Negroes should not be considered citizens, were mere chattel, and should once again be enslaved. He also advocated repeal of the 15th amendment, which gave blacks the right to vote.[695]

In sports, it was announced that Sam Fitzpatrick had taken Jack Johnson under his managerial wing. The *Freeman* said Fitzpatrick was a credit to the profession, for his word was as good as some men's bond, and he had never been associated with a job or fake in his life. At various times, he had been connected with fighters such as Peter Jackson, Kid Lavigne, Tommy Ryan, Bill Hanrahan, and Tom Sharkey, amongst others. "Johnson was lucky in securing a man of Fitzpatrick's ability and standing to manage him, and the big colored fellow will now be in a position to command the recognition that his ability seems to entitle him."[696]

Fitzpatrick said that all of the top fighters were avoiding Johnson.

> I have been watching Johnson's work for a long time, and I think he is the best colored heavyweight since the days of Peter Jackson. He never was given a chance at Jeffries, Jack O'Brien, Bob Fitzsimmons, Kid McCoy, Jim Corbett or Tom Sharkey, but was forced to meet the men with smaller reputations, but who were strong and dangerous just the same.

Fitzpatrick would try to get the big-name bouts to show that Johnson could do just as well with those men. He was ready and willing to match Johnson against Tommy Burns, Jack O'Brien, Al Kaufman, Sam Berger, Mike Schreck, Gus Ruhlin, Bob Fitzsimmons, Marvin Hart, Bill Squires, Jack Sullivan, or any other heavyweight. He would accept any reasonable

[694] *Freeman*, October 6, 1906.
[695] *Seattle Republican*, October 26, 1906; *Hawaiian Star*, October 31, 1906.
[696] *Freeman*, October 6, 1906.

terms. Nobody seemed interested, either because they were afraid of losing, because they did not want to fight a black man, or both.

The *Los Angeles Express* said Johnson would make the best showing against Jeffries, but Jeff would not fight him on account of his color, "and it is said that this was one of the prime reasons for his retirement, as the Burbank man is opposed to entering the ring with negro." Jeff had hoped that one of the other white fighters would have put him away, so that he could meet Johnson's conqueror. However, the ones who had tried had failed, while the others had drawn the color line. Few truly believed that Hart had defeated him.[697]

However, not everyone agreed that Johnson would prove to be a sufficient challenge to Jeffries. The *Los Angeles Examiner* wrote, "Jack Johnson? They cannot build a fence high enough to keep the black-and-tan champion from climbing over and taking to the woods. Johnson is the best fighter in the bunch, but he has a yellow streak a foot wide."[698]

Of course, the claim that Johnson was yellow was a laughable statement, given that Johnson was willing to fight anyone, had boxed seven times in 1903, five times in 1904, and thirteen times in 1905. He would wind up boxing eleven times in 1906. In two years, from 1905 - 1906, he would box more often than Jeffries had in his entire career. Further, by fighting so often, he kept his name in the newspapers.

On October 2, 1906 in Los Angeles, in a highly entertaining hard-fought battle, heavyweight champion Tommy Burns scored a KO15 over "Fireman" Jim Flynn, who previously had fought a draw with Jack "Twin" Sullivan. Burns combined science with power to wear down the strong and aggressive Flynn, fighting him primarily on the inside, but also demonstrating his outside skills as well. Both fighters weighed around 170 pounds.

Shortly thereafter, Burns signed to meet Philadelphia Jack O'Brien for a $12,000 purse. The big fight was scheduled to be held in late November.

The *Police Gazette* claimed (erroneously) that Jeffries had declared an intention to return to the ring for one more fight. Despite all of the attention that O'Brien and Burns were receiving, the *Gazette* believed that the only fighter who really would have a chance against Jeffries was Jack Johnson, for O'Brien and Burns were too small to handle Jeff's bulk. Hence, it believed that Johnson was the best heavyweight in the world outside of Jeffries, not Burns or O'Brien.

It again questioned why Jeff would dodge a meeting with Johnson. "Johnson has a fine record, but it is not a terrifying one by any means." It cited the fact that men like Young Peter Jackson, Marvin Hart, Joe Jeannette, Sandy Ferguson, Jack Munroe, Sam McVey and Denver Ed

[697] *Los Angeles Express*, September 26, 1906.
[698] *Los Angeles Examiner*, September 28, 1906.

Martin had at one point lasted the full distance with him. Still, Jack was the best man available.

> The trouble is that most of the leading heavyweights have carefully avoided getting in a bout with the negro. ... Like Gans, he has probably been compelled to hide his real punching powers a bit in order to get contests. Johnson is a fighter of the Gans ilk. That is to say, he has everything a successful pugilist should have, including remarkable skill, endurance and the power to inflict punishment.
>
> Had he a cleaner list of knockouts to his credit Jeffries could never have avoided a meeting with him before taking to farming. As most of Johnson's important battles were merely won on points, Jeffries has not been very much criticized for passing the negro up....
>
> Jack Jeffries was an easy mark for Johnson. He gave him a terrible beating, and knocked him out cleanly in the fifth round. It was thought then that Jeffries would seek revenge, but Johnson's ability has evidently made a deep impression on his mind, for he never said a word about fighting the black, and drew the color line harder than ever.
>
> A meeting between Jeffries and Johnson would certainly be the greatest attraction possible in the ring today. ... Johnson is the only man with the right to face Jeffries today.[699]

The *Freeman* said that some believed Jeffries was not in as good a shape as he was when he left the ring. He had taken on too much flesh. However, its opinion was, "Jeff is as powerful as ever. Jack Johnson will have a great deal to do if he can stand those terrific blows that Big Jim can land on him should they meet. Jeffries is one of the greatest pugilists that has ever entered an American prize ring. Sullivan in his best days was never the equal of him as a fighter."[700]

A week later, a *Freeman* writer said there was not the least doubt that Johnson would "be successful in beating the boiler-maker clear out of the ring." However, Jeffries would easily beat men like Hart, Schreck, and Root. "Jack Johnson is the only one that would make a mouthful for the 'champ.'" Hart was called a monumental bluffer.[701]

Regardless, Jeffries said the statements attributed to him were false, that he had no intention of coming out of retirement. Talk of him fighting anyone was worthless, because it was not going to happen. The press liked to do it anyhow.

Jack Johnson said he would fight Burns, O'Brien, Berger, or Kaufman, winner take all. He also said that if he failed to whip any one of them

---

[699] *Police Gazette*, October 13, 1906.
[700] *Freeman*, October 13, 1906.
[701] *Freeman*, October 20, 1906.

decisively, he would drop out of the race for the title. Kaufman openly drew the color line and refused to fight Johnson.[702]

During October 1906, *The Clansman* was being performed in Philadelphia, where Jack Johnson was then residing. Race consciousness and prejudice throughout the country was alive and well.

Advertisement that appeared in the *Philadelphia Record*, October 21, 1906

The *Police Gazette* reported that colored boxers of the highest order gradually were becoming scarce, for white boxers were drawing the color line, and club managers did not care to match black and white. It said the only first-class black pugilists were Johnson and the lightweight and welterweight champion, Joe Gans. The next best crop of black fighters included Sam Langford, Dave Holly, Jack Blackburn, and Rufe Turner. Joe Jeannette was a comer, but wasn't getting enough opportunities. Joe Walcott and others of the past, like George Dixon, had been great fighters, but were past their primes. Of course, this overlooked the fact that many black fighters were fighting each other.

Johnson was compared with Peter Jackson. "Jackson was by long odds the best that ever put up his hands in this or any other country. He probably did not have much on Johnson as a scientific boxer, but as a clever, hard-hitting fighter he towered away over Jack."[703]

---

[702] *Police Gazette*, October 27, 1906.
[703] *Police Gazette*, November 3, 1906.

In Australia, the *Referee*, quoting the *New York Evening Mail* of October 20, reported that the American heavyweights had side-stepped Johnson.

> While Sam Fitzpatrick is wilting away collars in the rush to get somebody with nerve enough to fight Johnson, the big smoke is not worrying at all. He struts around Philadelphia togged out simply gorgeous, and rather seems to enjoy the prestige he gets from not being able to get a fight through fear on the part of possible opponents. Johnson really does seem to be in hard luck. Few men of his weight want any of his game.[704]

On October 31, 1906 in San Francisco, Al Kaufman scored a KO10 over another highly touted rising heavyweight contender in former Olympic champion Sam Berger. However, the *Police Gazette* said Kaufman did not have the right to fight for the title until he defeated Jack Johnson.[705]

Johnson even offered to contract to knock out Kaufman in 20 rounds or not take a cent of the receipts, but Al refused.

As a result of their refusal to face Johnson, the *Police Gazette* called the current crop of white heavyweights "yellow." It said Johnson had the would-be champions such as O'Brien, Berger, and Kaufman on the run, for all of them had drawn the color line on him. It interpreted drawing the color line as a sign of fear and respect for Johnson, and proof that the heavyweight contenders were a "very bad lot to say the least."

Some suggested that Johnson was receiving more ink and praise than his performances warranted, simply because of the fact that white heavyweights were refusing to face him. "In spite of all the boosting that Johnson has accumulated, much of it in these columns, there is no doubt a lot of sympathetic sentiment attached to it. We are prone to overrate the big negro out of sympathy for him in his loneliness." Certainly though, something about Johnson had top whites afraid, and the press did not believe it was simply a matter of race pride.

Matches for Jack Johnson had been arranged with Jim Jeffords and Joe Jeannette, the only fighters with the grit to meet him, but, "doubtless there is some kind of an insurance clause in the articles in order to make this pair sign."

Sandy Ferguson, who was then listed as 27 years old, 6'4 ¾" tall, and 230 pounds, was willing to fight Johnson, but no one wanted to back that fight, given how Sandy had conducted himself in their last bout.

There was no great demand to see Jeffries come back to fight any of the top white heavyweights, for the opinion was that he would knock them out quickly. One writer said the retired Jeffries was unbeatable on the night that he defeated Corbett in their rematch, and none of the past great fighters in their primes could have defeated him; Sullivan, Corbett, and Jackson included. "On that night big Jeff was at his very best, and I honestly believe

[704] *Referee*, December 12, 1906, quoting *New York Evening Mail*, October 20, 1906.
[705] *Police Gazette*, November 17, 1906.

he could beat any four heavyweights we now have in the same ring at the same time." Jeff was "in a class by himself." He had retired undefeated, and had never even been knocked down.[706]

Promoters in the state of Iowa were trying to get the legislature there to legalize the sport. Under the current statute, even moving pictures of a prize fight could not be displayed in the state. Yet, illegal fight cards were taking place there occasionally. Boxing was still struggling to obtain full legal acceptance, despite the fact that the public was eager to patronize the sport.

Although deaths and injuries in boxing were frowned upon more strongly than they were in other sports, this was changing. Still, even to this day, boxing struggles with public perception.

> It has been the custom lately to look on the deaths of boxers who are injured in the ring as being in line with that of jockeys, baseball players or others who are killed in following their chosen occupations. This, with the number of deaths which occur in other sports, such as football, gunning, etc., has made the public accustomed to fatalities, and there is not the hysteria over the death of a boxer now that there was a few years ago when they were less frequent and were heralded all over the country as something terrible. Everything has been done to make the sport of boxing as safe as possible, and yet fatalities will occur. The sport is better safeguarded than any other which the public patronizes.[707]

Australia was well aware of Johnson's growing reputation, as well as his struggle with the color line. They sympathized with him, for they remembered how their champion, Peter Jackson, had endured the same struggles. The National Sporting Club of Sydney, New South Wales, made an offer for Johnson to fight there, guaranteeing $1,500 for each of two matches, as well as transportation for two. "Johnson will probably accept the offer. He has about given up hope of getting any of the present crop of American heavyweights into the ring."

The thinking was that Johnson would fight Bill Squires and Peter Felix, the best heavies in Australia. If successful, it was Alex McLean's intention to take Johnson on a tour to South Africa and England. If he was successful in all of his bouts, McLean felt certain that the best American heavyweights would have to accept a challenge from Johnson, including for the title.[708]

Apparently, McLean was co-managing Johnson along with Sam Fitzpatrick. McLean was an amusement promoter from Chelsea, Massachusetts, and had managed Sandy Ferguson.

Alex Greggains, who refereed and decided the Johnson-Hart fight, and whose decision endured a fair amount of criticism, further discussed the bout. He likely was perturbed by all the criticism. He said,

---

[706] *Police Gazette*, December 8, 1906; *Philadelphia Record*, November 10, 1906.
[707] *Police Gazette*, December 8, 1906.
[708] *Philadelphia Record*, November 7, 8, 1906.

Hart was a little fellow beside the big coon, and he didn't know enough about fighting or boxing to cut any ice. All he did was to go at Johnson and rush him all over the ring. Johnson has a yellow streak. Hart's rushes scared him half to death, and all he could do was to put up his hands and catch Marvin by the shoulders. Once in a while he jabbed Hart, but most of the time he just caught him and held his arms. I didn't want to give a decision if I could help it. I wanted to see a knockout, which would make it easy. You always lose friends, no matter which way you give a decision. So when I was breaking them I said: "Get in and fight, you big dubs. What are you stalling around like this for?"

"Why, I's a-fightin', Mr. Greggains," says Johnson. "I'se a-fightin' scientific."[709]

The *Lancaster Daily Intelligencer* said the championship would be contested between Burns, O'Brien, and Kaufman. Johnson was not in the running because none of the top fighters would fight him, all drawing the color line. "While there is much discussion about the championship between Kaufman, Burns and O'Brien, the truth is that all of them are afraid of Jack Johnson, who appears at the Lancaster Athletic Club against Jim Jeffords Next Thursday night." It quoted an opinion in the *New York World*, which opinion it said was shared by nearly every writer of note in the country.

While these men are challenging and counter challenging one another, Jack Johnson, the negro, is issuing challenges to the entire world. He has not even hesitated to challenge Jeffries. He is the colored heavy weight champion of the world, and he says he can beat any fighter in the world whether he be colored or not. But his challenges have been unheeded. All the present day champions draw the colored line, and will not agree to fight Johnson. And there is method in their madness. Johnson is undoubtedly cleverer, faster and a heavier puncher than any of the men whom he is trying to get a match with. The only man in the ring today who would be able to make a creditable showing against Johnson is Jack O'Brien, and the Quaker is far too shrewd to risk losing what prestige he has gained after beating a long list of easy ones. O'Brien won't fight the colored man, as the chances are even he would meet with defeat. All the other heavy weights fear him. But that word 'colored' gives them all a chance to escape without admitting their fear. When Johnson challenges they pay no attention to his challenges and seek safety behind the color line.[710]

Johnson arrived in Lancaster, Pennsylvania, on November 5, a few days before the Jim Jeffords bout. Jack would be quartered at George B.

---

[709] *New York World*, November 2, 1906.
[710] *Lancaster Daily Intelligencer*, November 5, 1906.

Robinson's hotel at Conestoga Park, so that he could run on the boulevard. He would do his other exercise in the hotel pavilion. Jeffords was training at Merchantville, New Jersey.

Jim Jeffords

On Thursday November 8, 1906 in Lancaster, Pennsylvania, Jack Johnson boxed a 6-round no-decision bout with Jim Jeffords. Previously, Johnson had stopped Jeffords in the 4th round of their 1905 meeting. Since then, significant Jeffords bouts included: 1905 LKOby4 Larry Temple and LND6 Joe Jeannette; and 1906 WND6 George Gardner. The 26-year-old 6'4" Jeffords typically weighed well over 200 pounds.

The local *Lancaster Daily Intelligencer* reported that the largest audience of the season gathered at Prince street hall to witness the Lancaster Athletic Club's monthly boxing show. Men came from all over, and nearly as many strangers were present as the number of locals. The audience left well pleased, for they witnessed one of the best shows ever offered at Lancaster.

The star event of the evening was the bout between Johnson and Jeffords. The management went to great expense to secure the bout, which would have drawn thousands of dollars in any big city at high prices. The bout was "strictly on the level." Both men had everything to gain by being square. To win or even make a good showing would help Jeffords' career, while Johnson could not afford to trifle in the face of the fact that he was trying to obtain more significant matches.

Jeffords was in superb condition, for he had been training for some time, while Johnson was "never caught napping in that line." The local paper said of the fight,

> The bout was lively from the first tap of the bell, with Johnson the aggressor. While the big coon had the best of it, Jeffords deserves the greatest amount of credit for staying the limit, despite the vigorous efforts of Johnson to put him out. He took an awful lacing, but came back every time, and he was the favorite with the audience, even if he did get the worst of the match. There are a dozen other big men in this country who would not have stayed, for as Jeffords said after the match, he was never hit so hard before.[711]

The semi-local *Philadelphia Public Ledger* and *Philadelphia Press* had more detailed next-day reports. Over 1,000 spectators witnessed a hot battle between Johnson and Jeffords.

1 - The *Public Ledger* said that at first, Jeffords was decidedly nervous. He soon went at his opponent gamely, though he was ever on the alert to avoid Johnson's rushes. At several stages, when Johnson was roughing things in a serious manner, Jim clinched to escape punishment. Johnson's blows were of the "clean-cut, sledgehammer type," whereas Jeffords' punches lacked steam. The round was tame compared with the following rounds, though Johnson managed to land a heavy right to the jaw.

The *Press* said both sparred carefully, and it was just a feel-out round.

2 - The *Ledger* said Jeffords did most of the leading, but Johnson was the one who did the most telling work. The *Press* said Johnson had gotten Jeffords' measure, and started after him. He landed two blows to one.

3 - Johnson had Jeffords on the ropes several times. He put Jeffords' left eye out of commission. From that time on, he alternated between right swings to the suffering optic and left swings to the stomach. Jeffords was clearly outclassed. Johnson was comfortable at all times.

4 - A blow from Johnson turned Jeffords clean around, but Jeff then landed a heavy jolt on Jack's jaw.

5 - Johnson continued pounding on Jeffords.

6 - The round was decidedly in Johnson's favor, for he was still fresh, while Jeffords was "well blown." When the gong sounded, Jeffords' left eye was closed.

The *Philadelphia Public Ledger* said, "Both men worked hard from start to finish, but it required only a few rounds to demonstrate the negro's superiority. He was not only handier with his fists, but his superior strength told from the beginning."

---

[711] *Lancaster Daily Intelligencer,* November 9, 1906.

The *Philadelphia Press* agreed that Jeffords was outclassed at every stage of the proceedings. At the end of 6 rounds, "No decision was given, but the colored fighter was the only factor in the game."[712]

Joe Choynski told the Australians to bring Jack Johnson out to fight their champion, Bill Squires. Joe said, "They are all afraid of him here. I beat him once in three rounds. He is very clever, and will, no doubt, give you a good line on Squires' ability. He is a fine fellow, and can be got reasonably."[713]

On November 8, boxing manager Sig Hart wrote to an Australian,

> Jack Johnson...is going to Australia to fight someone. Now, if he lands on your side I want to tell you that he will beat any man you have there, for he can beat anyone we have here. He is better than Peter Jackson was in his palmiest days. He is clever, can hit hard, and can stand the gaff. Not one of our heavies here would box him. Be sure you have a bet on him if ever he comes to your town to fight, for, as I said before, he is the best big man in the world today, and I don't bar anyone. By the way, your old townie, Sam Fitzpatrick, is looking after him now, and Sam knows a thing or two about the fighters.[714]

One article noted that although Irish fighters predominated the ring, they were not quite as numerous as they were years ago, for fighters of all races and nationalities were participating in the sport. The potential for big money was a great lure.

> The champion prizefighter of the present day has a great earning capacity. If he engages in four or five important battles a year he can make more money than a bank president or the President of the United States. This has induced the other races to take up the game with the result that nearly every race is represented in the ring today.

Jim Jeffries was of Dutch origin. Kid Lavigne was of French Canadian ancestry. Frank Erne was Swiss. Kid Carter was of Swedish extraction. Denmark had Battling Nelson. Mexico had Aurelia Herrera. Jack Root was Austrian. "There are scores of Italian fighters, but for some reason or other they choose to conceal their nationality under Irish or American cognomens." Tommy Burns, born Noah Brusso, was one such fighter. Hugo Kelly was an Italian, born Ugo Micheli. Joe Grim was born Saverio Giannone. Jim Flynn, who was of Irish-Italian heritage, had changed his name from Andrew Schreiglione. Tony Ross was born Antonio Rossilano. Tommy Ryan was Jewish, despite his repeated denial that he was a representative of the race. Jews and Italians like Ryan and Burns were trying to avoid the prejudice that their races had to endure. Jews also included Joe

[712] *Philadelphia Public Ledger, Philadelphia Press*, November 9, 1906.
[713] *Referee*, December 19, 1906.
[714] *Referee*, December 19, 1906.

Choynski and Abe Attell. Jimmy Handler came from Russia and was a Hebrew. Irishmen included George Gardner, Jimmy Britt, Jack O'Brien, Jack Bonner, and Sandy Ferguson, amongst scores of others. Many fighters were born in England. Some were German. Name-changing in boxing was as frequent a tradition as would become name-changing by actors.

> Negroes who have shone conspicuously in the ring during the past ten years or so are George Dixon, Joe Gans, Jack Johnson, Frank Craig, the Harlem "Coffee Cooler;" Joe Walcott, Young Peter Jackson, Jack Blackburn, Fred Blackburn, Dave Holly, Hank Griffin, Sam McVey, Bob Armstrong, Frank Childs, Joe Butler of Philadelphia, Harry Styles, George Cole of Trenton, Rufe Turner of Denver and last but not least, the late Peter Jackson.[715]

That same day, another newspaper, the *Daily Eastern Argus*, which was based in Portland, Maine, where Jack Johnson would next fight, argued that the Caucasian and the Negro fundamentally were extreme opposites in evolution.

> The Caucasian, and more particularly the Anglo-Saxon, is dominant and domineering and possessed primarily with determination, will power, self control, self government and all the attributes of the subjective self, with a high development of the ethical and aesthetic faculties and great reasoning powers. The negro is in direct contrast by reason of a certain lack of these powers, and a great development of the objective qualities. The negro is primarily affectionate, immensely emotional, then sensual, and, under provocation, passionate. There is love of outward show, of ostentation, of approbation. He loves melody and a rude kind of poetry and sonorous language. There is undeveloped artistic power and taste – negroes make good artisans and handicraftsmen. They are deficient in judgment, in the formation of new ideas from existing facts, in devising hypotheses and in making deductions in general. They are imitative rather than original, inventive or constructive. There is instability of character incident to lack of self control, especially in connection with the sexual relation, and there is a lack of orientation or recognition of position and condition of self and environment. ...

> The white and the black races are antipodal, then, in cardinal points. The one has a large frontal region of the brain, the other a larger region behind; ... the one a great reasoner, the other pre-eminently emotional; the one domineering, but having great self control, the other meek and submissive, but violent and lacking self control when the passions are aroused; the one a very advanced race, the other a

---

[715] *Hawaiian Star*, November 9 1906.

very backward one. The Caucasian and the negro are fundamentally opposite extremes in evolution.[716]

Such views were common. One has to consider how a black man being the central figure in boxing and the best fighter in the business might serve to contradict such notions.

Next up for Jack Johnson was a seventh bout with Joe Jeannette. They fought in late November, this time in Portland, Maine, for a scheduled 10 rounds. They recently had boxed a 6-round no-decision bout in late September. This fight would be held just 18 days after Johnson had boxed Jeffords. Both boxers posted forfeits guaranteeing their appearances and also 10 rounds of work to the best of their ability.

BOXING.
Auteurorium, Monday Evening, Nov. 26.
10 ROUNDS.
Jack Johnson vs. Joe Jeannette
Tickets—50c, 75c and $1.   nov20-1w*

It would be Johnson's last appearance in the U.S. before sailing for Australia. The local *Daily Eastern Argus* said, "In this country the big negro has been the toughest nut the heavyweights have ever run up against and for some time all of them have been sidestepping a match with him." Therefore, Johnson had been forced to go to foreign countries to do business. The fact that it would be the last opportunity to see him in action for a while was an added draw.

Although Jeannette was not as prominent as the elite white heavys, he was the only good man not afraid of an encounter with Johnson. "Jeanette is a big fellow and a mighty hard hitter as proven by the fact that he stopped Sam Langford in nine rounds, a job which Johnson failed to do in fifteen." Jeannette was expected to give him a great run, as shown by their previous six contests. "Jeannette is the only man in the country that ever bothered Johnson to any great extent."

The local paper said Johnson was at the very zenith of his ring career, acknowledged by all as a peer in his class, whom all top contenders were afraid to tackle. His fame had spread to foreign lands. "Johnson is without doubt the most prominent star in the heavyweight class in the squared circle today and in spite of open defies to all the best men in the business, the alleged title holders as well as promising aspirants of the honor have sidestepped a meeting with the giant." Men like Jeffries, Kaufman, Berger and other class heavies flatly refused to meet Johnson, and had

---

[716] *Daily Eastern Argus*, November 9, 1906.

"conveniently drawn the color line when Johnson sought a match, which is a polite way of saying 'cold feet.'"

Daily hyping the fight, the *Argus* said word that the world-famous Johnson and the great Jeannette would meet had spread like wild-fire all over. The bout promised to have the biggest ever crowd of boxing followers from outside the city. The sporting fraternity was crazy about the bout, which brought the two famous fighters together.[717]

Jeannette, the husky New Yorker, with manager George Armstrong, arrived a few days before the bout. Johnson would arrive the next day. Jeannette was in perfect condition and had trained hard, for it would mean a lot to him if he did well with the man "whom all the rated top notchers have conveniently side-stepped." The local paper said Johnson and Jeannette had for the most part boxed with honors about even, although in fact Johnson had the edge in all but one bout, when he was disqualified for a low blow. Both men were confident. Tickets were selling fast, for 1 dollar, 75 cents, and 50 cents.[718]

On Monday November 26, 1906 at the Portland, Maine Auditorium, under the auspices of the Casco Athletic Club, once again Jack Johnson fought Joe Jeannette. It was a scheduled 10-round no-decision bout. Hence, if there was no knockout or disqualification, no formal points decision would be rendered.

There was a large and enthusiastic crowd of 1,200 to 1,500 people present. Martin Sullivan refereed. The local paper said Sullivan was a first-class local referee who would guarantee honest work.

Johnson climbed through the ropes first. He was described as a long, rangy colored gentleman. "All who looked upon the powerful negro understood why so many heavyweights have been sidestepping a meeting with him." After a short wait, Jeannette appeared and received a great hand from the crowd.

Referee Sullivan, when introducing Johnson, announced that Jack was willing to meet any man in the world at any place, Jim Jeffries preferred. Jeannette was introduced as a comer who would bear watching. The pugilists were ordered to break upon the referee's command.

1 - When they came together in the first clinch, it could be seen that Johnson had greater height, reach, and weight. That caused the crowd's sympathies to be with the clever and gritty Jeannette. They shouted for him all the way through the bout.

There were some lively exchanges. Joe did most of the leading, once pushing the big fellow to the ropes, which caused Johnson to smile. While sparring for an opening, Joe slipped partly through the ropes, but no damage resulted. The gong sounded just as they seemed to be getting warmed up to their work.

---

[717] *Daily Eastern Argus*, November 16, 20-23, 1906.
[718] *Daily Eastern Argus*, November 24, 1906.

2 - Joe started with a left to the face, while Jack sent his right and left to the wind. Joe was right after him. He would dive in with both hands and then clinch around the waist. Jack missed a vicious right swing. Joe had a faculty of getting inside Johnson's swings so that they rarely landed and did but little damage when they did. The gong sounded as Johnson swung a left that landed high on the ribs.

3 - Johnson began to crouch. He jabbed the face and followed with right and left to the body. He continued jabbing the face, although for most of the bout he played for the body. Joe clinched a good deal, and towards the end of the round, Johnson wrestled himself loose and kept on hitting.

4 - Jeannette rushed and then clinched. It was a whirlwind round all the way. Joe landed some good body blows. Jeannette again slipped and all but went through the ropes. Jack was calm and collected all the time.

5 - This was a fast round. Jeannette landed a number of left stabs to the face, while Johnson sent in a whirlwind of uppercuts, though Joe guarded his face well, so few landed.

6 - Johnson went at him with slashing uppercuts, trying to get to the point of the jaw, but Joe covered well. There was a lively mix-up in which Johnson jabbed the jaw and Joe sent a left and right to the ribs.

7 - Johnson fired a whirlwind of uppercuts and swings, and Jeannette was bleeding a little. It was the fastest round of the bout. Jeannette had the crowd wildly cheering when he landed a corking right over the heart.

8 - There was a lively exchange. Johnson wrestled a bit and the crowd hissed. Joe kept rushing in and worked both hands to the body. He worked in close to avoid Jack's left swings.

9 - This was a slashing round, for both mixed matters. Each tried to rush the other off his guard. Johnson jabbed the left to the face several times, but his swings went around his opponent, who went inside, but then Johnson worked the trip-hammer blow to the back. At the gong, Joe pushed the colored champ's head back with a left to the face.

10 - The final round started at a fast clip, and in the first mix-up, Johnson wrestled Jeannette to the mat. Near the round's conclusion, Johnson followed up a slight advantage with a left hook to the jaw and Jeannette went down to his knee.

Jeannette stayed down, waiting to take advantage of part of the count. Referee Sullivan had counted five when the gong sounded ending the bout.

The local paper called it one of the best if not the best cards in local history. Johnson and Jeannette boxed 10 fast rounds in a "corking good main event." The crowd left perfectly satisfied that they had received their money's worth. They were also satisfied that they had "seen one of the best heavyweights in the business and another boxer possibly not in Johnson's class, but who is fast coming to the front."

Although no formal decision was rendered, "we are inclined to believe that, though slightly outclassed by a man who had a marked advantage in weight, height and reach, Joe Jeannette fairly earned a draw by his clever exhibition." This writer also said, "Both men were strong at the finish and while Johnson showed himself the cleverer boxer and ring general Jeannette certainly deserved a draw for his work. No decisions are given, however, and it is only a matter of opinion at best." So the local paper half-heartedly called it a draw, though it also said that Jeannette was outclassed slightly by Johnson, who was the cleverer boxer and ring general. Johnson had drawn blood and had scored the only knockdown. So the feeling was slightly Johnson or no worse than a draw.[719]

Johnson, "the black and tan champion of the world," wanted to fight the winner of the upcoming Burns-O'Brien championship contest. His manager Sam Fitzpatrick said, "Johnson and the winner coming together would prove a real championship contest." The *Los Angeles Examiner* responded, "Yes, if people could forget Jack Johnson's canary streak, he might make a good match with the winner. But so long as the memory of his orange stripe lingers Jack Johnson will be a beggar for matches. That is where he figures." Not everyone supported Johnson's title challenges. Some thought Jack lacked gameness inside the ring, particularly on the West Coast, where Johnson had some dull or lackluster performances.[720]

The *Examiner*'s C. E. Van Loan said,

> If he disposes of Jack O'Brien there is no man in the country who will have the right to dispute Burns' claim to the championship.

> Jack Johnson still lingers about the scene and every little while he emits a small yellow growl, but Jack deserves his fate. He might have been a top-notch fighter, but he was cursed with a great display of citrus fruit and every time he got in a pinch he showed the lemon color. The championship lies between Burns and O'Brien, and by this time next week it is hoped that one man will have a clear title to Jeff's cast-off shoes.[721]

Of course, given that Burns-O'Brien was taking place in the Los Angeles area, local writers had an interest in hyping that fight as a real championship match as much as possible. Plus, these writers often had a twinge of racial animus towards Johnson, as well as dislike of his style, referring to him as yellow or cowardly for having defensive inclinations, even though Burns and O'Brien had often fought quite defensively themselves, yet received heaps of praise.

---

[719] *Daily Eastern Argus*, November 26, 27, 1906.
[720] *Los Angeles Examiner*, November 28, 1906.
[721] *Los Angeles Examiner*, November 22, 1906.

WHY TILLMAN DISCUSSES THE NEGRO

Could He Get Into the Senate by Advocating Any Other Question?

Freeman, December 15, 1906

On November 27, 1906 in Chicago, Senator Ben Tillman gave an address for the benefit of the Union Hospital. In his speech, Tillman talked of the race question in a manner which "shocked some and delighted the majority of 3,000 listeners." He said a "black curse" hung over every Southern home. When discussing the 15th amendment, which gave blacks the right to vote, Tillman said, "If this law was enforced it would result in two states at least being dominated absolutely by Negroes, while four other states would be so near being governed by the Negro that there would practically be an equal division of offices." When someone asked, "What about the law?" Tillman responded, "To hell with the law!" Tillman discussed how the negro was prevented from casting the ballot in the South. He said the white race never would allow itself to be dominated by the Negro, and that before any such thing took place in South Carolina, "we will make it red before we make it black."

Pointing to a black man in the audience, Tillman said, "Look at that nigger down there. He's as black as the ace of spades. Don't tell me you haven't got niggers up here." Continuing, Tillman said, "The negro must be kept in subjection. He is not capable of ruling a white population. ... I want to be fair with the negro, but we must protect ourselves first." He also said,

> God Almighty made the Caucasian of better clay than the Mongolian or the African or any other race. The Ethiopian is a burden carrier. He has done absolutely nothing for history, nor has he ever achieved anything of any great importance. There are no great men among the race. Yet this people has been picked out by the fanatics of the North and lifted up to the equality of citizenship and to the rights of suffrage. No doubt many of you have listened to the oratory of the greatest colored man of this country – Booker Washington. He had a white father, however, and his brains and his character he has inherited from that father.

Tillman further spoke of the alleged attacks of white women by Negroes in the South.[722]

TOMMY BURNS   PHILADELPHIA JACK O'BRIEN

[722] *New York World, New York Tribune,* November 28, 1906.

On November 28, 1906 in Los Angeles, before a crowd of over 10,000 spectators, former champion James J. Jeffries, acting as referee, ruled the Tommy Burns vs. Jack O'Brien heavyweight championship bout a 20-round draw, although most thought Burns had won. Burns attacked throughout, throwing the harder punches. O'Brien moved incessantly and threw few punches, which though not very powerful, were quick, and he would clinch whenever Burns drew close. Burns pummeled his body on the inside and broke O'Brien's nose with a right. O'Brien closed Tommy's left eye. Burns claimed he was robbed, and several newsmen and experts backed him. No official weights were taken, though estimates ranged from 163-170 for O'Brien and 168-174 for Burns.

In Sydney, Australia, the *Referee* reported that James Brennan of the National Amphitheatre had engaged Johnson to meet the best men available in Australia.

Alec McLean, Johnson's co-manager, wrote a November 28 letter to Brennan saying that he and Johnson would set sail from San Francisco on or about December 27 and arrive in Sydney on January 17. "Johnson will do some training on board the ship, so he will be able to go in the ring in good shape about February 1." An American newspaper said Johnson had been booked to fight Bill Squires and Peter Felix.[723]

The *Police Gazette* confirmed that in view of the fact that Kaufman, Berger, and O'Brien all drew the color line against him, Jack Johnson would be traveling to Australia on the R.M.S. Sonoma to fight in two bouts for the National Sporting Club for $1,500 each.[724]

Not every black fighter thought Johnson could whip Jeffries. Joe Gans said Jeff was the wonder of the world and could whip anyone, for he was far better than any other fighter.

> I am a colored boxer, but my color does not carry me away when it comes to picking out the best fighters. I have heard hundreds of people express the opinion that Jack Johnson can whip Jim Jeffries. I don't think so. Does any man for a second think that Jack Johnson could have whipped Corbett in his prime? No, never. Jeffries whipped Corbett on two different occasions, and both defeats were decisive ones. Johnson is a hard man to best, but he does not class with Jeff.

Gans said Jack O'Brien was the next best man around, but O'Brien had no chance with Jeff, for he was too small. Gans did not think Johnson could have whipped Peter Jackson in his prime. Both were clever, but "Jackson was a punisher and Johnson is not. The heavyweight championship is not in doubt. There is still a real champion, because no one has ever beaten him, and that man is James J. Jeffries."[725]

---

[723] *Sydney Referee*, December 5, 1906, January 9, 1907.
[724] *Police Gazette*, December 15, 1906; *Referee*, December 12, 1906; *Referee*, January 30, 1907.
[725] *Freeman*, December 1, 1906.

The *New York Sun* reported that Jack Johnson left New York on December 8, 1906, heading for Los Angeles, where he hoped to force either O'Brien or Burns into a match with him. Johnson said he would do the fight winner-take-all, or split the purse evenly, and even was willing to agree that if he failed to score a knockout inside of 20 rounds that he would forfeit his share of the purse.[726]

The *Sun* said the real interest at present was in a fight between Johnson and either O'Brien or Burns. If Johnson could beat both of them, then Jeffries might be forced to fight him.

> Jeff has already drawn the color line on Johnson, but at a time when the colored pugilist was not in a position to appeal to the sporting public for moral support. Just now, however, Johnson has a big following in his attempt to force these alleged heavyweight champions to fight or run.[727]

Bob Edgren said Tommy Burns was a peculiarly built athlete. He was short, but that made him harder to hit. However, he had the reach of a tall man at 74.5 inches, 7.5 inches more than his height, which meant that he could hit bigger fighters at long range. His reach was longer than Corbett's, and nearly as long as Fitzsimmons' and Jeffries'. He could fight on the inside or the outside.[728]

Although there were rumors that promoter Tex Rickard had offered Jeffries $50,000 to come back to fight Johnson or Burns, eventually Rickard denied them. Rickard said none of the top heavies were in the same class as Jeffries, and the ring was "without a man who could be considered to have a possible chance to whip Jeffries, or even to make him extend himself." Hence, there would be insufficient financial incentive to promote such a bout. He said,

> The stories printed in the east and all over the country about my offering $50,000 for a fight between Jeffries and Tommy Burns or Jeffries and Jack Johnson are all absolutely untruths. To even think of such a thing would be ridiculous. Sam Fitzpatrick, Johnson's manager, started all this talk and the eastern sporting papers aided him. I would not for a minute consider a match between these men.[729]

If Jim Jeffries was coming back, Tommy Burns wanted to fight him and earn the huge payday that would come with such a bout. He was concerned by the rumors that Jeff might fight Johnson rather than him. Tom said to Jeffries,

---

[726] *New York Sun*, December 9, 1906.
[727] *New York Sun*, December 10, 1906.
[728] *Freeman*, December 15, 1906.
[729] *Los Angeles Herald*, December 20, 1906.

Jim, I think that you are not as good as you were at one time, and I believe that if anybody would have a show with you I would have the best look-in, that is, if I get O'Brien this time, and I expect to do so. This fellow Johnson who is hollering for a match ought not to be considered so long as I am in the game. Marvin Hart beat him and you know what I did to Marvin.

Jeffries told Burns that he would not fight a black man. He also told him that if someone offered them $50,000 to fight, he would take him on. However, the offer did not materialize.[730]

Jack Johnson said he was so certain of victory over Jeffries that he would split the purse any way Jeffries wanted, and also would bet another $10,000 on the result. He was burning with a desire to fight Jeff.[731]

Johnson also said that O'Brien, Burns, Kaufman, or Berger had to fight him or ring in a cowardly excuse.[732]

On December 21, 1906 in Los Angeles, Al Kaufman scored a KO14 over George Gardner.

A Philadelphia club offered 60% of the gate receipts for a 6-round bout between Johnson and Tommy Burns. Jack was anxious for the bout.

Sam Fitzpatrick was no longer worrying about Johnson's future.

He sees the public clamoring more and more every day for the white heavies to try the chocolate colored heavyweight out, and knows that they cannot ignore Johnson much longer.

In fairness to Burns, it must be said he has never said anything about drawing the color line, and it may be that he will be willing to meet Johnson.[733]

Tommy Burns had not specifically drawn the color line, but eventually he did, at least temporarily. In December 1906, Burns said,

I wish someone would put an end to these stories that I ever intended meeting Jack Johnson. I am having a hard time with my wife now, as she wants me to cut out this business. I don't know what she would do if she heard I fought a negro. She's a southerner and I guess you know what southern folks think of negroes. They may say I am afraid of Johnson and anything else they want to, but I am never going to fight a negro. I have fought them, but am drawing the line now.[734]

The *Police Gazette* responded, "As was expected, Tommy Burns has drawn the color line in the direction of Jack Johnson."

[730] *Los Angeles Herald*, December 20, 1906.
[731] *Referee*, February 20, 1907.
[732] *Freeman*, December 22, 1906.
[733] *Police Gazette*, December 22, 1906.
[734] *Los Angeles Herald*, December 13, 1906.

Of course, Burns was making a great deal of money already, which made it less likely he would want to fight Johnson. The Burns-O'Brien fight drew over $26,500 in gate receipts. Burns wanted a rematch in order to solidify his claim to the championship, to prove that he was O'Brien's master, and to make another very big payday. On December 22, Tom McCarey secured the Burns-O'Brien rematch for an alleged purse of $30,000.[735]

The *Police Gazette* lobbied,

> Johnson is as much entitled to consideration as any of the others. Many an expert is of the opinion that he is the greatest fighter of his race since the days of Peter Jackson, and there hardly is any question on that score. But Johnson has been sidetracked by all the white heavies because of his color, they claim. As a matter of fact, they are afraid of him if they only would acknowledge the corn. Johnson has as much right to fight for the title as any of the prominent men, and if he is treated fairly he will be given a chance. Barring him will not settle the much-twisted heavyweight situation.[736]

There were some negotiations for a match between Jeffries and rising Australian star Bill Squires, but Jeff wanted $25,000, win, lose, or draw. Jeffries turned down $20,000 guaranteed. The Rhyolite club representative in Nevada said,

> Jeffries' demands are entirely unreasonable. He should understand that this fight will not be a great drawing card compared to a fight with Johnson. ... He can pretty nearly name his own purse if he will fight Johnson, but when he refuses to fight the only man for whom there is a really national demand, he cannot expect to get a gold mine for fighting someone else.[737]

On January 10, 1907 in Philadelphia, Tommy Burns boxed Joe Grim in an exhibition bout. Grim had gone the full 6 rounds with O'Brien, Fitzsimmons, and Johnson (barely). However, Grim refused to box Burns anything more than three one-minute rounds. Burns still managed to drop him several times. Afterwards, the local paper opined that Grim could never survive a regulation 6-round bout with Burns.[738]

The *Freeman* said, "Jack Johnson is recognized by all fair-minded and unprejudiced fans to be about as good or better than any except Jim Jeffries. ... Students of the game are confident that Johnson can whip the rest of the short top fighters like breaking sticks." However, at that time, none of the elite white heavyweights were willing to fight him. They all drew the color line.[739]

---

[735] *Police Gazette*, December 29, 1906.
[736] *Police Gazette*, December 29, 1906.
[737] *Philadelphia Inquirer*, January 4, 1907.
[738] *Philadelphia Record*, January 11, 1907.
[739] *Freeman*, January 12, 1907.

CHAPTER 22

An Introduction to Australia

In late December 1906, Jack Johnson and manager Alec A. McLean left San Francisco on a ship heading for Sydney, Australia. James Brennan of the National Sporting Club provided the transportation money, and had Johnson under contract to fight any two men that Brennan selected. The N.S.C. held bouts at the Sydney Amphitheatre.

Australia advertised Johnson as the cleverest and most dangerous aspirant for the world's crown, the man whom Jeffries refused to box, and who could not obtain matches with top fighters in the U.S. An American said, "With Johnson at his best, with the exception of Jeffries, there is not a man in the country who would have anything on him." Supposedly, Jack was matched to box Bill Squires and Peter Felix.[740]

On January 11, 1907 in Lawrence, Massachusetts, Joe Jeannette and Sam Langford fought to a 12-round draw.

Johnson was on board the incoming American mailboat, the Sonoma, which arrived at Auckland, New Zealand on Saturday January 19, and was heading to Sydney. He and McLean brought with them a copy of the Burns-O'Brien championship fight films/cinematograph pictures.

McLean cabled to Sydney, asking whether a match could be made between Johnson and Australian heavyweight champion Bill Squires. By wire, Squires said he would fight Johnson in the event of no match being arranged for him in America.,

The question was whether Squires would look for an excuse to duck Johnson, for Jack had a big reputation. The local press reported, "The famous black is said to be a very clever boxer, and by some is said to be as skillful an exponent of the game as Peter Jackson was. Jeffries and others have refused to meet him, alleging as an excuse that they 'have no use for colored men.'"[741]

The *Sydney Bulletin* reported that the newspapers of his own country said "Amurkan" heavyweight Johnson was equal to Peter Jackson at his best. "Jeffries and other top-notchers have drawn the color-line against Johnson, and it has been printed that their objection was not so much to his color as to his dirty right." It wondered whether the hype was true. "It is just possible that Johnson may be overrated – Amurkan papers have been known occasionally to exaggerate." Australians were about to find out.[742]

---

[740] *Referee*, January 9, 1907.
[741] *Sydney Daily Telegraph*, January 21, 1907; *Referee*, January 23, 1907.
[742] *Sydney Bulletin*, January 24, 1907.

When they meet who will win?

Johnson arrived in Sydney on the evening of Thursday January 24, 1907. He was advertised as the cleverest exponent of the game that America had ever produced. He was a "fine specimen of physical manhood," standing 6' ½" tall, and weighing more than 15 stone, which Jack said was about 211 pounds, though he also said that he would shed some weight before fighting. He said he would be fit to fight for his life at about 190 pounds. His special mission was to fight Squires, who occupied an exalted position in the minds of the local sporting community.

Jack quietly but confidently said,

> I am here to make as much money as I can, and add to my reputation if possible. I heard of your champion, Bill Squires, when Jack O'Brien disappointed Mr. Wren, and I have travelled a long way mainly to meet and beat him, provided I get the chance.

> I am the colored champion of the world, and I am proud of the fact, for there are more colored than white boxers where I come from. I was born in Galveston, Texas, 28 years ago, and I have had 65 battles during my career. … I tried hard indeed to meet Jeffries before he left off fighting, but he drew the color line on me, despite that he had already fought other colored men in the persons of Hank Griffin (twice), Bob Armstrong, and Peter Jackson. The latter match was a cruel thing, indeed, as Peter had long before started on the down grade, and had not fought for four years previously.

Johnson was disgusted by Jeffries' statement that he would not fight a black man for any amount of money, and Jack said that motivated him to leave for Australia.

Johnson also said that he had been prominent before the public for seven years. Although he lost to Marvin Hart, Jack said he had outpointed him two to one.

The local writers were impressed. "Johnson is a bright-looking fellow, able to talk very intelligently, and entirely free of the mannerisms and style of speaking so pronounced in the music-hall negro." Another opined, "A little chat discovered Johnson a bright, brainy fellow, able to talk intelligently, and as one who knew his subjects well, of American fighting and fighters, and the country's resources generally. ... Johnson spoke modestly and to the point."

There was a "lurking suspicion that Johnson is a better fighter than either O'Brien or Burns." Neither one appeared to be interested in boxing Johnson.

A telegram was read which said that Mr. Wren intended to take Bill Squires to England and America. At that point, Johnson straightened up and said,

> Say, here's a nice thing. I've journeyed thousands of miles to hear that your champion, who advertised himself ready to meet anyone in the world, is going to side-step me directly I set foot on Australian soil. Is this the guy that pretended such great anxiety to shape up to Jeffries? Let him go to America. I'll bet his cake'll be dough when he gets there.

Johnson's manager added that Burns and O'Brien would be fighting a rematch of their draw in May, and therefore, Squires would not be able to fight either one before then, nor would either one likely be willing to fight him immediately thereafter. Hence, he too questioned why Squires was so eager to leave Australia just when Johnson had arrived and was prepared to give him a challenge.

However, Squires' backers had been negotiating a potential lucrative bout with Jeffries for $30,000, and likely did not want to risk a loss to Johnson for less.[743]

The next day, on the afternoon of Friday January 25 at the National Amphitheatre on Castlereagh-street, upwards of 100 people attended a reception given to Johnson, which James Brennan arranged. Prominent sporting men made several speeches of welcome.

Johnson was surprised at meeting with so cordial a reception. He said he came there to fight, and looked forward to meeting the country's champion. He hoped that Squires would not leave without giving him a match.

Mr. W. F. Corbett, boxing editor for the *Referee* (who also wrote under the pen name, "The Amateur") said that W. W. Naughton had recommended Johnson as a high-class brand of fighter. "Bill Squires should remain in Australia and meet Johnson – he could do no good in America for some time, as that country's pair of champions – Jack O'Brien and Tommy Burns – were matched for a return battle in May next."

---

[743] *Sydney Daily Telegraph*, January 25, 1907; *Referee*, January 30, 1907.

The general desire was to see Johnson matched with Peter Felix first, as a trial, so Australians could see for themselves just how good Johnson was. In the event of Johnson's winning, he then would meet Squires.

Another speaker said that if Squires did go without facing the visitor, then they would know who to blame. This statement drew applause.[744]

Johnson's remarks about Squires, implying that Bill was afraid to meet him, which were printed in the *Daily Telegraph*, were also printed in the *Melbourne Age*. From Melbourne, Squires read the remarks and became so angered that he expressed a willingness to postpone his trip abroad and meet Johnson, provided that the latter could find sufficient backing for a substantial side wager, and also if a satisfactory purse was offered, either in Sydney or Melbourne.

Squires was upset that as soon as Johnson arrived that Jack used all of his available wind in a thunderous blast of denunciation of Bill for daring to think of going to America without first asking his permission. Johnson accused Squires of side-stepping him, and called Bill a 'guy' even before ever speaking to him. "Pretty breezy sort of behavior this, and quite unnecessarily rude, in my opinion." Squires said that he had been negotiating for a match in America for a considerable time. "I am a professional boxer solely and simply for the financial advantages accruing to the business, and I think that there is more money to be made in America at the game I have taken up than there is here." He said he would fight Johnson if the money was right.

However, Bill had agreed to box under John Wren's management for a certain term, and would do as he said. Wren thought they could make more money in the U.S. Squires would fight Johnson if assured that Jack could put up a substantial side wager and the purse would be as large as what he was assured of getting to box in America. Wren said he would make the match for 1,000 pounds.

Johnson's manager Alex A. McLean said they came 12,000 miles to make money, and he would put up the money if Brennan did not. He was willing to back his protégé for any amount from 1,000 pounds upwards, and the gate or purse could divided however Squires pleased, 60/40 or winner take all. They would fight with the clean break or fight with one hand free. They would accept whatever venue Squires wanted, though they preferred Sydney. McLean wanted two judges and the referee to decide the contest if it went the distance, so that the responsibility would not be entirely on one man's shoulders.

> Mr. McLean further stated that if Squires defeated Johnson he could very justly claim the championship of the world, as he reckoned neither Tommy Burns nor Jack O'Brien, between whom the title now rested, would have a chance with Johnson, and a large number of American people were convinced that the big negro could account

[744] *Sydney Daily Telegraph,* January 26, 1907; *Referee,* January 30, 1907.

for Jeffries were the latter to, at any time, emerge from his retirement, which was hardly likely, as Jeffries weighed over 18 stone [252 pounds], and found farming too profitable an occupation to be neglected for what, at best, would be a big risk, all things considered.[745]

On Monday January 28, 1907, under the direction of James Brennan, a packed house at Sydney's Queen's Hall watched the Burns-O'Brien fight films. The *Sydney Morning Herald* opined, "Judging by the various rounds Burns had all the better of the contest, and to many who saw it the decision of Jeffries, the retired champion [of a draw]...was almost inexplicable."

Also as part of the show, Jack Johnson gave a 3-round sparring exhibition with 6'1 ½" 180-pound Peter Kling, a well-known local boxer. The local press said, "The visitor showed much cleverness, and created a favourable impression." Another said, "Johnson is evidently a more skillful boxer than any we have seen here for many a year; he uses a clever left effectively and accurately, and is as nimble as a cat on his feet." Each night that week, the moving pictures would be shown and Johnson and Kling would give a sparring exhibition.[746]

John Wren said that as a result of legal advice regarding the contract with Squires, there was not the slightest probability of a match with Johnson. Some wondered whether Wren's 'thousand' side-wager offer had been a big bluff, or whether something else was at work. Squires had said that he would fight Johnson in the event of no match being made in America, yet none had been made. Still, it appeared that Wren thought he was going to obtain a very big purse for Squires in the U.S., and he likely did not want to blow it with a potential loss to Johnson for less.

Squires asked, "What has Johnson to boast of in his record. Has he ever beaten a first class man? If so, I have not heard of it; have you? His record is that he lost to Marvin Hart, fought six rounds with Jack Munroe, a man that Jeffries stopped in two rounds." Squires said he would leave it up to his manager regarding whether or not he fought Johnson.[747]

The *Sydney Bulletin*, a weekly paper, summarized the situation. Managers Brennan and Wren had "pulled the leg of the daily press to some purpose. Never before was public interest in two bruisers so beautifully flogged up, and so cheaply." It wondered whether Squires really wanted to fight Johnson. "Squires persists that he is going to America, is in a great hurry to gather in scalps, has no time for Johnson's scalp." Someone then says, "Yah! Yer afraid." John Wren of Victoria, Squires' manager, said that Squires would stay and fight if sufficient inducement was offered, such as 1,000 pounds. Johnson's manager, Alex McLean, said that they traveled

[745] *Sydney Daily Telegraph*, January 28, 1907; *Referee*, January 30, 1907.
[746] *Sydney Morning Herald*, January 29, 1907; *Referee*, January 30, 1907. Significant bouts on Peter Kling's record included: 1905 KO3 Jim Griffin and KO9 Bill Smith; 1906 KO3 Smith, KO4 Peter Felix, LKOby1 Bill Squires, and LDQ5 Bill Lang.
[747] *Referee*, January 30, 1907.

12,000 miles to fight. If Brennan would not put up the money, he would, as much as Squires or his backers cared to cover. They were not particular about terms. Public interest was at a "fever heat."[748]

However, excuses prevailed. Despite McLean's acceptance of the offer to back the fight for the amount Wren demanded, "A couple days later, however, Mr. Wren discovered, so it was telegraphed, that a match could not take place, because of some obstacle found in a written compact between him (Mr. Wren) and Squires when the document had been submitted for legal opinion." It appeared that Wren did not want the bout to take place. Therefore, the press shamed Squires.

Given that the Squires side didn't really want to fight Johnson, therefore James Brennan matched Australian black Peter Felix to box Johnson for the colored heavyweight championship of the world, set to be held at Sydney's Gaiety Athletic-hall on February 19.

However, after Johnson-Felix was made, Squires, perhaps trying to save face, then said that he would put up the money on his own, 1,000 pounds, which represented his life savings, if the winner would take the entire gate receipts, and as long as the fight took place in Victoria prior to February 18, when he was scheduled to leave for San Francisco. "I will take my money up in three days if it is not covered, and will pay no further heed to Johnson."

It appears that the Squires side had used the trick of seeming interested in a fight when they knew that they would not have to fight, given that Johnson already had signed and begun preparations to fight Felix.

Furthermore, Brennan and McLean felt that a little more than two weeks was insufficient time to prepare for a man of Squires' reputation. If Squires was willing to delay a bit longer, Johnson would fight him. Of course, delay would mean that Squires actually might have to fight him.[749]

Squires said,

> I went to Mr. Wren this morning. He is negotiating with people in San Francisco on my behalf. There may be an answer any day which would clinch things. I am bound to him by agreement, and he tells me that I must carry out my undertaking to hold myself ready to sail in the Ventura on February 18. Meanwhile I want to meet this Mr. Johnson, and everything I can do to secure a match shall be done. I'll extend the challenge till Saturday week, February 9.[750]

Johnson was training at Sir Joseph Banks' Hotel in Botany. On the afternoon of Friday February 1, 1907, he put in a couple hours of hard work, boxing with all who cared to do so with him, and also engaged in rope skipping and shadow sparring. The large number of visitors "looked on with astonishment."

[748] *Sydney Bulletin,* January 31, 1907.
[749] *Sydney Daily Telegraph,* January 31, 1907.
[750] *Sydney Daily Telegraph,* February 1, 1907.

42-year-old Mick Dunn, ex-Australian middleweight champion, sparred 3 rounds with Johnson in a fine set-to.[751]

Larry Foley, retired ex-Australian heavyweight champion, was also persuaded to spar with Johnson. Foley was a legend in boxing. He had started his career back in 1871 and was a famous bareknuckle and gloved pugilist who had run a boxing hall where top boxers trained. He was a well-respected trainer who had sparred with the likes of Jem Mace, William Miller, Mick Dooley, Tom Lees, and Peter Jackson. The 58-year-old Foley and Johnson gave a very fine display. The *Sydney Daily Telegraph* said,

> The bout proved a treat indeed, and set the company talking of the old and the new methods. Johnson showed himself to be a very rangy boxer, quick to make the most of an opening, and up to all the tricks of the game, while his adversary skillfully eluded some cleanly delivered punches, and came back immediately to score a point.

Foley did surprisingly well, considering his advanced age and inactivity for years. Of course Johnson probably was just working with him.

The *Referee* said, "Johnson showed himself a good rangy fighter, with a cool head and very intelligent methods – more defensive than offensive. He has a fine and a very strong left, which he knows how to use well." Johnson was much taller than Foley.

It was noted that Johnson stood with his weight mostly on the front foot, and only the toes of the back foot, the right, on the boards. That was opposite to Australian methods, which put the weight more on the back foot. "Johnson rarely steps in with a blow. How could it be otherwise, standing as he does; and he frequently stretches his legs wide apart, and gets very low down in consequence." This too was in opposition to the Australian school which taught a man to make the most of his height.

> But all this notwithstanding, Johnson is a great boxer, and a fine fellow, and one only has to see him going to understand why Jim Jeffries sheltered behind that cowardly protection, the color-line, and also why the admitted cleverest boxer in the world this moment had to come all the way to Australia.

Squires' conditions for a fight were discussed. Johnson listened attentively, stood up with his gloved hands on his hips, and then said,

> Say, look here, I think I know myself better than other people know me. Sooner than let Squires go away to America without the match he pretends such anxiety to make I will meet him on the 15th of this month for any amount of money he likes. I think that is definite

---

[751] Mick Dunn had been boxing since 1890, and his record included: 1892 LKOby2 Dan Creedon; 1895 LKOby8 Joe Walcott; 1897 L25 Billy Edwards; 1900 LKOby7 Otto Cribb; 1901 KO9 Cribb (who died as a result of his injuries); and 1903 D6 Jim Scanlan. The retired Dunn had been inactive since 1903.

enough, isn't it, and if Squires is really genuine in his professions the contest will surely take place.

James Brennan said that although Johnson was only half fit, he would back him for 1,000 pounds and give a purse of similar value, but the meeting had to take place in Sydney. He said Squires could make as much money fighting Johnson as he would make in America, particularly since cinematograph pictures would be taken of the contest and Bill could have an interest in them as well.[752]

Every afternoon, Johnson entertained spectators at the Sir Joseph Banks Hotel by engaging in a set-to with anyone who came along wanting or willing to spar with him. "He is undoubtedly a great glutton for work. Johnson side-steps, sprints in and away, swings round in a 10 or 12 feet circle, and changes front with the rapidity of a lightning flash." He shadow sparred and practiced his footwork.

The *Referee* scouted the upcoming bout. Johnson and Felix both stood over six feet, and "both are first-class boxers." "The visitor is, as was Peter Jackson, essentially a jabbing, and consequently safe, fighter, so that even if he does triumph over Felix – a happening which certainly cannot be written sure – there'll be some time of good boxing, and, in my opinion, great excitement, before the referee is called upon to make his announcement."[753]

The Saturday February 2, 1907 *Sydney Morning Herald* again advertised that at Queen's Hall, both in the afternoon and the evening, Mr. James Brennan would exhibit the cinematograph pictures illustrating the 20-round fight between O'Brien and Burns. There would also be a 3-round spar between Jack Johnson and Peter Kling.

On February 5, at 1 p.m., Brennan deposited 1,000 pounds on Johnson's behalf at the office of the Sydney *Referee*. He expressed a hope that there would be no further talk, that the Squires side would cover the money as quickly as possible. Brennan said Johnson would be ready to face Squires upon 24 hours notice. He said his additional purse offer of 1,000 pounds was still good, provided the match took place in Sydney.[754]

The *Bulletin* said the business methods of fighters and/or their managers were the same as always.

> Challenges and counter challenges in the old days were rarely calculated to find acceptance, every hero being bent on getting credit for a red-hot eagerness to meet somebody whom he didn't expect to turn up. The Johnson-Squires interchange of defiances (through the press) is a mere demonstration of bruisers' bluff. When Johnson arrived in Australia he found that Squires had already booked a passage for America by a boat leaving three weeks later. Therefore he

---

[752] *Sydney Daily Telegraph,* February 2, 1907.

[753] *Referee,* February 6, 1907. It was also reported that Bill Lang was prepared to meet Johnson.

[754] *Sydney Daily Telegraph,* February 6, 1907.

posed as a bitterly disappointed man, and called Bill Squires a "guy." ... For a whole week Squires said nothing. Then he bounced upon the scene with £1,000 in his hand, and an announcement that the nigger could win the money by meeting and beating him any time within the next 16 days, after which he (Squires) would be bound to leave Australia, because Mr. Wren (salute!) wanted him to go away and challenge people in America. Obviously 16 days' notice was too short for Johnson, who in the meantime had fixed up a fight with Peter Felix. Of the two bluffs, the bluff of Johnson was the more reasonable, for it implied the question as to why the departure of Squires couldn't be delayed, considering that Mr. Wren (salute!) professes to be looking for blood (on Bill's account), and Johnson's gore might be collected in a jug before an American fighting engagement could happen. Squires evades this question. He talks about his blessed contract to fight for Mr. Wren (salute!) in America, as though it prohibited him from again appearing under the same management in Australia. Does he expect darkie Johnson to go back to America in pursuit of him? ...

Bill Squires is making a most deplorable exhibition of himself in the matter of meeting Johnson. So far his tactics have been those of a man who is anxious to escape a meeting, and who is trying to bluff the public that it is the other fellow who is afraid. To ask a man to fight within three weeks of the completion of a voyage from 'Frisco to Sydney is absurd. Writer saw Johnson stripped last week, and unhesitatingly declares that it is impossible for him to get into proper condition to meet a born fighter like Squires in the time. ... If he shoots off to 'Frisco now he will arrive there loaded with the suspicion that he was afraid to meet the colored champion. He is treating "this Mr. Johnson" as though the colored man was a mere nonentity. As a matter of fact he is a bigger man than Squires. He was considered good enough to meet the champion of the world, when that champion was in his prime, and the fact that Jeffries drew the color line does not detract from that fact, but rather emphasizes it.

The *Bulletin* felt that whipping Johnson would add to Squires' reputation, such that when he did arrive in the States, immediately he would be regarded as a serious opponent. Hence, only fear could explain his failure to make the fight.[755]

The next supposed obstacle to Johnson-Squires was the venue. Johnson and Squires were willing to fight, allegedly, but their respective promoters could not agree on a venue. Melbourne promoter Wren wanted to host the match there, whereas Sydney's Brennan wanted the bout held in his neck of the woods.

---

[755] *Sydney Bulletin*, February 7, 1907.

POSSIBLE HAPPENINGS IN A FIGHT BETWEEN SQUIRES AND JOHNSON.

WHAT "THE AMATEUR" SEES WITH HIS MIND'S EYE.

Referee, **February 6, 1907**

Eventually, negotiations fell through. Squires intended to head to the U.S. to try to make an even more lucrative match with Tommy Burns or Jack O'Brien. His hope was to win the world championship.[756]

The *Referee* said Squires' claim that it was Johnson's fault that the match did not take place was nonsense. Johnson had been eager for the match all along, but wanted a reasonable time to prepare. Squires himself was not fit for a fight.[757]

The *Bulletin* said, "There will be no fight – except with mud. … Squires' successful dodging of that fight with Johnson is his least creditable

[756] *Sydney Morning Herald*, February 6, 1907.
[757] *Referee*, February 6, 1907.

performance up to date." However, it understood why he had avoided the bout. "A trip to the States is an experience that any man might hanker after, and a defeat by Johnson might have seriously imperiled that trip. They have no time for beaten men in the States." A loss would diminish Squires' reputation and economic value.[758]

Australia Regrets They Will Not Meet.

JACK JOHNSON.   BILL SQUIRES.

On Saturday, February 9, the *Sydney Morning Herald* advertised that there would be a matinee and evening showing of the Burns-O'Brien films, followed by a 3-round sparring match between Jack Johnson and Soldier Thompson. This might well have been Soldier Jack Thompson, an Australian middleweight trial-horse.[759]

---

[758] *Sydney Bulletin*, February 14, 1907.
[759] *Sydney Bulletin*, February 14, 1907. Soldier Jack Thompson's record included: 1903 L20 and LKOby17 Arthur Cripps; 1904 LKOby5 Peter Felix, KO2 Al Neil, and LKOby6 Cripps; 1905 D20 and LKOby7 Al Neil, LKOby1 Jack Blackmore, KO16 Danny Hiam, and LKOby14 Cripps; and 1906 LKOby10 Jim Griffin, amongst others.

Reading from left to right :—**Top Row :** F. DORRINGTON, STEVE HYLAND (Johnson's trainer), A. A. MAC-
LEAN (Johnson's manager). GEORGE RIGNOLD, GEORGE DARRELL, and FRED PARKER. **Bottom Row :** JAS.
BRENNAN, JACK JOHNSON, LARRY FOLEY, and W. F. CORBETT ("The Amateur," Sydney "Referee").

The *Referee* reported that both Johnson and Felix were training hard. Felix stood perhaps an inch taller than Johnson. It anticipated that both men would tip the beam at about the same weight.

Johnson and Bill Lang also had been matched to fight in Melbourne at the Richmond racecourse by electric light on Monday March 4 for a 500-pound purse given by Jack Wren.[760]

Back in the U.S, Johnson had not been forgotten. The *Freeman* wrote, "Jack Johnson and Jack Blackburn are greatly liked. More sympathy has been extended in the behalf of these two fighters than any others known in the sporting world, because of the great handicap they have been placed in so far as getting matches with top notchers."[761]

On Tuesday, February 19, 1907 under the auspices of the Gaiety Athletic Club, held at the National Amphitheatre on Castle-reagh and King streets, which was leased by Mr. James Brennan for the occasion, Jack Johnson made his debut before an Australian audience in a formal fight. Admission was 10/(reserved chairs), 7/6/5, and gallery 2/.

Johnson was scheduled to box 20 rounds in defense of his colored heavyweight crown against "well-known coloured heavy-weight, Peter Felix.

---

[760] *Referee*, February 13, 1907.
[761] *Freeman*, February 16, 1907.

The latter is one of our cleverest boxers, and the contest to-night should be as skillful as one could wish to see." Both had undergone strong preparations, and the bout was anticipated to give patrons a good idea of the visitor's abilities. Mr. Harry Beckett would referee.[762]

40-year-old Peter Felix had about 40 fights of experience, and the ex-Australian heavyweight champion's record included: 1892 W4 Pablo Fanque; 1895 W10 Joe Goddard (Felix 188 pounds); 1896 LKOby2, W8, and W10 Mick Dooley, and W15 Edward Starlight Rollins; 1897 D20 Dooley; 1898 D20 James Tut Ryan and D20 Bill Doherty; 1899 KO7 Doherty; 1900 L20 and D20 Doherty; 1901 KO2 Mick Dooley; 1902 LKOby13 Doherty; 1903 L20 Doherty and WDQ15 Jim Scanlan; 1904 KO5 Soldier Jack Thompson, LDQ5 Bill Smith, LDQ11 Bill Squires, D20 Arthur Cripps, and LKOby1 Squires;

Peter Felix

1905 LKOby2 Gunner Moir and LKOby7 Squires; 1906 WDQ17 Cripps (Felix 184 pounds), LKOby4 Peter Kling, and LDQ5 Tim Murphy. A 1905 report said Felix weighed 14 stone, or 196 pounds, and stood 6 feet tall.[763]

The Gaiety Athletic Hall was packed with a very large crowd.

After the preliminary, loud calls for Squires brought him to his feet, and cheers were heard. Harry Beckett gave a little speech saying that Squires was dodging no one, for he intended to go to America to fight Jeffries. The *Bulletin* said that Squires had side-stepped Johnson adroitly.

With Johnson were his trainer Steve Hyland (brother of Fighting Dick Hyland), manager Alec McLean, and sparring partner Peter Kling. Felix had men named Newlyn, Frazer, and Jack Athorn. Both Johnson and Felix were well received, though Felix found himself to be the more popular idol with the fans, "for the Australian ring-sider is patriotic even with his black man when the opponent is a foreign colored man."

The pair presented an attractive picture; both appearing muscular and athletic, standing over six feet tall. Physically, they seemed well matched, though Johnson showed much better muscle development, especially about the shoulders and arms, "which were of a size rarely seen with a boxer." The *Bulletin* said Felix appeared to be at least half a head taller than Johnson,

---

[762] *Sydney Morning Herald*, February 19, 1907.
[763] Boxrec.com; *Philadelphia Record*, June 25, 1905.

but agreed that his shoulder and arm development were not in the same class as Johnson. "Felix is, as everybody knows, as black as a parson's new hat, while Johnson is merely brown, and of a build which suggests that somewhere in the generations a-rear was a white ancestor."

The *Referee* and *Bulletin* agreed that those conversant with Felix's cleverness felt confident that he would provide at least 6 to 8 rounds of a rousing scrap. Dispatches to America said Felix had a host of admirers willing to bet that he would stay at least 10 rounds.

When he gazed at Johnson, Felix seemed to have a worried expression. He commenced the bout "with his tail most obviously between his legs." Johnson led a few times, and when Felix evaded the blows, Jack smiled, showing his gold-encased ivories. He was evidently amused at something.

Felix poked a left out half-heartedly, which Johnson easily evaded and then immediately swung an effective left hook into the stomach – a pet blow of Johnson's – and Felix went down to the boards, falling over the punch and describing a half somersault as he went down.

Up again, Felix tried to make use of his long reach, but only succeeded in barely tapping Johnson's chest and gloves in a feeble manner. As Johnson closed in, Felix smothered, and Johnson, with a playful right, sent him to the boards. A couple writers did not even see the punch, wondering whether he had slipped.

Up once more, Felix tapped Johnson on the forehead with the tip of his glove, and the brown man, smiling, fired a left uppercut as Felix came in a trifle closer. It caught Felix on the extreme point of the chin, and down he went. Another writer said it was a right uppercut that jolted in while they were smothered. Yet another said the uppercut did not appear to carry a great amount of force, but nevertheless, Peter sunk down to the floor. He turned over on his stomach and Referee Harry Beckett counted him out.

Peter staggered to his feet after 11 seconds, amidst a storm of hoots and jeers from all quarters. The spectators were badly disappointed by how easily and quickly Johnson had stopped him. Felix had been down three times in 1 round, and had put up no opposition.

The *Sydney Daily Telegraph* said,

> The contest (if such it may be termed) calls for little description. Felix made no sort of a stand, and Johnson appeared more tolerant than he need have been. ... Not once during the 2 min. 20 sec. of time occupied in his defeat did Felix land a blow.

The *Sydney Morning Herald* simply said, "The display was not a good one."

The *Sydney Bulletin* said, "It was an awful fiasco, and a shocking finish to Felix's bruising career."

The *Referee* said Felix made no show at all. He never landed a glove on Johnson other than to brush an arm aside once. This account said there were only two worthy punches landed, and both came from Johnson.

Concluding, the *Referee* said, "Many good judges were much impressed with Jack Johnson's fighting power, and voted him a high-class one, which is probably a correct estimate, but nothing that occurred last night justified such a rating, for Felix has never done his capabilities such scant justice."[764]

Afterwards, Bill Squires said he was heading off to America, that to meet Johnson he would have to break his agreement, and he would not forgo his foreign trip for anything he could think of.[765]

Johnson was advertised to box 4 rounds with Sid Russell at the novice tournament at the Gaiety Athletic Hall on Friday, February 22, 1907, just three days after the Felix fight.[766]

The day after boxing with Russell, on Saturday evening, February 23, Johnson exhibited in Newcastle, at the Victoria Theatre. The Burns-O'Brien films were shown. Bill Squires was present, and he was impressed with O'Brien's cleverness and Burns' forceful hitting. After the show, Squires visited Johnson in his dressing room, and the two had a friendly chat, showing nothing but good will, not hinting at the acrimonious words previously exchanged.[767]

Johnson next traveled to Melbourne, Australia, to give exhibitions there and to fight Bill Lang. Lang was of French-Italian descent, and his original name was Langfranchi. Lang's known record to that point only contained about ten bouts, which included: 1905 LDQ9 Bob Fraser and L20 Ed Williams; 1906 WDQ3 Malley Jackson, L20 Bob Fraser, KO14 Tom Fennessey, and WDQ5 Peter Kling. To his credit, Lang had not yet been stopped in a fight, and twice had gone 20 rounds. The 6'1" 23-year-old Lang later claimed to have weighed about 174 pounds for the Johnson fight, which appears consistent with some known weights for him around this time.

The *Referee* opined that now that Squires was about to leave the country, Lang would become the resident champion and defend his title against Johnson at the Richmond racecourse by electric light on Monday March 4, two weeks after the Felix fight. "Lang is a big, husky, ambitious giant, a strong and vimful fighter, who has a chance with any heavyweight in the land. He is not at all scared at Johnson's fine record."

American lightweight Dick Cullen was on his way to Australia, and via letter he advised the Australians to bet on Johnson against any man, "for he is a great fighter, and will out-point any heavyweight in the world. Jack O'Brien and Jeffries know this, and that is why they bar him."

---

[764] *Sydney Daily Telegraph, Sydney Morning Herald, Referee*, February 20, 1907; *Sydney Bulletin*, February 28, 1907.

[765] *Referee*, February 20, 1907.

[766] *Sydney Morning Herald*, February 22, 1907. Australian heavyweight Sid Russell's record included: 1906 LKOby5 Jim Griffin, W20, D20, and L20 Jack Willis, and LKOby17 Ted Nelson. Three days after sparring with Johnson, Russell won a 20-round decision over Bob Fraser.

[767] *Referee*, February 27, 1907.

Johnson was scheduled to exhibit at the Melbourne Cyclorama for three nights, in connection with the exhibition of the O'Brien-Burns bioscope pictures.[768]

On February 28, 1907, Johnson made his first public appearance in Melbourne. He exhibited at the Melbourne Cyclorama and made a very good impression. He was undoubtedly the biggest man seen in an Australian ring. He sparred 8 rounds, 4 rounds each with "Starlight" Ed Rollins, who was an experienced veteran black fighter, and Sid Russell. Jack simply played with them, and "made it very apparent that he is a man of unusual versatility."[769]

The *Melbourne Argus* said,

> All that nature and art can do for the making of an ideal athlete has been done for Jack Johnson. Tall, reachy, willowy, with the smooth, swift action of a perfectly constructed machine, a variety of dazzling punches, acquired by long experience in the great American modernized schools; careful to a degree, patiently playing a safety game, he will prove a revelation in boxing science to the aspiring young Australians, whose idols are of the aggressive 'big punch' hit-'em-out-quick order. Jack Johnson as a scientific boxer stands today without an equal in the universe.[770]

Johnson and Lang were scheduled to box 20 rounds for a 500-pound purse. Admission would be 10/, 5/, and 2/. Johnson was called the lightning-like giant black. Lang was the dogged, defiant, stalwart white.

Lang said,

> There is no Felix streak in my composition. I'm going to fight a winning battle or a losing one, it's all the same. I'm going to fight. Squires kindly advised me before he left Melbourne. He said, "Stand off and you'll be outgeneraled and licked for a certainty. Fight close and fight hard and if Johnson can skip as fast on the retreat as you can advance to the attack then you're too slow for a funeral, and had best get out of the game." So, win or lose, I'm going to fight. Many think I'm going to be a target for a sharpshooter. I may be; but I'm going to be a moving target. I'm going to hustle. I'm going to fight, a minute or the limit. I'm just going to fight, and if confidence begets victory I'm just as surely going to win.[771]

---

[768] *Referee*, February 27, 1907.

[769] *Melbourne Argus*, March 1, 1907. Ed "Starlight" Rollins had been boxing since the 1880s, and his record included: 1889 LKOby20 and LKOby5 Jim Hall; 1890 LKOby9 Bob Fitzsimmons and LKOby5 Hall; 1891 LKOby7 Dan Creedon; 1895 LKOby5 Joe Goddard; 1896 L15 Peter Felix; 1901 D20 and 1902 LKOby7 Jim Scanlan; 1902 LDQ4 Bill Squires and LKOby3 Scanlan; and 1904 LDQ4 Squires.

[770] *Melbourne Argus*, March 1, 1907. That same day, on February 28, 1907 in Sacramento, CA, Sam McVey scored a KO16 over Denver Ed Martin.

[771] *Melbourne Age*, March 1, 1907.

On Friday March 1 at the Olympic Athletic Club, Johnson handled giant Tom Fennessy "just as easily as a boy" in their 3-round sparring exhibition. It appeared that with the exception of the Australian champion, "none of our boys seem to be in the negro's class." Admission to the exhibition was 3/, 2/, and 1/. Ladies were admitted. The Burns-O'Brien fight films were shown as well.[772]

The *Melbourne Age* said the local Victorian devotees of boxing were taking an especial interest in the contest because Lang was the first native aspirant to the crown that Victoria had produced in many years. He would enter the ring in the best possible physical condition.

On Saturday, March 2, 1907, Johnson exhibited at the Melbourne Cyclorama, Victoria-Parade. Admission was 3/, 2/, and 1/. He met Melbourne heavyweight Dick Kernick for 3 rounds of sparring. Those who saw the bout thought that "Johnson is not only a master of the art of boxing, but the possessor of an immense reserve of strength." As usual, the sparring was conducted as part of an exhibition of the Burns-O'Brien bioscope films.[773]

On the day of the big fight, the local *Melbourne Argus* said Lang had shown pluck in taking up the challenge to fight Johnson. "Lang is a much-improved man since he met and defeated Peter Kling, and good judges predict that the coloured champion will need to fully extend himself before he can claim the purse of £500 which the winner of tonight's contest will receive."

On Monday March 4, 1907 at the Richmond racecourse in Melbourne, the scheduled 20-round Jack Johnson vs. Bill Lang fight took place. They were set to

---

[772] *Melbourne Age*, March 2, 1907. Tom Fennessey's record included: 1905 LKOby10 Dick Kernick and LKOby5 Bill Squires; and 1906 LKOby14 Bill Lang.
[773] *Melbourne Age*, March 2, 1907. Dick Kernick's record included 1897 LKOby7 Tim Murphy; and 1905 KO10 Tom Fennessey and LKOby4 Bill Squires.

box at 9 p.m. The ring and grounds would be brilliantly lit with electric light so that night would seem like day. The ring was elevated so as to assure an uninterrupted view of the proceedings. A train would leave Prince's-bridge railway station for Burnley, which was only a five-minute walk from the grounds. The Richmond City Contest Band would perform during the evening. The gate would open at 7 p.m., and the admission prices were 10/, 5/, and 2/.

Bill Lang

John Wren was the promoter. Mr. M. McInerney would referee. Dr. Barrett and Mr. George Watson would judge. The arena was big enough to seat 30,000.[774]

A huge crowd was in attendance. The *Melbourne Argus* said there were nearly 15,000 people. It was a bigger crowd than that which had seen Squires-Kling or Squires-Williams. The *Melbourne Age* said there were between 15,000 and 20,000 men.

Unfortunately, the weather did not cooperate. Torrents of rain fell during the bouts. The spectators were soaked. The first bout started late, and it was not until after 10 p.m. before the main event was ready.

The immense crowd waited patiently. The spectators stood the rain, obediently lowering their umbrellas in response to the yells of those behind them who could not see. The fact that they withstood pelting rain showed how strong a hold the fight game had on the public.

There was a big curiosity to see Johnson, who appeared first. He received a good reception The *Argus* said he entered the ring in a dressing gown covered with faded hues of gaudy embroidery, with the hood pulled over his head, and a towel flung over his shoulders.

The *Age* said Johnson's entrance was "as theatrical as it was funny." A roar of laughter could be heard as an "elongated figure, attired in a duchesse

[774] *Melbourne Argus*, March 4, 1907.

robe, made of chintz or cretonne, besprinkled with damask roses and hlac sparys, with frills around the hem and a hood attachment similarly figured with flowers, stepped through the ropes." A humorist in the crowd yelled, "We don't want to see Mrs. Johnson. Go away woman, and send your husband; this is no place for ladies." The crowd entered into the spirit of matters, and Johnson was chaffed unmercifully. Jack's white eyes peered out at the crowd and he smiled. "At this stage it was hard to say whether Johnson looked most like a hoodoo man from the Congo or Red Riding Hood's grandmother." When he finally lifted his skirts and showed his sinewy black shins, the crowd encored him.

When Jack stripped, he appeared to be a "beautiful physical specimen, saving only for a falling away in the legs." His muscles were great, magnificent in contour, hard and solid. He wore his hair cropped so closely that he appeared almost bald. He had a wide, constant smile, which displayed a gleaming mass of gold fillings.

The local Melbourne man, Lang, delayed matters for nearly 10 minutes. The rain was coming down in torrents, and the mass of people commenced singing "Auld Lang Syne," as they waited for Lang to arrive. Messengers came back at intervals saying it was too wet to fight. The song "Waiting at the Church" was then chorused for five minutes, with particular emphasis put into the concluding bar, "My wife won't let me." They were taking jabs at Lang for making them wait.

When Lang finally entered the ring, the floodgates of the heavens opened, and the rain fell in a veritable deluge. The heavy downpour drenched everybody to the skin. Lang's entry was the signal for wild cheering and shouts of "Good boy, Bill."

The next ten minutes were filled with orators. Frustrated by all the delays, Johnson leaned over the ropes and remarked, "Dere all squabblin' over sompin. Ahm getting' a misery waitin' here; it's too bad." He then inspected the gloves made especially for the contest and remarked, "Ah! Dese are good mitts; maybe we'll warm each oder wid 'em when all the rest is don fightin' wid der tongues."

When the fighters stood near one another it became evident that Johnson's size and weight had been stated inaccurately. He was an inch taller and outmeasured Lang everywhere except for the calf, and had at least a stone (14 pounds) more weight. Another source said Johnson was much bigger, appearing to be at least a stone and a half heavier and an inch or so taller. "His shaved shiny black head radiated the beams of the electric lights like a policeman's helmet." Lang seemed nervous and moved stiffly.

1 – 2 - The *Argus* said Lang made vain but vigorous rushes, while Johnson displayed his remarkable defensive skill. Jack avoided blows in every way possible; by letting his head give way, by taking them on his glove, or by turning them aside with his right arm which thoroughly guarded his face, while his long left was ready to shoot out or up.

The *Age* said that for the first two rounds, Lang did the leading, but Johnson stood in a quiet, indolent, relaxed attitude, and foiled all of the attacks with ease. As he went to his corner, Johnson smiled and said, "Oh! Dis is a joke." The *Argus* said, "The smile made the crowd very angry before the fight was over."

3 - Only once, in this round, did Johnson seem in the least degree rattled by Lang's attack. Lang began fighting hard and swung in some heavy body blows, and occasionally reached the face. However, Lang rarely landed to either the body or head, and never with great effect. Johnson always just grinned, signaling that he was all right. Some thought it was a bluff smile.

However, it soon was apparent that Lang was not in his class, when a straight flash of Johnson's left opened up a cut on Lang's forehead. Once or twice in the round Johnson let himself out and Lang showed the effects of the blows in red rills that trickled down from his forehead. Yet, Johnson was not making any serious attempts at retaliation.

4 - Lang fought with more violence than skill, and Johnson uppercut him hard and often. Jack frequently followed with straight drives.

5 - The men were splish-splashing around the wet ring, for the water accumulated on the tarpaulin floor. As a result, Lang was often off his balance.

6 - When Lang was in a corner, Johnson ripped in three or four lightning uppercuts which showed what he was capable of doing when he so desired.

7 - Johnson showed how utterly outclassed Lang was. Johnson swung his left up to the body, and Lang went down.

Lang rose at six, but a smashing blow on the jaw sent him down for another seven seconds. "Johnson pranced across to his corner in a dancing cakewalk step." The crowd, which already was showing resentment towards Jack's theatrical attitudes and his obvious disregard for his opponent, hooted vigorously.

Lang paid the penalty for the hoots. Johnson again came in, this time with an angry face. Jack brought him down over and over again with blows, right and left, which swept away all of Bill's efforts at guarding.

8 - This round once again saw Johnson "in a lazy mood," and he decked Lang only once.

The *Age* summarized that the 7th and 8th rounds saw Johnson "lam" his man around as he liked, knocking him down a dozen times, opening his forehead in two or three places with heavy left and right uppercuts, which were his best and most efficient blows.

9 - The *Argus* said Johnson swung left and right to the face and body, and the white man crumpled down in his own corner. Lang's seconds threw in the towel.

The *Age* said Lang was down several times, and towards the close of the round, his corner threw in the towel.

Summarizing the bout, the *Argus* said it hardly could be called a match. Lang fought with remarkable gameness, extraordinary earnestness and determination, but had no chance of coping with Johnson. Bill forced matters, but his assaults were in vain.

Lang lasted 9 rounds, but only because Johnson was content to stop Lang's rushes without attempting to make any reply to them. "He could not have held himself more in reserve had he guaranteed to allow his opponent a few rounds of practice before going in to finish him."

The *Argus* called it a fight "farcical in its one-sidedness." "Johnson was as much his superior as Squires has proved over the rest of Australian fighters. How Johnson and Squires would compare is the question which every man in the 15,000 was asking as he left the racecourse."

The *Age* said, "The general impression Johnson made on the spectators was that he is a strong, clever, powerful fighter, far too good for any of our present heavyweights, with the exception of Champion Squires, who, on last night's showing, would probably have outed him."[775]

The *Sydney Bulletin* reported that Lang put up a vigorous fight, but was "over-reached, out-classed, and out-weighted." By the end of the 3rd round, Bill had shot his bolt, and thereafter became a "receiver-general." "Johnson smote him how and when he liked, he upper-cut him, he short-jolted him on ribs and diaphragm," and Lang endured it round after round, "vainly hoping for a chance to knock out his good-natured antagonist."

Like some in the American press who were critical of Johnson for not rushing in to stop his opponents quickly, some criticized Johnson for failing to stop Lang sooner.

> The fighting community is generally of the opinion that the fight has discounted Johnson's prowess considerably. He should have knocked out Lang in three rounds, say the cognoscenti, and if it takes him nine rounds to finish Lang he has no hope of walking over Squires, although he might beat him on points – always provided that Squires didn't get in close and "hit him with me hand on the jore!" As there is apparently no one in Australia of his class just at present, Johnson's manager is considering the advisability of letting him take on two men, one after the other, in quick succession. Which will be rough on the first man of the pair.[776]

Of course, the logic was flawed. Just because Johnson took several rounds to stop Lang did not mean that he would not or could not beat Squires or anyone else for that matter. Plus, most thought that Johnson could have

---

[775] *Melbourne Argus, Melbourne Age*, March 5, 1907. In 1907, Lang would win the vacant Australian heavyweight crown with a KO12 Peter Felix. In 1908, Lang would deck Tommy Burns in the 2nd round before being dropped several times himself until knocked out by Burns in the 6th round. Lang would defeat Bill Squires several times, including: 1909 KO17 and KO20, 1910 KO7, and 1911 KO5. Lang would score a 1909 KO12 Bob Fitzsimmons, but also had a 1910 L20 Tommy Burns.

[776] *Sydney Bulletin*, March 7, 1907.

stopped Lang sooner had he tried to do so. Johnson was content to beat his foes in his own way. It worked for him. Further, when Johnson stopped Peter Felix quickly, in one round, the press criticized the opponent's performance and the fight. So this time Johnson gave them more rounds, but still took some criticism.

The *Referee* reported that Johnson played with Lang in the drenching rain and sloppy conditions. The bout was 9 rounds on sufferance. "The contest does not call for much description, for Lang was like a novice in the hands of his skillful opponent, who, in a happy-go-lucky style, punched Lang at will and apparently where he pleased." Throughout the entire contest, Johnson was grinning like a schoolboy.

The Victorian Lang frequently was on the floor, partly from the effects of blows and partly from slipping on the wet floor. He fought with dash and determination, but never once was dangerous, for he never landed anything to disconcert Johnson. "The end came at the close of the ninth round, when Lang, having been a good deal knocked about, returned to his corner, and the towel was skied in token of defeat."

During the fight, the crowd subjected Johnson to a running fire of comment in respect to what Squires would have done with him had he been in Lang's place. Many felt that although Johnson would give Bill a very stiff fight, Squires' wonderful ruggedness and hard hitting would win it for him. This writer felt that only Jeffries could beat Squires.

Another writer observed,

> Johnson 'cake-walked' all over his opponent. His theatrical style did not please the crowd, which hissed him. This made Johnson angry, and he sent Lang down several times by way of getting even with the crowd. It is an open question whether Squires would have beaten the colored champion, and a good many people think that Bill was wise in getting away to America before his career was cut short.

Johnson and his manager intended to return to America in order to try to force a match with Squires.[777]

The *Referee* said, "Jack Johnson, who has made a splendid impression everywhere, both as a boxer and a man, desires me to tell the people of New South Wales and Victoria how highly he appreciates the many kindnesses extended him." Johnson said, "Everywhere I have been treated capitally. The hand of goodfellowship has been put forth in a free and genuine manner, and I think I have made many good solid friends here."

The Colored Progressive Association, a solid influential Sydney body, would tender Johnson a farewell before he left. Jack was billed for a display of ball punching.[778]

---

[777] *Referee*, March 6, 13, 20, 1907. It was later said that Johnson-Lang drew 800 pounds or $4,000 at the gate, which seems low given the massive reported attendance. The purse was 500 pounds or $2,500, cut 350 pounds to the winner ($1,750) and 150 pounds to the loser ($750). *New York World*, November 25, 1908.

Ultimately, when Squires left Australia, the *Bulletin* said, "Squires did refuse, or Johnson refused; the thing was so confused that nobody knows really who refused." The bulk of the evidence demonstrates that it was Squires who was not interested in a Johnson match. After all, it was Johnson who had fought twice in the span of a couple weeks.[779]

As it turned out, Johnson did not leave Sydney as planned. He was supposed to be on board the Ventura, the same ship that Squires was taking to the U.S. However, Jack and his manager, McLean, had a dispute that first would need to be dealt with in the local courts.

On or about March 18, McLean, accompanied by the sheriff, served a writ upon Johnson in an effort to enforce a claim for £112 alleged to be due in accordance with a signed agreement that had been generated before they sailed to Australia. After accepting the writ from the sheriff and McLean, Johnson punched his manager in the nose, breaking it and badly damaging McLean's face. Johnson was arrested immediately, but then bailed out by promoter James Brennan.

The next day, at the Police Court, it was said that McLean had called Johnson a vile name, though Johnson said nothing about that when explaining what took place. He said what aroused his ire was seeing his manager "acting the policeman." However, the evidence of the abusive name caused Magistrate Smithers to take a more lenient view of the case than he might otherwise have done, and Johnson got off with a £5 fine.

The alleged breach of agreement would have to be dealt with separately, which meant that Johnson would have to remain in Australia longer. McLean said Johnson would remain there for a very long time, unless and until he paid the 112 pounds owed.

> Johnson unquestionably made a very big hole in his manner, and lost a great number of friends, when he so far forgot himself. A pugilist should be even more forbearing than an ordinary citizen. ... McLean gave no provocation at all, beyond accompanying the Sherriff's officer – this according to Johnson himself. If McLean felt he had a claim upon Johnson, he had a perfect right to take legal action. Johnson could defend it, as every orderly, law-abiding citizen defends such matters – at the proper place and time. As it was, he made himself appear a brute, and played well into the hands of the enemies of the game of which he is such a great exponent.[780]

Back in the U.S., the *Freeman* said that colored fighters were popular, but always had to give their white opponents the better of everything, including the purse. Some had even agreed to lay down, but fewer were doing so recently, finding that doing so hurt them more in the long run than it helped them.

---

[778] *Referee*, March 13, 1907.
[779] *Sydney Bulletin*, March 14, 1907.
[780] *Referee*, March 20, 1907.

White fighters were so fearful of losing to colored fighters that they were drawing the color line more and more. "Afro-Americans are made of sterner stuff." Hence, several top black fighters were going overseas to find matches. This writer dreamed of blacks becoming champions in the welter, middle, and heavyweight divisions. "Wonder will that dream ever come true. We would like to see such be the case, as Negro pugilists have had a hard road to travel on."

The *Freeman* thought that Squires would not fight Johnson, because Bill would be so quickly and decisively beaten that his expectations of ever coming to America to fight for a championship and a big purse would be dashed.[781]

Freeman, April 6, 1907

Allegedly, Johnson and his manager had cleared close to 400 pounds for the two bouts, even after paying all of their expenses, so the trip had been financially successful.

However, the scuffle between Johnson and McLean, which led to McLean's nose being broken, face badly damaged, and Johnson jailed and fined, led to the *Bulletin* saying that "the departing nigger, whose refreshment bills here were very large, departed in a halo of recrimination."[782]

A week later, the *Bulletin* reported,

> The latest development in the McLean-Johnson upheaval is that McLean (now out of bed) will not allow Johnson to fight Bill Smith, as the colored bruiser intimated he would do. Johnson came to Australia pledged to fight under McLean's management, and McLean has an agreement with Mr. Brennan, so he says; and he 'reckons' that, under these circumstances, Johnson's name, as far as any fighting without his consent is concerned, is just plain slush.[783]

781 *Freeman*, March 16, April 6, 1907.
782 *Sydney Bulletin,* March 21, 1907.
783 *Sydney Bulletin,* March 28, 1907.

On March 31, 1907, Jack Johnson turned 29 years of age.

Some local experts were debating just how good Johnson was, and how he compared with past greats. Former fighter Mick Nathan said,

> Johnson is a wonder. Slavin, Goddard, and Jackson would have all been pie for him. He is as quick as lightning, and as nimble as a cat. Yes, I think he would prove more than a match for Jem Mace, whom I regarded as the greatest pugilist I had ever seen. If they have any as good, let alone better than Johnson in America, I am afraid Bill Squires will not have a pleasant trip in the States. I am an Australian, and would very much like to see a countryman of mine champion, but I'm afraid my wish will not be consummated.

The *Referee* criticized Nathan's opinion. It opined that Jackson, Slavin, or Goddard would have stopped Lang much faster than Johnson did. If Johnson looked so good, it was only because Lang was slow and not a top fighter. "Put a first-class boxer before Johnson, and I'll be bound he would be found very much wanting. ... I am satisfied from what little I have seen of Johnson...that he is a defensive boxer pure and simple, and by no means a top-notcher at that."

The *Referee* noted that when Johnson was training he bragged, "I can make any man in the world lead." When he sparred Foley, the ex-fighter asked Johnson to lead his left, just to see how Johnson went about it. However, Jack refused to do so, and upon being urged, said, "No; if I do you'll cross me with your right." The *Referee* responded, "Just imagine a champion speaking that way! Little wonder the onlooking crowd laughed."

This writer also criticized Johnson's weight being on the front foot, spreading the legs too wide, and dragging his feet when he wanted to shift instead of stepping.

Also noted was the fact that Goddard twice stopped Choynski when both were at their best, but when Choynski was a "has been" he stopped Johnson in 3 rounds. Hart beat Johnson but Burns beat Hart. Johnson had not been able to stop Jeannette. Jeffries stopped Griffin, but Johnson could do no better than obtain a draw with Hank. Clearly, the *Referee* was perturbed by Nathan's favorably comparing Johnson with Australia's great fighters of the past.[784]

Nathan later countered that he gauged his opinion by watching Johnson spar with the best heavy-weights in Victoria, and though they were not of the same class as the past greats, they gave Johnson ample opportunity to display his power as a boxer. "He stood well up to his man, and blocks leads in such a scientific manner that it created in my mind the impression that he was the cleverest big man I have ever seen. Surely I am entitled to my opinion." He argued that when Johnson was beaten by Choynski, he was relatively new to the sport and knew much less about the finer points of the game than he had learned in the six years that had passed since them.

[784] *Referee*, April 10, 1907.

Bill Farnan had stopped Peter Jackson early in Peter's career, but no one thought Farnan could beat Jackson six years later. Nathan also thought that Larry Foley in his best days was not in Johnson's class. He believed Jeffries had side-stepped Johnson for fear of being beaten.

Nathan noted that the Amateur, the *Referee's* writer, previously had spoken well of Johnson's exceptional merits. Nathan asked, "Why this sudden change of front?" Perhaps it was personal. In conclusion, Nathan said that he would be pleased if an Australian boxer could beat Johnson, "but I am not going to allow my national pride to run away with my judgment."

The *Referee* countered again, saying that the present crop of Victorian heavyweights was very poor. Johnson was no more than a defensive fighter unless opposed to a third-rater. It noted that Greggains awarded Hart their fight because, as Greggains said, "Hart made all the fighting - Johnson was invariably on the defensive."[785]

Malley Jackson, a "quadroon aborigine," tentatively was matched to fight Johnson at Wren's Athletic Pavilion on April 24 for a purse of 200 pounds to the winner and 50 to the loser. However, for whatever reason, the Jackson fight fell through.

Perhaps the terms of the Jackson fight did not suit Johnson, or maybe it had something to do with his dispute with McLean. Possibly he just wanted to return home, for on April 12, 1907, Johnson left Australia via the Sonoma and returned to the United States.[786]

CREEPING

Prejudice Against the Dark Races Seems to be Assuming a World-wide Scope

---

[785] *Referee*, April 24, 1907.

[786] *Sydney Bulletin*, April 18, 1907; *Referee*, April 17, May 1, 1907. Malley Jackson had knocked out Tom Fennessy in 4 rounds, but had lost to both Lang and Felix on fouls. In late April 1907, Peter Kling, the 6'1 ½' 12-stone, 12-pound fighter (180 U.S. pounds) would knock out the 6-foot, 13-stone 12-pound Jackson (194 pounds) in the 3rd round.

CHAPTER 23

Putting A Big Name
On the Resume

In early 1907, well-known New York sportswriter Tad Dorgan said that sportsmen were still hoping for a Johnson-Burns fight.

> It would be about the oddest match ever pulled off in the heavy-weight division if it should ever come to a head. On one side we would have the short, chunky Burns, a man standing 5 ft. 7in. and weighing about 170 pounds. On the other we have the giant Johnson. He stands over 6 ft. and weighs in condition about 195 pounds.

However, it was difficult to tell just how good Johnson really was, particularly given some inconsistency in his performances. Tad wrote,

> No one knows whether Johnson is a demon or not. He is an in-and-outer, like Herrera, but if some big fellow would only hook up with him and let us know there would be a big load off the minds of the sports who follow the fighting game. Burns showed up splendidly against the giant, Marvin Hart. Why not the same with Johnson.[787]

The *Freeman* opined that Jeffries had drawn the color line because he was "afraid that if the doors are thrown wide open, the whites may not be able to retain the championship." Jeff said, "If I were not champion I would fight a Negro at any time. I would be specially willing to meet one were he the champion." Meaning that he would want to recover the title for the white race, but would not risk losing the title to a black man. The *Freeman* responded, "Surely the white man's claim to superiority lacks ground to stand upon when those who are in a position to defend that claim are compelled to put up the bars to keep another race out of the charmed circle. Yet he has only confessed what others have felt all along."[788]

When asked whether he would have a chance with James Jeffries, Tommy Burns said that all champions get beat if they keep fighting long enough. Burns had been fighting and winning regularly, and was in perfect physical condition. "I know I am fast, and I have some cleverness. Moreover, I am not afraid to fight any man living." Conversely, Jeff was in the same physical condition as Sullivan was when he fought Corbett. "The biggest and toughest man living can't drink raw whisky the way Jeff does

---

[787] *Referee*, April 17, 1907.
[788] *Freeman*, April 20, 1907. On April 15, 1907 in New York, Joe Jeannette won a 10-round no-decision bout against Sam McVey.

and keep his vitality. It didn't hurt Jeffries for a few years, but it has him going now. Jeff is terrible heavy. ... He can't train down the way he used to." Tom said Jeff would underestimate him, regarding him as an easy mark who was too small for him, and therefore would not train in the same manner. "And there he'd make a mistake. I look small, but I weigh just what Sharkey weighed at his best. And I'm faster and a more clever boxer."[789]

On May 8, 1907 in Los Angeles, the Tommy Burns vs. Jack O'Brien championship rematch took place. Burns weighed about 178 pounds, while O'Brien weighed a little over 170 pounds. Before a crowd of 4,000, O'Brien ran and grabbed and barely threw any punches, much to the crowd's chagrin, which hooted and taunted him, as did Burns as well. This time, the referee awarded the clear 20-round decision to Burns. The gate receipts were just over $22,000.

There was a bit of a scandal when Burns subsequently revealed that O'Brien had refused to rematch him unless Tommy would agree to throw the bout. Burns indeed agreed to throw the contest, but then double-crossed O'Brien, who upon realizing it, fought purely to survive. Promoter Tom McCarey backed Burns' claims. Because of his prior knowledge, he had told referee Charlie Eyton to call off the bets just before the fight began, which he had done. At that point, O'Brien realized the game was up. James J. Jeffries further revealed that O'Brien had once offered him $80,000 to lie down to him. Burns' reputation took a hit for being involved in such a fiasco, though O'Brien's reputation took an even bigger blow.

Another story claimed that O'Brien had once been offered $42,000 to lay down to Joe Gans in Nevada, but O'Brien would not accept because "he did not want to stand the jibes of the world by losing in any way to a 'nigger,' according to his own alleged words." Many fighters drew the color line in part for fear that if they lost, they would be ridiculed and their reputations tarnished worse than if they had lost to a white boxer.[790]

Regardless of the scandal, San Francisco promoter James Coffroth offered Burns an $8,000 guarantee to fight Australian champion Bill Squires in a fight to be held on July 4, and Tommy accepted.

Jack Johnson was perturbed by the fact that Squires had avoided him after Jack had come all the way to Australia, and now Squires obtained a title shot as his de facto reward.

> Jack Johnson is running around San Francisco in an effort to make disturbance directed at Sir William Squires. Not for a while, Jack. Tommy Burns may celebrate the national holiday by attending to Mr. Squires' downfall. But, Tommy, what if you win and Jeff says no? A certain big black shadow will be looming above Thomas. How about it, Tommy? Yes? No?[791]

---

[789] *Los Angeles Herald*, March 3, 1907.
[790] *Los Angeles Times*, May 12, 1907
[791] *Los Angeles Herald*, May 17, 1907.

Johnson also made it clear that he wanted to fight Burns, and was not happy about the fact that he was not able to obtain an opportunity at the title. Jack told Tommy so, in person. "When matters were clinched, Johnson spoke to Burns in reference to a match to follow the one with Squires, and hot words, which nearly brought about an impromptu scrap, were indulged in." Johnson clearly was frustrated. His race and his ability were freezing him out.[792]

Jim Jeffries, who was going to referee the Burns-Squires match, promised to come out of retirement if Squires won, in order to bring the title back to America. If Burns won, he would remain retired. However, Jeffries was "not particularly anxious to fight again. Jim is a man who hates the grind of training – possibly because he trained harder than any fighter that ever conditioned himself." Jeff said it would take seven to nine months to get back into fighting trim.[793]

On May 30, 1907 in Tonopah, Nevada, Mike Schreck defeated Marvin Hart in the 21st round of their bout when Hart's corner threw in the towel. Hart had suffered a broken right hand/wrist in the 6th round, which hampered him. Thereafter, Schreck took over and administered punishment, despite Hart's fierce aggressiveness. They slugged throughout, and despite his injury, Hart almost knocked out Schreck in the 18th round. However, Schreck recovered, and in the 20th round, only the gong saved Hart from the onslaught. In the middle of the 21st round, Hart's corner threw in the towel.[794]

In a letter to famed sportswriter Tad, one man from Missouri offered advice on how the press and promoters should treat black fighters. He said,

> If you editors would drop the name of Gans, or, if you did mention him, say that he is a faker, the public would soon forget him, the way they did that other black gent, Mr. Jack Johnson. Keep them in the background. That's the way to treat them, and after a while, if they do fight, they will be old and stale and will get their black blocks knocked off. …

> The clubs are doing their part by not letting them fight, and if they do fight, they make them meet some man of their own color, and thereby keep them from getting any more championships. Now let the press do its work. Draw the color line on them. … I am a Southern man, and believe that it is the place of the white man to beat the black man, and not the reverse.

---

[792] *San Francisco Examiner*, December 25, 1908.

[793] *Los Angeles Examiner*, May 12, 1907. C. E. Van Loan said, "Jim Jeffries was the greatest heavyweight fighter this country ever saw. He was probably the greatest fighter of modern times. At the time of his retirement he was at the top of his physical perfection."

[794] *Los Angeles Herald*, May 31, June 5, 1907. Hart's right hand indeed was injured badly. In July, he would undergo an operation upon it. An x-ray had revealed two bones not only fractured but badly splintered. It had been bothering him ever since the Schreck bout. *Philadelphia Record*, July 18, 1907.

Tad responded,

> What is a champion, unless he can beat every man in the world of his weight, regardless of color? … The trouble with the black men is that they are too good. If they were easy and lost every fight there would be no such thing as the color line. … I don't like to see a black man wallop a white myself, but if they are in the game to show their skill it is coming to them.[795]

The *Freeman* again bemoaned the color line. "Sport followers want to see the best fighters, be they black or white, given a chance and the white fake pugilist does not want to see it that way."[796]

THE ARKANSAS MOVEMENT

The Arkansas Movement will doubtlessly stimulate race enterprises in that section.

Freeman, June 8, 1907

Bill Squires was the betting odds favorite over Burns, who found little confidence from gamblers. That made Burns the underdog in four out of five of his championship contests. Tommy had been the odds underdog

---

[795] *Freeman*, June 8, 1907.
[796] *Freeman*, June 29, 1907.

against Hart, and O'Brien in both of their championship contests, though he had been a slight favorite over Flynn. Having heard great things about him from Australians, many thought the hard-punching Australian champion Squires would be the next Bob Fitzsimmons. Some suspected that Burns had been paid to throw the fight so that the more lucrative Jeffries-Squires match could be made. Several respected experts and fighters either picked Squires to win or predicted an even match. However, Harry Pollock said, "My pal, Jack Johnson, tells me that Burns will win."[797]

On July 4, 1907 at Colma, California, in the San Francisco Bay area, before an estimated 9,000 spectators, 25-year-old 176-179-pound Tommy Burns scored a 1st round knockout over 28-year-old 182-185-pound Bill Squires. Burns lightly and quickly bounced around and circled the attacking Squires, timing him with jabs and crisp rights, dropping him three times in all. Observers said that Burns was a shifty, intelligent fighter with a terrific punch, and had been underestimated by many.

The gate receipts totaled $25,251.50. Burns earned his $8,000 guarantee, plus a $5,000 side-bet with Squires' backer, Barney Reynolds. The fight was filmed.

Referee Jim Jeffries said he would remain retired:

If Squires had been the victor, it would have meant $100,000 to me. I would have gone into the ring and would have defended the title. As long as I am able to fight it will be kept in this country. Burns can have the title, unless he should be defeated by some foreigner. That's the only chance to get me back in the ring.[798]

Regardless of his impressive victory, Tommy Burns still struggled to obtain respect as a fighter and firm recognition as champion. The *San Francisco Call* said,

The status of Tommy Burns as the successor to Jim Jeffries has not been firmly fixed by his victory yesterday. It is conceded that no foreign boxer has a chance with him, but Jack Johnson is to be reckoned with in this country. Burns undoubtedly has been underestimated by many and the full measure of his ability is still a mystery, as it was not brought out by his fight yesterday. One thing was settled beyond doubt, and that was his ability to deliver a hard blow.

Former lightweight champion Battling Nelson felt that Burns needed to defeat other men, like Hugo Kelly and Mike Schreck, to clinch his claim to the world title.

If successful in defeating these two men he should take on the only real legitimate candidate for the championship honors, Jack Johnson.

---

[797] *San Francisco Bulletin*, July 3, 1907.
[798] *San Francisco Chronicle*, July 5, 1907.

If Burns can defeat Johnson, the colored heavyweight champion, he will be proclaimed the undisputed heavyweight champion of the world beyond the question of a doubt, now that the only real heavyweight champion, James J. Jeffries, has retired.[799]

Jack Johnson, who was in Atlantic City training for a scheduled mid-July 6-round fight in Philadelphia with Bob Fitzsimmons, said,

Didn't I tell you Squires was the biggest sucker that they ever sent over? Why, Jack Palmer could lick him. He never did anything, never had anything and never will amount to anything. ... I will fight Burns any way he wants – clean break, straight rules, cut the purse or winner take all. He is not a champion until he beats me, and I am recognized as the best big man in America today.

Fitzsimmons? Well, I'll put him away before the limit – you'll see.[800]

When the question about fighting Johnson was raised to Burns, he said that he was not sure whether he would be able to do so. Tom was willing to fight him to show the world that he was the "dusky" fellow's master, but his wife and family had something to say about it. They did not want him to engage in a mixed-race title fight.[801]

Jim Jeffries said Burns was being underrated.

Burns can have the title of champion if he wants it and I think he will take care of it in a satisfactory manner. It will take a good man to whip him. He has unlimited confidence since he has whipped O'Brien and Squires and confidence counts more than many pounds of weight. Burns has ability to back his confidence. He can take a punch and can deliver a punch such as will win fights. Besides, he is clever and fast. He'll stay on top for a long time, barring accidents.[802]

Burns said he would be willing to rematch Squires in Australia if he was guaranteed $10,000. Barney Reynolds felt that Australians would want to see the man who could defeat their idol so quickly. "The prestige he gained by his sensational victory would make him a big drawing card." Reynolds said the folks out there, upon seeing Burns, would be shocked that he was the man who had defeated their respected champion. They would say, "That's the man who beat Squires! What! That little fellow?"

Burns would earn easy money on the vaudeville stage, and was considering a match with England's heavyweight champion, Gunner Moir.

Some called Burns the "one and only real active heavyweight champion," while others called him the "near champion."[803]

---

[799] *San Francisco Call*, July 5, 1907.
[800] *San Francisco Call*, July 8, 1907.
[801] *San Francisco Evening Post*, July 9, 1907.
[802] *San Francisco Call*, July 9, 1907.
[803] *Los Angeles Herald*, July 21, 1907.

The *Freeman* wrote that Squires or his manager had known that Johnson would beat him, which would have cost them the loss of a chance for a bigger purse against Burns or Jeffries. Hence they had avoided him, because the payment for fighting Johnson would have been smaller and the punishment a good deal greater.

Famed promoter and gambler Tex Rickard declared that Johnson was the best heavyweight in the ring, and if given the chance, easily would become the champion.

Joe Jeannette also wanted to fight for the championship. "Many sports consider Jeannette one of the best men of his weight in the country today." In mid-April in New York, Jeannette had won a 10-round no-decision bout against Sam McVey.[804]

Jack Johnson's next fight was against a legend. 44-year-old Bob Fitzsimmons had been boxing longer than the 29-year-old Johnson had been alive. His amateur career dated back to the 1870s, and his professional career spanned over 27 years, since the early- to mid-1880s. Major fights in his nearly 80-bout career included: 1891 KO13 Jack Dempsey (world middleweight crown); 1892 KO12 Peter Maher; 1893 KO4 Jim Hall; 1894 KO5/D5 Joe Choynski (police stoppage when Joe all but out) and KO2 Dan Creedon; 1896 KO1 Maher and

Bob Fitzsimmons feeds his pet lion

LDQby8/KO8 Tom Sharkey (Bob stopped him but was disqualified controversially); 1897 KO14 James J. Corbett (world heavyweight championship); 1899 LKOby11 James J. Jeffries; 1900 KO6 Gus Ruhlin and KO2 Tom Sharkey; 1902 LKOby8 Jeffries; 1903 W20 George Gardner (world lightheavyweight championship); 1904 ND6 Jack O'Brien; and 1905 LKOby13 O'Brien. Only Jeffries and O'Brien had actually defeated Bob. Although Fitz was old and coming off a long layoff, he was a big-name fighter, one of the biggest in boxing, and a former three-division world champion who still was highly respected. His reputation preceded him. Bob had that special aura and charisma that made fans want to see him no matter what; and suspend their disbelief about his age and inactivity.

[804] *Freeman*, July 13, 1907.

San Francisco said the East was crazy over the bout. Despite his advanced age and fact that he was well past his best days, the legendary Fitz was conceded to have a chance against Johnson. When the match was first made, some made light of it "on the ground that Fitz was too old and physically unfit" to engage a young man like Johnson. However, as the bout grew closer, many were giving Fitz a chance. Several writers boosted the bout. Fitz was full of confidence and said he believed that he could defeat Johnson. Bob Edgren said,

> Fitzsimmons surely has the courage of his convictions. His fight with Jack Johnson will squelch those howlers who claim white men fear the big smoke. Bob Fitzsimmons never feared any man. … And when Jack sees the icy glint in Bob's blue eyes it's a good bet that he will feel less like fighting than like running a hundred yards in 9 3/5 seconds.

After all, Fitz was crazy enough to keep lions as pets. He feared no man.

Dick Kain said many criticized the match on account of Fitz's advanced age, inactivity, lack of fitness, and bad hands. However, there was nothing weak about Bob's heart. True, Johnson was clever and much younger. "But that lets the colored man out. If there is anything yellow about him Fitz will not be long in finding it out and then the way things will come to Johnson will be sure to surprise him."

After their rematch, Jeffries said,

> I never believed a man could hit so hard. I had eight stiches taken under my right eye after the fight and eight over it. My left eye had to be sewed up. My nose was pushed flat on my face and my teeth were loosened. Fitz was the greatest fighter I ever saw. These little fellows fighting now wouldn't have classed with him for a minute.

Kain asked, "The question now is, how much steam and strength does Fitz sill possess?" Fans were willing to pay to find out.[805]

Fitzsimmons said he was just as good as young men, for he had taken care of himself and lived a temperate life.

> I figure that Johnson, who has gained a lot of prominence in the ring because the white men have refused to meet him, will be so busy blocking that he won't be able to hit me. I may step in with a shift and land one of my 57 varieties. One, I think will be enough. I expect to win with a knockout.[806]

Regardless of any hype or excitement, Fitzsimmons had boxed in only one fight in each of the past three years, although occasionally he boxed in some exhibition bouts. Most writers were calling upon him to retire after he defeated Gardner at age 40 in 1903. He was still tricky, clever, and powerful,

---

[805] *San Francisco Bulletin*, July 8, 1907.
[806] *San Francisco Call*, July 8, 1907.

but did not hit quite as hard, as rapidly, or as often, and grew tired much more quickly. At that point, Fitz had agreed, saying, "I did well for an old man, but my ring days are over." Two years later, when stopped by O'Brien in 1905, many said that Fitz was done for as a fighter and that only father time had beaten him. Fitz again agreed, saying that he was slow of hand and foot, and no longer could respond to the openings. At that point, Fitz once again retired. Yet, like many retired fighters, he came back again and again. He had scored a 1906 KO4 Charles Haghey, and in March 1907 had boxed a 4-round exhibition with Tony Ross.

Fitz trained at Dunellen, New Jersey. Bob had been sparring with Joe Rodgers and Kid Cutler, but the Kid left, for he "did not relish the walloping he was getting."

On July 14, just three days before the fight, Bob trained with Joe Rodgers and Joe Jeannette, who was added to the camp as a substitute for Kid Cutler.

On hand to see Bob train were Tex Rickard, Bat Masterson, Tom O'Rourke, Bob Edgren, Kid McCoy, who would second Bob, George Considine, and Tom Sharkey. Many came by automobile.

Fitz boxed 4 fast rounds with Rodgers, putting him to his knees in the 2nd round. He then boxed 4 more rounds with Joe Jeannette. "They slugged hard all the way, but neither let out his best."[807]

The *Philadelphia Record* said the upcoming bout had the fight critics guessing. Some took it as a joke and declared that it was nothing but a frame-up, believing that Johnson would carry Fitz. Others took it seriously and declared that old Fitz was due to get an awful lambasting unless he landed one of his famous solar plexus blows early in the contest.

> Bob's hands have been broken too many times to allow him to think of trying to knock Johnson's head off, even were Jack less clever than he is, for a negro's skull is harder than a white man's broken hands, and Bob would surely get the worst of it.

> Johnson is a fast boxer, and it is likely that he will pepper Fitzsimmons pretty much at will unless he gets a smash that slows him up.

Some speculated that Johnson had agreed not to stop Fitz, but he denied it. The gate receipts would be divided based on an agreed-upon percentage, regardless of result. Still, both were motivated to do well.

> A decided victory for either man will do him a lot of good. It would be a great feather in Fitzsimmons' cap to knock out the man whom all the other white heavies have been dodging. ... Johnson, by putting Fitz away in a decisive manner, can strengthen his claim for a fight

[807] *Philadelphia Record*, July 15, 1907.

with Burns or any other white heavyweight who claims the championship.[808]

Jim Corbett picked Fitzsimmons to win. He knew how Bob could punch, and "he also knows that the big negro heavyweight dislikes body blows. The bout has excited unusual interest, and it is likely that all attendance records will be broken at the clubhouse."[809]

On Wednesday night, July 17, 1907, at the Washington Sporting Club on 15th and Wood streets in Philadelphia, Jack Johnson fought former three-division world champion Bob Fitzsimmons.

The day of the fight, the *Record* called Fitzsimmons "the daddy of them all at mixing it up," and Johnson "the big black, whom they all have passed up as too hard a game." Both were in good condition, having trained for the past four weeks.[810]

Among the 2,500 men and one woman present, most were Fitz fans and friends. The spectators paid from $1 to $5 each for tickets. The house generated $8,000. The fans, which completely filled the building, sweltered in the heat for two hours, first watching two preliminary bouts.

Although Johnson was the odds favorite, the old warrior's backers' almost inexplicable confidence made some wary and refuse to bet.

Yet, before they entered the ring, it was rumored that Fitz had a very sore arm from a blow received in training.

It was 10:30 p.m. when Johnson skipped over the ropes. There was feeble and scarce applause. Deputy Sheriff Billy Leedom served a writ upon him. Obviously, someone was claiming that Jack owed them money. Johnson was seconded by Sam Fitzpatrick, Barney Furey, and Black Bill. Spectators amused themselves by throwing money at Bill, who was holding down Johnson's chair. Earlier that evening, Morris Harris had knocked out Bill in the 3rd round.

Two minutes later, Fitzsimmons came down the aisle. Bob was received with deafening cheers from nearly every man in the house, which continued for several minutes. Fitz had Tom O'Rourke, Young Corbett, and heavyweight Joe Rodgers in his corner.

Joe Jeannette and Sandy Ferguson were both on hand to challenge the winner or any man in the world. They were introduced, as were Jack Blackburn, Dick Hyland, and Frankie Neil.

Johnson wore blue trunks. Fitz had a long pair of trunks and a belt made of an American flag. Upon his introduction, when he stood up, Bob received another rousing cheer. Johnson was almost ignored.

The first shock of the evening came when Referee Tommy Keenan announced to the crowd, "Gentlemen: The majority of you don't know, but I have a little reputation to sustain. I hear from a very reliable source that

[808] *Philadelphia Record*, July 16, 1907.
[809] *Philadelphia Public Ledger*, July 16, 1907.
[810] *Philadelphia Record*, July 17, 1907.

Fitzsimmons has broken his right arm. Now unless Fitz will stand for a physical examination, I am done." Keenan then left the ring.

Fitz, Johnson, and their seconds were in the ring at the time, with their gloves on, ready for the bout.

Fitzsimmons raised his hand to ask for quiet, and said,

> I did meet with a little accident. On Monday last when sparring with Joe Jeannette he hit this arm (holding up his right), forcing it a little farther than it ought to go, and since that time the doctor has taken out three ounces of blood and pus from the elbow. But at that it is in pretty good shape now and, since I am willing to take a chance, I don't see why any one else should worry over it.

Another quoted him as saying,

> Gentlemen and friends: In sparring with Joe Jeannette last Monday he hit my old bum right arm and forced it back. I have had two operations performed on it, and a doctor in Paterson took the blood and pus out. If I am willing to take a chance I don't see why the public isn't.

This seemed to satisfy the spectators. There was a yell of "good for you, Bob, go on." The crowd wanted to see them fight, regardless.

Another paper reported that Fitz had torn the ligaments of his right elbow on Monday afternoon (the 15th), two days before the fight, sparring with Joe Jeannette.

Apparently, Fitz was having some financial difficulties and was not about to pull out of a payday. The same day as the fight, George Considine obtained a judgment against him for $4,200 on a note dated July 1. Considine executed an attachment summoning the Washington Athletic Club as garnishee. So, injured or not, Fitz needed the money to pay his debts.

Club manager and matchmaker Billy McCarney settled all questions by jumping through the ropes and announcing that he would referee. McCarney called the men to the ring center. He signaled to Timekeeper Lew Derlacher and the bout began.

1 - The round was slow and tame, with little to it, for both men appeared very cautious. There were numerous clinches and some pretty left-hand work by both. Fitz boxed entirely with his left, keeping his right over his chest in close. Bob only used his right for defense, moving it up and down whenever he saw a blow coming. Bob ducked a number of blows and repeatedly made Johnson jump away by a strong feint.

No one looked for anything resembling a fight. However, Johnson was the faster man and occasionally landed a left or right. Fitz landed two or three times, once bringing cries of "that's the place" from the crowd when he reached for the stomach. Fitz kept dancing away, and when Johnson got close, Bob made passes with his left. There was feeble applause at the end of the round. Neither man had landed an effective blow.

More specific descriptions of the round said they sparred for several seconds. Fitz missed a swing and clinched. Johnson landed a light left to the body and they clinched. Johnson hooked a left to the face and swung a hard left to the body. There was a lot of fiddling, with Fitz dancing away. Johnson twice landed his left to the body. They sparred again, Fitz landed a left hook on the ear and the crowd yelled. Jack jabbed the face with his left and uppercut him on the check with his left. Bob ducked and danced away. Fitz hooked a light left to the ear, and Johnson jabbed the face and threw the left to the wind at the bell.

2 - Johnson was more determined and rushed in, endeavoring to make short work of Fitz. Each local source had its own version of what happened:

Record: Upon the first clinch, Johnson sent Fitz down hard with a left hook followed by a twist that made Bob fall very heavily.

Inquirer: Johnson swung a right to the face and then threw Fitz to the floor, an act for which the referee warned him.

Public Ledger: Fitz ducked two vicious left swings and ran into a clinch. Johnson picked him up and threw him to the floor.

Press: Fitz started to shift but stopped. Johnson swung his right to the face and threw him down hard. Fitz took a five-count and rose.

Fitzsimmons seemed to be jarred and unnerved considerably, and he took his time in rising. He was still full of fight, though, and went after Johnson hard. Bob landed a short left hook to the body, which Johnson returned in kind. Each local paper had its version of the end:

Record: A Johnson left and right sent Fitz down again, and he failed to rise in the ten seconds. While down, "Bob rolled about on the mat as though doing a circus stunt, and some thought he rather overdid the matter, for he was on his feet, apparently strong, two seconds after McCarney had counted him out."

Inquirer: Johnson jolted him with a right. Fitz went down and tried to rise at nine, but fell over sideways and the referee stopped the fight.

Public Ledger: Johnson fired off two right uppercuts, one landing under the heart, and the other opening a gash on Bob's left cheek bone, sending Fitz down. He rolled over onto his back. At the count of five he got up onto one knee, but then his head went down onto the mat and he fell over gracefully as the referee counted him out.

Press: Johnson swung his right to the body and when they came together with a hard collision Fitz fell to the floor without being struck by a blow. He rolled over and over on the floor, and, being in such a helpless state, Referee McCarney put his arms around him and led him to his corner.

The *Philadelphia Record* reported that Fitz had been counted out in the 2nd round after making a weak showing against the burly negro. The fight was "only a farce," and the fans were "handed a lemon." Johnson was "in his prime" and in perfect condition. It further said, "The fight, if such it could be called, did not amount to much. Fitzsimmons, who is only a poor imitation of his former self, was no match for the big black, who could probably have stopped Bob in the first round had he gone at it with a little more determination."

Afterwards, Johnson said the crowd wanted him to allow Fitz to last the 6 rounds, but he was taking no chances with Bob, treating him with as much consideration as he dared in justice to himself. He was not about to allow Fitz to land a devastating blow on him, and figured that getting him out as soon as possible was the best course of action.

The *Philadelphia Inquirer* told a slightly different version. It said Referee McCarney stopped the bout in order to save Fitzsimmons. The blow that dropped him in the 2nd round did not appear hard enough to have done much damage, but the crowd made no fuss. It was evident that Fitz was too old to have a chance. Most of the spectators were glad that he was not completely knocked out cold.

The *Philadelphia Public Ledger* said Johnson's victory was clean-cut, but there was little credit attached to it, for Bob's right arm was practically useless. Fitz put up no competition, and the crowd received little action for their money. However, the fact that before the fight Bob had addressed the spectators as "fellow Elks" had "acted as a balm, and they were apparently willing to stand for anything." They liked him.

The *Philadelphia Press* said Fitz attempted to box with a useless crippled right arm but practically collapsed after a round and a half of boxing. The pitiful spectacle was a farce and nearly a fake. During the four and a half minutes of fighting there were not three hard blows struck.

The crowd saw two big men wander around the ring. In the 1st round, it was apparent that Johnson was inclined to be merciful. Typically, when the crowd has paid good money to see men box, it would urge the fighters on, but this time, the spectators fell into the colored man's whim and were happy that he was merciful. They wanted to see Fitz survive. However, in the 2nd round, Johnson threw him down and then bumped him down, and the referee, seeing that feeble Fitz was helpless, stopped the bout.

The fight was called a lemon and a big barney, with Fitz to blame for handing it to his followers. He had no excuse to enter the ring when he knew that physically he was unable to defend himself. He should have called off the affair. He permitted the public to pay the exorbitant prices of $1 to $5 to see him with the expectation that he would put up a good contest. That he did not and could not do.

Johnson escaped censure because of his apparent effort to be merciful. Tom Keenan proved his honesty and willingness to protect the public. His reputation was sustained.

There was some censure for the club, but as it had gone to big expense to bring the men together, it was understandable why it still supported the bout in spite of the injury.[811]

The *Freeman* reported that the 1st round was tame. It was apparent that Johnson would at least win on points, but the knockout was not looked for, at least not so early. Fitz was not in the same class as Johnson, but showed flashes of his old form.

Fitzsimmons claimed that Johnson deliberately fouled him by wrestling and throwing him to the floor in the 2nd round. That dazed him and left him vulnerable to the subsequent punches. "He wrestled me to the floor. I fell flat on my back and the blow hurt me." Some said there was a right or a left hook that landed before he was wrestled down, which might have had something to do with Bob being dazed.

After rising, a quick, snappy right hook to the chin sent Fitz down like a sinking ship, lifeless, hopelessly beaten and outclassed. Johnson, the man whom every other top white fighter had avoided for over a year, seemed as surprised as the crowd. Bob tried to rise at nine but fell over sideways. The packed crowd sat in a numbed and pitying silence.

Even Johnson gave no signs of exultation. "He seemed to feel as the crowd did - that he was viewing the wreck of the greatest fighter that the game ever saw." There were no cheers. It had the feel of a funeral for a great fighter.

Many said it would have been a totally different fight if the Fitz of ten years ago had been present. Some said Johnson would not have lasted 6 rounds. Tom Sharkey said Bob had seen his day and was no more a fighter. He still had cleverness, but the speed and snappiness was no longer there. "He was willing, but the colored fighter, young and active, as quick as a cat, was too good." Tom O'Rourke said Bob's age told. "He was a kingpin in his day, but his days are over." Young Corbett, who seconded Bob, said, "The old man tried once too often." His age caused his strength to give out early on. It might have been a slightly better fight if Bob had not been injured coming into the bout.[812]

Fitzsimmons did not give Johnson much credit as a puncher, even though he had stopped Bob in 2 rounds, when the fastest Jeffries had managed to stop him was 8 rounds. Of course, they had met two totally

---

[811] *Philadelphia Record, Philadelphia Inquirer, Philadelphia Public Ledger, Philadelphia Press,* July 18, 1907.

In the preliminary, Morris Harris stopped Black Bill in 3 rounds. Black Bill knocked Morris Harris out of the ring in the 1st and 2nd rounds, but both were very tired in the 3rd, when Harris hit Bill in the stomach and Bill went down and out.

In the second preliminary, Kid Cutler, John L. Sullivan's sparring partner, knocked out Jim Jeffords in the 3rd round. Jeffords had all the best of matters until the point in the 3rd round when Cutler landed a punch to the jaw that dropped Jeffords to the mat. A few moments later, a punch in the stomach ended the bout.

[812] *Freeman,* July 27, 1907.

different versions of Fitz. Bob said the hardest puncher he ever met was Choynski. He ranked Jeffries second.[813]

It was the first time that a black man had defeated a former world heavyweight champion. Although Fitzsimmons was a shell of himself, as has proven to be the case in boxing, names sell tickets, and putting names with reputations on one's record helps build a fighter's reputation. Ironically, although in a competitive boxing sense, it meant very little, this win actually helped boost Johnson's reputation much further.

Years later, Johnson said he realized that Fitz was only a shadow of his former self. He normally allowed fighters to last rounds in order to give the crowd their money's worth, but he could not afford to compromise his reputation, given that Bob was so old. Therefore he decided to take him out quickly. Johnson took little credit for beating a man so far past-it. However,

> The oddest thing about the entire affair was that this knockout earned me a huge leap in everyone's esteem. He knocked out Bob Fitzsimmons! This Johnson must be a real boxer! ... This goes to show how reputations are made. For years I had been fighting the best men who ever put on the gloves and all of those bouts put together did less for my reputation than knocking out poor old Bob Fitzsimmons!

The fact was that Fitzsimmons was still a very big name to have on the resume, and history has proven that fight fans often foolishly care more about name and reputation than anything else.

In his later autobiography, Johnson said, "I do not take much credit to myself for this bout, but it seemed necessary at the time in clearing the course that was before me."[814]

All of the top white heavyweights were sidestepping Johnson. Some said that Tommy Burns had to defeat Johnson to become the real champion.

Mike Schreck made his case as a top contender with his stoppage of Hart, but "Johnson is more entitled to a match than Schreck."

Schreck's wife did not want him to fight Johnson. She said, "No, I do not approve of Mike fighting a colored man, unless he held the title. Then I would insist on Mike's fighting him. But there is no chance for Mike to meet Jack Johnson as long as Johnson is not the champion." So Schreck drew the color line as well.[815]

Johnson signed to fight two white boxers who were seeking to boost their reputations with a strong performance against the top contender: Kid Cutler, the bout to be held in late August, and Sailor Burke, the bout to be held in mid-September.

165-pound Sailor Burke was "a middleweight of little reputation." Some called the bout a joke. However, Burke was positive that he could win,

---

[813] *Freeman*, August 3, 1907.
[814] *My Life and Battles* at 60-61; *In the Ring and Out* at 55.
[815] *Freeman*, August 3, 1907.

saying, "I will secure a decision over Johnson as sure as we fight." Jack was training for Cutler in Atlantic City. He would train for Burke at New Dorp, Long Island.[816]

In late August 1907, Tommy Burns told promoter Jim Coffroth that he was willing to fight Jack Johnson if offered $25,000. Scouting the potential bout, one wrote of Johnson, "Few better built big men have ever put on a boxing glove. He stands six feet two, and weighs well over 200 pounds. … Johnson is a remarkably clever boxer. His quickness and great strength give him ability to hit a heavy blow."

Sam McClintick, Dick Hyland's manager, said,

> Johnson is game enough. He has no yellow streak. The only trouble with him is that he isn't aggressive enough. He is too careful. He stalls along all through his fights, taking good care of his face and letting the other man do the work. It's almost impossible to reach him. He doesn't take any chances. He has faked a lot of fights. Perhaps that was because he couldn't get the matches without promising to be good. Tommy Burns has faked a fight or two as well as Johnson. But neither Johnson nor Burns has ever 'laid down.'

Heavies Who Are Carded for Next Big Battle.

TOMMY BURNS

JACK JOHNSON

Burns was said to be a great fighter for his inches. He was half a foot shorter than Johnson, but he had as long a reach, and his arms were just as thick. He was broad-shouldered, very tough and enduring, would likely tear into Johnson, and could take a world of punching without losing any courage.

Burns said, "I am not afraid of Johnson, as so many people seem to think. While the husky Negro is clever, he has a streak of yellow in his makeup that will

[816] *Freeman*, August 10, 31, 1907; *Philadelphia Record*, August 28, 1907.

show itself in short order when he gets into the ring with me."[817]

On August 28, 1907 in Wilmington, Delaware, at the Farmer's Fair, U.S. Senator Benjamin R. Tillman of South Carolina delivered an address. Several thousand persons were on hand to hear him talk about "The Race Problem From a Southern Standpoint." Tillman said, "The race problem is threatening the civilization of the South." Tillman declared that the negro was a menace, and the problem the negro created was greater now than at any time since the civil war. He "dwelt upon the sad fact that the Civil War cost the nation a half million lives of the very flower of its manhood, yet, he asserted that the race question has to-day more aspects of danger than prior to the opening of the war."

Tillman declared emphatically that he did not believe that education would succeed in solving the race question, and ridiculed that idea which black leader Booker T. Washington had advanced. Tillman declared that all the brains Washington had were due to the white blood in his veins. His father was white and his mother a negress. "There are 10,000,000 negroes in the country and one Booker T. Washington." He said that one of the worst things in connection with the race problem was the education of the negro, for it would lead to a dreadful war of the races.

He was critical of Pennsylvania, where white and black children went to school together. Tillman abhorred the idea of mixed-race schools, feeling that they would cause a contamination.

Tillman said the negro vote was venal and purchasable, and was the controlling vote in many Northern States. "The worst of all creatures is the mean, low, white man who puts himself on the level with negroes in order to secure their votes and for political purposes. They are worse than the negroes themselves." Continuing, Tillman said, "I despise a man who for the sake of securing the franchise of negroes placed them on their level."

He pleaded for the annulment of the 15th amendment, for it had only led to the pollution of the ballot. "The remedy and the solution of the question lies in the repeal of the Fifteenth Amendment. Unless this is done there will be a race war eventually, and what can now be settled by the ballot will be settled by the bullets."

Tillman related the experience of South Carolina and other Southern states during the reconstruction period, when negroes had held political offices. "How would you like to be ruled by negroes?" In response, there were cries from the audience of, "No, no." He said that all acts designed to disenfranchise blacks were necessary in order to preserve civilization. He would take away the negro vote. Tillman further said,

> Therein lies the root of the trouble, the doctrine that a negro is as good as a white man. I make this prediction, that the time will come when the two races will be engaged in a deadly conflict. You will wake up some morning and read of the slaughter of whites and

[817] *Freeman*, August 24, 31, 1907.

blacks, and a race war in all parts of the South. But we shall be able to take care of them. And I have no doubt that the white men of the North, even from Pennsylvania, would come to the help of the Caucasians of the South if their help were needed. But we want the long-nosed Yankees to keep their hands out of it and let us settle the problem.

And the cause of this feeling between the races in the South? We have been spending our money to educate the negroes. We have been educating them so that many of them can read and write. ... But the fanatics and negroes of their North are sending down their papers to the South Carolina and other Southern negroes, and this incendiary stuff inflames them. They believed from reading it that they are oppressed and deprived of rights which they are told were given them as an outcome of the civil war. This flame of hatred fanned by the Northern fanatics will cause the outbreak that will bring bloodshed to the South and a war of the races.

The negro can never be the equal of the white man because he is by nature the inferior. You can't make a white man out of a negro by sending him to school. The negro race has not the necessary moral fibre in it.

After his speech, members of the Democratic League presented him with a handsome gold-headed ebony cane. "Tillman held the attention of the large crowd from beginning to the end of his speech, which was frequently interrupted by applause. Many of his hearers were women, who were particularly demonstrative when he made some of his most effective points."[818]

That same day, on Wednesday August 28, 1907, in an open-air arena on the Atlantic League baseball grounds at Lauer's Park in Reading, Pennsylvania, Jack Johnson fought Charles "Kid" Cutler.

For a year and a half, Cutler had traveled with John L. Sullivan as his sparring partner. Cutler also gave wrestling exhibitions, for he was a wrestler turned pugilist. He had met all-comers during the season, and of the 215 wrestlers that he had met, only 5 of them were able to stay 15 minutes with the young giant. He was recognized as one of the best wrestlers in the country. Cutler knew that defeating Johnson would catapult his reputation even further.

According to secondary sources, Cutler's only known bouts to that point were 1907 ND6 John Ferrili, KO3 Jim Jeffords (on the undercard of Johnson-Fitzsimmons), and LKOby9 Jim Barry. The Barry bout took place just 19 days prior to the Johnson fight. Cutler was fairly inexperienced to be going up against such a boxer as Johnson. However, Sullivan believed in him and hailed Cutler as the coming champion.

---

[818] *Philadelphia Press, Philadelphia Record*, August 29, 1907.

The Minnesota native Cutler was 23 years old, stood 6 feet tall, and was a muscularly-built 197 pounds. Johnson stood over 6 feet tall and weighed 210 pounds.

Johnson presumed his victories, for already he had his schedule mapped out. After Cutler, Jack's next bout would be with Sailor Burke at Bridgeport, Connecticut. He then planned to go to California to try to obtain fights out there. Johnson was advertised as the man who was being side-stepped by champion Burns and nearly all the other top heavies.

The fight was scheduled for 6 rounds. A crowd of over 600 witnessed the bout, which was the main event.

The ring was erected near home plate, and all present had a good view of the bouts. The baseball grounds were illuminated with four large electric lights. 12 women were amongst the big crowd, and by their cheering, they must have enjoyed the fights.

According to the local *Reading Eagle*, when the bell rang, Cutler stepped to the center of the ring and fired a blow at the jaw which Jack ducked.

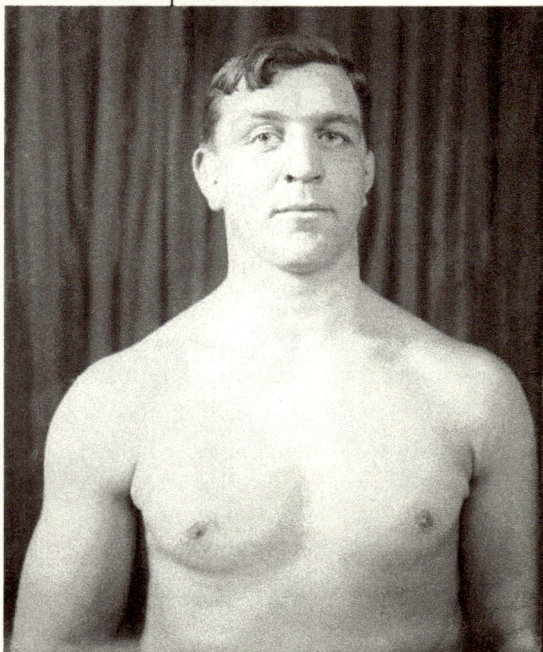

Kid Cutler

They sparred for a half-minute. Johnson was studying his opponent. Suddenly, Jack landed a terrific blow on Cutler's jaw and he fell like a log. Referee McNealis counted him out. The quick end surprised the crowd. The fight had lasted only a minute.

Despite being counted out, Cutler wanted to continue, but he was done for. He too was surprised and greatly disappointed. He had wanted to stay the full 6 rounds with the colored man.

> For a big fellow, Johnson is very clever. He is six foot tall and has immense shoulders, but his legs are almost as thin as those of ex-Champion Bob Fitzsimmons. People who saw how quickly he disposed of Cutler think he would have a good chance with Champion Jeffries. Cutler is one of the best built fighters that ever donned fighting togs.[819]

[819] *Reading Eagle*, August 28, 29, 1907; *New York World*, August 28, 1907.

The *Philadelphia Press* reported that Johnson led in the fighting, and after landing a few blows, he decked Cutler with a stiff uppercut to the jaw, and Referee McNelius of Philadelphia counted him out.

The *New York World* said that as soon as the bell rang, Johnson slammed a left on Cutler's nose. Three punches were struck, and Cutler received them all in the face. After one minute of fighting, Johnson landed a blow on the jaw and Cutler fell to the floor like a log. It took several minutes for him to revive, and when he did, he wanted to continue fighting. Cutler was quite discouraged, for he had been promised a number of bouts had he stayed the 6 rounds.

The *Freeman* reported that Johnson ripped a wicked right to the jaw, and Cutler went to the canvas like a cherry dropping from a tree. He rose just as the referee reached the count of ten, but Referee McNeals had spoken the final number.[820]

Years later, Johnson explained why he had stopped Cutler so quickly. John L. Sullivan had been declaring that Johnson didn't have a champion's punch, and that his young sparring partner, Kid Cutler, was better than Johnson. Hence, Jack took the fight and saw to it that Sullivan's protégé got little glory out of the match, for Jack decided to show his punch and take him out quick. "That was the last I ever heard of John L. Sullivan's opinions."[821]

The *Freeman* predicted that Johnson had about as slim a chance to fight Burns as O'Brien had to convince the public that his bouts were on the level. "Burns has no idea of taking on Johnson, and when he gets ready to fight again he will sidestep big Jack and take on one of the white men."[822]

Although Mike Schreck was coming off his KO21 over Marvin Hart in late May, on August 29, 1907 in San Francisco, Al Kaufman knocked out Mike Schreck in the 7th round. This win made Kaufman a strong contender.[823]

On September 2, 1907 at Colma, California, 150-pound Stanley Ketchel scored a KO32 over Joe Thomas in a brutal, lengthy war that saw both men down. Ketchel's original name was Stanislaw Kiecal. He was born in the U.S., though his parents were from Poland.

Johnson was scheduled to box Sailor Burke fifteen days after the Cutler KO. The approximately 22-year-old Sailor Burke's record included: 1905 KO2 Eddie Haney; 1906 KO2 Peter Maher, KO3 and W6 Joe Grim; 1907 WND6 Jim Jeffords, KO3 Andy Walsh, WND6 Grim, and KO3 Dave Holly, amongst others. Burke was known as a good puncher. He had scored 9 knockouts in 17 wins, which included newspaper decision victories.

---

[820] *Philadelphia Press, New York World*, August 29, 1907; *Freeman*, September 7, 1907.

[821] *My Life and Battles* at 61.

[822] *Freeman*, September 7, 1907.

[823] *San Francisco Call*, August 30, 1907. Kaufman's victory over Schreck was significant because Schreck had been on a hot streak, with results that included: 1906 KO8 Dave Barry; 1907 KO19 John Willie, KO13 Tony Ross, and KO21 Marvin Hart.

However, many of those were only 3-round bouts, the most allowed in New York at that time. He had no official losses, though he had lost a couple 3- and 4-round newspaper decision bouts, and had a couple newspaper draws as well. He had 21 known fights, and had never been stopped.

The *New York World*'s Robert Edgren said the bout was another opportunity for Johnson to prove just how great a fighter he really was. Burke was a local light heavyweight. "Johnson will have to beat Burke quickly or else he will never get a chance of getting on a match with any of the big fellows. None of the club managers would offer him 30 cents unless he acts quickly."

Edgren opined that Johnson should have little difficulty in disposing of Burke, for Jack was two inches taller, had a several-inch reach advantage, and weighed 20 pounds more.

Still, despite the handicaps, many thought that Burke had a good chance to beat Johnson. Burke was confident, and claimed that one of his great right swings to the jaw would do the trick. He realized that Johnson was very scientific, so he did not intend to box with him. He would sail right in and let both hands fly for the jaw.

Johnson said he would meet the sailor's rushes with a left jab and a short right uppercut to the body or a right swing to the jaw.

Both had been training for the past few weeks and were in the best condition possible. One of the largest crowds ever to witness a contest at Bridgeport was expected. Every seat had been sold.[824]

On Thursday September 12, 1907 at Bridgeport, Connecticut, under the auspices of the Liberty Athletic Club inside Smith's Opera-House, the Jack Johnson vs. Sailor Burke bout took place. 5,500 people attended, including prominent sporting men from New England, New York, and Philadelphia. Smith's theater was packed to capacity, from cellar to dome. Sports were even packed into the aisles. About 1,500 New Yorkers paid $2.30 each for railroad fare and from $2 to $5 each for seats. Nearby towns such as New Haven, Waterbury, and Hartford were also represented Joe Humphreys/Humphries said at least $6,500 was in the house.

The afternoon of the fight, Burke said he would knock out Johnson, while Johnson said he would win in 3 rounds. Jack was the favorite. The local Bridgeport gamblers were surprised and delighted that so many strangers were willing to bet that the Sailor would go the scheduled 6-round distance. However, little betting was done. Burke's backers demanded 8 and 10 to 1 odds. Some small wagers were taken at 2 to 1 that the fight would last the entire scheduled 6 rounds.

Various national dispatches reported that Johnson weighed about 182-185 pounds to Burke's 163-165 pounds, though no official weights were taken.

---

[824] *New York World*, September 12, 1907.

At close to 10 p.m., Johnson appeared, arrayed in a big gray blanket and a bathrobe "from which his long legs projected like the stilts of a camera under the focusing cloth." He climbed into the ring, followed by seconds Larry Temple (who likely was his sparring partner), trainer Herbert Furrey, and manager Sam Fitzpatrick. Jack was greeted with a roar of applause as he walked over and shook hands with Joe Humphreys, Burke's manager. Jack took a chair, pulled it over close to his manager's seat, and engaged him in a friendly chat.

There was a wait of at least a half-hour, until the crowd began to whistle and stamp. Burke was a no show. The crowd wondered audibly what had become of Burke. Some thought he had grown cold feet. Joe Humphreys explained, "He can't get on his shoes." A spectator asked, "Are his feet frozen?" Humphreys simply winked. Some thought he was making Johnson wait, so as to get the big fellow's nerves on edge. At last, Humphreys said, "I'll get him," climbed through the ropes, and then almost immediately appeared with Burke.

Burke finally entered the ring, dressed only in white trunks. He was attended by Jim Savage, Frank McElroy, Joe Mulvihill, and Joe Humphreys. Despite making everyone wait, he was given a tremendous ovation.

Referee Dan Walker called the men to ring center, where the comparison in their size "made the bout immediately appear farcical." Burke looked like a bantam next to the "colossal negro." Another said the Sailor looked as strong and as well-built as Fitzsimmons in his prime, but Johnson, with smooth-gliding muscles, towered over him as they shook hands. Johnson had advantages in height, reach, and weight. They agreed to break at the referee's order.

They started for their corners, but Humphreys began a loud discussion of the rules. Fed up with the long wait, Johnson interrupted, impatiently saying, "Oh! Fight! Fight! We'll just fight!" There was drama in the moment. "Spectators held their breath at these ferocious words of the great Zulu, and looked pityingly at his victim." In awe, Humphreys left the ring.

A reporter was on the scene from the nearby *New Haven Evening Register*, as well as Robert Edgren of the *New York World*. The former perceived Johnson as doing all that he could to stop Burke, while Edgren thought Johnson was holding back and carrying him.

1 - When the bout began, the "dinge with a broad smile" immediately used kidding tactics. He greeted Burke with, "Hello little sailor boy." Burke responded with two prettily timed vicious rights to the head and followed with a left to the stomach. This caused Johnson to change temper immediately.

Johnson rapped Burke on the stomach with a resounding thud. He used a bull-like rush and pushed the sailor violently to the ropes and then dropped him to the floor with two heavy rights to the ribs.

Burke rose and Johnson pushed him down again. Burke jumped to his feet and ran into a clinch. On the break, the sailor crossed a slow right to the "cloud's jaw." Johnson fired a hard right to the wind that sent Burke down and almost through the ropes. He took a five-count.

When Burke rose, Johnson began slapping his hands into Burke's stomach. The sailor began falling without being hit, and appeared afraid. At the bell, Burke was hanging on, though apparently still strong.

2 - Johnson went right after Burke with terrific rights and lefts to the stomach, which had the sailor visibly distressed. After Johnson had battered him in his first rush, Burke slipped to the floor and took a nine-count.

After rising, Burke landed a right to the stomach that plainly hurt Johnson. However, the "ink person" started battering Burke with leads to the head. Burke clinched to survive.

3 - This round saw the last vestige of aggressiveness taken from Burke. As they broke from an early clinch, the sailor landed a left to the jaw. As a result, Johnson nearly put him out. Jack responded with continual rushes, pounding him all over the ring, sending in terrific blows.

Starting half-way into the round, three times Johnson forced Burke to drop and take a nine-count, each time the result of hard body blows. Burke groaned from the punches.

Robert Edgren saw matters differently, for he believed Johnson was carrying Burke. He said that perhaps "conscience-stricken," Johnson stopped slapping Burke on the body and "only pushed him down gently to let him take the count. He even urged the sailor in a soft whisper to stay down as long as he could. But amiable Mr. Johnson's distress was relieved when the bell rang after that two minutes, cutting the round one minute short."

A national dispatch disagreed with Edgren, saying that Johnson smiled at Burke in this round and said, "Stand up and fight; I can't knock you out when you are on the floor. Here, how do you like this one? Go ahead, shoot one at me; I want to see if I can catch it." At the bell, Burke was hanging on desperately, evidently in a bad way.

4 - This round was like the prior one, except it went the full three minutes. The bout degenerated into a pitiful stall on Burke's part. He continually rushed into clinches and held on as often as possible. On each break, Burke shifted and dropped, taking nine seconds to rise, making it impossible for Johnson to stop him, in spite of desperate attempts to land successive effective blows.

When Burke did essay to send over a lead, he was totally unable to land or sting his opponent, and after missing, would generally slip down for a rest and at least half of the count.

5 - According to Edgren, Burke, knowing that Johnson "wouldn't take a chance by hitting him anywhere else, covered his blushing stomach with his forearms" and left his jaw exposed. "Johnson flapped and slapped Burke on the crossed wrists, but never, never risked hitting him on that open and

exposed jaw." Johnson finally hit him hard on the chest and Burke went down for a nine-count.

The *New Haven Evening Register* said clinch after clinch marred the bout. As the referee attempted to separate them, Johnson would hold his hands high above his head to show who the offender was.

Burke staggered about and made a sorry spectacle. Time and again but a single blow was needed to drop him. After the most terrific body punishment, even though his face was contorted with pain, Burke would survive and continue, showing his condition and desire to last.

6 - To start the last round, they shook hands. Burke soon fell and took a count. Johnson smiled pleasantly, and then hit the sailor on the ribs a couple of times with an open hand. Burke stood with his stomach drawn in and his arms crossed over it. Edgren said, "It puzzled Johnson to think out some way of getting at him without hitting his jaw by accident. Burke's jaw was so near that it was always getting in the way. It was a nuisance." Johnson seemed intent upon working the body.

Burke swung at Johnson's jaw and fell down when he missed. He took only four seconds to rise this time, and Johnson said in a jokingly reproachful way, "Aw, why didn't you take nine?" The crowd began to hiss and yell. After the last round ended, the theatre emptied out in two minutes.

Since it was a no-decision bout, no formal decision was rendered, though everyone knew that Johnson clearly won every round.

Summarizing, the *New Haven Evening Register* said Johnson beat up Sailor Burke with ease, completely outclassing him. Johnson landed at will, and only Burke's clinging and dropping kept him from being stopped. Clinching marred the bout. After the 1st round, the only interest in the fight was the question of whether the sailor would stay the full 6 rounds. In order to last, Burke was compelled to resort to all the stalling methods known to the game. He retained his reputation as a game and resourceful fighter, while Johnson "simply remains the foremost active heavy."

Light Heavyweight Who Was Outclassed by Jack Johnson at Bridgeport Last Night.

SAILOR BURKE.

Afterwards, Johnson said that he failed to discover the alleged speed and hitting ability that had been touted for the sailor. "I tried hard to get him, but he was there to stay and he did it. He just wouldn't stand up and fight."

Unlike the *New Haven Evening Register*, which thought Johnson was trying to do all he could to stop Burke, but could not do so as a result of all the clinching and flopping, the *New York World's* Robert Edgren strongly believed that Johnson was carrying Burke. He reported that Johnson faked in the fight and never had any intention whatsoever of putting Burke away. Burke appeared to be there only to make a reputation as a man who could stick for 6 rounds. He flopped frequently, and Johnson helped by refusing to hit him in the head. The fans knew it, and therefore left in disgust. A few minutes later, Burke showed up in Fred Bullen's café, and did not even have a flush on his face to show for the "fight."

At 2:15 a.m., as the New Haven Railroad "special train" dropped off the New York fans "in the wilderness that lies just above Harlem River," the spectators swore, "Never again."[825]

SCENES AT RINGSIDE WHERE WOULD-BE 'CHAMP' WAS PRINCIPAL IN RAW FAKE

New York World **cartoon by Robert Edgren, September 13, 1907**

The *Washington Times'* next-day report said the bout was "rank," because in order to survive and kill time, the Marine Burke went to his knees several times without being hit. Still, Johnson gave him a hard beating and Burke proved his gameness, for he ate all the wallops that came his way. For 6 rounds, "he took a whaling that would have torn the heart out of an ordinary fighter," but his great condition and toughness pulled him through.

Burke went down 17 times. He was knocked down many times, and at other times, like Joe Grim, when things got too warm and a knockout seemed to be on its way, Burke dropped down to the canvas and took a nine-count to recover before resuming.

In the first couple of rounds, Burke tried once or twice to fight, and swished by Johnson's jaw with rights and slashed his left at the body, but the blows were either cleverly blocked or missed by an inch or two.

---

[825] *New Haven Evening Register, New York World*, September 13, 1907.

Johnson invariably would come back with a rush, knocking Burke down, or belting him so hard in the body that he was forced to the floor for a respite.

Many cheered Burke for continuing to try even though he faced certain defeat. In the 3rd and 4th rounds, however, when Johnson smashed his body and attempted to follow up, Burke would drop to the canvas, whether or not he was hit. When he dropped three times in succession, the crowd got sore at him, and some hissed and howled at his actions. They told him to get up and fight or quit.

Johnson played with him, but landing the one solid finishing blow was not that easy, given Burke's tactics.

In terms of their boxing abilities, there was no comparison. It was no contest. Johnson merely exhibited what a clever boxer and accurate hitter he was. He was infinitely cleverer than Burke, much too strong for him as a mixer, and far too fast for the sailor even to hope to compete with him.

The *Day*, a newspaper based in New London, Connecticut, said Johnson entirely outclassed Burke in every way. By the end, the Sailor was on his feet, but very wobbly and hanging on to Johnson for support.

It was more an exhibition than a contest. Burke was knocked down or wrestled to the floor fourteen times. He hit the floor about five times more often than his glove landed on any part of Johnson's anatomy. The pitiful exhibition only served to show that Burke could take a lot of punishment. After the 1st round, nearly every time that Johnson hit him he sent the Brooklynite to the floor. Burke took the full nine seconds each time.[826]

Jack O'Brien sat at ringside and observed that it was merely an act of charity on Johnson's part to let Burke stay the full 6 rounds. "I think Jack Johnson is a wonderful boxer, puncher and fighter. I believe he could whip Jeffries and I don't blame any of the big fighters for ducking him."

Most disagreed with O'Brien's opinion that it was charitable to let Burke stay. "They were of the opinion that it would have been much more charitable if the colored heavyweight had ended the 'exhibition' quickly and not cut poor Burke up so much."[827]

In early October 1907, there again were indications that Tommy Burns would be willing to cross the color line if he was offered enough money. Burns once again told San Francisco promoter Jim Coffroth that he would fight Johnson if he was paid $25,000. Although this was quite a large amount of money, "under present conditions they would undoubtedly draw a big house and at top prices, too." However, at that point, no promoter was willing to put up that much money for the fight.[828]

Burns wanted to solidify further his claims to the world championship, so he decided to travel to England to fight the British champion, Gunner Moir. Burns was willing to fight the white Moir for a third of what he demanded to fight Johnson.

---

[826] *Washington Times, Day*, September 13, 1907.
[827] *Freeman*, September 21, 1907.
[828] *Los Angeles Herald*, October 2, 6, 1907.

CHAPTER 24

Convincing the San Franciscans

On October 15, 1907, Jack Johnson arrived in San Francisco with manager Sam Fitzpatrick to sign articles to fight former heavyweight title challenger Jim Flynn. "Fireman" Jim Flynn's 34-bout career included: 1902 W20 Willard Bean and D20 Joe Cotton; 1903 LKOby8 Jack Root; 1904 D20 Andy Walsh, KO9 Fred Cooley, and D10 George Gardner; 1905 KO8 and KO9 Mike Rowan; 1906 KO4 Morgan Williams, D15 Jack "Twin" Sullivan, and LKOby15 Tommy Burns. Against Burns, Flynn put up a game, grueling, thrilling, and entertaining bout, so his stock rose even in defeat. Fans admired him, and enjoyed watching his aggressive hard-punching style.

Since being defeated by Burns, Flynn had not lost a fight. His subsequent record against respected fighters further justified the good opinion of him: 1907 W20 and D20 Jack "Twin" Sullivan, KO18 George Gardner, KO7 Dave Barry, and WDQ13 Tony Ross.

Flynn fought like Marvin Hart, and they were fighting in the San Francisco area, where Johnson felt he was robbed of the decision against Hart. This would be Johnson's first bout in San Francisco since that late March 1905 fight, two and a half years prior.

As soon as Johnson arrived in San Francisco, Zick Abrams announced that he had Jack under contract, and said that Johnson owed him a "couple of hundred." The former poolroom man wanted to be paid. He had a document signed by Johnson, dated May 27, in which Johnson authorized him to make all of his matches.

Regardless, Johnson and Flynn signed articles with promoter Jim Coffroth for a 45-round encounter to be held at Coffroth's Mission street arena at Colma at 3 p.m. on Saturday November 2, for 55% of the receipts, to be divided 55% to the winner and 45% to the loser. Billy Roche was named as referee.

A 45-round fight was long enough such that Johnson would not have to worry too much about a bad decision. Someone likely was going to be stopped in that length of time.

Johnson would immediately start training at Joe Millett's, near Colma, under the watchful eye of manager Sam Fitzpatrick. He would spar with Denver Ed Martin and Joe Willis. Flynn already had been training at San Rafael for the past week.[829]

---

[829] *San Francisco Call*, October 16, 1907.

Johnson began training with Ed Martin on October 16. The local *Call* said, "Johnson is conceded to be the cleverest of the heavy weights and all he needs is to back up his quality with fighting spirit and he should prove invincible."[830]

A few days later, the *Call* said,

> With Tommy Burns en route to England in search of some easy money, Jack Johnson looms up as the star of the heavy weight division. He has not always been taken seriously here, as he has shown too much timidity in the ring to suit the taste of the local fans. The latter want lots of action together with the spilling of some blood, and this Johnson did not care to provide.[831]

On October 20, the large gymnasium where Johnson usually worked was too small to accommodate the nearly 800-person crowd which came to see him train, so he did his boxing outdoors on an open-air platform instead. He boxed 6 rounds with Denver Ed Martin, and their work was greatly admired. Johnson exhibited all of his skill, as well as his huge proportions. He was never far out of condition. He liked roadwork, having completed 12 miles that morning.

Jack Johnson and sparring partner Ed Martin

At Shannon's, near San Rafael, the Pueblo fireman Flynn also worked before an admiring crowd. In the morning, he ran to Kentfield and back. In the afternoon, he boxed with 217-pound Charles Miller, showing no fear. He worked for 45 minutes, and trainer/manager Frank McDonald was satisfied.[832]

---

[830] *San Francisco Call*, October 17, 1907.
[831] *San Francisco Call*, October 20, 1907.
[832] *San Francisco Call*, October 21, 1907.

Johnson advertised that he would have a ladies' day at his training quarters on Thursday the 24th. "The fair members of his race are expected to appear in numbers, as 'Arthur' is popular with his people." Jack had been seen on Fillmore street with his bulldog and "his swaggering walk." Johnson had no worries about the upcoming fight's outcome, and was advising all of his friends to get a bet down on him.

Owing to his size and cleverness, the "big smoke" opened as the 7 to 10 favorite. The confident underdog Flynn advised his friends to bet on him, as he intended to wager on himself.

Gallery admission would be $1, the lowest amount charged since the great fire. Hence, Coffroth expected a large gallery attendance. Reserved seats would be $3 and $5, and box seats $7.

On October 24 at Shannon's, fight fans saw Flynn go 3 hard rounds of sparring with Charles Miller, who was larger than Johnson, but proved to be nothing better than a punching bag for the aggressive Colorado native. Flynn roughed him as though he were an infant. But for trainer Frank "Mollie" McDonald's intervention, Flynn "would have flattened Miller just as sure as fate." The general impression was that a rougher, tougher fellow than Flynn never tied on a padded mitt.

The *Evening Post* said, "Before making a bet on Johnson, it would be well worth while to look this fireman-fighter over." The *Post* was impressed. "As a gymnasium worker, Flynn is in a class by himself." Jim never rested. "He is constantly on the move – he really works."

The *Call* said, "Flynn seems to have every qualification for a fighter, his only possible deficiency being in the length of his arms." He was well-proportioned, heavily muscled, lively on his feet, and could hit hard.

Flynn's friends did not think his 20-pound smaller size would be a big factor. Flynn would offset the weight, reach, and height advantages with his aggressiveness, an area in which he outclassed Johnson. Plus, other comparatively smaller men had gone rounds with Jack.

> Johnson has not been a success as a knock out hitter, but this time it seems he must stop his aggressive opponent or suffer the humiliation of being knocked out himself. Johnson has the skill and the strength, but when he is stung he prefers to keep away rather than take a chance. It will be hard to keep away from Flynn, who seems to be most effective at infighting.[833]

A number of women visited Johnson's camp on the 24th for ladies day. Johnson sparred with Ed Martin.[834]

That same day, Tommy Burns set sail for England for his scheduled match with Gunner Moir. Before he left, Tom said that he intended to fight Jack Johnson when he returned to the U.S. Burns said of Johnson,

---

[833] *San Francisco Call*, October 22 - 25, 1907.
[834] *San Francisco Evening Post*, October 25, 1907.

I haven't much regard for him. He is big, but he isn't as big as he looks. ... His body isn't strong, and I'm satisfied that he has a yellow streak. ... I'll give Johnson a fight, but I'll make terms. Gans demanded and got 80 per cent with Memsic, win, lose, or draw. I won't be that hard on Johnson, but I'll get mine.[835]

The *Call* said Johnson was alleged to be big enough to beat Jeffries, yet had "never lived up to his formidable fighting appearance." Johnson promised to upset all precedent in his engagement with the rugged Flynn by carrying the fight to him. "In the past Johnson has been willing to let well enough alone and has been content to go along and trust to getting the decision at the end of 20 rounds." He could not do that for two reasons. First, the bout was scheduled for 45 rounds, so someone likely would get stopped along the way. Second, Flynn was the type of fighter to keep on top of Johnson every minute of the bout, so he would have to fight hard.

Jim Coffroth was amongst a large crowd that visited Johnson's training quarters at Colma on the 25th. Johnson scoffed at the idea of Flynn beating him. He offered to wager Coffroth a suit of clothes that he would land 22 blows on Flynn's nose before the latter could land twice on him. Coffroth was willing to make the bet with Johnson if Jack would take another bet. He wanted to bet that the couple blows Flynn landed would do more damage than the 22 that Johnson landed. Jack wanted to think about it, and busied himself with his Boston terrier.

That day, because the roads were muddy, Jack did not do his usual road work, but doubled his boxing time with Denver Ed Martin.

Harry Pollock felt that Johnson had a large contract on his hands. "Flynn's style, which is aggressive, is just the kind of fight which Johnson does not like and if he lands some of those short arm blows on Johnson's body the latter is expected to show unusual speed in getting out of range."

Frank McDonald, who was training Flynn, had run out of sparring partners. He was extending invitations to heavyweights to come to Shannon's to work with his man. Few wanted to stand the beating that Flynn would give them.[836]

The *Call* said Johnson would have to show gameness in order to beat Flynn. It believed that the fight would force Jack out into the open. "Many excuses have been made for Johnson in the past as to why he lacked aggressiveness, but this time there can be no excuses. Either he is a fighter or he is not." Flynn had as much fighting spirit as a bundle of tiger cats, and this quality likely would force Johnson to bring out all of his ability, both as an offensive and defensive fighter.

Still, it opined that when comparatively lighter men like Gardner and Langford had been able to hold their own and last the full distance with

[835] *New York Evening Word,* October 24, 1907. Burns was set to meet English champion Gunner Moir for a $5,000 purse and a $2,500 side wager. *Call,* October 27, 1907.
[836] *San Francisco Call,* October 26, 1907.

Johnson, "there must be some weak spot hidden beneath that big physique." Yet, Johnson had won those fights clearly and had dropped both of them more than once, so the criticism appears a bit harsh and picky.

Flynn was said to be looking even better than Marvin Hart in training. Hence, some bettors were wagering on him. Still, on form and career history, Johnson figured to be the strong public choice. Regardless of how a fighter looked in the gym, the past had shown that gymnasium form is one thing, and fighting form quite another. "A man may be a veritable bear in training and then prove lamblike when he steps into the ring."

Johnson would have a 2.5-inch height advantage, 5.5-inch reach advantage, and 20 pounds in weight. Still, his advantage in power was said to be slight. Flynn was 22 years old, while Johnson was 29. Johnson was listed as 6'1" and 195 pounds to Flynn's 5'10 ½" and 175 pounds. Regardless, Flynn was expected to make Johnson move some and it was up to Johnson to protect himself and at the same time take some of the fighting spirit out of Flynn.

On the 27th, Johnson worked out in front of a big crowd, sparring with Ed Martin. The *Call* again harped on its theme: "Johnson works like a champion in his gymnasium, but in the past he has seldom lived up to this promise when in the ring. When the fighting pace quickened Johnson invariably showed a tendency to avoid the rough work and thus earned the reputation of being faint hearted." It believed that on the day of the fight, Johnson "seems to lose this confidence and it is then that an opponent who knows nothing but fight gets on his nerve." The upcoming contest would demonstrate whether this defect had been corrected.[837]

Flynn's appearance and performance in training impressed many of the bettors. They liked his aggressiveness, and banked on it, combined with Johnson's defensive and cautious showing in the majority of his fights, to return Flynn the winner. Johnson "likes to stand off and box, while posing in statuesque attitudes." Flynn bettors believed that when foes carried the fight to Jack, as Flynn undoubtedly would do, Johnson did not fight up to his formidable appearance. At least that was his record in his San Francisco fights, according to the *Call*.

Yet, for all the denigration of Johnson, the odds still remained at 10 to 7, with Flynn the underdog. On appearance and confidence, the *Call* said Johnson should have been a 1 to 2 favorite.

Given that he and Ed Martin had sparred strenuously the day before, Johnson took matters more easily on the 28th. Instead of boxing with Martin, he took on welterweight Jim Hayward. Johnson's nose was slightly sore from his bout with Martin, and he did not think Hayward could add to his injury. The little fellow tried hard to land, but had to leap into the air to do so.[838]

---

[837] *San Francisco Call*, October 28, 1907.
[838] *San Francisco Call*, October 29, 1907.

On October 29, Johnson opened up the day as a 2 to 1 favorite over Flynn. "The wise bettors figure that Johnson's class will carry him through." Flynn was a live underdog though, for the fight was scheduled for 45 rounds, and he was a well-conditioned, rough, tough, rugged fellow who was willing to take blows in order to land his own. It was believed that his chances would increase if he could make it past 20 rounds.[839]

More than a few fight folks were taking notice of Flynn and boosting him, saying that he was the real goods. He was in great shape, ready to go the full scheduled 45 rounds if necessary.

> Scrappers of the Flynn type, especially among the heavyweights, are exceptionally scarce these days, for never since the days of Tom Sharkey has the American prize ring seen so slashing a husky among the big fellows. With Flynn it is a case of rip and tear from the sound of the first gong until somebody hits the canvas, and his mixing methods are bound to win him a home with the fans.

A big crowd was anticipated, judging by the size of the crowds which had been visiting the training camps.[840]

Gamblers were wagering that Johnson would stop Flynn in about 20 rounds. Johnson had all the physical advantages and was conceded to be the cleverest boxer in the division. The fact that Flynn was much more aggressive did not sway their opinion. Johnson remained a 1 to 2 favorite.

Short-enders would find the odds tempting. Flynn had the reputation of being just the kind of fighter who had a chance with Johnson, for in the past the latter proved to be a boxer who liked to stand off and peck at his opponent. Jack did not do as well with rough and tumble fighting, the kind of mixing that Jim liked to do. Johnson represented the clever Jim Corbett boxing school, while Flynn was another Sharkey, "with more skill than the sailor could boast." Flynn felt sure that Johnson could not stop him.

> It is almost a tradition of the ring that Johnson does not like the game when it reaches that point where the sporting blood of the spectators commences to sizzle. He has shown a tendency to act on the defensive entirely. ... During his fight with Marvin Hart Tim McGrath, who was seconding him, pleaded with him to try to land at least once on his opponent. Johnson was willing to let well enough alone and finished out the twenty rounds, only to lose the decision for his lack of aggressiveness.

Trainer Sam Fitzpatrick, "who knows a fighter when he sees one," vouched that Johnson would put up a fight and surprise even his friends. Johnson wanted a match with Burns, and felt that stopping Flynn would make it hard for Burns to ignore him.[841]

---

[839] *San Francisco Call*, October 30, 1907.
[840] *San Francisco Evening Post*, October 30, 1907.
[841] *San Francisco Call*, October 31, 1907.

Tiv Kreling had spoken with Flynn. "If Flynn is as courageous in the ring as he appears to be in his talk, he stands a very good chance of beating the black scrapper. I don't think I have ever talked to a fighter who seemed to feel so absolutely sure of winning as this Flynn. Furthermore, one can see at a glance that he's in great condition."[842]

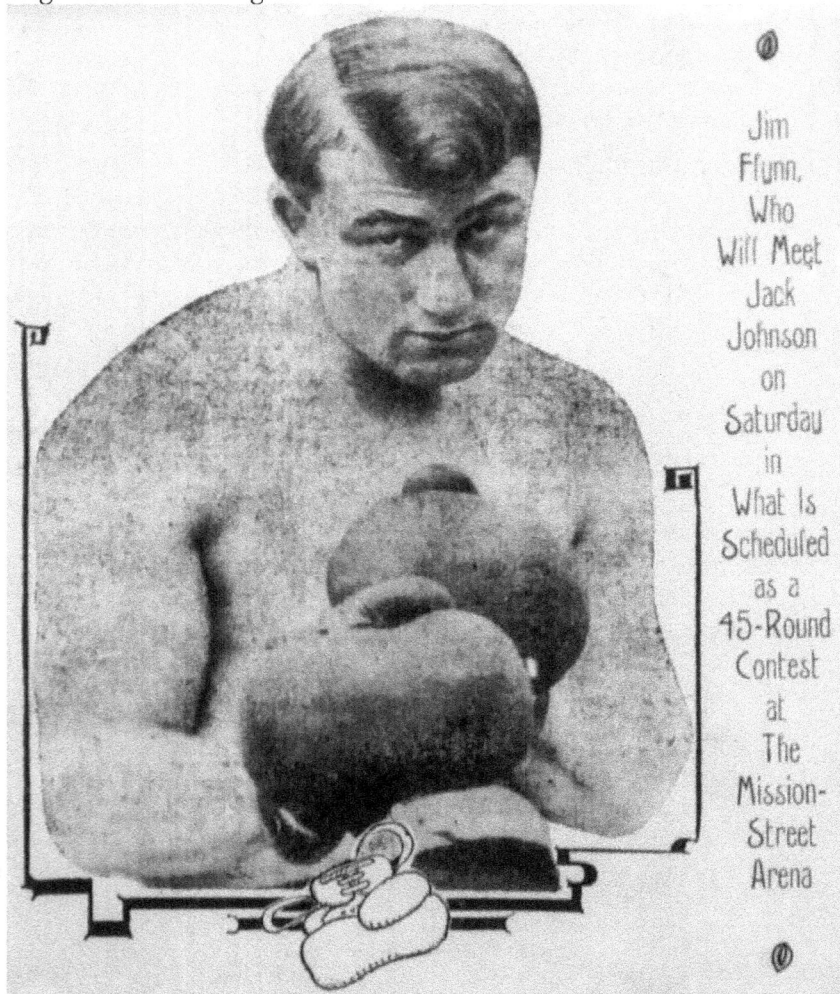

Jim Flynn, Who Will Meet Jack Johnson on Saturday in What Is Scheduled as a 45-Round Contest at The Mission-Street Arena

Though Johnson remained a heavy odds favorite with the sporting fraternity, Frank McDonald, Flynn's trainer, said there was a big surprise in store, for Flynn was being held too cheaply. Johnson had the newspaper reputation as being the man that both Jeffries and Burns were afraid to fight, "and this has given him a lot of prestige that he hasn't really earned." McDonald said Flynn had been asking him for a year to make a match with Johnson. He was confident that Jim wanted the fight, and wasn't taking it simply for a payday or because there wasn't anything else in sight for him.

---

[842] *San Francisco Evening Post*, October 31, 1907.

Sam Fitzpatrick said the fact that Flynn was a game, aggressive fellow with a faculty for assimilating punishment did not bother him at all. He said those very qualities would make him a sure mark for Johnson's punches, and his durability would simply prolong the agony before Flynn was knocked out. He said it was not often that a man became champion by allowing the other fellow to hit him. "If Flynn starts in as bravely as he says he will, Johnson will pick him to pieces very quickly." Fitzpatrick promised

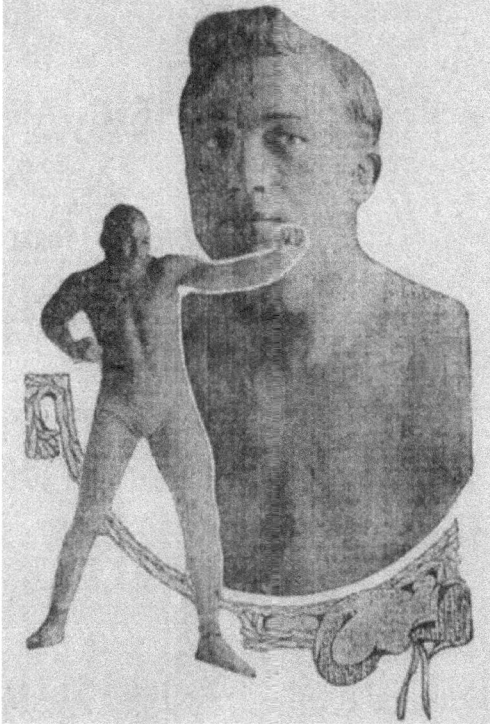

that Johnson would show a lot of aggressiveness in this match, which the *Call* said was "a quality he has not shown in any of his fights here."

It was even money that Johnson would stop Flynn within 20 rounds. Bettors expected Jack to reverse his usual way of fighting and win decisively, particularly given that it was scheduled for 45 rounds, so he could not just coast to a 20-round decision, and also because he wanted to create further demand for a Burns fight.

However, some of Flynn's followers were so enthusiastic that they wanted to bet that *he* would stop Johnson within 10 rounds. They also wanted to wager that Johnson would jump over the ropes when Flynn started after him in earnest. Flynn had a lot of dash and intended to take the fight out of Johnson from the start.

Johnson already was figuring himself to be the winner, and said he wanted to meet both Kaufman and Burns. "Johnson declares that he has the promise of Tommy Burns that he will fight him upon his return to this country and that is the one match he wants."

Both men talked bravely, so one was in store for a surprise.

Jim Coffroth said there would be none of the former difficulty in reaching the arena, for the transportation facilities were now good. On the day of the fight, the street-car service would be increased, and after 11 a.m., the Valencia street cars would run to the arena under a four-minute headway.[843]

---

[843] *San Francisco Examiner, San Francisco Call,* November 1, 1907.

Sports-writers could not understand why Flynn was such a heavy underdog. However, gamblers felt that Johnson's physical advantages gave him the edge. "This mill is especially interesting to local fans, as it will give the patrons of the game the proper dope on the gameness of the negro, who has never been called upon to go above the twenty-round mark before a rough and hustling fighter of the Jim Flynn variety."

San Francisco Examiner, **November 2, 1907**

The day before the fight, Johnson ran 6 miles. He had trained for three weeks. Flynn had been in training for four weeks.

Fitzpatrick and McDonald, the respective managers, were both satisfied with their fighters' condition. McDonald said Flynn was fit and ready to go 100 rounds if necessary. Jim was in such splendid fix that it would require a world of beating to put him down for the count. Fitzpatrick said his fighter never allowed himself to get out of shape, and Johnson was as well physically as for any of his former battles.

Flynn said, "I can only say that I am in condition to make good on the many previous statements made by me in regard to this fight. I have said that I would make Johnson stop and still believe I can do it."

Johnson said, "I think about ten rounds at the outside will be enough for Flynn. I'm going to show the public that when it comes to rough work, I'm there. They tell me that Flynn will come to me in every round. That will make it still easier. I don't think there is a heavyweight in the ring that I cannot beat if he forces the fighting."[844]

Principals in today's heavyweight fight at the Mission street arena. Jim Flynn is shown on the left, while Johnson, with his "I should worry!" smile, is the man with the open countenance.

San Francisco Call, **November 2, 1907**

The day of the fight, each of the local papers gave their final thoughts and analysis. The *Call* said the fight would determine whether Johnson could prove his right to compete for the world's championship or whether he would jump over the ropes when the going got tough.

> In the past Johnson has an almost unbroken record of being a fighter who would not take a chance and this has won for him the reputation of being faint hearted. He has shown this quality in practically all of his fights here, and although he has won some of them he would have had a much brighter record had he shown some aggressiveness.
> . . .
>
> If he had Tom Sharkey's heart, coupled with his own strength, he would easily beat Jeffries for the championship. Without the courage he would present the spectacle of a black man turning white if he ever faced Jeffries in the ring.

---

[844] *San Francisco Bulletin*, November 1, 1907.

Johnson promised to "upset all precedent," saying that he would show the spectators that he had all the gameness and aggressiveness required.

Flynn was a bundle of aggressiveness and confidence. He liked short-range up-close work, while Johnson preferred the long-range. Jack would have decided advantages in height, reach, weight, cleverness, and experience.

Although even-money was being wagered on Johnson's chances to stop Flynn within 20 rounds, that was "something he has seldom done in the past. The majority of his fights have gone the limit of rounds. ... Smaller men than Flynn have held their own with the big black." Sam Fitzpatrick smiled when broached on the subject of "Johnson's timidity" and said that none of that quality would be shown this time.

The day before the fight, on November 1, *after* their final training, Flynn weighed 174 ½ pounds, while Johnson weighed 192, giving him the 17 ½-pound weight advantage. All of the local papers reported these weights. Given that both men took the scales after training, and would not work again until the fight the next day, it was likely that both would be a bit heavier when they entered the ring.

Johnson said he would arrive at the arena early, in order to sit in his sparring partner Denver Ed Martin's corner, to coach him in his fight with Spider Kennedy. Jack had faith in Ed, and wagered $100 on him.

Al Kaufman said he would be at ringside to challenge Flynn if he won, but was passing up Johnson. He continued to draw the color line.[845]

The *Examiner* reported that Johnson, "who disputes Tommy Burns' right to call himself champion of the world," promised to stop Flynn within 10 rounds. Johnson declared that he would redeem himself for past performances and create demand for a Burns match. Flynn responded that Johnson was talking in order to bolster up his weak heart, and would be most surprised by the end of the afternoon's battle.

They would fight straight Queensberry rules, meaning that they would have to protect themselves in the clinches and when breaking away.

Johnson said,

> No man with sense will try and stall through forty-five rounds. If he does he will be merely trying to make a test of condition of it, and that's a dangerous game. Forty-five rounds means a finish, and the best plan is to keep your eyes open, get busy and try for a knockout.
> ...
>
> If there should be any need for it the crowd will find me gaited for a long, hard fight. I don't look for anything of that kind. I expect to finish this fellow in ten rounds at the furthest and then if there is nothing in sight I will go to New York. I will be at the dock to meet Tommy Burns when he returns from England. If he has defeated Gunner Moir I will extend my congratulations and at the same time I

[845] *San Francisco Call*, November 2, 1907.

will slip him a challenge to box me for the championship of the world.

Flynn said, "I always fight close. I don't try to nurse myself along. I start in as briskly for a finish fight as I do for one of six rounds, and if the other man is as willing as I am there is no fear of the crowd becoming tired."[846]

The *San Francisco Chronicle* said Johnson was the logical favorite. In some ways, it was an unequal match in Johnson's favor, but Flynn's punching power and aggressiveness and the element of uncertainty in boxing made the fight intriguing. Johnson would match his science against Flynn's "animal strength." Flynn wanted to prove that Johnson would stop if he took a few hard punches. Jim's supporters relied on his power and aggressiveness to discomfort Johnson and make him quit almost to the stopping point, and finally allow himself to be defeated. "With a forty-five-round route over which to travel, the pair ought to be able to demonstrate to the satisfaction of the crowd which is the correct line of reasoning."

> While it is true that in a number of his fights Johnson has been a disappointment to the spectators, it is a question whether it is right to attribute to him the so-called streak of yellow. There are many men who, when not hard pressed to win, take matters too leisurely. This was unquestionably the case with Johnson when he fought Marvin Hart. Laying all over Hart in the earlier rounds, Johnson slowed down and more because of that than because he was outpointed the decision was given against him.

Flynn would bring the fight to Johnson and make him fight, which actually "should be a distinct advantage to the black. If he will stand his ground he should be able to stop Flynn's rushes and at the same time wear him down."

However, Flynn was a hard puncher, and when he landed "his punches are going to hurt and the spectators will then have an opportunity to find just how much punishment Johnson will stand." Flynn was confident that he had figured the correct way to beat Johnson.

> If Johnson expects any future in the heavyweight division he must win this fight. Flynn was defeated by Tommy Burns in Los Angeles in fifteen rounds and for Johnson to go under, or fail to win decisively, would be to put him out of the running.

Flynn would leave San Rafael at about 11 a.m. Johnson would leave Millett's at an early hour and go to the arena with Ed Martin for the 2:15 p.m. preliminary fight. The main event was to start at 3 p.m.[847]

The *San Francisco Evening Post*'s pre-fight analysis said, "Flynn is something after the style of Kid Carter, but seems to have more class as a

---

[846] *San Francisco Examiner.* November 2, 1907.
[847] *San Francisco Chronicle,* November 2, 1907.

boxer and a fighter." Supporters of Johnson, the prohibitive favorite, figured that he was much the cleverer of the two, that he would be able to "jab the white man to pieces," and "is somewhat of a mixer when the milling is not too fast."

Most felt that the fight would be on the square, because the loser's end was small. Both had plenty of incentive to fight hard. "The winner will be matched with Tommy Burns for the world's heavyweight championship."

The fight was considered a tryout for Johnson, to give some sort of a line on the respective merits of Burns and Johnson. After all, Burns had given Flynn "a merciless beating, putting him away in the fifteenth round after battering away at him for three minutes in the fourteenth with Flynn practically helpless."[848]

On Saturday November 2, 1907 at Jim Coffroth's Mission street arena in Colma, California, in the San Francisco bay area, the Jack Johnson vs. Jim Flynn fight took place. It was a fine, sunshiny day.

The fight drew an unusually large attendance, much larger than expected. The bleachers were crowded and many spectators had to stand. Some women were present. There was also the usual smattering of professional men.

Billy Roche refereed both bouts on the card. Billy Jordan was the announcer.

At 2:15 p.m., there was a scheduled 10-round preliminary between Johnson sparring partner Ed Martin and Spike Kennedy of Kansas, whom the *Examiner* called the two tallest pugilists "in captivity." Each stood 6'4". Referee Billy Roche stopped the fight after the conclusion of the 6th round and awarded the bout to Martin. Kennedy was taking an awful one-sided beating, and the referee and Kennedy's cornermen decided he had enough. Martin showed all of his old-time cleverness.

The scheduled 45-round main event was set to start at 3 p.m. Johnson was first to enter. With him were Sam Fitzpatrick, Harry Foley, Denver Ed Martin, and Jim Haywards. Jack wore an air of confidence and smiled about the arena.

As Flynn climbed through the ropes, Johnson put out his hand to shake, but Jim rudely thrust it to one side with a vicious scowl on his face.

Flynn's seconds included Frank McDonald, Eddie Hanlon, Charlie Miller, Billy Shannon, and Martin Murphy and/or Johnny Murphy.

Challenges were read out in various weight divisions. Jack "Twin" Sullivan challenged Kaufman, who accepted. Various other challenges were made.

Billy Jordan announced "the negro" as the heavyweight champion of the world by default. Flynn was announced as the Colorado fireman and cyclone.

---

[848] *San Francisco Evening Post*, November 2, 1907.

1 - Before the contest, Flynn said that he would go right after Johnson, and he kept his word, setting a fast pace from the start. From the opening bell, Flynn rushed to close quarters and tried for the stomach with both hands. Johnson stood his ground, and each man landed body blows before

clinching. Johnson was very cool. He showed his wonderful cleverness by landing a right and left to the head without a return. He met the next rush with a left jab and right, while Flynn landed an overhand blow. Flynn worked his arms in windmill fashion and the crowd egged him on. Johnson stood away and hooked two lefts to the jaw. Flynn responded with short-arm blows and they clinched. Johnson uppercut Flynn and landed short jolts to the heart. Flynn dashed in and landed to the body, making Jack look serious for a moment.

In some of the clinches, Johnson tried to hold, but could not prevent the strong Flynn from beating at his body with short punches. Johnson landed two good rights to the body and missed a terrific right uppercut. Flynn landed both hands to the kidneys, while Jack got him with a hard left hook to the stomach.

At the next rush, Johnson landed a vicious straight right that landed just beneath the left eye, gashing the fireman's cheek. It also started to raise a lump that rapidly swelled and eventually grew as big as a walnut. This one punch momentarily dazed Flynn, but the gong rang, which prevented a follow-up.

2 - Despite the swelling to the left eye which almost entirely closed it, Flynn was not daunted, but rushed in with his head down. He reached the ribs with a right and landed an overhand left hook on the neck or jaw that made a loud noise, but did not seem to bother Johnson. The Pueblo man was full of fight and Johnson had hard work baffling him at close quarters. They clinched and fought all over the ring.

When they broke from a clinch and Flynn rushed again, Johnson swung his left twice in succession on the ear and jaw and then crossed over with a right that caused Flynn's head to wag. After stalling for a few seconds, Flynn went in, and again "the big smoke" met him with clean rights and lefts to the face and body.

Undaunted, Jim charged again and jammed Jack into a corner. As he had the colored fighter off balance against the ropes, the crowd cheered. Johnson forced his way to ring center and let go a savage right for the head that missed. Flynn then swung his left to the cheek. Johnson put in a heavy left to the ribs at the gong. The *Call* said, "It was all Johnson."

3 - Flynn bounded at the "black boy" and took a straight left to the face. They exchanged rights and lefts to the jaw. Flynn then landed a left to the body but took a right and left to the jaw in return.

Throughout the round, ringsiders encouraged Flynn with shouts and yells. Flynn kept after Johnson continuously. Johnson blocked his swings and placed lefts and rights on the face. In one rush, Flynn butted Johnson, but immediately apologized.

In another rush, Flynn took a left jab and slipped to his knees, but was right up and after his man again. Still, the fact that he went down caused some to feel that the punishment was having some effect on him. The *Examiner* and *Call* said it was a slip, but the *Chronicle* called this a clean knockdown. It said Johnson had landed a right to the jaw. Flynn took the count coolly, but the body punches that followed did him no good.

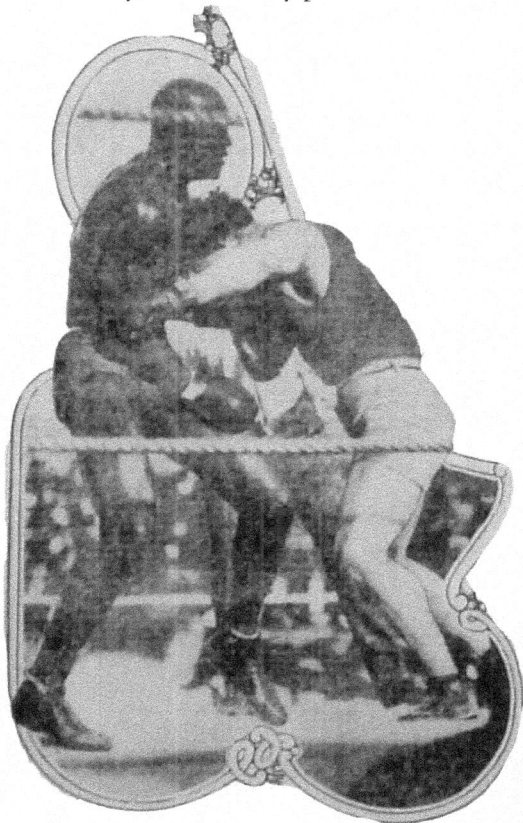

When Flynn came in again, Johnson landed a left uppercut to the jaw. Flynn piled Johnson into a corner and reached the neck with an overhand right, bringing a wild hoorah from the gallery. At the gong, Flynn was boring into the body and the crowd was rooting wildly for him. Johnson's lips showed traces of blood as he went to his corner.

4 - They clinched and Flynn forced Johnson around the ring, trying to land short blows to the body. Johnson held himself together splendidly and baffled Flynn at every point. He drew back from a body punch and dealt out a hard right to the ribs. They exchanged body blows.

Flynn crowded Johnson to the ropes and glanced an overhand right off his head. Jim was short with a right to the body and Johnson caught him in the pit of the stomach with a savage right.

Flynn kept after Johnson, but took some hard left hooks to the jaw. Johnson clouted his man around the ears and ribs and avoided every return. After breaking from a clinch, Johnson swung a mean left hook to the face, but Flynn was not daunted and bore in again. Johnson landed another hard left to the face and followed with a right uppercut.

Flynn kept coming and landed a choppy left to the jaw. Johnson was clinging on as the bell rang. The spectators stood and cheered Flynn.

5 - They missed left leads. Flynn tore in, but Johnson grabbed his arms and laughed. Jack broke away from the clinch and landed left hooks on the ear and a few rights on the ribs. Flynn returned with body blows. Johnson landed a left jab that tilted Flynn's head far back. Jack's corner commended him on the punch and Jack repeated the assault. After another clinch, the "smoke" whipped in a couple more nice hooks.

Flynn was very willing, but found it hard to reach his elusive opponent. He rushed but Johnson held him off with his long reach. Flynn fought hard, as if nothing could stop him, which endeared him to the crowd. Johnson saw he had a lead and for the remainder of the round showered light rights and lefts on Jim's jaw. Flynn rushed vainly.

Towards the end of the round, Flynn gathered himself for a desperate rush, and he crowded Johnson into a corner and hammered away at the body, causing the crowd to cheer.

6 - Flynn bounded across the ring and rushed Johnson to the ropes, landing two clean lefts to the jaw. Johnson worked himself loose and hooked his left to the face. Flynn tried to rush again, but Jack sidestepped.

Johnson began to goad Flynn. With a broad grin, he said, "Come right on Flynn. They're asking you to do it. Step right in, my boy." As Flynn rushed he ran into a right uppercut which increased the swelling below his left eye. Flynn went at Johnson like a wild man.

Roche broke them from clinch after clinch, and each time Flynn charged in again. He smashed Johnson on the neck with a left and the crowd rooted for him harder than ever.

Johnson snuck in a shower of rights and lefts to the head. Flynn's right ear commenced bleeding from the frequent lefts which Johnson had landed there. Flynn went in again and whipped a good left to the ribs at the close of the round.

7 - Flynn started with his usual rush and they clinched. Johnson played a waiting game, but still scored cleanly and often. Jack stung him with three

lefts to the face without a return. Flynn went at Johnson desperately and wrestled him about the ring.

Once, while awaiting Flynn's inevitable rush, Jack drew his left elbow far back and then gave him the full force of a straight left on the nose as Jim came on.

Flynn waded in, landing three times with jolty rights and lefts to the stomach that made Jack wince. Johnson worked himself loose and uppercut his left to the body. Flynn landed rights to the ribs and Johnson repaid him with right uppercuts.

Flynn tore in like a whirlwind and carried Johnson to the ropes, landing short left hooks to the body while Jack held on. They parted from the clinch and Johnson swung a punishing left into the stomach and left to the face at the bell.

8 - When the round began, Johnson seemed to remember that he had told his friends to bet on a 10-round finish. He loosened up more than usual, allowing his head to roll with Flynn's overhand blows and lashing out in a free-fisted way. Still, Flynn rushed Johnson all over the ring, landing a couple of telling rights to the body.

In one lively rally in Jim's corner, Johnson wrestled Flynn down to the floor, and the crowd jeered and hooted Jack. Flynn's seconds claimed a foul, but Jim rose and Roche motioned the fighters to go on as though nothing had happened.

After a series of clinches, Johnson bent down and waited for the next rush. He caught the incoming Flynn with a fierce left swing on the temple that sent him staggering. Johnson landed several times to the head and body with rights and lefts. Flynn tried again and again and each time a swift left crack disarranged his attack.

Flynn made a great rally at the close of the round, sending Johnson against the ropes and shooting short jolts to the body and a left to the head, while the crowd shouted itself hoarse for him.

9 - The start of the round saw Flynn tearing in again. Johnson stabbed him between the eyes with jabs. Flynn finally worked in close enough to hammer at the body, but then Johnson clasped him and held on. As they swayed together, Flynn bent down and hoisted Johnson clear to the ropes, where Roche interfered and parted them.

Flynn tore in again and was soon struggling in Johnson's arms. Jack suddenly pulled away and met him with a hard right on the ribs as Jim rushed. Johnson blocked a couple of high lefts and then mixed it in a fierce rally in which Flynn got much the worst of it.

The *Examiner* said Johnson staggered Flynn with a right on the jaw, and in trying to recover his balance, Jim slipped to the floor. The *Call* described this sequence by saying that after Johnson had shot in two hard lefts to the stomach, Flynn rushed him to the ropes, but again stumbled and slipped down. He jumped to his feet in an instant.

Flynn immediately came at Johnson again. The *Examiner* said Jack blocked a high right and then ripped in a right uppercut which brought Flynn to the floor. It landed one second before the bell rang. Of this sequence, the *Call* said that as they came out of a clinch just before the gong, Johnson whipped a right uppercut into the stomach and Flynn fell to his hands and knees.

Saved by the bell, Flynn's seconds carried him to his corner and revived him during the one-minute rest. The *Examiner* opined that had the punch landed 30 seconds sooner, Johnson's friends might have collected on the 10-round money.

10 - Flynn showed wonderful recuperative powers by coming out at the start of the round still full of fight. He was game to a fault. His left eye was of no service to him and his peculiar glare made it appear as if he was seeing double. He kept attacking though, and Jack just stepped aside and laughed. Flynn went after Johnson but his attack was stopped with a left jab to the head. Jack began putting his left to the jaw.

Johnson repeatedly tried for a knockout. He measured Flynn with his right several times but as a rule missed the chin. Flynn bore in but received a right and left to the jaw. Johnson followed with a shower of blows, meeting every rush of his opponent without breaking ground.

Flynn reeled more than once but always rallied and rushed again. Occasionally, Johnson laughed over Flynn's shoulder. Flynn was becoming desperate, so he butted Johnson severely with his head. The referee warned him.

Johnson continued landing right and left frequently to the head and body, but Flynn kept on trying. Just before the bell, Johnson whipped in a hard straight right to the jaw. However, as they parted from a clinch, Flynn laughed and said, "Gee, but you're a tough nigger, ain't you?"

11 - They fiddled around a bit at the start. Johnson

yelled derisively, "Come on Flynn. They're telling you to." Flynn needed no urging. His left eye was closed tight from the repeated visitations of Johnson's gloves. Still, he glared savagely with the good eye and rushed. Johnson led cleanly with his left and they clinched. After breaking, Flynn came in again, rushing continually.

Johnson caught him with a left hook and then their bodies bumped together, each hammering at the ribs with both hands. Referee Roche parted them. Flynn shook his head and laughed good-naturedly, saying,

"You're a clever nigger. I wish I knew as much as you." Johnson replied, "That's what I am."

Flynn lowered his head and rushed again. The *Examiner* said Jim tried an overhand left for the face and the next instant Johnson dropped Flynn with a swift, perfectly-timed, well-placed counter right uppercut to the jaw. Flynn went down on his face and became fair prey for the timekeeper's watch.

The *Call's* version of the final sequence said that as Flynn started in, Johnson was waiting for him and shot a straight right to the point of the jaw, and Flynn went down in a heap.

After momentarily glancing nonchalantly at Flynn's prostrate body, Johnson walked leisurely to his corner, feeling sure the blow had brought the fight to an end.

Even before the ten-count had concluded, Jim's seconds were in the ring acknowledging defeat. They went to help bring Jim to the corner. However, Flynn remained out cold for several minutes. He finally recovered and was able to leave the ring unassisted. The end of the fight came after 1 minute and 30 seconds of fighting in the 11th round.

The *San Francisco Examiner* said Flynn was no match for Johnson. Jim put up a rushing fight. Johnson battled cautiously, but floored Flynn in the 9th and finished him in the 11th with "as neatly placed a right uppercut as ever crashed against the fighter's chin."

> The contest was full of action, but to the practiced eye it looked as though Johnson held his man safely at all stages of the affair. The negro did not slug indiscriminately. In the main he stood over Flynn like a big black hawk over a plump partridge, and waited for the white man's attack. The crowd rebuked Johnson for being too eager to hold and blanket Flynn in some of the rounds, but the end justified the means. Johnson has been criticized for failing to finish his opponents in a workmanlike manner in former contests in this city and he kept cool and bided his time yesterday. It was as plain as daylight that he figured on dropping the fireman with a right hand punch. He told his friends he would accomplish his task in ten rounds and he made a fairly good forecast, for it took him about one minute longer.

The *San Francisco Chronicle* said the colored man outboxed, outfought, and outroughed the Coloradan at will. Johnson outclassed Flynn in every point of the game. The contest was never in doubt. With one eye cut open in the 1st round and closed in the next, the fireman took a beating all the way. He had strength and gameness, and put up the best fight he could, but "his best was a farce so far as Johnson was concerned. Had he been minded to take a chance, Johnson could have finished his man earlier than he did." Flynn's vaunted punch never had a chance to land cleanly. Johnson blocked his rushes and blows at will and literally pecked him to pieces about the head and dealt out punishment to the body. Jack dropped Jim in the 3rd, 9th, and 11th rounds.

As a heavyweight contest, it was well worth watching. Although each round was one-sided and Flynn was not able to land, he showed his willingness to mix. The crowd enjoyed his spirit, and there were few slow moments from start to finish. Flynn's only chance was to mix and land in the clinches, and even then he found very quickly that Johnson had the upper hand. When he so desired, Johnson could rough it too.

Flynn's confidence carried him over a longer route than he might otherwise have gone. It was no child's play to take the blows that Johnson sent to his face and body and still come back for more. Jim did it round after round.

The rounds were much the same. Johnson showed his class from the start, and not only maintained but increased his lead. For the first half of the fight, Johnson let Flynn set the pace. Johnson fought at distance, waiting for Flynn to come in. Jack could land whenever he desired. Jim would wade in with the evident desire to clinch and rough it, wrestling his man around the ring. Johnson would fire the right to the stomach or slap the left to the face and send Flynn back. In the 6th, he taunted, "Come on, Flynn, come right in." At the times when he saw that Jim had no particular desire to come in, Jack took the initiative and forced the fighting a bit. Referee Bill Roche had his work cut out for him at stages, as Flynn persisted in holding to save himself.

During the 9th round, his seconds called on Flynn to do anything to win, and Jim butted Johnson as they clinched, and hit him low twice. Just before the close of the round, Johnson pushed Flynn to the floor. When the white man got up, Johnson shot over a right to the jaw that sent Flynn down for the second time, a true knockdown. The gong rang as Flynn hit the canvas. Only the bell saved him. He had to be dragged to his corner.

Just to show that he was okay, when the 10th round ended, Flynn danced to his corner.

The 11th round lasted a minute and a half. Flynn said, "You're a clever big nigger. I wish I was as clever as you." Johnson replied with his right straight to the chin and toppled Flynn, who was already weak and discouraged. At the count of four, Jim's cornermen Eddie Hanlon and Frank McDonald went through the ropes to carry the defeated pugilist to his corner.

Johnson impressed, raised his stock, and garnered more momentum for his championship challenges. "That Johnson fought better yesterday than at any time during his career, so far as his record is known in California, is admitted." Flynn was a rough and ready fighter not to be held cheaply, and Johnson showed his caution and cleverness, but also his fair share of aggressiveness and readiness to fight. "That he must be reckoned with when the heavyweight championship is discussed Johnson proved to the satisfaction of the crowd that was present." He was willing to mix it in close, although he could have won easily at long range. In the clinches, he landed far more than Flynn expected. "It was not the same Johnson who stalled through with Marvin Hart when he had that worthy licked. Fighting like that and Tommy Burns must give him a battle or be considered as unwilling to take his chance with Johnson." Johnson had accomplished "far more than Burns" by stopping him in 11 rounds, for Burns had required 15 rounds to end matters with Flynn.

Another *Chronicle* writer said Little Arthur Johnson was no longer a dark joke. It was a lucky thing for Jeffries that he was retired. But as for Burns, "he must come out of the cyclone cellar and take a look at this black cloud that is waiting for him. He must drop the festive stall and cease the airy bull and fight Little Arthur or forever hold his peace."

Flynn was a game man to stay in the ring as long as he did with "that big cannibal." Anyone else would have picked out a soft spot on the ground after the first round. All he had was gameness, but against weight, reach, height, and cleverness he had as much chance "as a Prohibition candidate in Kentucky."

In the opening round, Flynn looked the part of the Colorado Cyclone until Johnson landed a piledriver downward right on his lamp. During the remainder of the fight, Jim's view was obstructed. "It was Johnson all the time. … Flynn did not land one punch that hurt the Ethiopian." Jim ate the wallops, and though they came fast, he was still hungry for more of them at the finish.

Before the 11th round, his seconds told Flynn to "go and get the big shine any way he could." Flynn remarked, "I wish I was as clever as this coon." They embraced in a clinch, and Johnson entered his objection to the remark by landing his right uppercut with the speed of a sixteen-inch shell, and it exploded right on the point of the jaw. Flynn dropped down and out. "The wallop would have made a class A re-enforced concrete structure look displeased." It took about ten minutes to revive him.

> If Johnson has any of that yellow streak, he left it at home yesterday or he must have thought that the ropes were too high to jump over. Those who expected him to bark or show other symptoms of the dog breed that is in him were disappointed. The gold mine he uses for teeth was flashing all the time as the fight went on, for the coon was grinning like a black Cheshire cat. Jack will never be broke as long as he retains his dentistry. There is enough of the root of all evil in his face to support him comfortably in his old age.
>
> After the battle everything black or tan adjourned to the Rue Pacific, where the countrymen of the winner indulged in the dances of their native jungles in sunny Africa. The attendance of the "cullud" population at the show was a large one, and very few of the chickens in the vicinity of Colma ventured out of their apartments until long after the backers of "Lil Arthur" were well on their way to the Rue Pacific.
>
> Tommy Burns, please write.

One of the jingles that the happy black crowd at the Rue Pacific sang included,

> There am music, there am dancing on Pacific street tonight.
>
> Golly, chile, dem coons am crazy, yes sah, crazy wif delight.
>
> Hey, you niggahs, swing yo' partners, shake a leg there, Sam and Mose;
>
> Dee dem yaller gain a smiling in their go-to-meeting clothes?
>
> Mistah Flynn, jes' patch you' optic, then jes' sort of take a roam.
>
> Bang dat banjo, on you Sambo – Johnson brought the bacon home.

JACK JOHNSON KNOCKS OUT FLYNN IN ELEVEN ROUNDS

San Francisco Chronicle, **November 3, 1907**

The *San Francisco Call* said Flynn was the gamest fighter of his inches in the world, and the worst matchmaker. This was apparent from the 1st round on until he was knocked out with a straight right to the jaw. Johnson had too many advantages in height, reach, weight, and skill. Flynn only had indomitable courage and spirit, which could not be subdued until he had reached the limit of his physical resources.

The *Call* was also impressed with Johnson.

> It was a different Johnson who stepped to the center of the ring yesterday from the one who had been seen in action here on other occasions. He had all the qualities which go to make a great fighter. His hitting was true and clean, and every time he landed he took some of the steam out of Flynn's rushes. Johnson's favorite blows were a left hook to the head and a right to the body. He waited for Flynn to come in and the Coloradan proved to be so slow that Johnson was able to set himself and thus put all the tremendous power of his arms and shoulders into the blow.

Flynn looked like a "small boy" alongside the "big, rangy colored man." He was unfortunate enough to receive a hard blow on the left eye just at the close of the 1st round, and this was a decided handicap for the remainder of the bout. Instead of bleeding, it began to puff up and assumed the size and color of a plum. Johnson frequently used it as a target. The eye gradually closed as the fight progressed, until Flynn could not see out of it at all.

Flynn administered virtually no punishment. His most effective blows were to the body, but they did not stop Johnson. Jack stood erect, and at all times ready to bring his wonderful skill into play. With his enormous reach, he was able to hold Flynn at arm's length, so Jim found it difficult to reach the body. Flynn showed his aggressiveness, and kept Johnson on the move.

Flynn's only hope was in landing a chance blow. But the hope vanished in the 9th round. Flynn stumbled down early in the round, "which is the sign of a tired athlete." He was up in an instant, but just before the bell sounded the end of the round, as they were breaking out of a clinch, Johnson shot in a jolty right to the solar plexus. Flynn went to his hands and knees, and a deathly pallor spread over his face. Flynn's seconds rushed in and carried him to his corner. From then on, it was a hopeless fight on his part until he went down before Johnson's superior science.

After the fight, Johnson said,

> Well, that yellow streak they have all been talking about has not shown in me yet, and I want to say right now there is not a man living who can bring it out. I met Flynn every time he started and I beat him at his own game. He could not begin to hurt me with any of his rushes. He is a good tough fellow, but I had him all the time and was only waiting to hang the haymaker on his point.

> Now I will fight any of them. They can not bring them up too fast. Burns is my meat and I am going to keep after him until he consents to meet me. He will have to fight me sooner or later, and when he does he will get the same as Mr. Flynn got this afternoon. In the meantime, I am willing to take on any of them, so let them step forward.

Johnson was also quoted as saying,

> I did just what I said I would do. I finished Flynn up in short order. Now I want a fight with Tommy Burns. I think I have earned that much after my showing with Flynn, and I want to force Tommy to meet me for the championship. Flynn is a good, tough fellow, but he was easy for me all the way through and never caused much trouble. If I can get a fight with any of the heavyweights in the country I am willing to stay in California; but if there is no chance I will go East and wait for Burns to come back from England. Nobody is barred. I am willing to meet any of them. Guess I showed the people that I can be aggressive and that I have improved.

Flynn said,

> I admit that he knocked me out clean and cold and I am not going to make any excuses. I was game and I thought that I could make him quit until he hit me in the stomach in the ninth. That weakened me and took a lot of the fight out of me.

> I am the only one of these fellows who is game enough to take a chance with Johnson and I ought to get some credit for the fight I put up. He is so big that I could not reach him. If I had ever got in right I would have made him quit. Let some of the others go after him now. I am satisfied that I gave the San Francisco people a good run for their money the first time I started here.

No, I am not through fighting. As soon as I am rested I will look around for another good match.

Flynn was also quoted as saying,

> He was too big for me, that's all there was to it. Just say for me that he is too much for any of the white fellows, bar none. I've tried them all, and I know that if Johnson can get me this way he can take care of any of them. I just want to see him go up against some of those fellows. They'll find out for themselves what I found out. I wish I was as clever as he is. Of course I will fight again. I am not going to get out of the game just because of this fight. As soon as my eye gets well I'll be at it again. Take it from me, Johnson is a wonder and the best of them all.

Referee Billy Roche praised both fighters, saying,

> Johnson put up the best fight of his ring career and Flynn is not disgraced in losing to him after such a struggle as they went through. Flynn was outboxed, outfought, and outroughed and never had Johnson in trouble. All the advantages of height, reach and weight were with the winner, and Flynn's wonderful gameness and desire to fight could not offset all these advantages. The crowd was given a good run for its money, as there was never a moment when Flynn was not trying. He hoped either to tire or discourage Johnson with his rushes, but the big colored man had so many natural advantages over him that Flynn could make no headway. Flynn was willing and must be credited with having done the best he could.[849]

The *San Francisco Bulletin* was impressed with Johnson as well. It said he had shown his class. Burns was the only fighter in the field for Johnson, and even he might be no match for Jack. "Tommy Burns was wise in picking Gunner Moir for his next opponent for the probability is that if he had tackled Jack Johnson prior to taking on the Englishman, the trip to King Edward's country would have been indefinitely postponed." Johnson's fight with Flynn showed that "he is in a class by himself so far as the heavyweights of the present day are concerned."

After he had been knocked out, Flynn gave a short statement that summed things up. "Just let these other white fellows go up against that nigger, is the best compliment that I can pay him. I have met all of the top-notchers and have managed to hold my own with them."

The *Bulletin* summarized,

> Johnson surprised the veterans at the ringside by his aggressiveness and his wonderful improvement since the Marvin Hart fight. The people on this coast had looked upon Johnson as a quitter and a man who would slow-up under punishment, and while Flynn didn't reach

---

[849] *San Francisco Examiner, San Francisco Chronicle, San Francisco Call,* November 3, 1907.

him very often, he was always after the big black fellow and forced him to fight. Of course, Johnson looked a winner all over from the very outstart and while he didn't take any unnecessary chances he never backed away from the fighting fireman and not only outgeneralled and outboxed his adversary, but outfought him in the clinches, where Flynn was supposed to shine.[850]

San Francisco was finally fully convinced. Jack Johnson had fought six times in 1907, and had been far superior to all of his opponents.

JACK JOHNSON, WHO KNOCKED OUT FLYNN

---

[850] *San Francisco Bulletin*, November 4, 1907.

CHAPTER 25

Chasing the Champ

After defeating Jim Flynn, the prospect for Jack Johnson to find opponents was looking dim. Tommy Burns was fighting in England, and Al Kaufman and others drew the color line. Therefore, "the husky negro will be obliged to await Burns' return from England. Even then it is no cinch that he will be able to get a match, as Burns doesn't appear very anxious to meet the 'ding.'"[851]

Jim Ryan said, "Since his defeat of Jim Flynn, Jack Johnson's smoke has increased in volume and has received such recognition that the chances are Tommy Burns will be forced into a meeting with him when he returns from England." There likely would be a good house, too, for people were paying to see both Burns and Johnson. Therefore, unless affected by racial considerations, promoters would be more likely to try to make the match. "It may be that Tommy has been dodging Johnson, but that does not prove that he is afraid of him. It is probable that if he could see any prospects for a good house he would take on the big black in a hurry." Tom thought that Johnson was being overrated. He said Flynn lacked class, such that Johnson's victory over him did not mean as much as the critics all over the country were saying. Ryan continued:

> Jack is a very clever fighter. He has had a few chances and, although he has won, he has not done the work stylishly enough to warrant the belief that he is a whirlwind. He may have been cheated out of a verdict over Marvin Hart, but if he is as good as many people claim he is he should have put Hart out or at least beaten him so badly that Marvin could not possibly have been given the decision.

Of course this discounted the fact that Hart was a tough cookie, known for his aggressiveness, strength, endurance, and ability to absorb punishment.

Ryan opined that Burns was better than Hart, and that if he met Johnson, Tommy would stop the black champion in 15 rounds or less.[852]

In his third title defense of the year, on December 2, 1907 in London, England, the alleged 171-pound Tommy Burns knocked out supposed 182-pound British champion James "Gunner" Moir in the 10th round. The fight was filmed, and showed Burns to be adept both as an attacking inside fighter, as well as a clever outside boxer, with speed and power. As a result of beating title claimants Hart and O'Brien, Australian champion Squires,

---

[851] *San Francisco Bulletin*, November 4, 1907.
[852] *Freeman*, November 23, 1907.

and British champion Moir, several newsmen said Burns had to be given firm recognition as the heavyweight champion of the world.

Talk of a Tommy Burns vs. Jack Johnson bout continued.

> Burns is under promise to come back to the United States and give battle to the negro heavyweight. Johnson, who doesn't bank altogether on what Tommy has said in the connection, says he will be waiting at the dock. ... [T]he Johnson-Burns match now seems inevitable.[853]

The champion was not ruling out the possibility of such a match. Burns said, "I hope now to arrange a match with Jack Johnson upon my return to America.... I am also willing to box Roache [sic], the Irish champion, if there is money enough in it.... What I want just now is to take a vacation trip through France, Germany and Italy with my friends."[854]

There were those who felt that Jack Johnson was the best heavyweight in the world, and that Burns would not fully earn undisputed recognition as champion until he defeated Johnson. Tommy Ryan said, "Tommy Burns, a good fighter, is a joke for a champion. Really I must consider this fellow Johnson as a sure enough black peril. I doubt if there is a heavy today that can stand him off. He is getting better all the time, too."[855]

Jack O'Brien tentatively scheduled a match with Johnson, but then called it off with a claim of a hand injury. The *Freeman* believed that like Burns, O'Brien feared Johnson and would make any excuse not to fight him. "They all fear Johnson, because they are satisfied Johnson is the real superior of them all in the heavyweight division."

Regarding Sam Langford, who on December 17 clearly won a 10-round no-decision bout over 190-pound Jim Barry, the *Freeman* said, "He may not be the man that Jack Johnson is, but it is safe to say that should he be matched against Johnson, he would put up a stiff fight."[856]

On December 20, 1907 in Bakersfield, Jim Flynn knocked out Bill Squires in the 6th round. Flynn proved that he was a very effective fighter against those not as formidable as Johnson.

Regardless of the earlier talk, Tommy Burns was not about to return to America to fight Johnson any time soon. He was receiving too many lucrative offers to fight against lesser foes abroad. Burns was happy to collect what he perceived as easy money, for he was in the business to make as much money as possible. Hence, he decided to remain overseas. From England, Burns wrote,

> I just got through reading a bunch of American papers and it's certainly funny the bunk writers hand out but I guess it's all in the business to get knocked at times. It sure won't hurt me as I'll have

---

[853] *San Francisco Examiner*, December 3, 1907.
[854] *San Francisco Examiner*, December 4, 1907.
[855] *Los Angeles Herald*, December 8, 1907.
[856] *Freeman*, December 28, 1907, January 4, 1908.

mine when I get through fighting and I ain't handing anybody any money for boosting me either. ...

Yes, I'm getting the easy money and anybody who wouldn't take this easy money would be a fool. ...

You can gamble that I'll fight Johnson when I return, and I'll demand the big end too. ... Of course somebody might knock about this division, but that knock won't cut any ice with Tommy Burns.

We sign articles...to fight Roche in Leinster Hall, Dublin for a £1,500 ($7,500) purse, cut 80 and 20, and a side bet of £500. This fight alone will net me $8,500, but I figure a lot of bets on the side as the Irish are confident that Roche will beat me. I am almost sure of $10,000 for the Palmer fight Feb. 10, as I am working on 80 per cent of the gross, which I figure to come out at £3000 ($15,000), as seats are being sold from £5 5s. (over $25) down to a half guinea (equal to $2.50), and the big price seats are going good already.

Don't blame me do you? This beats gold mining.[857]

From New York, Johnson said he intended to sail out to meet Burns. "I won't give him a chance to turn around again. ... I certainly am anxious to meet that man." Regarding Flynn, Johnson said, "Oh, he was made to order for me. Yes, I know Burns took a few rounds longer to beat him, but I'll lick Burns in the same time that it took to trim Flynn. All I want is the chance. That's all, just the chance."[858]

Joe Gans was willing to bet $5,000 that Johnson would defeat Burns with ease. "I think Johnson can beat Burns, not because he is of my color, but because he is the best heavyweight in the world, barring, of course, James J. Jeffries. Jeffries, I think, could take two or three of the leading heavies and defeat them one after the other, with a rest between each bout." Gans later picked Johnson to beat Burns in a limited-rounds bout, but Burns to win in a fight to the finish. "I think Jack Johnson is the cleverest heavyweight in the world today. He is as clever as Jim Corbett was in his prime." However, "Tommy Burns is a better man than the public gives him credit for being. ... Burns, besides being clever, is a rugged fellow. In a finish fight he would wear down the other fellow and win out."[859]

On February 10, 1908 in London, Tommy Burns knocked out Jack Palmer in the 4th round.

Johnson made an offer to stop Burns within 20 rounds or forfeit his share of the proceeds if he failed to do so.

Well aware of the fact that he had all of the negotiating power, at that time, Burns insisted on receiving 75% of the total proceeds, guaranteed, win

[857] *New York World*, January 10, 1908.
[858] *Freeman*, January 11, 1908.
[859] *New York World*, February 3, 1908; *Freeman*, March 14, 1908.

or lose, for a Johnson bout. However, Johnson and his manager wanted their fair share. Initially, Sam Fitzpatrick rejected those terms.[860]

W. W. Naughton wrote, "The American public will forgive Tommy for taking on these easy marks if he will keep his promise and come home within a reasonable time to fight Jack Johnson." A Burns acquaintance said Tommy wanted to meet several men of different nationalities so that there was no doubt as to his right to call himself world champion when he finally met and defeated Johnson.[861]

The *New York World* said,

> Johnson will give Tommy a battle, but in spite of the great difference in height and weight, it is no cinch that the champion will turn his title over to the big smoke. Probably a battle between Kaufman and Burns would be a far better drawing card than one between Burns and Johnson, for people have not yet forgotten the fact that Johnson is a faker of the Jack O'Brien school.[862]

New York World cartoon by Robert Edgren, February 25, 1908

Regarding the possibility Johnson fighting Burns in England, Sam Fitzpatrick said,

> Sure I'm willing to let Johnson fight in England. He can fight in China if he wants to so long as he gets a crack at Burns and gets a fair share of the purse that he is entitled to according to his reputation and fighting ability. No, I'm not going to put up a $2,000 forfeit on any indefinite proposition. I'll wait for more news and if the Englishmen have anything worth while to offer you can bet we'll take it up.[863]

---

[860] *San Francisco Examiner,* February 10, 1908.
[861] *San Francisco Examiner,* February 11, 1908.
[862] *New York World,* February 1, 1908.
[863] *New York World,* February 25, 1908.

The *New York Sun* said Burns had avoided Johnson by traveling abroad, and then remaining there. Many believed that "with the big negro Burns will have the fight of his life."

From England, Burns said,

> This fellow Jack Johnson is the first man I'll fight when I return to America, if shown the money, as he does not look any harder to beat than some of the fighters I've already defeated, such as Marvin Hart, who beat Johnson in San Francisco several months before I trimmed Hart.

Burns claimed Johnson offered to bet him $10,000, which Burns accepted and immediately wrote out a check, but Johnson was not able to put up the money. Jack said he only had $700, but would put up the rest by the next day or Burns could have the money. Well, the next day came and Johnson withdrew the money, for he could not come up with the rest.

> I then told him I would show the people present what kind he was. I asked him to step into a room, lock the door and fight me for nothing. But the big black was not game. I called him in a way that I wouldn't take from any man even if I knew I was going to be killed the next minute. All yellow fighters are alike. Give then an inch and they'll try to grab the whole world. I am going to force him to fight or crawl just as soon as I get back to the States.[864]

Johnson offered to fight Burns winner-take-all, and claimed that Burns was a liar who did not want to fight him. The war of words was on.

The fighters' representatives laughed at an English offer of $5,000 for Johnson-Burns. Fitzpatrick said Coffroth would put up $25,000 for a fight at Colma, while Tex Rickard would match or exceed that amount for a fight at Goldfield, Nevada. However, formal American offers never materialized, and negotiations never bore fruit.[865]

On March 3, 1908 in Boston, in an exciting bout, Sam Langford and Joe Jeannette fought to a 12-round draw.

Mrs. Burns said her husband and Johnson would sign articles to fight just as soon as Tom landed in New York, "and he will make Johnson jump out of the ring before the fight is over." However, she didn't want him to fight a black man.

> He would never fight Johnson if I had a chance to decide it, for I don't like him to fight colored men, and he promised me when we married that he would never fight a Negro. But he's sore about what has been printed about him and Johnson, and I'm positive that he will have to sign up for the battle just as soon as he gets in America and leave the explanations with me later.

---

[864] *New York Sun*, March 1, 1908.
[865] *New York World*, March 2, 1908.

Sam Fitzpatrick expected Burns to return from England shortly after his St. Patrick's Day fight in Dublin with Irish champ Jim Roche. "I don't think he intends to dodge Johnson this time. In fact, I do not see how he can."[866]

Although initially not satisfied with the terms that the English offered, Johnson changed his mind and said he would be willing to fight Burns for $5,000 cash as his end of the purse. He would accept whatever conditions Tommy wanted. Jack said,

> Burns can make the ring ten feet square and select a private ring and throw the key out of the window if he dares. I know I can beat him and I think he knows it, too. If he backs down on the proposition, I will go over to London anyway and shame him out of King Edward's islands.

> When the offer was first cabled from the other side it seemed so unfair to me that I naturally balked. We could get more money in California, and money is what we are both after. But I am so anxious to get him into a ring that I will waive everything within reason to make the match. By betting the $5,000 I can double my end of the purse. ... If Burns can beat me, I am willing to quit the game. Any number of rounds will suit, from one to a thousand. ... Burns can name the terms.[867]

The *Freeman* thought that Johnson would be given fair treatment in England, for there was less race prejudice there. "Prejudice has grown so strong in this country that a majority of the sporting element can barely stand to see the black boy defeat the white."

The *New York Sun* reported that several matchmakers were trying to induce Johnson to fight Joe Jeannette again, given that Joe recently had fought Sam Langford to a 12-round draw. "Johnson has tackled Jeannette on several occasions, but has never won decisively. When asked yesterday if he would fight Jeannette again Johnson said that he would make a match providing he could get a side bet of from $500 to $2,500."[868]

Sam McVea/McVey was a hit in Paris, fighting for good money there. He recently had knocked out Henry Shearing in the 4th round. A crowd of 3,000 paid from 30 francs down to 5 francs for admission ($7.50 to $1.25). His string of victories in Paris made him comparatively affluent. He would continue living and fighting there for several years to come – until 1911.[869]

Jim Corbett was noncommittal in picking the likely winner of Burns-Johnson. Although he had sparred with Burns when Tom was just a middleweight, he had not seen him in an actual fight. "I have seen Johnson and he looks good in a pugilistic way. He has it on Burns in height and

---

[866] *Freeman*, March 8, 1908.
[867] *Freeman*, March 8, 1908.
[868] *New York Sun*, March 13, 1908.
[869] *Freeman*, March 14, 1908. While in Paris, he was known as Sam McVea, not McVey.

reach and he is stronger. Johnson has a wicked punch and he is clever, there is no denying that."[870]

On St. Patrick's Day, March 17, 1908 in Dublin, Ireland, 168-pound Tommy Burns scored a 1st round knockout against 177-pound Irish champion Jem Roche. The fight only lasted 88 seconds.

In the U.S., Jack Johnson agreed to fight Jim Barry in Wisconsin. However, the bout was called off after Sam Langford knocked out Barry in the 2nd round on April 7.[871]

In early April 1908, Tommy Burns' manager Billy Neil said Burns would remain in Europe for several more months, for the money there was too good to turn down. He claimed that Tommy already had made $53,125 in fight purses, side-bets, and theatrical engagements.

Neil was also in the process of negotiating a potential future match with Jack Johnson. Burns would fight for any club that paid him $30,000 as his share of the prize money, regardless of the result. He preferred a fight to the finish or one of 45 rounds. Burns was making easy money, so if he was going to take a risky fight, he wanted to make a bundle. He was also willing to bet Johnson $5,000 that Jack could not stop him within 20 rounds. Neil claimed that when he put $5,000 in front of Fitzpatrick that Sam backed down from the offer.[872]

In mid-April it was reported that articles for a fight between Burns and Johnson were to be signed. The agreement was for Burns to receive $30,000, win or lose, and for Johnson to be guaranteed at least $5,000. The biggest impediment would be finding a promoter willing to pay that amount, and one willing to promote a mixed-race heavyweight championship, something which never had been done in the gloved era. The *Chronicle* asked, "It is an easy matter to sign articles, but what promoter is going to offer $35,000?"[873]

Some criticized Burns' large monetary demand as a way of pricing himself out of the market, so as to avoid the fight, fearful of losing to Johnson. However, Burns believed the fight was worth that amount. Before the end of the year, he would be proven correct.

On April 18, 1908 in Paris, France, Tommy Burns stopped the husky Jewey Smith in the 5th round.

Burns agreed to meet Sam McVey *if* the money was right. The Parisians liked McVey, who had scored knockouts in all of his fights there, and they wanted to see him fight Burns.[874]

Sam Fitzpatrick was negotiating a possible 6-round bout for Johnson with Jack O'Brien in Philadelphia. Johnson said he might not be able to

---

[870] *Freeman*, March 21, 1908.
[871] *New York World*, March 20, 1908, April 8, 1908.
[872] *Los Angeles Herald*, April 11, 1908; *New York World*, April 11, 15, 1908.
[873] *San Francisco Chronicle*, April 14, 1908, April 15, 1908.
[874] *New York Herald, New York Daily Tribune, San Francisco Chronicle*, all April 19, 1908.

knock him out over that distance, but he'd do some damage, and O'Brien would not be able to hit him with anything significant.

Speaking of how badly he wanted to fight Burns, Johnson said,

> Say, there's one thing in this world I'm crazy for and that's fried chicken, with corn muffins on the side. Would you believe me if I told you that I'd fast for three days with that outside my window if I thought I could fight Burns the next day? Burns isn't treating me right, and I don't think he's treating himself right. Suppose he beat me – why, he could go round the world and be just twice as big a drawing card as he is. People think he is afraid to fight me, and is picking the quinces. Why, my golly, if he can beat me, why don't he come back and do it? He said that right after the Moir fight he was coming back to muss me up, but I see now that he has two more fights up. Well (sigh), everything comes to him who waits, they say.[875]

In late April, Jack Johnson and manager Sam Fitzpatrick set sail for England in order to go after Burns. Sam said Tommy should be satisfied with a 2/3 guarantee of the purse. He noted that even Fitzsimmons only got a 65% guarantee against Jeffries when he first defended the crown.[876]

Bob Fitzsimmons picked Johnson to defeat Burns.

> I did not take much stock in Johnson as a fighter until he beat me at Philadelphia. I thought I could beat him easily. ... Before we had been at it a minute I saw I was up against a big, strong, clever fighter, and really was not surprised when he knocked me out. I must admit Burns is a good little man but Johnson is a good big man and therefore should beat him.[877]

On April 27, 1908, Johnson and Fitzpatrick arrived in London, England, hoping to arrange a meeting with Burns in Europe. However, neither the English nor the French were willing to meet Burns' financial demands for such a fight. At that time, Burns was in Paris.[878]

Fighter Willie Lewis offered his thoughts on Burns, Johnson, and McVey, saying,

> [Burns] played with [Jewey] Smith and he would occasionally drop over a left hook or a right cross, and down would go 200 pounds of English beef. Believe me, Burns is a terrific puncher. He dropped this fellow Smith with little hooks that didn't travel six inches. He's a corking good puncher, and the fastest big man I ever looked on. If you want my opinion, he'll whip Johnson to death certainly. Anyone who picks Burns for a sucker is a sucker himself for doing it. ... He is a large edition of Terry McGovern when Terry was 'Terrible Terry.'

---

[875] *New Zealand Truth*, April 25, 1908, quoting the *San Francisco Bulletin*.
[876] *New York World*, April 21, 1908.
[877] *Freeman*, May 9, 1908.
[878] *New York World*, April 27, 1908.

He carries a sleep pill in either mitt, and fights with a crouch that makes it hard for an opponent to get to his jaw.

He is very short and put together compactly, but he's got an awful reach. That's the secret of his fighting. His reach is 74 ½ inches, about the same as Bob Fitzsimmons. He is a fast puncher, quick to take advantage of an opening, and he is the jollying kid in the ring, for while fighting Smith he kept encouraging the latter to fight by saying, "That's right, Jewey, keep coming," and "Oh, you forgot to block that one," and "That's right, put more steam in it." This got Smith's goat, and he had barrels of confidence when he entered the ring.

You may be surprised to know that Sam McVey, the big Los Angeles negro, is the Parisians' fighting idol, and as soon as Burns got to Paris he was pestered to death with challenges from McVey and his followers. They offered a purse of $20,000 for the match, and Burns said to me:

"I had made up my mind that I would fight only one negro – that's Johnson – but I hate like the deuce to let this money get away from me." At the fight Saturday McVey and his backers again challenged Burns, and Tommy replied:

"Give me a purse of $25,000, split $20,000 to the winner and $5,000 to the loser, and a side bet of $5,000, and I'll fight McVey here." If they fight the scrap will draw an awful mob. Everybody in this town is crazy over McVey. They never saw anything else as big and ugly. ... You ought to see that coon. He's got clothes that would make a Sixth avenue darkey dude look like a rag picker. Last time I saw him he wore a cream-colored suit that looked like silk – sort of a pajama rig. He goes to fights in a carriage with a dress suit on and a bouquet in his hand, and they say society has taken him up, and he is taken around to dinners in the swell houses, and let sit at the table without putting a muzzle or a chain on him.

The frogs will go crazy when Johnson comes home. And they will think we're a dingy nation for fair when those two big smokes go down the boulevard at the same time.[879]

The *Manchester Guardian* reported that there was little hope for a Burns-Johnson bout, for Burns had declined the National Sporting Club's offer of 2,500 pounds ($12,500), insisting upon $30,000 guaranteed, win or lose.[880]

Burns-McVey was not going to happen either, because French promoters were not willing to pay Burns what he demanded for that fight.

The British were upset by Burns' financial demands. "Burns is fast losing favor with the general public, owing to his excessive demands. Johnson has

---

[879] *Los Angeles Herald*, May 6, 1908.
[880] *Manchester Guardian*, May 6, 1908.

the general sympathy of the English sporting world, and many are already calling him the world's champion, saying that Burns has lost the title by default."[881]

Scouting a Burns-Johnson bout, the *New York World's* Robert Edgren opined that Burns would win. Johnson would have the size advantages, but "he will be up against a rough, clever, determined fighter with speed, head, gameness and wallop.' Johnson was the biggest and cleverest of the heavies, and he could hit. However, Edgren believed that he was only game as long as he was winning. "But let a tough-looking proposition appear in front of Johnson and he becomes the most careful and retiring fighter in the world." He thought that a few drives into Johnson's stomach and ribs from Burns would suffice. "No black fighter ever entered a ring who was game when he got a body lacing."[882]

One man who was being discussed as a potential future Burns opponent was world middleweight champion Stanley Ketchel, whose recent KO20 victory over Jack "Twin' Sullivan had been impressive, given Sullivan's vast experience and credentials.

On May 19, 1908 in Boston, Sam Langford won a 12-round decision over Sandy Ferguson.

In late May, from London, Burns sent a cablegram to Jack Curley accepting an alleged offer to fight Jack Johnson on Labor Day in Nevada for a $30,000 guarantee, win or lose.[883]

The *New York World* reported,

> The opinion that Tommy will beat the big black man is growing in favor. Burns is fast and clever, and has a punch. Johnson has all of these things – added to his great bulk. But Burns is game, and that is where Johnson falls short of the mark. Of course, Johnson may have improved in the matter of gameness. They say a man can improve. Ring history shows such a thing to be possible.

It was also speculated that Johnson might have so many physical advantages that he might not "suffer from his usual attack of heart failure when the champion comes to him."[884]

The *Los Angeles Herald* wrote,

> Tommy Burns may be stalling in his long drawn out negotiations with Jack Johnson, and again he may be in earnest. Far be it from the humble layman to decide the matter at this distance from the present scene of action. One thing is sure, however, and that is that the rotund Thomas is as clever as they go in the fight game. Probably no other fighter at present in the ring would be tolerated if he procrastinated about the match as has Burns. He is the legitimate

[881] *Freeman,* May 23, 1908.
[882] *New York World,* May 12, 1908.
[883] *Los Angeles Herald,* May 20, 1908.
[884] *New York World,* May 20, 1908.

champion, however, and he is making good use of his title to bring in the shekels.[885]

When for four days there was no reply to his cablegram accepting the Johnson fight, Burns told the press that in view of Curley's silence, he decided to accept an Australian offer to fight Bill Lang in Sydney during the visit of the American fleet. He would earn $10,000 in Australia, regardless of result, with the possibility of another $7,500 for a second fight.[886]

The *Los Angeles Herald* wrote, "Tommy Burns, of course, stands out as the leading light in the heavyweight class, though the dark cloud created by the appearance on his trail of Jack Johnson has somewhat dimmed his star. The title seems to lie between these two, however, and should be so confined for some time."[887]

TOMMY BURNS FEELS SAFE IN HIS NEW CYCLONE CELLAR

Los Angeles Herald, **June 7, 1908**

While in England, Johnson gave some sparring exhibitions. In June, he possibly boxed a 4-round exhibition with Al McNamara, heavyweight champion of the Royal Navy since 1907.

Johnson also engaged in several sparring exhibitions with Fred Drummond in London in late May, during early June in Neuilly, France, and back in London again in mid-to-late June and early July.[888]

Sam Fitzpatrick wrote that he and Johnson had been in England for four weeks, doing their best to force Burns into a match. "The British public know full well that we have placed no obstacle whatever in the way of Burns." Sam said that Burns all along had been putting forward obstacles which he knew could not be surmounted so he could avoid the Johnson match and take on easy opponents. Tom was scheduled to rematch Squires in Paris, a man whom he had defeated already in a single round (and whom Jim Flynn had stopped after Johnson had stopped Flynn). There was also

---

[885] *Los Angeles Herald*, May 23, 1908.
[886] *Los Angeles Herald*, May 24, 1908; *New York World*, May 28, 1908.
[887] *Los Angeles Herald*, June 7, 1908.
[888] Cyberboxinzone.com.

talk of Burns fighting Lang in Australia, a man whom Johnson had handled and stopped easily. Fitzpatrick saw these bouts as a way to get Burns out of England, where he was taking criticism for his financial demands, and again avoid Johnson. Sam further said,

> In the face of all this, there is surely no question as to who is today the genuine champion of the world. Johnson is, as he has been all along, prepared to box, and Burns fails to come forward. There is, therefore, only one inference to be drawn, which is that Burns is afraid. From this date I therefore feel justified in claiming the championship for Jack Johnson, who, I may add, is ready to defend it at all times, and against all comers, giving Burns the first chance.[889]

Burns continued insisting on $30,000 (6,000 pounds). The *Freeman* reported, "Johnson claims that it is a get-out on the part of Burns, a way of evading a meeting, and I must say this opinion is shared by many."

Burns said,

> Johnson strolled into the National Sporting Club yesterday, lording it in a disgusting way, and I turned him down cold – wouldn't shake hands with the big dub. I'll beat him just as sure as my name is Brusso – that is, if I can get him into a ring with me. ... I am going over to Paris to trim Squires. ... I have a tempting offer to run down to Australia, where I will find another lemon. I know I have been regarded as a joke during all my fighting career, but I am getting the money, so what's the difference? Thirty thousand for mine, though, don't forget that.

The Brits took Johnson's side and called Burns a bluffer. They believed that Tommy was just out for the easy money; scoffing at real tests.[890]

Johnson's brother went to England to join him as a sparring partner.[891]

In the meantime, in his second fight in Paris, on June 13, 1908, in a rematch, Tommy Burns stopped Bill Squires in the 8th round. Jack Johnson was sitting at ringside. The plan was not to allow Burns or the sporting public to forget about Johnson and his rightful challenges.

Within days of their rematch, it was announced that an Australian sporting syndicate had arranged a third bout between Burns and Squires for a very large $15,000 purse. It made no economic sense for Burns to fight Johnson for less, when he could make very good money fighting a man whom he had defeated twice already.[892]

The *Los Angeles Herald* said,

> Burns is the most pronounced globe-trotting champion the world ever knew. No other champion undertook the worldwide tour that

---

[889] *Freeman*, June 20, 1908.

[890] *Freeman*, June 27, 1908.

[891] *Freeman*, August 1, 1908.

[892] *New York World*, June 15, 1908; *Los Angeles Herald*, June 16, 1908.

the Los Angeles fighter has undertaken, and the great success he is experiencing in mopping up with all the ambitious heavyweights in Europe, after cleaning out the American stable of would-be champs, justifies him in his hunt for easy game, big money and a glorious good time. ...

When he returns to America next fall he undoubtedly will be ready to take on Jack Johnson and all other fighters who want his game. Never lacking in cool courage, he is not afraid of any of them, and his good judgment in passing up the hard game for the soft money engagements should not be construed as cowardice on his part. It merely is an exhibition of good sense in taking easy money where no chance is involved, in preference to taking the same money where a materially greater chance of losing exists.[893]

Johnson wrote an article that was published in London, entitled, "I Am Getting Very Tired." In it, he discussed his Tommy Burns hunt. He was convinced that Burns was anxious to avoid meeting him at anything other than an absurd price that no one would pay. He noted that Burns did not draw the color line, but used financial reasons as his excuse to avoid him. And yet,

[N]ot content with wriggling out of a match with me, he adds insult to injury by declaring that I have a 'yellow streak,' which, in everyday language, of course, means that I am afraid, or am not game, which, all things considered, seems hardly justified, since every sporting man in England knows that, for some time past, I have been chasing Burns half round the world in order to get a match with him.

Johnson said that when he came out East to try to get a match with Burns, Kaufman, Berger, or O'Brien, all of them left and went West again. When he went West, they all scattered about. Then he went to Australia to get a match with Squires, but then Bill sailed away to America. The "white fellows were beating it faster than ever to keep out of my way."

Jack noted that several splendid offers had been made to fight in England, but Burns preferred matches with "dead easy" men instead and was looking to go to Australia. "'Pon my word, this sort of thing is enough to drive any ordinary man just crazy. ... I suppose I shall have to continue my 'Burns-hunt.'"

Regardless, Johnson said he did not wish to underrate Burns for a moment. "I consider Burns is a great boxer, for he is both clever and game." He noted that Burns had power and skill combined.[894]

One man who had seen Johnson box exhibitions in Birmingham, England with British welterweight Curly Watson, said,

---

[893] *Los Angeles Herald,* June 22, 1908.
[894] *Penny Illustrated Paper and Illustrated Times* (London, England), June 27, 1908.

The champion gave the impression of being a tremendous hitter. Against such a small man as the ex-sailor, he, of course, let up considerably, but even at that could not disguise the fact that when on real business bent he would prove a most dangerous opponent. He has the reach and the power behind it to make a championship position secure for a long time. It is difficult to imagine it possible for a human being to withstand for long a pounding this colored heavyweight is capable of bestowing upon a rival. Burns may be a good glove fighter – indeed, is one – but against such a mountain of sinew and muscle which constitutes the body of Johnson, it does not seem to me that he could prevail for long. I saw the Canadian's contest with Gunner Moir at the National Sporting Club, and consider him physically and scientifically the inferior of Johnson.[895]

On July 4, 1908 at Colma, California, Battling Nelson knocked out Joe Gans in the 17th round to win the world lightweight championship.

The *Los Angeles Herald* noted in a headline that the Negro fighter was passing away, and had been eliminated from championships, which were now held by all white fighters. George Dixon, Joe Walcott, and Joe Gans all had been defeated and lost their world titles, having fought once too often. "The negro of today in the ring occupies a decidedly less conspicuous position and will find it remarkably difficult to get engagements. Jack Johnson alone stands in a position to command the admiration of the fight world for his prowess, real or imaginary, as it may be."

Despite the push by some for a Burns-Johnson fight, there were many who did not want a mixed-race championship bout to happen. No American promoter put up the money necessary to make the Burns-Johnson match. Fewer and fewer were promoting mixed-race championship bouts in any weight class, at least not after whites had recovered the titles.[896]

On Friday July 31, 1908 at the Cosmopolitan Club in Plymouth, England, Jack Johnson took on Big Ben Taylor, "the Woolwich Infant," who had about 40 fights under his belt, including: 1900 KO1 Woolf Bendoff; 1901 LKOby3 George Chrisp and W5 Sandy Ferguson; 1902 KO3 Arthur Morris, L10 and D6 Sandy Ferguson, and L10 Jack Scales; 1903 LKOby12 Jack Palmer and L20 Charlie Haghey; 1904 L6 Charlie Wilson, L10 Gunner Moir, and L10 Jack Scales; 1905 L6 Geoff Thorne; 1907 LKOby3 Sam McVey, L6 Jack Scales; and April 15, 1908 LKOby11 Sam McVey in Paris. Taylor was tough, experienced, and unlike most, was willing to fight Johnson. Jack had not fought since early November 1907, nearly nine months earlier.

The *London Sporting Life* said Johnson came to the country in company with Sam Fitzpatrick three months earlier. It appeared that their visit would be fruitless, as far as arranging contests was concerned.

---

[895] *Freeman*, August 15, 1908.
[896] *Los Angeles Herald*, July 6, 1908.

However, Ben Taylor came forward. He did not care what color a man was. He had been boxing 7-8 years, was 28 years of age, stood 5'11 ½" and weighed about 14.5 stone (203 pounds). Taylor's losses usually were the result of a lack of condition. One of his best contests was with Sandy Ferguson. When Taylor fought Moir he was out of condition at 18 stone (252 pounds), but he still lasted the full 10 rounds and lost on points. His last bout with Sam McVea was one of the finest contests seen in Paris. It was his display on that occasion that made him considered to be the best local representative that could be pitted against Johnson.

Ben Taylor

The *Sporting Life* helped make the match. The Cosmopolitan Club agreed to pay the boxers 80% of the gate receipts for a 10-round bout of 2 minutes each, fought with 6-ounce gloves, to be held on July 31. The parties signed "Sporting Life" articles. The gloves would be supplied by the *Sporting Life*, which also had the power to appoint a referee.

After articles were signed, Taylor began training immediately, and got himself into splendid condition. The day of the fight, he said he never felt better in his life.

In the meantime, Johnson was completing music-hall engagements. In addition to his exhibitions, Jack had been doing road work at Regent's Park and gymnasium exercise at the National Sporting Club in London.

When Johnson arrived in Plymouth the day before the fight, he met with a great reception.

The contest had been the sole topic in the town. Advance booking had been exceedingly heavy, with many seats secured by Londoners and sportsmen from all over. Never before had a contest in West England aroused so much interest. The next-day *Manchester Courier* said the bout attracted a crowd of 3,000.

Plymouth's well-known Cosmopolitan Club formerly was known as Hancock Winter Gardens on Mill-street.

On hand to witness the bout was a writer known as Chronos, of the Manchester-based daily *Sporting Chronicle* (which was known fondly as the "Chron"), who had seen Johnson exhibit in various music halls.

After some preliminary contests, at nearly 10 p.m., Johnson entered the ring first, wearing a long loose dressing gown. He bowed gracefully in response to the cheers that greeted him. His seconds were Sam Fitzpatrick, Young Lippo, Charley Jenkins, and Sam French.

Ben Taylor soon followed, seconded by Tom Bridgeman, Jim Leonard, and George Rowlands. He too received a warm welcome.

Both looked to be in fine condition. Johnson was taller and also appeared to be slightly heavier than Taylor, who was a big man himself.

Mr. John T. Hulls, whom the *Sporting Life* appointed, refereed. Mr. E. Cloud was the timekeeper. Sgt-Maj. Coulon was the M.C.

The *Sporting Chronicle* and *London Sporting Life* offered round-by-round descriptions:

1 - Johnson immediately began forcing the work, and smashed right and left to the face. Taylor retreated and attempted to counter, but received a hard left to the body, which Johnson followed up by scoring heavily with both hands on the face. Ben's head shook noticeably. He raised his guard and Johnson landed a left to the ribs. Jack laughed and forced Ben all over the ring. Ben fired three blows in combination, but Jack drew his head back from the first punch, cleverly parried the second with his left glove, and stopped the third with his right. Johnson then drove his left flush on the mouth and drew blood. Ben clinched, but Jack hooked the ribs with lightning speed until Taylor broke away. Jack forced the fighting and put in a lot of two-handed work. Ben fought back and landed a good one to the face, but Jack remained busy with both hands until the gong.

2 - Johnson again set a fast pace, gliding after his man, always seeming to be within striking distance, though he never was there when Taylor threw his punches.

After working into range, Johnson landed a right hook to the side of the head that dropped Taylor to his knees.

Taylor quickly rose and Jack stood back to let him put up his guard. Taylor moved around, keeping out of range. Suddenly Ben tried to mix matters, but Johnson neatly parried. The smile vanished from Jack's face and he sailed in, landing a hard left to the nose that shook the Englishman down to his toes. Ben looked all but beaten, but Johnson stepped back to allow him to recover until the gong sounded.

3 - Taylor gamely rushed, firing his left at Johnson, who nimbly side-stepped and then countered to the ribs as he passed, staggering him. Attacking strongly, Johnson fired several hard left hooks, and then staggered Taylor with a right jolt to the jaw. Jack came after him like a shot and caught and held Taylor up, actually preventing him from falling.

There were loud shots of encouragement for the plucky Taylor. In response, he made a fierce rush and hit out, but was met by Jack's vicious left full on the mouth, causing the blood to stream down to his chest. Johnson stepped back to survey his handiwork, feinting a left to the head, and then driving a hard right to the body that made Ben wince. Taylor rushed in again and attacked with great fury, but Jack smiled, stepped back, and parried the blows with ease and nonchalance.

4 - Johnson waited for Taylor to attack. Ben attempted a left lead to the body but Jack avoided it and countered with a right to the head. Johnson struck out with both hands, using skill, precision, power, and judgment, until a final bruising right to the jaw dropped Taylor.

Upon rising at the count of eight, Taylor rushed in with his head down, but Johnson cleverly eluded danger and sent in a volley of forceful uppercuts. Taylor gamely took the blows and kept coming back for more, showing tremendous pluck.

5 - For half a minute, little was done. Then Johnson went in like a whirlwind, showing his real quality as a fighter. His speed and power left the spectators aghast. Jack banged three lefts to the face, and then sent a pile-driving right into the ribs. Ben staggered back from the fearful bombardment, his legs wobbling and arms hanging low from fatigue and weakness. However, Johnson made no effort to land a finishing blow, and was content to spar at long range until the bell. Taylor made a good show, but Johnson's body blows were telling.

6 - Johnson fought fast again, working his way into range, smashing his left to the face and then sailing in, hitting out smartly with both hands. One punch sent Taylor reeling backwards six feet. Quickly moving in, Johnson dropped Taylor with a nasty right to the head followed by a left hook to the chin.

When Taylor rose at nine, he was half dazed. He wandered about as Johnson punched him at will. Ben's defense was gone, and he was knocked about by the smiling black champion, who finally landed a heavy right to the chin that sent Taylor down once more.

Ben rose at nine, but was very groggy. Yet, he managed to last to the end of the round.

7 - Johnson punched Taylor from pillar to post, dropping him no less than five times; for two, nine, seven, eight, and nine seconds respectively, twice being sent through the ropes.

Ben gamely tried to fight back, but was like a child in Jack's hands. It was clear that the end was near, and had the round been of regular three-minute duration instead of two, Taylor would not have lasted.

8 - Obviously, the end was near. Johnson walked up to Taylor and knocked him down with a left hook to the chin. Ben struggled to rise at nine, looking like a beaten man. A tremendous clean right to the chin floored the brave Britisher again. Seeing that he was done for, the referee stopped the bout and declared Johnson the winner.

Johnson had dominated, dropping Taylor in the 2nd, 4th, 6th (twice), 7th (five times), and 8th (twice).

The *Sporting Life* said that from the outset, Johnson had matters his own way. "Johnson's display was that of an accomplished boxer, and those critics who asserted that he was as clever as the late Peter Jackson were by no means wrong in their assertion."

Taylor made a game stand, which was appreciated greatly. He took the blows without flinching, and by the time the referee stopped the bout in the 8th round, he had taken sufficient punishment to stop half a dozen men. After the contest, Johnson kindly paid tribute to Taylor, saying that he had never met a gamer man in his career.

Chronos of the *Sporting Chronicle* said that "to say that Johnson's victory was complete and decisive is a mild way of describing his somewhat easy task. Taylor had no chance against the black champion of the world, yet Ben knew no fear and stood up to his man until nature forsook him."[897]

The next-day *New York Journal* reported that Johnson fought Ben Taylor, "one of the best English heavyweights," for a $500 side-bet and a percentage of the gate. When Johnson hurt Taylor badly several times, he let up. Jack then played defense as Taylor wore himself out trying to hit him. Afterwards, Johnson said he allowed Taylor to stay as long as he did just to give the spectators a run for their money.

English experts who had seen both Johnson and Burns in action claimed that Johnson was Tommy's master at all aspects of the game. One said Johnson was 100% better than Burns. "He is cleverer, can hit harder, can stand more punishment, and is just as cool under fire."

Johnson said,

> I will probably return to America within a few days. Of course, if I am offered any more matches I will stay, but I am afraid that none of the fighters over here have any more use for my game than Tommy Burns, who persists in avoiding me.

> When I return to the United States I shall claim the heavyweight title of the world, and I am sure that everybody will agree with me that it rightfully belongs to me now that Burns refuses to fight me.[898]

The National Sporting Club was looking for a white fighter who was both willing and able to face Johnson, for it "was not the desire of the club managers to put two black men into the ring." However, it was obvious that no white man in England could cope with Johnson. Mike Schreck's name was mentioned as a potential opponent. However, the fight did not materialize, which is not surprising given that Schreck drew the color line.[899]

On August 7, 1908 in New York, Sam Langford stopped Italian Tony Ross in the 5th round. Ross had knocked out Mike Schreck in 7 rounds, George Gardner in 5 rounds, and had stood off Flynn for 16 rounds before

[897] *Sporting Chronicle*, July 31, 1908; *London Sporting Life*, *Manchester Courier*, August 1, 1908.
[898] *New York Journal*, August 1, 1908.
[899] *Freeman*, August 29, 1908; *New York World*, August 6, 1908.

being stopped. Langford was coming off knockout victories over Jim Barry (KO3) and John Willie (KO2).

Langford was being called one of the best fighters in the world. Many fans were of the opinion that Sam could beat anyone, including Burns. Langford intended to challenge Johnson when Jack returned from England. His manager, Joe Woodman, said, "Langford has grown heavier since he last fought Johnson, and I think it will be a cinch for Sam to beat him."[900]

Writer Robert Edgren described Burns, whom he highly respected. "He is a white Langford in build, but twenty pounds heavier, twice as fast, twice as clever, fully as hard a hitter, and a man of keen active intelligence."[901]

Before he left Rome, Italy, to travel to Australia, Burns wrote, "Give my regards to Spring street and tell the doubting ones to cage Johnson and hold him until I get back. I don't want this mess of gravy spilled before I return."[902]

On August 11, 1908, Burns arrived in Sydney, New South Wales, Australia. Promoter Hugh D. McIntosh said that if Burns' bouts there were successful financially, his enterprise would make the Burns-Johnson fight. "Of course he demanded a large sum, but after he had fought all the best whites offering he believed Burns was prepared to meet Johnson for the largest sum obtainable."[903]

The black-owned *Washington Bee* noted that from 1906 - 1907, 122 negro lynchings had taken place under the supposed U.S. democracy, all in states under Democrat rule.[904]

Starting on August 14, 1908, in the Northern town of Springfield, Illinois, home of Abraham Lincoln, a three-day riot took place, initiated by a white woman's claim that a negro had violated her (which she later admitted was false). Inflamed by newspaper sensationalism, and fueled by mounting economic and racial tensions, crowds of whites gathered around the jail demanding that the arrested black man be lynched.

When the sheriff transferred the accused and another black man to a jail in a nearby town, white mobs instead headed for Springfield's Negro section and attacked and destroyed homes and businesses. Two blacks were lynched, while others were dragged from their houses and streetcars and beaten.

By the time National Guardsmen reached the scene, seven persons were dead—five whites and two negroes. The Northern race riot shocked white liberals. By year end 1908, at least 89 black Americans would be lynched.

In Sydney, while preparing for his third match with Bill Squires, Tommy Burns told the Australian press that it was well within probability that he

---

[900] *New York World*, August 7, 1908.
[901] *New York World*, August 11, 1908.
[902] *Los Angeles Herald*, August 5, 1908.
[903] *Sydney Daily Telegraph*, August 12, 1908.
[904] *Washington Bee*, October 17, 1908.

and his colored challenger, Jack Johnson, might decide their differences in Australia.

It was also said that Burns might meet world middleweight champion Stanley Ketchel, who was on a meteoric rise. The 22-year-old's recent victories included May 1908 KO20 Jack "Twin" Sullivan, June W10 Billy Papke, and late July KO3 Hugo Kelly.[905]

On August 24, 1908 at Rushcutters Bay in Sydney, Australia, before 15,000 - 18,000 spectators, Tommy Burns stopped Bill Squires in the 13th round. The fight had been highly entertaining, and Australians were impressed with Burns. "Added to his scientific precision of boxing is a capacity for taking punishment which is almost superhuman. It may be possible to hurt Burns with a battle-axe, but most of those who witnessed his performance of yesterday would be inclined to doubt it."[906] Burns was a skilled boxer-puncher who could stick and move from the outside or rough it in the clinches on the inside, and he could also take a punch. "This power Burns has of dealing terrific hits with either hand at a distance of about a foot, combined with his amazing footwork, make him the wonder he is." He also was well-conditioned and calm under fire.

The *Sydney Bulletin* said,

> The man who beats Burns will be either too quick or too scientific for him. He will either get his blows in so quickly that Burns cannot dance away from them or destroy the aim by tapping the biceps or shoulder, or he will have such marvelous dexterity that he will be able to feint a blow, draw Burns' defence, and then, while Burns is tapping the firing arm, cross suddenly with the other and land on the jaw. And that man doesn't seem to be on deck just now.[907]

Bill Squires said,

> Burns is a good hard fighter, and one who will take a whole heap of beating, no matter who he faces. ... Burns is a man in thousands. He is very quick on his feet, a hard puncher, a shrewd fighter, and has a frame of iron [908]

Burns said he hoped McIntosh would bring him and Johnson together. Once their fight took place, he would retire and fight no more, for he had made ample money, sufficient to live very comfortably.[909]

On August 25, 1908 in Los Angeles, Al Kaufman scored a 9th round knockout over Jim Flynn, stopping him faster than had either Burns or Johnson.[910]

---

[905] *Sydney Daily Telegraph*, August 19, 1908.
[906] *Sydney Morning Herald*, August 25, 1908.
[907] *Sydney Bulletin*, August 27, 1908.
[908] *Referee*, August 26, 1908.
[909] *Referee*, September 2, 1908.
[910] *Los Angeles Herald*, August 26, 1908.

Speaking of the reasons why Burns had not yet fought Jack Johnson, one Australian writer opined, "Racial pride counts for something in pugilism, and one great reason why Burns would not give Johnson a chance to wrest the championship of the world from him was a ferocious hatred of the idea of the negro being the bruising monarch of the earth."[911]

However, racial prejudice aside, given that Burns had drawn very well for the Squires fight, and that Australians had seen Johnson defeat Peter Felix and Bill Lang the previous year and were well aware of his prowess, it was within the realm of possibility that Hugh McIntosh might be able to meet Burns' financial demands for a Burns-Johnson title fight.

From London, Johnson said his original offer to stop Burns in 20 rounds was still good. He was willing to fight Burns anywhere in the world.

Apparently, negotiations had been ongoing between McIntosh and Johnson via McIntosh's London representative. In order to meet Burns' guarantee, McIntosh had to pay Johnson a relatively smaller amount.

The *Referee* quoted James Jeffries, who called Johnson's talk "guff" and a "feeble effort to talk big." Jeffries said Johnson "has no call to talk about knocking any clever man out. Not once in his career has he been guilty of such a thing." He noted that every time Burns had posted 1,000 pounds as a wager to be covered, Johnson's side had failed to do so. "As far as one may judge on form in boxing, Johnson should prove a certain victim for Burns." Burns was improving with every fight, was fighting frequently, and therefore would not be rusty, "while it is the other way about with Johnson." Continuing, Jeffries said,

> Tommy Burns will defeat Jack Johnson if they ever meet, provided Burns can get in a couple of good punches in the midsection of the Senegambian. ... Jack Johnson is the biggest quitter that ever entered a prize ring, and has a streak of yellow in his system as wide as a street. This is the kind of man who does lots of talking, but in actual work does nothing. I think Tommy Burns is as game as they make them, quick on his feet, clever, and able to stand a world of punishment. This last is what Jack Johnson cannot do. I think this talk about Burns being afraid of Johnson is more or less a fable. Burns is afraid of no man, white or black, and has taken chances that no other man in the world would have taken. He fought Marvin Hart when the latter was a 5 to 1 favorite over him, and has never balked at fighting any man. Tommy probably sees a chance to get a lot of Press agent matter out of this controversy, and is working both ends against the middle with good results.

Jeff also said the National Sporting Club's paltry offer of 2,500 pounds was a ridiculously poor inducement, given that even a Burns-Squires match

[911] *Sydney Bulletin*, August 27, 1908.

was worth 3,000 pounds. Jeffries agreed that promoters were sorely undervaluing the Burns-Johnson fight.[912]

SAM LANGFORD

Sam Langford, who since his loss to Johnson had victories over Young Peter Jackson (winning rematches after being defeated by Jackson), a couple of 12-round draws with Joe Jeannette, and victories over Sandy Ferguson, John Willie, and Tony Ross, was also challenging Burns and middleweight champion Stanley Ketchel.

On September 1, 1908 in New York, Langford nearly knocked out Joe Jeannette. Langford twice dropped Jeannette in the 1st round and once in the 5th round en route to the unofficial 6-round no-decision win.[913]

A *Freeman* writer opined that by the time Burns returned to America, Langford likely would be a stronger candidate for his attention than Johnson, despite the fact that Sam was more of a middleweight in size. "Langford is a marvel as a fighting machine. He has the gorilla build and tremendous power of Fitzsimmons. ... Langford is a legitimate candidate for a match with Jack Johnson. .... There are many experts in New York today who believe Johnson would be no match for Langford now."[914]

Regardless, increasingly the American press was warming up to Burns, and some even took his side against fighters who were challenging him:

> Jack Johnson is making a big noise about claiming the heavyweight championship from Tommy Burns, because Tommy deemed it his duty to keep his contracts with the Antipodean promoters to go to Australia and whip all the heavy crop in that neighborhood. These big blacks consider themselves of extreme and exclusive importance any time they desire to talk and evidently believe that because they are black they should have first call on any of the champions they desire to fight. If they are as anxious to fight as they proclaim themselves to be, why in the world do they not arrange a match between themselves? Both Langford and Johnson are hotfooting it after Burns.... It is a cinch that Burns and Ketchel will mop up with the fighters who are in line for their titles, as neither is afraid of any fighter in his class, black or white. In the meantime, it would be an

---

[912] *Referee*, September 2, 1908.
[913] *San Francisco Chronicle, New York World*, September 2, 1908.
[914] *Freeman*, September 5, 1908.

excellent idea for Langford and Johnson to prove themselves in the heavyweight division by an elimination contest.... Johnson never has whipped a real classy fighter when that fighter was in his prime, unless his decision over Langford can be so termed. Langford has whipped a few classy men. If Langford is the demon he claims to be, he should trim the big black noise without trouble. ... Black fighters have the same fault they charge to the white fighters. They draw the color line. ... [N]obody ever has heard of Langford chasing Johnson all over the country with defis, although both Langford and Johnson are hurling challenges every hour at Burns and Ketchel. If either is sincere in his desire to fight for championships, it will be no great trouble to arrange a Johnson-Langford match, and this fight would draw almost as well as a Langford-Ketchel fight. And if Langford ever gets the big saffron in the ring, the fight world will have heard the last yawp from this noisy individual whose mail is addressed to Jack Johnson. ...

Those who are criticizing Burns for going to Australia to pick the lemon crop in that country are making an error that they readily will admit any time they think it over without prejudice. Burns has had a hard climb to the top rung. Easy money is the rule now, instead of small purses and hard fights, as he experienced in his climb up the ladder. Having attained that prominence that is the goal of all fighters ... he has the right to accept all the emoluments of his office, and a few easy scraps and big money are among them. Nobody ever has accused Tommy of being a coward, as he has accepted fights with bigger and heavier men and whipped them, and has done all that has been asked of him since he claimed the championship. He has begun a fighting tour of the world, in order that he may become a legitimate world champion, and has whipped everything in sight of any consequence. ... He will return to America in November or December, and after he gets home there will be considerably less talk by fighters who now are seeking matches (in their minds) with him.[915]

Regarding a potential fight with Johnson, Burns said,

All that is needed to fix that battle is Johnson's signature, and that has yet to be obtained. My terms have been stated, and they go. I shall not alter them. ... This I now wish the world to know – my fight with Jack Johnson will be the last fight of my life. ... I want to meet Johnson, and have done with it; but I don't want to have done with it till I meet Johnson, or till he says he will not meet me.[916]

Just ten days after the third Burns-Squires bout, on September 3, 1908 in Melbourne, Australia, before a crowd of 7,000 to 10,000 spectators, Tommy

---

[915] *Los Angeles Herald*, September 1, 1908.
[916] *Melbourne Age*, September 3, 1908.

Burns took on current Australian heavyweight champion Bill Lang. Since his March 1907 KOby9 loss to Jack Johnson in Melbourne, Lang had been undefeated for nearly two years, having won 13 fights in a row, including KO9 Peter Kling, KO1 Mike Williams, KO12 Peter Felix (vacant Australian heavyweight title), KO8 Arthur Cripps, KO7 Felix, KO1 Bill Smith, and July 1908 KO5 Jim Griffin. The *Sydney Bulletin* said of Lang, "He was quite a novice, as he says, when he stood up against Johnson, the tall nigger whom Burns, thus far, has avoided." Lang had grown larger since the Johnson fight, and was weighing 186-189 pounds. Burns allegedly weighed 174 pounds.[917]

Although Lang decked Burns in the 2nd round with a left hook, Burns rose and fought back well, dropping and hurting Lang several times throughout until he knocked him out in the 6th round.

The *Melbourne Age* said, "There is probably no boxer alive who has been more perfectly equipped by nature for the game he follows than Tommy Burns. He is a big man packed into the smallest possible space, and overflowing with strength and endurance." On the inside, "It was the force, the speed and the roughness of these close range attacks that wore Lang down." Burns was a "ring general and a brainy fighter." The *Referee* said, "I have seen all the best men Australia has known during the past quarter of a century, but I can't recall one who had the combative instinct so strongly prominent. Burns would beat a cleverer man." Trainer Pat O'Keefe said Burns had a great chin, and never would be beaten until someone knocked him limp. "I don't think the man lives who has the necessary weight in his punch."[918]

The next day, Burns said he was not going at top speed at any time in the Lang fight. "I had a lot of energy in reserve all the time, but I dare say I'll put it all into the Johnson encounter whether it is needed or not – that is, of course, if I have the good luck to meet him, and I hope to meet him here."[919]

The *Sydney Bulletin* said the reports about Burns before he came to Australia were misrepresentations. He had been pictured as a small-sized champion dancing around his adversaries like a cat on hot bricks. His strength was less noticeable than his agility and ring-craft. This paper felt that in fact, Burns was a big, very strong, aggressive fighter, willing to mix it up on the inside. He had a bull neck, heavy shoulders, and thick waist. "To be clinched by Burns was to be punched in the region of the heart, kidney, liver, lights or spleen." He was stronger than the larger Lang. "Tommy is a 'born fighter,' to be sure, and God gave him a stocky figure and a quick eye and more brains than most men in the stoushing business." In fact, Tommy Burns could be a bull-like attacker or a fancy dancing boxer.[920]

---

[917] *Sydney Bulletin*, August 20, 1908.
[918] *Melbourne Age*, September 4, 1908; *Referee*, September 9, 1908.
[919] *Melbourne Age*, September 5, 1908.
[920] *Sydney Bulletin*, September 10, 1908.

The Burns-Squires fight drew 13,700 pounds, or $68,500, not including the motion picture rights. When Burns fought Lang in bad weather, the gate was 4,400 pounds, or $22,000. Burns had generated $90,500 in two fights in ten days. He was a very big revenue generator in Australia, which increased the likelihood that McIntosh would offer him what he wanted to fight Johnson.[921]

Burns wanted a rest. He already had defended the title successfully six times in 1908 alone.

> No more work for me for two months, anyhow. I've been working now for nine months on end, fighting and giving theatrical displays, and to finish up with I have fought two world's championship battles in ten days. I think I've earned a spell, and I will leave Melbourne on Monday to take a rest in the mountains.[922]

In America, there were rumors that Johnson and Burns had been signed to fight in Australia. The rumors were doubted, for,

> [I]t is the biggest sort of a cinch that if Johnson had been signed the big black would be making so much noise about it that the news would come by word of mouth from him in London, instead of by cable or telegraph. They may be matched, but if so, Burns has been shown considerably more money than he could get in America or England for fighting Johnson. … Burns is not afraid of Johnson, but he realizes that a match with the saffron streak would be worth more to him, financially, than any half a dozen fights in which he could engage, and he means to make the club that stages it stand a tap. And he is right as a fox, too.[923]

However, in Australia it was reported that negotiations were at an impasse, for "it has now been found impossible to get Johnson to suggest terms on which he will consent to meet Burns." Jack wanted to be paid as well. He had been doing music hall turns in England.

When interviewed, Burns said,

> Johnson has been running about England making a big boast of what he would do, and trying to make out that I was afraid of him. I never avoided Johnson, and he knows it; but he has religiously avoided me. I have always been ready to meet him, insisting, of course, that a certain amount would have to be guaranteed me, win or lose. I did not care what he made out of the encounter. … He is a great bluff. … He made a statement that he had deposited 2500 dol. with a New York journal as a forfeit that he would stop me in 20 rounds. I at once sent Billy Neil to New York from London with 5000 dol. to cover it, and to bet him as much more; but Johnson would have none

[921] *New York World*, November 25, 1908.
[922] *Melbourne Argus*, September 4, 1908.
[923] *Los Angeles Herald*, September 3, 1908.

of it, and furthermore we found that he had never deposited a cent. Afterwards in London he stated that he had put up £100 with the 'Sporting Life' to bind a match with me, but when I went with the cash to cover it there was no money there. Johnson then said that he had put up £1250 with the National Sporting Club that he wagered against £1000 of my money that he could beat me, but when I made inquiries of Mr. Bettinson, secretary of the club, he knew nothing whatever of Johnson's money. This is the way this fellow has been going on. He is simply living on my reputation. While I was in France Johnson was in Paris, showing at the Bowling Palace Music Hall, and he was no draw. As a matter of fact, I know that he drew just exactly 179 francs for one week, and of that he got 50 per cent, and his trunks were seized. Seeing that this is the kind of living he is making it seems strange that he would not jump at the chance of a match with me if he was really wanting one. As a matter of fact, I don't think Johnson wants to be any closer to me than he need be. He knows how he fared at the hands of the game, gritty Marvin Hart, who is not clever, but certainly is courageous. Johnson doesn't like rough usage. ... I particularly want to meet Johnson and get out of the boxing game forever. I want to meet Johnson, firstly, to make it plain that I draw no color line, that I do not bar any man in the world; and secondly to establish my own opinion that I am Johnson's superior, and thirdly, to quit the game as champion of the world. And if Johnson refuses to meet me then I will retire for good and all, for a match with him is the only one I desire. ... When I quit the professional ring I will settle in Australia, at least for some years.[924]

The *Sydney Bulletin* supported Burns, saying that Tommy had proven himself to be in the world-beater class, unlike Johnson, whom it called a talkative "Galveston nigger."

If there is one defect common to prizefighters...that Burns lacks it is loquacity. He has fought more fights in his brief career than any other champion in the world's history, and always he has maintained a practically dead silence before, during, and after the disagreement. If there is any loquacity about, Johnson, whom the British papers laud as a sort of ringside Crichton, is guilty of it.[925]

The *Bulletin* said Johnson was backed by a section of the U.S. press that jeered at Burns for "running away" from Johnson, the "murky person" who recently described himself as champion of the world and accused Burns of "having fled from the glare of his countenance."

However, it also reported that Fitzpatrick/Johnson were negotiating for more money, and were reluctant to come to Australia. Johnson was piling

---

[924] *Melbourne Age*, September 7, 1908; *Referee*, September 9, 1908.
[925] *Sydney Bulletin*, September 10, 1908.

up dollars on the Parisian music-hall stage. It believed that "Johnson's diffidence about bruising with Burns is due, not to fear of Tummas, but to reluctance to come to Australia and get half-killed for £1000, when he can make twice as much by staying in Paris and keeping an undamaged countenance."[926]

Regardless of all the talk, on September 16, 1908, Jack Johnson signed articles to fight Tommy Burns in Australia in late December for the championship. Hugh McIntosh had made the fight. Burns would receive $30,000 guaranteed, and Johnson $5,000, a mere one-sixth of what Burns would make.

> Johnson has practically chased Burns around the world in an effort to get a match. The champion has long evaded the negro, although he has frequently said he would fight him in good time when sufficient financial inducements were made. ...
>
> Where American and English sporting men have failed the New South Wales people have succeeded.

Johnson booked passage on the steamer Ortona for Sydney.

> When the black man meets the Canadian-American in the ring there will be a battle for generations to remember, unless the general acceptance of the respective abilities of the two men is all wrong. Burns is a thick set, heavy hitting, never-say-die fighter of the Sullivan type, while Johnson is a scientific ring general, with all of Corbett's cleverness and possessing greater hitting ability than the present actor ever had.
>
> Burns does not lack cleverness either, and is as light on his feet as a mountain goat. All that those who follow the fighting game can see for either man is a knockout after a bruising, punishing fight.[927]

Before having made the Burns fight, Johnson had agreed to fight Sam Langford in England, the fight to take place on or about February 22, 1909 for a £1,000 purse ($5,000), with 1/3 of the interest in any bioscopic pictures taken.

According to a cable from London, before Johnson left, he agreed to return to London in February to fight Langford, regardless of whether he won or lost to Burns.[928]

[926] *Sydney Bulletin*, September 17, 1908.
[927] *New York World, New York Tribune, Los Angeles Herald*, September 17, 1908.
[928] *Freeman*, November 14, 1908.

CHAPTER 26

Preparing for and Promoting
the Big Fight

Scouting the upcoming Tommy Burns vs. Jack Johnson heavyweight championship bout, Jay Davidson of the *Los Angeles Herald* wrote,

> If this is to be a finish fight Burns should win. If it is to be a 20-round affair, as at first reported, Johnson may outpoint him. The big saffron streak will have the time of his life at knocking out the world champion, and I still am a Missourian on the subject. I rather prefer to predict that before the fight has gone twenty rounds the Antipodean sportsmen will witness a new kind of an airship, as a combination black-yellow streak makes an aerial flight out of the ring to escape annihilation. There is a vast difference between Burns and the mutts that Johnson has been putting away in his ring career.[929]

The *Herald* complimented Burns' business sense in holding out until he got the $30,000 the match was worth. "Burns has proved his own good, calm judgment in this affair in holding off from other offers of a match with Johnson until he got the terms he desired, although he has been subjected to a grilling, the like of which no fighter ever has been forced to accept." He had proven that he was not afraid of Johnson. "Burns is the only fighter with a title who will fight a negro nowadays, and after he whips Johnson, as he surely will, he probably will draw the color line, as his wife strenuously objects to her hubby fighting negroes." Burns was receiving more for a single fight than any previous fighter, and Johnson in making $5,000 would earn more than he ever had for a fight as well.

The *Herald* and Jim Jeffries thought that the longer the fight lasted the better it would be for Burns, for he had staying qualities, gameness, a strong jaw, a cool head under fire, a terrific wallop, ability to finish a man, aggressiveness, and cleverness. "Tommy may have had a few enemies in the world before this match was made, but practically every fight fan in the world will pull for him to win, as it will be a case of a game fighter against a big coward, and no fighter with the yellow label on ever had much of a following."[930]

When again asked for his opinion of the Johnson-Burns championship match, James Jeffries said, "I think that it will be a great fight, and I look to Burns being returned the winner. He is too clever, too strong, and too

---

[929] *Los Angeles Herald*, September 20, 1908.
[930] *Los Angeles Herald*, September 25, 1908.

courageous for the black fellow. Burns is better than he is given credit for being."[931]

In a letter dated October 9, 1908, Burns said he was about to fill a theatrical engagement, four nights a week for £500 ($2,500) and transportation for three, which would make him a little over £10,000 ($50,000) earned in Australia up to the date of the Johnson fight, not including motion picture revenues. Tommy said it was pretty good for a poor kid who started out with nothing. Tom also said Hugh McIntosh was an honest and fine fellow and the greatest promoter ever. The purses, pictures, and transportation were costing McIntosh about $40,500.

Johnson would arrive in Sydney at the end of October. Tommy noted, "He says he is going to stop me in twelve rounds of the twenty rounds." Burns was willing to bet up to $10,000 that Johnson could not do it, and he did not think Jack would cover his wager. "Believe me, I'll fight for my life to beat this black man…and I'm sure I have it figured out so I'll win. It's the ambition of my life to whip Johnson."[932]

Burns evidently had no misgivings about the result of the fight, for he deposited a cheque for £1,000 as a wager that Johnson could not stop him in 20 rounds, let alone 12, as Johnson had boasted he would. Burns also deposited another like amount wagering that he would win the fight. All Johnson had to do was cover the amounts and the bets were on.

Burns said it would be his last fight, as he was retiring in deference to his wife's wishes. He would settle in Australia. "He is an anachronism in pugilism, a man who regards the whole business with sovereign contempt." Tom discovered that he was good at boxing and could make a lot of money in the sport, more than any other profession, so he did it.

Hugh McIntosh deposited with Sydney *Referee* sporting scribe W. F. Corbett "cheques" for £7,100, the stake for the Burns-Johnson fight, set to take place on Boxing Day, December 26. Many boxing scribes looked at the huge checks "with watering mouths and wondered why their misguided parent hadn't brought them up to be world-famous bruisers."

Boxing Day was not in honor of the sport. It was the day in which the English gave their servants presents, which came to be known as Christmas boxes. It was a legal holiday in Australia, which would allow the biggest turnout possible to the fight.

Johnson would earn 1,000 pounds ($5,000) plus an extra 100 pounds ($500) for the motion pictures, plus three round-trip tickets from London ($1,200 in expenses). Burns' end was 6,000 pounds in cash, regardless of the result, which was about $30,000. He would also receive a motion picture film, valued at 350 pounds ($1,750), plus $1,000 in expenses.

The *Sydney Bulletin* believed that Burns would enter this fight with a personal feeling against his opponent, for Johnson had pursued him with

---

[931] *New York World*, October 3, 1908.
[932] *New York World*, November 25, 1908.

irritating talk. Tom's reputation was at stake. "The other side has sneered at his reputation as a paper one, made by sweeping through a crowd of mediocre fighters." It was the current fashion to regard fighters of the past, like Jeffries, Sharkey, Ruhlin, and Fitzsimmons as superior to anything at present. However, this writer opined that had they been on deck now, that Burns would have fought them all, and "considering the anatomical subtleness of his fighting methods, would also have held his own."

Johnson would give Tommy a taste of the old-school methods, for he too used mighty swings and bone-smashing blows. Burns represented the new school of "short, quick jab on the vital spot, repeated over and over again, till the other man crumples up." He also had a unique defence. He went with blows, depriving them of their force like a swinging door. Rather than simply blocking or dodging, he paralyzed the attack by delivering short, quick taps on the shoulder or arm which diverted the blow and destroyed its force. Of course, anyone who watched Johnson knew that he did the same.[933]

The *Freeman* noted that Johnson had ordered a new batch of stationery in London that said under his name, "Heavyweight Champion of the World." He claimed to hold the title by default. "Why not? World's titles are now found in such large quantities that they are cheap. Scan the list and pick the fighter who is not champion of something." If they thought they had a lot of titles back then, they might be shocked by modern-day boxing.

Johnson was fairly popular in England. When he left Charing Cross Station in London, heading off on his trip to Australia, frantic fight fans almost mobbed him.[934]

Sam Fitzpatrick, writing from Naples just before he and Johnson sailed for Australia, said the match seemed too good to be true. He wouldn't believe that Burns was going to fight Johnson until he saw him in the ring and heard the first bell ring. They were set to box with four-ounce gloves.[935]

In late October, the *New York Sun* said the "big negro has long chased the so-called heavyweight champion." Johnson, who scaled 200 pounds, had been trying to make a match with Burns for two years. He always had maintained that he could beat Burns and repeatedly offered to stop him in 20 rounds or forfeit his share of the purse. At first, Tom drew the color line; then he left the U.S. to escape Jack's thick and fast challenges; and finally when Johnson arrived in England, Burns insisted that he would not fight him for less than $30,000. "Johnson had him cornered, and with public opinion behind him the negro actually drove Burns out of England. It did not take long for the leading British sporting authorities to hail Johnson as the real champion and Burns as counterfeit."

---

[933] *Freeman*, October 31, 1908, November 7, 14, 1908.
[934] *Freeman*, October 17, 1908.
[935] *Freeman*, October 17, 1908.

Burns is fast, aggressive and a hard hitter. He possesses science and is a ring general of conceded skill. His best fighting weight is about 170 pounds and he will shape up at least six inches shorter than Johnson. The negro is said by expert judges of pugilism to be the cleverest big man in the world today. He can punch, but whether he is dead game or not under grueling punishment remains to be seen. Few negro fighters as a rule relish a beating, and for that reason some wise men think that Burns, with his rushing tactics and heavy hitting, will take the heart out of Johnson.

Tom O'Rourke said Johnson would beat Burns to a certainty. Sam Fitzpatrick said that if Johnson ever got Burns into the ring, he'd "beat the white man to death."[936]

As a result of all his talk, Johnson had been "held up to scorn, hatred, ridicule and contempt as a loud-mouthed braggart." Yet, such publicity had garnered sufficient momentum and financial interest to get the Burns fight made.

However, when he arrived in Australia in late October, Johnson denied having boasted about what he would do to Burns. He claimed that the newspaper men were trying to foster ill feeling between the boxers; that it was all newspaper invention. The *Sydney Bulletin* writer had met Johnson when he was in Australia before, and confirmed that he "certainly saw nothing of the boaster about him."[937]

The *Freeman* reported that upon his arrival at Fremantle, Australia, Johnson had said, "I have chased the 'Liddle' chap from his nursery in 'Amurka.' I followed his 'Liddle' footsteps in Paris, and chased him over to the 'big smoke' and then succeeded in chasing him back to Australia." Sam Fitzpatrick chimed in and said he still did not know whether or not they had Burns, and wouldn't bet on it until he heard the bell. He called Burns a bluffer. Johnson replied, "A bluffer he is, and yet that is the man who has called me quitter. He is the man who is going to play for my body all the time, and win out." Grinning, Johnson held his huge fists above his head and asked, "And am I going to keep my hands above my head, so, while Burns is playing for my body? No sir. I have been fighting for sixteen years now, and I reckon I know more about the game than any other man. I am a larger man than he, and I am cleverer."

Johnson was a man of great stature, with broad shoulders and a commanding presence. He stood over six feet tall and appeared to weigh about 15 stone, or approximately 210 pounds. The impression was that it would be futile for a man of 5'7" to try to penetrate his defense.[938]

It was noted that Johnson had failed to cover Burns' wagers on the fight. "And all the killing of Burns with his mouth that has been accredited to

[936] *New York Sun*, October 25, 1908.
[937] *Sydney Bulletin*, October 29, 1908.
[938] *Freeman*, December 19, 1908.

Johnson does not make up for that little oversight." Of course, it is possible that Johnson did not have enough money to cover the wagers, or he did not say those things, or he said them in order to garner publicity and generate pressure in order to obtain the fight, without actually intending to place any wagers. However, some took his failure to cover the bets as a sign of who really had the confidence and who was just a talker.

In late October in Australia, Johnson was welcomed at the Café Francais. He seemed very fit. "The colored man is accompanied by his wife, a white woman, somewhat addicted to jewellery."

Johnson would train at the Joseph Banks Hotel at Botany, New South Wales. He would spar with former opponents Bill Lang and Joe Grim, amongst others.

Burns would prepare for the fight at a resort called Medlow Hydro in the Blue Mountains, New South Wales.

On October 26, 1908 in Melbourne, Burns seconded his sparring partner Pat O'Keefe in a fight for the Australian middleweight crown against Ed Williams, won by Williams via 15th round knockout.[939]

Johnson trained before admiring crowds, including a fair sprinkling of females. "There is a touch of Louis XIV about Johnson, and as far as possible he lives in the glare of publicity."

Burns was training privately at Medlow, where he had a cottage to himself, and "scours the rugged country on foot all day."

The *Bulletin* questioned the logic of paying visiting pugs £6,000 for a couple months of training and one hour's battling when the country's own prime minister only earned £2,100 for an entire year's work. "Go into the ring, young man, go into the ring."[940]

Writing from Australia early in his training, Burns said,

> I am finishing my training at Medlow Baths, in the Blue Mountains. It's a fine place, with everything I could want. They went to the expense of building me a handball court the other day, and I have a fine twelve-room house to myself. My wife is with me, and before the hard work began we enjoyed taking trips on the road. I've been swimming a good deal. The water and the air are ice cold. That was before I began hard work.

> Johnson is at St. Joseph's Bank Hotel, Botany. He has a fellow by the name of Williams as sparring partner, and is getting Bill Lang also – the last fellow I fought. They tell me that Joe Grim, the iron man, is Johnson's pal out there. Johnson is as flash as ever and looks flash, and he sure is holding me cheap by his talk. That suits me fine, as those fellows are the kind I like to fight.

---

[939] *Sydney Bulletin*, November 5, 1908.
[940] *Sydney Bulletin*, November 12, 1908.

I toured the Tasmanian Island for ten days, and got very good receptions everywhere. ...

Johnson wants Gene Corri, from London, to referee, but not for mine this time. Corri is a good fellow and all that, but he had Johnson to dinner at the Thieves' Kitchen, where I was entertained a month before. He is too friendly to Johnson and Fitzpatrick. I want Jeff, but Johnson says he won't stand for him, as he beat his brother, and Jim is sore at him (what a joke!). Leave it to me – I'll get an honest fellow. ...

I'll win this battle, unless I'm badly mistaken in Johnson's ability. I weighed 199 pounds with my clothes on yesterday. Of course, I let myself get a little fat, as I have a long time to work it off, and it won't hurt me. I am feeling very good. The people sure are grand in this country.[941]

In mid-November, the *Sun* reported that Australians did not see how Johnson would have a chance with Burns, whom they considered invincible. However, Johnson was far better than anyone Burns had beaten since leaving the U.S. Tom O'Rourke said Burns was a counterfeit champion and was not Johnson's equal as a slugger, boxer, or ring general.[942]

Bill Delaney, while agreeing that Burns was best entitled to claim the championship, acknowledged that many felt he needed to defeat Johnson to have the undisputed claim to being the best heavyweight in the world. However, Delaney believed the next best fighter was actually his boxer, Al Kaufman. He picked Burns to defeat Johnson.

Johnson's claims never have bothered me. He never has done anything to justify the suspicion that he is the best man in the heavyweight division, as he never has defeated any of the near-champions of that division. His claim upon the consideration of other heavyweights is based upon the suspicion that seems generally held by the sporting public that he can do things that he never has done and that he will show class that no fight he ever put up really would justify.

It is my opinion that Burns will whip Johnson if they are to fight to a finish. ... Johnson has not the class that is desired in a champion. He is accused on all sides, and not without justification, of being the possessor of a yellow streak. If he has that streak Burns will develop it.

Delaney said Burns had greater stamina than Johnson, was courageous, clever, quick, and a puncher. Even though Johnson also had cleverness,

---

[941] *New York World*, December 22, 1908. It usually took a long while for letters from Australia to arrive.
[942] *New York Sun*, November 14, 1908.

speed, and a punch, Delaney doubted he had a sufficient punch to knock out Burns. Plus he felt that the game fighter usually won in a long fight, and Burns was much gamer than Johnson. "Burns has my best wishes for his success in the battle with Johnson because I want him to eliminate the negro from the contention. I do not believe in the recognition of the negro as a contender for any championship." Delaney's fighter, Kaufman, drew the color line, which pleased Bill.[943]

Despite a liberal offer, Bill Squires turned down an offer to spar with Burns.

Tom wanted Jeffries to referee the fight, but "Jeff's unholy terms make him just about impossible." Jeff wanted too much money. Besides, Johnson did not want Jeff anyhow.

Some members of the clergy came out with anti-fight rhetoric. One speaker for the Anglican-Synod denounced the professional contest as dangerous and brutal; although he did not object to amateur boxing, for he once had been an amateur himself. The *Sydney Bulletin* humorously suggested, "The best thing that McIntosh can do is to send along free seat tickets to the ex-amateurs of the Synod in double quick time."[944]

The fight was set for 11 a.m. on December 26, but most New Yorkers would be able to learn about the result on the evening of the 25th, owing to the time difference of 14 hours and 40 minutes. "Most New Yorkers who follow the game think they know the ultimate result now – Burns will win."[945]

Apparently, speculators had purchased the Australian rights to the motion pictures for 4,000 pounds, or $20,000. The stadium cost 2,000 pounds to erect, equal to the land value, making the arena cost $20,000. Seats were selling for £ 10, 5, 3, 2, 1, and 10s. That was $50, $25, $15, $10, $5, and $2.50, which was fairly expensive for the era.

The fight was advertised in Sydney as Burns (World's Champion) vs. Johnson (Colored Champion) for the Absolute World's Boxing Championship, to be held at the Stadium at Rushcutter's Bay in Sydney, which was known popularly as the Stadium. Hugh D. McIntosh, Director of Scientific Boxing and Self Defense, Ltd., Challis House, Sydney, was the promoter.

Jim Corbett thought that Johnson would defeat Burns.

Some did not want to wager too much on the bout, fearing that Burns would induce Johnson to lay down. However, Fitzpatrick said Johnson would fight to win and score a clean knockout inside of 20 rounds.[946]

In a November 23 letter, Sam Fitzpatrick told W. W. Naughton that Burns was in for a beating. Australians were boxing mad at the present, so a very large attendance was expected. It was a scheduled 20-round bout.

---

[943] *Los Angeles Herald*, November 15, 1908.
[944] *Sydney Bulletin*, November 19, 1908.
[945] *New York World*, November 21, 1908.
[946] *New York Sun,* November 25, 1908; *San Francisco Chronicle*, December 6, 1908.

I want to tell you that I never wanted to come out here, but Johnson was crazy to get at Burns and there was no holding him. I wanted to keep Burns until we could get a fair share of any purse that was offered. As long as he was somewhere handy, we had a chance of forcing him into a fight in America, for, although he claims to be thick-skinned about criticism, he hates being panned. However, we had to follow him and now that we are so close on his heels, I feel that Master Tommy is in for the whaling of his life.

This climate surely does agree with Arthur. He is bigger and stronger than he ever was in his life and unless we get one of those Fitzsimmons-Sharkey decisions, I cannot see where Burns has a look-in.

Tommy is a slight favorite in the betting at present, but that will not last. It is the general opinion among thinking sports that Jack will start a strong favorite. The men are supposed to be in the ring at 11 a.m. December 26th, and ready for business.

In conclusion, I want to tell you that those who see Johnson at work for the first time go away feeling sorry for Burns. We are looking forward to Johnson winning well inside the twenty-round mark, and we expect to be in San Francisco in the early part of March.

The *Examiner* noted that clearly Fitzpatrick did not consider the contract to meet Langford in February or March in England to be a binding one.[947]

Johnson was working hard, "perspiring profusely and beaming brilliantly after a series of three-round bouts with his trainers and the best the local field could produce." He liked visitors, and always made a point of issuing a bulletin to the press. Johnson said,

I will enter the ring on the 26th of December feeling ready to undertake the contest of my life. I have had ample facilities for training, and the best of treatment accorded to me by Mr. McIntosh, the promoter for the syndicate. I don't wish to boast, but if my present feelings are any indication, I think you can announce to James J. Jeffries that he better get ready to come out of retirement. Mrs. Johnson is enjoying the best of health an' I am learning to hit like the native kangaroo kicks!

Johnson was taking some tremendously long walks in Botany. He also ran through National Park. In total, allegedly he was averaging around 20 miles a day, in addition to his usual sparring and other exercises. He was only about four pounds above his fighting weight.

At the "Medlow Hydromajestic" in the Blue Mountains, Burns did not take as lengthy excursions as did Johnson, but he was working hard nevertheless.

---

[947] *San Francisco Examiner*, December 24, 1908.

McIntosh was receiving abusive letters from both sexes, upset that Burns had been sent so far away to train. They demanded that something be done, for they wanted to see him. McIntosh decided that in the future, on Wednesday and Saturday afternoons, Burns would train before the public at the Stadium in Sydney.[948]

One month before the fight, on Wednesday November 25, 1908 at the Stadium at Rushcutters' Bay, Burns gave his first public exhibition of training. A crowd of around 2,000 people attended, including 200 ladies, generating a gate of over 90 pounds. A nice arrangement of palms was placed on tables, lending an attractive appearance to the scene.

Clad from neck to heels in a tight-fitting red woolen costume, Burns jumped into the ring at 4 p.m. and was received with cheers. Tom did leg and stomach exercises, rope skipping, and shadow boxing. He then sparred middleweight Les O'Donnell, as well as Irish light heavyweight Pat O'Keefe. In a fast engagement, Burns demonstrated considerable skill in evading O'Donnell's very clever left. Burns occasionally remained inert for a moment or two, allowing his man to punch away as hard as he could. During the O'Keefe bout, Burns caught him with a swinging right to the temple and Pat went down, but he quickly rose, shook the champ's hand, and resumed. "The champion already looks in splendid condition." Tommy would continue working with them on a daily basis.[949]

Johnson wanted two judges to be appointed to decide the bout along with the referee. This was an unusual request, for most important battles were decided by the referee only.[950]

Burns was opposed to Johnson's idea, responding, "Say Mac, what's the matter with the man?" Johnson had claimed that he would knock out Burns. The fact that he was concerned about having judges gave Burns and the *Sydney Bulletin* the impression that Johnson was a talker and not really all that confident that he would knock out Burns, but rather intended to win on points.

Despite the fact that Johnson was the slight odds favorite in the U.S., and all the pros in Sydney declared that Johnson would win, and that "on paper, Johnson ought to win easily," the *Sydney Bulletin* still felt that Burns would win as a result of his superior brain. Most local gamblers agreed, for Burns was the local betting odds favorite.[951]

Some reported that Jeffries said that if a black man won the championship, that he would emerge from retirement to recover the title for the white race.

> All this talk is very fine, but "emerging from retirement" usually means coming out to get a violent hiding. Jeffries is not improving

[948] *Sydney Bulletin*, November 20, 1908.
[949] *Daily Telegraph*, November 25, 1908.
[950] *Daily Telegraph*, November 27, 1908.
[951] *Sydney Bulletin*, December 3, 1908.

physically during these days that he is piling up money, and long ere this the once mighty boilermaker has got fat inside. There is no certainty that James could have walloped Johnson when he was at his best, although the impression is in James's favor. Still, it is only an impression, and so many general impressions have turned out to be wrong when tested. But it is almost a certainty that if the big man with the 24 inch neck does "emerge from his retirement" to face Johnson, he will get a bad beating.[952]

On Saturday November 28 at the Stadium, upwards of 5,000 attended Burns' training. As part of their admission, Mrs. Burns presided over the afternoon tea to which ladies were treated. Smart waiters served the ladies with complimentary tea and pastry. Ladies would not be admitted to the title fight, so they had to see Burns in training instead.

Johnson was training at the Olympic Recreation Grounds at Botany. He sparred with three strong fellows in well-known hard-fighting middleweight Ranji Burns, amateur heavyweight Paddy McTigue, and plucky welterweight Bob Bryant. Every afternoon at 3:30 p.m., Johnson trained publicly.

McIntosh announced a cable from New York that said Johnson was the slight betting favorite in several American cities. Opinion was equally divided regarding his ability to stop Burns in 20 rounds.[953]

Arriving from Vancouver, lightweight Rudolph Unholz spoke highly of Johnson, whom he said Americans looked upon as the likely winner of the coming engagement. Jack was big and clever, and if there was a yellow streak in him, no man had yet succeeded in finding it. In his opinion, the match would be a close one.

Canadian middleweight champion Joe Summer opined that although Johnson was bigger, he was not as quick as Burns, who would win.

Burns' brother-in-law noted that white boxer Battling Nelson had defeated the considered-invincible black lightweight champion Joe Gans (KO17 and KO21 in July and September 1908) by working the body, and said that Burns would use similar tactics.[954]

On the afternoon of Tuesday December 1, 1908 at the Queen's-hall, Pitt-street, an invitation exhibition of the moving pictures of Burns and Johnson in training was given. The 1,000 spectators appreciated the show very much, bursting with applause. It was the era's version of pre-fight hype, like today's 24-7 show on HBO.

On December 2, upwards of 2,000 people, including 200 - 300 ladies, watched Burns' afternoon training at the Stadium. The ladies were again treated to tea.

That evening, at the Stadium at Rushcutters' Bay, Jack Johnson refereed a boxing bout between Jack Blackmore and George Stirling, won by

[952] *Sydney Bulletin*, December 3, 1908.
[953] *Daily Telegraph*, November 30, 1908.
[954] *Daily Telegraph*, December 2, 1908.

Blackmore when Stirling's corner threw in the towel at the conclusion of the 12th round.[955]

From New York, Robert Edgren said Burns had proven himself to be a great businessman as well as fighter. The bout likely would break all gate receipt records. By waiting to fight Johnson, Burns was making much more for the fight than he would have if he had taken it a year prior. He already had made $50,000 in Australia, and would make another $30,000 for the big fight. "Foxy Tommy intended all along to fight Johnson when it became worth while. He delayed simply to boom Johnson's reputation and make him a drawing card."[956]

Announcing upcoming bouts, on December 9, Burns sparring partner Pat O'Keefe, who allegedly had won a 6-round no-decision bout with Billy Papke, would fight Jack Blackmore. Burns would second O'Keefe, and instead of a preliminary, the Burns-Johnson training pictures would be exhibited. On December 14, Burns would spar 4 rounds with Snowy Baker at a benefit to Baker. On December 15, Burns sparring partner Les O'Donnell would fight Johnson sparring partner Bob Bryant. Burns would second O'Donnell, while Johnson would second Bryant. Instead of a preliminary, the Burns-Johnson training pictures would be exhibited.[957]

On December 5, a crowd ranging from 7,000 to 8,000, including 1,000 ladies, came to see Burns train at the Stadium. In addition to his usual routine, Burns sparred with an amateur named Page. "Burns looked bright and well, and is evidently in splendid condition, despite the worry of his wife's illness, which is causing him no little concern. Mrs. Burns has had three doctors in attendance upon her, and it is quite possible she may have to spend a week or two in a private hospital."

That same day, a crowd of about 1,500 watched Johnson train at the Sir Joseph Banks Hotel. He sparred 4-round bouts each with Bob Bryant, Soldier Thompson, and Bill Lang, for a total of 12 rounds. Johnson showed good skill and fine condition in dealing with each man.

Both fighters had motor cars at their disposal, to take them wherever they wanted.[958]

On December 9, Burns was scheduled to box 4 rounds with Dave Smith, the current Australasian and New South Wales amateur heavyweight champion.[959]

A cable from Burns dated December 9 said interest in the fight was remarkable, that 6,000 people paid to watch him train daily (making him even more money). He also said the betting was even, and the referee had not yet been chosen.

---

[955] *Daily Telegraph*, December 3, 1908.
[956] *New York World*, December 3, 1908. Burns also sent Edgren a copy of the motion pictures from the recent Squires fight.
[957] *Sydney Daily Telegraph*, December 5, 1908.
[958] *Sydney Daily Telegraph*, December 7, 1908.
[959] *Sydney Daily Telegraph*, December 9, 1908.

Also on December 9 at the Sydney Stadium, Pat O'Keefe fought Jack Blackmoore to a 20-round draw.

The *New York World's* Robert Edgren said Burns had made a tremendous hit in Australia. "And Johnson, by his gigantic stature and his panther-like skill in boxing, has no doubt made himself an object of awe to the natives, although he has been training there only a month or so." That Jack had made a good impression was borne out by the fact that the betting was even. Johnson's "size has offset to a degree Burns's easy victories over Australian fighters." Edgren called Burns the Rockefeller of fighters. "As a money-maker he is a marvel." If he "whips this big negro, who has been a bugaboo to all the heavyweights for a year past, he'll be as popular a champion as even the great John L. Sullivan." "People who think that Burns hardly qualifies as a heavyweight champion because he is a pigmy compared with the great Jeffries might remember that Burns is an exact duplicate of the Sailor [Tom Sharkey] in stature – in height and weight – but has a reach just equal to that of Jeffries and Fitzsimmons, and is as clever as Jim Corbett."[960]

Burns wrote, "I will surely be in shape for the big Negro – better than I ever was, as it is the ambition of my life to beat him." Burns felt that many writers had not been fair to him.

> I have never drawn the color line. There was never a champion before me who gave a Negro a chance to win the title, and I simply named a good stiff price for my end of the match. I am getting it, too.
> ...
>
> Those who said that I was a careful matchmaker want to remember that I am about the only world's champion who went clear around the world, meeting and beating my challengers in the countries they belong in.
>
> When I boxed Squires here the house drew $67,000, so you see this country is going some. There were 17,000 persons present and a fine crowd to box in front of. About 9,000 people saw me defeat Lang ten days later.[961]

Given the strong level of advance ticket sales, which already had exceeded those for Burns-Squires, predictions were that the world's record would be outdone. A $100,000 audience was expected.[962]

Johnson transferred his training quarters from Botany to Manly.

Burns gave an exhibition on December 12 before a crowd of 1,000. He would exhibit at the Tivoli on the afternoon of the 14th.[963]

---

[960] *New York World*, December 10, 1908.
[961] *Freeman*, December 12, 1908.
[962] *Melbourne Age*, December 14, 1908.
[963] *Sydney Daily Telegraph*, December 14, 1908.

JOHNSON
READY FOR A
MATCH

Rumors that the men were to box to a draw intentionally for the sake of the moving pictures were disavowed. The pictures would be worth much more if the bout was on the level and had a decisive victor.[964]

On the afternoon of December 15, Johnson gave his first exhibition at the Stadium, before a good gathering that included ladies. He sparred with local middleweights Arthur Cripps and Soldier Thompson, in addition to shadow sparring.

That evening, Bob Bryant and Les O'Donnell, respective sparring partners for Johnson and Burns, engaged in a bout at the Stadium which resulted in a 20-round draw.[965]

The local *Bulletin* argued that on close inspection, the much-boomed physical advantages that Johnson had over Burns were not advantages at all. Burns was three years younger at age 27, so he had youth over the 30-year-old Johnson. Although Johnson had height and reach advantages, Burns increased the difference with his crouch, which actually would work to his advantage. "Johnson will have to hit down, which is a disconcerting thing, and, worse than all, his tender spot...his solar plexus, will be right opposite to Burns' main battery." Johnson had fought only once in the past year, whereas Burns had scored seven knockouts in the past 12 months, so Tom would have the superior fight sharpness.

There were some "disquieting rumors" floating about that Johnson would refuse to enter the ring unless two judges were appointed in addition to the referee. Another rumor was that if Johnson won, he would draw the color line against whites. "And there is no earthly reason why he should not. If it is a fair and reasonable thing for a white fighter to refuse to allow a

---

[964] *Melbourne Age*, December 15, 1908.
[965] *Sydney Daily Telegraph*, December 16, 1908.

black or colored man to compete for the championship, a colored champion is quite within his rights in refusing to meet 'white trash.'"[966]

The *World's* sports-writer, Robert Edgren, said Burns was the best of the white heavies and Johnson the best of the negro aspirants. Hence, the winner would be the world's best fighter. "Burns and Johnson have cleaned them all up." Al Kaufman perhaps would be next in line. "After that there'll be little chance for anyone to mix in for a while unless Jeffries himself should take up the game again."[967]

Burns and Johnson continued giving public sparring exhibitions about every other day or so.

Those who saw Johnson spar Arthur Cripps were impressed immensely at the improvement Jack was showing over anything he did when in Australia on his previous visit. "Good judges who have followed the training of both men very closely are now veering to the opinion that the odds on the black, so freely offered in America, are a pretty shrewd tip as to the actual result."

However, Burns was calmly confident, saying,

> I have never been better. ... I am now fitter than I have ever been to defend the title. I am not a bit scared of the tall talk that comes out of Botany, and I am absolutely confident that I will win. I'm certain I'll win, and if Johnson lets me get near him, I'll knock him out. I don't say this in any spirit of bravado. You ask me what I think, and I simply give you my firm conviction.

Despite being over five inches taller than Burns, as well as having weight and reach advantages, and despite Burns' reputation for being a dangerous infighter, Johnson said that he would give Tommy every opportunity to get in his deadly work. He was willing to fight, and fight on the inside. Jack said,

> I know that Burns expects me to fight at arm's length, keeping him off. He's going to get a surprise, good and early. I'm going to sail right in, and I will keep little Tommy real busy from the jump. Do I think I'll win? Well, in London, I offered to take absolutely nothing for my end of the purse if Burns was on his feet at the end of 20 rounds.[968]

John L. Sullivan was upset that Burns was going to break the color line as champion, something no other reigning heavyweight champion of the gloved era had done. Excoriating him, Sullivan said of Burns,

> He is money mad. His every instinct is for the coin. He is shameless in his degradation of the great game of boxing in favor of the commercial side of it. ... Shame on the money-mad champion! Shame on the man who upsets good American precedents, because

[966] *Sydney Bulletin*, December 17, 1908.
[967] *New York World*, December 17, 1908.
[968] *Melbourne Age*, December 19, 1908.

there are Dollars, Dollars, Dollars in it! Burns may lose his title to this black man. But I don't think he will. … He is a 'sure thing' man, but I must say a better fighter than people give him credit for.[969]

As a result of the Burns-O'Brien II scandal, some feared a fake. Still, "Johnson wants the championship, and it would take a good sum of money to 'fix' him, even should he agree to such a proceeding. Burns as well understands the value of the title and would be loth to part with it."

There was no evidence that Johnson had ever thrown a fight. The most that could be said was that he carried some of his opponents, but he had never intentionally allowed them to win. The betting in the U.S. was 10 to 9 in Johnson's favor. "Johnson is unquestionably clever, but many Americans believe that Burns will be able to outgame him."[970]

The *New York Herald* would have famous author Jack London on scene to report on the fight.

Five days before the bout, on December 21, the *Herald* reported that in Australia, Burns was the 5 to 4 favorite over Johnson.

Summarizing the history of how the fight got made, the *Herald* said,

Since James J. Jeffries retired and Burns defiantly flung his banner to the breeze and announced that he would defend the title against all comers, barring colored men, Johnson has camped on his trail, denying the right of Burns to draw the color line, and no little amount of public opinion has sided with the big negro.

Burns instead had been picking up easy money against second and third raters. "Nobody, however, doubted Burns' ability to give Johnson a good fight." "While up to the present time there is nothing in the record of either man that stamps him as anywhere near the class of the champions of bygone days – men like Jackson, Sullivan, Jeffries, Corbett or Fitzsimmons – they will doubtless put up a great battle before one of the largest crowds that ever witnessed a glove contest."

It was estimated that over 20,000 people would be on hand to see the fight. 10,000 tickets already had been sold. Contracts for the motion picture rights were being made in all parts of the world.

Both men were in the pink of condition. Burns was quartered at Darling Point, still being trained by Pat O'Keefe and Les O'Donnell.

Johnson was at Manly, a seaside suburb. Jack Mullins was his trainer. Bill Lang had been sparring with him for a few weeks, to give him points on Burns' style. Johnson was described: "He is as big and rangy and quick as the proverbial cat in his movements." He was the showiest boxer since Corbett, but hit harder.

---

[969] *Freeman*, December 19, 1908.
[970] *San Francisco Chronicle*, December 20, 1908.

Both had been giving training exhibitions twice a week at the Stadium, and thousands, including women, had watched them work, making both fighters even more money.

The fight was set to be held in a 24-foot ring in the open air.[971]

The entire $37,500 for purses and expenses had been deposited with the Sydney *Referee*. Photographs of checks for 6,000 pounds ($30,000) for Burns and 1,100 pounds ($5,500) for Johnson were produced to various sportswriters to prove it. Burns had also deposited $5,000 as his side-bet with Johnson and an additional $5,000 as his forfeit guaranteeing his appearance. The large side-bet proved that Burns expected to win.

Both men had fought in Australia, and each had his supporters, but Burns was better liked and the odds favorite. The *Los Angeles Herald* reported,

> The antipodean sports argue that Burns is gamer, has a better wallop, is more aggressive and is sound and in perfect health and condition, while Johnson is accused, and very rightfully, of being a big yellow streak with great cleverness, height and weight in his favor, but not possessed of that deadly wallop that has made Burns the greatest heavyweight now in harness.

Another article said,

> Burns is admitted to be the greatest fighter, thoroughly game, willing to take a beating and never flinching under fire. He is aggressive to the superlative degree, fights all the time without stalling, and hits like a battering ram.
>
> On the contrary, Johnson is recognized as the cleverest heavyweight in the harness. He has several pounds the better of the weights, is taller and probably has a longer reach. But his cardinal feature is of the yellow hue, and he will not take a beating. Burns' supporters refer to Johnson's yellow streak and his inclination to 'dog' it when pressed too hard as proof that they are correct in picking out Burns as the winner. They argue that Tommy will go after the big black-and-yellow streak like a flash and fight him off his feet, giving Johnson little chance to do anything except defend himself. Owing to the difference in their height, Burns will find it easy to get to Johnson's vital spot, his stomach, and a brief pounding in that region should make Johnson 'dog' it until Burns puts over the dreamland wallop. It is a finish fight, and Burns looks like the goods.[972]

The *Los Angeles Herald* ultimately said, "It will be quite disappointing to local fans if Burns fails to keep up his winning streak."[973]

---

[971] *New York Herald, Los Angeles Times*, December 21, 1908.
[972] *Los Angeles Herald*, December 21, 1908. Some said it was a fight to the finish, while others reported that it was scheduled for 20 rounds, the latter being correct.
[973] *Los Angeles Herald*, December 22, 1908.

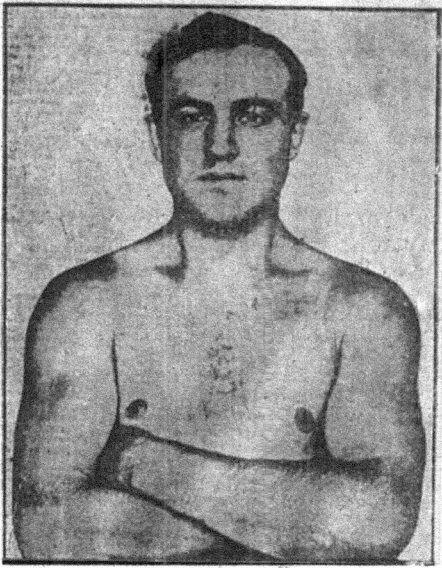

TOMMY BURNS.

Burns was quite popular in Australia, and he liked the Australians. He had been driven from city to city in an automobile, and dined with various sporting celebrities. Tom said he had never met a better bunch of sports. The crowd was always fair to him, even though he had fought Australians. He again said the Johnson fight would be his last, for he had promised his wife that he would quit the ring. Tom called attention to Johnson's claim that he would stop him in 20 rounds and said that he was willing to wager otherwise, wanting to call Johnson's bluff. "You can gamble that I am going to fight the battle of my life."[974]

On December 21, 1908 in San Francisco, Sam Langford, who weighed in the neighborhood of 168 pounds, knocked out the similarly-sized Jim Flynn at two minutes and fourteen seconds of the 1st round. "As for Langford, enough was seen of him to suggest that he will be a holy terror, no matter how big the man he is sent against." His upper body was as big as a heavyweight's and he had immense strength and punching power. Flynn said every punch that landed hurt him. A local writer opined, "He seems to carry guns enough for big Jack Johnson, even." Another said that Langford had the strength of a gorilla and the intelligence of a human being. He was a "bone breaker," the master of the ring, such that white fighters now would have reinforced concrete color lines.

Langford said he wanted to meet any man in the world, "bar Jack Johnson." Johnson was the only man in the world whom Langford conceded was better than him. "Just tell them that I will fight any man in the business save Jack Johnson, and that I'll let Stanley Ketchel name the weight if he will only meet me." Langford's greatest desire was to meet Ketchel for the world middleweight championship.[975]

The *Examiner* said Langford wanted to meet Ketchel, but Ketchel wanted to fight Burns.

There is some little surprise at the fact that Langford in challenging the world has barred big Jack Johnson. ... It was understood that

[974] *Los Angeles Herald*, December 21, 1908.
[975] *New York World, San Francisco Examiner, San Francisco Chronicle*, December 22, 1908; *San Francisco Chronicle*, December 5, 1908.

whether Johnson won or lost with Burns he was to fight Langford at the National Sporting Club in London next February. This report was published in the English sporting papers, and Langford ratified it at his training quarters less than two weeks ago. Under the circumstances Langford's motive in barring Johnson at this time is not understood, but it is just possible that Sam wants to keep Johnson in abeyance until he has fought himself out among the middleweights and light-heavies.[976]

However, the next day, perhaps after being informed of the promotional error of his ways in making such a statement, Langford said it was a mistake to credit him with the desire to bar Johnson. He said he would rather meet Ketchel than anyone, and Johnson was his second choice. He was expecting to meet Johnson before the National Club if Johnson won from Burns.[977]

Of the upcoming championship fight, the *World* said, "The winner will have a title to the crown that only Jeffries himself can come out and question."[978]

Burns and Johnson met at McIntosh's office on the 22nd to discuss and decide the referee issue. What happened in that meeting was revealed a couple months later by Fitzpatrick and McIntosh.

Sam Fitzpatrick said that when they met with McIntosh at his office, Burns and Johnson could not agree on a referee. Without warning, Burns reached over for a large ink stand to throw at Johnson, but McIntosh grabbed his hand. Tom then picked up a chair and told Johnson that he would kill him before he left the room. McIntosh then took the chair from him, and Burns then put his hand in his hip pocket and again said that he would kill Johnson. "All this time Tommy was pouring out a line of abuse on Jack that would not look good in print." Johnson remained calm, and replied, "Tommy, you're a gentleman." Burns kept going, and Mac held him back. Burns tried to instill fear in Johnson, telling him that whether he won or lost, the crowd would mob Jack. In reply, Johnson said that he would just as soon die in Australia as anywhere else. Burns persisted. Finally, Johnson said, "Don't hold him, Mack; let us see what he will do." However, McIntosh would not let go of Burns. He opened the door and got Tom out of there.[979]

Hugh McIntosh later said that when Johnson and Burns met in his office prior the battle, Burns was in an excitable mood. He made several slurring remarks about Johnson, calling him a "nigger." Johnson strenuously objected to the name, but remained cool until Burns grabbed a chair and rushed at him. Mac jumped between them. Johnson told Burns that he'd eat him up. Burns appeared to be trembling.[980]

---

[976] *San Francisco Examiner*, December 23, 1908.
[977] *San Francisco Examiner*, December 24, 1908.
[978] *New York World*, December 22, 1908.
[979] *Tacoma Times*, February 17, 1909.
[980] *New York Sun*, March 13, 1909.

The *World* quoted McIntosh as saying,

I never saw any sign of a yellow streak in Johnson. In fact, Johnson showed particular courage in a near-fight with Burns right in my office. Burns was going to do him up and Johnson said coolly: "Let him. Let him come, man. Don't interfere with him." Burns was shaking like a leaf It was all about a referee.

In an apparently friendly way the two men met in my office on the Tuesday before the fight. Johnson was not in a bad temper. Burns was whittling a stick, sitting back in his chair. He was surly.

"If I go into the ring I shall have one point the worst of it," said Johnson.

"Yes," growled Burns, "they don't like niggers in this country, do they?"

"What do you mean by nigger?" said Johnson. "O, niggers, that's all," Burns replied surrily. I smoothed it over. "It means a colored gentleman," I said. "You don't want to fight," sneered Burns.

There was a little girl in the office, the daughter of an actor, a friend of mine, a child named Fitzpatrick. Johnson is very fond of children.

"Take that kiddy out of the room," said Johnson. Then to Burns: "Now if you are chasing a fight. I'm ready."

Burns grabbed a folding chair. "I'll slip it over on you," threatened Burns. Then Burns grabbed an inkwell and attempted to hurl it at Johnson with a trembling hand. "You've spilled ink on your hand, haven't you, Tommy?" remarked Johnson, laughing.[981]

In his autobiography, Johnson said that at that meeting Burns told him, "You used to be a good fighter, but you are all shot now; you might as well take your medicine." Johnson smiled at this and other insults, but when Burns started to use profanity and become obscene, Jack warned Tom to stop. "Burns, the newspapers are describing you as a gentleman, so be careful what you say. If you swear any more before this child, I shall give you a lacing right here." Burns grew angrier and made a gesture as if he was going to pull a gun. Johnson moved towards him and Burns grabbed a chair, which McIntosh snatched from him. Tom then grabbed an inkwell, but Mac grabbed his arm. Johnson said to McIntosh, "Let him loose. He's tame and harmless." Jack then said to Tommy, "I'll remember this when I get you into the ring."[982]

On December 22, at a benefit boxing tournament at the Manly Skating Rink, Johnson was scheduled to box 4 rounds with Larry Foley. He was also set to spar Bob Bryant and Bill Lang that day. The musical portion of

---

[981] *New York World*, March 15 1909.
[982] *In the Ring And Out* at 162.

the programme was to include items by Mr. Jack Johnson's orchestra. An exchange to America said that Johnson also boxed with a kangaroo.

The weather was very hot. Boxing Day was supposed to be the hottest day on the calendar in Australia, for the American winter was the Australian summer season. Fitzpatrick did not want Johnson working too long in the heat. "The big tar baby is watched like a hawk by his wise old owl manager, Sam Fitzpatrick," who was concerned that Jack might be overtraining.[983]

On December 23, Burns gave his final show at the Stadium before a large crowd of about 3,000, including the usual percentage of ladies. The champion appeared to be in splendid condition. He skipped rope, punched the ball, shadow boxed, and sparred with New Zealand athlete Harry Sandow or Sandown, and Pat O'Keefe.[984]

Tom said he was down to the weight at which he met Bill Squires in America. He never felt better or fitter in his life. He would rest on the 24th, and do some light work on Friday the 25th before the fight on the 26th.

Burns anticipated a long struggle, similar to his bout with Hart. He would rely on infighting and his hitting powers.

Johnson replied that it was foolish for Burns to let him know what methods he would use.

In response, Burns said, "Johnson's answer has tickled me to death, for if he thinks I'm telling him how I'll fight, well, he's a 'huge guy.'"

Johnson gave his final training exhibition at Manly on the 23rd.

Some thought that Johnson had not trained hard enough, but others said he had paid careful attention to his training. Jack's frequent motor car trips into the city caused some to wonder. "Johnson has peculiar ideas about training, and he has shaken the confidence of his most ardent admirers to such an extent that they have been laying off." However, "Johnson boasts that he has forgotten more than Burns ever knew."[985]

On December 23, 1908 at the Stadium, Johnson sparring partner Arthur Cripps won the Australian middleweight title with a KO11 over Jim Griffin. Johnson had been scheduled to referee the bout, but did not do so, saying that he was afraid of catching a cold.

The *New York Sun* noted that Burns was the first heavyweight champion to meet a negro for the title. Public opinion had forced him to do so. Johnson finally accepted the most unfair terms, $30,000 for Burns and only $5,000 for Johnson, just 1/6 of what Burns would earn. Johnson wanted the title so badly that he was willing to take the short end.

Some thought the fight would not be on the level because Johnson did not leave England for Sydney until Burns sent word to him to come. However, both men had sent telegrams to friends saying that they were sure they would win.

---

[983] *Sydney Morning Herald, Daily Telegraph, San Francisco Examiner*, December 22, 23, 1908.
[984] *Sydney Daily Telegraph*, December 24, 1908.
[985] *Melbourne Age*, December 24, 1908.

Tom Sharkey, who years earlier had sparred with him, picked Johnson. "I never saw a faster man, and Johnson will win. I said some time ago that he would be the world's champion and I still think so. I believe Johnson is the greatest fighter in the ring today." He called Burns overrated.

Sharkey said Johnson trained him back in 1901 in Denver, "and even then I thought him a comer. He was big, clever and strong." He thought Johnson would outpoint Burns. Sharkey said there weren't any good heavyweights now, that they were all jokes compared to the old-timers. He said that men like himself, Fitz, and Jeff eight years ago would stop all of the top fighters of the present time. He argued that current fighters did not have the strength, stamina, and vitality of his era's fighters.

From Oakland, Burns' brother said that if Tommy won, the champ would fight Stanley Ketchel next.[986]

As of the 24th, two days before the fight, the referee question still hung in abeyance. Without providing details, the local press simply said there had been some stormy meetings between McIntosh, Burns, and Johnson. "The colored pugilist is reported to be very obstinate." He wanted Harry Beckett. Burns wanted Snowy Baker. McIntosh interviewed W. C. J. Kelly, Burns' acting co-manager, and Fitzpatrick, but they were not able to agree. "There is every likelihood of Mr. McIntosh himself being called upon to referee the fight. It is stated that both contestants are favorably disposed towards him."[987]

When Jim Jeffries was asked if Johnson won and challenged him, what he would do, Jeff said,

> If that coon comes around here and challenges me to fight him, if he wins from Burns, I'll grab him by the neck and run him out. ... I have repeatedly declared that the ring would never know me again, yet some simple-minded stiff in the east wired me today asking if I would meet Johnson in case the smoke won. I didn't take the trouble to answer, for every one knows that I have made up my mind.

Allegedly, on a previous occasion when Johnson challenged Jeff, "Johnson was told that he could accompany Jeff into the cellar, lock the doors and let the best man come out when he was ready. This did not appeal to Jawn Arthur's heart, so there was no Jeffries-Johnson scrap to go down on the book."

Jeff said that if Johnson won, there were other heavys to keep Jack busy, like Al Kaufman.[988]

Jeffries was also quoted as saying that he was retired for all time. He was swamped constantly with telegrams asking him whether or not he would box again if Johnson won. "In the event of the negro winning I realize full well that there will be a powerful demand, or rather series of demands,

---

[986] *New York Sun*, December 23, 1908; *New York World*, December 24, 1908.
[987] *Sydney Daily Telegraph*, December 24, 1908.
[988] *Los Angeles Herald*, December 24, 1908.

made upon me to meet Johnson and re-take the heavyweight title." However, Jeff said he had fought his last ring battle and was fortifying himself in advance to resist any influence brought to bear on the issue. He hoped never again to be bothered with such a question.

> To begin with, I doubt whether or not I could even, by long and conscientious training, get myself into such condition that I could do myself and the American public justice. I have been out of the ring for over four years. During the major portion of the time I have indulged in no gymnasium exercise at all. This is a long time for an athlete to be out of training, as any expert will testify, and it is a serious question in my mind whether I could ever train to a semblance of my former fighting form again.[989]

Tom Corbett said San Francisco wagering had Johnson the favorite at 10 to 9, even though Burns was the favorite in Australia. San Franciscans remembered the manner in which Johnson disposed of Jim Flynn. That, combined with the fact that Burns insisted on a large guarantee, win or lose, raised a suspicion as to whether Burns truly believed in his own ability to whip Johnson.

> While Johnson is more clever than Burns, the Canadian has a clever style of his own. Whether he will be able to outgame Johnson remains to be seen. ... Jim Corbett, when he was in San Francisco not long ago, gave it as his opinion that Burns would be the winner, and when asked why, said; "I think that Burns will outgame the negro. Johnson is more clever, but Burns is a game boy, and will stick it out."[990]

The *Sydney Bulletin* said the air was full of disquieting rumors about Johnson's training. Some said his training largely consisted of champagne and female society, "interlineated with streaks of terrifically hard work." However, many of the rumors were due to the fact that another black man named Johnson was in the city and was being mistaken for the fighter.

> Writer knows personally that the colored champion has done tremendously hard work. ... His strength is at any time abnormal, and with the exercise he has been taking it is now almost phenomenal. ... Sparring with Lang, the Australian champion is a baby in his hands, and could be laid out at any moment. In the clinches, he has a curious lock-action, by which the Australians who have sparred with him have found their arms rendered powerless and in-fighting made an impossibility. Not a boxer in the city but says Johnson must win, and win easily. In all sparring exhibitions he has shown amazing skill in defending his head and face, and not one of

---

[989] *San Francisco Examiner*, December 24, 1908.
[990] *San Francisco Chronicle*, December 24, 1908.

the sparrers could land a really effective blow in the neighborhood of his jaw.

However, Tommy was also very well trained and impressive. This same writer felt that Burns compared favorably with Johnson. "Judging by the exhibitions given by both men, Burns is faster on his feet, and hits more quickly and with much more weight behind the blows. Johnson hits with his arm, Burns with his whole weight. The difference is tremendous." Johnson would not have to defend his head against Burns, but his body, which would be "exposed to the quick, savage, jerky blows behind which Burns will put his whole 13 stone [182 pounds]." Burns' body appeared to be protected by a coat of thick, hardened muscle, while Johnson's midriff appeared vulnerable and soft-looking. Johnson's most effective blow would be the uppercut, but it would "probably be met on Burns' glove." And when Jack threw the uppercut, his body would be exposed.

Ultimately, this writer opined that Burns would win the contest between the 9th and 13th rounds. He had displayed better form than Johnson in their public exhibitions. "Barring the random swipe, Johnson, if he is to win, will have to show a degree of skill and speed not so far indicated in any of the exhibitions that he has given." It was also noted that Johnson had not covered the 2,000-pound side-wager that Burns had deposited.[991]

After three days of wrangling, at the request of both fighters, Hugh McIntosh finally agreed to be the referee. He would be the sole arbiter of the bout. The referee issue had been so contentious that Johnson at one time even declared that he would not fight. Burns wanted Snowy Baker, but Johnson would not agree. Other suggested names included Mr. Harry Nathan, Larry Foley, and Professor William Miller, but all nominees were rejected by one or the other. Some time ago, both Burns and Johnson had asked McIntosh to officiate, but he had refused, preferring that someone wholly unconnected with the contest be elected. However, since matters were at a deadlock, he consented.

MR. H. D. McINTOSH.
Promoter and Referee of the Big Battle.

MR. SAM FITZPATRICK.
Jack Johnson's Manager.

[991] *Sydney Bulletin*, December 24, 1908.

TOMMY BURNS AND JACK JOHNSON

As the fight approached, some said Burns remained the 5 to 4 favorite. The *Chronicle* said Burns was a 10 to 7 favorite in Australia. Others said the odds had shifted to 2 to 1 with Burns the heavy favorite, but most experts thought that 6 to 5 on Burns was more accurate. "The long odds are attributed partly to the preference for the white man, but more to a rumor that Johnson is not training properly." However, physicians examined both men and declared them to be in perfect physical condition.

Because Johnson was seen in town and drank a glass or two of wine or beer, folks took that to mean that he was not taking the fight seriously. That affected the odds. Some also said Johnson did his best to knock out a smaller and less experienced version of Bill Lang than Burns had fought, and yet Burns had stopped the bigger and better version much faster. Therefore, amongst other reasons, the week before the fight, odds of 7 to 4 and even 2 to 1 were offered against Johnson.

Of course, if one read the local primary sources, they said that Johnson could have stopped Lang much sooner had he so chosen. Also, history has shown that just because A stops B much faster or easier than C stopped B does not mean that A beats C. However, how fighters did against common opponents had its use amongst gamblers.

There was some logic to Burns being the slight betting favorite, even putting race aside. Tommy had won the heavyweight title in early 1906, and had defended the title successfully four times that year, three times in 1907, and six times in 1908. With over 50 fights of experience, including 8 bouts that went 20 rounds (that's 160 rounds in just 8 fights), as a heavyweight, Burns was undefeated at 14-0-1 with 11 KOs. He had victories over Hart, Flynn, O'Brien, Squires, Moir, and Lang. Against common opponents, Johnson had "lost" to Hart while Burns had defeated him. Johnson stopped Flynn faster, though Burns did it first. Burns stopped a larger and more experienced version of Lang faster than did Johnson. However, Tommy got decked by Lang, whereas Johnson just toyed with him. In O'Brien, Burns had defeated the man considered to have the fastest hands and feet in the business, who also was supposed to be the cleverest. In Hart, Burns had defeated the man considered to be the toughest, roughest, strongest, and most well-conditioned fighter. Hence, he had beaten slick, clever, fast, and fleet-footed men, and strong, hard-hitting, rushing men. Burns had defeated several bigger heavyweights, spotting weight to Hart, Squires, Moir, Smith, Lang, and several others, so he had proven that he could defeat larger men.

Although Johnson had mixed success early in his career, he had improved steadily, and had fought more often against good boxers in lengthy bouts on his way to the championship than had any other boxer who became champion. He had honed his skills over time, had developed one of the toughest defenses to penetrate that ever had been seen, and like Burns, could fight both on the inside and outside. He had ducked no one and clearly was the top contender to the crown.

The stadium would hold 20,000, and it was thought that some might have to be turned away, the demand was so great. The advance sale of seats already had eclipsed $40,000. It had been many years since a heavyweight championship fight had attracted such an extreme world-wide interest.

The *Sun* said the bout was scheduled for 20 rounds in a large 24-foot ring, and the pugilists would wear 4-ounce gloves. New Yorkers would know the result at about 11 p.m. on the 25th.

Johnson was listed at about 195 pounds to Burns' 180 pounds. Burns stood 5'7 ¾" to Johnson's 6'1 ¾". Johnson's reach was about the same as Burns, who had a 74.5 inch reach. Jack was 5.5 inches taller.[992]

James J. Corbett said there had been a tendency in America to underrate Burns. "My sympathy is all with Burns, as it always has been where a white man has met a negro. If the Canadian tries to beat the negro in a give and take encounter he might win. Johnson possesses every advantage over Burns one can mention except when it comes to nerve."

---

[992] *New York Tribune, New York Sun, San Francisco Chronicle,* December 25, 1908. Victories listed on Johnson's record included W15 John Lee, KO2 Charley Brooks, KO3 Horace Miles, KO10 George Lawler, all at Galveston, KO10 Dan Murphy at Waterbury, KO4 Ed Johnson at Galveston, and W15 Bob White.

Battling Nelson, lightweight champion, picked Johnson as an easy winner. Others of like opinion included Bob Fitzsimmons, Tom Sharkey, Sam Langford, and Joe Gans.

Marvin Hart, who had fought both, said Johnson would whip Burns in short order. He had a fight scheduled with Mike Schreck, and if he won, he would challenge Johnson.[993]

Burns was confident, advising his friends to bet on him. "I will win and will put the colored man out before the twenty round limit is up."

Burns also wired, "Johnson insisted promoter referee. Feeling confident will beat alligator. Am two-to-one favorite. Advance sale over ten thousand pounds."[994]

One writer noted the acute tension in the air, in part because of race. "There is bitter feeling between the principals. Public sympathy is almost wholly with Burns, owing to color prejudice. There is some fear of a row in the stadium, especially if Johnson should win. Consequently a big force of police has been ordered to be present." Australian racial sympathies were with the white man.

THE TAIL OF THE KANGAROO.

In Australia the prejudice to Negro labor is extremely great.

Freeman, April 4, 1908

---

[993] *New York Herald,* December 25, 1908; *Melbourne Age,* December 26, 1905.
[994] *San Francisco Chronicle, San Francisco Examiner,* December 25, 1908.

CHAPTER 27

Finally - The Championship

The morning of the Jack Johnson vs. Tommy Burns world heavyweight championship fight, the *Sydney Morning Herald* reported that hundreds of people were camping in the vicinity of the grounds.

The gates would open at 7 a.m. The men would enter the arena at 10:30 a.m. for the convenience of the moving picture photographers. The 20-round bout would start at 11 a.m.[995]

The *Melbourne Age* said no athletic event ever had taken place in Australia that caused anything like the excitement engendered by this fight. "Practically nothing else is talked about in the city." References to the battle were made in Christmas sermons. Even women seemed interested.

The day before, on Friday December 25, as Burns and his wife exited St. Mary's Cathedral, thousands congregated around the main entrance and cheered him. The general desire was to see Burns emerge victorious. However, even his well-wishers admitted that he had undertaken one of the hardest tasks any athlete had ever essayed, for "it is just now that the public are learning the solid truth concerning what a formidable man Johnson is and how cutely he has been 'hiding his light under a bushel.'"

Burns, as the white man, was the clear favorite. but Johnson was by no means without friends among the sporting community.

There was suspicion that the rumors that Johnson had not been training properly were generated by Johnson and his own camp so that they could obtain better betting odds when wagering on Johnson. Although Jack remained the slight betting favorite in the U.S., in Australia, Burns remained the odds favorite all the way up to the opening bell.

Burns had trained in his usual steady, conscientious, hard-working way, and crowds of thousands had marveled at his activity, strength, and endurance. Aside from training, Tommy remained at home, living quietly, reading, and conversing with friends. There was a "strong, almost unanimous prejudice in his favor," though "Johnson, as a matter of fact, has been quite as assiduous in his work as Burns."

250 policemen had been engaged for duty around the Stadium, including a force of mounted men. They would ensure order.

Regarding the weighs, the day before the fight, "Burns was weighed in the buff today [December 25], and turned the scales at 12 stone ½ pound

---

[995] *Sydney Morning Herald*, December 26, 1908. The fight took place on Saturday the 26th. Since most local papers did not print on Sunday the 27th in observation of the Sabbath, their fight reports came out on the 28th.

[168 ½ pounds], which is nearly 3 pounds less than when he fought Squires the first time. Johnson is expected to lower the beam at nearly 14 stone [196 pounds]."[996]

THE STADIUM EMPTY.

The Tommy Burns vs. Jack Johnson world heavyweight championship contest took place on Saturday December 26, 1908 at the Stadium at Rushcutters' Bay, in Sydney, New South Wales, Australia. The following account is an amalgamation of the *Sydney Daily Telegraph, Sydney Morning Herald, Sydney Referee, Sydney Bulletin,* and *Melbourne Age* (which had a special reporter on scene).[997]

The fight wound up generating enormous telegraphic cable business, for folks from around the world were interested in the bout. The U.S. Deputy Postmaster-General said 46,362 telegraphic wires passed over the lines from Sydney on the day of the fight.

Although it was a fight between the world's best two heavyweights, both in the prime of their lives, many of those who were interested in the result, particularly Americans, were not simply interested in it as a mere prize fight or because they enjoyed boxing, but because of the racial and social implications that the bout had. Interest in the fight was huge. The *Sydney Morning Herald* said,

> We should probably be right in saying, however, that that interest has not had its root exclusively in the love of a prize fight for its own sake. On the American side, for instance, there would be the 'colour' consideration – a consideration of tremendous import to many millions of Americans, both white and black, and one which would have held sway in any supreme encounter between a white man and a black, whether in a prize ring or on any other species of trying ground. In England the 'colour' question would not appeal in the same intense way.

Australians were biased towards the white man as well, but they could be generous and just to a black man, as had been the case with Peter Jackson. Allegedly, they also liked Burns because his demeanor merited commendation in a way that Johnson's had not. They liked Tom more. Plus, there was a natural sympathy for the smaller man.

---

[996] *Melbourne Age*, December 26, 1905.
[997] *Sydney Daily Telegraph, Sydney Morning Herald, Melbourne Age*, all December 28, 1908; *Sydney Referee*, December 30, 1908; *Sydney Bulletin*, December 31, 1908.

Folks were so eager to see the bout that as early as 2 a.m., masses of passionate fans gathered themselves up near the 10-shilling entrances. Some slept in the adjacent park in order to obtain good positions when the doors opened. Others said these claims were "mere newspaper yarn." Large crowds were awaiting the opening of the doors as early as 6 a.m. At 6:30 a.m., Superintendent Mitchell appeared, in charge of 250 policemen who positioned themselves.

The crowd was allowed to enter just after 7 a.m. Within five minutes of the doors opening, the cheap seats were filled with 4,000 - 5,000 people. The flow of people was continuous and ever-increasing. Trams, buses, cabs, and motor cars formed a great procession leading towards the Stadium. Loads of humanity kept coming. Many thousands walked as well.

After one hour, the entire section of cheaper seats was occupied, and those who entered after this were forced to stand or were turned away. The demand was so great that there was not space enough in the huge arena to take in all those who wanted seats, even though the tier of benches went up to 20 feet off the ground.

For a couple of hours, the Newtown Brass Band, stationed in the ring, provided some excellent music to entertain the big audience.

By 10 a.m., an hour before the fight, nearly every seat in the arena was occupied, except for just a few of the higher-priced £10, £5, and £3 reserved seats immediately around the ring. The crowd was wonderful in size and temper, for the most part being orderly and well behaved. Men of every station in life were present.

About 20,000 people filled the stadium to the brim, making it an impressive sight. By fight time, there was not a vacant seat. Probably another 1,000 or so more than capacity were crowded into the arena. 5,000 were unable to obtain admission. Another 15,000 or more just wanted to be in the vicinity of the arena. Over 20,000 people filled the South Head-road. They eagerly waited outside to hear any news that might be passed through.

Photographer Kerry had purchased the sole right to take pictures of the contest, but some pirates had commandeered the platform and refused to come down. The police did not want to climb up there to get them down. Instead, Kerry enlisted the services of these pirates as a body-guard against those who were drawing near and also thinking about climbing up. They hoisted up Kerry and his machinery and threatened to kick the heads off any others who attempted to follow.

At 10 a.m., the band music was stopped temporarily while the cinematograph took pictures of the crowd, which rose to its feet and cheered wildly. The cinematograph was placed on a well-built platform, canvas covered, and roped in with ropes drawn through well-padded stanchions, or upright supports. The cinematograph films would be a great advertisement for the country, and a wonderful source of revenue.

The sky was overcast with dark clouds, and rain threatened to fall. Just before the men entered, there were some drops, but that was all. Ultimately the fight took place under ideal weather conditions. The day was dry and warm and there was no bright sunlight to affect anyone's vision.

At 10:40 a.m., Jack Johnson climbed into the ring with his attendants. Jack was grinning, clothed in an old, long, grey dressing gown/smoking jacket/bathrobe and cap. After climbing through the ropes, he removed the cap from his shaven head. With him were manager Sam Fitzpatrick, Jim Brennan, trainer Duke Mullins, Joe Grim, Bob Bryant, Bill Lang, and Rudolf Unholz, known as the Boer.

The crowd faintly cheered Johnson. Jack bowed and smiled north, south, east, and west. "He didn't get much homage, but made a lot of what he did get." He then pirouetted around, and again smiled towards the crowd, finishing by kissing his hand to the cinematograph.

Jack created an impression that was never destroyed, of confidence and cheerfulness. He waved his hand. "Perhaps the most prominent feature of the whole business was Johnson's smile. ... Johnson's smile made a tremendous impression. It fascinated and filled all beholders with amazement." He seemed unconcerned, "bored even." Burns advocates were puzzled by his confidence. He took a seat in the south-east corner, beaming.

A few minutes later, the thick-set Burns approached the ring in a dark tweed suit – trousers, a loose blue sac suit, and a green sweater. His appearance set the crowd alight, rising and showing their sympathies. He was hailed with loud, roaring, invigorating applause, cheers, and cries of "Good boy, Tommy." The sounds that thundered from the crash of applause and cheering mass of humanity nearly blew Burns out of the stadium. It made the earlier cheer for Johnson seem like a whisper by comparison. The local *Daily Telegraph* said, "Mainly it was White against Black with them, and they roared defiance to the 'coon', and frantically cheered Burns." The local *Bulletin* agreed, saying, "[T]hat huge crowd was aggressively white in its sympathy." They came not to see a fight but to "witness a black aspirant for the championship of the world beaten to his knees and counted out."

However, Johnson was not worried, and acted unconcerned, as if he had expected such a demonstration. He maintained his grin. Leaning over the ropes, he asked one of his attendants whether he had got "that bet on." Johnson seemed relieved that he had.

Despite the cheers, Burns looked cross, and his smile was not really a friendly one as he acknowledged the crowd with bows. He looked game and determined, but anxious. With Tommy were manager W. C. J. Kelly, Tom's brother-in-law L. C. Keating, Pat O'Keefe, Pat Burke, Les O'Donnell, Arthur Scott, and Jimmy Russell (Squires' trainer). They brought the inevitable suitcase of items.

Tommy's looks were far less cordial when Johnson rose from his seat and crossed the ring from the southern corner smiling broadly, showing his heavily gold-filled teeth as he approached, and said, "Tahmy," holding out his hand to shake. Burns hesitated, looked his opponent up and down, then daintily just barely touched the big black hand with the tips of his fingers and let it drop, in sullen silence, in a "no-love-lost sort of fashion." He gazed at Johnson as he walked back to his corner. Not disconcerted, Johnson smiled more pleasantly. His smile later became a feature of the proceedings. The crowd sensed that there would be razors in the air shortly.

Burns sat in the corner he used for the Squires fight, seeming serious. An announcement was made that Bill Squires was willing to fight either man, or Bill Lang, with Lang preferred.

Hugh D. McIntosh was introduced as the referee. W. T. Kerr, who had acted similarly for Burns-Squires, was the timekeeper. The gloves were placed on the scales in the ring and declared to be the correct weight (four ounces). Dr. Maitland examined all four gloves and declared them genuine.

Final preparations were made. Tom's shoelaces were given an extra pull, his belt was loosened, and his gloves were fitted. In his corner were placed smelling salts, cotton wool, and various chemicals, making it a small chemist's shop. Resin was placed on the floor at the corners.

McIntosh brought them together to discuss the rules. They followed the *Referee* rules, which apparently were straight Queensberry rules.

Tom wore maroon-red trunks with an old-gold belt, and a Stars and Stripes American flag was knotted at his hip. Johnson was attired in dark sky-blue trunks and was similarly belted with an American flag.

After the several announcements, Johnson objected to Burns wearing elastic rubber bandages on each of his elbows, which had been used as a protective measure as a result of prior injuries. The rubber bands were "as delicate as the costume of a ballet dancer." Still, Johnson insisted that they be removed, declaring that he would not fight unless they were. The referee, Hugh McIntosh, examined them and said they were not against the rules. Johnson said, "Take them right off – you don't see any of those on me," holding up his two brown arms. Burns would not comply, saying, "I ain't going to take them off – I wore them with Squires and Lang both." Johnson replied, "Don't care. I'll sit here an hour, and more if necessary, but he must take them off." He then squatted in his corner in his dressing gown. "All right. I'll sit here till he takes 'em off. They must be there to do him some good, and if he don't take 'em off there'll be no fight."

Mr. Westmacott announced to the crowd that Johnson refused to fight until Burns removed his elastic arm bandages, and a storm of hoots and howls from the impatient spectators went through the air, particularly at Johnson. Some urged Burns not to give way to the "black cow" and other animals. Johnson sat, grinning at the crowd.

Old expert Larry Foley came to the ringside and said that custom dictated that Burns must remove the bandages, "though the whole thing was so trivial that Johnson need not have bothered about it." At last, with a stamp of annoyance and look of defiance, at 11 a.m. Burns conceded the point and allowed his seconds to wrench off the offending elastic bands from his arms. There was some applause, cheers, and yells of "Good boy, Tommy." Conversely, "The colored man was soundly hooted."

It was announced to the crowd that if the police stopped the contest that McIntosh would immediately declare the winner. McIntosh told the fighters to shake hands, and he dragged their hands together to get them to do so. He then made a few remarks.

The two men posed for the photographers and the moving picture camera. It only lasted a few seconds, but Burns cast a look of hatred at his towering opponent. The absence of good feeling between the two was evident. Burns in particular showed his aversion to Johnson in every glance. His face wore a heavy frown whenever it turned in Johnson's direction. Johnson was the opposite. He simply wore an "ominous" smile. The excitement was intense.

The *Daily Telegraph* said Burns was short, broad-chested, muscular, and hard looking. Johnson towered over him by many inches, lithe and athletic-looking.

However, it also said Burns looked very finely drawn, and was very much lighter than his opponent, a good deal more than the weights given might have indicated, which were Burns 12st. ½ lb.; (168 ½ pounds), and Johnson 13 st. 10lb. (192 pounds), but "as neither was placed on the scales because there was no necessity for it, the information must be taken for what it is worth." No one knew for sure exactly what they weighed.

Johnson was obviously much bigger. "The Ethiopian towered over the Canuck." He was taller, heavier, and stronger looking. Burns looked like his announced weight, while Johnson looked even bigger than the weight given. Their physical disparity provoked an all-around murmur of comment, and immediately some were heard calling out wagers on Johnson, though prior to that the betting had been all in favor of Burns.

The *Morning Herald* said Burns looked like a little boy beside the "giant negro." He looked fat and flabby, and his face yellow. However, he looked exactly the same way as he did before he fought Squires, and before that day was over he showed that his appearance was deceptive. Hence, the *Morning Herald* said there was no reason to believe that Burns did not enter the ring in form.

The *Referee* opined that Burns looked too light, and his face was pitched and drawn, an indication that he might be stale or overtrained.

The *Melbourne Age* said that when Burns peeled off his clothes he was seen to be as fit as a man could be. "His short, husky frame was powerfully hewed from top to toe, but he did not move around with his customary springy gait."

The local odds remained with Burns as the favorite, shortening to 7 to 4 just before the fight. At one point, odds as much as 3 to 1 and 2 to 1 had been offered in some local places, Tom was such a favorite.

They returned to their corners to await the bell. "At last the two men who had lashed each other into a fury with stinging words across oceans and continents were going to have it out."

1 - At 11:05 a.m., the gong sounded the start of the fight. Burns assumed his usual crouch and approached Johnson, who stood still near his corner, smiling with supreme confidence. Still smiling, Johnson sneered, "Carm ahn, Tahmmy." Another quoted him as saying, "Aal right, Tahmmy!"

They moved warily around one another for a moment, until suddenly as Burns drew near, Johnson fired a light feeler left, but Burns was alert and moved away. Thousands yelled, "Good boy, Tommy." Johnson again stepped in with a left jab and they clinched and scuffled, fighting fiercely at close quarters while the referee frantically endeavored to separate them. Tom hit the ribs with his left.

Johnson dragged his right free from the clinch and, just as the referee was breaking them, like a flash, Johnson smote Burns on the chin with a tremendous right uppercut so heavily that he was lifted off the floor and fell hard to the canvas in a sitting posture. Since they had agreed to straight rules, meaning they had to protect themselves at all times, the blow was perfectly legal. Johnson taunted him, saying, "What you want to lie down so soon for, Tommy?" The round had barely just begun.

Some thought the fight was over already, but they did not know about the stuff of which Burns was made. Tom rose after eight seconds. He immediately moved into the inside and attempted to work the body. Johnson demonstrated his wonderful kidney blow, which was assisted by his superior height. He landed three heavy blows over the kidneys, roughed Tom badly in holds, and blocked nearly every effort by Burns to land his famous short solid body shots that had been so telling against Squires. The few body punches that Tom did land had no effect. Johnson would not budge. There was more clinching until the referee broke them again.

Johnson landed his right swing to the jaw heavily enough to trouble nine out of ten men, but Burns only shook his head and came in like a Trojan.

Some clinching and scuffling followed, in which Burns hit the body until Johnson gripped both of his arms and held them as if in a vise. Johnson attempted uppercuts.

After being freed, they went back at it again, each holding an arm and trying to fight with their free member.

As they broke, Johnson crashed a heavy short right to the chin or ear and Burns went down to the boards again, the second knockdown of the round.

Burns rose quickly, bouncing up even before the count commenced. They sparred at long range. Johnson missed a right when Tom ducked. Thousands roared their delight. Johnson again swooped down upon him but Burns held one arm and blocked the other from uppercutting. Tom again ducked and the bell ended the round. Great cheering was heard as the men went to their chairs.

Summarizing, the *Daily Telegraph* said already it was "plain that Johnson was much too big and heavy and strong for Burns, and besides, he fought very coolly."

The *Referee* said, "Johnson had certainly done the better work right through the round, and he fought coolly and methodically all the time."

The *Bulletin* said the right uppercut that caused the first knockdown was the really decisive blow of the fight. Burns obviously was dazed. He lost his ring craft, hitting power, and his speed. Still, he went at Johnson like a tiger. But it was a blind, dazed fury that Johnson met with straight lefts and rights until Tom succeeded at clinching.

Johnson uppercut him again and again. Tom tried to respond, but Johnson locked his arms and Burns had no strength. Johnson would push him off and smash him on the jaw as he did so. Jack had demonstrated that Tom's defence was useless against him, and that he was so much stronger that he could hold the champion helpless until he was ready to punch him.

At the gong, Burns went to his corner in a very bad way, and his attendants rubbed him with champagne and combed his hair.

Johnson sat in his corner coolly, laughing and talking. He asked for water and drank. He gargled and spat it out, with a fair amount splashing over the furious pressmen.

Up aloft, the cinematograph man was turning his handle.

The *Morning Herald* slightly disagreed with the *Bulletin*, saying that Burns showed no signs that the first knockdown blow had troubled him seriously. However, Johnson prevailed throughout, and in fact the round was so much in Johnson's favor that it indicated that "Burns had no chance of winning the fight." Yet, Tom was still full of fighting spirit, so the inevitable end was delayed.

2 - Johnson talked at Tommy and grinned. The crowd did not like it, and many rose and protested by jeering at Johnson. Burns landed a left to the temple, which riled Johnson so that he gripped and roughed him, and then hit with his right and left three or four times. Tom cleverly ducked most of the blows.

In a clinch, a Burns blow on the chin only provoked a smile from Johnson, as well as a half-dozen heavy short jolts that tilted Tom's head backwards. Johnson crowded Burns onto the ropes and hammered him sorely. Burns shot back a left jab to the nose, but made no impression.

There were several clinches between each of their exchanges. The referee often had to break them. Johnson talked and sneered again, and blocked a left. Then he rushed in close and swung his big powerful left to the ribs twice in quick succession, and the blows had to hurt. Johnson lost his balance in throwing a left but cured matters by twice landing his right-cross to the ear. Burns drove rights into the stomach. He stopped a couple of lefts. Johnson landed a couple rights to the ear and they clinched. Burns managed to sneak in a couple of rights to the stomach. He ducked a left and blocked a couple of others before the inevitable clinch.

Summarizing, the *Daily Telegraph* said Tommy's friends were better pleased with him in this round.

The *Melbourne Age* said that at the gong ending the round, Burns went to his corner apparently still fresh and full of fight.

The *Referee* said, "If Burns didn't have a little the better of this round he certainly had none the worse of it."

However, the *Morning Herald* said the round was a record of continued success by Johnson and one light, useless hit by Burns that evoked tremendous cheers but which had no effect other than to make Jack grin and start off in his remarks, which he continued throughout the fight.

The *Bulletin* said Burns came in with determination and landed a few useless blows to the face. Tom had recovered some of his speed, and showed wonderful skill at evading some rights and other blows, but overall, the round was not much better for him than the 1st. The audience sighed as it realized that the fighters were not in the same class. Burns got into clinches and Johnson held him helpless.

Repeatedly, Jack rose on his toes and brought down his right with an awful smash on Tom's kidneys, then pushed him off and uppercut him on the jaw as he did so. The referee was busy parting them. Once Johnson held Tom with his left and hit him with his right, receiving a warning.

3 - Burns rushed in at once and landed a left on the neck. Johnson missed a left jab as Tom ducked. The crowd cheered, "Good boy, Tommy!" They also cheered every time Burns made any contact. Tom landed two smart telling rights into the stomach. He landed left and right to the body and ribs in the clinches.

Burns worked, but his blows did not have their wonted power. Johnson sneered, "Carm ahn." Burns landed the right to the ribs, but Johnson simply grinned "like a chimpanzee," showing his gold teeth, which irritated Burns.

Tom bore in close and punched a couple of heavy blows to the stomach before Johnson landed a right to the head. Johnson eluded a right uppercut, and he looked more serious for a while.

Burns landed a right to the neck and Johnson locked both of his arms. When Burns clinched, Johnson showed the value of his immense strength, moving freely in Burns's grasp. "The grip of the white man was no more to him that the pressure of an ordinary elastic band would be about the arm of an average athlete. He simply changed his position at will and punished Burns every time he moved."

In a clinch, Johnson knocked Burns about with right uppercuts and a hard left to the ribs. The referee was working hard to separate them from several clinches.

Tom got clear and jabbed his left to the mouth but received a jab to his chest. There was some inside scuffling. Tom landed right and left to the stomach, but the ginger was not there. Johnson grinned "that grin which was so much and so objectionably in evidence that one sighed for a Peter Jackson so that it might be wiped out forever."

Johnson landed left and right swings to either side of Tom's body, and they must have hurt.

On one occasion Burns landed three blows at long range, but their power was spent before they reached the head. Yet the spectators cheered wildly.

Burns continued working both hands to the stomach. Tom landed a right to the mouth and smiled. They finished the round in a give-and-take rally. At the bell, Johnson drove a heavy right to the ribs that would have hurt any other man.

The *Daily Telegraph* said there had been a lot of good punching in this round.

The *Morning Herald* said this was the only round that Burns made any kind of a showing, "and regarded without prejudice, it cannot be denied that even in this the third round Johnson was ahead on points."

The *Referee* said, "There were several solid punches in this round, and the brave white-skinned fighter received much more than a fair share of them."

The *Bulletin* said Johnson defended his stomach and avoided uppercuts with the greatest ease. "A more one-sided struggle it would be impossible to imagine." Burns was plucky as a lion, but Johnson was as strong as a locomotive. The only bright feature was how heroically Burns took his smashing and came in again and again. Tom's face was in a very bad way. His mouth was bleeding, his cheek beginning to swell, and his eyes growing puffy. He made no impression on Johnson, who occasionally stood still with his hands down, talking and jeering at Burns. Tom skirted around looking for an opening that never came. Jack let Tom do the fighting.

4 - Johnson again said, "Carm ahn, Tahmy!" Folks in the crowd hollered in response, "Why don't you go on yourself?" Goaded into it, Johnson missed some swings, but in a clinch, a nasty powerful right uppercut nailed Burns on the chin. Still, Tom took it well. A follow-up right and left to the ribs did not improve matters for the champ. On the outside, Johnson jabbed his left, and on the inside, landed his right to the ribs while the referee was trying to separate them. Burns showed grit and pluck, fighting back as hard as he could. As they parted, Johnson jabbed to the chin and swung a right to the neck. He feinted, and drawing Tom in, pounded hard with the right over the kidneys and onto the ribs.

There was much talk during this round. Burns's seconds started their secret calls, using numbers to tell Tom what punches to throw.

Johnson landed good lefts to the chin and neck. He feinted, drew Burns, and landed a left on the neck. Burns landed his left to the ribs, and Johnson landed his right to the head and jaw. Clinches were frequent, taking place after every couple of blows. Both were eager to get to the other at in-fighting. Johnson's right landed hard on the face, and his left to the forehead shook Burns a bit. Jack's footwork beat Tom's left several times, making him miss.

For the most part, the round was a series of clinches, with Johnson scoring heavily during the infighting, his ripping uppercuts landing on Tom's face hard and often. When Burns crouched, Johnson hammered down hard on his back and loins, the heavy blows sounding like the beating of a drum.

Burns made a slight rally, catching Johnson over the heart with a heavy left, and, hauling him off, landing a right on the jaw. Johnson was quieter for the rest of the round but it was his round all the same.

The *Morning Herald* opined that the round was similar to the previous one, with Johnson's superiority being comparatively slight.

The black man stood like a tower.

5 - Johnson taunted Tom with a sneering invitation to "Come right in, Tommy, and stay a while." Burns then dashed madly to close quarters, where he met with a veritable storm of smashing blows.

The *Daily Telegraph* said Johnson fired his left and right to the ribs and forced Burns down. The *Morning Herald's* description said that a few seconds after the round opened Burns was down again, partly as a result of a slip and partly due to a blow at close quarters. The *Referee* said Johnson again jeered at Burns and swung left and right to the ribs with considerable force, sending Tom down.

It was later said that Burns sprained his ankle when he went down.

Burns rose immediately and advanced. Johnson fired blows that went every which way - up, down, and across. Burns emerged with his face showing many marks, and his left eye had developed a mouse under it.

Johnson then appeared to hold and hit, and some cried foul. Burns said, "You are holding and hitting, you cur!" Tom then danced back out of range. Johnson replied, "Now, don't stand talking to the people, Tommy. Come back here till I finish."

Johnson stood his ground and allowed Burns to do the leading. Jack uppercut the cheek. Burns ducked a left and missed a weak counter which brought Johnson's ever-ready grin. Tom's supporters would cry out, "Let him do the fighting, Tommy." Burns was doing most of the leading. In this round, Johnson appeared to be more anxious to wait, counter, and clinch. Tom said, "Why, you won't fight at all."

Burns's characteristic attitude.

Burns came in again like a shot, and Johnson again dealt out heavy punishment. Jack would make remarks to the ringsiders and then punctuate his statements with powerful short jolts.

Johnson varied his tactics slightly by using his straight left, and he found it to be as effective as his other punches.

As the round finished, Burns hit Johnson on the right eye with a heavy overhand clout, but Johnson merely shook his head and said, "Why! Durn you, Tommy, be careful!"

6 - Again Johnson urged Burns to come in. As Tom did so, Jack then said, "Look! He's gaht me now." They roughed each other across the ring. While they were locked together, Johnson hammered a half dozen rights to the ribs and kidneys. A moment later, Tom suffered from Johnson's deadly right cross, which shook him to his feet. Jack narrowly missed an uppercut to the sound of "Ooh!" from the crowd.

Johnson stood straight up and grinned while Tommy weakly hit his right onto the ribs. At close quarters, Burns landed a few blows, but there was no weight behind them.

Jack landed a left uppercut and smiled. Johnson's left uppercut hurt Burns very much, but he stood the punishment remarkably well.

Rushing in, Tom dealt a few blows to the ribs and stomach. A hard Burns right to the ribs put Johnson off balance a bit and a left over the heart in the clinch scored well. Jack shut his mouth, which caused ringsiders to laugh. Tom looked better than at any previous time.

Burns made a fine effort, but Johnson had too much over him. Jack's left jab to the mouth was more of a poke than a punch, but he still grinned and talked. Jack drove another left to the mouth. Three times in the clinch Burns prevented the left uppercut from landing.

Jack ripped one of those terrific lefts to the stomach, then came with a right to the body as well, followed by a left to the neck which almost floored Tommy, who went into the ropes.

However, Burns again rushed in and hit the body. While Johnson leaned on the ropes, he took several blows to the body.

Jack grinned derisively. He stepped in and swung a heavy right and left onto Tom's mouth that sounded "squashy," as if there was weight behind them. Tom cleverly ducked a follow-up rush.

Burns went to his corner with his lips puffed and his right eye swollen.

7 - The round began with a tremendous smashing rally. Johnson hit hard with both hands to the head and body, intending to do some real damage.

Burns' capacity for punishment proved to be truly wonderful. The expression on Tom's face indicated that he was determined to do or die, and another heavy right saw him still coming on while his right eye bled.

Bleeding from the mouth and with his eyes and cheek looking swollen, Burns stood his ground and was still inclined to be the aggressor. He fought back with game courage. During a clinch, Tom's right to the ribs and head brought applause from the thousands.

Johnson uppercut his jaw with the right, which seemed to shake Burns. Tom's right eye bled in a couple of places. It was difficult to see all of the work up close in the clinches, for often they were very close to one another.

Burns dashed in again and fired his right to the ribs and head. Johnson uppercut his right to the jaw, and that whale of a blow landed often. Jack also fired short rights to the head and left rips into the stomach.

Tom was tossed from side to side as Johnson's mighty fists thundered in on him. Tom missed a left swing and Jack crossed a right to the ear. Burns broke away from a clinch with his face roughed.

Johnson remarked to the crowd, "Now, look, see, I thought Tahmy was an in-fighter." He smiled and then complained humorously about Burns' holding. "Look at him now," appealed Johnson to the referee as he held his arms up. Then Johnson fired his left into the stomach.

According to the *Daily Telegraph*, as Burns came in again, Johnson sent home a stinging left to the stomach and Tom fell to the floor. The *Referee* description of this sequence said Tom rushed, missed a blow, and fell down. The *Age* said Johnson jumped after him and sent Burns down with a heavy left swing to the body.

Burns rose quickly and rushed in again. Johnson brought his ever-handy right up to the chin and they clinched. Tom pumped his right to the ribs and Jack grinned his usual grin. However, Jack also protested Tom's holding and hitting. Someone in the crowd shouted, "He's quitting." When the gong sounded, Burns skipped to his corner, seemingly still strong and fresh in his demeanor. He had to be in tremendous shape.

Summarizing, the *Daily Telegraph* said, "Johnson dealt out a very great amount of punishment in this round." The *Referee* agreed, saying, "Poor Burns assimilated a great many hard knocks in this round."

However, the *Morning Herald* offered a different perspective. It said Johnson seemed to ease off slightly in this round. Only on one occasion did he inflict serious punishment. However, just as it looked as if Burns could no longer withstand his attack, Jack allowed Tom to rest in his arms and recover himself. "There was little doubt that Johnson had no desire to have the fight over too soon." He enjoyed belabouring Burns. "He relinquished fighting for insult, and proceeded to taunt Burns afresh, and pass asides to the spectators." The writer thought he was carrying Burns. Jack also could have been pacing himself.

8 - Johnson asked Burns, "Do you hear them telling you to come right along, Tom? Do as they tell you, Tahmy!" Jack then closed in and bore down on Burns, swinging three or four lefts. A ringsider said, "Stick to him, Tom. That yellow streak's there. You'll find it!" Johnson retorted, "You can't find it."

After breaking and sparring, Johnson bore in and ripped his left to the ribs. In the midst of landing some effective body blows, Johnson asked, "Aren't I clever?" The crowd replied by hooting vigorously. In an infighting rally, Johnson shook up Burns badly.

The *Daily Telegraph* said Johnson continued to make things warm throughout the round, and "it now looked certainly only a matter of time when he must win, but Burns kept going bravely, and here and there scored a good blow, but his punching didn't appear to have anything like the power expected."

Tom came in again with his usual pluck that won admiration. Johnson clinched. Tom tried hard to smash his right to the chin but it was thwarted by the octopus that clung to him. Johnson talked and missed a right and ducked a counter. Jack hooked a right to the head.

Johnson grinned and swapped remarks with the other corner, something he had been doing for some time. Tom landed a right and left into the stomach that made the challenger seem more serious. Johnson clinched for a while.

Burns tore in so fiercely that Johnson gave ground. A Burns left banged flush on Jack's mouth, and Johnson was seen to be bleeding slightly from his mouth.

Johnson bore in with blind fury, for the toreador had goaded the bull. Burns ducked and clinched. The crowd cheered. Johnson drove blows to the body, then drove his left into Tom's face, staggering him.

During most of the rest of the round, Burns held Johnson close to avoid the uppercut.

When the bell rang, Johnson smiled and waved his hand at Burns as if to say "ta-ta." Some in the crowd responded, "The cur!" "The brute!" Burns was cheered for making a game fight. Regardless of the punishment, Tom went to his corner looking strong.

9 - Burns missed a big right that made the spectators say "Ooh!" Johnson's left poked the nose. They again clinched and were separated, but then clinched again. Tom eluded a jab and stepped in to land a body shot. Jack ripped his left into the stomach. Tom drove in his right and there was more clinching.

Johnson appeared to be resting again in this round. He allowed Burns to do the work. Johnson evaded Burns' powerful blows and then clinched. Tom said, "You're holding again, you cur! You're always holding." Burns was fuming with rage and disgust.

Goaded, Johnson charged in wildly and missed some swings and then clinched again. After the referee separated them, Burns missed a right uppercut, and as Tom bent to reach the stomach, Johnson landed a right cross to the neck.

Burns' pluck, endurance, gameness, and persistence evoked admiration. Some thought that Tom would wear him down. There were many volleys from the crowd of "Good boy, Tommy!" Every now and then the champ did something that encouraged his friends to hope that he might yet succeed, "but the odds were too great." Burns was fighting strong and frequently landed to the face, but did no harm.

Johnson was content to put in an odd blow now and then and reflect on his adversary. Still, even the few blows he landed had their effect on Burns. Tom's face became more and more swollen.

Johnson tapped the nose with his left. He was a very careful fighter. Tom's right went around the neck. Jack planted a right on the jaw. In response to "Thirteen now, Tommy," from Tom's corner, Jack said, "Here's fourteen!" Burns' seconds called out "thirteen" and "twenty-three" quite often.

Johnson closed in, and while Tom was hammering away at his body, Jack coolly raised up his arms, intentionally allowed Burns to strike his body, and nodded to several acquaintances around the ringside. He was showing everyone that he could take it to the body, something whites claimed black fighters could not do. In his autobiography, Johnson said he invited Burns to hit him, saying, "Find that yellow streak. You have had much to say about it; now uncover it." The local primary sources said Johnson then held Burns and posed and looked at the cinematograph. Tom broke free and swung a vicious right but Jack ducked it.

The *Daily Telegraph* said the fight was still very much Johnson.

10 - Early in the round, Burns rallied. He had recovered sufficiently to make a serious attack, and bustled Johnson. Then, for the first time, he stood off and dodged several of Jack's attacks.

However, eventually Johnson really got to work again. He hooked the right to the eye, which puffed up immediately. Johnson nailed him a hook to the chin and right to the jaw, and then resumed talking to him. Tommy replied, "Say, you can't fight a lick!" Jack came in with a rush, jerked the left to the body, swung the right to the head, and then held him. When he got free, Tom landed a left on the nose and collided with the referee while springing clear.

Johnson saw that his foe was taking big risks in forlorn hope, so he paused his speech-making, attacked and forced Burns into a corner and landed hot head and body blows. Johnson pummeled away with both hands, but Tom stood it all. Johnson crossed the right to the head twice. His blows sent the white man helpless to the ropes and left him rattled and groggy when time was called.

The *Referee* said Burns was a comparatively easy mark. The *Daily Telegraph* said that although Burns had landed some fine punches, it was mostly Johnson who put in some great work in this round. Burns was fortunate that the round ended when it did, for at that point he appeared on the verge of going down.

11 - Burns emerged from his corner with his face looking badly punished. The *Age* said it was "evident that he had not the ghost of a chance, while Johnson was as fresh as paint and quite unmarked." However, Tom was still full of fight, and dashed in just as eagerly as ever, appearing to be recuperated from the prior round. The fighting was still vimful and exciting.

Johnson rushed and whipped a left to the body. He did a lot of damage with his uppercuts and short-arm jolts to the head and jaw. Some missed, but the ones that landed were effective. Tom hit the ribs with the left and landed a couple of rights to the ribs while they were locked. Jack held around the neck and fired right uppercuts while the crowd hooted uproariously. Those punches troubled the champ. Jack then held on tightly. He loosened up to land a light right cross. While the clinch was on, Johnson pounded four rights on the ribs and kidneys as a butcher might chop at a carcass. Burns again fell against the ropes.

Tom came back and swung his right to the head. He also jolted his right to Jack's ribs. Tom danced a bit, as he did with Squires and Lang. The crowd applauded the evidence that there was still life in Burns.

The *Referee* said Burns returned to his corner apparently as strong as ever. The *Daily Telegraph* agreed, "With all the wear and tear he had suffered Burns still seemed strong." However, the *Morning Herald* said, "It was obvious that, barring accidents, the fight was over." The *Age* said that without wincing, Burns had taken all that he received, and it was plenty. Johnson could do what he liked with him. There were numerous calls from the crowd of, "That's enough; it's no use beating a beaten man." The *Age* opined, "The referee could reasonably have given a decision at this point, but Burns was still hopeful that he might land a winning punch."

12 - Johnson poked his left to the face, crossed a right to the eye, uppercut the jaw, and chopped the chin with another right as Tom moved away. Jack followed with left jabs flush in the face. Tom's face was badly swollen.

Johnson poked the left on the nose and landed several right and left uppercuts to the chin.

During the round, Johnson's left was seldom out of Burns' face. With his left he maneuvered Tom's head into position for a right which always landed square and rattled Burns badly, but Tom still fought back with rare gameness. However, the terrible battering was sapping Tom's strength.

Burns made a fine effort, but either he missed or his blows did no damage. Tom darted in with vim, but Jack got away. Tom countered a left with a blow flush on the mouth. He then landed a left to the body, but Johnson fired good left and right hooks to the face.

A Johnson left to the chin was so hard that people marveled at how Burns not only continued but still attacked. The round closed with Johnson retaliating, swinging one after another on the champ. The bell found Burns falling onto the lower rope, enduring a torrid time, being belted mercilessly.

The *Morning Herald* said Burns was at his mercy, and would have been knocked out had the fighting continued. The *Referee* said Burns had endured a perilous period, yet, despite this, he never winced and actually hopped to his corner. The *Daily Telegraph* said the round was similar to the prior one, with Burns trying hard, but taking a lot of punishment.

13 - After finessing for a couple of moments, Johnson rushed and banged left and right to either side of the head with sufficient severity so as to overbalance the recipient. Jack then held Tom and rested.

Burns eluded and blocked some blows. Johnson chopped his right at the ribs, and subsequently jolted the right to the ear and chin. He planted a left on the face, which caused Tom to come in furiously and they clinched. Jack held with the left and punched with the right. Tom missed a right. Johnson landed a right cross to the head and another at close range.

The blows only aroused Burns to more effort. A left hit Jack's ribs. Stung, Johnson waded in and landed four right uppercuts to the chin. Burns took it and fired a left to the face and right to the body.

Johnson fought fiercely, attempting to finish Burns with a quick succession of heavy punches. One of them, a particularly severe blow, caused Tom's already badly swollen face to become worse. Tom's face presented a sorry spectacle. His mouth bled freely. Half a dozen jolting uppercuts made him look like a wreck. Although Johnson hammered him with a terrible battery, Burns' courage was undiminished and his fighting instinct was still there.

14 - Johnson immediately went in to fight because he felt satisfied that there was nothing to fear. He quickly rushed in and seemed to be making a genuine effort to end it. Johnson opened with a couple solid crosses, one on the face and the other to the ribs. There was a clinch and a few kidney hits. He landed a right uppercut to the chin but missed another. A solid jab to the face caused Burns some pain, and the blood flowed from his lips. Jack hooked a right to the side of the head and followed it up with blows to either side of the face, making the blood spurt from the right eye.

Johnson was slaughtering him, landing his left to the side of the head and right uppercut, each of which were telling. A rousing left rip to the ribs preceded a clinch of Johnson's own making.

Burns continued to rush, lead, clinch, and infight to the best of his ability, and even demonstrated some speed and evaded some blows. However, ultimately his efforts were fruitless. Through it all, Burns received the worst of it. Burns was "too far gone, and could not guard. He was just a plaything in the hands of the negro, who was as fresh and strong as a horse." Jack continued to taunt Burns, who "took his gruel with a courage that earned him the whole hearted admiration of everyone."

Eventually, Burns became quite helpless and clung to the ropes. The left side of his face puffed out further, and the sag in his mouth convinced some that his jaw was broken. Johnson aimed for it and followed up with sudden ferocious rushes. Jack served out punishment at a fast rate and in heavy doses.

A hard right reached Tom's injured-looking jaw. Johnson landed a heavy left to the body and then measured off his distance and landed a right cross to the chin that dropped Burns with such force that he rolled over twice.

Johnson retired to his corner and complacently watched the count with his hands resting on his hips. McIntosh counted, waving time with his right-hand forefinger extended. Most agreed that the two hard rights had sent him down.

Burns scrambled up to his feet at the count of eight and staggered towards Johnson.

Johnson bounded from his corner like a panther. His second yelled, "Finish him, Jack!" Johnson swept down like a cyclone on the staggering, almost helpless champion. He smashed away with a fusillade of successive left hooks and right uppercuts to the head, nearly all of which landed. A left smash landed on the forehead, knocking Tom against the ropes. A right landed on the swollen cheek again. One said that Burns swayed to and fro, making it appear as if a touch would send him down. Another said that Burns was able to absorb the punishment and remain upright, though staggering. Still another said one blow would make it seem as if Burns was about to drop, but another blow would keep him from going down.

Police Superintendent Mitchell entered the ring and waved his hands aloft, commanding cessation of the bout. He had seen enough. McIntosh said, "Stop, Johnson!" Jack went to ring center, and McIntosh pointed to him and said, "I declare Johnson winner on points." There was a new world heavyweight champion. The crowd remained silent. Johnson waved his hands to a crowd that did not cheer him.

Of the finish, the *Morning Herald* said, "There was no need to continue. The fight was over, and nobody in the Stadium was sorry to see Superintendent Mitchell, who was in command of the police arrangements, scramble through the ropes, and wave the giant back to his corner." The *Referee* opined, "Burns was not done; he could certainly have gone on; how long one can hardly guess; but there was no help for it, and Mr. McIntosh had, in accordance with an understanding arrived at beforehand, to declare the winner on what had taken place up to the moment of interference."

Burns was led to his corner. He had been down twice in the 1st, and again in the 5th, 7th, and 14th rounds.

THE LAST FEW SECONDS OF THE FIGHT.

The spectators were not happy about the black man's victory, for Burns was the fan favorite. There was little cheering. Mostly there was sad silence. The heartbroken crowd quietly put on their hats and quickly streamed out. onto New South Head road. In twelve minutes, the stadium was empty. They had wanted Burns to win, but when it was over, they admitted that he was never in it.

The *Sydney Bulletin* said Johnson had won "from start to finish." "To the writer it seemed that he could have knocked Burns out at any time after the seventh round."

> When Burns fought Squires this writer opined that the man who would eventually beat Burns would be the one who could draw his defence with one hand and then cross with the other to the jaw. And just because this was precisely what Johnson succeeded in doing at the opening of the struggle, the first round was the really decisive one of the battle.

According to the *Sydney Morning Herald*, "[T]he more powerful fighter won. That Johnson won fairly and decisively enough hardly anyone questions, although Burns believes that, had not the police interfered, he still had a chance." However, "No one who witnessed the affair will agree with the ex-champion that the police intervention was ill-timed or unjustified. Burns was outclassed by an opponent who, in addition to skill, had on his side very much greater size and weight."

During the fight, several men who were perched at the top of the 10-shilling seats supplied details of the fight to the crowd outside the stadium. At one point, one said, "Burns has no chance with the black fellow. He is simply playing with him."

The *Sydney Daily Telegraph* said Burns was outclassed completely. "The contest was one-sided throughout. Burns was outmatched in every round, and was severely punished, while Johnson seemed quite unharmed." Each round was similar - one-sided for Johnson - with the chances for Burns to win becoming more and more remote as each round passed, until finally they vanished altogether. Ugly rumors about Johnson's inability to stay and his indifferent training were proven to be untrue.

Another *Daily Telegraph* writer said the scene provided a great human drama. On one side was Johnson, the black man full of humor, almost tickled to death with the situation, lively as a kitten, dancing and prancing, showing the strength of a lion, and magnificent physical abilities. On the other side was Burns, a sallow-looking, huge-shouldered, terribly determined, steely-eyed white man. "It was a joke to one, a tragedy to the other." Johnson battered his way to the championship with a smile on his face and a joke on his lips, while Burns received terrible punishment with a sullen, stony silence that sent the crowd's sympathy out to him, as it usually did when a man took his grueling without wavering or complaining.

> Only once was there a gleam of hope for Burns – he winked at his faithful attendants after striking the nigger somewhat hard, and the crowd were not loth to encourage him to repeat it. But it was all in vain – there was too much strength and skill in front of him – he was a hopelessly beaten man.
>
> In the character of the fighting there was nothing sensational. They would shape up, Johnson would make a few speeches, there would be a smashing rush by the negro, and they would hold on to each other for minutes at a time. But in these clinches there would be thud after thud, and the clicking sound of a man's teeth being rattled. The victim was Burns. His face began to look pulpy, his left eye had lost 50 per cent of its usefulness, while internally he must have suffered from the terrific slogs of the black man as he crashed through his defence and smashed his right-hand glove into the Canadian's stomach.
>
> So the contest went on, hopelessly for Burns, treated as a joke by Johnson. The champion was being slowly pounded. Smash after smash he received in the face, until one side of it looked as if it didn't belong to the other. He was sent down with cruel smacks several times, and there was the anguish of a beaten man in his eyes. Game to the last, he poked his tongue out at the swarthy giant who was steadily teaching him to taste the bitterness of defeat by a process of

battering that only a brave-hearted man with a tremendous capacity for taking punishment could have withstood so long.

The *Morning Herald* said,

> Johnson won in every department of the game and at every stage of the fight. He represents a class in himself. Burns was very badly punished, while Johnson was unmarked and practically unhit. ...

> Except to those who had seen the remarkable capacity of Burns for taking punishment in his fight with Squires, the issue was not in doubt from the first clash of blows. Within five seconds of the commencement, Johnson chipped Burns a nasty right uppercut on the chin, knocking him down, and keeping him on the floor for six seconds. A few moments later he sent the champion to the boards again, and from this out Burns was hopelessly outclassed. Every round terminated in favour of the negro, and long before the police entered the ring in the fourteenth round, and compelled a cessation of hostilities, Burns was plainly a beaten man. Throughout, however, he displayed the courage and capacity for taking punishment.

The *Morning Herald* said that with his longer reach, Johnson was able to avoid all of Burns' attacks, using similar methods that Burns had used on others, striking the biceps or arms and taking the fire out of the blows.

Johnson carried and toyed with Burns.

> Johnson was greatly the superior of Burns; in fact, it seemed possible that he could have beaten him in half the time had he so chosen. ... His superiority as a boxer was undeniable, and his height and strength served him in good stead. ...

Both engaged in the American practice of hitting in the clinches. In fact, most of the fighting was done in clinches. Johnson's display was "magnificent." All the tricks that Burns had used to hit Squires in the clinches were circumvented by Johnson's strength and skill.

> When Burns's arm locked his own in a clinch, so that he could not deliver a blow, Johnson simply shifted it to where he wanted it, and then struck. Summed up, the position was that, in out-fighting, Burns could not reach Johnson, while every time they got into holds, he received one or more solid punches before they broke free, and was himself powerless to display his ability in the line of boxing in which he had hitherto been regarded as pre-eminent.

Burns fought with a sprained ankle from the 5th round on, but it seemed to affect him but little, for even in the closing rounds his footwork was excellent and his poise perfect, even when the upper part of his frame was clearly weak.

From start to finish, Burns did not have a look-in. Those who saw him for the first time might think he knew nothing about infighting, whereas those who saw him in the Squires fight afterwards looked upon him as the last word in the art.

In holds, Johnson was able to deal out severe blows to the head with his right shot from beneath Tom's left elbow, or if he was more to one side, he would swing heavily with his right over Burns' back. Tom landed a few short hits on the body but they lacked force. It was like a man and a schoolboy. "Johnson simply toyed with Burns, and the latter was beaten at every point of the game." Jack so obviously was the superior in physique, skill, and tactics, such that "it would have required a battleship and not a man to defeat him."

Though they sympathized with the defeated man, "there was not one in the vast concourse who could deny that Johnson is the finest fighter who has been seen within the memory of living Australians, if not living men." They credited Burns for suffering untold pain.

The *Morning Herald* opined, "Johnson is probably the best fighter of modern times – possibly of all time. … He has everything in his favour except his over-confidence; and unlike many of his race, is conscientious in his training." Although his long record showed relatively few knockouts, causing some to think he had a lack of hitting power, "the fallacy of such a theory required nothing beyond Saturday's performance to reveal it."

The only word of hesitance was that it felt that athletes, and especially pugilists, have their primes early in life. It thought that Johnson already was past his prime at age 30. Except for Fitzsimmons, no other champion had obtained the honor so late in life. Of course, Johnson had to be frustrated for years by his inability to obtain a title shot when he was younger. If he had been allowed to fight Jeffries from 1903-1905 and won, his reign likely would have lasted several more years. Regardless, even at age 30, Johnson was in top shape and very sharp. He could maintain that level if he continued to take care of himself.

The *Referee* said Johnson looked good physically. On the other hand, Burns looked too light, and his face was pinched and drawn. "Stale suggested itself to me at once, and his fighting bore that assumption out, for he completely lacked the vim and speed of the Lang battle." He had trained longer than he did for Squires or Lang; perhaps too long.

Burns was not as active on his feet as he was in his other fights, perhaps owing to the ankle injury suffered during the fight. Although the blow he endured in the opening round affected him, it did not totally account for all of his falling off.

The *Melbourne Age*'s special on-scene reporter said the fans witnessed "the white champion humbled and beaten silly by the negro giant." Johnson hammered Burns for 14 rounds. The spectators wondered how on earth or by what extraordinary means Burns beat the much larger 200-pound Marvin Hart. Johnson was just as big as Hart, but Burns could do nothing with him.

The local press summarized the fight. Burns started the 1st round with his crouch, seeming calm, but alert, strong, and agile, showing his fierceness when punching. Johnson was more upright. They danced about in nimble fashion. Their arms were up and down. Johnson bounded in with strength and skill.

They clinched, broke loose, and like a flash, Johnson with a tremendous right uppercut caught Burns under the chin, lifted him off his feet, and sent him to the floor in a sitting posture. The sound of the punch landing on the jaw made a clicking sound. The blow shocked Tom and stunned his party. Johnson smirked. Thereafter, Jack was in total control.

Johnson demonstrated that Burns' defence was useless against him, and that he was so much stronger that he could hold the champion helpless until he was ready to punch him. The round ended with some grinding punches on Tom's jaw.

In the 2nd round, Johnson became an orator. He grinned and talked to Burns incessantly, taunting him, chaffing him, and patronizing him. Burns said nothing, but fought on with silence and determination, though it was hopeless. Johnson laughed over Tom's shoulder. He passed the time of day to someone in the crowd he called "Patsy," and commented about the good weather.

The *Bulletin* said it wasn't until the 4th round that Burns made any kind of a really dangerous attack. It was still Johnson's round though.

Thereafter, Johnson "commenced a most beastly exhibition of rubbing it into a man who was fighting a game battle but was altogether overmatched." He did just as he liked, and did it in good humor, "goading the white man on with sneering remarks, laughing at the hardest body blows, and replying with quick retort to the incessant comments and advice of the attendants in the Burns corner."

Johnson was "determined to impress the fact on this crowd of white trash" that he was quite unruffled by anything Burns did. He looked down at a photographer and asked, "Did you get that? Anyhow, I'll give you a good picture." Then he suddenly sprang in on Burns and smashed a left to the stomach and right to the jaw, and hurled Tom against the ropes. He frequently held Burns against himself, helpless, while he exchanged gibes with the crowd, grinning as he did so. Then he would twist Burns into a position that he wanted so he could smite him.

Johnson talked and joked at or about Burns with a tireless fluency. He even spoke with ringside spectators. When the gong rang to start a round, Johnson would grin at him and address Tom as a mother would an impatient child. "All right, Tahmy," he soothingly said. "Come along, Tommy, my boy." Or Johnson would say, "Come on, leedle Tahmmy," as he laughed. "Come right here where I want you!" Then he swung Burns into his corner, where Tom broke loose and attempted a feeble uppercut. Johnson teased, "No good, Tahmmy! I'll teach you!" Then he threw Burns off and uppercut him twice with his right and bashed him on the side of the head with the left. Later on he again invited Burns to "come in." His eyeballs rolled and the row of gold and white teeth shone. Johnson coaxed him to lead, saying, "Take a chance, Tahmy."

When Burns clinched, Johnson taunted him by asking, "Why don't you fight, Tommy?" McIntosh ordered Tom to break, but he was too dazed to hear, and feebly hit the stomach. McIntosh said, "Let go, break, Tommy!"

Jack also inquired scornfully about all the talk of Tommy's infighting, of which he had heard so much. When Tom's seconds called to him, "Get away from him, Tommy; get away from him!" Johnson drew Burns in close and said to the Burns corner, "I thought Tahmmy was an in-fighter." While Burns was punching his ribs, the unphased Johnson asked, "Do you call this in-fighting?"

Johnson criticized the champ's lack of hitting power, replying to Tom's punches by saying, "He can't hurt, he can't hurt," as he smashed Burns over the kidneys. "Why, I thought you could hit, Tahmy," he said in "tones of shocked pleasantry." Jack also asked, "What's that rib hit of yours, Thomas?" Burns would not respond, so Johnson turned his attention to the Burns corner and to the spectators.

Burns' seconds directed his tactics by means of a code of secret signals. They would call out "33" or "15," depending on the situation. They reminded Burns to cover certain points, to step in and mix it, or to be wary. Someone in Tom's corner told him to give him a "Twenty-three, lower down," or they cried out, "Thirteen, good boy, Tommy."

However, "all the strategy in the world was powerless against the irresistible battery of the giant negro." Johnson rolled his eyes, grinned, welted Burns, and said, "Fourteen – put that down." Or Johnson might respond with "Look out, Tommy; here comes 24!"

When the angry spectators resented his talk, Jack glared at them over Tom's shoulders and grinned. In the 8th round, Johnson chaffed the crowd with his question to Burns' seconds, "Ain't I clever? Yah!" There was no response from Tom's cornermen.

All the pleasantry was with Johnson. He was cool and collected, and showed very few signs of wear and tear. The boxers would rush and smash and clinch, but it was the smaller fighter who suffered pains.

Between speeches, and sometimes accompanying them, Johnson administered terrific punishment. Occasionally Johnson dropped his grin and ferociously smashed both hands into Burns. This was his response to the charge that he had a yellow streak, the accusation which had caused much bitterness. His enraged response was a surprise to the disappointed spectators, who had expected less from him. "The big negro distributed some sickening punches in the stomach. They sounded like a well-kicked football banging against a wall – whoomph. Then there would be a sharp, grinding click – that was the grinner sending his long, brawny arm jolting upwards to the Canadian's chin." While clinched, Johnson would use his long reach to have free play over the smaller man's back, battering the kidneys. "Human endurance has its limits, and Burns had to be beaten."

Burns suffered badly round after round. His eyes were bruised and cut, his mouth was swollen and distorted from the constant terrific right uppercuts on his left jaw, and his body was bruised and almost bleeding from the terrible punishment.

In about the 10th round, Burns made a fine rally. Johnson ducked a right in time to allow the blow to go over his neck. As they crashed together, Johnson gurgled, "Ah, that's what I like," and smashed Burns heavily in the ribs with his right.

After every round, a Burns attendant combed his hair. "He might lose his championship, the supremacy of the white race might go to the Devil, Burns himself might be slowly battered to pieces or suddenly killed outright, but at least he should die with his hair properly parted."

After 11 rounds, Burns was in a horrible plight. His face was all puffed out on one side, his jaw hung down as though it were broken, and the blood oozed from his battered mouth. "Outgeneralled, over-reached, overmatched in strength, insulted and treated like a helpless mouse by a great black cat, he came up heroically to take his punishment." He was willing to fight to the bitter end. Tom did all that he could against such odds. He kept trying to attack and force the fight.

For 12 rounds, Johnson was ascendant, and still ascending. Despite the terrible punishment, Burns was remarkably fresh, and his footwork delightful. But, towards the end of the round, Johnson roughed him into a corner and landed three swinging blows in succession. One caught him on the ribs and the others to the face. That Burns felt their effect was shown when he came to his corner.

The *Morning Herald* said the fight really ended in the 13th round. Johnson scored solidly to the face and body, and also landed half a dozen blows to the kidneys. Burns clinched for safety. As they broke, Jack swung a strong left to the ear which sent Tom staggering. Johnson dashed in and delivered a left on the abdomen and a right cross to the jaw. Burns shook like a reed in the wind. His knees trembled, and Johnson swung another solid left on his neck. Burns clinched, and when they broke, Tom seemed about to fall from sheer weakness, but the gong saved him.

When Burns went to his seat, one side of his face was so swollen and distorted that many spectators thought his jaw might be broken. His seconds literally plastered him with Vaseline.

Between rounds, police superintendent Mitchell and Dr. Maitland consulted. Mitchell remained close to the ring so he could monitor the situation carefully.

When the 14th round began, Johnson lost no time, but hit Burns in the head and they clinched. After the referee broke them, Burns swayed on his feet like a drunken man. Johnson stepped in and measured him and landed a heavy blow on the ear. Burns dropped his hands. Then Johnson threw in blows of great weight, any one of which could have knocked Burns down, but before he had time to fall, the impact of another blow made him recover his balance. A moment later, a right swing on the jaw dropped Burns for eight seconds.

After Burns rose, as they came together again, Johnson swung a heavy-sounding left to the mouth, and the champion tottered again. Then the law stepped into the ring and stopped the one-sided battle that had been 14 rounds of suffering for Burns.

And yet for all we know and feel,
For Christ and Shakespeare, knowledge, love,
We watch a white man bleeding reel,
We cheer a black with bloodied glove.

—"Nemo," in "The Daily Telegraph."

The *Daily Telegraph* said Johnson became the champion of the world "on an award of points which would have been quite unnecessary had the police held back another minute." But that was the point. They did not want to allow Johnson to knock him down and out for the count.

Another *Daily Telegraph* writer said that in the 14th round, Johnson smashed Burns' jaw some more and he "sank hopelessly to his knees." Johnson walked to his corner grinning. Burns rose at eight. Another crash on the jaw made Burns wobble. Tom was helpless, for nature had done all it could for him. A man in uniform made for the ringside and the referee stopped the fight, awarding the championship to Johnson. Jack bounded to the ropes and said, "What did I tell yar?" He grinned again.

Another writer said the sun was mostly behind the clouds, but it came out near the end.

With the sun came the end. It was the setting of the sun for the White man, and the rising for the Black. Down went the champion, thudded on the jaw, to struggle to his feet, dazed, bruised, and beaten, to receive another. Then the Law humanely stepped in and saved Burns from further partial disfigurement; the left side of his face was then considerably out of shape.

Unlike the *Daily Telegraph*, which opined that Burns would have been knocked out within another minute, the *Referee* said that when the police stopped the fight,

> Tommy was enduring a rather parlous period, but there was still plenty of vitality left, and the black had been puffing some during the previous few rounds, so that though appearances were against the likelihood of Burns seeing the 20 rounds through, I wouldn't attempt to say he could not have done so, as many and many a time men just as desperately situated have survived, and in not a few cases knocked their opponents out.

The *Melbourne Age* said Johnson proved incorrect the assertions that he would show a yellow streak against Burns.

> If Johnson has a 'yellow streak' he showed no evidence of it. He did not need to, as he was always safe. If it exists, it will take a man who carries more guns than Burns to expose it. The opinion formed by good judges is that Johnson is a splendid fighter of considerable resource, and probably courageous.

Summarizing the bout, it said,

> As for the contest, it was no fight; it simply amounted to the terribly severe chastisement of Burns. There was little science shown, and none at all was needed. Johnson, through sheer weight and strength, could have beaten Burns had he possessed little more than the mere rudiments of boxing. ... The plucky little white man, full of courage, and quite oblivious to consequences, fought the black colossus in quite the wrong way. He rushed him time after time, and hurled himself up against the huge mass of bone and brawn towering up over him, only to be beaten back without ever leaving the slightest impression of his visit upon his foe. The white man was hopelessly outclassed, and from the first round his efforts to hurt his big antagonist were absolutely futile. Blows that would have knocked down a man of his own grade fell upon the black man's body with no more effect than the fists of a boy would fall upon a horse. ... Burns's favorite overhand punch in clinches was mere amusement for Johnson. ... Burns's attempts to drop a hot shot on Johnson's jaw were almost invariably deflected by the muscle embossed shoulder to glance harmlessly off the top of the hard bullet head, while all Burns's most strenuous endeavors to beat some hurt into the bulky, muscle

clad body were wasted efforts. Johnson, after the first clinch, knew and felt that he was Burns's master, and knowing it he became offensive and flash, taunted his game little antagonist, and riled him to rush into close quarters, where Johnson was able to hold and beat him as he pleased. ... Burns had been told that Johnson's weakness lay in his inability to take punishment about the body. ... As a matter of fact Johnson is as strong as a bull about the body, and he was just delighted when he could lure Burns right in, and get him with head down flogging away violently, but harmlessly, at his ribs and loins. ... [Johnson would then] rip everything upward in irresistible, smashing, short range uppercuts [that] sent him reeling and dazed back across the ring or down to the boards. Often he would follow up his favorite upper cuts in quick left and right half-arm cross blows that buffeted Burns from side to side like a bundle of straw, and through it all he taunted his game little antagonist. "Come on Tommy, come right in here, and show the folks some of that infighting of yours! I want you, ma honey, an' I'll give you the best I've got! I've been keeping it so long, Tommy, an' I'm jest crazy ter hand it out to yer!"

Johnson would alternate his flash remarks with awful wallops and grins. As Burns worked away like a bull terrier, an irate spectator remarked, "He'll knock the smile off you directly, you flash nigger." Johnson coolly turned and said, "Well! He's jes' doin' his little best, but I can't help smilin'. He's ticklin' me to death! Why, deary me, I thought he wuz de little man wat wuz goin' to make ma head swim!" Turning back to business, Johnson would whirl in half a dozen hooks and uppercuts that would drive back Burns' head and toss it from side to side. Often Johnson would hold Burns in a clinch, pause from hitting the kidneys, and kiss his mitten to the cinematograph. "This sort of thing soon made him unpopular, and he was subjected to a running fire of hoots and adverse comment, which, however, seemed to affect him as little as Burns's blows." Johnson beat Burns, "but he might just as easily have accomplished his task without recourse to such an amount of quite unnecessary flashiness."

None of the local writers or fans appreciated Johnson's flashiness. The *Morning Herald* said that unfortunately, Johnson's "fine boxing was disfigured by a display of bombast that is happily seldom seen in any sporting arena." It felt that Johnson's verbal taunts had robbed himself of personal acclaim.

The *Bulletin* noted that a depressing feature of the bout was Johnson's "flashiness." Jack was not loathe to publish his delight in himself.

Had his nods, becks, wreathed smiles, etc., occurred in America, a prominent citizen would inevitably have risen impressively somewhere about the close of the fourth round, and, amid encouraging cheers, have drawn a gun upon Johnson and shot that immense mass of black humanity dead. In the ensuing murder trial counsel for the defence would have put in the cinematograph film as his sole exhibit and evidence, and on its testimony alone secured a verdict of 'justifiable homicide.'

The *Daily Telegraph* said the most noticeable feature of the bout was that Johnson grinned throughout.

> The first thing that struck the huge assemblage about the big negro was his grin – an everlasting, confident, self-possessed, defiant grin. He took it into the ring with him, he carried it unimpaired through the fight, mixing it up occasionally with some terrific blows, and an almost ceaseless chatter of a deep, husky voice – and when the depressed crowd last saw him, he still had it; and there was something else with it – the triumphant gleam of the victor. It was not a savage, ferocious grin, but the simple, good old painstaking, faithful smirk of the negro that would not leave its native home. Times have been when the multitude has roared its sides out at that type of grin, but on Saturday morning it gave thousands the heartache. And Burns could not drive it away, and therein was the despondency of the people.

The *Morning Herald* opined that it was a pity that Johnson was not content to let his boxing do its own talking. "He is so fine a fighter that advertisement is unnecessary, and people who attend fights appreciate the points of the game without having their attention directed to them by their author." However, Johnson did not obey the axiom that a fighter should keep silent. He kept up a running fire of remarks that either directly insulted Burns or were intended to express indirect contempt. He had won the talking championship as well.

The local papers failed to note Burns' history of verbal taunts and insults directed toward Johnson (and others), either because they were unaware or because they did not care. It was clear that Jack intended to get his revenge on this day. However, in general, whites felt that blacks should endure insults from whites with solemn silence.

Certainly, race factored into the feelings regarding Johnson. The *Bulletin* said, "But the victory, fairly won as it was, was wholly unpopular. That crowd was white to the core. It had given the brown man a fair deal, and didn't feel called upon to do more."

The *Daily Telegraph* said that although many were sympathetic to Johnson's struggles to obtain a title shot owing to his race, there still was strong race sympathy with the white man. Yet, the spectators were fair to Johnson. "Jack Johnson, who was favorite with comparatively few, had an absolutely fair field on the color line. If the people did not rejoice in his systematic and regular punishment of the white man, they certainly did not manifest any resentment. But the crowd was sorry – it was sad."

The *Morning Herald* said the 20,000 fans were sadly disappointed, in part because for the first time in history, a black man was the world heavyweight champion. In the gloved era, Jack Johnson was the first black man to challenge for and the first to win the heavyweight championship.

The weekly *Referee* headline said the top notchers of the white and colored races had met. "The past must be dug very deeply into before an occasion may be discovered when accredited representatives of the Caucasian and colored peoples of the earth contended for anything approaching the distinction involved" in this fight.

The *Referee* also commented on Johnson's conduct during and after the fight.

> No man the world over has been a greater supporter than myself of the colored boxer's claims for consideration; but after last Saturday's happenings, and the subsequent exultation and gloating of the winner over the fall of so brave a foeman, and such a clean-living fellow as Tommy Burns, I am satisfied there is a great deal more than most of us suspected behind America's prejudice against the black.

When an American previously had said that Johnson was "as flash as chain-lightning," the writer put it down to racial hatred existing throughout the U.S. "Johnson's actions and bearing on Saturday have, however, had such an effect upon me that I never want to see a white and a black man face each other in the ring again." Peter Jackson had suffered the same racial slurs and indignities, but conducted himself in a sportsmanlike, gentlemanly, modest, and chivalrous fashion nevertheless. Johnson was different. He grinned, bitterly taunted, and waved "ta-ta" to his opponent.

The Australian perspective was that the black man was required to suffer indignity in silence and not retort. That was not Jack Johnson. Hence, the question was asked, "Who will dethrone him?"

The *Melbourne Age* also said the crowd was not happy about Johnson's victory. They wanted to see the white man win.

> A general feeling of antagonism to Johnson permeated the crowd inside and outside the Stadium. It was there, and there was no gainsaying it. Deep down beneath the spirit of fair play it made itself felt – people could not help manifesting it. The 'white Australia' color prejudice cropped up.

Even those who had predicted a Johnson victory said things before the fight like, "Well! I've backed the nigger, but I won't be sorry if I lose my money."

Hence, despite the Australians' fairness regarding the color line, they still had their own racial prejudices and rooting interests. They wanted to see the white man win. And they did not want to see the black Johnson vengefully taunt the white man who had called him "yellow" and "nigger."

Some said that prejudice against the colored fighter explained the odds which had Burns as the strong betting favorite in Australia. The only other explanation was a belief that all was not well with Johnson. Mr. Bettinson, manager of the National Sporting Club in England, said the result was not a surprise in English and American boxing circles. The betting in San Francisco and London was 10 to 9 on Johnson.

Misters Kerry and Co. of George Street had purchased the sole photographic rights of the contest. They had four working cameras at the stadium. Some footage was taken with the camera resting on the edge of the platform. It was so close, that on one occasion when Johnson threw Burns, the camera had to be pulled from under his foot. Johnson, looking down, asked, "Did you get it?" The negatives were developed rapidly.

A rumor was published in London that Burns had died as a result of his injuries, which obviously was false.

Referee and promoter Hugh McIntosh received compliments for his performance as referee, particularly for not getting involved very much. Other referees might have ruined the fight by breaking the fighters constantly and hampering their work. He had permitted the bout to be fought along the lines of American rules interpretation. Hitting in holds prevailed almost throughout, although when one held and hit, McIntosh would disengage the holding hand and permit the men to fight without breaking them apart. McIntosh did better in his first bout as a referee than some referees do today even after hundreds of fights.

The referee question was not settled until the day before the fight. Johnson would not accept Snowy Baker because of something Jack's wife had overheard at a restaurant, though he declined to divulge what it was. Burns did not want Harry Beckett because Harry was close friends with some men who had backed Johnson heavily. Both fighters wanted McIntosh, so he gave in.

McIntosh said it was his first time acting as a referee, but he was not nervous because he was not new at the boxing game. He said, "Both men fought with scrupulous fairness. Neither made an appeal to me on a foul, and no foul occurred on either side."

When asked what he thought of the battle, McIntosh said, "Burns put up a splendidly game fight, but it was against great odds. He met a man who was 5 ½ inches above him in stature, and 2 stone [28 pounds] better in weight. That was a considerable handicap, and I think he did remarkably well under the circumstances." He also said Burns' display of pluck must have won admiration. "Tommy was strong when the police commanded a halt, and their actions surprised me, but Johnson would surely have won in the end bar a knock-out, which didn't seem likely." He said Johnson fought and won fair and square. When asked if Johnson's victory was a surprise, McIntosh declined to comment.

The fight was not only memorable for the racial angle but also because the gate amounted to £26,200 ($131,000), easily a world's record. The previous best was Nelson-Gans, another interracial fight, at $69,715. Well before it took place, the fight had been discussed and debated all around the world in a manner without parallel. The purses totaled £7,500, showing that McIntosh had made a wise investment, and that Burns' £6,000 ($30,000) purse demand was not unreasonable, something of which Johnson took note when it came to his own future purse negotiations. Payment was made the next day. Johnson earned £1,500 ($7,500), including expense money.

McIntosh said over 20,000 people were admitted into the grounds. 2,000 who had purchased tickets were not admitted, lest there be overcrowding. Their money would be refunded.

McIntosh said he would cable an offer of £10,000 ($50,000) to Jeffries to fight Johnson. "Jeffries stated that he would re-enter the ring if a colored man or a foreigner won the championship. Now he is morally obliged to come back."

However, Jeffries declined to fight Johnson or anyone else. When subsequently told of Jeff's position, McIntosh replied, "Which is just what I expected. Jeffries is a sensible fellow. He has been out of the game too long, and is doing well enough."

After the interview, McIntosh hurried off to telephone the news of the result to each of the fighters' spouses.

In his dressing room, where he seemed as strong and as well as when he began the fight, new heavyweight champion Jack Johnson said,

> I never had a doubt regarding the outcome of the battle since the match was made. Burns fought a better battle than I anticipated, and took a lot of punishment. He is a very plucky fellow. ...

> Some of them have been talking about me being yellow – having a yellow streak, and all that sort of thing. Well, he looked as 'yaller' as I did, I reckon. When I got him in the ring I made up my mind I'd not only win, but I'd give him a beating he'd remember into the bargain. I beat him proper, and I did it on purpose. I wanted to beat him down bit by bit, and show him and the public how much yellow there was in me. I could have won sooner, only I wanted to beat him so he'd remember me. ...

> I could have beaten him a lot quicker, but I did not desire to. I wanted to get even. He and those with him had spoken very slightingly of me, and I laid myself out to make the drubbing as severe as possible. Wonder if they think I have a yellow streak now.

> None of the blows delivered by Burns troubled me much, and I was not concerned at any stage of the fight. I just wanted to give it him in small doses, and he got it, and I'm satisfied.

Johnson further explained,

> I just laid myself out to beat him all the way, and not too quickly. He fought much gamer than I expected, but never seriously troubled me at any time. I wanted to show Tommy Burns and all you people looking on that that yellow streak was not in me. I waited a long time for that chance and now I am champion others will have an opportunity of locating the weak spot. Burns only hit me a few hard

punches all through, but I guess I handed out a big bunch of them to him. It was a longer fight than I looked for.

Another quoted the elated, smiling Johnson as saying,

I told you so. ... Confident? Yes, I felt very sure bar accidents, and they happen anywhere. Burns is a game fighter, but I had it on him too much. No, he never troubled me at any time, and as for in-fighting – well, I don't think he showed me any points.

Speaking of the end, grinning, Jack said,

P'raps it was just as well it was stopped. Little Tommy was jes' too easy, an' he would have got hurt badly later on. I'm too big and strong for him, but he's a game, good little fighter, mind you. I gave him a bad hiding, and spun it out on purpose, but we shook hands and I hope there's no more bad blood between us. I could have won sooner if I had cut lose.

A local writer said, "Johnson was inclined to exult over his victory at the expense of the defeated man, and said things which, it is to be hoped, he regrets today."

The unmarked new champion said he would endeavor to hold the title for as long as he could by fair fighting.

Can't say exactly what I'm going to do yet. I'm going to put in a five weeks' engagement with Mr. Rickards in sparring appearances at the Tivoli. After that I'll think about what else I'm going to do. Of course, I've got to fight Sam Langford at the National Sporting Club in London on Derby night. That match is arranged.

Johnson was willing to fight Squires if Bill could come up with a £2,000 side bet ($10,000). Continuing, Jack chuckled, "That is, mind you, in case he still wants to." It was not likely that Squires would be able to find a backer for that amount, given how unbeatable Johnson had looked against Burns, a man who had defeated Squires three times.[998]

The *Referee* disagreed with Johnson's claim that he did not try to beat Burns quickly. It felt that had he the power to end matters, he would have done so.

From what I saw of Johnson's punching, I feel satisfied it had no extraordinary amount of sting in it. He battered away at Burns' head with uppercuts, crosses, hooks, and short-arm jolts, and walloped that

---

[998] Johnson intended to pick up a considerable sum of money on the vaudeville stage, earning $1,750 per week, or more than what most folks made in a year. His five-week Sydney music hall act under Harry Rickards' management would consist of bag punching and demonstrating his training methods. The engagement would commence the following week.

Sam Fitzpatrick said that after the vaudeville concluded, Johnson would return to America. Fitzpatrick confirmed that Johnson would fight Squires for a side bet if Bill really wanted the fight and was confident enough to put up the money.

much-talked-about left rip to the stomach and ribs times out of number, and when they were clinched Johnson on dozens of occasions literally pounded away at the ribs and kidneys as if he were endeavoring to smash a rock, and still the sturdy little Canadian had strength and fight in him, despite the great shaking he got right at the outset of the battle.

The writer said Johnson was the best two-handed fighter at close quarters seen in many a day, but his left was not the terrible thing one had been led to believe it was, at outfighting especially. Peter Jackson's left jab was harder. Johnson's best weapon was his right, and he did most of the damage with it, as demonstrated by Burns' swollen left side of his face.

The *Referee* said the fight neither proved nor disproved the assertion that Johnson had a yellow streak, because he was more or less the master of the situation throughout the bout, and therefore had not been put to the test. Conversely, Burns had proven his grit because he took the pounding and kept fighting. This writer wanted to see Johnson in with someone of his own height, weight, and strength.

Sam Fitzpatrick said, "Well, I told you so. Johnson is the greatest heavyweight in the world. He won easily. Burns got very few really solid punches home. Tommy proved a better fighter than I thought him." He was also quoted as saying, "As for Johnson, he proved to be what I knew he was – the greatest fighter in the world. He had no trouble throughout. Burns hit him only one solid punch from the start."

According to one local source, the day after the fight, Burns' face was only slightly puffy, and showed few traces of the bout. He practically had recovered from the effects of the severe contest. Burns told the *Daily Telegraph*,

> I wasn't so badly punished as people imagined, and I am sure Johnson could never have stopped me inside the 20 rounds we agreed to go over; he is by no means a hard hitter. I am as well as ever I was about the body, despite those frequent visitations from the black fellow's left, particularly.

> There is very little doubt in my mind but that I might have won had the police not interfered, for I could feel Johnson tiring, and hope had risen high within me at the moment. In the majority of my other fights I took much more real punishment than Johnson administered, and then succeeded. ...

> I had begun to pick up from about the tenth round, and though Johnson landed a great number of blows I felt that I only had to bide my time.

Burns explained how and why he lost.

> That blow in the first round settled my chances. I would have given Johnson a great shaking but for his lucky punch. A round or two later

my ankle went badly, and endeavoring to hide the fact handicapped me a lot, because of the pain. No, I never really felt myself. I was lighter than I have been for a long time. He can't hit worth a cent. He had me dazed all the time, and got his favorite blows home often, but I was there till the police interfered, and would have been there through the other six rounds, and might have won, because the big nigger was tiring fast.

Burns also said,

I am satisfied with the decision given by the referee. It was fair beyond all doubt. I tried to win. Even up to the time when the police stopped the contest I thought I had a chance; but I fully realize that up to that stage I was fairly beaten. I do not wish to say a single word to depreciate Johnson's victory. He won, and I lost, and he deserves the credit.

Having said so much, however I may point out one or two things in justice to myself. I gave away 2 ½ stone in weight. That is a very big handicap. My actual weight on entering the ring was 11 st. 12 lb. [166 pounds]. That is 8lb or 10lb below my proper fighting weight. The fact is that I was too anxious in regard to this contest, and I overtrained. I did too much work, with the result that I was stale. ... [T]hen, at an early stage of the fight I had the misfortune to strain the sinews of an ankle. That handicapped my footwork — a very big handicap to me, because I depended upon it so much. ... It was very painful.... It was a great difficulty, but I still thought I had a chance, and, notwithstanding those handicaps, I would have fought on had the police not interfered.

However, Johnson won, and deserves the full credit of his victory. I did my best under the disadvantages, and I believe that those who saw the fight fully recognized my efforts.

I stated before this fight that win or lose I would retire from boxing. That I intend to do; but I would like to say to the people of Australia how much I appreciate their kindness. I am very thankful to them. Their generosity, both before and after the fight has greatly touched me. ... I intend to reside in Australia and become an Australian citizen.

Burns said he had promised Johnson early the previous year that he would fight him as soon as all the top-notch white fighters in sight were accommodated, and he had honored his promise.

I need not have done that. As you are aware, the color line was drawn very strongly by all modern champions who preceded me, and had I followed suit none could or would have raised the slightest objection.

When I signed to meet Johnson I did so with my eyes open. I knew his size, bulk, skil, and strength, but I had faith in the powers that landed me where I was, and, while anticipating the toughest job of my career, it seemed to me that it might be faced successfully.

Johnson is exulting, is he? Well, that's nothing to his credit, and will certainly give him no lift in popular favor, nor add lustre to the title he has won from a man half a foot shorter and much over 2 stone lighter than himself. Men who should know tell me Johnson weighs every ounce of 15 stone [210 pounds], but I am not offering any excuse. I only wish to show that there's nothing for the big fellow to throw bouquets at himself about. ...

No; I certainly did not think I did myself justice in the fight. That punch in the first round had me rattled badly for a time, and I never really recovered from its effects. Again, on one or other of the earlier rounds the ankle you saw Patsy Burke rubbing just now screwed under me, and I couldn't get a fair rate of speed on. Once, after letting the trouble spell for a while, I tried to liven the pace, but had to give it up, the pain was so severe. ...

I am through with boxing, and no one is more pleased than Mrs. Burns.

No, there's no one man in sight with a chance against Johnson; he is sure to hold his position for a long time if he takes after himself.

Although Burns thought Johnson was capable of holding the championship for a long time, he hoped that a white man would regain the title.

Mrs. Burns remarked, "Tommy couldn't have been very bad when he ate half a chicken and some broth at his tea, and an hour afterwards enjoyed six ice creams." They both attended church that morning, the day after the fight.

Larry Keating, Tom's brother-in-law, said he had never seen such a big crowd in his life, and he had attended Jeffries-Fitzsimmons and Jeffries-Sharkey. Tom deserved credit for the way he fought, giving up nearly three stone. "I have seen men in far worse condition than Tommy was on Saturday pick themselves up and win. Burns would have fought on. Johnson's right-hand punch to the jaw in the opening round was a terrific blow; it practically settled matters. But Johnson was too big for Burns and that proved the main factor in the result."

Tom's manager W. C. J. Kelly echoed that Tom was up against great odds with the size difference, the terrible blow in the opening round, and the subsequently sprained ankle in the 5th round, which greatly affected his speed and footwork. Yet, "a strong boxer always has a chance of winning till he is counted out."

Burns' trainer Pat O'Keefe said, "Johnson is a great fighter or he wouldn't have beaten Tommy as he did, in spite of his big pull in weight, height, and reach." He said Burns had been beaten fairly and squarely.

Bill Squires said Johnson was a good big man and Burns a good little man.

> Johnson is certainly a better fighter than lots of people think he is; but I must say Burns is a game chap. He takes a lot of punishment and is pretty hard to silence. From what I saw, it was a very fair fight on both sides and as far as generalship goes there was not much to choose between them. Burns is certainly a brainy fighter, and I can see Jack Johnson fights with his head quite a bit, too. Johnson is a big puncher, too, and he is a better in-fighter than people give him credit for. He hits awfully hard in close quarters, getting his punch in with a lot of stuff behind it.

Squires also said,

> A good big man ought to beat a good little man, and that's the summing up of the whole thing. Johnson showed better than a lot of people thought him. Tommy is as game as anyone, and there was just as good generalship on his side as on Johnson's. Jack puts a lot of weight behind his blows, but I'd like to fight him. He won't have the weight and the height over me much.

Squires' trainer, Jimmy Russell, said, "I knew Johnson to be a very stiff proposition, and thought Tommy Burns was up against it, but he is such a shrewd fighter and so plucky that it did seem as if he might get through. Burns wasn't near done, when the police interfered."

Bill Lang, who had fought both, said, "There was only one in it right through. Burns never had a hope of hurting Johnson, for the big fellow seemed to take everything just as Burns wanted to give it to him without worrying. This chap is a champion, I tell you, and I don't see where he is going to be beaten." He also said, "Johnson didn't trouble about his punching. Jack is the best one I know anything about, and someone to lick him will want a heap of finding."

Snowy Baker said it was a case of the big man being too big. "It was the strength and height that did it. There was only one in it all the time, and that was the big fellow."

Well-known referee Harry Beckett said, "The better man undoubtedly won. Burns did not have a look-in from the world 'go.' Burns was never in it." Beckett had refereed the Johnson-Felix bout, and had gauged the probable winner of the big fight. "When I saw Johnson beat Felix I marked him a great fighter. I thought then, and said so, that the black man was the best big boxer the world ever saw – giving Mace in. He is a second edition of Griffo as regards cleverness."

Larry Foley said it simply was a matter of strength, weight, and height telling its tale. "Johnson's strength and terribly long reach were with him all the time, but his in-fighting gave him the day. He was too big for Burns, and gave him such terrible punishment in the first round that he never seemed to recover."

L. H. Nathan, who refereed Burns-Squires III in Australia, was very high on Johnson, who was too skillful, big, and strong for Burns.

> Johnson is undoubtedly the cleverest big man I have ever seen in the ring, even excelling Burns at in-fighting – the latter's strongest point. So far as condition went, I am of the opinion that Burns was the better of the two. He took terrific punishment with the greatest pluck that any man could possibly show, and it was a pity that his skill was not equal to his gameness and powers of endurance. Every round belonged to Johnson, and the end would assuredly have come in the round the contest finished or at latest the next.

Mr. J. Bain, who worked with James Brennan, the one who had first brought Johnson to Australia, said,

> Johnson passed the remark to me last week that he would make Burns look like a sparring partner. And he did, too. It was absolutely one-sided from the jump. And the in-fighting – you ought to have seen it. "I thought you called yourself an in-fighter, Tommy," Johnson would say as he'd hustle Burns and upper-cut him with his right, and then push him off, and hit him again. There's nothing more to be said. The result was never in doubt from the first blow. Burns was absolutely outclassed.

Charles Campbell, an old Gaiety Athletic Club sport, echoed the sentiment that they were both clever but Johnson the cleverer, and he also had the physical advantages. Burns was game, but did not have a look-in.

> He would have stood up to Johnson again had the police not interfered, but my own opinion is that the battle was won much earlier.

> I think there is no man alive at the present time who can beat Johnson. I think he is the real champion, and well deserves the honor he has won. He is the cleverest boxer I have seen since Peter Jackson, and the man who beats him will have to be a top-notcher. I think that now he has got the championship he will hold it for a considerable period.

Frank Hewitt said, "I've seen them all. Tommy Burns worked when he should have been resting, and went into the ring palpably stale, and was consequently beaten before he started. Jim Brennan made no secret that Johnson would win. He told me on Friday morning it was a certainty."

Fighter Arthur Cripps said, "It surprised me. The men fought a good fight, but there was only one in it all the time. Burns showed uncommon grit, and Johnson proved too clever as well as too big."

Professor William Miller, the veteran boxer/wrestler, said, "Burns was never in it, but only Johnson's weight and height beat him. The black is a good puncher with the right, but his left is nothing to rave about."

Despite the prohibition against the admission of women, half a dozen eluded the gatekeepers by disguising themselves as men or hiding by using an overcoat and hat. Jack London (author of *The Call of the Wild* and *White Fang*) and his wife occupied ringside seats. Apparently, his wife was given special permission to attend. Mr. London said, "You seem to reverse the position here. In America, ladies attend the fights, but don't go to see the men training. Here you let them go to the training quarters, but bar them out at the finish. It seems strange to me. Now, it's up to somebody to dig Jim Jeffries out of his alfalfa patch." Mrs. London said, "I didn't think Johnson would have done as well, judging by his form in training. But Burns, well, he's the grittiest man I've ever seen."[999]

Jack London famously reported back to America for the *New York Herald*. He wrote, "The fight! There was no fight. No Armenian massacre could compare with the hopeless slaughter that took place in the Sydney Stadium today. It was not a case of 'Too Much Johnson,' but of all Johnson. A golden smile tells the story, and a golden smile was Johnson's." London said it was like a Colossus and a toy automaton, a playful Ethiopian against a small and futile white man, a grown man cuffing a naughty child, a monologue by Johnson, "who made a noise with his fists like a lullaby, tucking one Burns into his little crib in Sleepy Hollow." Johnson was the undertaker, gravedigger, and sexton at Burns' funeral. When Johnson smiled, a "dazzling flash of gold filled the wide aperture between his open lips, and he smiled all the time. He had no trouble in the world."

When he entered the ring, Burns looked pale and sallow, as if he had not slept all night, or as if he had just pulled through a bout with fever.

Johnson refused to fight unless Burns removed the tape from his skinned elbows. "Nothin' doin' till he takes 'em off." The crowd hooted, but Johnson smiled his happy golden smile.

When the fight began, the monologue began. With an exaggerated English accent, Johnson said, "Tahmy," and talked throughout the bout when he was not smiling.

The fight barely had begun when Johnson caught him with a fierce uppercut, turning Burns over completely in the air and landing him on his back. "There is no use giving details. There was no doubt from the moment of the opening of the first round. The affair was too one sided." It was a case of a plucky, determined fighter who had no chance for a look-in at any moment of the fight.

There was no fraction of a second in all the fourteen rounds that could be called Burns'. So far as damage is concerned Burns never

[999] *Sydney Daily Telegraph, Sydney Morning Herald, Melbourne Age*, all December 28, 1908; *Sydney Referee*, December 30, 1908; *Sydney Bulletin*, December 31, 1908.

landed a blow. He never phased the black man. It was not Burns' fault, however. He tried every moment throughout the fight except when he was groggy. It was hopeless, preposterous, heroic. He was a glutton for punishment, and he bored in all the time. ... Burns had no opportunity to show what he had in him. Johnson was too big, too able, too clever, too superb. He was impregnable. His long arms, his height, his cool seeing eyes, his timing and distancing, his footwork and his splendid outsparring and equally splendid infighting kept Burns in trouble all the time. ... He was smothered all the time.

As for Johnson, he did not have to extend. He cuffed and smiled and smiled and cuffed, and in the clinches whirled his opponent around so as to be able to assume beatific and angelic facial expressions for the benefit of the cinematograph machines.

Not Burns, but Johnson, did the infighting. In fact, the major portion of the punishment he delivered was in clinches. At times he would hold up his arms to show that he was no party to the clinch. Again he would deliberately and by apparently no exertion of strength thrust Burns away and clear of him, and yet again he would thrust Burns partly clear with one hand and uppercut him in the face with the other, and when Burns instantly fell forward into another clinch would thrust him partly clear and repeat the uppercut.

Once he did this five times in succession as fast as a man could count, each uppercut connecting and connecting savagely, but principally in the clinches Johnson rested and smiled and dreamed. This dreaming expression was fascinating. It seemed almost a trance. It was certainly deceptive, for suddenly the lines of the face would harden, the eyes would glint viciously and Burns would be frightfully hooked, swung and uppercut for a bad half minute. Then the smile and the dreamy trance would return as Burns effected another clinch. ...

Johnson play-acted all the time, and he played with Burns from the gong of the opening round to the finish of the fight. Burns was a toy in his hands. ...

"Hit here, Tahmy," he would say, exposing the right side of his unprotected stomach, and when Burns struck Johnson would neither wince nor cover up. Instead, he would receive the blow with a happy, careless smile, directed at the spectators, turn the left side of his unprotected stomach and say, "Now here, Tahmy," and while Burns hit as directed Johnson would continue to grin and chuckle and smile his golden smile.

One criticism, and only one, can be passed upon Johnson. In the thirteenth round he made the mistake of his life. He should have put Burns out. He could have put him out. It would have been child's play. Instead of which he smiled and deliberately let Burns live until the gong sounded, and in the opening of the fourteenth round the police stopped the fight and Johnson lost the credit of a knockout.

But one thing remains. Jeffries must emerge from his alfalfa farm and remove that smile from Johnson's face. Jeff, it's up to you.[1000]

However, Jeffries said he had no intention to come back:

I refused time and again to meet Johnson when I was in the ring and now I am out of it for good. I'll never fight again, no matter who holds the championship. Of course, I may spar for a benefit or something of that nature, but as for appearing in a ring to fight, never again.

Tommy Burns' mistake, the one big mistake of his career, was in letting Johnson have a chance to fight for the championship. When I was holding the title I refused to let him have a chance, although I knew I could defeat him. I surely would not return to the ring to fight a negro now.

The best man won in that Australian fight, and I can't for the life of me see who Johnson is going to fight now. ... All night last night and all day today I was besieged with telegrams asking me if I would re-enter the ring. I answered them now as I have answered hundreds of times before. I have fought my last ring battle. I am through with the game.

Another paper quoted Jeffries, who previously had hinted that he might come back if necessary to prevent a negro from holding the championship, as saying that he would not come back unless and until there were no more qualified top white contenders with a good chance to dethrone Johnson. He said men like Kaufman and Jim Barry were to be reckoned with. "I don't expect to fight him until he has disposed of all the legitimate aspirants for the championship. ... [I]t is not for me to butt in when there are men who probably can defeat Johnson."

Regarding the championship fight, Jeffries said he thought Johnson would win unless they had tied his hands and legs. He expected no other result, though he had not expected the fight to last so long. Of course, this contradicted several of his prefight statements predicting a Burns victory.

Jeffries criticized Burns for crossing the color line. "Burns had no right to fight Johnson for the heavyweight championship."

Like Jeffries, contradicting his pre-fight prediction, John L. Sullivan also claimed that he was not surprised, saying, "The fight came out very much as I had predicted. Even with his victory over the so-called champion – though in my opinion Burns never was the champion – the negro can't assume that title, for the present day bouts cannot be styled prizefights." He

---

[1000] *New York Herald*, December 27, 1908.

also said, "I can't see where Johnson will be given a high position in the opinion of the general American public. I am of the opinion that the American public is fast losing interest in the manly art of self-defence."

Burns' mother, Mrs. Kuhlman, was gloomy. She said, "I didn't want him to fight Johnson, and his wife tried to persuade him not to fight a colored man."

Stanley Ketchel said he would challenge Johnson. "Until now I have always said I would draw the color line. Now it is different. I had expected to meet Burns in San Francisco July 4th." The fight's outcome was a surprise to him, for he had expected Burns to win.

Joe Gans had predicted a Johnson victory. He said, "I told you so."

> I know and have boxed with Johnson, and the result bears out my prediction. There is no doubt that he will hold for a long time the heavyweight championship, for I do not think that there is a man living who can defeat him. He has cleverness equal to the best James J. Corbett ever showed, and besides he is a giant in stature and as quick as a flash.

He further said,

> I boxed him in New York eight months ago and saw in him the science, endurance, and strength which he maintained in today's battle. ... He has demonstrated he is the best colored fighter in his class in the world.[1001]

Several American newspapers had same-day or next-day reports, based on cabled dispatches.[1002]

The *New York Herald*, *New York Daily Tribune*, and *San Francisco Examiner* had similar reports. They said Johnson badly whipped and outclassed Burns, who was unable to defend himself from the savage blows. Johnson won from the opening bell.

There was a great deal of kidding indulged in, Johnson doing so as a result of his confidence, while Burns' talk was the result of sheer desperation. Johnson treated Burns' punches as a joke. When Burns landed, Johnson would laugh outright in his adversary's face, make sarcastic remarks; turn to his corner and wink. Johnson deliberately took some of Burns' best blows just to show the public that he was not yellow and that Burns could not hurt him. They continued hurling abusive epithets towards one another. In the 9th round, Jack said, "Come on, Tommy; swing your right!" Burns responded by calling him a "yellow dog."

Burns was almost out in the 13th round. He was in such bad condition at the end of the round that the police threatened to interfere. They consulted

---

[1001] *Chicago Tribune*, December 26, 1908.
[1002] *New York Herald*, *New York Daily Tribune*, December 26, 1908; *San Francisco Examiner*, December 26, 27, 28, 1908; *San Francisco Chronicle*, December 26, 27, 1908; *Los Angeles Times*, December 27, 28, 1908.

about stopping the unequal affair. Burns was interviewed, and declared that he was still quite strong and eager, and implored the police not to interfere. McIntosh pleaded with the police to give him one more round.

After Johnson dropped Burns in the 14th round, when Tom rose after eight seconds, Johnson rushed in to end it. Burns was tottering and unable to defend himself, so the police, realizing that he was a beaten man, mercifully swarmed into the ring and stopped the battle in order to save the champion from suffering unnecessary punishment and the humiliation of a knockout. "Burns could not possibly have lasted the twenty scheduled rounds." Johnson won the bout on points.

Afterwards, Johnson appeared fresh, while Burns' eyes were badly puffed and his mouth was swollen to twice its normal size. The Canadian fought a game battle full of indomitable pluck, but was no match. Tommy admitted that his rival was too much for him.

The *Los Angeles Times* reported that after the fight, Burns was in good condition, except for discolorations about his eyes and a swollen jaw. It wasn't broken; only badly bruised. Burns claimed to have made $200,000 in his career, more than enough to allow him to retire.

Some years before, Sam Fitzpatrick had come into the *New York Herald* office and tried to obtain attention for Johnson, whom he called a wonderful, remarkable boxer with the physique of a giant who someday would be world champion. He finally had been proven correct. "Long and lithe, he is as graceful as a dancing master and as true as an arrow in placing his blows. Especially deft is he with his left hand, and few boxers, unless they have great skill, are able to keep the big black man from beating their faces to tatters."

Regarding rumors of a potential fix before the fight, McIntosh said that Johnson would not have chased Burns nearly 12,000 miles to get a match and then throw it, and Burns would not lay down to a negro. There seemed to be such concerns before every big fight.

The *San Francisco Chronicle* said Burns had kept Johnson waiting for more than sixteen months, and paid for it in the ring. Johnson's victory was spectacular and decisive. "He toyed with the pudgy white man; held him at arm's length and beat him where and when he pleased."

The day after the bout, Johnson showed no signs of the battle, but admitted that he was sore about the stomach. Jack said, "Burns got to me often, but he did not hurt me at any time. It was when the muscles around the stomach got sore this morning that I felt the punches. I can lick him any day in the week, but I must say he's a game enough fellow." He also said, "I never doubted the issue from the beginning. I knew I was too good for Burns. I have forgotten more about fighting than Burns ever knew. I was sure I would win from the start. The referee was fair, and I have no complaints to make."

Regarding potential future matches, Johnson seemed to be in much the same position as Jeffries was before he retired. Jeff was out of the question, for he insisted time and again that he was retired and would never fight again. "Even could he be induced to re-enter the ring, it would take a year to put the big Californian in shape."

Jim Coffroth wanted to promote a fight between Al Kaufman and Johnson. However, his manager Bill Delaney declared that he never would let Al fight a colored man, and would draw the color line. Bill said, "When I managed Jeffries, I would not allow him to fight Johnson or any other negro, and the same holds good for Kaufman." However, some thought he might change his mind, given that he wanted Al to be champion.

Another potential contender mentioned was Langford, who "might be induced to fight Johnson, but the majority of people would remember that Langford is a middleweight." Sam would have all the same size handicaps that Tommy Burns had. Plus, Johnson had handled Langford easily once already. "Langford is in no haste to get a fight with Jack Johnson, although he declares that he is not unwilling to meet the big heavyweight, and that when the proper time comes he will sign articles."

Furthermore, Langford's manager Joe Woodman said that they were chiefly trying to obtain a middleweight championship fight with Stanley Ketchel, whom Sam most wanted to fight. Woodman said, "Langford wants to be the middleweight champion of the world, and a little later it will be time enough to talk business with Johnson or any heavyweight in the business. ... We want to whip Stanley Ketchel, acquire the middleweight title and then go after the boys higher up in the division." Hence, the Langford team showed no eagerness to fight Johnson, despite the fact that both parties previously had signed to fight in London.

The next day, the *Examiner* said that some were discussing the possibility of a Burns-Johnson rematch. It quoted Johnson as saying,

> I can lick Burns every day in the week and twice on Sunday. Of all the men I have ever met he is the easiest. I could have knocked him out much sooner had I wished. I wanted to take a good revenge and had my satisfaction. Fight him again? Well, count me in.

> Now that the shoe is on the other foot, I just want to hear that fellow come around whining for another chance. I'll give him a real live taste of my match-making genius. See how he will relish the chances of a beating for bare expenses. Ha! Ha!

Johnson was prepared to give Burns the same financial treatment that he had received.

Burns was quoted as saying,

> I have no excuses. Johnson beat me and beat me fairly, I will acknowledge. I did not think he had such a punch or things might have been different. I made up my mind to rush him from the start and was somewhat careless. That first punch won the battle for him. I was not myself at any time after that. Indeed, I have little recollection of what followed. Though he beat me and beat me badly, I still believe I am his master.

If Johnson is not too arbitrary, I might meet him again. I do not have to fight; but I feel the sting of defeat doubly because of the fact that my fall allowed a colored man to usurp the title for the first time in ring history.

W. W. Naughton of the *Examiner* said the betting world had forgotten the negro's fighting power. Burns was the favorite in spite of the fact that most everyone felt that Johnson was the greater ringster. "The real truth of the matter is that the fighting part of the men was lost sight of." Burns was called a "common or garden variety of money hog, nothing more."

Naughton believed that Jeffries had made a big mistake by not fighting Johnson when he had the chance, when he was at his best. It would be quite difficult for him to refuse to do so now.

> My, what a jacketing is in store for big Jim Jeffries. He took time by the forelock to the extent of declaring ahead of things that no earthly consideration could induce him to give battle to Johnson, but if Jeff remains of that way of thinking in the face of the clamor that will arise and the pressure that will be brought to bear, he is more adamantine in his resolves than I have any suspicion of.

> And even those who are not hounding him to gird his loins and give the negro battle are blaming him for existing conditions.

> "Why did Jeffries refuse to fight this fellow when Jeffries was at his best," they are saying. "If he had done so Johnson would have been put aside for all time, and he wouldn't be going around, as he is now, saying, 'I licked Tommy Burns, and I can lick Jeffries, too.'"

> And meanwhile, Johnson is the undisputed world's champion and fully entitled to the title, black skin or no black skin. He is of the world all right. If you prick him he will bleed, and if you hit him hard enough he will tumble. And if there's any one can lick Johnson, say the smart fellows, it is Sam Langford, also colored.

> Verily the negro is a power in pugilism at present. And it might have been worse. Had Johnson and Langford happened along when Dixon, Gans and Walcott were on top, championship row would have looked like a spade flush.

However, when told of the $50,000 offer to fight Johnson, Jim Jeffries said, "I have said that there was not one chance in ten million that I would ever fight again, and I meant it. Why can't the public take what I say as final and let it go at that?" Already Jeff was annoyed by the persistent attempts to get him to agree to fight Johnson. One writer said, "Jeffries is fat and out of condition, and it is thought by his associates that he never could be got into condition to enter the ring, even if he had the inclination to re-enter."

Yet, for whatever reason, the possibility of Jeff coming out of retirement would be a hot ongoing topic of discussion. Jeffries would be hounded to death by a white press and public that could not stand the idea of a black man holding the world heavyweight championship.

Jimmy Britt said the result was as he expected. Other than from a financial point of view, he thought the match had been a mistake to make on Burns' part. He said Johnson had whipped better men than Burns, and had done it repeatedly. "While I do not like to see a negro whip a white man, I did not think Burns had a ghost of a chance against Johnson."

The *Los Angeles Times* said all the available pugs were afraid of Johnson. The white scrappers would have to fight each other in elimination contests, although doing so was not likely to develop a white man capable of making any kind of a showing against the new champion. Johnson "could probably beat any two of them in the same ring, the same night." He was in a class by himself. The only white man who approached Johnson was big Al Kaufman. However, what Johnson would do to him "would be a crime."

Mike Schreck said that Burns' loss served him right. He was glad to see Burns get a dose of his own medicine.

> When he was champion he would not give any of us big fellows a chance and now he is on his knees begging for another whack at the negro. It must certainly be humiliating to the puffed-up ex-champion. I have several witnesses that I can produce with affidavits at any time, that he wanted me to post $5,000 for a fake fight with him not so very long ago, the money to become the property of Burns in case I did not carry out the part he had picked out for me. He suggested that I pretend to be knocked out some time after the tenth round.

When they learned that a black man was now world heavyweight champion, most blacks were jubilant. Speaking about black folk in the "black belt" of Chicago, the *Chicago Tribune* wrote,

> Of course all wore expressions of unmixed joy, but there was a total lack of arrogance in their manner towards white men and many of them politely tried hard to conceal the delight they could not help showing.

> It was purely pride of race that made them joyful, for in the matter of betting not a single wager of any size, as far as could be ascertained, was made by them upon the fight. The betting men were not at all confident of Johnson's ability and kept away from the affair altogether.

> With Langford, however, it would have been different. Sam is the colored boxer who commands the confidence of the race and many an argument was advanced that Sam was a better man than Johnson.

Both the black-owned *Freeman* and the *Richmond Planet* offered black newspapers' perspectives. The *Freeman* wrote, "Dopesters who made the spread that Jack Johnson would show a yellow streak, lay down, and do a hundred other things to lose his fight with Tommy Burns are now speechless." The *Planet* said Burns believed Johnson would lose his courage if hit in the stomach, but Johnson had proven him wrong. Tom soon learned that Johnson was as stout-hearted as any elite fighter, and there was no quit in him.

Johnson was like a cat playing with a mouse. Jack jabbed, slammed, hammered, and mercilessly slaughtered him, showing the cleverness of Corbett and the punishing powers of Fitzsimmons.

Burns was game, for although he was no match and dropped several times, dazed and reeling, with his face puffed to twice its size, he continued trying in the unequal fight. In the 14th round, Johnson decked Burns with a stiff right to the jaw. He rose at 8 but was careening around the ring. The police interfered and stopped it in order to prevent unnecessary punishment and save Tom from being savagely beaten into helplessness.

Without hesitation, McIntosh awarded the fight to Johnson, for it had been agreed that if the police interfered that a decision should be rendered on points, and Johnson had been Burns' master throughout. Although technically it was a referee decision victory, regarding the bets, Johnson's win would be treated like a knockout. Today, it would be called a technical knockout.

Jack Johnson was the era's most wonderful fighter, regardless of what some said. "The sports are beginning to see now why Burns held off Johnson so long before making a match with him."

Most top fighters had used the silly color-line as a subterfuge to avoid meeting Johnson. He had whipped everyone who dared to meet him. There was nothing but admiration for Jack's patience in obtaining his title shot. Frustrated at how he was avoided by the champions and top contenders, Johnson once said, "It makes my blood boil to think that I am being treated this way by men who are supposed to have courage. I can whip any of these heavyweights if they give me a chance. They are trying to keep me down, but it won't last forever. They'll have to recognize me some time, and then you'll see Mr. Johnson on top." Jack Johnson was the first of his race to win boxing's top prize - the world heavyweight championship.

Before the fight, Burns said, "I will win. I know that Johnson is a clever boxer, but I will show him before the fight is over that I am gamer than he, and I expect to knock him out."

Johnson said, "I will beat Tommy. He's a good one, but not in my class. Bet your money on me."

After the fight, Burns said,

> I did the best I could and fought hard. Johnson was too big and his reach too great. That punch he landed in the first round won the battle for him. Had the fighting been allowed to go on I might have had a chance, but I am willing to acknowledge that I was in bad shape when the police stopped the bout. I am through with the fighting game now forever. I would like to fight Johnson again, but am not

willing to wait for months for the chance. He will, of course, go after the easy money now.

The *Freeman* reported that Burns was a sorry sight. His eyes were almost closed; his face was puffed up to almost twice its size, while his body bore evidence of the heavy punishment. Johnson hardly showed any marks.

Johnson said, "It was even easier than I expected. ... I really could have put Burns away earlier in the battle, but I knew I had him whipped after the first round and simply played with him. I am now ready to fight anyone who aspires to the title and won't draw the color line."

Jack Johnson had chased Tommy Burns around the world and had been forced to accept the vastly smaller end of the purse. However, it proved to be a wise business move. Now that he was champion and in a position of power, he would have no trouble obtaining good purses, and the money would not be split so unevenly. The man who for years had agreed to any financial terms, including ones unfair to him in order to get fights, was finally in the position to do the dictating. Now he had the chance to make a fortune.

Most experts picked Johnson to win, but there were constant unwarranted fears that he would be bought off and throw the fight. Some speculated that by making the financial terms so strongly in his own favor, Burns would have the leverage to induce Johnson to throw the fight, perhaps offering another $10,000 if he would do so. However, Johnson might have double-crossed him even if he had agreed. Of course, that was just rumor and speculation.

The *Planet* said it was difficult to think of a fighter who was qualified to face the new champion. Langford had declared that he would not go out of the middleweight class to take on such a formidable adversary. Kaufman and Ketchel previously had drawn the color line, but might withdraw their objections to fighting a black man in order to recover the title for the white race. Some suggested that Jeffries would emerge from retirement to put the title back in the hands of a white man. "This is scarcely considered probably, for Jeffries has been inactive so long that he realizes that he could never come back. In his prime Jeff would have been a redoubtable foe for the Negro, but he is now slow and overweight, and would be hacked to pieces by the speedy Negro, who is the fastest big man the ring has known since the days of James J. Corbett."

The *Freeman* opined that Johnson would have no trouble obtaining lucrative fights now that he was champion. It said,

> Prejudice is so great against a black man holding the championship title that there are many right at this moment who would take a chance, be it ever so desperate, to grasp the title from Johnson because of his shady hue. Even Jeffries, who once declared he would never again fight a battle, is considering a go with Johnson. Prejudice, that's all. ...

Johnson deserves recognition and will get it. He is the most wonderful fighter of the day, regardless of what the gossipers say in reference to his being a second rater. He is a giant in size and in knowledge of the fistic art, as perfect as any. Although he has lost fights to some second raters, they dare not fight the Jack Johnson of today with the idea of defeating the champion.[1003]

The *Richmond Planet* noted the joy of colored folk, which was the greatest since Emancipation. The result had great meaning to them.

No event in forty years has given more genuine satisfaction to the colored people of this country than has the signal victory of Jack Johnson. … The cause of this is not to be found in the satisfaction of knowing that a colored man can whip a white one, for that species of superiority could be demonstrated in every day life, due primarily to the physical superiority of the average citizen of color, who is bent in the performance of his exacting duties, which tend to develop bone and muscle, but in the superior skill in training to that definite degree of excellence that caused the white referee to decide that Johnson, the Negro, won on points scored as well.

The further cause for this satisfaction is the action of President Roosevelt and the War Department in black-listing 167 soldiers in the United States Army and of creating the impression that they were inefficient, lawless and a positive menace to the service. The report from the United States Military Academy at West Point, N.Y., coupled with this victory at Sydney, Australia will tend much to rehabilitate the race in the good opinion of the people of the world.[1004]

Two days after the fight, on Monday evening, December 28, the fight films were shown on a big screen at the Sydney Stadium, and close to 8,000 people watched. The films showed the men in training, ball punching, shadow boxing, and sparring. The crowd cheered Burns and groaned at Johnson's every move and counter move.

During the fight, when the reels were being changed, the screen was momentarily lowered, and Burns spoke.

Ladies and gentlemen, I am very sorry that many, perhaps all of you, saw me beaten by Johnson for the championship. While admitting, however, that the negro fought well, I may say I was by no means done up in the fourteenth round, and had the police not interfered I think I might have won. I would consequently like to have another try to win the championship.

[1003] *Freeman,* January 2, 1909.
[1004] *Richmond Planet,* January 9, 1909.

Burns received cheers. Someone in the audience called, "Don't go yet, Tommy. Have a look at the pictures and see how the big fellow scored; it will be useful in the future." The popular Burns was cheered everywhere he went.

Tom offered a novel opinion as to why the police stopped the fight. "He thinks Johnson's seconds spread a report that his (Burns's) jaw was broken, and that was the reason the police stepped in. He would like to meet Johnson again, but it rested with his wife, as he had promised her that Saturday's fight would be his last."

The remaining pictures were then shown, except one or two reels were missing. It was said that they had not yet been developed. Every evening that week, the films were shown at the Stadium.

Today, only selected rounds and portions of the films have been found or are still preserved. Most versions do not show the knockdowns, either because they were deleted for political and racial reasons, or because it just so happens that those were the portions of the films which disintegrated.

The films show that Johnson would launch quick, somewhat long swinging lead punches as he quickly stepped in with fast footwork. He would then place his hands on Burns' arms and shoulders so he couldn't get off with anything substantial. Johnson remained relaxed as Tommy attempted to punch. Burns mostly focused on the body. Johnson didn't move much, standing with his legs bent, well balanced and alert, occasionally feinting or pumping in a long stiff left jab. His clear height and reach advantages allowed him to stand his ground on the outside, choose when to attack, and catch and smother Burns. He kept his hands down, but from a distance, knowing when to punch, lift his arms to block, or reach out to grab. Between rounds, their attendants waved towels to cool them off.

Generally, on the inside, the patient Johnson ripped vicious fast right uppercuts and occasional sweeping hooks and rights, followed by grabbing and pushing Tommy off. The much smaller Burns leaned in too much, leaving him vulnerable to the sneaky fast right uppercut.

Burns often lightly bounced and moved around and Johnson moved forward and initiated more than one might have been led to believe from the written accounts. Jack calmly stalked him and decided when to step in with a blow. Burns also clinched quite often, more than the written accounts indicate.

Other times, Johnson stood still and awaited Tom's attack so that he could time it by striking first, or he would counter the lead blow.

Throughout the bout, Jack smiled and spoke to Tommy, teasing and taunting him in retribution for all the insults that Burns and others had hurled at him. Inside the ring was the one arena where Johnson could seek revenge for the race hatred he endured outside the ring. Both Johnson and Burns were known as "mouthy" fighters who liked to engage in insults. This was in part strategic, in order to upset the opponent, make him tense and fail to think, or destroy his confidence.

In the 8th round, after firing right uppercuts and left hooks in combination, Johnson clinched and smiled at ringsiders, not appearing to be bothered by anything Burns did on the inside. Johnson spoke to Burns and ringsiders both. After the round, Johnson smiled at Burns and waved at him. It was his way of letting Burns know that nothing he did was affecting him.

Overall, the pace was slow, with Johnson throwing one or two punches at a time before they clinched. He fired combinations only occasionally.

However, in the 14th round, after methodically breaking down Burns with a poised attack and allowing Tommy to wear himself out trying to land, Johnson began attacking with some ferocity. Johnson staggered and overwhelmed Burns with a hard nonstop series of punches, mostly right uppercuts and left hooks to the head, but with a couple rights as well (and possibly even dropped him, although it remains unclear whether this sequence was before or after Burns was decked). At that point, things were not looking good for Burns, so the police terminated the bout to save him from further punishment and the impending knockout, though the limited existing films do not show this. Burns clearly was beaten and outclassed.

Hugh McIntosh would sail for London and take with him the moving pictures of the fight.

In the days following the fight, as Johnson whirled about Sydney in his motor car, he met with a mix of cheers and hoots.

Starting just two days after the fight, Jack exhibited before large crowds at the Tivoli on Monday December 28 and Tuesday the 29th. His appearances there also were greeted with both cheers and hoots. Johnson demonstrated some ball punching and then sparred 2 rounds each with Bob

Bryant and Bill Lang. Bryant rushed more energetically than Lang, but Johnson did not exert himself with either man, for he did not need to do so.

Johnson deposited a 2,000-pound wager at the *Referee* office, for a match with anybody who cared to cover it.[1005]

The *Examiner* noted that notwithstanding reports which quoted Tommy as saying that he was beaten fairly, that Johnson was too big and strong for him, Burns had changed his tune. Burns' telegram to Naughton said, "Johnson's seconds influenced police in stopping contest. Was strong; had chance, as Nelson with Gans. Johnson was tiring. Pictures show everything. Willing to fight Johnson again. Can beat him. Pictures arrive in two months. Tommy Burns."[1006]

Johnson felt that the newspapers were biased for Burns and had skewed their reports against him in Tom's favor. They mostly printed his taunts, but did not print what Burns had said to and about him.

> Johnson complains that he has not been treated fairly by some newspapers. They have, he says, been a little bit too one-sided, and language that Burns has used to him and about him has never been allowed to get out, while a few things he has said playfully have been made the most of, to make it appear as if he did not play the game fair. "The strange thing the public did not notice," observed Johnson, "is that Burns has always been saying he wanted a big man against him – that the bigger the man the better. Well, he got a big man on Saturday, and bless me if he did not turn round and say then I was too big. …. I will fight him again on the same terms as he fought me, and that is £6,000, win, lose or draw. I think that is only fair, as he was allowed to get his own terms."[1007]

Johnson said he would give Burns a rematch if he really wanted it.

> I will fight him any day this week he likes. I have sent £2000 to the *Referee* office today, and let him cover that and come along and fight. I am ready to give him another beating. I am going away to Melbourne on Sunday night to keep my engagements, but if he likes I'll fight him in private or public on Saturday night. It seems to me that all Burns is doing is trying to turn the public against me, and what have I done? I asked for a fair deal, and that is all I have ever asked for. Burns goes about whining and crying about his ankle and about his family, and he would do certain things if it were not for family reasons. Well, I did not come out here to fight his family. I came here to fight him and I beat him, and I can beat him again any time he likes to come on. Why, do you know what Burns said to me in Mr. McIntosh's room before the fight? He said, "You used to be a great fighter, but

[1005] *Referee*, December 30, 1908 *Melbourne Age*, December 29, 1908.
[1006] *New York Herald, San Francisco Examiner*, December 29, 1908.
[1007] *Melbourne Age*, December 29, 1908.

you're not now. I have been kidding you for two years until I got you where I wanted you. Now you are all shot to pieces, and I will lick you." "Well," I said simply, "is that so?" But Mr. McIntosh will tell you that Burns used language to me, and raised a chair to strike me. Mr. McIntosh had to interfere, and then Burns, when he was prevented with the chair, tried to hurl an inkstand at me.

When told of what Johnson said, Burns said he would cover Johnson's money and fight him as soon as his ankle got well. Regarding the row in McIntosh's office, Burns added, "Johnson said things to me that it would not do to print. He said something about my wife in the ring, and if the public had heard him they would have lynched him."[1008]

Burns subsequently visited the *Referee* office and discovered that Johnson's money had not been deposited there as claimed.

Regardless, Hugh McIntosh said that there was no likelihood at all of Burns and Johnson meeting again for a good while, if ever.

On December 29, Burns signed an agreement with Harry Rickards for a five-week engagement at £225 weekly, commencing the following Monday.

When asked about what sort of man Sam Langford was, Johnson replied, "A really good man, but I will beat him just as easily as I beat Burns. Langford has beaten all the best men we have over in the States, and I think he is the best man in America."

Johnson said he had won only a couple thousand pounds on the Burns fight, and he had no interest in the pictures. He likely was going to take Bill Lang with him to London, as well as his trainer, Duke Mullins. He had opened up negotiations with Mr. Bettinson of the National Sporting Club for Lang to fight Moir.

A report out of London said that as a result of Burns' lack of popularity in England (owing to his financial demands for a Johnson fight), sportsmen were glad at the result.

A New York correspondent informed Australians that white Americans disliked Johnson's victory and were depressed by it, but negroes were greatly delighted and jubilant, welcoming the announcement with great enthusiasm.

American reporters were saying that the way Johnson dominated proved that Burns had no right to be classed with the best champions of the past. Perhaps Johnson was just that good, as opposed to Burns being that bad. Race politics affected interpretation.[1009]

Jack O'Brien said he wanted to fight Johnson. "Jack O'Brien is the most likely man to fare at all well with the colored man." However, "the general opinion seems to be that no man at present known in the pugilistic world has a chance of beating the big black fellow."[1010]

[1008] *Daily Telegraph, Melbourne Age*, December 30, 1908.
[1009] *Daily Telegraph*, December 29, 1908.
[1010] *Daily Telegraph, Melbourne Age*, December 30, 1908.

At the Stadium on the evening of December 30, 1908, a crowd of 10,000 witnessed a fight between Rudolf Unholz and Frank Thorn for the Australian lightweight crown. Johnson accompanied Unholz, and when he entered the ring, the crowd hooted. During the 2nd round, Burns put in an appearance, and he was cheered for some minutes. After the 8th round, Johnson left the grounds, and as he made his way to the exit, he was the recipient of hoots that were mingled with some cheers. Unholz lost a 20-round decision to Thorn.

An advertisement for Johnson's exhibitions at the Tivoli said he would exhibit ball punching, shadow fighting, various training exercises, and 4 rounds of boxing with sparring partner Bill Lang.[1011]

In its weekly analysis, the *Sydney Bulletin* was not sure whether to give Burns credit for being able to absorb vicious bombs, or to criticize Johnson for lacking power.

> Either Burns is an abnormally tough man or Johnson's blows are not nearly so heavy and forceful as they appear. Had they been what they seemed, Burns' jaw must have assuredly been broken. He received 17 right smashes on exactly the same spot in the first three rounds – and was not knocked out. Talk about the man with the iron jaw! Had those blows been anything near what they looked like, iron itself should have been bent if not broken by so much accumulated shock. He received 19 right-hand smashes over the left kidney, and was not bent, let alone broken in two. After the fight the place showed practically no sign of injury. Therefore, either Burns is gifted with

---

[1011] *Sydney Morning Herald, Sydney Daily Telegraph*, December 31, 1908.

tissue like no other man on earth, or Johnson's tremendous-looking smashes are more showy than effective.

The *Bulletin* felt that Burns fought the wrong fight, and might win a rematch. Burns should have played a waiting game and allowed Johnson to do the work, so that Johnson's "moral fibre would crumple up" once he tired out.

> He should have allowed Johnson to do all the running after the title and all the hard work, and have saved his strength to administer the *coup de grace* when the black man was worn out. Of course, he could only play that game if his speed was superior to that of Johnson; and on Saturday's showing it wasn't, although in the training operations it certainly was. Even in the fight, and despite the sprained ankle, we saw flashes of velocity, and those flashes were good to see. Had there been a steady blaze, Burns would not have received the punishment he did.

> Notwithstanding the published opinions of the critics, headed by Jack London and Larry Foley, this writer fails to see that there is any particular reason why Burns should not have beaten Johnson.

The *Bulletin* felt that despite the size differences, if Tommy had fought a smarter tactical fight and moved about and allowed Johnson to do the work and tire himself out, that Burns would have won. However,

> Burns was not as he ought to have been. His nerves had given way; he was over-trained, and had gone stale. To beat Johnson, or even hold his own, it was necessary that he should have superior speed, should keep off, and should lead the inky antagonist round the ring for a dozen rounds or so till those thin spindle-shanks of the top-heavy blackfellow began to tire. Also, it was necessary that he should give up all idea of hurting Johnson's head. That head is too hard, anyhow, and too far away, and to reach it he had to come within the bear-like grip of a man who was strong enough to hold him and twist him into any position which was most suitable for the receipt of damage.

After Burns got dropped in the 1st round, he forgot all his "beautiful maxims, and threw all his own published tactics to the winds." Instead, Johnson followed Burns' methods. He let Tom do the leading and hard work. He succeeded in making him wild and turning him from a wary, cunning master of ringcraft to a rushing fury who offered a target for Johnson's long drives and tremendous right swings and crosses. Burns even forgot his crouch.

Another *Bulletin* writer gave Johnson a lot more credit. He said,

> I have no love for the Black Agony, but feel insulted as to my intelligence at the majority of the press reports, which give Johnson little credit as a fighting expert, but simply state that he was 'too big

and too strong' for Burns. The fact is, he was in a still greater degree too good a boxer for his adversary. From the world 'go' the ink-bottle spilled himself all over Burns and put his fire out. The spectacle was comparable to that of a gorilla toying with a light meal. ... If Lang or Squires is allowed to have a go at the present champion there'll as likely as not be an elegy-writing job for some white poet shortly after. Johnson is (1) a better boxer than Burns or anyone else in these parts; (2) he is as strong as a cast-iron elephant. And there is no earthly sense in burking these obvious facts.

Another said that Burns was in obvious denial about his defeat, having come up with several excuses.

When Burns was interviewed, immediately after the fight, he said that Johnson was 'too big and strong for him.' A while later he said he was unlucky in spraining his ankle. Then he began to feel better and talked of wanting another fight, because he hadn't been really beaten at all. Then he sent a wire to the *Sporting Life* in London, stating that Johnson's seconds had asked the police to stop the fight, lest Johnson (who was tiring) should be beaten, he (Burns) being full of vigor when the police interposed. By this time Tahmmy has probably persuaded himself that he knocked Johnson out in the first round.

Fighters' egos made them masters of denial and spin.

James J. Jeffries had declined to fight "Massa Johnsing." The *Bulletin* understood why. He was fat inside and nearly 20 stone in weight (280 pounds).

By the time he got all that surplus tissue off him he would be a very limp man to try and recover a championship. The chances are that if he did fight Johnson, Jeffries would get an unholy licking, unless the brown champion turned cocktail. And James is making so much money in other ways that he is under no necessity to earn a big purse by taking a walloping from any negro.[1012]

[1012] *Sydney Bulletin,* January 7, 1909.

CHAPTER 28

The Aftermath and the Start of the White Hope Era

In the wake of the Burns-Johnson fight, in Australia, the sport of boxing came under a great deal of criticism, which also brought out its defenders. Much of the ill-will was the result of the fact that a black man had defeated a white man for the heavyweight title, though for some it might have been subconscious. The fact that there was such a great outpouring of anti-boxing sentiment following this particular fight, when other fights had not brought forth such strong feelings, certainly lends some credence to the position. However, the anti-boxing sentiment was also consistent with the general anti-boxing views of many in the religious community. The local Sydney newspapers printed several editorial letters.

Some lamented the influence such a spectacle would have upon the general tone of the community. They argued that boxing bouts served to stimulate the brute in those who witnessed them, as well as the lower class of society to whom the bruiser was a hero. "The effect is to glorify brutish practices in quarters where the brutish instinct is already an anti-social force."

Another letter agreed that boxing fights, newspaper accounts, and cinematographic pictures do infinite harm, for they stimulated the fighting spirit.

Several, including clergy, said the fight and boxing had a degrading, demoralizing, and dehumanizing influence. A reverend said, "A huge crowd of men would evidently have seen a fellow-creature pretty well battered to death if it had not been for the interference of the police. ... The only satisfaction I have in the whole business is that the despised black man proved to be the superior animal."

Another reverend said he was ashamed and humiliated that such a disgraceful exhibition should be held in Sydney.

The *Sunday Observer*, a British paper, characterized the fight as a degrading spectacle.

Some called for the law to prevent fights. They said gloved boxing was far more dangerous and brutal than old-time bareknuckle bouts. Decent people of the community were "filled with loathing and disgust at what has transpired," and hoped that the Ministry would do its duty in connection with "the fighting evil," as it had with the evils of gambling and drinking.

One countered, "The men were not forced to fight, and the public were not forced to watch them. It was done at their own free will. In my opinion the people who watched the fight last Saturday saw no more brutality than they would in a game of football."

Several writers noted the inconsistency of those who extolled football and rugby yet condemned boxing, despite the fact that there were many more injuries in the former. "The list of injured at Rugby football reads like a battle, while as for the good feeling in the game, I cannot remember of any instance where a pugilist knocked down and kicked an adversary." Football matches contained so much more brutality than boxing that "if anyone attempted to do what is often done on the football ground in the public street he would be charged with attempted murder."

One writer echoed that there was much more "inhumanity" going on affecting more people on a daily basis than was the case with boxing, yet all the church leaders were silent regarding those more serious concerns while they preached about the evils of boxing. For example, schoolchildren were being "shockingly sweated on dairy farms," "young girls were working in city factories for a shilling and even nothing a week," and "doing heavy manual labour for long hours – practically men's work."

Another agreed that the fight was not brutal if Burns, within 24 hours, was attending church and spending the day picnicking at National Park with his wife. His jaw was not broken as rumored, for he had given a vigorous speech at the Stadium. He had made a great deal of money from the contest and was a well-trained athlete. The crowd was orderly and civilized. "The point which most people seem somehow to evade is that many worse things are in our midst daily than boxing contests for money of which but little notice is taken." Examples included cigarette-smoking.

> The police who were there do not state that they stopped the display for its brutality, but simply because they considered that Burns had no chance of winning, and would only get punished more. They have the power, and in what safer hands could that power be placed? The promoters are prepared to obey the police, not defy, as in the days gone by. The crowd was satisfied that the correct thing was done.

Noted was the fact that Burns had suffered more severe punishment in other contests, including ones in which he had won. Johnson received some blows too, but his color prevented them from showing as prominently as they did on white skin.

Some argued that boxing was good for the Anglo Saxon race in general, for it kept it tough and able to defend itself. "These boxing contests, in the normal man, appeal to that bulldog nature – that desire to be on top, that in our forbears has placed the Anglo-Saxon race in the pre-eminent position it occupies today. To keep this position in the struggle for existence these instincts must be fostered. Real war is a merciless game, and to the strong in mind and body is given the victory." Another argued, "Once the science of self-defence is made punishable by Act of Parliament, then good-bye to the good old adage of Britons never shall be slaves." Yet another wrote,

"Boxing is for manly men (may we have more of them), not for ladies, nor for effeminate degenerates."

One writer flatly opined that race motivated the anti-boxing sentiment.

> They are hurt because a black man has won, and they howl, "Stop the game, the colour line should have been drawn." They are not sportsmen in any sense of the term.

> And there are others whose feelings are lacerated because they know that the downfall of the white man before the coloured will be told, sung, and cinematographed everywhere where there is a black skin; because they know that the victory of black over white will be preached among every coloured race; because they know that the story of the fight will help to promote unrest and sedition; and because they see in the triumph at the Stadium on Saturday last a grinning savage with his foot on the neck of White Australia and exclaiming, "What did I tell yah?"

Hence, the fight's result could have worldwide racial and political implications. Many whites of all nationalities were concerned about the larger symbolic impact, particularly given that most white nations had conquered and colonized most non-white nations, and had instituted racial caste systems. The whites did not want the non-whites to get any ideas that they could be victorious over whites, or that white dominance might not be the result of the natural and automatic order of things.

Another writer agreed that race motivated the anti-boxing sentiment, saying,

> If Burns had won there would have been none of this outcry. ... They listened readily to every bit of idle tittle-tattle about Johnson. ... They speak of Mister Johnson 'spitting venom' when they know well the insults he himself had to submit to. Did Burns not taunt the despised black man? ... Read Burns's book, and you will find the advice there to 'make your opponent wild.' What has Mr. Simpson to say about the gross insult by Burns that Johnson was a cur with a yellow streak? That sounds to me somewhat venomous, but I am old-fashioned. ... I was at the fight, prepared to cheer the best man, irrespective of colour or creed, and when I observed the masterful demeanour of that magnificent black man, dominating the whole of that hostile, one-eyed crowd, I was lost in admiration. ... As soon as the boomed American gets a drubbing, fairly and squarely, then the cry is raised that Australia is in danger from the aggressive coloured races. Not a word of this before the fight.

> Is it not the very limit of hypocrisy? All this new and well simulated abhorrence of prize-fighting is entirely due to the fact that the Burnsites are smarting over the defeat of the courageous man whom they were gulled to believe was supernatural.

A clergyman told his congregation that the Christmas season had been marred by a brutal prizefight with 4-ounce gloves, in contravention of the season's spirit of peace and good will towards man. His statements also demonstrated the cognizance of the significance of race, even in Australia.

> A ray of sunshine was in the hope that the triumph of the colored man over the white would lead here to a truer conception as to the power of the non-European peoples. Believers in a White Australia – and he was one – should recognize the danger and sin in pushing that doctrine to the extreme. The asiastic neighbor as well as the negro had some marvelous capacities when trained, and Johnson was an illustration in one line of action.

Another Australian Methodist clergyman denounced the fight and boxing as a carnival of savagery which had undesirable racial and political implications.

> After all the boasting, bragging, and betting, those 20,000 raving white Australians beheld their white champion beaten by the despised black man. Racial hatred had been set on fire. There would be racial reprisals and recriminations. They have by this deed put back the clock of history. There was not one redeeming feature in the savagery and brutality. God grant that the defeat of Saturday may not be the sullen and solemn prophecy that Australia is to be outclassed and finally vanquished by these dark skinned people who everywhere are beginning to realise their immense possibilities.

One writer urged that Burns' performance had been a credit to the white race.

> We read daily of these 'croakers' of the supposed brutality of this great contest, which proved the grit, determination, and bravery of our white race, in the person of Tommy Burns, and which was an object lesson to all those present to follow Burns's example of pluck and endurance against great odds. ... If he should meet Johnson again I am sure he would make a better show, and use other tactics to regain his title; and I hope, should this ever take place, that he will have the satisfaction of erasing that 'dirty smile' off a 'champion' full of his own conceit and self-importance. Away from Johnson's personality, he is a wonderful boxer, and any man that goes down to him has nothing to be ashamed of.

Noted was the fact that most of the anti-boxing outrage came out *after* the fight, not before it. "This fight should be a lesson to all, for it has exhibited the superiority of the despised black over the white, and brings into satirical relief the law appropriating this large continent to one race only." Another said, "The signal victory for one of the black races may 'give us pause' amid our dithyrambics about a 'White Australia.'"

Yet another writer said, "I should very much like to have seen Burns win, because he is a white man; at the same time I have no antipathy to the dark man. Black people have taken high positions in various walks in life."

Further highlighting the racial aspects of the analysis, one noted,

> There is one phase of this brutal struggle to which I would desire to call attention. Now may we not see why there is such a spirit of hostility to the colored race (the negro race) of the States? All Americans have a true and genuine respect for men like Frederick Douglas or Booker Washington. Allowances must be made for a people so recently recovered from the barbarism of darkest Africa. As we count history our black brothers are only infants in the progress of civilization. The wonder is that so much has been accomplished. ... On the other hand, I have met large numbers of a very different style of man. Johnson is not simply unpopular at the present time, he is the subject of a race hatred much more intense than the Judenhetze of the Germans. Perhaps our white people are to blame for it, for there is, apart from any idea of race superiority, a wisdom in drawing the color line. ... And so have we appealed to savage brute force as a test of superiority, we must be content with the consequences. The black man won in the war of brute force, and the cheer which followed, though restrained, was his due. And yet how humiliating!

The Cabinet would discuss whether to make pugilistic encounters illegal.

Hence, Johnson's victory had social, political, and racial meaning and relevance even in Australia. Australia had its own racial issues, particularly with Aborigines and Asian immigrants. Johnson's victory made Australians' true feelings regarding race more noticeable.[1013]

The *Freeman* reported that there were some schemes afoot in the U.S. to boycott the new champion. It asked, "Why should the Americans be prejudiced against Jack? Is he not an American? And did he not represent America in his fight? Tommy is a Canadian. But still home was and is against Johnson as master of the fighting game."[1014] Clearly, race trumped nationality.

The *New York Age*, another black-owned newspaper, quoted Bat Masterson as saying, "Jack Johnson, like most of the Negroes in this country, is genuinely American, and if we have no white native capable of holding and defending the championship title it is far more in line with American patriotism to have it defended by a black native than an imported American whose skin happens to be white."

[1013] *Sydney Morning Herald, Daily Telegraph*, December 30, 1908. *Sydney Daily Telegraph, Sydney Morning Herald, Melbourne Age*, all December 28, 1908; *Sydney Referee*, December 30, 1908; *Sydney Bulletin*, December 31, 1908.
[1014] *Freeman*, January 9, 1909.

However, for the most part, Masterson's feelings were not shared. The *Age* said,

> Such should be the opinion of every American with reference to the result of the Burns-Johnson bout; but race prejudice is an affliction that renders the patient totally unconscious to merit, justice and fair play. As it is, we have but few white Americans to express through the press such sentiment as 'Bat' Masterson recently made in the *New York Telegraph*. There is Tad, of the *New York Journal*, who is one of the fairest writers that ever pushed a pencil and who has always evinced an inclination to judge a fighter on his merits – be he white or black – but after the two above-mentioned scribes you will find them writing, as does Edgren, of the *New York Evening World*, with a pen that has been dipped in gall and wormwood whenever a Negro fighter is the subject for discussion.

A *New York Telegraph* writer, Charles Meegan, expressed the sentiment of the majority of white Americans when he said,

> Sportsmen generally did not approve of Burns risking the loss of a title to a Negro when the match was made, and the defeated champion will get little sympathy. While censuring Burns, sportsmen do not extend open arms to the new champion by any means. Johnson never will be a popular champion, although his title to the honor is clear and clean. He won it in a fair, hard battle, proving that he is the better man, but the sporting world is not enthusiastic at the spectacle of a Negro occupying the position of its former idols – Sullivan, Corbett and Fitzsimmons.

The *Age* went on to say,

> It is perfectly true that the white sporting world does not relish the spectacle of a Negro being the champion fighter of the world. Every Negro, from the lad large enough to sell papers to the old man who is able to read the paper (if he can read) is happy today, but it is not natural that the white man should be. How many Negroes were happy July 4, when the news, sad to us, came from the West that Joe Gans had been beaten by 'Battling' Nelson? The writer doubts that there was one in America. Then we should not expect to see the white Americans enthuse over a Negro becoming champion of the world. However, we do expect all white Americans to show a spirit of fair play.

The *Age* noted that as a result of race prejudice, the majority of white writers had opined that Johnson had a yellow streak, regardless of whether they truly thought it. Johnson was disproving that theory.

> This same 'yellow streak' is generally attributed to all colored fighters until they prove otherwise in decisive fashion. Johnson has stopped all talk about having a 'yellow streak' by giving Burns such a beating it

took all the police in Australia who could be hastily summoned to the ringside to pull him off his white adversary before a tragedy was committed.

Now the white writers are staying up late at nights trying to figure who can wrest the championship from Johnson. The best they can do is to resurrect a bunch of 'has beens.' They talk of Jim Jeffries, but he drew the color line several years ago after he saw Johnson send his brother to the 'Land of Dreams.' He would be the champion's most troublesome white contender. ...

But Edgren speaks truthfully when he declares Johnson will be champion for some time. In the opinion of the writer, Johnson's strongest rival is a Negro – Sam Langford – and the champion has defeated him.

Several months earlier, at Madison Square Garden, where the Negro Elks were giving an entertainment, Johnson had been introduced as the next champion. In a speech, he had told members that he was going abroad to chase Burns until he secured a match with him, that when he returned he would occupy a position in the pugilistic world that would cause every Negro to feel proud.

He has not only kept his word but has also shown to the world that the theory of a Negro possessing a 'yellow streak' is only a piece of imagination on the part of many white writers, who have unfortunately had too high a regard of the white fighters' ability of ring generalship and too low an opinion of the Negro's. ...

Every time Johnson knocked down Burns a bunch of prejudice fell, and at the same time the white man's respect for the Negro race went up a notch.

Christmas in America was truly a great day for the sable contingent of our great population, and it is natural that we should assume an a la peacock pose whenever we think that for the first time in the world's history a Negro is champion over land and sea.[1015]

Clearly, Johnson's victory uplifted the black spirit and served to refute many racial myths and stereotypes.

In Australia, when Johnson was asked about another fight with Burns, he said,

Another go with Burns? Look here, I don't mind telling you that Burns is absolutely no good. He is popular, certainly, here, but in England and America he is looked upon merely as a bluffer. Why, the man was a mere child in my hands on Boxing Day. I could have beaten him in two rounds, but I was in a merry mood that day, and

---

[1015] *New York Age*, December 31, 1908.

just gave him little bit by little bit so that in case he ever fought anybody else he might know a wrinkle or two. Wasn't that friendly?

Burns beat me! Why, I could beat Burns at any line of sport! We hear daily bulletins about Tommy in his motor-car; how he drove from Medlow or went to National Park and other places in so many minutes! Bah! I met Burns the other day on the road to Tom Ugly's. … The struggle was short. I simply left Tommy as if he'd been walking, and I did so by skillful and superior handling of the motor, as the old crock I was on was decidedly slower than his.

But that is not the only thing I can beat Tommy at. I can beat him at any line of sport he chooses to name. I will deposit £20 that I can wallop him as easily as I did in the fight at cycling, running, swimming, tennis baseball, or golf. At bowls, I am an adept, and would like a match even with any local champion. … As for sculling, I know a little bit there, too. … I feel so sick of hearing the opinions of Sydney people about Burns's merits that I want to show that I can beat him at anything. You ask him, will he play me a game of billiards…? Find out if he will tackle me on the piano, the guitar, the fiddle, or the banjo, or even the concertina.

Johnson said he would remain some weeks in Sydney before visiting Melbourne and Adelaide. "I like this country, and do you know, I spend most of my spare time in the art galleries and the museums. My principal hobby is archaeology. … I'm real interested in aeronautics. I have an idea of a new kind of flying machine, which will turn out, I think, a fine success."

Four days after the championship fight, on December 30, 1908 in Australia, New South Wales Chief Secretary William H. Wood said the government would not allow a Johnson-Burns rematch any time in the near future, and if they did try to fight, the police would interfere and the principals would be arrested and prosecuted. He said the contest had savored more of the brutal and repulsive than of the scientific, and that the American invention of infighting would have to be eliminated if boxing was to continue.

Of course, the government had not been as concerned when it came to less prominent fights that were much more brutal, nor when it was a white fighter pounding on a black one.

Amongst the spectators in attendance at the Burns-Johnson fight were the Australian Attorney General, the state government premier, and the chief secretary. They had no problem with boxing's brutality before the white man was beaten.[1016]

Jack Johnson's victory was viewed along racial lines. It cannot be underestimated how significant an occurrence it was for a black fighter even to be allowed the opportunity to attain the status of heavyweight champion,

[1016] *Sydney Morning Herald, Sydney Daily Telegraph*, December 31, 1908.

let alone win it. Many believed blacks had no right to challenge for the heavyweight championship, regardless of ability. It offended notions that blacks and whites should occupy separate existences and never intermingle in a competitive way. In the U.S., Burns drew criticism for violating the norm.

Boxing champions had been revered as symbols of skill, intelligence, courage, as well as racial and national superiority. For a black man to represent the ultimate symbol of those values was a threat to the existing social order. Either the representative would have to be changed or the image of the champion boxer would have to be altered in order to satisfy the dominant ideology.

Immediately the call for a white man to regain the title and remove Johnson's golden smile began. The "golden smile" in the face of white defeat was a sign of black pride; something blacks were not supposed to show. This began the era of the search for the "White Hope." Johnson noted that the hunt for the white hope began "with ill-concealed bitterness."[1017]

Some even attempted to inoculate themselves from Johnson's victory by claiming that since Jeffries had never been defeated in the ring, he still was the champion, not a black man. Johnson laughed at the idea, saying that when a champion leaves the ring, like a politician who leaves office, he is an ex-champion.

Joe Woodman, Sam Langford's manager, said he would put Langford in with Johnson for a 12-round bout, but not 20 rounds. He would not allow him to fight more than 12 rounds, because he felt that in a 20-round fight, Johnson's superior weight and strength eventually would tell.

> Because of Johnson's giant physique and his ability as a boxer, and as Langford would not go into the ring much over 160 pounds, his natural fighting weight, Woodman doesn't think it would be advisable to send his hard hitting boxer against the champion over a distance longer than the twelve-round mark.[1018]

On December 30, 1908 at the Jeffries arena in Burbank, in the Los Angeles area, before a crowd of about 4,000, 198-pound Al Kaufman stopped 185-pound Jim Barry in the middle of the 39th round, when Barry's chief second tossed the towel into the ring. Barry was all but gone. Kaufman had dropped him in the 37th round with a right to the jaw, and pounded on him at will thereafter, with little return.[1019]

[1017] Johnson, *In the Ring and Out*, at 58-59.

[1018] *San Francisco Examiner*, December 30, 1908.

[1019] *San Francisco Chronicle, Los Angeles Times*, December 31, 1908. Barry had the best of matters for about 25 rounds, but claimed that his hands had given out on him. Others said Kaufman's strength and stamina began to tell, and gradually he wore down Barry. Kaufman had both cheek bones swollen, his eyebrows puffed, and his upper lip bunched up.

Joe Jeannette, who wanted to fight Johnson, was matched with Sam McVea.

Previously, world middleweight champion Stanley Ketchel had claimed that he would draw the color line. He would not fight a black man as long as there was coin in his pocket and potential white opponents. He thought a white man lowered himself in the respect of his associates when he fought a colored man.

However, Ketchel had changed his mind, and continually would make it known that he would cross the color line in order to regain the heavyweight title for the white race. His manager said that he was willing to allow Ketchel to fight a negro, including Langford, if the money was right. However, initially, his manager thought it would be foolish to give up so much weight to Johnson.[1020]

Ketchel said,

> I had made up my mind before the Burns-Johnson fight never to fight a colored man, but now that the great bulk of the American sporting public seems to be incensed over the fact that Johnson is the recognized champion, I am thoroughly willing to fight him, but all other negroes I will bar. ... The fact that I am willing to fight Johnson is proof positive that the talk of my being afraid of Langford is all bosh.[1021]

Ketchel also said, "I was against fighting colored men, but since there is a public demand to dethrone Johnson, I am ready to comply with the demand of the people."

Baltimore's *Afro-American Ledger* noted that Jim Corbett and Bob Fitzsimmons were discussing potentially fighting Johnson. Although not formally challenging the new champion, Corbett said that other than Jeffries, he had the best chance with Johnson. Of course, he was 42 years old and had not fought since 1903, so he was delusional. Corbett said, "I simply feel badly to see a colored man champion." Although retired for several years, his prejudice had him considering re-entering the ring.

Yet, despite his age and inactivity, perhaps blinded by prejudice, several respected experts said that Corbett would have a shot to win if he had six months to train. Those experts included Jim Coffroth, Spider Kelly, Tim McGrath, Tiv Kreling, Sam Berger, Eddie Graney, Eddie Hanlon, Jim Jeffries, and Sam Langford, though Langford's manager Joe Woodman said that Johnson would stop Corbett. They all said that an in-shape Corbett was the cleverest man who ever lived. Johnson had knocked out the totally shot Fitzsimmons already.

> They cannot abide a Negro being the heavyweight champion of the world.

[1020] *San Francisco Chronicle*, December 31, 1908.
[1021] *Tacoma Times*, January 6, 1909.

Ever since the days of Peter Jackson, the white heavyweights have absolutely refused to fight with a colored man. Johnson ran Burns almost all around the world to get a crack at him. Burns said he was going to do things to Johnson whenever he got the chance, but he was no more to Johnson than if he had been a lightweight amateur. Now if any of the big fellows think they have got any fight in them left, all they will have to do is to call up the long distance, and Johnson will, no doubt, be found on the other end listening for what they have to say.

The secret of the whole matter is that these fellows think there will be big money in a chance at Johnson, and it is more that than anything else.[1022]

The *Freeman* noted that there was a tendency to view boxing battles between white and black fighters from a racial standpoint. Hence, whites wanted Johnson dethroned. Johnson had the world stirred up because he was a black man holding the title.

By Jack being master of the heavyweights means that a Negro is at the lead of his class. There seems to be a sentiment predominating whenever a colored man meets a white man in the ring that it is a question of race superiority. ... The fact that it is a question of the best man winning, regardless of color, is lost sight of.

Regardless of the white desire to see him dethroned, the *Freeman's* expert believed that Johnson would be champion for a long time.

Jack Johnson seems destined to hold the heavyweight championship of the world for some time to come. Just think for two years he has been chasing Burns for a match and in return he got nothing but insulting remarks from the 'fourflushing' champion. Burns called him a 'quitter,' a 'yellow dog,' and other choice names. ... Now that Johnson is the champion there isn't a fighter in sight capable of giving him anything better than a reasonably stiff argument.[1023]

The following week, the *Freeman* again observed that the hunt was on to find a white fighter who could dethrone Johnson.

Since Johnson has become champion, the sporting circles have been busy looking over the list of the 'ex's' and fighters of the day...to fight a man who can dethrone the black man. So ambitious are some of the old men of the fistic game to bring the laurels back to the white race that there have been a number of replies of willingness to

[1022] *Afro-American Ledger*, January 9, 1909. *Salt Lake Herald*, *Los Angeles Herald*, January 4, 1909; *San Francisco Call*, January 10, 1909.
[1023] *Freeman*, January 16, 1909.

re-enter the ring on Johnson's return home and defeat the colored wonder.[1024]

Most whites wanted Jim Jeffries, for they felt that he was the only man who could return the title to the white race. In January 1909, Jeffries started some light training under the auspices of vaudeville exhibitions.

Jeffries started saying things that gave the impression that he was at least considering a comeback:

> It's awful to think that a big negro can lord it over all the white men. Maybe I'll see my way clear to make him go yet. I'll never fight again unless I am sure that I can get right. ... I must be in condition to fight if I ever return to the ring. I'd look nice taking a beating from a big coon after fighting my way right to the top. A man is not like whisky. He don't improve with age. I never considered Burns a heavyweight champion. He always looked like a big, well developed middleweight to me.[1025]

How About Johnson?

THE RECEPTION.

JAMES JEFFRIES' PREDICAMENT.

NEW YORK EVENING JOURNAL.

[1024] *Freeman*, January 23, 1909.
[1025] *San Francisco Call*, January 17, 1909.

John L. Sullivan declared that Johnson never would have the prestige of a white champion. Sullivan said it was foolish for anyone to think Corbett had any chance to defeat Johnson. However, "As for Jeffries, if he can get into shape he has a good chance."

Unlike whites, the colored population was wild with enthusiasm over Johnson's victory. They were "dippy with delight." "Negroes are proud of Johnson. He is the Corbett of his race. He is fast on his feet, has a world of strength and knows how to keep his brain clear when in action. He is the best fighter the black race has ever produced, and I think even the white followers of the ring are disposed to give him credit."

The white prejudice against blacks doing well in life was nothing new. At that time, Senator Ben Tillman was giving speeches saying that he was opposed to the higher education of negroes, for it might do away with the white man's supremacy. When addressing teachers at Columbia, South Carolina, Tillman insisted that negroes should not be allowed to have higher education because it meant the final undoing of white people.

The *Afro-American Ledger* noted that there had been 101 lynchings in 1908, the largest number since 1903. 98 of them were in Southern States. The Night Riders had lynched and burned both colored people as well as whites. All were made to feel its power. Even some women had not escaped.

Since the 1905 race riots in which most blacks were driven from the town, the remnants of the Harrison, Arkansas black community lived a tenuous existence. However, in late January 1909, Harrison's transformation into an all-white town was completed by yet another violent riot, brought on in the wake of the January 18, 1909 arrest of a black man on the charge of raping a white woman. The continuing presence and activity of the mob resulted in another mass exodus of black citizens from Harrison. Unprotected, most left on the night of January 28, 1909, and their property quickly was declared forfeit and seized by the town's whites.[1026]

In Australia, the *Sydney Bulletin* said Jack Johnson was the first "colored bruiser" to hold the heavyweight championship, and "already they are talking of his wiping out." Al Kaufman was looked upon as the most likely man to do the job. He was bigger, heavier, and taller than Johnson, "and when the eminent black Methodist meets that white giant we shall see what sort of a losing fight he can put up."[1027]

Sam Langford suddenly wanted to fight Johnson, and said he would fight any man in the world, barring Jeffries, whom he considered the greatest living fighter.

The *Freeman* lamented, "Sullivan has been continually poisoning the minds of the sporting world with the dope that a Negro has no right to hold the championship over white men."

[1026] *Afro-American Ledger*, January 9, 1909; *Freeman*, January 23, 1909.
[1027] *Sydney Bulletin*, January 28, 1909.

The *Freeman* said racial prejudice had caused many to predict Johnson's defeat to Burns as a result of his yellow streak. Now that he had proven them wrong, whites were taking an interest in the heavyweight division as a result of racial envy. It had predicted this would occur in the event of Johnson's victory. It said many whites engaged in all kinds of slander and schemes to deny Jack's ability and right to hold the title.

> So strong has the desire to dethrone the Negro champion become that James J. Jeffries, the only man who is thought to have an equal chance with Johnson – the retired champion who has said "Let it be understood that I will never fight again"; - has been brought back into the limelight as being the last hope for white supremacy. There is now no doubt of Jeffries' intention to re-enter the ring. He is getting into shape while on a theatrical tour. Believing it to be a certainty that the big Californian will step back into the roped square, although he strenuously denies the charge, the fans have already begun to wager on the prospective bout.

Johnson's victory was making Jeffries big money, for it brought him before the public more strongly than ever before. He could make good money giving stage exhibitions, owing to the fact that he was a potential prospective opponent for Johnson, one who had a chance to win back the title for the white race. That made folks want to see Jeff more than ever.[1028]

The *Sydney Bulletin* noted the inconsistency of Americans, particularly its reporters. One minute they were hard on Burns for not fighting Johnson, and the next they were hard on him for having fought him. It was a matter of better watch what you ask for.

> The Americans are marvelous people. Three months ago, they were yelping at Tommy Burns with one united yelp to drop his nonsense about the color line, and face Brother Johnson like a man. Jim Jeffries yelped in this regard as loudly and as persistently as any of them. When the U.S. heard that Thomas was really going to meet the Black Agony they were pleased. They started forecasting the result of the event, and many of their forecasts favored the white champion. Jim Jeffries, for example, went into details on the subject, and gave Burns the decision six weeks before the fight on his superior footwork, his infighting ability, and his gameness. Now the fickle James says this, which is what 90 per cent of the other fight fans in Hamland say: -

> "Tommy Burns' mistake, the one great mistake of his career, was in allowing Johnson the opportunity to fight for the title. I refused time and again to meet Johnson while I was holding the title, even though I knew I could beat him. I would never allow a negro a chance to fight for the world's championship, and I advise all other champions

---

[1028] *Freeman,* January 30, 1909.

to follow the same course. Tommy Burns has been vastly overrated as a fighter. This has always been my belief."

Of a verity, N. Brusso spoke sooth when he remarked after the Johnson chastisement, that "Americans have no use for a beaten man." They are the world's worst sportsmen.[1029]

In early February, Roscoe Johnson, one of Jack's brothers, who lived in New York and was about 19 years old, died of pneumonia.[1030]

On February 12, 1909 in New York City, W. E. B. Du Bois founded the National Association for the Advancement of Colored People (NAACP), which was dedicated to promoting equality of rights for colored people and eradicate caste or race prejudice.

Jack Johnson cabled a friend in the U.S., saying that he would leave Brisbane, Australia on February 17 and head for Vancouver, Canada. He would then tour the Canadian colonies before returning to the U.S.[1031]

Jim Corbett said it would be a crime for Jeffries to meet Johnson any time soon, for the ex-champ had taken on a lot of weight during his years of inactivity. He thought that Jeff would need at least one to two years of work to be prepared properly.

> There is too much at stake – a Negro has the championship and it must be won back by a white man, to whose race it belongs. Jeffries must be right in every sense of the word before he takes the chance, and he can not hope to be right until he undergoes a long course of training. The American public and the fight promoters are making a big mistake by endeavoring to force Jeff into a match.[1032]

Jeffries had signed a contract to appear on the vaudeville stage for 20 weeks at $2,500 a week, which was big money. He would do some light sparring with Sam Berger and have time to do a little training and think over a potential fight with Johnson.

Jeffries said he feared no man, and felt that he had nothing to fear from Johnson, but wanted to be sure that he could get right again before agreeing to take him on. Jeff said,

> Who said that interest in the boxing game was on the wane? After my experience of the last week I am led to believe that the gloves are more popular with the public than ever before. It may, of course, be possible that the fact that Jack Johnson, a Negro, holds the heavyweight championship of the world is responsible for the Queensberry revival. ...

[1029] *Sydney Bulletin*, February 4, 1909.
[1030] *New York World*, February 4, 1909.
[1031] *Tacoma Times*, February 4, 1909.
[1032] *Freeman*, February 6, 1909.

Everybody and his neighbor appears to believe that it is their honorable duty to ask me if I am going to fight again. ...

W. W. Naughton and other experts have been kind enough to place themselves on record as saying that I have nothing to fear from Jack Johnson. That just about expresses my sentiments. I don't fear the Negro or any other being who walks on two feet.

My performances with Berger during the first week of my theatrical engagement has been most satisfactory to me. ... I am fat, no mistake about that.

It will take many a long run on the road to get rid of this fat and to put my mind in anything like first-class condition. My general health is of the best, and if anybody thinks that I haven't got my punch left, let him come up and put the gloves on with me.

Followers of pugilism are an inconsistent lot. When I was in this city last summer...everybody was criticizing Tommy Burns because the Canuck would not fight Jack Johnson. ... Now these fellows are howling out of the other side of their mouths, and they are howling longer and louder than ever. "This man Burns is a disgrace to the ring," they say. "He should never have crossed the color line. Had he refused to meet Johnson, the white people would never have been disgraced by having a Negro as the heavyweight champion."

I am wondering day by day what my fate would be were I to meet Jack Johnson and be defeated. The sporting world is crying at me now to go in and fight the Negro. In some instances the criticism hurled at me is not of the kindest nature. I get letters calling me a coward and all that sort of rubbish. I pay no attention to them. I have Burns' example in front of me.[1033]

Jack Kipper, a partner with Jeffries in a Los Angeles saloon business, thought that Jeff would fight again if he could condition himself.

And, believe me, that negro will be the worst whipped coon that ever crawled from the ring when Jeffries gets after him. If it took the black man, with all his vaunted cleverness and tremendous hitting power, 14 rounds to stop Tommy Burns, a man by no means as large as he is, what will Jeff do to him?[1034]

Eventually, that question would be answered.

Jack Johnson's story continues in:

In the Ring With Jack Johnson – Part II: The Reign.

[1033] *Freeman*, February 6, 1909.
[1034] *Tacoma Times*, February 10, 1909.

Appendix: Jack Johnson's Record

(Up to the Championship)

Born: March 31, 1878, Galveston, TX
Died: June 10, 1946, Franklinton, NC, age 68

W Jackie Morris	Galveston, TX	street fight
W Dave Pierson	Galveston, TX	street fight

? Johnson alleged he knocked out his brother-in-law in the 3rd round of a bout for money.

?	Bob Thompson	Galveston, TX	ND 4

Johnson earned money for lasting 4 rounds with Thompson.

1895?

?	John Lee	Galveston, TX	KO 15, 16, or 17
?	Curlin	Galveston, TX	W

Johnson sparred in New York with Joe Walcott and Bob Armstrong.

Jul 25	Julius Mack	New York, NY	NC

Police stopped the bout while in progress.

Johnson was a sparring partner for a black fighter named Scaldy Bill Quinn in Massachusetts and/or New York.

Johnson became Joe Walcott's sparring partner for two months in Boston.

1897

Sep/Oct Johnson likely served as a sparring partner for Joe Choynski.

Nov 1	Charles Brooks	Galveston, TX	KO 2

Scheduled 15-round bout for the Texas middleweight championship.

Nov 20	Ed Johnson	Galveston, TX	KO 5

1899

Apr 19 Johnson won a battle royal at Springfield, IL. One fighter was named George Williams.

Johnson sparred with Joe Bonansinga.

May 6	Klondike John Haines	Chicago, IL	L 5 or 6

Johnson dropped Klondike in the 2nd round, but grew fatigued and held incessantly until the police lieutenant requested that the referee stop the bout. Hence, it was somewhat of a DQ or TKO. There is a divergence in the reports regarding what round the bout was stopped.

Johnson sparred with Dan Creedon, Tom Tracy, and Frank Childs. He possibly also sparred Jack Root and Tommy Ryan.

Johnson claimed to have fought in Pittsburgh. He might have also served as a Joe Walcott sparring partner for a couple of months in Boston around that time as well.

Jul   Johnson sparred with Kid Conroy in New Haven, Connecticut.

?	Dan Murphy	Waterbury, CT	KO 10?

Some later sources reference a possible KO3 Horace Miles and W15 Bob White, dates, locations, and order unknown.

A later source references a possible knockout over Charley Strong in 7 rounds at Trenton, N.J., date unknown.

1900

In January, Johnson was in Chicago.

Mar 21	Jack McCormack	Galveston, TX	ND 15

Apr 9	William McNeill	Galveston, TX	ND 4

Apr 20	Jack McCormack	Galveston, TX	WDQ 6

Jun 25	Klondike John Haines	Galveston, TX	D 20

Pre-fight agreement of a draw if both on their feet at the end.

?	George Lawler	Hot Springs, AK	KO 10 ?

This fight likely took place sometime after the 9-8-1900 Galveston flood.

?	Howard Pollar		W

One source listed an unconfirmed draw with Al Weinig in 20 rounds at Hot Springs, Arkansas. Another also listed an unconfirmed knockout over Thunderbolt Smith in 3 rounds in Memphis.

Nov 28	Josh Mills	Memphis, TN	TKO 7

Mills failed to answer the bell starting the 7th round.

Dec 27	Klondike John Haines	Memphis, TN	TKO 14

Klondike failed to answer the bell starting the 14th round.

1901

Jan 14	Jim Scanlan	Galveston, TX	D 7

Originally called a no contest, the referee subsequently called it a draw. He had terminated the bout early owing to excessive fouling. Regardless, Johnson was the superior pugilist.

Feb 25	Joe Choynski	Galveston, TX	LKOby 3

In April and May in Colorado, Johnson sparred with Tom Sharkey.

Apr 26	Billy Stift	Denver, CO	D 10

May 7	Bob Armstrong	Cripple Creek, CO	ND 4

Aug 14	Mexican Pete Everett	Victor, CO	D 20

Oct   Johnson allegedly engaged in a tryout with black welterweight Dixie Kid in Los Angeles, CA.

Nov 4   Hank Griffin   Bakersfield, CA   L 20

Dec   At Croll's Garden in Alameda, in the San Francisco area, Johnson was acting as a sparring partner for Kid Carter.

Dec 27   Hank Griffin   Oakland, CA   D 15

1902

Jan   Jack Johnson sparred and trained with Jack Root.

Feb   Johnson sparred with Billy Woods to prepare for the Kennedy match.

Mar 7   Joe Kennedy   Oakland, CA   KO 4

May   Johnson sparred with Billy Woods to prepare for the Jack Jeffries fight.

May 16   Jack Jeffries   Los Angeles, CA   KO 5

Jun   Johnson sparred Bob Jones in preparation for the Hank Griffin bout.

Jun 20   Hank Griffin   Los Angeles, CA   D 20

Oct 21   Frank Childs   Los Angeles, CA   TKO 12
Colored Heavyweight Championship

Oct   Johnson trained and sparred with the Dixie Kid and Black Muldoon for the Gardner fight.

Oct 31   George Gardner   San Francisco, CA   W 20

Johnson sparred with Dan Long for a short period of time in preparation for the Russell fight.

Dec 4   Fred Russell   Los Angeles, CA   WDQ 8

1903

Jan   Johnson sparred with Hank Griffin to prepare for the Martin fight.

Feb 5   Ed Martin   Los Angeles, CA   W 20
Undisputed Colored Heavyweight Championship

Feb   In preparation for the McVey fight, Johnson sparred with Jack Lavelle, Jack Laplace, and Tom Kingsley.

Feb 26   Sam McVey   Los Angeles, CA   W 20
Johnson said that while in Los Angeles he met and trained with world featherweight champion Young Corbett II (a.k.a. William Rothwell), when Corbett was preparing for his fight with Terry McGovern, which took place in San Francisco on March 31, 1903.

Apr 16   Sandy Ferguson   Boston, MA   W 10

May 11	Joe Butler	Philadelphia, PA	KO 3

Jul 31	Sandy Ferguson	Philadelphia, PA	W/D ND 6

Some said Johnson won, while others called it a draw.

Oct 27	Sam McVey	Los Angeles, CA	W 20

Dec 11	Sandy Ferguson	Colma, CA	W 20

1904

Feb 6	Sandy Ferguson	Philadelphia, PA	NC 5

Feb 15	Black Bill	Philadelphia, PA	WND 6

Apr 22	Sam McVey	San Francisco, CA	KO 20

Jun 2	Frank Childs	Chicago, IL	W 6

Sep	Johnson was sparring with Jack "Twin" Sullivan.

Oct 18	Ed Martin	Los Angeles, CA	KO 2

1905

Mar   Johnson sparred with Billy Woods, Denver Ed Martin, Jim Haywards, and Jim Gallagher to prepare for the Hart fight.

Mar 28	Marvin Hart	San Francisco, CA	L 20

Apr 25	Jim Jeffords	Philadelphia, PA	KO 4

May 2	Black Bill	Philadelphia, PA	KO 4

| May 9 | Joe Jeannette | Philadelphia, PA | WND 3 |
| May 9 | Walter Johnson | Philadelphia, PA | KO 3 |

Jun 26	Jack Munroe	Philadelphia, PA	WND 6

| Jul 13 | Morris Harris | Philadelphia, PA | KO 1 |
| Jul 13 | Black Bill | Philadelphia, PA | WND 3 |

Jul 18	Sandy Ferguson	Chelsea, MA	WDQ 7

Jul 24	Joe Grim	Philadelphia, PA	WND 6

Oct	Johnson sparred with Jack "Twin" Sullivan in Los Angeles.

Nov 25	Joe Jeannette	Philadelphia, PA	LDQby 2

Dec 1	Young Peter Jackson	Baltimore, MD	WND 12

Johnson won every round, but had contracted to give Jackson the larger share of the purse if he could last the distance, which he did. No formal decision was rendered.

Dec 2	Joe Jeannette	Philadelphia, PA	WND 6

1906

Jan 16	Joe Jeannette	New York, NY	WND 3
Mar 14	Joe Jeannette	Baltimore, MD	W 15
Apr	Johnson was sparring with Jack Murray.		
Apr 16	Black Bill	Pittston, PA	KO 6 or 7
Apr	Johnson sparred with Jack Murray and Joe Walcott to prepare for Langford.		
Apr 26	Sam Langford	Chelsea, MA	W 15
Apr 28	Sam Langford	Boston, MA	EX 3
Jun 18	Charles Haghey	Gloucester, MA	KO 1
Jun 18	Jimmy Murray	Gloucester, MA	EX 5
Sep 3	Billy Dunning	Millinocket, ME	D 10
Sep 20	Joe Jeannette	Philadelphia, PA	WND 6
Nov 8	Jim Jeffords	Lancaster, PA	WND 6
Nov 26	Joe Jeannette	Portland, ME	W/D ND 10

1907

Jan 24	Johnson arrives in Sydney, NSW, Australia.		
Jan 28	Peter Kling	Sydney, NSW	EX 3

Johnson and Kling would exhibit each night in conjunction with the exhibition of the Burns-O'Brien fight films.

Feb 1	Mick Dunn	Botany, NSW	EX 3
Feb 1	Larry Foley	Botany, NSW	EX 3
Feb 2	Peter Kling	Sydney, NSW	EX 3
Feb 9	Jack Thompson	Sydney, NSW	EX 3
Feb 19	Peter Felix	Sydney, NSW	KO 1
Feb 22	Sid Russell	Sydney, NSW	EX 4
Feb 28	Ed Starlight Rollins	Melbourne, Vic.	EX 4
Feb 28	Sid Russell	Melbourne, Vic.	EX 4
Mar 1	Tom Fennessey	Melbourne, Vic.	EX 3
Mar 2	Dick Kernick	Melbourne, Vic.	EX 3
Mar 4	Bill Lang	Melbourne, Vic.	KO 9
Jul 17	Bob Fitzsimmons	Philadelphia, PA	KO 2
Aug 28	Kid Cutler	Reading, PA	KO 1

| Sep 12 | Sailor Burke | Bridgeport, CT | WND 6 |

Oct 16   In preparation for the Flynn fight, Johnson sparred with Denver Ed Martin, his primary sparring partner. He also on occasion worked with Joe Willis and Jim Haywards.

| Nov 2 | Jim Flynn | Colma, CA | KO 11 |

1908

Apr   Johnson sparred with Joe Gans in New York.

Apr 27   Johnson arrives in London, England.

Johnson engaged in several sparring exhibitions with Fred Drummond in London in late May, during early June in Neuilly, France, and back in London again in mid-to-late June and early July.

In June (?) in London, Johnson gave a 4-round exhibition with Al McNamara. He also exhibited with Curly Watson.

| Jul 31 | Ben Taylor | Plymouth, ENG | KO 8 |

Two-minute rounds.

Johnson continued giving exhibitions in England and France.

Sep 16   The Johnson-Burns fight is made and signed by the principals.

After arriving in Australia in late October, for the next two months, at various times Johnson sparred with Bill Lang, Joe Grim, a man named Williams, Ranji Burns, Paddy McTigue, Bob Bryant, Soldier Thompson, and Arthur Cripps.

| Dec 26 | Tommy Burns | Sydney, NSW | W/TKO 14 |

Referee stopped fight at request of police. Decision rendered, pursuant to prefight agreement.

On December 28, Johnson began an exhibition engagement in Sydney, which also would extend to places like Melbourne. Johnson sparred 2 rounds each with Bob Bryant and Bill Lang.

Jack Johnson's record continues in *In the Ring With Jack Johnson – Part II: The Reign.*

Bibliography

Primary Sources

Afro-American Ledger
Anadarko Daily Democrat
Bakersfield Daily Californian
Baltimore American
Baltimore Sun
Bangor Daily News
Billings Gazette
Boston Daily Globe
Boston Evening Standard
Boston Herald
Boston Post
Brooklyn Daily Eagle
Butte Intermountain
Butte Miner
Chicago Daily News
Chicago Chronicle
Chicago Times-Herald
Chicago Tribune
Chicago Record-Herald
Clarion-Ledger
Colorado Springs Gazette
Colored American
Cripple Creek Evening Star
Daily Alta California
Daily Eastern Argus
Daily Illinois State Register
Daily Inter Ocean
Daily Picayune
Day
Denver Daily News
Denver Post
Denver Times
Detroit Free Press
Evening Times
Freeman
Galveston Daily News
Gloucester Daily Times
Grand Forks Daily Herald
Guthrie Daily Leader
Hawaiian Star
Houston Free South
Lancaster Daily Intelligencer
London Sporting Life
Los Angeles Examiner

Los Angeles Express
Los Angeles Herald
Los Angeles Times
Louisville Courier-Journal
Louisville Times
Manchester Courier
Manchester Guardian
Melbourne Age
Melbourne Argus
Memphis Commercial Appeal
Minneapolis Tribune
Muskogee Cimeter
National Police Gazette
Newark Evening News
New Haven Evening Register
New York Age
New York Clipper
New York Daily Tribune
New York Herald
New York Journal
New York Sun
New York Times
New York World
New Zealand Truth
Oakland Enquirer
Oakland Times
Oakland Tribune
Oxnard Courier
Penny Illustrated Paper and Illustrated Times
Philadelphia Evening Bulletin
Philadelphia Inquirer
Philadelphia Press
Philadelphia Public Ledger
Philadelphia Record
Pittsburgh Courier
Pittsburgh Press
Reading Eagle
Referee
Reno Evening Gazette
Richmond Planet
St. Louis Republic
St. Paul Appeal
Salt Lake Herald

San Francisco Bulletin	*Sydney Referee*
San Francisco Call	*Tacoma Times*
San Francisco Chronicle	*Times-Democrat*
San Francisco Evening Post	*Topeka Daily Capital*
San Francisco Examiner	*Topeka Plaindealer*
Saskatoon Star-Phoenix	*Topeka State Journal*
Scranton Republican	*Toronto Evening Telegram*
Seattle Post Intelligencer	*Trenton Times*
Seattle Republican	*Utica-Herald Dispatch*
Sporting Chronicle	*Washington Bee*
Springfield Journal	*Washington Post*
Sunday News Tribune	*Washington Times*
Sydney Bulletin	*Wilkes-Barre Record*
Sydney Daily Telegraph	*Wilkes-Barre Times*
Sydney Morning Herald	*Williamsburg Journal*

Secondary Sources

Corbett, James J., *The Roar of the Crowd*, (G.P. Putnam's Sons, NY, 1925).

Fleischer, Nat, *50 Years at Ringside*, (Fleet Publishing Co., NY, 1958).

Harper, Kimberly, *White Man's Heaven: The Lynching and Expulsions of Blacks in the Southern Ozarks, 1894 – 1909*, (University of Arkansas Press, 2012).

Johnson, Jack, *In the Ring and Out*, (National Spots Publishing Co., Chicago, 1927).

Johnson, Jack, *My Life and Battles*, translated and edited from the 1911 and 1914 French versions by Christopher Rivers, (Praeger Publishers, Westport, CT, 2007).

Purday, Richard, ed., *Document Sets for the South in U. S. History*, "Speech of Senator Benjamin R. Tillman, March 23, 1900," Congressional Record, 56th Congress, 1st Session, 3223–3224, (D.C. Heath and Company, Lexington, MA, 1991).

Roberts, Randy, *Papa Jack*, (The Free Press, NY, 1983).

Rucker, Jr., Walter, and Upton, James Nathaniel , *Encyclopedia of American Race Riots*, (Edited by Greenwood Publishing Group, 2006).

Runstedtler, Theresa, *Jack Johnson: Rebel Sojourner*, (University of California Press, 2012).

Ward, Geoffrey C., *Unforgivable Blackness*, (Alfred A. Knopf, New York, 2004).

Zangrando, Robert L., *About Lynching*, excerpt from article in *The Reader's Companion to American History*, Editors Eric Foner and John A. Garraty, (Houghton Mifflin Co., 1991).

Acknowledgments

I want to thank all those who helped in some way with the research, photographs, promotion, or general support of my endeavors:

Clay Moyle

Sergei Yurchenko

Tracy Callis

Steve Gordon

Katy Klinefelter

Gregory Speciale

Robert Snell

Evan Grant

Paul Hindley

Jeff Baker

Anna Bruno

Dan Cuoco

Dave Bergin

Tony Prignits

Miles Templeton

Steve Lott

Anthony Reader

Zachary Daniels

Chris LaForce

Joe Botti

Kevin Smith

Steve Compton

Cyberboxingzone.com

Boxrec.com

Eastsideboxing.com

University of Iowa

University of Iowa Interlibrary Loan

Index

Roche, Billy, 51, 168, 193, 196, 198, 200, 207, 211, 253, 350, 524, 536, 546, 550

Roche, Jem, 558

Roche, William, 51, 166, 168, 170, 193, 196, 198, 200, 207, 211, 253, 350, 524, 536, 550

Rollins, Ed, 49, 484, 487, 688

Roosevelt, Theodore, 43, 85, 86, 281, 443, 445, 660

Root, Jack, 49, 50, 75, 79, 89, 92, 102, 103, 105, 106, 130, 139, 141, 148, 150, 179, 183, 249, 266, 304, 332, 373, 374, 379, 380, 418, 424, 460, 524, 684, 686

Ross, Tony, 460, 506, 517, 524, 569, 573

Ruhlin, Gus, 49, 52, 58, 63, 65, 75, 79, 81, 88, 90, 92, 99, 100, 101, 102, 105, 111, 127, 161, 183, 188, 190, 191, 218, 219, 237, 241, 245, 246, 255, 266, 275, 300, 301, 304, 354, 362, 363, 383, 401, 402, 403, 442, 451, 504, 581

Russell, Fred, 7, 65, 75, 77, 79, 80, 83, 103, 105, 130, 131, 133, 134, 152, 153, 154, 155, 156, 157, 158, 159, 160, 161, 166, 167, 168, 170, 176, 242, 269, 371, 395, 486, 487, 608, 648, 686, 688

Russell, Jimmy, 608, 648

Russell, Sid, 486, 487, 688

Ryan, Tommy, 46, 49, 75, 77, 79, 80, 92, 103, 297, 451, 460, 553, 684

San Francisco Athletic Club, 320

Savage, Jim, 519

Sayers, Governor Joseph, 67, 68, 69, 70, 71

Scanlan, Jim, 55, 58, 61, 75, 95, 478, 484, 487, 685

Schmitz, Mayor Eugene, 129

Schreck, Mike, 148, 363, 402, 435, 442, 451, 500, 502, 512, 517, 569, 504, 657

Schreiber, Belle, 68

Scott, Dred, 25, 33

Segregation, 8, 11, 26, 28, 34, 43, 159, 417

Shannon, Billy, 525, 526, 527, 536

Sharkey, Tom, 51, 52, 53, 55, 58, 65, 75, 76, 77, 79, 80, 81, 83, 84, 92, 99, 101, 105, 127, 152, 159, 183, 188, 190, 244, 249, 273, 275, 300, 301, 305, 312, 356, 359, 362, 374, 375, 378, 381, 418, 422, 451, 499, 504, 506, 511, 529, 533, 581, 586, 590, 599, 604, 647, 685

Shaughnessy, Mark, 163, 172, 200, 227

Shrosbree, George, 248

Siler, George, 44, 45, 47, 101, 268, 382, 401, 405, 445

Slavery, 8, 13, 24, 25, 26, 27, 29, 30, 31, 33, 35, 69, 243, 281, 283, 327, 444

Slavin, Frank, 80, 180, 371

Smith, Charles, 11

Smith, Denver Ed, 65

Smith, Ed, 57, 65, 96, 109

Smith, Eddie, 226

Smith, Hoke, 450

Smith, Thunderbolt, 142, 685

South, 18, 19, 20, 21, 22, 25, 26, 28, 29, 30, 31, 35, 43, 53, 54, 59, 67, 69, 82, 85, 86, 226, 280, 281, 282, 283, 288, 295, 301, 302, 304, 311, 331, 354, 360, 399, 400, 402, 417, 429, 440, 444, 456, 466, 467, 493, 500, 514, 515, 570, 578, 583, 589, 606, 607, 630, 675, 680, 690, 691

Spanish-American War, 43

Squires, Bill, 307, 451, 456, 460, 468, 471, 472, 473, 474, 475, 476, 477, 478, 479, 480, 481, 484, 486, 487, 488, 489, 492, 493, 494, 495, 496, 499, 500, 501, 502, 503, 504, 552, 553, 562, 563, 564, 570, 571, 572, 574, 576, 585, 589, 590, 598, 603, 606, 608, 609, 611, 613, 626, 630, 632, 633, 644, 648, 649, 667

Stelzner, Jack, 105

Stift, Billy, 49, 52, 57, 61, 75, 76, 77, 78, 79, 95, 98, 103, 113, 130, 148, 244, 303, 304, 319, 373, 396, 685

Strong, Charley, 49, 52, 80, 131, 142, 180, 371, 685

Stuart, Harry, 117, 118, 119, 123, 125, 126, 132, 133, 139, 154, 156, 157, 163, 166, 167, 168, 172, 174, 254

Sullivan, Dave, 312

Books By Adam J. Pollack

In the Ring With John L. Sullivan

In the Ring With James J. Corbett

In the Ring With Bob Fitzsimmons

In the Ring With James J. Jeffries

In the Ring With Marvin Hart

In the Ring With Tommy Burns

In the Ring With Jack Johnson – Part I: The Rise

In the Ring With Jack Johnson – Part II: The Reign

In the Ring With Jack Dempsey – Part I: The Making of a Champion

Adam J. Pollack is a boxing referee and judge, attorney, and member of the Boxing Writers Association of America.

www.ingramcontent.com/pod-product-compliance
Lightning Source LLC
Chambersburg PA
CBHW020409100426
42812CB00001B/260